THE INDIANIZED STATES OF SOUTHEAST ASIA

THE EAST-WEST CENTER—formally known as "The Center for Cultural and Technical Interchange Between East and West"—was established in Hawaii by the United States Congress in 1960. As a national educational institution in cooperation with the University of Hawaii, the Center has the mandated goal "to promote better relations and understanding between the United States and the nations of Asia and the Pacific through cooperative study, training, and research."

Each year about 2,000 men and women from the United States and some 40 countries and territories of Asia and the Pacific area work and study together with a multinational East-West Center staff in wide-ranging programs dealing with problems of mutual East-West concern. Participants are supported by federal scholarships and grants, supplemented in some fields by contributions from Asian/Pacific governments and private foundations.

Center programs are conducted by the East-West Communication Institute, the East-West Culture Learning Institute, the East-West Food Institute, the East-West Population Institute, and the East-West Technology and Development Institute. Open Grants are awarded to provide scope for educational and research innovation, including a program in humanities and the arts.

East-West Center Books are published by The University Press of Hawaii to further the Center's aims and programs.

THE INDIANIZED STATES OF SOUTHEAST ASIA by

G. COEDÈS *Edited by Walter F. Vella*

Translated by Susan Brown Cowing

AN EAST-WEST CENTER BOOK
THE UNIVERSITY PRESS OF HAWAII
HONOLULU

This translation was done under the auspices of the Research Publications and Translations Program of the Institute of Advanced Projects, East-West Center.

Library of Congress Catalog Card Number 67-29224

ISBN 0-8248-0368-X

Manufactured in the United States of America

NOTE ON SECOND EDITION

A first edition of this work appeared in Hanoi (Imprimerie d'Extrême-Orient) in 1944, under the title Histoire ancienne des états hindouisés d'Extrême-Orient. *It was soon out of print in Indochina.*

Insofar as possible, this second edition takes into account the relatively few works that were published during the time Indochina found herself isolated and deprived of relations with Europe and America. Many pages dealing with Funan, pre-Angkorian Cambodia, and early Champa have been rewritten in order to take into account the recent Sinological and epigraphical studies, still unedited, that will be published in the Bulletin de l'Ecole Française d'Extrême-Orient *or elsewhere.*

Paris, November 1947

NOTE ON THIRD EDITION

The second edition having in turn gone out of print in 1962, a third edition has become necessary. I have taken advantage of this opportunity to bring up to date a work that was greatly in need of it. Since the end of the war, numerous studies devoted to Southeast Asia have greatly advanced our knowledge of its past. I was thus obliged to enlarge the bibliographic references and, above all, to rewrite completely a number of sections that, as originally written, no longer reflected the present state of research. I hope that, in fifteen years or so, this third edition will in its turn be made obsolete by the progress made by an increasing number of scholars attracted to the study of the Indianized states, whose history I believe I was the first to synthesize.[1]

Paris, November 1963

EDITOR'S NOTE

It would be difficult to overestimate the contribution of George Coedès to the field of Southeast Asian studies. He is revered by other scholars in the field as the unchallenged dean of Southeast Asian classical scholarship. Since 1904 a truly prodigious and uninterrupted flow of articles, books, and papers on various aspects of early Southeast Asian history has issued from his pen: he has discovered and translated primary materials (inscriptions and annals in Pali, Sanskrit, Cambodian, Thai); he has interpreted the meaning of these materials in approximately two hundred scholarly articles; and he has synthesized his own work and that of his colleagues by writing integrated, readable accounts for specialists and the general public. Any one of his many epochal discoveries would be regarded as the proudest achievement of many a scholar.

Coedès' primary interest has been in the history of the Khmer Empire. His contribution here has been to supply a reliable historical chronology and an incisive delineation of the nature of Khmer kingship and other traditional Khmer institutions. What we know of ancient Cambodia stems predominantly from the work of Coedès. In other areas of Southeast Asia, Coedès is most famous for his pioneer depiction of the origin of Sukhothai, the first historical kingdom of Thailand, and his dramatic identification, in 1918, of the name, geographical scope, and importance of the ancient Indonesian empire of Śrīvijaya. His discovery of Śrivijaya has been called, by Paul Wheatley, "possibly the most significant contribution ever made to the progress of Southeast Asian history."

Coedès' major work of synthesis is his study *Les États hindouisés d'Indochine et d'Indonésie,* here translated, that covers the period from approximately A.D. 1 to A.D. 1500. This work has been universally acclaimed and—the surest proof of its impact—heavily relied on by all later scholars. Revised by Coedès in 1964, it is the basic text for all those who seek to understand

Southeast Asia—not only its ancient past but also its immediate present—for the Southeast Asia of today cannot be understood without a knowledge of the traditional values and institutions, which remain vital and which present leaders seem increasingly to esteem as a guide to the future.

A few notes on editorial policy may be in order for those who wish to compare the translation with the French original. The aim throughout has been to adhere scrupulously to the meaning of the original text. The format of Coedès' footnotes has been modified: full citations of sources have been provided for first references in each chapter; titles frequently referred to have been abbreviated, and a key to all abbreviations has been supplied. All quotations from English sources have been searched and supplied as they appear in the original quoted material. A few minor editorial changes have been made for the sake of clarity. Finally, the entire English text has been submitted to Professor Coedès, and approved by him.

A note on the system of transliteration used: An attempt has been made to adhere to the spirit of Coedès' transcription of Indian, Chinese, and Southeast Asian words and names—that is, to use as simplified a system as possible consistent with good usage. Many common geographic and other terms (e.g., Mekong, Vishnu, Mahayana) have been given in the spellings that appear in standard dictionaries. Tonal marks are not indicated for Chinese, Vietnamese, Burmese, or Thai. For most words and names the following systems were used as guides: for Chinese, the Wade-Giles system; for Vietnamese, the standard *quoc-ngữ;* for Thai, the system recommended by the Royal Institute of Thailand in 1941; for Sanskrit and Pali, the system used by most Indologists.

WALTER F. VELLA

Honolulu, Hawaii
July 12, 1967

CONTENTS

ILLUSTRATIONS

endsheets

other maps and charts following text

INTRODUCTION

The present volume complements the one which Louis de La Vallée-Poussin contributed to the *Histoire du monde* series in 1935 under the title *Dynasties et histoire de l'Inde depuis Kanishka jusqu'aux invasions musulmanes* (Vol. VI, Part 2). The present work is announced there (p. 296) and is to some extent anticipated there by substantial notes and bibliographic references (Appendix 2: *Navigation et colonisation,* pp. 291–97). Perhaps I should have followed the same method as La Vallée-Poussin, offering readers a simple outline accompanied by critical notes and, when possible, glimpses of the whole. The historical study of Southeast Asia is even less advanced than that of India, and it might seem premature to attempt to produce an unbroken and coherent narrative from incomplete information.[1] I have, nevertheless, tried to do this, for my purpose is less to produce a history presenting all the details than to offer a synthesis showing how the various elements of the history are related.

The geographic area here called "Farther India" consists of Indonesia, or island Southeast Asia except for the Philippines; and the Indochinese Peninsula, or India beyond the Ganges, including the Malay Peninsula. Excluded are Assam, which is simply an extension of India and Bengal, and northern Vietnam, whose history developed outside Indian influence.

The natural riches and geographic position of the region thus defined confer on it a place of primary importance. Around the beginning of the Christian Era, Southeast Asia was the "land of gold" toward which the Indian navigators sailed; a few centuries later, it (especially Indonesia) became the land of spices, camphor, and aromatic woods for the Arabs and Europeans; more recently, the region has become one of the most important producers of rubber, tin, and oil. Moreover, the position of the Malay Peninsula and of the Sunda Islands makes them a necessary port of call for seamen going from the West or India to China and vice versa—hence their importance in maritime commerce.

Culturally speaking, Farther India today is characterized by more or less deep traces of the Indianization that occurred long ago: the importance of the Sanskrit element in the vocabulary of the languages spoken there; the Indian origin of the alphabets with which those languages have been or still are written; the influence of Indian law and administrative organization; the persistence of certain Brahmanic traditions in the countries converted to Islam as well as those converted to Singhalese Buddhism; and the presence of ancient monuments which, in architecture and sculpture, are associated with the arts of India and bear inscriptions in Sanskrit.

The expansion of Indian civilization "to those countries and islands of the Orient where Chinese civilization, with strikingly similar aspirations, seemed to arrive ahead of it,"[2] is one of the outstanding events in the history of the world, one which has determined the destiny of a good portion of mankind. "Mother of wisdom," writes Sylvain Lévi, "India gave her mythology to her neighbors who went to teach it to the whole world. Mother of law and philosophy, she gave to three-quarters of Asia a god, a religion, a doctrine, an art. She carried her sacred language, her literature, her institutions into Indonesia, to the limits of the known world, and from there they spread back to Madagascar and perhaps to the coast of Africa, where the present flow of Indian immigrants seems to follow the faint traces of the past."[3]

The great importance of the civilizing activity of India can be measured by a simple fact of observation. On the basis of somatological, or physical, characteristics a Cambodian peasant scarcely differs from a Pnong or a Samré. But the Pnongs, like the Mois of Vietnam, have remained in a stage of tribal organization; they settle their differences by means of an oral tradition; they have no religion but a rather crude animism, the elements of which vary from one tribe to the next; their cosmology is rudimentary; they have no system of writing their language. The least advanced Cambodian, on the other hand, is caught up in the wheels of a strongly hierarchical state; he is subject to courts that judge according to a written code; he fervently practices a religion that possesses dogmas, sacred writings, and a clergy and that, at the same time, gives him coherent views of the world and the hereafter that are shared by a large part of Asian humanity; finally, he uses a system of writing that gives him access to a vast literature and enables him to communicate from a distance with his fellow men. All this he owes to India. To reduce these facts to a rather crude formula, it can be said that the Cambodian is an Indianized Pnong. If we vary the terms of this formula, it can be applied to the Burmese, to the southern Thai, to the ancient Chams, to the Malays,[4] and to the Javanese before Islam.

From this Indianization was born a series of kingdoms that in the beginning were true Indian states: Cambodia, Champa, and the small states of the Malay Peninsula; the kingdoms of Sumatra, Java, and Bali; and, finally, the Burmese and Thai kingdoms, which received Indian culture from the Mons and Khmers. Through reaction with the indigenous substratum, however, each of these states developed according to its own genius, although their cultures never lost the family resemblance that they owed to their common origin.

Curiously, India quickly forgot that her culture had spread over such vast domains to the east and southeast. Indian scholars have not been aware of this fact until very recently; it was not until a small group of them, having learned French and Dutch, studied with the professors of the Universities of Paris and Leyden that they discovered, in our works and those of our colleagues in Holland and Java, the history of what they now call, with justifiable pride, "Greater India." [5]

A first chapter entitled "The Land and Its Inhabitants" presents a very brief geographic outline, as well as a résumé of present knowledge of the prehistory and ethnology of Farther India.[6] It is certainly important to have some notion of the substratum over which Indian civilization spread. The second chapter examines the causes, the times, the methods, and the first results of the progressive Indianization of the area defined in the preceding chapter. The twelve following chapters recount the important facts in the ancient history of Farther India, up to the arrival of the Europeans.

The simplest method of dividing such a vast and complex subject into chapters seemed to be to cut it up, so to speak, into vertical, or geographical, segments, as René Grousset, for example, has done in his works; [7] and to summarize, in the light of the most recent research, the works of Etienne Aymonier,[8] Paul Pelliot,[9]

Georges Maspero,[10] Bijan Raj Chatterjee,[11] Ramesch C. Majumdar,[12] and Lawrence P. Briggs[13] for Funan and Cambodia; those of Georges Maspero[14] and Ramesch C. Majumdar[15] for Champa; of Arthur P. Phayre[16] and Godfrey E. Harvey[17] for Burma; of William A. R. Wood[18] and Phanindra N. Bose[19] for Siam; of Paul Le Boulanger[20] for Laos; of Gabriel Ferrand,[21] Ramesch C. Majumdar,[22] K. A. Nilakanta Sastri,[23] Richard O. Winstedt,[24] Roland Braddell,[25] Lawrence P. Briggs,[26] and Paul Wheatley[27] for Malaysia; and of Nicholaas J. Krom,[28] Frederik W. Stapel,[29] Bernard H. M. Vlekke,[30] and Hermanns J. de Graaf[31] for Indonesia.

This method requires constant repetition in all cases of relations between states or even of facts that pertain to more than one country. I prefer to treat Farther India as a whole and divide the subject into horizontal, or chronological, segments.

Such a division is simpler than one would suppose, for the various countries of Southeast Asia that were civilized by India also moved in the political orbit of China because of their geographic position. Most of them experienced the great shocks that shook the Indian Peninsula or the Middle Kingdom. The conquests of Samudragupta in the Ganges Valley and southern India in the fourth century, the expansionistic policy of the Choḷa emperors of Tanjore in the eleventh century, had repercussions on the other side of the Bay of Bengal. Moreover, events in China clearly influenced the history of Farther India. The Chinese never looked with favor on the formation of strong states in the southern seas, and it is a fact worth noting that the periods of the greatest strength of Funan, Cambodia, and the Javanese and Sumatran kingdoms correspond in general to the periods of weakness of the great Chinese dynasties. In addition, the countries of Farther India are bound together by geographic and economic ties, and any revolution in the interior of one, by stirring up the populace, has had repercussions on the others. The disintegration of the Funan empire, the birth of the Sumatran kingdom of Śrīvijaya, the accession of Anôratha in Pagan or Sūryavarman II in Angkor, the founding of the Thai kingdom of Sukhothai, all had distinct effects beyond the borders of the countries in which these events took place. There are, then, critical dates which constitute real "turning points" in the history of Farther India and which make it possible to delimit a certain number of epochs, each having its own characteristics, each marked by the imprint of a strong personality or by the political supremacy of a powerful state.

A concluding chapter attempts a brief evaluation of the heritage left by India in the countries that benefited from its civilizing activity for more than a thousand years.

Far more often than I would like, this account will assume the nature of dynastic annals and give the impression of a skeleton without flesh. This is because of the nature of the sources used—Chinese annals, epigraphy—and also because of the relatively unadvanced state of Southeast Asian studies. The most important task facing researchers at the outset is to identify the ancient place names and establish the reign dates—in other words, to sketch a geographical and chronological framework. This work is very nearly complete for most of the countries, and reasonably complete for many of the others. The religions and arts of the countries are beginning to be better known, but much remains to be done on the history of their political institutions and their material culture. Epigraphy may furnish much information on these questions, as soon as the interpretation of texts in the vernacular—often difficult work that attracts only a small number of scholars—becomes more advanced.[32]

Another defect that the reader cannot help but notice is the difference of tone, I would say almost of style, between various sections of the same chapter. Thus, when the Burmese kingdom of Pagan comes on the scene in the eleventh century, one has the impression that its history is infinitely more lively than that of Cambodia; thus, furthermore, the history of Cambodia in certain periods appears much less rich in precisely dated political facts than that of Champa. This lack of unity among the diverse parts of the account is, again, due to the nature of the sources used. The history of Cambodia at present is founded chiefly on epigraphy, whereas that of Champa profits from abundant documentation in Chinese and Vietnamese annals and that of Burma relies on chronicles. If there were the same romanticized chronicles for Cambodia as for Burma, it is probable that the hazy figures of a Yaśovarman or a Sūryavarman II would become much clearer and would come to life as vividly as the kings of Pagan. Proof of this is found in the case of Jayavarman VII: because his inscriptions depart from the usual mythological bombast to relate precise biographical facts, his personality immediately has a concreteness that makes it possible to trace a living portrait.

The documents on which the history of the Indianized states of Southeast Asia is founded—inscriptions, local chronicles, foreign accounts (Chinese, Arab, European)—are enumerated in the general works mentioned previously. The two great sources of information are the Chinese annals and the inscriptions. The chief value of these sources lies in their chronological accuracy, but they have many deficiencies. They report only certain kinds of facts, such as religious endowments and the diplomatic or commercial relations of China with countries to the south. The abundance of these sources in a certain epoch or their scarcity in another may often give a false impression, and argument *a silentio* in the case of an absence of sources is still more dangerous. For example, Jayavarman II, king of Cambodia from 802 to 850, did not leave a single inscription, but it would be a misinterpretation to infer from this that his reign was without interest. As for the Chinese sources, their silence with regard to a particular country does not necessarily signify its eclipse, but is often the result of a momentary weakening of Chinese foreign policy.

From the time that Europeans began to take an interest in the countries of Farther India, chiefly for colonial reasons, they have studied the archaeology and history of the area. But these studies have been pursued unequally in the different territories.

Those who have undertaken the archaeological exploration of Cambodia, Champa, and Java deserve praise; however, the work is far from complete, and each year new inscriptions are dug up from the soil of Angkor. Excavations have scarcely begun in Sumatra, are just beginning in Siam and in the Malay Peninsula. Epigraphy has progressed quite satisfactorily everywhere except in Burma, where it consists of only a very insufficient number of translations.[33] The examination of Chinese sources, completed for Funan, Champa, and certain parts of Indonesia, is still very incomplete for Cambodia, Burma, and the Thai countries.

The unevenness in research and in the utilization of documents is an inevitable consequence of the division of Farther India into several states or colonies, which have been subject to different regimes and have developed unequally. This, in addition to the disparate character of the sources mentioned above, renders difficult, and perhaps premature, the attempt—undertaken here for the first time—to produce a historical synthesis of the countries of Farther India.

I hope I will be forgiven for offering for Cambodia a generally more detailed account, with more numerous references to original sources. It is not that, by a sort of professional distortion, I accord an exaggerated pre-eminence to the history of the Khmer people. But whereas for Champa and for Java one can use the historical treatises of Georges Maspero and Nicholaas J. Krom, who give a complete résumé of present knowledge, there is no parallel for Cambodia.[34] I have thought it advisable to fill this gap to a certain extent by dividing among the various chapters of this work the elements of a summary of the ancient history of Cambodia that take the most recent studies into account.

Since I am not writing exclusively for the general public, but also for those historians, philologists, and ethnologists who lack a background in the history of this part of the world, I have not hesitated to give a sketch of current discussions concerning controversial matters when the occasion presented itself. The narrative is thereby interrupted, but silence or, on the other hand, too pat an affirmation would risk giving a false idea of the state of knowledge. If this work proves useful by summarizing what has been learned so far[35] and by indicating the points on which research ought to be encouraged, I hope it will be pardoned for its faults.

THE INDIANIZED STATES OF SOUTHEAST ASIA

CHAPTER I

THE LAND AND ITS INHABITANTS

1. GEOGRAPHIC SKETCH

There will be no attempt made here to give a detailed geographic description of the vast and complex area over which Indian civilization spread from the east coast of India. An excellent description of this area of the globe can be found in the second volume of *L'Asie des moussons,* by Jules Sion, under the heading "Quatrième partie: L'Indochine et l'Insulinde."[1] It will suffice here to indicate some of the general features that give the area a certain unity and that must be known in order to understand the historical events that took place there.

The Indochinese Peninsula and the islands of Indonesia are among the tropical lands dominated by the monsoons. Although there are some variations from one year to the next—variations which can be disastrous for wet rice culture, the only method of cultivation that assures an abundant supply of grain—in general there is an alternation of dry seasons and rainy seasons that conditions the life of the sedentary populations and an alternation of dominating winds that determines the direction of navigation by sail.

From Burma, the Malay Peninsula, and the island of Sumatra, the western face of Farther India is turned toward the Indian Ocean, where, to quote Sylvain Lévi, "the pattern of currents and the pattern of periodic winds that govern navigation have long fostered a system of trade in which the African coast, Arabia, the Persian Gulf, India, Indochina, and China continually contributed and received their share."[2]

On the other side of the natural barrier formed by the Malay Peninsula and the islands that extend from it, there is a veritable Mediterranean formed by the China Sea, the Gulf of Siam, and the Java Sea. This enclosed sea, in spite of its typhoons and reefs, has always been a unifying factor rather than an obstacle for the peoples along the rivers. Well before the arrival of foreign navigators, these peoples had their mariners, and although the remote origins of these peoples were probably quite diverse, they had developed, through continual trade, a certain similarity of culture that will be discussed later. This pre-Indian culture developed near the sea: in the valleys and deltas of the great rivers, the Mekong, the Menam, the Irrawaddy, and the Salween; in the low plains of Java; and in the basins of the coastal rivers of Vietnam, the Malay Peninsula, and Sumatra, which are scarcely suitable for navigation, but excellent for irrigation. "The civilized man of that area," writes Jules Sion, "is essentially, uniquely a man of the plains; he leaves to the aborigines the high places, which are not necessarily poor, for the aborigines have long been able to utilize them thanks to millet, certain kinds of rice, and herds."[3] This retreat of the aborigines and of the "less civilized" to the mountains is undoubtedly a very ancient phenomenon; the process has continued over the centuries and must have been particularly evident during the period of Indianization. It explains to a large degree the ethnic stratification of the countries of Farther India. The mountains of these countries have remained the province of peoples who are sometimes nomadic, who practice hunting, gathering, and slash-and-burn agriculture, and who, in the midst of the twentieth century, seem scarcely to have evolved from Neolithic life.

2. PREHISTORY

In spite of the works of Henri Mansuy,[4] Madeleine Colani,[5] Etienne Patte,[6] Jacques Fromaget and Edmond Saurin,[7] and Paul Lévy[8] for Indochina; of Ivor H. N. Evans,[9] H. D. Collings,[10] M. W. F. Tweedie,[11] Pieter V. van Stein Callenfels,[12] A. N. J. Thomassen à Thuessink van der Hoop,[13] G. H. Ralph von Koenigswald,[14] and H. R. van Heekeren[15] for Malaya and Indonesia; of Fritz Sarasin,[16] Pierre Teilhard de Chardin,[17] and H. R. van Heekeren[18] for Siam; and of J. Coggin Brown,[19] T. O. Morris,[20] and Hallam L. Movius, Jr.,[21] for Burma, the prehistory of Farther India is still in the exploratory stage, and the brilliant attempts at synthesis by Robert von Heine-Geldern[22] and Jean Naudou[23] can only be considered working hypotheses. We must be content here with a factual treatment that will give an approximate idea of the cultures and ancient distribution of the ethnic groups over which India was to exert a civilizing influence by means of a process to be discussed in the next chapter.

From earliest times, the population of Farther India was composed of very diverse elements, some of which were related to the Negritos and Veddas, others to the Australoids and the Papuan-Melanesians, and still others to the Indonesians.[24] This fact leads to a clear conclusion: that the earliest inhabitants of Farther India are related to those who inhabit the islands of the Pacific today, and that the Mongolian element in Farther India is of very recent origin. But races are less important for our purposes than types of culture.

These ancient peoples have left stone, bone, and metal implements, pottery fragments, glass trinkets, and, in certain regions, megaliths. The chronology of these remains has by no means been satisfactorily established. Not only is it difficult to fix absolute dates, but even the order of succession of the various types of implements has not yet been established. The fact that polished stone is often found with iron objects shows that the prehistoric period lasted much later here than in Europe. One can say without great exaggeration that the peoples of Farther India began to use metals widely, under the influence of their neighbors, only in the last century before the Christian Era. This was the period during which the historic civilizations of China and Aryan India began to exercise their profound influence.

We must disregard the Pleistocene remains discovered in Java (Pithecanthropus of Trinil, Neanderthaloid of Solo, Proto-Australoid of Wajak), which are outside the framework of this book because they are too ancient, and limit ourselves to an indication of the principal periods of the prehistory of Southeast Asia.

Paleolithic industry, in the sense meant by the term in European prehistory, is represented in Burma by the "ancient Anyathian," characterized by pebbles shaped into axes, specimens of which have also been found in Siam (Fing Noi) and in upper Laos (Ph'u Loi). This industry was the work of the proto-Australians, who have also left traces of the "Chellean" type in Java.

Remains of the following period, characterized by stone chopper tools and the almost complete absence of pottery, have been found in Tongking (Hoa-binh Province) and in North Vietnam, in Laos (Luang Phrabang), in Siam (Chiangrai, Lopburi, Ratburi), and in Malaya (Gua Kerbau, Perak). On the eastern coast of Sumatra, axes ground on one side seem to date from the same period. This civilization, commonly called "Hoabinhian," is classified by some authors as Mesolithic.

In some deposits, the chipped stones are mixed with sharply polished instruments characteristic of Bacsonian industry (discovered in the mountainous mass of Bac-sơn, Tongking) along with a little cord-marked pottery and some bone implements.

Some of the human remains found in the Hoabinhian and Bacsonian sites exhibit characteristics that relate them to the Australian and Papuan-Melanesian races;[25] others are of Indonesian type, already showing some of the Mongoloid characteristics that were later to increase.

However, the human remains that are associated with an industry marked by an abundance of chips and microliths and seen in Sumatra, Java, Borneo, and the Celebes, seem to be connected with Negrito and Veddoid types.

Finally, a last form of late Paleolithic or Mesolithic culture characterized by bone artifacts and seen in Indochina, Siam, Malaya, and from Sumatra to Japan through Java, the Celebes, Borneo, the Philippines, Taiwan, and the Ryukyus, is perhaps the result of the emigration or expansion of a race yet to be determined.

Neolithic industry, traces of which have been found all over the Far East, may have been introduced in part by newcomers—undoubtedly the Indonesians, who at present constitute the majority of the population of Farther India. Rich in pottery with designs that sometimes recall those of ancient China[26] and of the West, Neolithic civilization did not disappear with the introduction of metals; we could almost say that its spirit lives on today among certain backward groups of the mountains and the interior.

In the Neolithic period, we notice a split between the northern and southern regions of the geographic area studied here, perhaps caused by a migration of the first Mongoloid or Mongolized ethnic elements. Mainland Southeast Asia, southern China, and northeast India are the region of the axe with a shouldered tenon, the characteristic utensil of peoples speaking languages of the Austro-Asiatic family,[27] while the region of the Indonesian languages, situated to the south, is scarcely familiar with anything but the chiseled axe that is semicircular or triangular in cross section.

It is apparent from the implements associated with them that the megaliths found throughout Farther India had already appeared by the age of metals, that is, in the proto-historic epoch. The oldest of the megaliths, in association with which we find only bronze and no iron, are the dolmens of eastern Java, from which the Balinese sarcophagi trace their descent. These dolmens and the vaults of central Java, southern Sumatra, and Perak,[28] the monolithic jars of upper Laos, and the menhirs of upper Laos, Malaya, Sumatra, and Java are always funerary monuments, related to the worship of ancestors and departed chiefs. This fact has led to some very bold theories.[29]

There is some question about whether it is proper to speak of a "Bronze Age" in Farther India. The use of stone continued very late there, and iron appeared almost simultaneously with bronze. We must not forget that in China under the Han, in the last two centuries before the Christian Era, weapons were still made of bronze, and iron had only recently been imported.[30] There are no remains from Dongson civilization—which corresponds to the age of bronze in Tongking and North Vietnam [31] (probably the centers of diffusion of bronze drums)—that can be considered to have preceded the last centuries before Christ. Pieter V. van Stein Callenfels has proposed placing the arrival of bronze in Indochina around 600 B.C.; in the archipelago, around 300 B.C.[32]

In most cases, we pass without transition from the late Neolithic to the first Indian remains. On the coast of Vietnam and in Cambodia, there is nothing between the Neolithic strata of Sa-huynh [33] and Samrong Sèn [34] and the Xuân-lôc megalith on the one hand [35] and the first monuments of Champa and Cambodia on the other. The Indian establishments of Oc Eo [36] (in Cochin China) and of Kuala Selinsing (in the state of Perak in Malaya),[37] from which come seals engraved with Sanskrit names in the writing of the second to fourth centuries, have also yielded instruments of polished stone. In the Celebes a bronze Buddha of the Amarāvatī school was found at Sempaga above a Neolithic layer.[38] So we can say, without great exaggeration, that the people of Farther India were still in the midst of late Neolithic civilization when the Brahmano-Buddhist culture of India came into contact with them.

3. AUSTRO-ASIATIC CIVILIZATION

But this late Neolithic contact was not the first contact. The extensiveness of the diverse types of culture just enumerated and, notably, the abundance of glass beads of Indian origin found in the Neolithic strata of Farther India prove that from prehistoric times maritime relations existed not only between the various parts of Farther India but also between the latter and India proper.

This is also indicated in the remarks of Arthur M. Hocart[39] and of Paul Mus[40] concerning the similarity of some fundamental beliefs and certain essential rites in all of monsoon Asia. It appears from implements[41] and vocabulary[42] that there was a community of culture between pre-Aryan India on the one hand[43] and Farther India on the other.

According to some scholars,[44] one or more ethnic waves originating either in the Indochinese Peninsula or in the islands spread throughout India before the Aryan invasion. According to others,[45] the Dravidians or the Aryans, entering India from the northwest, pushed the aboriginal populations into eastern and southern India; these peoples spread to Southeast Asia, where they brought about a sort of pre-Aryan Indianization, while the Indonesian peoples in their turn left the continent to populate the islands.[46] It will be best for the moment not to attempt to be too precise, but to use the prudent formula of Jean Przyluski,[47] who says that "during the second Bronze Age [in Europe], the Indochinese Peninsula entered the orbit of a maritime civilization comprising both the mainland and the archipelago of Southeast Asia."

Whatever its origin, this civilization was carried all the way to Madagascar by the Indonesians, either before[48] or after their Indianization.[49] It is possible that it also touched Japan; relations between Japan and the countries to the south have been indicated in various ways by prehistoric implements,[50] language,[51] and folklore.[52]

One scholar has proposed[53] linking the Austro-Asiatic cultural complex with the "Austronesoid" cycle, characterized by the use of the bow, the practice of the matriarchate, and totemic beliefs. We must be on guard against the dangers of forcing a flexible reality into too rigid categories.[54] At the same time, we can indicate what seem to have been the characteristic traits of this pre-Aryan civilization: with regard to material culture, the cultivation of irrigated rice, domestication of cattle and buffalo, rudimentary use of metals, knowledge of navigation; with regard to the social system, the importance of the role conferred on women and of relationships in the maternal line, and an organization resulting from the requirements of irrigated agriculture; with regard to religion, belief in animism, the worship of ancestors and of the god of the soil, the building of shrines in high places, burial of the dead in jars or dolmens; with regard to mythology, "a cosmological dualism in which are opposed the mountain and the sea, the winged race and the aquatic race, the men of the heights and those of the coasts";[55] with regard to linguistics, the use of isolating languages with a rich faculty for derivation by means of prefixes, suffixes, and infixes.[56]

To a great extent it was undoubtedly this unity of culture that led the Chinese to group the diverse peoples of Farther India together under the name *K'un-lun*.[57] This name, it is true, did not appear until after Indianization, and we may well wonder if the unity of Indian culture explains the term. This opinion could be argued from the fact that the Chinese speak of "*K'un-lun* writing," and writing was a basic Indian contribution. But when they speak of "*K'un-lun* language" and of "*K'un-lun* merchants and pirates," they seem to apply this term to an ethno-linguistic entity.[58] The word *K'un-lun* has been interpreted in various ways. The researches of Gabriel Ferrand indicate that the word must have been used to transcribe many different indigenous terms that had become confused in Chinese usage. Sylvain Lévi has interpreted the term as the equivalent of the Sanskrit expression *dvīpāntara,* "the people of the islands."[59] Nicholaas J. Krom has indicated the possibility of equating *K'un-lun* and *Malaya,*[60] and the recent hypotheses of Ramesch C. Majumdar,[61] even if we allow for what is a little superficial in his comparisons, give some consistency to this view in that they assign a preponderant place to the "Malay" element, that is, the Indonesian element developed in contact with the foreigners of Mongoloid origin, as the vector of Austro-Asiatic civilization.

Thus, the Indians found themselves among not uncultivated savages but organized societies endowed with a civilization (notably Dongson civilization)[62] that had some traits in common with their own. Some peoples of the mountains and back country of

Indochina and Malaya today can give us an approximate idea of these societies.

The apparent unity of the elements known to us, of which language is the most important, certainly conceals a great racial diversity, in spite of the conclusions drawn from certain measurements by Father Wilhelm Schmidt.

Austro-Asiatic culture has obscured the culture of peoples who have long existed, and still exist in small pockets, by borrowing from them or by assimilating some of their material and spiritual elements. What there is in common among the various ethnic groups of the area in question is very often the contribution of one of them or of a common substratum that has now disappeared. And the remarks of P. Rivet concerning the common traits of the languages he calls "oceanic" [63] appear applicable not only to the languages but also to other elements of the civilization of the Austro-Asiatic complex.

4. ETHNOLOGICAL OUTLINE

Now let us discuss the peoples, more or less impregnated by this culture, over whom Aryan India had a civilizing influence.[64]

At the time when the Indianization of Southeast Asia began, that is, around the beginning of the Christian Era, the great prehistoric migrations of the Melanesians, Indonesians, and Austro-Asiatics had come to an end; in the south of the Indochinese Peninsula and in the archipelago, the principal ethnic groups occupied approximately the areas they do now. Indeed, from the time of the appearance of the first vernacular inscriptions we see the use of Khmer in Cambodia, of Cham in the Cham provinces of Vietnam, of Malay in Sumatra, and of Javanese in Java. In the central and northern peninsula, however, we see during historic times the retreat of the Chams of central Vietnam from the Vietnamese and of the Mons of the Menam and of the Irrawaddy from the Thai and the Burmese.

This "push to the south," [65] caused by the attraction of the deltas and the sea, is an ancient phenomenon. It explains the present distribution of ethnic groups in the Indochinese Peninsula and, to a certain extent, in the islands, since, as has been said above, they received their populations and their cultural complex from the continent.

Even if it were true that the migrations could have penetrated Southeast Asia only by the narrow valleys of rivers originating in China and the confines of Tibet, it would nevertheless be wrong to represent these movements of populations as a series of outpourings leading to superficially contiguous ethnic formations; this would, I believe, be a false idea, unfortunately fostered by the appearance of ethnographic maps registering present population patterns. Once these waves reached the mainland plains or the islands, they spread and overlapped.

Moreover, it is necessary in some cases to view this process as the expansion of a culture or of a language rather than as an actual migration.

Apparently the actual migrations resulted usually not in the annihilation or complete eviction of the old occupants of the soil by the newcomers but in the adoption by the former of the language and customs of the conquerors or new ruling class. The expansion of the Thai, for example, was not necessarily the result of the displacement of a large human mass, especially in the south of the peninsula; a military aristocracy was able to impose its language, which spread among the other racial groups.

Moreover, the successive ethno-linguistic waves did not completely mask one another. In some cases a later wave extended beyond the preceding one in a certain direction while not reaching as far in another direction and skipping over some peaks, some small pockets, and certain fringes of territory. The Mon-Khmers did not thoroughly impose themselves on the Indonesians and, in their turn, were not completely overlapped by the Thai; the Vietnamese worked their way along the coast and streams, settling only in the deltas; the aborigines, related to the Negritos, Veddas, or Dravidians, still roam the mountainous interior of the islands and of the Malay Peninsula.

Wherever there were migrations to already settled areas, intermarriage took place, from which physical and cultural characteristics associated with the oldest groups survived.

These considerations suffice to explain the great wealth and variety of Southeast Asian ethnological material. This book is devoted to Farther India insofar as it was culturally dependent on India proper; it will not deal with the backward tribes driven into the mountains where Indianization could not reach them. By treating only the ethnic groups touched by Indian civilization, we can represent their distribution and their geographical situation toward the beginning of the Christian Era in a systematic fashion.

Given the direction of the "push to the south," the ethnic groups situated farthest to the south are most likely to have lived in their present habitat longest. In fact, the Indonesians, who constitute the basis of the island population,[66] have undoubtedly been there since Neolithic times. "The Indonesians," writes Jules Sion, "were the proto-Malays, whose sojourn in the interior of the large islands permitted them to better conserve their racial purity, in spite of mixture with the aborigines—for example, the Bataks of Sumatra, the Dyaks of Borneo, the Alfurs of the Celebes and the Moluccas. The Malays were simply Indonesians of the coasts, who became much less pure racially because of very diverse cross-breeding . . . ; it is a mixed race, great in its diffusion and multiple in its varieties." [67] We have seen that it was undoubtedly these Malays of the coast to whom the Chinese and Indian seamen applied the names *K'un-lun* and *Dvīpāntara*. These are the Malays of Sumatra, the Sundanese, Javanese, and Madurese of Java, and the Balinese, who were the principal agents for the reception and diffusion of Indian culture in the archipelago. In his Indo-Javanese history, Nicholaas J. Krom [68] has presented a picture of Malay civilization, particularly of Javanese civilization, before Indianization that consists largely of hypotheses, for it is based chiefly on the present ethnology of the non-Indianized Indonesians; thus he enumerates among the characteristic elements of their material culture the irrigation of rice fields, the dyeing of fabrics by the process called batik, and the development of the gamelan orchestra and the *wayang* shadow theater.[69] Documents of inestimable value for the study of Indonesian social organization are the collections of customary law diligently compiled by the Dutch in the archipelago.[70]

On the peninsula, in those areas where Malays now constitute the majority because of relatively recent migrations from Sumatra and Java, the Indians undoubtedly encountered on the coast proto-Malays—Indonesians already strongly Mongolized, whose descendants are known today by the name *Jakun*.[71]

On the Indochinese Peninsula, the Indians found: on the coast of central and southern Vietnam, the Chams, whose language was Malayo-Polynesian, and whose last descendants still occupy some districts of South Vietnam (Phan-rang, Phan-thiêt); in the delta of Cochin China, present-day Cambodia, and the basin of the central Mekong, the Khmers, who were subsequently supplanted in part of Cochin China by the Vietnamese and driven from the north by the Thai; [72] in the Menam Valley and Lower Burma, the Mons, also called Peguans or Talaings,[73] linguistic relatives of the Khmers, who today are confined to the Irrawaddy Delta and to Tenasserim, or pushed back in Siam; in the basin of the Irrawaddy and the Sittang, the vanguard of the Tibeto-Burman peoples, of whom the most important element, then still kept in check by the Mons, was the Pyus, who have disappeared or been assimilated by successive waves of Burmese or Thai immigration.

These are the ethnic groups upon which we shall see India exercising its civilizing influence.

CHAPTER II

INDIANIZATION

1. DEFINITION OF INDIANIZATION

The history of the expansion of Indian civilization to the east has not yet been told in its entirety. We are beginning to be familiar with the results of this expansion in the various countries considered separately, but we are reduced to hypotheses concerning its origins and its processes. I do not pretend to solve these problems in the pages that follow. I shall only attempt to assemble the results that have been established and to set down some general traits common to all the Indianized kingdoms of Farther India.

I have so far, for the sake of convenience, used the terms "Indianization" and "expansion of Indian culture" as if they referred to a simple historical fact that took place in a specific epoch. This concept must be made more precise. As has been seen in the preceding chapter, the relations between India proper and Farther India date back to prehistoric times. But from a certain period on, these relations resulted in the founding of Indian kingdoms on the Indochinese Peninsula and in the islands of Indonesia. The oldest archaeological remains these states have left us are not necessarily evidence of the first civilizing wave. It is probable, a *priori,* that the priests who consecrated the first Brahmanic or Buddhist sanctuaries and the scholars who composed the first Sanskrit inscriptions were preceded by seamen, traders, or immigrants—founders of the first Indian settlements. These settlements, in turn, were not always entirely new creations; in many cases (Oc Eo in Cochin China, Kuala Selinsing in Perak, Sempaga in the Celebes, etc.), they were built on Neolithic sites that the seamen from India had frequented perhaps from time immemorial.

The coming of the Indians to Southeast Asia cannot be compared to the arrival of the Europeans in America, for in this part of the world the newcomers were not strangers discovering new lands. At some time that we must try to date, following circumstances that we can attempt to determine, the sporadic influx of traders and immigrants became a steady flow that resulted in the founding of Indian kingdoms practicing the arts, customs, and religions of India and using Sanskrit as their sacred language.

"It seems," writes Alfred Foucher,[1] "that the numerous emigrants—like those who still swarm into eastern Africa—encountered only savage populations of naked men. They implanted in these rich deltas or favored islands nothing less than their civilization or at least its copy: their customs and their laws, their alphabet and their scholarly language, and their entire social and religious establishment, with as close a likeness as possible of their castes and cults. In short, it was not a question of a simple influence but, in the full meaning of the term, a true colonization." We will see later that this "colonization" did not involve political ties with the mother country.

The nudity of the natives, mentioned by Foucher, is no more a criterion of "savagery" in this case than it is in the case of the hill tribes of Laos or Vietnam. We have seen before that the Indians were not confronted by uncultured "savages" but, on the contrary, by people endowed with a civilization that had traits in common with the civilization of pre-Aryan India. The speed and ease with which the Aryanized Indians propagated their culture is undoubtedly explained in part by the fact that, in the customs and beliefs of these immigrants, the natives discovered, under an Indian veneer, a base common to all of monsoon Asia.

It is then neither a question of a contact between strangers or of a first contact. If the Indianization of Farther India around the beginning of the Christian Era seems to be a new development, it is because the Indians—who were not on their first voyage, but were arriving in greater numbers—were accompanied for the first time by educated elements capable of spreading the religions and arts of India and the Sanskrit language. The Indianization of Farther India is the continuation overseas of a "Brahmanization" that had its earliest focus in Northwest India and that "having begun well before the Buddha, continues to our day in Bengal as well as in the south."[2] And, in fact, the most ancient Sanskrit inscriptions of Farther India are not much later than the first Sanskrit inscriptions of India itself.

Indianization must be understood essentially as the expansion of an organized culture that was founded upon the Indian conception of royalty, was characterized by Hinduist or Buddhist cults, the mythology of the *Purāṇas,* and the observance of the *Dharmaśāstras,* and expressed itself in the Sanskrit language. It is for this reason that we sometimes speak of "Sanskritization" instead of "Indianization."

This Sanskrit or Indian civilization, transplanted into Southeast Asia and called, according to the country, "Indo-Khmer," "Indo-Javanese," etc., is the one we are able to recognize in the epigraphical or archaeological documents. Perhaps the only difference between it and the "Sanskrit civilization" of Bengal and the Dravidian countries is the fact that it was spread by sea while the other was spread by land and, in a sense, by "osmosis." The Indian civilization of Southeast Asia was the civilization of an elite and not that of the whole population, whose beliefs and way of life are still very insufficiently known. Since nothing more is known, it would be vain to try to arbitrate the conflict between those who hold that the indigenous societies have preserved the essence of their original character under an Indian veneer and those who believe they were integrated into a society of the Indian type.[3]

2. THE FIRST EVIDENCE OF THE INDIANIZATION OF FARTHER INDIA

An attempt has been made to find in a passage of the *Arthaśāstra*—the treatise on politics and administration by the Brahman Kauṭilya, minister of Chandragupta (end of the fourth and beginning of the third century B.C.)—proof that the colonization of India dates back at least to the Maurya emperors. Louis Finot[4] has justly disposed of this theory, which is based on a text that, in its present form, is of uncertain antiquity. And regardless of its age, the *Arthaśāstra,* which simply recommends to the king that he "people an old or new country either by taking the territory of another or by sending forth the excess inhabitants of his own," cannot prove much and is less explicit than the *Jātakas,* with their tales of seamen, and the *Rāmāyaṇa,*[5] which mentions Java and perhaps Sumatra. The *Niddesa,* a Pali canonic text which dates at the latest to the very first centuries of the Christian Era, is even better informed; it enumerates a number of Sanskrit or Sanskritized place names that Sylvain Lévi has suggested may be identified with localities of Farther India.[6] In our present state of knowledge, neither archaeological and epigraphic documents nor foreign sources can be dated any farther back than the *Niddesa.* Let us anticipate the following chapter somewhat and seek the oldest evidence of the existence of Indian kingdoms in Farther India.

In Burma—apart from the religious mission of the Buddhist monks Soṇa and Uttara which Emperor Aśoka sent in the third century B.C. to Suvaṇṇabhūmi, the "Land of Gold" (generally identified, rightly or wrongly, with the ancient land of the Mon, and especially with the town of Thaton)—there is no trace of Indian penetration before about 500 A.D., the date of the fragments of the Pali canon found at Môza and Maungun, on the ancient site of Prome.[7]

In the Menam Basin, the site of Phra Pathom and, farther to the west, the site of Phong Tưk[8] on the Kanburi River have yielded the substructures of edifices and Buddhist sculptures in Gupta and post-Gupta styles,[9] and also a bronze statuette of the Buddha that was first considered to belong to the Amarāvatī school[10] and therefore to date back to the third or fourth century A.D. but that really is considerably later.[11]

The Brahmanic statues of Si Thep on the Nam Sak are perhaps not as old as I believed when I first wrote about them in 1932,[12] but inscriptions found at the same site cannot be more recent than the fifth or sixth century A.D.[13] A bronze statuette of the Buddha that shows Gupta influence and possibly dates back to the fourth century has been found in the region of Khorat.[14]

In Cambodia, the Chinese place the founding of the kingdom of Funan by the Brahman Kauṇḍinya in the first century A.D. China entered into relations with Funan in the third century A.D., and the oldest of the four Sanskrit inscriptions that this country has bequeathed to us dates back to this time.[15] The bronze statuette of Poseidon found at Tra-vinh (Cochin China), which was inspired by the famous statue by Lysippus on the Isthmus of Corinth,[16] and the various objects that came from the excavations at Oc Eo in western Cochin China, south of Phnom Bathé—the most ancient of which is a gold medallion bearing the likeness of Antoninus Pius, dated 152 A.D.[17]—obviously do not constitute evidence of Indianization. But this Roman medallion from Oc Eo was found near other objects that are definitely Indian, notably intaglios and seals with Sanskrit inscriptions which date from the same epoch and from following centuries.[18]

The Chinese begin to speak of the kingdom of Champa, on the coast of present-day Vietnam, in 190–93 A.D. The most ancient archaeological vestige found to date in the Cham territory is the Đông-dương (Quang-nam) Buddha, which is one of the most beautiful specimens of Buddhist art. It has been identified with the style of Amarāvatī,[19] but it is in reality of Gupta influence and dates at the earliest back to the fourth century.

On the Malay Peninsula, the Chinese mention petty Indian states from the second century A.D. Sanskrit inscriptions do not go back any farther than the fourth century.[20]

In the archipelago, the Sanskrit inscriptions of Mūlavarman in the region of Kutei, Borneo, date back to the beginning of the fifth century A.D. and those of Pūrṇavarman, in the western part of Java, to the middle of the same century. But certain images of the Buddha are more ancient; the most notable of these are the one discovered in the Celebes,[21] which is the oldest and corresponds to the tradition of Amarāvatī and of Ceylon (fourth to fifth centuries?), the one found in southern Jember Province (eastern Java),[22] which shows Singhalese influence (fourth and fifth centuries), and the Buddha of the hill of Seguntang at Palembang (Sumatra).[23]

In summary, none of these findings can be dated before the time of Ptolemy (second century A.D.).[24] Ptolemy's geographical nomenclature for trans-Gangetic India was full of place names with Sanskrit correspondences. In the preceding century, Pomponius Mela, Pliny the Elder, and the *Periplus of the Erythrean Sea*[25] were still only vaguely aware of a country of gold, "Chryse," lying beyond the mouth of the Ganges.

Yet, Gabriel Ferrand, erroneously believing that Java was already Indianized in 132 A.D. and supposing "that the Indianization of the Javanese was effected only slowly, during the course of many years," concluded that "the beginnings of Indianization in trans-Gangetic India and in Indonesia must have been before our era."[26] This conclusion is not supported by the evidence if we recall what has been said about the antiquity and permanence of the contacts between India proper and the countries beyond the Ganges. A greater flow of traders and immigrants, including some religious leaders and scholars, would have sufficed to start the rapid founding of Indian kingdoms in Southeast Asia where there had previously been only aboriginal tribes. The oldest Sanskrit inscription of Funan is no later than a century and a half from the date fixed by the Chinese for the founding of Funan by the union of a Brahman and a naked woman. It seems to me prudent to say simply that Indian colonization was intense in the second and third centuries of our era and came to fruition in the fourth and fifth.

We could add that the presence of Buddha images of Indian origin on the coast of central Vietnam and in the Celebes before the fifth century is proof of the extensiveness of the voyages which, during the first centuries of the Christian Era, carried the Indians to the farthest limit their colonization was to attain.

3. THE CAUSES OF INDIAN EXPANSION

How can we explain this maritime drive of a people who regarded crossing the "black water" and contact with the Mlecch'a barbarians as bringing defilement and pollution?[27] Remote causes have been sought in the bloody conquest of Kalinga on the eastern coast of India by Aśoka in the third century B.C. and the exodus of population it presumably provoked, but we might well ask why the effects were not felt until three centuries later. At most, we can suppose that the fugitives, if there were any, opened the way to a more important later emigration.

One theory is that pressure was exerted on the mass of the Indian population by the invasions of the Kushans in the first century A.D.,[28] an idea chronologically more acceptable. But this is nothing more than a hypothesis, still not supported by any precise fact.

Another hypothesis is that high-caste Indian adventurers were allowed to seek their fortunes overseas.[29] But this is only a hypothesis.

On the other hand, there are a number of indications that the Indian expansion in the first centuries A.D. was commercial in origin.

The contact that was established between the Mediterranean world and the East following the campaign of Alexander, the founding of the empire of Aśoka and later that of Kanishka in India, and the birth in the West of the Seleucid Empire and the Roman Empire caused an increase in the luxury trade that was deplored by the Latin moralists of the first century.[30] Gold, spices, aromatic woods (sandalwood, eaglewood), and fragrant resins (camphor, benzoin) were among the products of the countries and islands beyond the Ganges. The names Takkola ("market of cardamom"), Karpūradvīpa ("the island of camphor"), Narikeladvīpa ("the island of coconut palms"), and many other similar Sanskrit place names show what attracted the Indians to these regions.

But perhaps the attraction of these countries would not have been so great if they had not also had the reputation of being endowed with a richness in gold, a reputation that is echoed in the Greek and Latin geographic names.

"I would like," writes Sylvain Lévi,[31] "apropos of Kanakapurī, 'the city of gold' in Dvīpāntara, to stress the role played by the search for gold in the Indian expansion in Farther India; it is not only the classical appellations of Survarṇabhūmi and Suvarṇadvīpa that give evidence of this. The names of rivers and streams recorded by Ptolemy in his tables evoke the 'fabulous metal' which the sands of Indonesia still bear. The multiple dialectic alterations of these names may reveal the origins of the seekers for gold. It was gold that attracted India to the Eldorado of the Far East."

To us, for whom the nineteenth century has revealed the rich veins of California and South Africa, the gold capacity of Farther India does not seem to justify a parallel "rush." But gold was much rarer then and—an important fact that does not seem to have been considered in relation to the Indianization of Farther India—India had just lost its principal source of the precious metal shortly before the beginning of the Christian Era. India had obtained gold from Siberia by way of caravans that crossed Bactria, but the great movements of the peoples of Central Asia in the last two centuries before the Christian Era [32] had cut this route and deprived India of the gold it needed. India therefore imported a great number of coins from the Roman Empire in the first century A.D., as is shown by the fact that, although some coins must have been melted down for current use, many of these old Roman coins have been found in Indian soil.[33] The emperor Vespasian (69–79 A.D.), however, succeeded in arresting this flight of currency, which carried a grave threat to the imperial economy, and it is possible that the desire to find another source was one of the reasons for the exodus of adventurers toward the "Golden Chersonese."

Their distant voyages abroad were to be favored, moreover, by two circumstances of very different character.

The first was material: the development of the Indian and Chinese navies [34] and the construction of seaworthy junks that were capable of transporting from 600 to 700 passengers. These junks were constructed by a technique in use in the Persian Gulf.[35] A detailed description of this technique given in a Chinese text of the third century A.D.[36] shows that the fore and aft rigging may have made possible sailing "close to the wind," a major innovation in the art of navigation. We know, moreover, that around the middle of the first century A.D. the Greek pilot Hippalos discovered the periodic alternation of the monsoons, which the Muslims knew but had kept secret. From this discovery resulted a prodigious increase in maritime commerce between India and the ports of the Red Sea, door of the West. "We must come down fourteen centuries later," writes Sylvain Lévi,[37] "to encounter an economic revolution comparable to this one, when the Portuguese revolutionized the commercial routes of all Asia." Communications by sea between India and the lands and islands of the East could not help but be affected.

The other circumstance, of a moral nature, was the development of Buddhism. By abolishing, for the Indians converted to the new religion, caste barriers and exaggerated concern for racial purity, it removed, with one stroke, the shackles previously placed on their maritime voyages by the fear of being polluted by contact with barbarians.

We are thus led to represent the eastward expansion of Indian civilization at the beginning of the Christian Era as the result, at least to a considerable degree, of commercial enterprises—as the result of a continual outflow of seamen, originally recruited from among "merchants of the sea," of whom many types are depicted in ancient Buddhist literature and who seem to have had a particular devotion to the Buddha Dīpankara, "Calmer of the Waters."[38] "A great number of Jātaka tales," says Sylvain Lévi, "have dealt with maritime adventures; the sea and seafaring clearly occupied an important place in the life of India at the time when these tales were conceived."[39]

4. HOW THE FIRST INDIAN ESTABLISHMENTS WERE FORMED

By what process did traders in quest of spices and adventurers in search of gold succeed in constructing communities homogeneous enough and strongly enough organized to give birth to veritable Indian kingdoms?

We can only attempt to give an idea by observing what happened in similar circumstances in other places and at other times.

Gabriel Ferrand has written many pages about the Indianization of Java that undoubtedly contain a good deal of guesswork but that can be applied with some reservations to other countries of Farther India.[40] I will cite a few extracts:

> The true picture must have been something like this: two or three Indian vessels sailing together eventually arrived at Java. The newcomers established relations with the chiefs of the country, earning favor with them by means of presents, treatment of illnesses, and amulets. In all the countries of primitive civilization where I have lived, from the Gulf of Aden and the east coast of Africa to China, the only effective means of peaceful penetration is the same: welcoming gifts, distribution of curative medicines and of preventive charms against all ills and dangers, real and imaginary. The stranger must be or pass for a rich man, a healer, and a magician. No one could use such procedures better than an Indian. He would undoubtedly pass himself off as of royal or princely extraction, and his host could not help but be favorably impressed.
>
> Immigrants to this *terra incognita,* the Indians did not use interpreters. Thus they had to learn the native language which was so different from their own, thereby surmounting the first obstacle to acquiring the freedom of the city among the Mlecch'as. Next came union with the daughters of the chiefs;[41] only then were the strangers able to use their civilizing and religious influence with any chance of success. Their native wives, instructed for this purpose, became the best propaganda agents for the new ideas and faith; since they were princesses or noble daughters, if they affirmed superiority over the manners, customs, and religions inherited from the ancestors, their compatriots could scarcely contradict them.
>
> The Javanese had no equivalent terms to use in transmitting these social, moral, and religious innovations. It was therefore necessary to impose Indian terminology in all these domains, terminology that is still being used in Indonesia after two thousand years.

Ferrand bases this hypothetical reconstruction on his personal experience of the Islamic penetration among the Sakalava of Madagascar. R. O. Winstedt, an expert on the Indonesian world, paraphrases this passage in his *A History of Malaya*[42] and adds other parallels: "In time," he writes, "a few [of the Indians] married into leading Indonesian families and brought Hindu ideas of kingship, just as more than a thousand years later the Muslim Tamils married into the families of the Sultans and Bendaharas of Malacca. The coming of the Hindu appears to have been very similar to the later arrival of the Muslim from India and the Hadramaut, the Brahmin and the Kshatriya taking the place to be usurped by the Sayid."

This was without doubt the first stage of Indianization. It consisted of individual or corporate enterprises, peaceful in nature, without a preconceived plan, rather than massive immigration which would have resulted in greater modification of the physical type of the Austro-Asiatic and Indonesian peoples than has occurred. This is, basically, the opinion of N. J. Krom,[43] to which it has been objected that it would have been difficult for the Indians assembled in coastal settlements to establish the sort of contacts necessary for exerting any cultural influence whatever over the indigenous societies in the interior.[44]

But after the merchants, and in a sense in their wake, came the cultivated elements, belonging to the first two castes. We must assign a large role to these elements, without which we could not understand the birth of these civilizations of Farther India, so profoundly impregnated with Indian religion and Sanskrit literature. In this regard, one scholar has come forward with the hypothesis that the Brahmans, whom the merchants described as famous for their magic powers, were summoned by the native chiefs to augment their power and prestige.[45] We have, moreover, proof of this, for in Funan, the first kingdom about which the Chinese give us precise information, some officials were Indians, as is shown by the fact that their family name was the ethnic term *Chu*[46] by which the Chinese designated people native to India. It is not certain that all of these immigrants, of a much higher social class than the first seamen, were pure Indians of ancient Aryan stock, however. Among them there were undoubtedly a good number of non-Aryans who, in these new lands and in their relations with the natives, had a good chance for pretending to belong to social classes that had rejected them in India proper.

I have already indicated the influence of Buddhism on the increase in maritime commerce, and we have seen that, in many cases, the most ancient evidences of Indianization are the images of the Dīpankara Buddha, who enjoyed great favor with the seamen frequenting the southern islands. The role of Buddhism is undeniable; it seems to have opened the way, thanks to its missionary spirit and lack of racial prejudice. But most of the kingdoms founded in Farther India soon adopted the Sivaite conception of royalty, based on the Brahman-Kshatriya pairing and expressed in the cult of the royal linga.[47] K. A. Nilakanta Sastri writes that ". . . just as in classical times the Greek colonists carried with them the fire from the sacred hearth of the city, a token of their filial relation to the land they left in search of new abodes, so also the Hindu colonists carried a cult with them, the cult of Śaivism in which Śiva played the role of the guardian of the state, thanks to the kind offices of his chief devotee. . . ."[48]

The founding of these kingdoms, the transformation of a simple commercial settlement into an organized political state, could come about in two different ways: either an Indian imposed himself as chief over a native population that was more or less strongly impregnated with Indian elements, or a native chief adopted the civilization of the foreigners, strengthening his power by becoming Indianized. The change must have occurred in both ways. In cases of the first type, however, where the dynasty was purely Indian in origin, it is hardly possible that it could long remain so because of the mixed marriages the Indians of necessity entered into. A marriage of this kind was the origin of the dynasty of Funan, as reported by the Chinese. But the elevation of native chiefs to the level of Kshatriya by means of the *vrātyastoma,* the Brahmanic rite for admitting foreigners into the orthodox community,[49] must have been the rule, and epigraphy furnishes examples. The king Mūlavarman, who left Sanskrit inscriptions in Borneo at the beginning of the fifth century,[50] was the son of Aśvavarman, whose name is purely Sanskrit, but his grandfather's name was Kuṇḍunga, which is certainly not. Sanjaya, founder of the Javanese dynasty of Matarām in the eighth century,[51] was the nephew of a certain Sanna, whose name sounds like the Sanskritization of a Javanese name.

Generally speaking, the social structure of India, dominated by the caste system, seems to have undergone profound modifications upon contact with native societies. The genealogies of ancient Cambodia often present a curious mixture of Sanskrit and Khmer names, a fact that prompted Auguste Barth to say that the Brahmans of Cambodia "do not appear to have been very scrupulous about racial purity."[52] It seems, rather, that these Brahmans were obliged to stretch the rules of endogamy considerably if they wanted to found a family. The occurrence of such mixed marriages has been contested.[53] However, a Chinese text of the fifth century[54] affirms that "in the kingdom of Tun-sun there are more than a thousand Brahmans of India. The people of Tun-sun practice their doctrine and *give them their daughters in marriage;* consequently, many of these Brahmans do not go away." [55]

On this point we can evoke the example of South India, where the strictest Brahmans are, physically speaking, pure Dravidians. Louis de La Vallée-Poussin has outlined, with supporting bibliographic references, a living picture of the role assigned to the Brahmans among the tribes of Bengal "in the process of Brahmanization" and shows that "the Brahmans put themselves in the service of the clan for all spiritual matters; either the hardships of the Iron Age forced the worst concessions on them, or the clan truly adapted itself to the exigencies of an obliging orthodoxy." [56]

For his part, Sylvain Lévi [57] notes that Brahmanism, "an amorphous religion without a leader, clergy, orthodoxy, or program," which nevertheless unified India, is still carrying on its work before our eyes. "It recruits new converts relentlessly. Even jungle tribes aspire to possess their own Brahmans. The Brahman, who is brought in through enticement or by raids, begins to recognize in the fetishes of the clan the disguised avatar of his divinities; he then discovers that the genealogy in use by the chief of the clan has a relationship to the epic cycles; in return he imposes his practices, especially the respect for the cow, the initial article of his credo." It may be added that the particular character of Indian civilization, "in which the way of life is bound up with a certain philosophic-religious doctrine, inevitably led to its adoption *en bloc* by the native elite which it attracted. The adoption of Hinduism brought in its train the Indian way of life, and the adoption of the Indian way of life brought in its train the practice of Hinduism. The Indians brought the native chiefs not only a complete administration but an administrative technique capable of being adapted to new conditions in foreign countries." [58]

The inferences we can draw from what still goes on before our eyes in India [59] tend to confirm the evidence in the ancient Chinese sources that the common traits of the countries of the Southern Seas are not those of colonies Indian in population but those of Indianized native societies.

"Thus," says W. F. Stutterheim, speaking of Bali,[60] "small domains appeared, governed by Indian or Indianized princes, in which only the members of the court had to have Indian blood in their veins. The mass of the population remained Indonesian.

Today the *trivaṃśa* (the three highest castes) constitute 7 per cent of the population; the rest are called *kaula* (servants) or *śūdra.*"

This process continued over many centuries by means of the commercial interchange that the founding of the first Indian kingdoms of Farther India favored and intensified, an interchange that may be inferred from Chinese texts. I say "interchange" advisedly, for it is true that, parallel with the voyages of the Indians to the countries of the Orient, there were, after a certain date, voyages of Southeast Asian traders to India, and these Southeast Asian traders settled in "colonies" in a few large ports in India. In analyzing the penetration of Indian civilization, we must consider another element which seems to have been forgotten: that is, the activity of the natives of Southeast Asia who, on returning from a sojourn abroad, must have contributed a great deal to the spread of Indian customs and beliefs in their countries. This assumption seems justified if it is permissible to judge the past by what has happened recently in Asia: Western styles, customs, dress, external signs of good breeding, and taste for certain forms of art, literature, and amusement have been introduced more quickly and easily by Asians returning from Europe or America than by Europeans themselves. It must have been the same at other times in the countries of Farther India, where the penetration of Indian culture was perhaps in part the work of natives impressed by a superior civilization.

Finally we must take account of the propensity of the Indians to reduce to treatises (*śāstras*) the various aspects of their civilization, from law (*dharmaśāstra*) and politics (*arthaśāstra*) to the search for pleasure (*kāmaśāstra*). Without claiming, as has been done,[61] that "the whole of Indian culture in Indonesia was acquired through books and manuals, the Indians themselves playing a quite insignificant or even negligible role," it is certain that all this technical and didactic literature in Sanskrit must greatly have facilitated the penetration of Indian culture abroad.

To conclude these paragraphs on how the Indian establishments were formed, I think it would be well to repeat what I have said elsewhere: [62]

> Indian-style kingdoms were formed by assembling many local groups—each possessing its guardian genie or god of the soil—under the authority of a single Indian or Indianized-native chief. Often this organization was accompanied by the establishment, on a natural or artificial

mountain, of the cult of an Indian divinity intimately associated with the royal person and symbolizing the unity of the kingdom. This custom, associated with the original foundation of a kingdom or royal dynasty, is witnessed in all the Indian kingdoms of the Indochinese Peninsula. It reconciled the native cult of spirits on the heights with the Indian concept of royalty, and gave the population, assembled under one sovereign, a sort of national god, intimately associated with the monarchy. We have here a typical example of how India, in spreading her civilization to the Indochinese Peninsula, knew how to make foreign beliefs and cults her own and assimilate them—an example that illustrates the relative parts played by Indian and native elements in the formation of the ancient Indochinese civilizations and the manner in which these two elements interacted.

5. THE POINTS OF DEPARTURE AND THE ROUTES OF INDIAN EXPANSION

What routes did the voyagers follow, and what were the centers in India from which this civilization radiated over the Indochinese Peninsula and the islands of the south?

It is obvious that the penetration of the archipelago was by sea, but we must wonder if land routes did not also play a role on the peninsula.[63]

Mainland Southeast Asia, extending down through the Malay Peninsula, and island Southeast Asia have been described as constituting a natural "barrier"; "it is only by means of relatively narrow passes like the channel of Singapore or the Sunda Strait that boats coming from the west by way of the Indian Ocean, or from the east by way of the China Sea, can pass from one side to the other." The author of these lines, Father H. Bernard,[64] adds: "The territorial shortcuts were formerly impracticable because the deltas of the Irrawaddy, the Salween, the Menam, the Mekong, and the Red River, sometimes obstructed by tropical vegetation, were backed up by a rugged and inhospitable interior which was not easily crossed until the advent of aviation."

But the Indochinese deltas and their mangroves did not altogether stop the adventurers in search of gold, just as the deserts of Central Asia or the snows of Pamir did not stop the silk merchants or the Buddhist pilgrims in search of sacred texts. Geographic obstacles were sometimes less formidable than the pirates of the sea; it was the growth of piracy in the straits, and later the tyrannical commercial policy of the kingdom of Palembang,[65] that made the land routes so very important, as is demonstrated by archaeological finds.

What could be more tempting, moreover, than to avoid the long way around through the Strait of Malacca and profit by the narrowness of the Isthmus of Kra and of the Malay Peninsula to carry merchandise by one of those natural routes which to our day allow one to go "easily by bicycle from one sea to another in a few hours"?[66] (I do not speak of the Sunda Strait, much farther south in relation to India, which, although sometimes used in antiquity, only achieved real importance after the great sailings by way of the Cape of Good Hope.)

Those seamen who, proceeding from southern India to the countries of gold, did not coast along the shores of Bengal but risked crossing the high seas were able to make use of either the 10-degree channel between Andaman and Nicobar or, farther south, the channel between Nicobar and the headland of Achin. In the first case they would land on the peninsula near Takuapa; in the second, near Kedah. Archaeological research has uncovered ancient objects at these two sites.[67]

One passes without difficulty from Kedah to Singora; from Trang to Phatthalung, to the ancient Ligor, or to Bandọn; from Kra to Chumphọn; and especially from Takuapa to Chaiya. The importance and antiquity of these routes have been revealed by archaeological research.[68]

It was, moreover, possible for travelers coming from central India and for those who sailed along the coast to approach the Gulf of Siam and the China Sea by the route that, from Tavoy, crosses the mountains at the Three Pagodas Pass and descends to the Menam Delta by the Kanburi River. It was on the shores of this river that we noted earlier the very ancient site of Phong Tůk, which is near that of the equally ancient Phra Pathom. Farther north, the approach to the Menam Basin is passable from the west by the route that now joins the port of Moulmein to the town of Rahaeng on one of the branches of the Menam.

Finally, one scholar has postulated the existence of a route connecting the Menam to the Mekong by way of the Khorat Plateau via Si Thep, another ancient site, and the Mun Valley.[69] The cradle of the Indian kingdom of Kambuja, founded in the region of Bassac in the middle Mekong,[70] separated from the lower Mekong and the sea by the unnavigable rapids of Khon, constituted in a sense the terminus of this route.

Still farther north, there was a route connecting India and China through Assam, Upper Burma, and Yunnan. There is clear evidence that this route was used from the beginning of the second century A.D.,[71] and its use probably dates back to the second century B.C. By this route Indian influence, after affecting Upper Burma, reached Nanchao.[72]

Whence came the Indians who emigrated to Farther India, and where did they embark? Much research has been done on this subject. Unfortunately, those who are most involved in this research, the Indian historians, have not always approached it with the desired objectivity: if they were natives of Madras, they attributed the honor of having colonized "Greater India" to the Tamil lands; if they were from Calcutta, to Bengal.

Apart from a Tamil inscription in Sumatra[73] and two on the Malay Peninsula[74]—which allow the Madras school to score a point, although none of these inscriptions date back to the beginning of Indianization—the colonists did not leave vernacular documents abroad that could inform us of their place of origin. Our sources of information on this point are the texts of geographers and of European and Chinese travelers, Indian texts alluding to navigation, and finally the place names, traditions, scripts, and plastic arts of Farther India.

"All the eastern ports of India up to Tāmralipti (Tamluk) contributed to this Indian expansion," writes La Vallée-Poussin,[75] "but the South played the greatest role."

In fact, although the *Periplus of the Erythrean Sea* (§60) indicates that Kamara (Khabari of Ptolemy, i.e., Kāviri-paṭṭinam in the Kaveri Delta),[76] Podoukê (Pondicherry?),[77] and Sōpatma were the three large neighboring ports whence the great ships named *kolandia*[78] set sail for Chryse, Ptolemy (VII, 1, 15) locates the port of departure (*apheterion*) of the voyagers to the Golden Chersonese farther north, near Chicacole.[79] It was at Tāmralipti (Tamluk on the mouths of the Ganges) that the Chinese pilgrims Fa-hsien, in the beginning of the fifth century, and I-ching, at the end of the seventh century, embarked on their return from India to China. It was undoubtedly also at Tāmralipti that merchants starting from Benares or Champa, in the valley of the Ganges, took to the sea in the direction of Suvaṇṇabhūmi, the Land of Gold, from the time of the composition of the *Jātakas*.[80] Finally, it is certain that the large ports of the western coast—Bharukacch'a (Greek Barygaza, modern Broach), Śūrpāraka (Souppara, Sopara), and Muchiri (Greek Muziris, modern Cranganore)—were in touch with the Golden Chersonese.[81]

The information we can draw from the Indian place names transplanted into Farther India is not very conclusive, for these names often appear for the first time in writings of a later date, and the choice of names like Champa, Dvāravatī, Ayodhyā, and other famous cities of Puranic legend does not necessarily prove the Gangetic origin of those who transplanted them into foreign lands. Place names that are less well known offer better evidence. One can, for example, establish a relationship between Tārumā, which the earliest inscription of Java places on the western part of that island,[82] and a locality of the same name located near Cape Comorin. Likewise, the use of the term Ussa (Odra, i.e., Orissa) for Pegu and of Śrīkshetra (i.e., Purī) as an old name for Prome in Burma[83] certainly indicates a relationship between these states and Orissa. The name Kalinga resembles that of Kling used by the Malays and the Cambodians to designate the Indians. The appellation Talaing, applied to the Mons by the Burmese, seems to indicate that at a certain epoch Telingāna, or the Madras region, was in particularly active relations with the Mon country.[84] Following the same line of thinking, we can recall the presence of ethnic names originating in Dravidian India among the Karo Bataks in Sumatra: Choḷa, Pāṇḍya, Pallava, Malayālam.[85]

Dynastic traditions can furnish precious data. An attempt has been made to establish a relationship between the Śailendras of Java and Sumatra and the Śailas of Orissa,[86] but a more satisfactory comparison can be made between the dynastic tradition of the sovereigns of Funan and that of the Pallavas of Kānchī (Conjeeveram).[87] Both the founder and the great Indianizer of Funan were of the Brahmanic clan Kauṇḍinya, a clan that originated in northern India, one branch of which exerted great influence over Mysore around the second century.[88] Various references to the sage Agastya and his cult in Farther India suggest a contribution of the Pāṇḍyas of southernmost India[89] to the work of Indianization.

The paleography of inscriptions furnishes useful particulars: for example, a wave of Bengali influence from the end of the seventh century to the beginning of the ninth century has been attested to by the short-lived use of a pre-Nāgarī script.[90] Unfortunately, the various types of Indian writing are less clearly differentiated the older they are. R. C. Majumdar has tried to show[91] that the script of the oldest Sanskrit inscription of the

Indochinese Peninsula (which dates back to the third century and which came from Funan, not Champa) [92] is derived from the script of the Kushans, used in the central part of northern India. But this revolutionary opinion has been opposed with good arguments by K. A. Nilakanta Sastri,[93] defender of the classic thesis that the alphabets of Farther India originated in southern India, with the influence of the script of the Pallavas predominating.[94]

The plastic arts are of no great help, because the most ancient remains are generally several centuries later than the beginning of Indianization. An exception are the Buddhas called Amarāvatī—in reality of Gupta or Singhalese influence—whose presence in various parts of Farther India has been noted above. They give evidence of a southern preponderance at the beginning of Indianization, although the subsequent influences that have been noted in sculpture—that of Gupta art, then of Pāla and Sena,[95] and the influence of Orissa on images of Burma and Java [96] —give an idea of the diversity of the sources that contributed to the formation and evolution of the plastic arts.

The same conclusion would undoubtedly be revealed by a study of architecture, if we possessed remains dating before the sixth century. In the present state of documentation, the monuments of Farther India are so differentiated from and already so far from their Indian prototypes that one scholar was able to write: "The relationship between the earliest of these edifices and those of India, present or past, is far from striking; without their images, their inscriptions, and various texts that have now disappeared no one at first glance would dream of relating them to Indian temples. At most one senses among them a family likeness, by no means a direct kinship." The author of these lines [97] attributes this fact to the disappearance of an architecture that used light and perishable materials which, if we were familiar with it, would undoubtedly supply the connection we seek. It is generally believed that the monolithic temples of Māmallapuram, constructed at the beginning of the seventh century by the Pallava sovereigns, show the closest affinity with the ancient Indian monuments of Farther India. But southern India is not the only region of India that can claim to have influenced the Indian architecture of Southeast Asia; we cannot help but be struck by the resemblance of the brick towers of pre-Angkorian Cambodia or of ancient Champa with certain brick monuments of central

India,[98] and especially with the temple of Bhitargaon of the Gupta era in the Ganges Valley,[99] possibly a descendant of a common ancestor of the brick towers of India and of Farther India.

From this brief and incomplete review of our sources of information on the origins of Indian expansion toward the east, we derive an impression that can be stated by summarizing with slight modifications the formula of La Vallée-Poussin already cited: all regions of India contributed something to this expansion, and it was the south that played the greatest role. We have perhaps had a tendency to magnify the role of southern India by attributing an exaggerated influence to the Pallavas.[100] Except in Funan, the appearance of the first epigraphic texts and the most ancient archaeological remains coincides with the ascension of the Pallava dynasty; this is probably a coincidence, but it has been transformed into a cause-and-effect relationship. We will see in the following chapter that, at least for Funan, there may be reason to take into account influences from Northwest India, scarcely considered up to now. Nevertheless, the influence of southern India, on the whole, was preponderant[101] and that of Ceylon was far from negligible.[102]

But the Indian expansion was not, I repeat, a historical fact clearly delimited in time and space. It was a phenomenon that touched vast and diverse regions and lasted several centuries; it involved successive waves, local currents of various origins. It was aided by the centers of diffusion constituted by the first Indian kingdoms of the Malay Peninsula, which served, in effect, as relay stations between India proper and the rest of Farther India. The Brahman Kauṇḍinya, second Indianizer of Funan, came from the kingdom of P'an-p'an located on the peninsula.[103] In the south of Sumatra, a great center for the diffusion of Buddhism in the seventh century was Palembang, where foreign scholars like the Chinese I-ching[104] came to study.

Finally, in the research on the origins of this expansion, we must not forget that our sources consist for the most part of data from Farther India, which tell us about the result but rarely about the chain of events that produced it.

Given the nature of the documents on the Indianization of Farther India in the first centuries of the Christian Era—epigraphy, archaeology, and foreign sources—we can write about the evolution and transformation of Indian culture upon contact with indigenous societies and about the retreat of Indianization, but we can say very little about the history of the expansion of Indianization itself and even less about its origins.

6. THE DEGREE OF PENETRATION OF INDIAN CIVILIZATION IN THE AUTOCHTHONOUS SOCIETIES

To what extent did Indian civilization penetrate the mass of the population of Farther India or remain the privilege of an elite? Was the decline of this civilization in the thirteenth century caused by its adoption by a greater and greater number of natives, who caused it gradually to lose its distinctive traits? Or was it caused by the disappearance of a refined aristocracy, impregnated with a culture that remained foreign to the mass of the population? On these questions our sources—notably epigraphy, which especially informs us of the religions and the organization of the courts and ruling classes—do not furnish the desired information.

Historians agree that, under an Indian veneer, most of the population preserved the essentials of their own culture. This at least is the view of Nicholaas J. Krom with regard to Java; and with regard to Bali, W. F. Stutterheim tells us that "Hinduism has always been and still is the culture of the upper classes, but never became completely that of the masses, who were attached to Indonesian animism and to the ancestor cult." [105] It must have been the same in Cambodia, the decline of which in the fourteenth century seems to have been caused by the decline of the Brahmanic aristocracy in the thirteenth century, recorded in an inscription of Sukhothai.[106]

Hinduism, under the particular aspect of the royal cult that it assumed in Farther India,[107] was essentially an aristocratic religion which was not designed for the masses; this explains the ease and speed with which the masses adopted Singhalese Buddhism and Islam at precisely the time when the Indian world was shaken by the repercussions of the Mongol conquests and the Muslim invasions.

Even in the countries where indigenous traditions reacted most strongly and splintered the Indian veneer, however, such was the force of the penetration of Indian culture that its legacy is far from being negligible. We will see, in the Conclusion of this work, that this legacy includes the system of writing, a great part of the vocabulary, the lunar-solar calendar, the virtually unchanged cosmogonic myths, the great epic themes of the *Rāmāyaṇa* and the *Purāṇas,* certain artistic formulas, the administrative and legal framework, and a keen feeling of social rank, last vestige of the caste system.

It is astonishing that in countries so close to China—countries that entered into commercial and diplomatic relations with her from the first centuries of the Christian Era—the cultural influence of the Middle Kingdom has been insignificant, although it was intense in the deltas of Tongking and North Vietnam. We are struck by the fundamental difference of the results obtained in the countries of the Far East by the civilizing activity of China and India.

The reason for this lies in the radical difference in the methods of colonization employed by the Chinese and the Indians. The Chinese proceeded by conquest and annexation; soldiers occupied the country, and officials spread Chinese civilization. Indian penetration or infiltration seems almost always to have been peaceful; nowhere was it accompanied by the destruction that brought dishonor to the Mongol expansion or the Spanish conquest of America.[108] Far from being destroyed by the conquerors, the native peoples of Southeast Asia found in Indian society, transplanted and modified, a framework within which their own society could be integrated and developed.

The Indians nowhere engaged in military conquest and annexation in the name of a state or mother country. And the Indian kingdoms that were set up in Farther India during the first centuries of the Christian Era had only ties of tradition with the dynasties reigning in India proper; there was no political dependence. The exchanges of embassies between the two shores of the Bay of Bengal were made on the basis of equality, while the Chinese always demanded that the "southern barbarians" acknowledge Chinese suzerainty by the regular sending of tribute.

The Chinese commanderies of Vietnam were administered by Chinese governors, while the Indian kingdoms of Farther India were governed by independent sovereigns of native origin or of mixed blood, advised by Indian or Indianized counselors whose activity was chiefly cultural.

Thus, although China exercised a more or less successful political guardianship over these countries for centuries, her civilization did not spread beyond the area of her military conquests.

The peaceful penetration of the Indians, on the other hand, from the beginning extended to the limits of their commercial navigations.

The countries conquered militarily by China had to adopt or copy her institutions, her customs, her religions, her language, and her writing. By contrast, those which India conquered peacefully preserved the essentials of their individual cultures and developed them, each according to its own genius. It is this that explains the differentiation, and in a certain measure the originality, of the Khmer, Cham, and Javanese civilizations, in spite of their common Indian origin.

CHAPTER III

THE FIRST INDIAN KINGDOMS

From Their Origins to the Middle of the Fourth Century

The various factors analyzed in the preceding chapter resulted in the creation of small Indian states governed by leaders bearing Sanskrit names. These states began to appear at the beginning of the third century A.D., thus confirming the data of the tables of Ptolemy.

These states have left only a few archaeological or epigraphical traces from before the fifth century. We know very little about most of them before that date except for the names mentioned by Ptolemy, by the *Niddesa,*[1] and, most important of all, by the Chinese dynastic annals, which carefully register embassies from the countries of the South Seas. The locations of most of these states are uncertain or only approximate.

The smallest of these countries usually had to move in the orbit of the most powerful kingdoms—kingdoms destined for a brilliant future, the history of which we can outline from Chinese texts and epigraphy.

1. THE BEGINNINGS OF FUNAN (FIRST CENTURY A.D.)

The most important of these kingdoms was unquestionably the one the Chinese called Funan. This name is the modern Mandarin pronunciation of two characters once pronounced *b'iu-nâm,*[2] which is the transcription of the old Khmer word *bnam,* the modern form of which is *phnom,* "mountain." The kings of this country had as their title the term meaning "king of the mountain"—in Sanskrit *parvatabhūpāla* or *śailarāja,* in Khmer *kurung bnam.*[3] The Chinese came to designate the country by this royal title.

The center of the country was located on the lower course and delta of the Mekong, but its territory at its apogee must have encompassed southern Vietnam, the central Mekong, and a large part of the Menam Valley and the Malay Peninsula. Its capital for a time was Vyādhapura, "the city of hunters" [4]—in Chinese T'e-mu, which is perhaps a transcription of a Khmer term (*dmâk, dalmâk*) having the same meaning.[5] The city was situated in the vicinity of the hill of Ba Phnom and of the village of Banam, two places in the Cambodian province of Prei Vèng which, in their names, perpetuate to our day the memory of the ancient name. According to the *History of the Liang*[6] this capital was 500 *li* (200 km.) from the sea. This is approximately the distance that separates Ba Phnom from the site of Oc Eo,[7] where there was located, if not that port itself, at least an emporium where foreign merchants were established.

The first information about Funan comes from an account left by the mission of the Chinese envoys K'ang T'ai and Chu Ying who visited this country in the middle of the third century.[8] The original of their narrative is lost, but there remain fragments of it scattered in the annals and in various encyclopedias. These, along with a Sanskrit inscription of the third century, constitute our basic documentation on the first two centuries of the history of this kingdom.

According to K'ang T'ai, the first king of Funan was a certain Hun-t'ien, that is, Kauṇḍinya, who came either from India or from the Malay Peninsula or the southern islands.[9] This king, having dreamed that his personal genie delivered a divine bow to him and directed him to embark on a large merchant junk, proceeded in the morning to the temple, where he found a bow at the foot of the genie's tree. He then boarded a ship, which the genie caused to land in Funan. The queen of the country, Liu-ye, "Willow Leaf," wanted to pillage the ship and seize it, so Hun-t'ien shot an arrow from his divine bow which pierced through Liu-ye's ship. Frightened, she gave herself up, and Hun-t'ien took her for his wife. But, unhappy to see her naked, he folded a piece of material to make a garment through which he had her pass her head. Then he governed the country and passed power on to his descendants.

This is the Chinese version of the dynastic origins of Funan. It is without doubt a distortion of an Indian legend, reported more faithfully by a Sanskrit inscription of Champa.[10] According to this version, the Brahman Kauṇḍinya, having received a javelin from the Brahman Aśvatthāman, son of Droṇa, threw it to mark the location of his future capital, then married a daughter of the king of the Nāgas, named Somā, who gave birth to a royal line.[11]

This mystical union—which was still commemorated at the court of Angkor at the end of the thirteenth century in a rite mentioned by the Chinese envoy Chou Ta-kuan,[12] and of which the modern Cambodian annals have preserved the memory [13]—is identical with that from which the Pallava kings of Kānchī, in southern India, claim to issue.[14] Opinions differ, however, on the vague origin of this legendary theme.[15]

In any case, the historical events that were forced to fit this plot could not have occurred later than the first century A.D., for as early as the following century we find in Funan historical personages whose existence is documented by epigraphy and by Chinese historians.

According to the *History of the Liang,* one of Hun-t'ien's descendants, named Hun-p'an-huang in the Chinese, was over ninety years old when he died. He was succeeded by "his second son P'an-p'an who transmitted the care of his affairs to his great general Fan Man," [16] whose full name was Fan Shih-man, according to the *History of the Southern Ch'i.*[17] "After three years' reign, P'an-p'an died. The people of the kingdom all chose [Fan Shih-man] as king. He was brave and capable. Once more, with his powerful troops, he attacked and subjected the neighboring kingdoms; all acknowledged themselves his vassals. He himself took the title Great King of Funan. Then he had large ships built, and sailing all over the immense sea he attacked more than ten kingdoms, including Ch'ü-tu-k'un, Chiu-chih, and Tien-sun. He extended his territory five or six thousand *li.*" [18]

2. THE INDIAN STATES OF THE MALAY PENINSULA IN THE FIRST CENTURIES OF THE CHRISTIAN ERA

Rolf Stein believed that in the above text Ch'ü-tu-k'un ought to be read Ch'ü-tu, Tu-k'un, etc., and that Ch'ü-tu should be identified with Ch'ü-tu-ch'ien (or -kan), which he believed corresponded to the Kattigara of Ptolemy.[19] This country, founded by emigrants from Chu-wu (north of Quang-tri, between Cửa Tung and Cửa Việt), should be sought in Cochin China, where the most recent studies also tend to place Kattigara.[20] But Ch'ü-tu-k'un must probably be dissociated from Ch'ü-tu-ch'ien.[21]

Tien-sun is undoubtedly identical with Tun-sun, which a text of the fifth-sixth centuries describes as a dependency of Funan.[22] We can locate it with some probability on the Malay

Peninsula, and more precisely on the two shores of the Isthmus of Kra; [23] the sparse data available on the other countries lead in the same direction.[24] The conquests of Fan Shih-man should then in part have been carried out on the peninsula, where some other Chinese texts reveal the existence of small Indianized states at an early period.

The most ancient of these states appears to have been Lang-ya-hsiu, the founding of which the *History of the Liang* (502–56) places "more than 400 years ago." [25] This kingdom, which will reappear at the end of the seventh century under the names Lang-chia-shu, Lang-ya-ssu-chia, etc., is the Langkasuka of the Malayan and Javanese chronicles; [26] its name survives in modern geography as the name of a tributary to an upper reach of the Perak River.[27] It must have been situated astride the peninsula and have had access at the same time to the Gulf of Siam in the Pattani region [28] and to the Bay of Bengal, north of Kedah, therefore controlling one of the land transportation routes discussed in the preceding chapter.

Tāmbralinga, on the eastern coast of the Malay Peninsula between Chaiya to the north and Pattani to the south, had its center in the region of Ligor,[29] whence comes a Sanskrit inscription dating from the sixth century or afterward.[30] Mention of it in the Pali Buddhist canon (*Niddesa*) in the form "Tambalingam" [31] proves that this kingdom already existed around the second century.

It is the same with Takkola,[32] cited in another Buddhist text, the *Milindapaṇha;* it is generally agreed that this town was located at Takuapa on the west coast of the Isthmus of Kra or perhaps farther south.[33] As for the port whose name is transcribed by the Chinese T'ou-chü-li and which is sometimes identified with Takkola, Paul Wheatley [34] has shown that this name is in reality Chü-li and that it corresponds to the Kōli of Ptolemy, probably on the estuary of Kuantan. It was from here that the embassy sent by Funan to India in the third century embarked.

If we disregard the megalithic tombs of Perak and Pahang and the discoveries of Indian and "Roman" pearls at Kota Tingi in Johore,[35] which belong to the domain of proto-history, it is from the region of Kedah and of Perak that the most ancient epigraphical and archaeological remains of the Malay Peninsula come.

Those discovered at Kedah are from various periods. They attest to the antiquity of this site, which we will hear of again later under its Sanskrit name Kaṭāha and its Chinese name Chieh-ch'a. But, like the other inscriptions and archaeological discoveries,[36] they do not date as far back as Ptolemy, the *Niddesa,* or the Chinese texts, that is, as far back as the time of the conquests of Funan on the peninsula.[37]

3. FUNAN (SECOND TO THIRD CENTURIES)

It is difficult to be precise about the extent of Fan Shih-man's conquests. There is good reason to consider his name as a transcription of that of the king Śrī Māra mentioned in the venerable Sanskrit stele of Vo-canh (in the region of Nha-trang).[38] This inscription was long thought to be Cham,[39] but in 1927 Louis Finot attributed it to a vassal state of Funan.[40] If the identification of Śrī Māra[41] with Fan Shih-man is correct, the inscription—which emanates from a descendant of Śrī Māra who reigned, to judge by the script, in the third century—must be considered as one of the sources for the history of Funan. It is apparent from this inscription that at the time when it was engraved and in the region where it was erected (that is, present-day Khanh-hoa) Sanskrit was the official language of the royal chancellery.

The Chinese texts already cited inform us that the great conqueror Fan Shih-man died in the course of an expedition against the Chin-lin, or Frontier of Gold, which, there is cause to believe, corresponds either to Suvaṇṇabhūmi, the Land of Gold of the Pali texts, or to Suvarṇakuḍya, the Wall of Gold of the Sanskrit texts (Lower Burma or the Malay Peninsula).[42] A nephew of Fan Shih-man, named Fan Chan, murdered the legitimate heir, Chin-chêng, and usurped power. But about twenty years later, Fan Chan was assassinated by a son of Fan Shih-man named Ch'ang. This was vengeance without result, for Ch'ang was murdered in his turn by the general Fan Hsün, who proclaimed himself king.

These events took place roughly between 225 and 250,[43] and it is between these two dates, during the reign of Fan Chan, that Funan entered into relations with the Indian dynasty of the Muruṇḍas and sent its first embassy to China. I have emphasized elsewhere[44] that the significance of "this event, which has more to do with commercial preoccupations than with political ambitions, confers a certain importance on his reign. In this epoch, that of the Three Kingdoms, southern China (the Kingdom of Wu), finding it impossible to use the land route held by the Wei for its commercial relations with the West, sought to procure for itself by sea the luxury goods it wanted.[45] Now Funan occupied a privileged position on the route of maritime commerce and constituted an inevitable way station for the seamen who used the Strait of Malacca as well as for those, probably more numerous, who crossed the isthmuses of the Malay Peninsula. Funan was perhaps even the terminus for navigation hailing from the eastern Mediterranean, if it is true that the Kattigara of Ptolemy was located on the western coast of Cochin China."

"The reign of Fan Chan is important," writes Paul Pelliot;[46] "it was this usurper who was the first to enter into official and direct relations with the princes of India. A text of the fifth century tells that a certain Chia-hsiang-li, native of a country T'an-yang, which was located, it seems, west of India, reached India, and from there Funan. It was he who taught the king Fan Chan what marvels this country could show the visitor, but the voyage was long; to go and return might take three or even four years. Was King Fan Chan captivated by the report of Chia-hsiang-li? At least we know from a reliable source that he sent one of his relatives named Su-wu on an embassy to India. This person embarked from T'ou-chü-li, perhaps Takkola,[47] which indicates that the influence of Funan extended as far as the Indian Ocean at that time. The embassy arrived at the mouth of the Ganges and ascended the river to the capital of a prince who undoubtedly, as Sylvain Lévi has recognized, belonged to the Muruṇḍa dynasty. The Indian king took the foreigners on a tour of his country; he then took leave of them, entrusting them with four horses of the Indo-Scythian country as a present for their king and giving them the Indian Ch'en-sung as a companion. By the time Su-wu got back to Funan, four years had passed since his departure."

It was also Fan Chan, according to the *History of the Three Kingdoms,* who in 243 "sent an embassy [to China] to offer a present of musicians and products of the country."[48]

Was it also he who was author of the previously cited Sanskrit inscription, and whom this text designates as a member of the family of Śrī Māra? This is not impossible, for Fan Chan, son of the sister of Śrī Māra, might well have claimed to be related to his predecessor.

The usurper Fan Hsün, who succeeded Fan Chan after having murdered a son of Fan Shih-man, received some time about 245 to 250 the Chinese mission of K'ang T'ai and Chu Ying, who met an envoy of the Muruṇḍas at his court.[49]

This Chinese mission established relations with Funan that resulted in the dispatch by Fan Hsün of a series of embassies to China from 268 to 287. These embassies are mentioned in the *History of the Chin*.[50] The last three, those from 285 to 287, were perhaps a consequence of the resurgence of maritime commerce after the reunification of China by the Chin in 280, a reunification that stimulated an increased desire on the part of the court for the products and imported luxuries of the countries to the south.

It is undoubtedly to K'ang T'ai that we are indebted for the first information about the country: "There are walled villages, palaces, and dwellings. The men are all ugly and black, their hair frizzy; they go about naked and barefoot. Their nature is simple and they are not at all inclined toward thievery. They devote themselves to agriculture. They sow one year and harvest for three. Moreover, they like to engrave ornaments and to chisel. Many of their eating utensils are silver. Taxes are paid in gold, silver, pearls, perfumes. There are books and depositories of archives and other things. Their characters for writing resemble those of the Hu [a people of Central Asia using a script of Indian origin]."[51]

4. THE BEGINNINGS OF CHAMPA: LIN-YI (FROM THE END OF THE SECOND TO THE MIDDLE OF THE FOURTH CENTURIES)

The *History of the Chin* inserts a report in the biography of T'ao Huang, Chinese governor of Tongking, in which he complains, in around 280, of the raids of Lin-yi. This kingdom, he says, "touches Funan in the south. Their tribes are numerous; their friendly bands render mutual aid; taking advantage of the ruggedness of their region, they do not submit [to China]."[52]

Lin-yi was the first center of the Cham country, which enters into history at the end of the second century. In fact, Chinese texts place its foundation about the year 192.[53] A native official, Ch'ü-lien, profiting by the weakening of power of the later Han dynasty, carved a domain for himself at the expense of the Chinese commandery of Jih-nan (between Hoanh-sơn and the Col des Nuages) and proclaimed himself king in the southernmost subprefecture, that of Hsiang-lin, which corresponds roughly to the southern part of the present-day Vienamese province of Thừa-thiên. At first it was thought that Lin-yi, "the capital Lin," was an abbreviation of Hsiang-lin-yi, "the capital of Hsiang-lin," [54] but one scholar has proposed more recently that it is an ethnic name.[55] The creation of the kingdom of Lin-yi in 192 had been preceded a half-century before, in 137, by a first attempt to invade Hsiang-lin by a band of about a thousand barbarians from beyond the frontiers of Jih-nan; [56] their name Ch'ü-lien, although written with different characters, can scarcely be dissociated from that of the founder of Lin-yi.[57]

In any case, it is almost certain that these "barbarians from beyond the frontiers of Jih-nan" were, if not all Chams, at least Indonesians who, if they were not already Indianized, soon became so.

We will see, in the course of its history, that the Cham country was divided into a certain number of natural provinces corresponding to the coastal plains. Present-day Quang-nam, with the archaeological sites of Tra-kiêu, Mi-sơn, Đông-dương, is in a sense the holy land of Champa.[58] The beautiful bronze Buddha found at Đông-dương is evidence of the antiquity of Indian penetration in this region which bears—is it pure chance?—the name Amarāvatī. South of Amarāvatī, the principal centers mentioned in epigraphy are Vijaya in present-day Binh-định, Kauṭhāra in the plain of Nha-trang, and Pāṇḍuranga in the region of Phan-rang. The inscriptions show that in the eighth century Cham was spoken in the southern provinces. But originally these southern provinces were part of Funan. This is proved by the presence, in the region of Nha-trang, of the inscription of the third century emanating from a king of Funan—the descendant of Śrī Māra (i.e., Fan Shih-man) who perhaps was none other than Fan Chan.

We have no ancient evidence, like that for Funan, of the Indianization of the Chams and the dynastic tradition of their kings; the Chinese are silent on these two points, and it is not until an inscription of the ninth century that there appears for the first time the name of Maharshi Bhṛigu, personage of the *Mahābhārata,* eponymous ancestor of the dynasty of the Bhārgavas, from which the kings of Champa claimed they had descended. As for the name of Champa itself, whence is derived the name of the Chams, although it does not appear in epigraphy until the beginning of the seventh century, it may be much older.

The descendants of Ch'ü-lien took advantage of the dismemberment of China at the fall of the Han to expand to the north. Between 220 and 230, one of them sent an embassy to Lü Tai, governor of Kwangtung and Chiao-chih (Tongking), in connection with which the name Lin-yi, along with that of Funan, appears for the first time in a Chinese text. Lü Tai, says the *History of the Three Kingdoms,* "sent emissaries to spread Chinese civilization south beyond the frontiers. Also the kings of Funan, Lin-yi, and T'ang-ming (?) each sent an embassy to offer tribute." [59] This was purely a formality, for in 248 the armies of Lin-yi rose to pillage the villages of the north and retained from their raid, following a great struggle on the bay south of Ron, the territory of Ch'ü-su, that is, the region of Bađôn on the Song Gianh.[60] Finally the king Fan Hsiung, grandson of Ch'ü-lien in the female line,[61] renewed these attacks around 270, aided, it was said, by the king of Funan, Fan Hsün. It took ten years for the governor of Tongking, T'ao Huang, to force the people of Lin-yi back within their frontiers. From the beginning, their attempts at expansion toward the north clashed with the push of the Vietnamese toward the south. The battles fought by these two representatives of rival civilizations—the Indianized Chams and the Sinicized Vietnamese—were waged from Hoanh-sơn to the Col des Nuages; they were to result in the final retreat of the Chams in the fourteenth century.

In 284, Fan Yi sent the first official embassy to China—if we do not count the one sent to the governor of Chiao-chih between 220 and 230. During the second half of his long reign of over fifty years, Fan Yi had a certain Wen as his counselor. Wen is identified in various texts as a Chinese, native of Yang-chou in Chiang-su, who had settled in Lin-yi, but he may have been a Sinicized native.[62] He went to China in 313 and 316, and there learned various techniques; his knowledge of the material civilization of China was of great value to his master. By gaining the confidence of the old king, he managed to get himself named general in chief and then to brush aside the heirs to the throne. At the death of Fan Yi, which took place unexpectedly in 336, he succeeded him.

Fan Wen, whose capital was located in the region of Hué, pacified the savage tribes and in 340 sent an embassy to the Chin emperor requesting that the northern frontier of his kingdom be fixed at Hoanh-sơn Mountain. When the emperor hesitated to abandon the fertile lands of Jih-nan to him, he seized them in 347, thus giving his states the boundary he had desired. He died in 349 in the course of another expedition north of his new frontier.

CHAPTER IV

THE SECOND INDIANIZATION

From the Middle of the Fourth Century to the Middle of the Sixth Century

1. FUNAN: REIGN OF THE INDIAN CHAN-T'AN (357)

In 357, for reasons that are not known, Funan fell under the domination of a foreigner. In the first month of this year, according to the dynastic histories of the Chin and the Liang, "T'ien Chu Chan-t'an, king of Funan, offered tamed elephants as tribute."[1] T'ien Chu is the Chinese name for India, and the expression "T'ien Chu Chan-t'an" means "the Indian Chan-t'an."[2] Sylvain Lévi has shown[3] that Chan-t'an is a transcription of *chandan,* a royal title in use among the Yüeh Chih, or Indo-Scythians, and especially among the Kushans in the line of Kanishka. "Tien Chu Chan-t'an or Chu Chan-t'an," he writes,[4] "was thus a royal personage who originally came from India; his title Chan-t'an seems to connect him to the same stock as Kanishka. The connection is not at all surprising. A century before Chu Chan-t'an, in the time of the Wu (220–64), between 240 and 245 according to the calculations of Paul Pelliot, the king of Funan had sent one of his relatives on an embassy to India to the sovereign Mou-luan (Muruṇḍa) who reigned on the Ganges, and in return Muruṇḍa had sent four horses of the Yüeh Chih as a present to the king of Funan. We know what close lines united the Muruṇḍas with the Yüeh Chih; it has even been maintained[5] that Muruṇḍa was the dynastic title of the Kushans. We also know that the Kushans extended their domination over the Ganges, at least as far as Benares, where they installed a satrap. In 357, under the great emperor Samudragupta, all of northern India had submitted to the Gupta dynasty; the Scythian invaders had been driven back. It is possible that a branch of the Kushan family, driven from the banks of the Ganges, sought its fortune beyond the Bay of Bengal, in this Land of Gold (Suvarṇabhūmi, or Chryse) which had been opened to adventurers from India."

Perhaps the reign of this foreigner, coming after the exchange of embassies with the Muruṇḍas, accounts for some connections we are tempted to establish in several fields between Funan and ancient Cambodia on the one hand and the Iranian world on the other. We will see later[6] that at the end of the fifth century the servant of a king of Funan bore the name or title Chiu-ch'ou-lo, which could be identical with the title *kujula* in use among the Kushans. A little later, in the seventh century,[7] we see a Scythian (Śaka) Brahman arriving from the Dekkan and marrying the daughter of the king Īśānavarman I. The pre-Angkorian iconography of the images of Sūrya, with their short tunics, short boots, and sashes similar to those of the Zoroastrians, is clearly of Iranian inspiration.[8] Perhaps these images represent the sun considered as a Magian or Scythian Brahman, who is designated by the name Śakabrāhmaṇa in Angkorian epigraphy.[9] Even the cylindrical coiffure of the pre-Angkorian images of Vishnu can be regarded as showing Iranian influence. It is true that the immediate model for this hair style is found in the sculpture of the Pallavas,[10] but we know that one group of scholars is convinced of the northern origin of the Pallavas, maintaining that they are descendants of the Pahlavas, that is, the Parthians.[11] Finally, even the name of the Kambujas, heirs of Funan, may be related to that of the Iranian Kambojas.[12] It would be imprudent for the moment to push these comparisons too far, but they are worth pointing out, especially because the discovery at Oc Eo,[13] in western Cochin China, of an intaglio representing a libation to fire and of a cabochon with a Sassinid effigy[14] has furnished tangible proof of Funan's relations with the Iranian world.

The reign of the Indian or Indo-Scythian Chan-t'an constitutes a sort of interlude in the history of Funan. The date 357 is the only one we know for his reign, and we hear nothing more of Funan before the end of the fourth century or the beginning of the following century.

2. CHAMPA: THE FIRST SANSKRIT INSCRIPTIONS OF BHADRAVARMAN (THIRD QUARTER OF THE FOURTH CENTURY)

In Lin-yi the son of Fan Wen, named Fan Fo by the Chinese historians, continued the traditional policy of expansion to the north. But following unsuccessful campaigns in 351 and 359, he was obliged to restore Jih-nan to China and to send embassies there in 372 and 377.[15]

Fan Fo was succeeded by Fan Hu-ta, who was either his son or his grandson. Fan Hu-ta is ordinarily identified with Bhadravarman, whose Sanskrit name we know from the inscriptions he left in Quang-nam [16] and in Phu-yên.[17] This identification is based on the probable date of the inscriptions [18]—around the year 400 according to Abel Bergaigne [19] and Louis Finot.[20] But another author has advanced strong paleographic arguments that the inscriptions are several decades older; [21] we would then have to attribute them to Fan Fo, whose name could be an exact Chinese transcription of Bhadravarman.[22]

Rolf Stein [23] has suggested, as an explanation for the discrepancy between the Chinese and Sanskrit names of the kings of this epoch, that the kings of Lin-yi who were known to the Chinese, with their capital in the region of Hué, may in fact have been different from the kings with Sanskrit names living in Quang-nam, which was conquered later by Lin-yi.

Bhadravarman was the founder of the first sanctuary constructed in the cirque of Mi-sơn and dedicated to Śiva Bhadreśvara, whose name—following a custom we encounter constantly from then on—recalls that of the founder. This temple was destroyed by a fire two and a half centuries later.

Bhadravarman's capital was discovered east of Mi-sơn, on the site of present-day Tra-kiêu, whose environs have yielded stone inscriptions in a script identical with that of the inscriptions mentioned above. Two of them [24] mark the limits of the domain consecrated to Bhadreśvara, and the third,[25] which is the oldest known text in the Cham language or in any Indonesian dialect, contains an imprecatory formula ordering respect for the "nāga of the king"—undoubtedly a reference to the protective divinity of a spring or well. This vernacular text shows that in the fourth century the country was inhabited by a Cham-speaking population.

Did these representatives of the Indonesian linguistic group receive Indian civilization directly by sea or through the intermediary of already Indianized neighbors in territories to the west or south? It is as difficult to answer this question as it is to know whether the Ch'ü-lien, founders of Lin-yi at the end of the second century, were already Indianized. The discovery in Quang-nam of the famous Buddha of Đông-dương, a bronze statue of Gupta influence, perhaps of Indian origin, and dating in all probability from the fourth century, unfortunately does not prove much either about the origin of Indianization or about the possible priority of Buddhism in a country which, except for a Buddhist upsurge at the end of the ninth century, manifested an especially profound attachment to Hindu cults. Such images are easily transportable, and there is nothing to prove that the Đông-dương Buddha was brought to Indochina immediately after it was made.

Nor is it easy to say whether, as some believe, the east coast of the peninsula, on which the Indian expansion took place, was already impregnated by Dongsonian civilization, remains of which are found north of the natural frontier of Hoanh-sơn.

What is important is that, through the Chams, Indian civilization spread to this frontier—which, moreover, it never crossed. It was assimilated by the Chams. And, although their divided country was poorly suited for the building of a strong and centralized state, this civilization nevertheless resisted the pressure of Sino-Vietnamese civilization for centuries.[26]

The inscriptions of Bhadravarman are the first documents we possess dealing with the religion of the court. They reveal "the dominance of the cult of Śiva-Umā, without prejudice to the homage rendered to the two other members of the Trimūrti." [27] Later inscriptions found at Mi-sơn show us that the god Bhadreśvara was represented by a linga. It is the oldest known royal linga [28] in Farther India.

The following information on the customs of Lin-yi at this time has been extracted from Ma Tuan-lin: [29]

> The inhabitants build the walls of their houses with baked bricks, coated with a layer of lime. The houses are all mounted on a platform or terrace called *kan-lan.*[30] The openings are generally placed on the north side, sometimes on the east or west, without fixed rule. . . . Men and women have no other costume than a length of *ki-pei* cloth [31] wrapped around the body. They pierce their ears so they can suspend little rings from them. The distinguished people wear leather shoes; the common people go barefoot. These customs prevail equally in Funan and in all the kingdoms situated beyond Lin-yi. The king wears a tall hat decorated with gold flowers and trimmed with a silk tassel. When he goes out he mounts an elephant; he is preceded by conches and drums, sheltered under a parasol of *ki-pei,* and surrounded by servants who wave banners of the same material. . . .

Weddings always take place in the eighth moon.[32] It is the girls who ask for the boys in marriage, because the girls are considered to be of inferior nature.[33] Intermarriage among people who bear the same family name is not prohibited. These foreigners are of a bellicose and cruel character. Their weapons consist of bows and arrows, sabers, lances, and crossbows of bamboo wood. The musical instruments they use are very similar to those we use ourselves: the cithern, the violin with five strings, the flute, etc. They also use conches and drums to warn the people. They have deep-set eyes, noses that are straight and prominent, and black, frizzy hair. The women fasten their hair on top of the head in the form of a hammer.... The funeral ceremonies of a king take place seven days after his death, those of the great mandarins three days after death, and those of the common people the day after death. Whatever the status of the deceased, the body is carefully wrapped, carried to the shore of the sea or of a river accompanied by the sound of drums and by dances, and then burned on a pyre set up by those present. When a king's body is burned, the bones spared by the fire are put in a gold urn and thrown into the sea. The remains of mandarins are put in a silver urn and thrown into the waters at the mouth of the river. In deaths of completely undistinguished persons, an earthenware vase taken to river waters suffices. Relatives of both sexes follow the funeral procession and cut their hair before turning away from the shore; it is the only mark of the very short mourning. There are, however, some women who stay in mourning in another form throughout their lives: they let their hair hang loose and dishevelled after it has grown out. These are the widows who have vowed never to marry again.

3. THE STATES OF THE MALAY PENINSULA AND INDONESIA FROM THE FOURTH TO THE SIXTH CENTURIES

The appearance of the first inscriptions in the Sanskrit language in Champa, in the second half of the fourth century, slightly preceded that of similar texts on the Malay Peninsula and in Borneo and Java.

The fragmentary stone inscriptions found at Cherok Tekun, opposite Penang, have been attributed to the fourth century.[34] The inscription of Bukit Meriam at Kedah, which reproduces two Buddhist verses, dates from the same or a slightly later time.[35] Archaeological research in the vicinity of Kedah has brought to light an inscription of the fifth or sixth centuries containing three Buddhist stanzas.[36] A bronze statuette of the Buddha found in this region dates from the same era.[37]

The most interesting document comes from the northern district of Province Wellesley.[38] It is an inscription carved on the upper part of a pillar, on each side of which is delineated a stupa crowned by a seven-tiered parasol. The Sanskrit text consists of a Buddhist stanza and a prayer for a successful voyage formulated by the master of the junk (mahānāvika), Buddhagupta, of the Red-Earth Land (Raktamṛittikā). The script seems to date from the middle of the fifth century.

This Red-Earth Land,[39] known to the Chinese under the name Chih-t'u, must have been located on the Gulf of Siam, in the region of Phatthalung[40] or Kelantan.[41] The Chinese do not speak of it before 607,[42] but it had by then already existed at least a century and a half, since, as we have seen, it is mentioned in the inscription of Buddhagupta.

In Perak, the late Neolithic site of Kuala Selinsing, probably occupied at an early date by Indian seamen, has yielded a Cornelian seal, engraved with the name of Śrī Vishṇuvarman. This seal has caused much ink to flow;[43] the writing appears to be earlier than the sixth century and recalls that of certain seals of Oc Eo.[44]

On Tun-sun, which was discussed in the last chapter, a Chinese text of the fifth-sixth centuries gives us some information worth citing: "When they are sick they make vows to be buried by birds. They are led outside the city with songs and dances, and there the birds devour them. The bones that are left are burned and placed in a jar which is thrown into the sea. If the birds do not eat them, they are put in a basket. As for those buried by fire, they are thrown into the fire. The ashes are collected in a vase which is buried and to which sacrifices of unlimited duration are made."[45]

Lang-ya-hsü, or Langkasuka, which has also been discussed in the preceding chapter, first established relations with China in 515[46] under a king who bore the name Bhagadatta. "The inhabitants," says the *History of the Liang*,[47] "men and women, let their hair hang loose and wear sleeveless garments of a material they call *kan-man*,[48] whose fiber is *ki-pei* cotton. The king and the dignitaries of the kingdom add a piece of dawn-red material over their dress which covers the upper part of the back between the shoulders. They gird their loins with a cord of gold and suspend gold rings from their ears. The women adorn themselves with beautiful scarves enriched with precious stones. The walls in this country are built of brick. The houses have double doors and pavilions surmounting terraces. The king leaves his palace seated on an elephant, sheltered under a white canopy, preceded by drums and banners, and surrounded by ferocious-looking soldiers."

To the north, Langkasuka bordered on P'an-p'an,[49] a country located on the Gulf of Siam, very likely on the Bay of Bandọn. P'an-p'an's first embassy to China goes back to the period 424–53,[50] and others followed up to 635. At about the time of the first embassies, as we shall see, another Kauṇḍinya, second Indianizer of Funan,[51] came from P'an-p'an.

"Most of the people," writes Ma Tuan-lin,[52] "live on the shores of the sea. These barbarians do not know how to build defensive walls; they are content to set up palisades. The king half reclines on a golden couch shaped like a dragon. The important persons of his entourage go on their knees before him, bodies straight and arms crossed in such a way that the hands rest on the shoulders. At his court one sees many Brahmans, who have come from India to profit from his munificence and are very much in favor with him. . . . The arrows used in the kingdom of P'an-p'an have tips made of very hard stone; the lances have iron tips sharpened on both edges. In this country there are ten monasteries for monks and nuns who study the sacred books of Buddhism and who eat meat but do not drink wine. There is also a Taoist monastery. The rules of the latter are very strict; these monks abstain from both meat and wine."

Paul Wheatley[53] proposes to locate another state, Tan-tan, which sent ambassadors to China in 530 and 535, much farther south, in the region of Trengganu.

In Borneo, the seven inscriptions on pillars found in the sultanate of Kutei seem to date back to around 400.[54] They emanate from a King Mūlavarman, grandson of a certain Kuṇḍunga (whose name is perhaps Tamil or Indonesian,[55] but surely not Sanskrit) and son of the Aśvavarman who is considered the founder of the dynasty (*vaṃśakartṛi*). These inscriptions are associated with a sanctuary bearing the name Vaprakeśvara, in which must be recognized Siva or Agastya or a local divinity—unless, of course, the sanctuary is not a funerary monument at all.[56]

Furthermore, there are scattered over Borneo—along the Kapuhas, Rata, and Mahakam rivers—more or less clear traces of Indianization. A beautiful bronze Buddha of Gupta style has been found at Kota Bangun[57] in the province of Kutei. Aside from the inscriptions already mentioned, Kutei has yielded some Brahmanic and Buddhist images of undetermined date[58] in a grotto of Mount Kombeng and in an estuary of the Rata River.

Someone has proposed placing the Barhiṇadvīpa named in the *Vāyupurāṇa* (XLVIII, 12) on Borneo.[59] This name recalls, in fact, the name P'o-ni by which the Chinese designated Borneo from the ninth century.[60] But that is a very fragile connection. There is also a P'o-li in the Chinese, from which a king with the family name Kauṇḍinya sent embassies to China in the first quarter of the sixth century.[61] If this P'o-li does not refer to the island of Bali, it might refer to Borneo (unless, of course, it was not situated east of Java at all).

The island of Java is probably mentioned in the *Rāmāyaṇa* (*Yāvadvīpa*)[62] and in Ptolemy (*Iabadiou*).[63] But because of a curious phenomenon of inhibition, the scholars who are most audacious in other matters of phonetic relationships seem stricken with incomprehensible timidity when presented with a place name distantly, closely, or even very closely resembling Java. They use all pretexts to seek locations anywhere but on the island that bears this name. It is true that Java and Sumatra were often thought to form one island and that Marco Polo called Sumatra "Java Minor." But is this sufficient reason to brush Java aside and systematically relate all the evidence concerning countries denominated *Java, Yāva* (*dvīpa*), *Yeh-p'o-t'i,* and *She-p'o* to Sumatra, or, indeed, sometimes to Borneo or even to the Malay Peninsula?

In Java, aside from the Buddha of Gupta style found in the east that has already been mentioned,[64] the oldest traces of Indian penetration are the four stone inscriptions discovered in the westernmost part of the island, that is, the region commanding the Sunda Strait. "It is significant," writes the scholarly editor of these inscriptions,[65] "that these earliest records of Hindu settlement are found exactly in that part of the Island where the Dutch traders first established their 'factories' and which became the centre from which the power of Holland has spread over the whole of the Indian Archipelago. The geographical position of the Batavian coast with regard to the continent of India and Sumatra and the special advantages its configuration offers to shipping and trade are circumstances which will easily account for a coincidence that is certainly not due to mere chance."

Pūrṇavarman, king of the land of Tārumā, is the author of these Sanskrit inscriptions. The script can be dated around 450, a little later than that of Mūlavarman in Borneo. The name Tārumā, which is preserved to our day in the name of the river Chi Tarum, in the region of Bandung, is also encountered in southern India about twenty kilometers north of Cape Comorin.[66] The inscriptions reveal that Pūrṇavarman, who talks about his father and grandfather without naming them, observed Brahmanic rites and was engrossed in irrigation works in his kingdom. Two of the inscriptions reproduce his footprints; it has been suggested, not without some justification, that what we see here is a symbol of the taking possession of the neighboring region of Buitenzorg where the inscriptions were found.[67] The kingdom of Tārumā still existed in the seventh century, if it is this kingdom that the *New History of the T'ang* mentions under the name To-lo-ma as having sent ambassadors to China in 666–69.[68]

In Sumatra, as in Java and the Celebes,[69] the most ancient Indian archaeological vestige is a statue of the Buddha in Amarāvati style.[70] It was found west of Palembang, in the vicinity of the hill Seguntang. It is unusual in that it is made of granite, a stone unknown in Palembang; it must therefore have been brought from elsewhere. Perhaps it came from Bangka, an island off the east coast of Sumatra, which, if Bangka can be identified with the Vanga mentioned in the Pali *Niddesa,* was certainly frequented at an early date by Indian seamen.[71] The presence of this statue of the Buddha in Palembang is proof of the antiquity of the Indian penetration in the country.

There has been much discussion about whether three countries mentioned by the Chinese from the fifth century, Yeh-p'o-t'i, She-p'o, and Ho-lo-tan, were located in Java. Yeh-p'o-t'i is where the pilgrim Fa-hsien stopped in 414 on his return voyage from India to China and where he found ascetics but few traces of Buddhism.[72] She-p'o is where the monk Guṇavarman, early prince of Kashmir, preached Buddhism shortly before 424. She-p'o sent ambassadors to China in 433 and 435.[73] Ho-lo-tan is placed on the island of She-p'o by the *History of the Early Sung* (470–78). It also sent ambassadors between 430 and 452.[74] The most recent research tends to place these three countries on the Malay Peninsula,[75] marking, in this case, a regression with regard to the conclusions of Pelliot, according to whom they corresponded wholly or in part to the island of Java. Yet there seems to be better evidence for locating Yeh-p'o-t'i on the western coast of Borneo[76] than for identifying it with Java. As for Ho-lo-tan, the question is complicated by the fact that the king who promoted the embassy of 434 bore the name Shih-li-p'i-ch'o-yeh, which transcribes perfectly into Śrīvijaya. Since it is customary usage in this region for kings to lend their names to their kingdoms, one wonders if the name of this king was the origin of the name of the kingdom which appears at the end of the seventh century in southern Sumatra.[77]

Kan-t'o-li, first mentioned in the *History of the Liang* in connection with events occurring in the middle of the fifth century, is located by general agreement in Sumatra. It presumably preceded Śrīvijaya and may have had its center at Jambi.[78] Between 454 and 464, a king of Kan-t'o-li, whose name in Chinese characters can be restored to Śrī Varanarendra, sent the Hindu Rudra on an embassy to China. In 502 a Buddhist king, Gautama Subhadra, was reigning. His son, Vijayavarman, sent an embassy to China in 519.

4. THE RESUMPTION OF INDIAN EMIGRATION AND THE SECOND INDIANIZATION OF FUNAN IN THE FIFTH CENTURY

In summary, a wealth of Chinese and archaeological evidence indicates that the Indian penetration is as ancient in the islands as on the peninsula. And the inscriptions of Mūlavarman in Borneo and Pūrṇavarman in Java and the development of diplomatic relations with China indicate a sudden renewal of Indianization of Farther India in the first half of the fifth century that can be attributed, if not to an influx of immigrants, at least to the influence of cultural elements that we can assume, on the basis of various kinds of evidence, came from eastern and southern India.

The immediate causes of this movement have been sought in the history of India, and much imagination has been used to connect the new dynasties of Farther India to Indian royal houses. I shall not follow the authors who have ventured onto this shaky ground.[79] It does seem probable, however, that the conquests of Samudragupta (around 335–75) in southern India, and the subsequent submission of the Pallava sovereign with his viceroys,[80] produced serious perturbations that in turn resulted in the exodus of certain elements of the southern aristocracy to the countries to the east. We have seen that Lévi attributes the probable presence of an Indo-Scythian on the throne of Funan in 357 to the conquest of the Ganges Valley by Samudragupta. This episode was perhaps merely the prelude to a more general movement which, from the middle of the fourth century to the middle of the fifth, brought princes, Brahmans, and scholars to the peninsula and islands, which were already Indianized and in regular contact with India. These Indians were responsible for the introduction of Sanskrit epigraphy in Champa, then in Borneo and Java.

It was in the same period and doubtless for the same reasons that Funan was infused with a new dose of Indian culture, to which we owe the oldest inscription of Funan after the stele of Vo-canh.

The *History of the Liang* informs us that one of the successors of the Indian Chan-t'an was Chiao Chen-ju (Kauṇḍinya).[81] "He was originally a Brahman from India. There a supernatural voice told him: you must go reign over Funan. Kauṇḍinya rejoiced in his heart. In the south, he arrived at P'an-p'an. The people of Funan appeared to him; the whole kingdom rose up with joy, went before him, and chose him king. He changed all the laws to conform to the system of India. Kauṇḍinya died. One of his successors, Shih-li-t'o-pa-mo (Śrī Indravarman or Śreshṭhavarman), during the reign of the emperor Wen of the Sung (424–453) presented a petition and offered products of his country as a present." [82] This offering of products refers to the embassies that the *History of the Early Sung* places in 434, 435, and 438. It is without doubt this King Shih-li-t'o-pa-mo who is referred to in the same work in the passage stating that, in 431–32, "Lin-yi wanted to destroy Chiao-chou [Tongking] and borrow soldiers from the king of Funan. Funan did not consent."[83]

5. CHAMPA FROM THE END OF THE FOURTH CENTURY TO 472

Before going on with the history of Funan, which, from around 480, offers an almost continuous thread, we must say a few words about what was taking place in Lin-yi.

At the death of Fan Fo (Bhadravarman?), his son or grandson Fan Hu-ta, who had succeeded him in 380, invaded Jih-nan in 399, but suffered defeat. Encouraged by the anarchy that marked the fall of the Chin dynasty in China, he renewed his incursions in 405 and 407, then in 413 embarked on a new expedition in the territories situated north of Jih-nan, from which he did not return.

The son of Fan Hu-ta, whom the *History of the Liang* calls Ti Chen, succeeded him, but abdicated in favor of a nephew and went to India. Perhaps it is he whom an inscription of the seventh century[84] names Gangārāja, celebrated "for his qualities, among which knowledge and heroism were recognized as royal qualities. The royalty difficult to abandon [he abdicated it]. The view of the Ganges is a great joy, he told himself, and went from here to the Ganges." It seems that he was succeeded by a person who appeared in an inscription of the seventh century under the name of Manorathavarman[85] and who was perhaps his nephew.[86]

What happened following this is not very clear. Around 420 a king of obscure origin appeared who called himself Yang Mah, "the Prince of Gold." After an unsuccessful raid in Tongking, he requested investiture from the court of China in 421. At his death, which took place the same year, his young, nineteen-year-old son succeeded him under the same name and continued to engage in piracy north of his states. In 431 he sent more than a hundred ships to pillage the coasts of Jih-nan. The Chinese reacted vigorously and, while the king was absent, laid siege to Ch'ü-su (in the region of Bađôn on the lower Song Gianh). The Chinese, however, were hindered by a storm; they were unable to exploit their success fully and had to lift the siege. It was at this point that Yang Mah tried in vain to borrow troops from Funan "to destroy Chiao-chou [Tongking]." In 433 he requested from the court of China that he be given the government of Chiao-chou; this request had no success whatsoever. The Cham excursions having begun again stronger than ever, the new governor of Tongking, T'an Ho-chih, in 446 undertook strong repressive measures. Renouncing the negotiations in which the Chams had shown most remarkably bad faith, T'an Ho-chih laid siege to Ch'ü-su, which he took and sacked. Another battle delivered the capital, situated in the region of Hué,[87] to the Chinese; from it they withdrew 100,000 pounds of pure gold. The king died brokenhearted.

His successor was his son or grandson Fan Chen-ch'eng, who sent embassies to China in 456, 458, and 472. This king is probably none other than Devānīka, who left a Sanskrit inscription at Bassac near Vat Ph'u.[88]

6. THE LAST KINGS OF FUNAN (480–550); CHAMPA FROM 484 TO 529

Around 480 the *History of the Southern Ch'i* speaks for the first time of the Funanese king She-yeh-pa-mo (Jayavarman), whose family name is Chiao Chen-ju—that is, descendant of Kauṇḍinya.[89]

"This prince," writes Pelliot,[90] "sent merchants to Canton who, on their return, were thrown up on the coast of Lin-yi (Champa), as was the Indian monk Nāgasena, who was on board with them. Nāgasena reached Funan by an overland route and, in 484, King Jayavarman sent him to offer presents to the Chinese emperor and to ask the emperor at the same time for help in conquering Lin-yi. Several years earlier, a usurper had taken possession of the throne of that country; the texts on Lin-yi call him Tang-ken-ch'un, son of the king of Funan, but King Jayavarman represents him as one of his vassals named Chiu-ch'ou-lo.[91] The emperor of China thanked Jayavarman for his presents, but sent no troops against Lin-yi. Through the often obscure phraseology of Jayavarman's petition we distinguish at least two things: we see that Sivaism was dominant in Funan but that Buddhism was practiced at the same time. The petition is in great part Buddhist, and it was delivered by an Indian monk who had resided in Funan. Furthermore, it was during the reign of Jayavarman that two Funanese monks established themselves in China;[92] both knew Sanskrit quite well, for they had used it during their lives to translate the sacred books."

The same passage of the *History of the Southern Ch'i* from which Pelliot extracted his information adds some facts on the material civilization of Funan that merit reproducing:

> The people of Funan are malicious and cunning. They abduct and make slaves of inhabitants of neighboring towns who do not pay them homage. As merchandise they have gold, silver, and silks. The sons of great families cut brocade to make themselves sarongs; the women pass their heads [through some material to dress themselves]. The poor cover themselves with a piece of cloth. The inhabitants of Funan make rings and bracelets of gold, and plates of silver. They cut down trees to make their dwellings. The king lives in a storied pavilion. They make their city walls of wooden palisades. An enormous bamboo, with leaves eight or nine feet long, shoots up along the seashore. Its leaves are woven to cover the houses. The people also live in raised dwellings. They make boats that are eight or nine *chang* long.[93] These are hewn to six or seven feet in width. The bow and stern are like the head and tail of a fish. When the king travels, he goes by elephant. Women can also go on elephants. To amuse themselves, the people have cock fights and pig fights. They have no prisons. In case of dispute, they throw gold rings and eggs into boiling water; these must be pulled out. Or else they heat a chain red-hot; this must be carried in the hands seven steps. The hands of the guilty are completely scorched; the innocent are not hurt. Or else the accused are made to jump into the water. The one who is right enters the water but does not sink; the one who is in error sinks.[94]

A later text, the *History of the Liang*,[95] adds these details:

> There where they live, they do not dig wells. Several scores of families have a pond in common where they draw water.[96] Their custom is to worship the sky spirits. They make bronze images of these sky spirits; those that have two faces have four arms, and those that have four faces have eight arms. Each hand holds something—sometimes a child, sometimes a bird or a four-legged animal, or else the sun or the moon. The king, when he goes out or returns, travels by elephant; the same is true of the concubines and people of the palace. When the king sits down, he sits sideways, raising his right knee and letting his left knee fall to the ground.[97] A piece of cotton material is spread before him, on which vases of gold and incense-burners are laid. In time of mourning, the custom is to shave off the beard and hair. There are four kinds of burial for the dead: "burial by water," which consists of throwing the corpse into the river currents; "burial by fire," which consists of reducing it to ashes; "burial by earth," which consists of burying it in a pit; and "burial by birds," [98] which consists of abandoning it in the fields.

The reign of Jayavarman marks for Funan an epoch of grandeur which is reflected in the regard shown Funan by the Chinese emperor. On the occasion of the embassy of 503, an imperial order says: "The king of Funan, Kauṇḍinya Jayavarman, lives at the limits of the ocean. From generation to generation he [and his people] have governed the distant lands of the south. Their sincerity manifests itself afar; through their many interpreters they offer presents in homage; it is fitting to reciprocate and show them favor and accord them a glorious title. This is possible [with the title of] General of the Pacified South, King of Funan." [99]

We have seen that a son or vassal of Jayavarman who fled to Champa had himself proclaimed king there on the death of Chen-ch'eng and that in 484 Jayavarman asked the emperor of China in vain to help him punish the usurper.[100] We do not know what Jayavarman did. What is certain is that in 491 the usurper still reigned under the name Fan Tang-ken-ch'un and got himself recognized by the court of China as king of Lin-yi. But in the following year, 492, he was dethroned by a descendant of Yang Mah, named Chu Nong, who reigned six years and was drowned in the sea in 498. We know nothing about his successors, Fan Wen-k'uan, Fan T'ien-k'ai (perhaps Devavarman), and P'i-ts'ui-pa-mo (Vijayavarman), except the dates of the embassies of 502 to 527. In 529 there came to power a new dynasty whose origins and history will be traced in the following chapter.

Jayavarman, "Great King of Funan," died in 514. We have no inscriptions emanating from him, but his first queen, named

Kulaprabhāvatī, and one of his sons, named Guṇavarman, have each left us a Sanskrit inscription in the writing of the second half of the fifth century.

On a stele found in Cambodia in the southern part of the province of Takèo, Queen Kulaprabhāvatī, desiring to retire from the world, tells of the founding of a hermitage consisting of a dwelling and an artificial lake.[101] The prefatory stanza of the text is Vishnuite in inspiration.

It was also a Vishnuite inscription, in a script that appears to be slightly older, which was engraved by order of Guṇavarman, son of the king who was "the moon of the Kauṇḍinya line," on the pillar of a small temple at Thap-mưới, in the Plaine des Joncs in Cochin China. It commemorates the foundation "of a realm wrested from the mud," of which Guṇavarman, "although young," was chief, and of a sanctuary named Chakratīrthasvāmin[102] that contained the footprint of Vishnu. Whereas the footprints of Pūrṇavarman in Java perhaps marked, as has been said, the taking possession of a country after a military conquest, these prints of Vishnu mark a peaceful conquest, after drainage and partial raising of embankments in a region that is even today very marshy and inundated during part of the year.[103]

It is probable that the mother of Guṇavarman is none other than Queen Kulaprabhāvatī.[104] And it is not impossible that Guṇavarman was that son of Jayavarman[105] who, according to the *History of the Liang,*[106] was deprived of the throne at the death of his father in 514 and assassinated by his eldest brother, Liu-t'o-pa-mo (Rudravarman), the offspring of a concubine.

Rudravarman, who sent various embassies to China between 517 and 539, was the last king of Funan. A Sanskrit inscription of the province of Bati[107] tells us that he was reigning at the time the Buddhist monument mentioned in the inscription was constructed. That Buddhism was flourishing in Funan at this time is clear from a passage in the *History of the Liang* which states that a Chinese embassy was sent to Funan between 535 and 545 to ask the king of this country to collect Buddhist texts and to invite him to send Buddhist teachers to China. The king of Funan chose the Indian Paramārtha or Guṇaratna of Ujjayinī, who was then living in Funan, for this mission. He arrived in China in 546, bringing 240 bundles of texts with him.[108] A stele of the seventh century names Rudravarman as the predecessor of Bhavavarman I, the first king of pre-Angkorian Cambodia.[109] An inscription of the tenth century represents him as the founder of a line of kings tracing their origin to the couple Kauṇḍinya-Somā, who reigned after the successors of Śrutavarman and of Śreshṭhavarman, descendant of Kambu.[110] We will see in the following chapter how this genealogical tradition must be evaluated. It suffices here to say that the irregularity of the succession of Rudravarman to the throne seems to have provoked in the provinces of the middle Mekong a movement of unrest, directed by Bhavavarman and Chitrasena, that resulted in the dismemberment of Funan in the second half of the sixth century.

Funan was the dominating power on the peninsula for five centuries. For a long time after its fall, it retained much prestige in the memories of following generations. The kings of pre-Angkorian Cambodia, as we shall see in the next chapter, adopted its dynastic legend; those who reigned at Angkor strove to relate their origin to the Adhirājas, or supreme kings, of Vyādhapura; [111] and the Javanese sovereigns of the eighth century revived the title Śailendra, "king of the mountain."

I have already reproduced extracts from the Chinese dynastic histories that reveal what little we know about the society and customs of the inhabitants of Funan. From the point of view of religion, the various Indian cults are seen there successively or simultaneously. The two Kauṇḍinyas who Indianized the country were Brahmans; they stayed to implant Sivaite rites, which were certainly flourishing in the fifth century. The *History of the Southern Ch'i* states that during the reign of Jayavarman "the custom of this country was to worship the god Maheśvara (Siva). The god continually descends on Mount Mo-tan." [112] This undoubtedly refers to the sacred mountain from which the kings and the country itself got their name. Near the capital and marking the center of the kingdom, it was the place where the heavens communicated with the earth, which explains why "the god continually descends" there. He was no doubt materialized there in the form of the linga of Śiva Giriśa,[113] "frequenting the mountain." A passage of the *History of the Liang* cited earlier speaks of images with *two* faces and four arms, which must have been of Harihara —that is, Vishnu and Siva united in a single body. The existence of Vishnuite cults is clear from the inscriptions of Guṇavarman and his mother. Finally, the Theravada Buddhism that used the

Sanskrit language, of which we have evidence from the third century, was flourishing in the fifth and sixth centuries, during the reigns of Jayavarman and Rudravarman.

Apparently no architecture has survived. But, even if everything has perished, an interesting hypothesis [114] gives us reason to believe that at least certain edifices of pre-Angkorian art, covered with a series of minute terraces decorated with little niches, reproduce the principal characteristics of the monuments of Funan. In this hypothesis the *mukhalinga,* or linga with a face, is intimately associated with this architecture.

As for human sculpture, the statues of the Buddha in Gupta style,[115] the mitred Vishnus and the Hariharas of pre-Angkorian Cambodia,[116] and, most of all, the images of Sūrya found in Cochin China,[117] although not, strictly speaking, belonging to the art of Funan, give some idea of what its statuary may have been like.

7. THE OLDEST EVIDENCE OF THE PYUS OF THE IRRAWADDY AND THE MONS OF THE MENAM

Finally, we must say a few words about the Indianized states of the western part of the Indochinese Peninsula. Because of their geographical position it would seem that they ought to have been penetrated by Indian culture earlier and more profoundly than Funan, Champa, and the other kingdoms of Farther India; they offer, however, only rare and quite late archaeological and epigraphical remains for the period before the middle of the sixth century. It would be imprudent to conclude from this negative argument that they were Indianized later, for various circumstances may have caused the disappearance or delayed the discovery of older remains. The almost total silence of Chinese sources for the period in question is due to the fact that the envoys from China to the kingdoms of the south at that time used the sea route and the countries situated farthest from China for the seamen were the last to establish relations with her.[118]

It seems, however, that by the third century the Chinese had entered into contact via Yunnan with the kingdom of P'iao, which corresponded roughly with the Irrawaddy Basin. The name of this kingdom is the Chinese transcription of the word Pyu.[119] The Pyu tribe, which constituted the vanguard of the Tibeto-Burman migration and called itself Tirchul,[120] occupied the region around Prome. The ancient sites surrounding this town have yielded fragments of texts extracted from the Pali canon written in a script that goes back to around the year 500.[121] These documents prove the existence of a Buddhist colony of southern origin in a region which the Chinese pilgrims of the seventh century called Śrīkshetra and in which a dynasty of kings bearing Sanskrit names reigned in the eighth century.

The Pyus had for neighbors the Burmese to the north and the Mons to the south. Local chronicles trace the history of these peoples back to the time of the Buddha, who, according to the chronicles, himself came to the region. They give a long list of kings [122] which cannot be verified at all. The example of the Cambodian chronicle, which bears no relation to the reality revealed by epigraphy for the pre-Angkorian epoch, scarcely encourages us to consider the Burmese lists reliable. Moreover, the dates given in the Burmese lists differ extraordinarily from one text to another. For the period before the sixth century, all we can really learn from the local chronicles is that there existed in the north, in the rich rice-producing plain of Kyaukse and in the region of Pagan, clusters of Pyus who had received Buddhism from northern India [123] and that in Lower Burma there were colonies of Indians who had come from Orissa. Of these colonies the principal one was Sudhammavatī (or Sudhammapura)—that is, Thaton [124]—at the mouth of the Sittang, where a local legend has it that Buddhaghosa, the celebrated monk of the Singhalese church of the fifth century, was born and died.[125]

In the Menam Basin, the only sites that are earlier than the middle of the sixth century are those already mentioned: Si Thep,[126] Phra Pathom, [127] and Phong Tửk.[128] We are almost completely ignorant of the kingdoms that have left these remains: we know neither their names nor the names of their sovereigns. All we can say is that they must have recognized the more or less effective sovereignty of Funan. The Buddhist sites of Phra Pathom and Phong Tửk from the seventh century on were part of the Mon kingdom of Dvāravatī, which may or may not have existed already in the fifth or sixth century. As for Si Thep, where the images of Vishnu are preponderant, it was part of the Khmer territory—perhaps as early as the end of the sixth century, but in any case during the period when the Angkor kings extended their domination to the west.

In summary, in the first period of the history of Farther India, which came to an end around 550, we witness the birth of a series of Indian or Indianized kingdoms in regions like the Irrawaddy

Basin, the valley of the lower Mekong, and the plains of central Vietnam, which were to remain seats of powerful states through the centuries, and, inevitably, in sites such as Kedah, Palembang, and the western extremity of Java, whose contemporary history has confirmed their privileged economic, commercial, or strategic position.

In most cases, Buddhism seems to have opened the way for the cultural penetration of India: the statues of the Buddha found in Siam (Phong Tủk and Khorat), in Vietnam (Đông-dương), in Sumatra (Palembang), in Java, and in the Celebes mark, right from the start, the extreme limits of the domain reached by Indianization. State Sivaism with its cult of the royal linga is not witnessed until a little later. As for Vishnuism, it did not appear before the fifth century.

Too often we know nothing about these kingdoms other than their names, recorded by Chinese historians on the occasion of the sending of embassies. Only Funan and Champa, which entered into relations with China at an early date, have a fairly continuous history.

Even before their constitution into an organized state at the end of the second century, the populations of Indonesian language who formed the nucleus of the Cham people were seeking to expand to the north, into the Vietnamese provinces of the Middle Kingdom. This was the first act of a dramatic conflict between the pioneers of Indian culture and the representatives of Chinese culture, a conflict that lasted fifteen centuries.

As for Funan, which at times played the role of a true empire, the civilization that it developed in the valley of the Mekong prepared the soil for the efflorescence of Khmer civilization, one of the most beautiful flowers that Indian influence has produced in India beyond the Ganges.

CHAPTER V

THE DISMEMBERMENT OF FUNAN

From the Middle of the Sixth Century to the End of the Seventh Century

1. THE END OF FUNAN AND THE BEGINNING OF CAMBODIA OR CHENLA (550–630)

The last embassy to China from Rudravarman of Funan was in 539. Although the *New History of the T'ang* continues to mention embassies from Funan in the first half of the seventh century,[1] it indicates that meanwhile a great change had taken place in the country: "The king had his capital in the city T'e-mu.[2] Suddenly his city was subjugated by Chenla, and he had to migrate south to the city of Na-fu-na."

The oldest text that mentions Chenla is the *History of the Sui:* "The kingdom of Chenla is southwest of Lin-yi. It was originally a vassal kingdom of Funan. . . . The family name of the king was Ch'a-li [Kshatriya]; his personal name was She-to-ssu-na [Chitrasena]; his ancestors had gradually increased the power of the country. Chitrasena seized Funan and subdued it." [3]

The name Chenla, used consistently by the Chinese to designate Cambodia, remains unexplained: no known Sanskrit or Khmer word corresponds to its ancient pronunciation *t'sien-lâp*. But we can locate the center of this state on the middle Mekong, in the region of Bassac, which must have come under the domination of Champa by the end of the fifth century, since a stele has been found there bearing a Sanskrit inscription in the name of the king Devānīka, known to the Chinese by the name Fan Chen-ch'eng.[4]

Indeed, the *History of the Sui,* which gives information dating before 589 and so before the total conquest of Funan and the transfer of the capital of Chenla to the south, says: "Near the capital is a mountain named Ling-chia-po-p'o, on the summit of which a temple was constructed, always guarded by a thousand soldiers and consecrated to the spirit named P'o-to-li, to whom human sacrifices are made. Each year, the king himself goes to this temple to make a human sacrifice during the night."[5] The mountain of Vat Ph'u which dominates the site of Bassac bears on its summit a great stone block similar to that which earned Varella the Chinese name Ling (*Linga*parvata)[6] and its modern European name which, in Portuguese documents, is used to designate pagodas.[7] As for P'o-to-li, we can recognize here the first two syllables of *Bhadreśvara*, which was the very name of the god venerated at Vat Ph'u.[8]

According to a Cambodian dynastic legend preserved in an inscription of the tenth century,[9] the origin of the kings of Cambodia goes back to the union of the hermit Kambu Svāyambhuva, eponymic ancestor of the Kambujas, with the celestial nymph Merā, who was given to him by Siva. Her name was perhaps invented to explain that of the Khmers. This legend, entirely different from that of the Nāgī,[10] shows a certain kinship with a genealogical myth of the Pallavas of Kānchī (Conjeeveram).

A line of kings was born from this couple Kambu-Merā. The first of these kings were Śrutavarman and his son Śreshṭhavarman.[11] The latter gave his name to the city Śreshṭhapura, and this name still existed in the Angkorian era—at least as the name of a district located in the region of Bassac. This city may have been founded as a consequence of the taking over of the country from the Chams at the end of the fifth century or beginning of the sixth century. The memory of this conquest is preserved to our day in the oral tradition of the Cambodians, according to which their country was originally constituted at the expense of the Chams of Champasak (Bassac).[12] Kings Śrutavarman and Śreshṭhavarman, according to the tenth-century inscription mentioned above,[13] "broke the ties of tribute in the beginning"; that is, they attained a more or less genuine degree of independence from Funan, or, as the Chinese text says, "gradually increased the power of the country." They felt themselves strong enough, during the second half of the sixth century, to attack the empire to the south. The king of Chenla at that time was Bhavavarman, grandson of the universal monarch (*sārvabhauma*)[14]—that is, of the king of Funan. A late but reliable epigraphic text adds this important detail, that Bhavavarman was the husband of a princess issuing from the maternal family of Śreshṭhavarman,[15] Princess Kambujarājalakshmī, whose name means "fortune of the kings of the Kambujas."

Bhavavarman, whose residence, Bhavapura, must have been located on the northern shore of the Great Lake (Tonle Sap),[16] was thus related to the royal family of Funan and became king of Chenla through his marriage to a princess of this country. This fact enables us to understand why the tenth-century inscription cited previously says that the line of descent of Kambu unites the sun race, which it claimed as its own, with the moon race, that of Funan. We also understand why the line of descent after Śrutavarman and the descendants of Kambu shows reigning kings who traced their origin to Kauṇḍinya and the Nāgī Somā and who claimed Rudravarman of Funan as head of their line. Finally, we understand why the kings of Chenla, successors to those of Funan, adopted the dynastic legend of Kauṇḍinya and the Nāgī.[17] In fact, they were merely preserving their own heritage, since Bhavavarman was himself a prince of Funan.

What were the circumstances surrounding the successful transfer of sovereignty from Funan to Chenla? If, as is probable, the opportunity was provided by the irregularity of the accession of Rudravarman, son of a concubine and murderer of the legitimate heir, two hypotheses present themselves. Either Bhavavarman represented the legitimate branch and took advantage of the death of Rudravarman to make the most of his rights or else Bhavavarman was a grandson of Rudravarman and defended the rights inherited from his grandfather against an attempt at restoration by the legitimate branch. The second hypothesis is the more probable, for the first hypothesis, which makes Rudravarman the last sovereign of a fallen empire, is hard to reconcile with the fact that Rudravarman is later considered "head of the line" while the second hypothesis is in perfect accord with this fact, for it definitely makes Rudravarman the head of the line through which Bhavavarman and his successors connected themselves to the great Funan.[18]

Perhaps religious motives and an antagonism between the Buddhism of Rudravarman and the Sivaism of Bhavavarman also played a role. The Chinese pilgrim I-ching, who wrote at the end of the seventh century, said indeed that formerly in Funan "the law of the Buddha prospered and spread, but today a wicked king has completely destroyed it and there are no more monks." If we recall what has been said about the prosperity of Buddhism in Funan in the fifth and sixth centuries, and if we consider that the epigraphy of the conquerors of Funan and of their successor is exclusively Sivaite, we are tempted to identify Bhavavarman (or Chitrasena) with the "wicked king" of I-ching.[19]

In the second half of the sixth century, Bhavavarman and his cousin [20] Chitrasena attacked Funan and, judging by their inscriptions, pushed their conquest at least up to Kratié on the Mekong, to Buriram between the Mun River and the Dangrek Mountains, and to Mongkolborei west of the Great Lake. The capital of Funan must have been transferred from T'e-mu (Vyadhapura, i.e., Ba Phnom) to a locality farther south named Na-fu-na (Naravaranagara).[21] There are various indications that this city should be placed at Angkor Borei, an archaeological site very rich in ancient remains, the name and topography of which indicate that there was a capital there.[22]

The conquest of Funan by Chenla in the guise of a dynastic quarrel is really the first episode we witness in Cambodia of the "push to the south," the constant latent threat of which we have already seen.[23] There is the same opposition between the high lands of the plateau of the middle Mekong and the alluvial plains of Cambodia as between the upper and lower valleys of the Menam or of the Irrawaddy. The effort of the kings, in Cambodia as in Siam and Burma, has constantly been directed toward the unification of two geographically, economically, and sometimes ethnically antagonistic regions; the division between them tends to reappear every time the central power shows signs of weakness.

Bhavavarman I, says an inscription,[24] "took power with energy." Until recently we possessed only one epigraphic document concerning him, a Sanskrit inscription from the environs of Mongkolborei which commemorates the erection of a linga.[25] Another Sanskrit inscription recently discovered on a stele at Si Thep in the valley of the Nam Sak in Siamese territory tells of the erection of the stele by Bhavavarman on the occasion of his accession to power.[26] Bhavavarman's capital, Bhavapura—the name of which afterward seems to have designated the territory of old Chenla, and particularly of Land Chenla in the eighth century [27]—must have been located on the northern shore of the Great Lake, in the environs of the archaeological site Ampil Rolüm, about thirty kilometers northwest of Kompong Thom.[28] We do not know how long Bhavavarman reigned; we only know that he was king in 598.[29] But it was undoubtedly during his reign that his cousin Chitrasena had short Sanskrit inscriptions engraved telling of the erection of other lingas along the Mekong, in the regions of Kratié and Stung Treng,[30] and to the west of Buriram between the Mun River and the Dangrek Mountains.[31] And it is therefore clear that Bhavavarman bequeathed a vast domain extending west to the valley of the Nam Sak to Chitrasena, who took the coronation name of Mahendravarman at the time of his accession around 600.

Aside from the inscriptions he had engraved when he still called Chitrasena, Mahendravarman left others at the confluence of the Mun with the Mekong,[32] and at Surin between the Mun and the Dangrek Mountains,[33] that tell of the establishment of lingas of the "mountain" Siva (Giriśa) and the erection of images of the bull Nandin. Since these lingas and images were set up on the occasion of "the conquest of the whole country," we can conclude that Mahendravarman followed the expansionist policies of his predecessor. We know, moreover, that he sent an ambassador to Champa to "ensure friendship between the two countries." [34]

The successor of Mahendravarman was his son Īśānavarman. He managed to absorb the ancient territories of Funan, which led the *New History of the T'ang* to attribute the effective conquest of the country to him.[35] Although we have not found an inscription of Mahendravarman south of Kratié, we have some of Īśānavarman that come from the provinces of Kompong Cham, Prei Vèng, Kandal, and even Takèo.[38] To the west, territory accepting his authority extended at least to Čhanthabun.[39]

The earliest known date of the reign of Īśānavarman, a date that must not have been long after his accession, is that of his first embassy to China in 616–17; the latest certain date is that of an inscription which names him as the king reigning in 627.[41] The *Old History of the T'ang,* which mentions, one after the other, two embassies in 623 and 628, encourages us to think that he was still reigning at this latter date, and the *New History of the T'ang,* which attributes to him the conquest of Funan at the beginning of the period 627–49,[42] gives us some basis for supposing that his reign lasted until at least around 635.

Īśānavarman's capital was named Īśānapura; the great pilgrim Hsüan-tsang called Cambodia by this name in the middle of the seventh century.[43] This city has been identified with some probability with the group of ruins at Sambor Prei Kuk, north of Kompong Thom,[44] where the inscriptions of Īśānavarman are particularly numerous;[45] one of the inscriptions, moreover, mentions Īśānapurī.[46] Apparently the first buildings of Phnom Bayang in the province of Takèo date from the reign of Īśānavarman.[47]

Continuing the policy of his father, Īśānavarman maintained good relations with Champa—relations that were to be sealed, as we shall see, by a matrimonial alliance between the two royal houses.

2. CHAMPA FROM 529 TO 686

In about 529, a new dynasty began to reign in Champa—a dynasty that reigned for a little over a century. At the death of Vijayavarman around 529, the throne was occupied by the son of a Brahman and the grandson of Manorathavarman.[48] He was a descendant of the king who went on a pilgrimage to the shore of the Ganges, and he had only tenuous lines of relationship with his immediate predecessor. He took Rudravarman for his reign name and obtained investiture in 530 from China. In 534 he sent an embassy to China.

In 543, Rudravarman I of Champa, as his predecessors had done before him, attempted a raid to the north, but he was defeated by Pham Tu, a general of Li Bon who had just revolted against the domination of the Chinese and had made himself master of Tongking. The fire at Mi-sơn that destroyed the first sanctuary of Bhadreśvara probably took place during his reign.[49] We do not know the date of the death of Rudravarman I, but we are tempted to attribute the embassies to China of 568 and 572 to him[50] for fear of otherwise attributing an overly long reign to his son and successor, Śambhuvarman, who died in 629.

The new king Śambhuvarman (Fan Fan-chih in the Chinese texts) took advantage of the weakness of the Ch'en dynasty (557–89) "to liberate himself from every manifestation of vassalage to China. When he saw the power of the empire reborn in the hands of Yang Chien, who proclaimed himself emperor of the Sui (589), he thought it prudent to renew relations spontaneously and presented the emperor with tribute in 595."[51] But ten years later, the emperor ordered Liu Fang, who had just reconquered Tongking for him, to launch a campaign against Champa. The resistance of Śambhuvarman was in vain, and once more the Chinese armies occupied Ch'ü-su and the capital, then at Tra-kiêu,[52] whence they brought back great booty. After they withdrew, Śambhuvarman again assumed control of his country and begged pardon from the emperor. For a while he neglected the obligation of tribute, but after the accession of the T'ang (618) he sent at least three embassies—in 623, 625, and 628.

It was probably Śambhuvarman who received the minister Siṃhadeva from Cambodia, sent by Mahendravarman to establish friendly relations with Champa. In the course of his long reign, which came to an end in 629, Śambhuvarman rebuilt the temple of Bhadreśvara, which had burned during the reign of his father, and gave the new sanctuary the name Śambhubhadreśvara, thus uniting his name with that of his distant predecessor Bhadravarman.[53] Scholars for a long while identified this new sanctuary with the great tower of Mi-sơn,[54] but the revised chronology of Cham art established by Philippe Stern attributes a much later date to this tower.[55]

Śambhuvarman was succeeded by his son Kandarpadharma (Fan T'ou-li of the Chinese), whose reign was peaceful and who sent rich presents to the emperor T'ai Tsung of the T'ang in 630 and 631.

Prabhāsadharma (Fan Chen-lung), son of Kandarpadharma, succeeded his father at an unknown date. We know very little about him except that he sent embassies to China in 640 and 642 and that he was assassinated in 645 by one of his ministers.

After a relatively short reign by Bhadreśvaravarman, son of the Brahman Satyakauśikasvāmin and a younger sister of Prabhāsadharma, the throne returned in the legitimate line to another sister of Prabhāsadharma, the daughter of a wife of the first rank of Kandarpadharma. The *Old History of the T'ang* tells us that this princess was crowned, but the inscriptions do not breathe a word of it.[56] They say only that a daughter of Kandarpadharma had a grandson named Jagaddharma who went to Cambodia,[57] where he married the princess Śarvāṇī, daughter of King Īśānavarman. A son, Prakāśadharma, was born of this marriage; at his accession to the throne of Champa in 653 he took the name Vikrāntavarman.[58] This king used his long and peaceful reign to multiply the religious buildings in the cirque of Mi-sơn, at Tra-kiêu,[59] and in various other places in Quang-nam. Many of these buildings show the existence in Champa at this time of a cult of Vishnu which "seems to have been literary rather than sectarian in nature."[60] A stone inscription found in the province of Khanh-hoa, north of Nha-trang,[61] proves that Vikrāntavarman's domination extended far to the south. He sent missions to China in 653, 657, 669, and 670. Unless we wish to attribute an overly long reign to him, we must suppose that he had a successor around 686 bearing the same name, Vikrāntavarman; it was probably Vikrāntavarman II who sent about fifteen missions to China between 686 and 731.[62]

3. PRE-ANGKORIAN CAMBODIA (635–85)

After Īśāvavarman I, who ceased to reign around 635, the inscriptions of Cambodia tell us of a king named Bhavavarman whose lines of relationship with his predecessor are unknown. The only dated inscription we have from him is of 639 and comes from the region of Takèo.[63] We can probably also attribute to him an inscription from the great tower of Phnom Bayang[64] and one from Phnom Preah Vihear at Kompong Ch'nang.[65] It is undoubtedly he, and not Bhavavarman I as was long believed, who is mentioned in the first two inscriptions published in the collection of Barth and Bergaigne.

These two texts speak of a son of Bhavavarman who succeeded him. This must have been Jayavarman I, for whom the earliest known date is 657[66] and who perhaps began reigning some years before.[67] The inscriptions dating from his reign have been found in an area extending from Vat Ph'u in the north to the Gulf of Siam in the south; he built structures in the region of Vyādhapura (Ba Phnom)[68] and at the old sanctuary of Lingaparvata at Vat Ph'u.[69] As far as relations with China are concerned, the *Old History of the T'ang* speaks in very general terms about embassies from Chenla received by the emperor T'ang Kao Tsung (650–83); it gives no precise dates. The reign of Jayavarman I, which seems to have been peaceful, lasted about thirty years and ended after 690.[70] Perhaps it is he whom an inscription of 713 designates by the posthumous title "the king who went to Śivapura."[71] He apparently left no heir, for the country was governed at that period by a Queen Jayadevi, who complains of "bad times."[72] The first sovereigns of Angkor did not connect themselves with the dynasty of Jayavarman I, whose fall was apparently the determining cause of the division of Cambodia in the eighth century.[73]

From the conquests of Bhavavarman I to the end of the reign of Jayavarman I, we observe the progressive strengthening of power of the Khmer kings over the territories of ancient Funan situated in the valley of the lower Mekong and the basin of the Great Lake. Numerous archaeological remains—monuments, sculptures, inscriptions—survive from this "pre-Angkorian" epoch of the history of Cambodia. The architecture, characterized by single towers or groups of towers, almost always of brick[74] with doors framed in stone, has been studied exhaustively by Henri Parmentier in his *Art khmèr primitif*.[75] The statuary, of which there are some remarkable specimens, preserves certain traits of Indian prototypes,[76] but it already shows tendencies toward the stiffness and frontality that characterize the art of Cambodia as compared with that of other countries of Farther India. Decorative sculpture already shows a richness that anticipates the exuberance of the Angkorian period.[77]

The inscriptions on the steles and on the pillars of the doors are written in a very correct Sanskrit, and always in poetic language. The inscriptions in Khmer, which begin to appear in greater number, have preserved an archaic stage of this language, a language that has undergone much less change over fourteen centuries than have Indo-European languages during the same period. These epigraphic texts constitute the principal source of information on the history and institutions of the country. They reveal a strongly organized administration and a whole hierarchy of officials whose titles we know better than their duties.

These inscriptions are most informative on the subject of religion. Their prefatory stanzas, containing prayers addressed to the divinities who are invoked on the occasion of the erection of the monuments, are particularly instructive. The major Hindu sects seem to have co-existed in Cambodia as in India proper, and among those already mentioned we find the Sivaite sect of the Pāśupatas and the Vishnuite sect of the Pāncharātras,[78] each of which in its sphere played a leading role in the Angkor period. Both epigraphy and iconography[79] show the importance in this and the following century of a cult of Harihara, or Vishnu-Siva united in a single body, which we scarcely hear spoken of later. The cult of Siva, especially in the form of a linga, enjoyed royal favor and was already almost a state religion. There is little trace of Buddhism—aside from the Buddhas of Gupta style mentioned in connection with Funan[80]—except for a unique inscription naming two Buddhist monks (*bhikshu*).[81] Buddhism seems to be in regression, if we recall the favor it enjoyed in Funan in the fifth and sixth centuries. Although the report of the Chinese pilgrim I-ching refers to Funan (called by him Po-nan), it is undoubtedly Chenla that he has in mind when at the end of the seventh century he writes: "The law of the Buddha prospered and spread. But today a wicked king has completely destroyed it and there are no more monks."[82] The literary culture that the Sanskrit inscriptions give evidence of was based on the great Indian epics, the *Rāmāyaṇa* and *Mahābhārata,* and on the *Purāṇas,*[83] which furnished the official poets with their rich mythological material.

With regard to social structure, some epigraphic texts show the importance of descent in the maternal line[84] which we find again in the Angkor period with regard to the transmission of offices in many great priestly families.[85] The matriarchal family system is widespread throughout Indonesia[86] and is found among various ethnic groups of the Indochinese Peninsula.[87] In ancient Cambodia, it may have been imported from India, where it is seen among the Nayars and the Nambutiri Brahmans.[88]

For knowledge of the material civilization in Cambodia during the seventh century, we rely on a passage of the *History of the Sui* which gives an account of the reign of Īśānavarman. This passage has been reproduced in full by Ma Tuan-lin in his ethnographic study of the peoples outside China, composed in the thirteenth century, and, in the absence of any better information, I think it will be useful to quote this account here. I follow the translation of Marquis d'Hervey de Saint-Denis:[89]

> This prince makes his residence in the city of I-she-na, which contains more than twenty thousand families. In the middle of the city is a great hall where the king gives audiences and holds court. The kingdom includes thirty other cities, each populated by several thousands of families, and each ruled by a governor; the titles of state officials are the same as in Lin-yi.
>
> Every three days the king proceeds solemnly to the audience hall and sits on a couch made of five kinds of aromatic wood and decorated with seven precious things. Above the couch there rises a pavilion hung with magnificent fabrics; the columns are of veined wood and the walls of ivory strewn with flowers of gold. Together this couch and this pavilion form a sort of little palace, at the back of which is suspended, as in Chih-t'u, a disc with gold rays in the form of flames. A golden incense-burner, held by two men, is placed in front. The king wears a dawn-red

sash of *ki-pei* cotton that falls to his feet. He covers his head with a cap laden with gold and precious stones, with pendants of pearls. On his feet are leather, or sometimes ivory, sandals; in his ears, pendants of gold. His robe is always made of a very fine white fabric called *pe-tie*. When he appears bareheaded, one does not see precious stones in his hair. The dress of the great officials is very similar to that of the king. These great officials or ministers are five in number. The first has the title *ku-lo-you* [guru?]. The titles of the four others, in order of the rank they occupy, are *hsiang-kao-ping, p'o-ho-to-ling, she-ma-ling,* and *jan-lo-lou*. The number of lesser officials is very considerable.

Those who appear before the king touch the ground in front of them three times at the foot of the steps of the throne. If the king calls them and commands them to show their rank, they kneel, holding their crossed hands on their shoulders. Then they go and sit in a circle around the king to deliberate on the affairs of the kingdom. When the session is finished, they kneel again, prostrate themselves, and retire. More than a thousand guards dressed in armor and armed with lances are ranged at the foot of the steps of the throne, in the palace halls, at the doors, and at the peristyles. . . .

The custom of the inhabitants is to go around always armored and armed, so that minor quarrels lead to bloody battles.

Only sons of the queen, the legitimate wife of the king, are qualified to inherit the throne. On the day that a new king is proclaimed, all his brothers are mutilated. From one a finger is removed, from another the nose is cut off. Then their maintenance is provided for, each in a separate place, and they are never appointed to office.

The men are of small stature and dark complexion, but many of the women are fair in complexion. All of them roll up their hair and wear earrings. They are lively and vigorous in temperament. Their houses and the furniture they use resemble those of Chih-t'u. They regard the right hand as pure and the left hand as impure. They wash every morning, clean their teeth with little pieces of poplar wood, and do not fail to read or recite their prayers. They wash again before eating, get their poplar-wood toothpicks going immediately afterwards, and recite prayers again. Their food includes a lot of butter, milk-curds, powdered sugar, rice and also millet, from which they make a sort of cake which is soaked in meat juices and eaten at the beginning of the meal.

Whoever wishes to marry first of all sends presents to the girl he seeks; then the girl's family chooses a propitious day to have the bride led, under the protection of a go-between, to the house of the bridegroom. The families of the husband and wife do not go out for eight days. Day and night the lamps remain lit. When the wedding ceremony is over, the husband receives part of the goods of his parents and goes to establish himself in his own house. At the death of his parents, if the deceased leave young children who are not yet married, these children receive the rest of the goods; but if all the children are already married and endowed, the goods that the parents have retained for themselves go to the public treasury.

Funerals are conducted in this way: the children of the deceased go seven days without eating, shave their heads as a sign of mourning, and utter loud cries. The relatives assemble with the monks and nuns of Fo or the priests of the Tao, who attend the deceased by chanting and playing various musical instruments. The corpse is burned on a pyre made of every kind of aromatic wood; the ashes are collected in a gold or silver urn which is thrown into deep water. The poor use an earthenware urn, painted in different colors. There are also those who are content to abandon the body in the mountains, leaving the job of devouring it to the wild beasts.

The north of Chenla is a country of mountains intersected by valleys. The south contains great swamps, with a climate so hot that there is never any snow or hoar-frost; the earth there produces pestilential fumes and teems with poisonous insects. Rice, rye, some millet, and coarse millet are grown in this kingdom.

In sum, the civilization of pre-Angkorian Cambodia, which was the heir of Funan particularly in matters of agricultural hydraulics and also in religion and art and was influenced in architecture by Champa, assumed in the course of the seventh century a dynamism which enabled it, even after an eclipse in the following century, to dominate the south and center of the peninsula for a long time.

4. THE MON KINGDOM OF DVĀRAVATĪ

West of Īśānapura, i.e., Cambodia, the Chinese pilgrim Hsüan-tsang, in the middle of the seventh century, placed a kingdom of T'o-lo-po-ti.[90] This name, T'o-lo-po-ti, with its many variants,[91] corresponds to that of the country *Dvāravatī* whose name is preserved in the official names of the Siamese capitals Ayutthaya,[92] founded in 1350, and Bangkok, founded in 1782. We will see later[93] that Ayutthaya was founded following the abandonment of a town situated in the region of Suphan, and it seems reasonable to infer from this that the name Dvāravatī was originally applied to a city situated in this region.[94] Moreover, the lower basin of the Menam, from Lopburi in the north to Ratburi in the west and to Pračhin in the east, contains archaeological and epigraphical remains of Buddhist origin[95] which are similar enough to each other to lead us to consider them as vestiges of the same state: the kingdom of Dvāravatī.[96] The birth of Dvāravatī perhaps corresponds with the dismemberment of Funan. But we know virtually nothing about this state of Dvāravatī. The inscriptions of Phra Pathom and of Lopburi, in archaic Mon language,[97] prove that the population was basically Mon.[98] Furthermore, a legend having a certain historical character attributes the foundation of the city of Haripunjaya (Lamphun)[99] to a colony of emigrants from Lavo (Lopburi) led by the queen Chammadevī. We will see a dynasty known through many inscriptions in the Mon language[100] reigning in Haripunjaya in the twelfth century.

Dvāravatī poses a problem for which a solution is not yet in sight. The tradition of the Mons places the center of their race at Sudhammavatī (Thaton, at the mouth of the Sittang), a site that has not revealed a single important archaeological vestige; this tradition seems to be unaware of the Menam Basin, where, on the other hand, these remains are fairly numerous.

5. THE PYU KINGDOM OF ŚRĪKSHETRA

West of Dvāravatī the Chinese pilgrims Hsüan-tsang[101] and I-ching[102] place the kingdom of She-li-ch'a-ta-lo, that is, Śrīkshetra, which is the ancient name of Prome (in Burmese, Thayekhettaya).[103] We have seen in the preceding chapter that the site of the ancient capital of the Pyus is represented by the archaeological site of Môza near Prome.[104] The city was encompassed by a circular enclosure of brick. The Buddhist images found here are in the late Gupta style. We have in the seventh century, notably in the works of I-ching, proof that there existed at Śrīkshetra, concurrently with the Theravada Buddhism witnessed from the end of the fifth century by inscriptions in the Pali language, a Theravada sect that used the Sanskrit language; this was the sect of the Mūlasarvāstivādins, which probably came originally from Magadha.[105]

The environs of Prome have also yielded funerary urns containing human remains. The Pyus cremated their dead and kept the ashes in earthenware urns. In the case of kings, however, the urns were of stone and bore inscribed on them the names of the deceased.[106] The inscriptions that have been found deal with kings who reigned at the end of the seventh and the beginning of the eighth century, about whom we will speak in the following chapter.

6. THE STATES OF THE MALAY PENINSULA IN THE SEVENTH CENTURY

West of Dvāravatī and southeast of Śrīkshetra the great pilgrim Hsüan-tsang places the country of Kāmalanka,[107] which is "near a large bay" and is perhaps identical with the Lang-chia-shu (i.e., Langkasuka) of I-ching.[108] In any case it must be located on the Malay Peninsula. Hsüan-tsang gives no details on this region, which he did not visit, and other texts give us historical facts only sporadically.

The information presented by Ma Tuan-lin in his chapter on Chih-t'u, or the Red-Earth Country, mentioned in the last chapter, dates back to the beginning of the seventh century. Here are some extracts that give an idea of the civilization of the small Indian states on the peninsula at this period:[109]

> The family name of the king of Chih-t'u is Ch'ü-t'an,[110] and his personal name is Li-fu-to-hsi. To what period the history of the ancestors of this prince dates back we do not know. We are told only that his father, having abandoned the throne to become a monk, transmitted to him the royal position, a position he has held for sixteen years.[111] This king Li-fu-to-hsi has three wives, all of whom are daughters of neighboring kingdoms. He lives in Sêng-ch'i (or Sêng-che), a city supplied with three walls, the gates of which are about a hundred paces apart. On each of these gates, wreathed with small carved gold bells, are painted Bodhisattvas and immortals who soar in the air. . . . The buildings of the palace have only one story. All the doors are on the same level and face north. The throne, raised on a three-step-high platform, also faces north. The king appears there, dressed in a robe the color of the rising sun. His cap is adorned with golden flowers and pendants of precious stones. Four young girls stand at his side. His guards number more than a hundred. Behind the throne is a sort of large niche made of five kinds of aromatic wood encrusted with gold and silver, at the back of which is suspended a disc with rays of gold in the form of flames. On each side of the royal platform are placed two large metallic mirrors; in front of each of these mirrors is a vase of gold, and in front of each vase is an incense burner, also of gold. At the foot of the platform is a recumbent golden ox, sheltered by a canopy, and, in addition, some very valuable fans. Hundreds of Brahmans, seated in two rows facing each other on the right and left of the platform, attend the royal audience.
>
> The high dignitaries, charged with collectively handling the affairs of the kingdom, consist of a first minister with the title *sa-t'o-chia-lo,*[112] two officers with the title *t'o-na-ta,*[113] and three other assistants with the title *chia-li-mi-chia.*[114] The repression of crime is specifically entrusted to a great magistrate with the title *chiu-lo-mo-ti.*[115] Finally, each town is placed under the authority of two principal mandarins called *na-ya-chia*[116] and *po-ti.*[117]
>
> For marriages, first of all a propitious hour is chosen. The five days preceding the appointed date are spent in rejoicing and drinking. On the sixth day, the father places the hand of his daughter in that of his son-

in-law,[118] and on the seventh day the marriage is consummated. When the nuptials are completed, all take their leave and the newlyweds go to live by themselves—unless the husband's father is still alive, in which case they go to live with him.

Those who have lost their father, their mother, or their brothers shave their heads and wear white clothing. They build a bamboo hut over the water, fill it with small sticks, and place the corpse in it. Streamers are put up, incense is burned, conches are blown, and drums beaten while the pyre is set on fire and the flames consume it. At the end, everything disappears into the water. This ceremony never varies. Nothing distinguishes the funeral of a high official from that of a common man. Only for the king is care taken to perform the cremation in such a way as to collect the ashes, which are placed in a golden urn and deposited in a funerary monument.[119]

7. INDONESIA: HO-LING IN JAVA AND MALĀYU IN SUMATRA

We have seen the debate concerning the location of the country Ho-lo-tan, which sent its last embassy to China in 452.[120] As for Ho-ling, whose first three embassies are dated 640, 648, and 666,[121] a recent theory places it on the Malay Peninsula. This theory fits in quite well with certain geographic data from Chinese sources.[122] But in other respects it raises serious difficulties that do not present themselves if we agree that Ho-ling was located in the center of Java.[123] Besides, it is in the center of Java that the kingdom of Walaing was situated, and the name Walaing, according to L. C. Damais, is in all likelihood the source of the Chinese name Ho-ling.[124] The archaeological remains of this period are unfortunately quite rare; we can scarcely cite anything but the inscription of Tuk Mas, probably from the middle of the seventh century,[125] and perhaps the oldest edifices of the Dieng Plateau.[126]

Ho-ling, whose richness is praised in the *New History of the T'ang*,[127] was a center of Buddhist culture in the seventh century. It was the homeland of the monk Jñānabhadra, under whose direction the Chinese pilgrim Hui-ning, who came to the country in 664–65, translated the Sanskrit texts of the Theravada into Chinese.[128]

In 644–45, almost the same time as the first embassy of Ho-ling in 640, the *New History of the T'ang* mentions the first embassy of Mo-lo-yu.[129] This name refers to the country of Malāyu situated on the east coast of Sumatra and centered in the region of Jambi. The pilgrim I-ching stopped off there for a time in 671.[130] He informs us in his memoirs that between 689 and 692 Malāyu was absorbed by Shih-li-fo-shih (Śrīvijaya).[131] This name had perhaps already appeared in the faulty transcription *Chin-li-p'i-shih* in a text based on data earlier than the voyages of I-ching.[132]

CHAPTER VI

THE RISE OF ŚRĪVIJAYA, THE DIVISION OF CAMBODIA, AND THE APPEARANCE OF THE ŚAILENDRAS IN JAVA

From the End of the Seventh Century to the Beginning of the Ninth Century

The development of navigation, which was due in great part to Arab merchants [1] and is documented by the voyages of Buddhist pilgrims and the increasingly frequent exchanges of embassies between China and the countries to the south,[2] inevitably gave a special importance to the southeast coast of Sumatra, whose outlines then differed appreciably from those of today.[3] Since this coast was situated at equal distance from the Sunda Strait and the Strait of Malacca, the two great breaks in the natural barrier formed by the Malay Peninsula and Indonesia, it was the normal point of landfall for boats coming from China on the northeast monsoon. Moreover, the fall in the early seventh century of Funan, a state that had been the dominant power in the southern seas for five centuries, left the field open for the inhabitants around Sumatran estuaries and harbors to develop control of commerce between India and China. It was thanks to these circumstances that the rapid rise of the kingdom of Śrīvijaya took place in the eighth century.

1. THE BEGINNINGS OF THE KINGDOM OF ŚRĪVIJAYA (END OF THE SEVENTH CENTURY)

When the pilgrim I-ching made his first voyage from China to India in 671, his first port of call, less than twenty days after his departure from Canton, was Fo-shih, where he stopped six months to study Sanskrit grammar.[4] "In the fortified city of Fo-shih," he says, "there are more than a thousand Buddhist priests whose minds are bent on study and good works. They examine and study all possible subjects exactly as in Madhyadeśa [India]; their rules and ceremonies are identical with those in India. If a Chinese priest wishes to go to the west to understand and read [the original Buddhist texts] there, he would be wise to spend a year or two in Fo-shih and practice the proper rules there; he might then go on to central India." [5]

On his return from India, where he had spent ten years at the university of Nālandā, I-ching spent four more years at Fo-shih —the years between 685 and 689, during which he copied and translated Sanskrit Buddhist texts into Chinese. In 689, after a brief voyage to Canton, where he recruited four collaborators, he returned to settle in Fo-shih and there wrote his two memoirs, one "on the eminent monks who sought the law in the western countries" and the other "on the spiritual law, sent from the southern seas."

In 692 he sent his manuscripts to China, to which he himself returned in 695. During this last stay, he noted in the second of the above works that Mo-lo-yu, where he had stopped and stayed two months in 671, "is now the country of Shih-li-fo-shih."[6]

A group of inscriptions in Old Malay,[7] four of which were found in Sumatra (three near Palembang, another at Karang Brahi on the upper course of the Batang Hari) and a fifth at Kota Kapur on the island of Bangka, show the existence in 683–86 in Palembang of a Buddhist kingdom that had just conquered the hinterland of Jambi and the island of Bangka and was preparing to launch a military expedition against Java. This kingdom bore the name Śrīvijaya, which corresponds exactly to I-ching's (Shih-li-) fo-shih.[8]

The oldest of the three inscriptions from Palembang, the one that is engraved on a large stone at Kedukan Bukit, at the foot of the hill of Seguntang, tells us that on April 23, 682,[9] a king began an expedition (*siddhayātrā*) by boat, that on May 19 he left an estuary with an army moving simultaneously by land and sea, and that, a month later,[10] he brought victory, power, and wealth to Śrīvijaya. This text has caused much ink to flow. Some scholars have chosen to view this inscription as a statement that the capital Śrīvijaya[11] was founded by an armada from the outside, perhaps from the Malay Peninsula,[12] and some have even interpreted this inscription as meaning that the primitive site of Malāyu was at Palembang,[13] which took the name of Śrīvijaya following this expedition. It seems to me that this is building very fragile hypotheses on a stone that differs from other inscribed stones found in Palembang[14] and on Bangka[15] only in the personality of the author of the inscription and the circumstances under which it was engraved. All we can say is that the events commemorated must have been considered important enough to merit giving a considerable wealth of chronological detail which other stones of the same type do not give. The king who in 682 set up this votive offering in some sacred place near Seguntang did so on returning from a victorious expedition that earned Śrīvijaya new power and prestige.[16]

This anonymous king is almost certainly the Jayanāśa who founded a public park two years later, on March 23, 684,[17] at Talang Tuwo, west of Palembang and five kilometers northwest of Seguntang, and on this occasion had a text engraved expressing the desire that the merit gained by this deed and all his other good works should redound on all creatures and bring them closer to enlightenment.

As for the three other inscriptions, one of which is dated February 28, 686, we wonder if the conquests that they imply do not represent the continuation of the expansionist policy commemorated by the stone of Kedukan Bukit. These three texts, in part identical,[18] deliver threats and maledictions against any inhabitants of the upper Batang Hari (the river of Jambi whose basin must have constituted the territory of Malāyu) and of the island of Bangka who might commit acts of insubordination toward the king and toward the officials he had placed at the head of the provincial administration. The inscription of Bangka closes by mentioning the departure of an expedition against the unsubdued land of Java in 686.[19] The land referred to may have been the ancient kingdom of Tārumā,[20] on the other side of the Sunda Strait, which we do not hear spoken of again after its embassy to China in 666–69.[21] Tārumā may have become the nucleus of the expansion of Sumatran influence on the island of Java which is evidenced in the following century by the inscription of Gandasuli in the province of Keḍu.[22]

Although King Jayanāśa is named in only one of the five inscriptions, they probably all emanate from him: the military expedition in 682, the foundation of a public park in 684, the affirmation of authority in the northwest and southeast of the kingdom, and the sending of an expedition against Java—all these mark the various stages in the career of a king whom we are tempted to recognize as the conqueror of Malāyu. Perhaps it was also he who sent the embassy of 695 [23] to China, the first one from Śrīvijaya for which we have a definite date. Before this embassy we have only a vague mention of embassies beginning with the period 670–73; [24] after it, we know of embassies of 702, 716, and

724 in the name of the king Shih-li-t'o-lo-pa-mo (Śrī Indravarman) and of 728 and 742 in the name of the king Liu-t'eng-wei-kung.[25]

Śrīvijaya's expansion northwest toward the Strait of Malacca and southeast toward the Sunda Strait is a very clear indication of its designs on the two great passages between the Indian Ocean and the China Sea, the possession of which was to assure Śrīvijaya of commercial hegemony in Indonesia for several centuries.[26]

The inscription of 684, the first dated evidence of Mahayana Buddhism in Farther India, confirms what I-ching said about the importance of Śrīvijaya as a Buddhist center[27] and about the various Buddhist schools in the southern seas. He asserts, it is true, that the Mūlasarvāstivāda, one of the great sects of the Theravada Buddhism that used the Sanskrit language,[28] was almost universally adopted there, but he mentions followers of Mahayana Buddhism at Malāyu[29] and records the existence in Śrīvijaya of the *Yogāchāryabhūmiśāstra*,[30] one of the major works of Asanga, founder of the mystic school Yogāchāra, or Vijñānavādin.[31]

The prayer (*praṇidhāna*) of King Jayanāśa on the occasion of his founding of a public park—expressing as it does the desire that all beings should obtain a series of felicities, the first ones purely material, but the later ones rising gradually to the moral and mystical planes until enlightenment is achieved—gives Louis de La Vallée-Poussin "the impression that all of this is in keeping with Mahayanist Sarvāstivāda."[32] It has even been suggested that the doctrine reflected by this prayer was perhaps already tinged with Tantrism.[33]

The archaeology of the region of Palembang,[34] although quite scanty, especially in architectural remains, confirms the evidence of I-ching and epigraphic data. The sculptures that have been found are all Buddhist, with a definite predominance of Bodhisattva images. But on the whole they are later than the period under consideration here.

After 742, the date of the last embassy from Shih-li-fo-shih mentioned in the Chinese texts,[35] our sources remain silent until 775; at that date a Sanskrit inscription engraved on the first face of the stele of Wat Sema Mưang[36] reveals that the Sumatran kingdom had established a foothold on the Malay Peninsula at Ligor, where a king of Śrīvijaya, probably named Dharmasetu,[37] had built various edifices, including a sanctuary dedicated to the

Buddha and to the Bodhisattvas Padmapāṇi and Vajrapāṇi. However, from 732 on central Java becomes of greatest interest to us. But before telling what took place there, it is important to relate the little that we know about events that took place on the Indochinese Peninsula from the end of the seventh to the middle of the eighth centuries.

2. THE DIVISION OF CAMBODIA: LAND CHENLA AND WATER CHENLA (BEGINNING OF THE EIGHTH CENTURY)

The T'ang histories[38] tell us that shortly after 706 Cambodia came to be divided in two[39] and returned to the anarchic state that had existed before it was unified under the kings of Funan and the first kings of Chenla. "The northern half, a land of mountains and valleys, was called Land Chenla. The southern half, bounded by the sea and covered with lakes, was called Water Chenla."[40]

The breakup of Cambodia apparently originated in the anarchy that followed the reign of Jayavarman I, who died without a male heir. In 713, the country was governed by a queen named Jayadevī; we have an inscription of hers found at Angkor,[41] in which she complains of the misfortunes of the times and mentions donations to a sanctuary of Śiva Tripurāntaka. This sanctuary was founded by the princess Śobhājayā, a daughter of Jayavarman I who married the Sivaite Brahman Śakrasvāmin born in India. Jayadevī is named in another inscription from which we learn that she herself was a daughter of Jayavarman I.[42]

Around the same time, a prince of Aninditapura named Pushkara or Pushkarāksha became king in Śambhupura[43]—a site represented by the group of ruins at Sambor on the Mekong, upstream from Kratié[44]—where he had an inscription engraved in 716.[45] It has been suggested that he obtained this royal status "by marriage,"[46] but this is a gratuitous hypothesis; we can just as easily hypothesize that he seized power because the throne was vacant.

It is possible that it was this Pushkarāksha who received at his death the posthumous name of Indraloka, a name mentioned in an inscription of Sambor as that of the great-grandfather of a queen reigning in 803.[47] Be that as it may, his taking possession of Śambhupura seems to have marked the beginning of the breakup of Cambodia.

All we know about Land Chenla in the first half of the eighth century is that it sent an embassy to China in 717[48] and sent an expedition to Vietnam in 722 to aid a native chief in his revolt against China.[49] As for Water Chenla, it seems that this country was itself divided into several principalities. That of Aninditapura, in the south, had a certain Bālāditya as its chief at an undetermined date. Bālāditya perhaps gave his name to a city Bālādityapura mentioned by the Chinese, under the name P'o-lo-t'i-po, as the true capital of Water Chenla.[50] Bālāditya claimed to be descended from the Brahman Kauṇḍinya and the Nāgī Somā and was considered later by the kings of Angkor as the ancestor through whom they were related to the mythical couple;[51] he must, therefore, have somehow been related to the ancient kings of Funan. In view of the resemblance of the names, we can presume that his successors included a certain Nṛipāditya who left a Sanskrit inscription in western Cochin China.[52] This inscription is undated, but it may go back to the beginning of the eighth century—that is, to the beginning of the division of Cambodia.

3. DVĀRAVATĪ AND ŚRĪKSHETRA IN THE EIGHTH CENTURY

We have no precise data on Dvāravatī in the eighth century; all we can say is that remains of monuments and some of the sculptures rightly or wrongly attributed to Dvāravatī probably date from this period.

At Prome, legends in the Pyu language engraved on royal funerary urns give us the names and ages of three kings, with the dates expressed in an era system that is not specified.[54] If we assume that this era system was that of 638 (in which the first year is the equivalent of 638 A.D.)—a system that may have been of Indian origin but was first used in Burma before spreading later to the Thai and to Cambodia—we have the following dates:

673—
688, death of Sūryavikrama, at the age of 64
695, death of Harivikrama, at the age of 41
718, death of Sīhavikrama, at the age of 44

We know from elsewhere the names, but not the dates, of Prabhuvarman and of Jayachandravarman. In view of the fact that their names end in "varman," these two would seem at first glance to belong to a dynasty other than that of the "vikrama" kings.[55] But a Sanskrit inscription engraved on the pedestal of a statue of the Buddha[56] tells us that Jayachandravarman was the elder brother of Harivikrama and that, to end the rivalry between the two brothers, their spiritual master had two identical cities built for them where they resided separately.[57]

It is believed that the Buddhist monuments of Prome whose ruins bear the names of Bôbôgyi, Payama, and Payagyi were built during the eighth century. These stupas are of a cylindrical type with a hemispherical or pointed dome. The origin of this type of stupa is to be sought in northeast India and on the coast of Orissa; the relations of Orissa with the Burmese delta have already been cited.[58] The origin of another architectural form characteristic of the Pyu kingdom—an edifice with an inner chamber that supports a cylindro-conic superstructure (*śikhara*)—must also be sought on the coast of Orissa. This form was to undergo a remarkable development at Pagan. Theravada Buddhism, witnessed at Prome before the seventh century in the fragments of the Pali canon previously mentioned,[59] was either supplanted or at least relegated to second place by a school with the Sanskrit canon, perhaps the Mūlasarvāstivāda, whose predominance in Farther India I-ching has affirmed.[60] But farther north, at Pagan, it seems that Mahayana Buddhism was already firmly established and had assumed, under the influence of Bengal, an aspect that is sometimes said to be Tantric.[61]

4. JAVA: SANJAYA (732) AND THE BUDDHIST ŚAILENDRAS (END OF THE EIGHTH CENTURY)

Apart from the inscription of Tuk Mas of uncertain date and slight historical interest,[62] Java furnishes us with no epigraphic documents for some time after the inscriptions of Pūrṇavarman in western Java that date from the middle of the fifth century.[63] Java re-enters the scene with a Sanskrit inscription of 732 found in the central part of the island among the ruins of the Sivaite sanctuary of Changal on the hill of Wukir, to the southeast of the Borobudur.[64] Its author was the king Sanjaya, son of the sister of Sanna named Sannā,[65] whose name seems very much like the Sanskritization of a native name. The inscription tells of the erection of a linga on the island of Yava, "rich in grain and gold mines," in the country of Kunjarakunja.[66]

Although Java does not produce gold, the context prevents us from searching elsewhere for the island of Yava. Nevertheless, one scholar has proposed that Yava be identified with the Malay Peninsula and has worked out a story[67] concerning the Indian origins of Sanjaya, his reign on the peninsula, and his flight to Java, where he became the vassal of the Śailendra dynasty that was driven from Palembang by Śrīvajaya—a story that is pure fiction. The highly fantastic character of this story has been demonstrated by another scholar.[68]

As for Kunjarakunja, an inexact reader of the text thought that it was the name of a foreign locality from which the linga had been brought, and hypotheses about the relations between Java and the Pāṇḍya country in southern India have been built on this erroneous interpretation.[69] There is indeed a locality with this name near the frontier between Travancore and Tinnevelly, and at this exact spot is located the sanctuary of the sage Agastya, the Hinduizer of southern India who is greatly venerated in Java under the aspect of the bearded and pot-bellied Bhaṭara Guru. But the reconstruction of the true reading[70] has made it possible to prove that Kunjarakunja is the name of the country where Sanjaya built his sanctuary, that is, all or part of the Keḍu Plain. This true reading does not, of course, prevent us from relating the name of this Javanese district to an identical name in southern India.

A late text credits Sanjaya with incredible conquests in Bali, in Sumatra, and in Cambodia up to China.[71] An inscription dated 907 inspires more confidence:[72] it represents Sanjaya as a prince of Matarām (southern part of central Java) and as the first of a line. According to an inscription of Kalasan, the second in this line, Panangkaran, reigned in 778, under the suzerainty of the Śailendra dynasty.

The name Śailendra, "king of the mountain," is an equivalent of (Śiva) Giriśa, and perhaps expresses an Indian adaptation of Indonesian beliefs which place the residences of gods on mountains.[73] One scholar[74] believed that it indicated the Indian origin of these newcomers, whom he thought were related to the Śailodbhava kings of Kalinga. But serious objections have been raised to this theory.[75] In any case, the appearance in the southern islands of the Śailendras, with their imperial title *mahārāja,* was, we can safely say, "an international event of major importance."[76]

I wonder if these "kings of the mountain" were not, in fact, attempting to revive the title of the ancient kings of Funan, who were zealous adherents of the linga Giriśa[77] and set themselves up as universal sovereigns. This hypothesis has gained some ground since J. G. de Casparis identified *Naravarnagara,* the last capital of Funan in the southern Indochinese Peninsula,[78] with the variant *Varanara* in an inscription of the ninth century. This inscription mentions that the country Varanara was ruled by a king Bhūjayottungadeva, who appears to have been the founder of the Śailendra dynasty in Java.[79]

This dynasty increasingly assumed the aspect of a suzerain power, exercising its supreme authority over the local dynasty governing the Keḍu Plain. F. H. van Naerssen in fact has shown that, in the inscription of Kalasan, "the ornament of the Śailendra dynasty" was not the Maharaja Panangkaran, author of the monument and the inscription, but his suzerain monarch.[80]

The first known king of the local dynasty reigning in the Keḍu Plain seems to have been Sang Ratu i Halu, of whom we have evidence around 768.[81] Only one thing is certain: the coming of the Śailendras was marked by an abrupt rise of Mahayana Buddhism. In 778, Maharaja Panangkaran founded, at the request of his spiritual teachers, a sanctuary dedicated to the Buddhist goddess Tārā and consecrated the village of Kālasa to it;[82] this is the monument now called Chandi Kalasan, located in the plain of Prambanan, east of the city of Jogjakarta.[83]

In 782, during the reign of a Śailendra king known as "the killer of enemy heroes"[84] and crowned under the name of Sangrāmadhananjaya,[85] a teacher from the country of Gauḍi (western Bengal) named Kumāraghosha consecrated in Kelurak, not far from Kalasan, an image of the Bodhisattva Manjuśrī, who is a synthesis of the Three Buddhist Jewels (*Triratna*), the Brahmanic trinity (*Trimūrti*), and all the gods.[86] The temporary vogue for the script of northern India which was used in the inscriptions of Kalasan and Kelurak, and later in Cambodia,[87] was apparently owing to this influence of western Bengal and the university of Nālandā.

It was at the beginning of the establishment of the Śailendras in Java, roughly in the second half of the eighth century, that the great Buddhist monuments of the Keḍu Plain were built. The chronology of these monuments is still a bit shaky. Kalasan, temple of Tārā, dated 778 by its inscription, furnishes a point of reference for dating the other monuments. Chandi Sari, a monastic dwelling provided with a sanctuary, appears to be contemporaneous with Kalasan, while Chandi Sewu, with its 250 little temples, a veritable stone *maṇḍala,* must be a bit later.[88] As for the most dazzling of these monuments, the Borobudur—together with its subordinate structures, Chandi Mendut and Chandi Pawon [89]—the paleography of the short contemporary inscriptions on its foundation prevents us from considering it as dating from before the middle of the ninth century, that is, at the end of the Śailendras. The Borobudur, which is decorated with bas-reliefs illustrating some of the great texts of Mahayana Buddhism,[90] is a Buddhist microcosm, another stone *maṇḍala,* and it is perhaps also the dynastic temple of the Śailendras.[91] Chandi Mendut shelters a magnificent triad, the Buddha preaching between two Bodhisattvas, executed in post-Gupta style. From the religious standpoint, this architectural ensemble [92] belongs to the esoteric Buddhism of Vajrayāna that was codified later in the treatise entitled *Sang hyang Kamahāyānikan.*[93]

The advent of the Buddhist Śailendras seems to have provoked the exodus to the east of Java of conservative elements faithful to the Hindu cults. The prosperity of these Hindu elements in the seventh century and the first half of the eighth is attested to by the most ancient monuments of the Dieng Plateau and the inscription of Sanjaya. Evidence from Chinese sources, which place the moving of the capital of Ho-ling to the east and its transfer from She-p'o to P'o-lu-chia-ssu by the king Chi-yen between 742 and 755,[94] is confirmed by the presence at Dinaya, to the northwest of Malang, of a Sanskrit inscription of 760,[95] the oldest dated inscription coming from the eastern part of Java.[96] This inscription mentions the construction of a sanctuary of Agastya by a son of the king Devasiṃha, named Gajayāna,[97] who was reigning over Kanjuruhan.[98] Both Devasiṃha and Gajayāna, who were perhaps related in some way to Sanjaya, were devotees of Siva and the guardians and protectors of a linga named Pūtikeśvara, which embodied the essence of royalty. Here is a new example of the cult of the royal linga that was to become the great state religion of Cambodia in the Angkor period—the cult of which Bhadreśvara of Mi-sơn in Champa furnished us with the first certain evidence.

The interesting inscription of Dinaya throws some light on the history of eastern Java in the second half of the eighth century, but the light is only a single ray in the night.[99] In the last quarter of the century, interest is concentrated on the Śailendras in the center of the island.

The accession of the Śailendras, which is marked in the field of internal affairs by the development of Mahayana Buddhism, is marked in the field of foreign affairs by incursions of the Śailendras on the Indochinese Peninsula and attempts to install themselves there.

In 767, Tongking was invaded by bands that the Vietnamese annals say came from She-p'o (Java) and K'un-lun (the southern islands in general). The governor Chang Po-i defeated them near modern Sơn-tây and drove them back to the sea.[100] In 774 "men born in other countries," says a Sanskrit inscription of Po Nagar at Nha-trang,[101] "men living on food more horrible than cadavers, frightful, completely black and gaunt, dreadful and evil as death, came in ships," stole the linga, and burned the temple. They were "followed by good ships and beaten at sea" by the Cham king Satyavarman. In 787, "the armies of Java, having come in vessels," burned another temple.[102]

At about the same time, no earlier than 782, an inscription in the name of a king bearing the personal name Vishṇu, "destroyer of his enemies," was begun at Ligor but not finished. This inscription was carved on the second face of the stele erected in Ligor in 775 by the king of Śrīvijaya.[103]

The text of the inscription states that King Vishṇu "bore the title of *mahārāja* to indicate that he was a descendant of the family of the Śailendras." This king was undoubtedly the king of the inscription of Kelurak—that is, Sangrāmadhananjaya.[104]

For some time it was thought that the Śailendras reigned in Śrīvijaya from the beginning and that during the second half of the eighth century and a large part of the ninth central Java became subject to the Sumatran kingdom.[105] But although the Śailendras were, as we will see,[106] kings of Śrīvijaya in the eleventh century and undoubtedly also in the tenth, we have no proof that such was already the case in the eighth.[107]

R. C. Majumdar, who has the honor of being the first to distinguish between the two faces of the Ligor stele[108] on which the assumption of Śailendra rule in Śrīvijaya from 775 was based, accepts the possibility that the seat of the power of the Śailendras was on the Malay Peninsula.[109] But we scarcely know where to locate it, for in the eighth century Chinese sources are poor in information on this region.[110] Someone has suggested Chaiya, which seems to have experienced a period of prosperity in the eighth century, judging by the quality of the archaeological remains dating from this epoch.[111] In any case, there is no reason to doubt that in the preceding century Śrīvijaya had its center at Palembang.[112]

On the basis of the documents available at present, Java does not appear to be the native country of the Śailendras of Indonesia, who, as has been seen, claimed rightly or wrongly to be related to the "kings of the mountain" of Funan. Java is, rather, the place in the archipelago where they first made themselves known. But this does not imply, as has been believed,[113] that Śrīvijaya was a dependency of its neighbors to the east, for the evidence we can draw from the Charter of Nālandā, to be discussed later,[114] is valid only for the second half of the ninth century. According to this text, Suvarṇadvīpa (Sumatra with its possessions on the Malay Peninsula) was governed at this time by a Bālaputra, that is, a "younger son"—in this case the "younger son" of a King Samarāgravīra, who was himself a son of a king of Yavabhūmi (Java), who was called "the ornament of the Śailendra dynasty" and bore a name followed by the title of "the killer of enemy heroes." This Śailendra of Java seems to be the same as that of the inscriptions of Kelurak and Ligor (second face), and his son Samarāgravīra can be identified with the king Samaratunga who reigned in Java in 824.[115] Samarāgravīra's son, Bālaputra, undoubtedly governed Sumatra for and under the authority of his father, a situation similar to the one that we will find in Bali in the eleventh century, where we will see a younger son of the king of Java perform the functions of a viceroy.[116] We can conclude from all this that in the second half of the ninth century Java and Sumatra were united under the rule of a Śailendra reigning in Java, but nothing authorizes us to think this was already the case in the second half of the eighth century.

On the other hand, the Śailendras of Java may have had some claim over Cambodia in the eighth century, for in the following chapter we will see the founder of Angkorian royalty inaugurate his reign with a ceremony designed to completely liberate him from vassalage to Java. The vassalage of Cambodia to Java may have originated in an incident that an Arab author has given us a romanticized account of—an account dating from the beginning of the tenth century.[117] The Arab author tells us that a Khmer king expressed the desire to see the head of the maharaja of Zābag (Jāvaka) before him on a plate and this remark was reported to the maharaja. The maharaja then, on the pretext of taking a pleasure cruise in the islands of his kingdom, armed his fleet and prepared an expedition against Cambodia. He sailed up the river leading to the capital, seized the king of Cambodia and decapitated him, then ordered the Khmer minister to find a successor for him. Once he had returned to his own country, the maharaja had the severed head embalmed and sent it in an urn to the king who had replaced the decapitated sovereign; with it he sent a letter drawing the moral of the incident. "When the news of these events reached the kings of India and China, the maharaja became greater in their eyes. From that moment the Khmer kings, every morning upon rising, turned their faces in the direction of the country of Zābag, bowed down to the ground, and humbled themselves before the maharaja to render him homage."

It would be unwise to accept this account as a page from history. It is possible, however, that it was inspired by the recollection of some historical fact and that the Śailendras of Java did indeed take advantage of the weakness of Cambodia during its disunity to assert over it the rights of its ancient masters, the "kings of the mountain." But it is also possible that the exploit of the maharaja should really be attributed to King Jayanāśa of Śrīvijaya at the end of the seventh century.[118]

5. CAMBODIA: THE TWO CHENLAS (SECOND HALF OF THE EIGHTH CENTURY)

Land Chenla, which was also called Wen-tan and P'o-lou by the Chinese and which perhaps corresponded to the original territory of Chenla, in 753 sent to China an embassy led by a son of the king. In 754 this same prince or another son of the king accompanied the Chinese armies that were operating against eastern Nanchao, where a King Ko-lo-feng reigned. According to G. H. Luce,[119] the *Man Shu* mentions that, during the period of the division of Chenla, an expedition from Nanchao may have reached "the sea," perhaps the Great Lake. In 771 an embassy was led by the "second king," named P'o-mi; then a new embassy was sent in 799.[120] The itinerary of Chia Tan by land from China to India [121] places the capital of Land Chenla, at the end of the eighth century, at a point which was at first placed in the region of Pak Hin Bun on the middle Mekong [122] but which was undoubtedly located much farther south, around the center of early Chenla.[123] An inscription in the name of a King Jayasiṃhavarman found at Phu Khiao Kao [124] in the Chaiyaphum district of the province of Khorat may date back to this period.

As for Water Chenla, we have some inscriptions from the region of Śambhupura (Sambor). Two of them, dated 770 and 781,[125] emanate from a king named Jayavarman.[126] An inscription of 791 found in the province of Siem Reap,[127] which mentions the erection of an image of the Bodhisattva Lokeśvara, is the most ancient epigraphical evidence of the existence of Mahayana Buddhism in Cambodia. We do not know what dates to attribute to a series of princes, ancestors of the first kings of Angkor, on whom the genealogies confer the title of king; they were apparently the rulers of the various principalities into which central and lower Cambodia were divided.[128] A "senior" queen, Jyeshṭhāryā, granddaughter of Nṛipendradevī and great-granddaughter of King Indraloka,[129] made an endowment at Sambor in 803,[130] a year after the accession of Jayavarman II.

It would be a mistake to believe that at this troubled period in the history of Cambodia there was a corresponding eclipse of Khmer art. On the contrary, art historians agree that some especially interesting works of pre-Angkorian art, intermediate between the style of Sambor Prei Kuk and that of the Kulèn,[131] date from the eighth century.

6. SOUTHERN CHAMPA, OR HUAN-WANG (SECOND HALF OF THE EIGHTH CENTURY)

The middle of the eighth century, which was notable because of the advent of the Śailendras in the southern seas, was also a critical era for Champa.

In 749 the reigning king in Champa was Rudravarman II, an obscure personage whose name we know only because of an embassy he sent to China in that year.[132]

Until that time, the heart of the Cham kingdom had been located at Thừa-thiên and then at Quang-nam. In the middle of the eighth century, however, we see a movement of the center of gravity to the south, to Pāṇḍuranga (Phan-rang) and to Kauṭhāra (Nha-trang). At about the same time, in 758, the Chinese stop speaking of Lin-yi and substitute for it the name Huan-wang.[133] Moreover, the new dynasty reigning in the south inaugurates the use of posthumous names indicating the divine presence of the king after his death, the god with whom the deceased king has been united. We do not know the origin and the exact dates of the first of these kings, Pṛithivīndravarman, whose posthumous name was Rudraloka.[134] We do know, however, that he was succeeded by Satyavarman (Īśvaraloka), the son of his sister, and that the Javanese raid of 774 occurred during his reign. This raid destroyed the original sanctuary of Po Nagar at Nha-trang, which, according to tradition, was built by the legendary sovereign Vichitrasagara.[135] After repelling the invaders, Satyavarman built a new sanctuary of brick that was completed in 784.[136]

His younger brother, Indravarman, who succeeded him, is said to have been warlike. Indravarman, like his predecessor, was subjected to a Javanese raid; the one during Indravarman's reign occurred in 787 and destroyed a sanctuary of Bhadrādhipatīśvara, located west of the capital Vīrapura, near modern Phan-rang.[137] Indravarman sent an embassy to China in 793[138] and in 799 reconstructed the temple destroyed by the Javanese. He was still reigning in 801.[139]

7. BURMA: CONQUEST BY NANCHAO (AROUND 760) AND THE DECLINE OF PROME

The establishment in the first half of the eighth century of the kingdom of Nanchao,[140] which occupied the west and northwest of Yunnan, had serious consequences for the Pyu kingdom of Burma. The second king of Nanchao, Ko-lo-feng, who was allied with the Tibetans against China, was anxious to establish communications with the west, and to this end he had to secure Upper Burma. Between 757 and 763, he conquered the upper Irrawaddy Valley.[141] We may wonder if the capital of the Pyus remained at Prome in this period or if it was not transferred farther north, to Ha-lin,[142] but few facts have been established for this period of Burmese history. The introduction of Mahayana Buddhism, which undoubtedly dates back to the "vikrama" dynasty, is confirmed by the discovery of Bodhisattva images, some of which appear to date back to the eighth century.[143]

8. THE EXPANSION OF MAHAYANA BUDDHISM IN THE EIGHTH CENTURY

The expansion of Mahayana Buddhism in the countries of Farther India, which coincides roughly with the advent in India of the Pāla dynasty in Bengal and Magadha around the middle of the eighth century,[144] is the dominant fact of the period dealt with in this chapter.

Aside from the inscription of Palembang of 684, whose Mahayanist inspiration seems to remain on the plane of the Sarvāstivāda,[145] a sect of Theravada Buddhism that used the Sanskrit language, the facts that are known are as follows, in chronological order:[146]

775, on the Malay Peninsula, construction at Ligor of a sanctuary of the Buddha and the Bodhisattvas Padmapāṇi and Vajrapāṇi by the king of Śrīvijaya;
778, in Java, construction of a sanctuary of Tārā at Kalasan by Panangkaran;
782, in Java, erection of an image of Manjuśrī at Kelurak by a teacher from Bengal, perhaps also in the reign of Panangkaran;
791, in Cambodia, erection of an image of the Bodhisattva Lokeśvara at Prasat Ta Keâm.

These facts prove that in the last quarter of the eighth century, probably under the influence of the Pāla dynasty and the teachers of the university of Nālandā,[147] Mahayana Buddhism established a definite foothold on the peninsula and in the archipelago.[148] Its principal characteristics were: (1) a tendency toward the Tantric mysticism of the Vajrayāna, popular in Bengal from the middle of the eighth century; (2) a syncretism with Hindu cults which, already manifest in the inscription of Kelurak, was to become clear in Cambodia in the Angkor period and was to culminate later in Java in the cult of Siva-Buddha; and (3) the importance attached to the redemption of the souls of the dead, which gave Javanese and Balinese Buddhism the aspect of a veritable ancestor cult.[149]

CHAPTER VII

FOUNDATION OF THE KINGDOM OF ANGKOR; THE ŚAILENDRAS IN SUMATRA

First Three Quarters of the Ninth Century

1. THE BEGINNINGS OF THE KINGDOM OF ANGKOR[1]: JAYAVARMAN II (802–50)

The liberation of Cambodia from the suzerainty of Java was the work of Jayavarman II, founder of the kingdom of Angkor.

He was only distantly related to the ancient dynasties of pre-Angkorian Cambodia: he was the great-grandnephew through the female line of Pushkarāksha,[2] the prince of Aninditapura who became king of Śambhupura (Sambor),[3] and also the nephew of a King Jayendrādhipativarman about whom we know nothing.[4] An inscription from the beginning of the tenth century,[5] speaking of Jayavarman II's advent to the throne, says: "For the prosperity of the people, in this perfectly pure race of kings, great lotus which no longer has a stem, he rises as a new flower." Official genealogists used metaphors of this sort to veil the occasional disruptions of the regular succession in the dynastic order. Jayavarman II is almost unique among the kings of Cambodia in that he did not leave a single inscription; at least, none has been found. Fortunately, the principal episodes of his reign are related in some detail in an inscription of the eleventh century on the stele of Sdok Kak Thom.[6]

"His majesty," the text tells us, "came from Java to reign in the city of Indrapura." The family of Jayavarman II, which was linked with the dynasties of the eighth century, no doubt took refuge in Java during the disturbances over the succession—unless it had been taken there by force following one of the maritime raids discussed in the preceding chapter.

Jayavarman II's return from Java, perhaps motivated by the weakening of the Śailendras on the island, took place around 800, for we have abundant evidence that the effective beginning of the reign was 802.[7] The country was in a state of almost complete anarchy, apparently without a king[8] or divided among many rival principalities, and before he could obtain respect for his rights or his pretensions to the throne of Cambodia, the young prince had to conquer at least part of the kingdom.

He began by establishing himself in the city of Indrapura. Various epigraphical fragments make it possible to locate a city of this name in the province of Thbong Khmum, to the east of Kompong Cham,[9] where he perhaps had familial ties. The site may possibly have been Banteay Prei Nokor, the name of which ("Citadel of the Royal City") proves that there was an ancient capital there; its monuments of pre-Angkorian art manifest the style of the ninth century in certain details.[10] But the remains along the western bank of the Western Baray (to be discussed in a moment) are not excluded as a possible site of Indrapura.

It was at Indrapura, it seems, that the young king took into his services as royal chaplain a Brahman scholar, Śivakaivalya, who was to follow him in all his changes of residence and to become the first chief priest of a new cult, that of the Devarāja, or "God-King."

After remaining some time in Indrapura, Jayavarman II left this residence, accompanied by Śivakaivalya and his family, and made his way to a region north of the Tonle Sap, or Great Lake, that regulator of irrigation and inexhaustible fish pond. This region, where the first city of Angkor would be erected a century later, had constituted the fief of Bhavapura, as we have seen before.[11] "When they arrived at the eastern district," says the stele of Sdok Kak Thom, "the king bestowed an estate and a village called Kuṭi upon the family of the royal chaplain." The "eastern district" refers to the region to the east of Angkor. The name Kuṭi survives in the name of Banteay Kdei, a late monument which was built near a much earlier one.[12]

"Later," continues the stele, "the king reigned in the city of Hariharālaya. The royal chaplain also settled in this city, and the members of his family were appointed to the corps of pages."

Hariharālaya corresponds to a group of ruins called the "Rolûos group," situated some fifteen kilometers southeast of Siem Reap and including a monument, Lolei, the name of which is vaguely reminiscent of the old name Hariha*rālaya*.[13] On this site were many edifices belonging to pre-Angkorian art: Jayavarman II was, by and large, content to make repairs on them, although the construction of some new edifices can be attributed to him.[14]

"Afterwards," the inscription says, "the king went to *found* the city of Amarendrapura, and the royal chaplain also settled in this city to serve the king."

In 1924 Georges Groslier[15] attempted to revive an old hypothesis of Etienne Aymonier[16] and identify Amarendrapura with the great temple of Banteay Ch'mar, but it is now known that this monument does not date farther back than the twelfth century. The geographic arguments advanced for locating Amarendrapura in the northwest of Cambodia are still of some value; however, this region does not possess monuments that can be attributed by their architectural or decorative style to the reign of Jayavarman II. And it is not clear why, after having begun to establish himself in Angkor, he would have chosen another area that was so distant from the Lake and that must always have been relatively barren. On the other hand, the terrain along the western bank of the Western Baray has revealed a series of walls associated with edifices whose style places them at the very beginning of Angkor art, before the art of the Kulèn; it is possible that this group, if it does not represent the Indrapura mentioned above, corresponds in part to the city of Amarendrapura founded by Jayavarman II.[17]

"Then," continues the inscription, "the king went to reign at Mahendraparvata, and the Lord Śivakaivalya followed him, establishing himself in this capital to serve the king as before. Then a Brahman named Hiraṇyadāma, learned in the magical science, came from Janapada[18] at the king's invitation to perform a ritual designed to ensure that the country of the Kambujas would no longer be dependent on Java and that there would be no more than one sovereign who was *chakravartin* [universal monarch]. This Brahman performed a ritual according to the sacred *Vināśikha* and established a Lord of the Universe who was the king [Sanskrit: *devarāja*]. This Brahman taught the sacred *Vināśikha,* the *Nayottara,* the *Sammoha,* and the *Śiraccheda.* He recited them from beginning to end in order that they might be written down and taught to Lord Śivakaivalya, and he ordained Lord Śivakaivalya to perform the ritual of the Devarāja. The king and the Brahman Hiraṇyadāma took an oath to employ the family of Lord Śivakaivalya to conduct the worship of the Devarāja and not to allow others to conduct it. The Lord Śivakaivalya, the chief priest [*purohita*], assigned all his relatives to this cult."

Mahendraparvata (i.e., Mount Mahendra) has long been identified with Phnom Kulèn, the sandstone plateau that dominates the northern part of the Angkor Plain.[19] Recent researches [20] have revealed an archaeological group there that undoubtedly shows the skeleton of the religious edifices of the city of Jayavarman II, for its style [21] lies between that of the last pre-Angkorian monuments and that of the first edifices of Angkor art, grouped not so long ago under the designation of the art of Indravarman.[22] It is worthwhile to dwell a moment on what happened at Phnom Kulèn, the more so since Jean Filliozat [23] has shown recently that, in southern India, Mount Mahendra was considered the residence of Siva as king of all the gods (*devarāja*), including Indra Devarāja, and as sovereign of the country where the mountain stands.

We have seen in the preceding chapter that the Śailendras of Java appear to have claimed for themselves the title of universal emperor which had belonged in other times to the kings of Funan. This could explain the method that Jayavarman II, upon his return from Java,[24] used to restore his authority over Cambodia at the beginning of the ninth century. In order to free himself from the vassalage of the "king of the mountain," whose very title conveys the quality of *mahārāja* or *chakravartin,* it was necessary that he become one himself, receiving from a Brahman, on a mountain, the miraculous linga in which resided henceforth the royal power of the Khmer kings. This was why he established his capital on Mount Mahendra (Phnom Kulèn) and summoned a Brahman who instituted the ritual of Devarāja and taught it to the chaplain "so that the country of the Kambujas would no longer be dependent on Java and so that there would be no more than one sovereign [in this kingdom] who would be *chakravartin.*"

If the more or less effective sovereignty of distant Java had been nothing but the result of the expeditions at the end of the preceding century, there would have been no need, it would seem, for all these ceremonies to achieve liberation. But if the Śailendras of Java exercised sovereignty as heirs of the old owners of the soil, that was a different matter, and a new ritual associated with a new mountain became necessary.[25]

In the Indianized kingdoms of Southeast Asia, the Hindu cults developed even further a tendency they had already shown in India and eventually became royal cults. This was particularly true of the worship of Siva. The essence of royalty, or, as some texts say, the *"moi subtil"* of the king,[26] was supposed to reside in a linga placed on a pyramid in the center of the royal city, which was itself supposed to be the axis of the world.[27] This miraculous linga, a sort of palladium of the kingdom, was thought to have been obtained from Siva through a Brahman who delivered it to the king, founder of the dynasty.[28] The communion between the king and the god through the medium of a priest took place on the sacred mountain, which could be either natural or artificial.

Since the only monument at Phnom Kulèn that suggests a pyramid is Krus Preah Aram Rong Chen, it undoubtedly corresponds to the first sanctuary of the Devarāja. When Jayavarman II and his successors ceased to reside on Mahendraparvata, they built other temple-mountains at the center of their subsequent capitals.[29]

The ritual of the Devarāja established by the Brahman Hiraṇyadāma was based on four texts—*Vināśikha, Nayottara, Sammoha,* and *Śiraccheda*—which the Sanskrit portion of the stele calls "the four faces of Tumburu." Louis Finot, in publishing the inscription,[30] expressed the opinion that these texts were of Tantric origin; two Indian scholars [31] have confirmed this point of view by pointing out, in a bibliography of Nepal, a group of *tantras* that have titles somewhat analogous to these. They were supposed to have been uttered by the four mouths of Siva represented by the *gandharva* Tumburu, but we do not know their contents precisely enough to give us an idea of the ritual instituted on Phnom Kulèn. This does not prevent us from establishing a relationship, perhaps illusory, between the *Śiraccheda,* "the beheading," and the story of the decapitation of the king of Cambodia by the maharaja of Zābag reported by the Arab voyager.[32] If the suzerainty of Java originated in an act of this sort, we can easily understand that the essential act of the ritual designed to end the subjection of Cambodia was the decapitation in effigy of the suzerain king. But another explanation is possible. A rite of suicide by self-decapitation designed to obtain a favor for a third party from the divinity is known in India.[33] It is possible that such a suicide, real or simulated, formed a part of the installation ceremonies of the Devarāja. In any case, the magical role of decapitation, real or simulated, is too well known [34] for us to be surprised at finding it at the beginning of the kingdom of Angkor.

We might ask why Jayavarman II did not perform this rite at the beginning of his reign and why he waited until he had already resided in three capitals before declaring his independence. It was because he first had to conquer a part of the kingdom,[35] to "reassemble the land" divided among several chiefs, each of whom claimed to be a king, to strengthen his power, to defend himself against the Chams,[36] and to re-establish order before daring to let the miraculous linga, the source of sovereign power, descend onto the sacred mountain. His changes of capitals must have been accompanied by military operations, to which an inscription of the eleventh century alludes by saying that the king "ordered the chief officers to pacify all the districts." [37] Foremost among these officers was Pṛithivīnarendra, "burning like fire the troops of the enemies," to whom was entrusted the task of reconquering Malyang, i.e., the region south of Battambang.[38]

In succeeding centuries, the establishment of Jayavarman II on Phnom Kulèn was considered a historical event marking the beginning of a new era: Jayavarman II is most often cited in the inscriptions as "the king who established his residence on the summit of Mount Mahendra." A number of families were to trace their first ancestor back to his reign, and several charters of endowment of land ownership attribute their origin to his reign.

We do not know the duration of Jayavarman II's stay on Kulèn. "Afterwards," the inscription continues, "the king returned to rule in the city of Hariharālaya and the Devarāja was brought back also; the chaplain and all his relatives officiated as before. The chaplain died during this reign. The king died in the city of Hariharālaya where the Devarāja resided."

Several monuments of the Rolûos group seem to date from the second stay of Jayavarman II at Hariharālaya.[39] As for the location of the royal residence, there seem to be two possibilities. It could correspond either to the large quadrangle called Prei Monti, the name of which is derived from the Sanskrit *maṇḍira* meaning precisely "royal palace," or to the quadrangle in the eastern district from which rise the towers of Preah Kô, funerary temple of Jayavarman II and of the ancestors of his second successor, Indravarman. This temple, following a custom of which there are other examples, might have been erected on the site of a royal residence.

Jayavarman II died at Hariharālaya in 850, after reigning 48 years.[40] He received the posthumous name of Parameśvara; this is the first definite example of the use of a name indicating deification for a sovereign of Cambodia.[44]

Jayavarman II's reign made a profound impression on the country. Although his effective authority undoubtedly did not extend beyond the region of the Great Lake, Jayavarman II began the pacification and unification of the country. He sought the site of the future capital in a region near that inexhaustible fish-preserve that is the Tonle Sap, slightly beyond the limit of the annual inundations, about thirty kilometers from the sandstone quarries of Phnom Kulèn, and quite close to the passes giving access to the Khorat Plateau and to the Menam Basin. It remained for his grandnephew and third successor, Yaśovarman, to found there the city of Yaśodharapura, which remained the capital of the Khmer empire for 600 years.

Jayavarman II instituted the cult of the Devarāja in which the sanctuary in a pyramid, erected on a natural or artificial mountain and sheltering the linga of stone or precious metal in which the Devarāja of each reign resides, henceforth marks the center of the royal city: the Bakong at Hariharālaya (Rolûos), the Bakhèng in the first city of Angkor, the great pyramid at Koh Ker, the Phimeanakas, the Baphuon.[42]

Art during the reign of Jayavarman II, who came from abroad but apparently was anxious to renew his connection with the national traditions, shows the transition between the art of the pre-Angkor period, to which the king was still closely attached, and that of the Angkor epoch, which owed to him some of its new forms. These forms were particularly influenced by the art of Champa and Java.[43]

Jayavarman II was succeeded by his son Jayavardhana,[44] a great elephant hunter,[45] who continued to reside at Hariharālaya. This king, who reigned from 850 to 857 under the name of Jayavarman (III), did some building in the region of Angkor.[46] At his death he received the posthumous name of Vishṇuloka.

2. SOUTHERN CHAMPA: PANDURANGA FROM 802 TO 854

In Champa, the kings continued to reside in the southern provinces. Harivarman I succeeded his brother-in-law Indravarman I around 802.[47] In 803 he launched a successful expedition in the Chinese provinces; in 809 he renewed his campaign there with less success. Around the same time, that is, at the beginning of the reign of Jayavarman II, Cambodia also appears to have suffered from attacks led by a Cham military leader, the Senāpati Pār.[48] Harivarman I was still reigning in 813[49] and probably in 817, a year in which the Senāpati made endowments at Po Nagar of Nha-trang. He was succeeded by his son Vikrāntavarman III, about whom we know only that he made a few endowments at Po Nagar of Nha-trang and at Po Nagar of Mong-dưc (854).[51]

3. BURMA: KINGDOMS OF P'IAO AND MI-CH'EN; FOUNDATION OF PEGU (HAṂSAVATĪ) IN 825 AND OF PAGAN (ARIMADDANAPURA) IN 849

In Burma, China's subjection of Nanchao in 791[52] led to the establishment of relations by land between China and the Pyu kingdom. In 802, the king Yung-ch'iang, surnamed K'un-mo-ch'ang, sent an embassy to China led by his brother (or his son) Sunandana.[53] Another was sent in 807.[54] The information on the kingdom of P'iao given in the accounts of these two embassies in the histories of the T'ang and the *Man Shu* is summarized in the following paragraph.[55]

If the journey is short, the king travels in a palanquin of golden cord; if it is long, by elephant. He has several hundred wives and concubines. The wall of the capital, measuring 160 *li* in length, is made of green glazed brick and is protected by a moat lined with bricks; it is pierced by twelve gates and armed with towers at the corners. Its population includes several tens of thousands of families. The houses are roofed with lead and tin shingles. There are more than a hundred Buddhist monasteries, decorated with gold, silver, and many colors of paint and hung with embroidered cloth. In the palace of the king there are two bells, one gold and the other silver, that are struck in a certain way if the kingdom is threatened by invasion; the sounds the bells make are interpreted as presaging good luck or bad. Near the palace there is a statue of a large white elephant 100 feet high, in front of which all those who have grievances kneel, reflecting inwardly about the justice or injustice of their own causes. In case of public misfortunes, the king himself bows down before the elephant, burning incense and blaming himself for the offenses he has committed. The women pile their hair on top of their head, forming a large knot that they decorate with tin flowers, pearls, and various stones. They all carry fans, and those of the upper class suspend five or six of them from their girdles. Young boys and girls have their heads completely shaved at seven years of age and are then placed in the temples and convents. They live there until their twentieth year, studying the religion of the Buddha, and then they re-enter the world. Their clothes consist only of a white cotton robe and a girdle whose red color imitates the shade of the clouds that surround the rising sun. They spurn the use of silk because it is necessary to take life in order to procure silk. The inhabitants of the country profess a love of life and a horror of killing. Neither shackles, manacles, nor any instruments of torture are used on accused persons, who are simply tied up. Those who are found guilty receive lashes of bamboo on the back: five blows for grave offenses, three for those less serious. Only murder is punished by death. They use neither tallow nor oil, and make candles of perfumed beeswax. They have silver crescent-shaped money. They carry on commerce with the neighboring nations, to which they sell white cloth and clay jars. They have their own special music and refined dances. (The Chinese sources give considerable detail about these.)

During the entire first half of the ninth century, Nanchao was master of Upper Burma. In 832, it abducted three thousand Pyus from the population of the capital Ha-lin to populate the eastern capital of Nanchao, Cha-tung, which corresponds to the modern Yunnan-fu (K'un-ming). This was the beginning of the Pyu decline.

The depopulation of Prome profited Pagan (Arimaddanapura), a city formed by the union of several villages, well situated close to the confluence of the Irrawaddy and the Chindwin, at the crossroads of the routes leading to Assam, Yunnan, and the region occupied today by the Shan states,[56] and not far from the rice plain of Kyaukse, which was the cradle of the Burmese and the center of the expansion of these racial brothers of the Pyus who followed the Pyus down from the confines of Tibet at the end of the eighth and the beginning of the ninth centuries.[57] This was also the place where the Burmese entered into contact with the Mons, who were established there in considerable numbers. The Mons taught them their Indic script and introduced them to the religions of India. Native chronicles date the origin of Pagan back to the second century and give a long list of chiefs of undetermined authenticity; it was one of these, the monk usurper Poppa So-rahan, who is supposed to have founded the Burmese era in 638.[58] Charles Duroiselle[59] believes that the "Arī" Buddhist sect, rich in Tantric rites including erotic practices, had penetrated to Pagan as early as the eighth century. But we do not hear the *araññika,* or "forest monks," spoken of before the beginning of the thirteenth century, and nothing indicates that at this time they professed any Mahayanist belief or that they practiced Tantric rites; their nonconformity was limited to partaking of meat and alcohol on the occasion of certain festivals.[60] In 849, Pagan entered definitively into history, if not in epigraphy at least in the annals, with the construction of its city walls by the king Pyinbya.

According to native chronicles, Pagan began as a group of nineteen villages, each possessing its "Nat," or local spirit. When these villages were fused into a single city, the king, in agreement with his subjects, sought to establish the cult of a common "Nat" that would be worshiped by all, which would become superior to the local spirits and the worship of which would unify the various tribes into a true nation. Mount Poppa, an ancient volcano situated not far from the city and already enjoying the veneration of the Burmese, was chosen as the place for the establishment of a pair of spirits: they were a brother and sister who, after, having been unjustly put to death by a neighboring king, were incarnated in a tree. This tree was cut down and floated to Pagan, and the images of Min Mahāgiri, "Lord of the Great Mountain," and of his sister Taunggyi Shin, whose name has the same meaning in Burmese, were carved from its trunk. This legend is interesting because it shows the establishment of a cult of a spirit on a mountain in order to achieve religious and territorial unification and the birth of a nation.[61]

At the beginning of the ninth century, the *New History of the T'ang* mentions among the vassal states of P'iao the kingdom of Mi-ch'en, which sent an embassy to China in 805[62] and was a victim of Nanchao aggression in 835.[63] According to an itinerary given in the same text,[64] Mi-ch'en must have been situated on the Gulf of Martaban, perhaps in the region of old Pegu.[65]

In this period, the center of gravity of the kingdom of Rāmaññadesa, that is, the Mon country,[66] shifted to the west: a chronicle gives 825 as the date for the foundation of Pegu (Haṃsavatī) by Samala and Vimala, twin brothers from Thaton.[67] This date seems to be preferable to the earlier or later dates furnished by other texts.[68] The chronicles of Pegu, like those of Pagan, give lists of kings [69] which are impossible to verify. The importance of the Brahmanic remains in lower Burma proves that before this period Buddhism was not the dominant religion. The conversion of the heretic King Tissa to Buddhism was to be accomplished by the queen, who originally came from Martaban.[70]

4. THE MALAY PENINSULA

On the Malay Peninsula, the only document that can be attributed to the first half of the ninth century was found at Takuapa, not far from the Vishnuite statues of Khao Phra Narai, which are perhaps contemporaneous.[71] It is a short inscription in Tamil indicating that an artificial lake named Avani-nāraṇam was dug by Nangur-udaiyan (which, according to K. A. Nilakanta Sastri, is the name of an individual who possessed a military fief at Nangur, a village in Tanjore district, and who was famous for his abilities as a warrior) and that the lake was placed under the protection of the members of the Manikkiramam (which, according to Nilakanta Sastri, was a merchant guild) living in the military camp.[72] Since Avani-nārāyaṇa is a surname of the Pallava king Nandivarman III who reigned from 826 to 849,[73] we can deduce the approximate date of this inscription. The inscription merits mention, since it, along with the inscription of Labu Tuwa on Sumatra dated 1088,[74] is one of the few documents composed in one of the vernaculars of India that has been found in Farther India. These two inscriptions alluding to the commercial activities of guilds known in southern India provide an interesting indication of the nature and geographic origin of the relations between India and Southeast Asia.

5. THE ŚAILENDRAS IN JAVA AND SUMATRA FROM 813 TO 863

Chinese sources list the last embassies of Ho-ling in 813 or 815 and in 818; [75] embassies of 820 and 831 are attributed to She-p'o.[76] She-p'o, which in the fifth century, it will be recalled, designated all or part of the island of Java,[77] was in the eighth century the name of the capital of Ho-ling. This capital was abandoned between 742 and 755 for P'o-lu-chia-ssu, situated farther east.[78] This change of capital was the result of the rise of the Buddhist Śailendras in central Java. The reappearance of She-p'o in 820 can be interpreted either as the reunion of the center and the east under the aegis of the Śailendras or, more probably, as the return to power in the center of the island of Sivaite princes who had migrated to the east.

We know little about the successors of Panangkaran, founder of Kalasan, except their names. The inscription of Balitung of 907 already cited [79] lists, without telling us their genealogical relations, the Maharajas Panungalan, Warak, and Garung. Garung, about whom we have an inscription dated 819,[80] perhaps took religious vows, which would explain his name Patapān in an inscription of 850.[81]

In 824 the ruler was Samaratunga.[82] Samaratunga is not included in the list of the inscription of 907 because he was one of the Śailendra sovereigns of the Sanjaya dynasty of which Balitung was the heir. Perhaps, in view of the resemblance of the names, we can identify him with Samarāgravīra, brother of the Śailendra king of Java mentioned in the Charter of Nālandā.[83]

The next to the last king mentioned in the inscription of 907 is Pikatan, for whom we have an inscription dated 850.[84] According to J. G. de Casparis, he may have begun reigning around 842. He seems also to have been known under the names of Kumbhayoni and Jātiningrat.[85] He married the Princess Prāmodavardhanī, a daughter of the Śailendra Samaratunga, who was himself the husband of the princess Tārā of Śrīvijaya. The salient fact about the reign of Pikatan was his conflict with his brother-in-law Bālaputra, "younger son" of Samarāgravīra, also known as Samaratunga. Pikatan's victory over Bālaputra in 856 [86] was apparently the reason why Bālaputra moved to Śrīvijaya, the country of his mother Tārā. The Charter of Nālandā (*ca.* 860) informs us that Śrīvijaya at this time was governed by the "younger son" (*Bālaputra*) of Samarāgravīra.[87] Thus, the earliest mention of the maharaja of Zābag (Jāvaka) by an Arab author (Ibn Khordādzbeh) [88] refers to a Śailendra reigning in Java rather than to a Śailendra of Sumatra, as will be the case later.

But the decline of power of the Śailendras at the center of Java, accompanied by a renewal of Hinduist worship there that is indicated by an inscription coming from the vicinity of Prambanan (863),[89] resulted in the strengthening of the power of the Śailendras in Sumatra. This growth of Śailendran power in Sumatra is reflected in the Arab and Persian sources. It is certain in fact that in the tenth century Zābag corresponded to the San-fo-ch'i of the Chinese, that is, to the Sumatran kingdom of Śrīvijaya.

All that we know about Śrivijaya around the middle of the ninth century [90] is—and here I repeat some information from the preceding chapter—that the "mahārāja of Suvarṇadvīpa" was a "younger son" (*Bālaputra*) of the king of Java Samarāgravīra (i.e., Samaratunga) and a grandson of the Śailendra "king of Java and killer of enemy heroes" who was probably the Sangrāmadhananjaya of the inscription of Kelurak, that is, the Śailendra mentioned on the second face of the Ligor stele. Through his mother Tārā, he was grandson of a King Dharmasetu—a king whom one scholar has sought to identify with Dharmapāla of the Pāla dynasty of Bengal [91] but who was much more probably the king of Śrīvijaya who built the sanctuary that prompted the inscription on the first face of the Ligor stele.[92] This Bālaputra was undoubtedly the first Śailendra sovereign of Śrīvijaya. He had a monastery built in India, at Nālandā,[93] to which the king Devapāla, in the thirty-ninth year of his reign (*ca.* 860),[94] offered many villages. This donation was the subject of a charter containing the genealogical information that has been incorporated in the preceding pages.

CHAPTER VIII

THE FLOWERING OF THE KINGDOMS OF ANGKOR AND ŚRĪVIJAYA

From the End of the Ninth Century to the Beginning of the Eleventh Century

1. THE KINGDOM OF ANGKOR (877–1001)

After the somewhat surprising silence of Jayavarman II and Jayavarman III, Indravarman, who came to power in 877, resumed the epigraphic tradition of his predecessors of the pre-Angkorian period. Perhaps we owe this fortunate circumstance to the influence of his spiritual master, the Brahman Śivasoma, a relative of Jayavarman II [1] and a disciple of the famous Hindu philosopher Śankarāchārya, the restorer of orthodox Brahmanism.[2] Apparently, Indravarman was not related to his two predecessors. Genealogists of the following reigns tried after a fashion to make him the grandson or grandnephew of the parents of Jayavarman II's wife,[3] but this claim did not appear in any of his inscriptions. He was son of a King Pṛithivīndravarman and, on his mother's side, great-grandson of a King Nṛipatīndravarman; we know nothing else about these so-called sovereigns.[4] Through his wife Indradevī, descendant of Pushkarāksha, he undoubtedly acquired rights over Śambhupura, where his two predecessors may not have exercised effective sovereignty. He continued to reside at Hariharālaya (Rolûos), and in the first year of his reign, in 877, he undertook to construct north of the capital the Indrataṭāka, the great artificial lake, which is now dry and in the center of which the monument of Lolei was later built. The lake served practical as well as ritual purposes: it was a reservoir for irrigation during the dry season. Thus, Indravarman set an example for his successors, whom we will see exercising great care in the planning of larger and larger reservoirs designed to retain running water during the rainy season and to distribute it at the proper time to the rice fields surrounding the capital.[5] In 879, he dedicated the six stuccoed brick towers of Preah Kô [6] to statues of his parents, his maternal grandparents, and Jayavarman II and his wife, deified in the forms of Siva and Devī.[7] Finally, in 881, he inaugurated the first great monument in stone, built for the royal linga Indreśvara, the name of which linked, according to custom, the name of the god Īśvara (Siva) with that of the founding king. This was the pyramid of Bakong,[8] south of Preah Kô.

Indravarman's rather short reign seems to have been peaceful. His authority extended from the region of Chaudoc, where he dedicated a *vimana* to Siva in the old sanctuary of Phnom Bayang,[9] to the region northwest of Ubon, from which comes a Buddhist inscription of 886 mentioning him as the reigning king.[10] His teacher Śivasoma affirms that with regard to external affairs "his rule was like a crown of jasmine on the lofty heads of the kings of China, Champa and Java," [11] a claim that is certainly greatly exaggerated but gives some idea of the diplomatic horizon of Cambodia in this period.

At his death in 889, Indravarman received the posthumous name Īśvaraloka. He was succeeded by his son Yaśovardhana, whose mother Indradevī was a descendant of the ancient royal families of Vyādhapura (Funan), Śambhupura, and Aninditapura. The new king thus restored the pre-Angkorian legitimacy [12] which had been interrupted by the reigns of Jayavarman II and III and of Indravarman. Moreover, his teacher was the Brahman Vāmaśiva, who belonged to the powerful priestly family assigned by Jayavarman II to the cult of the Devarāja [13] and who was connected, through his master Śivasoma, to the great Hindu philosopher Śankarāchārya.

The reign of Yaśovarman I lived up to the promises of this double ancestry, and the building program he realized was later to serve as a model to his successors.

The very year of his accession, 889, he had about a hundred monasteries (*āśrama*) built in the various provinces of his kingdom, near ancient sanctuaries or at places of frequent pilgrimage. Each monastery had a royal pavilion (*rājakuṭī*) reserved for the sovereign during his travels.[14] We know a dozen locations of these lightly constructed monasteries, each marked by the presence of a stele bearing a Sanskrit inscription in ordinary characters on one face and on the other face the same text in a script of northern India (pre-Nāgarī) similar to the script introduced in Java a century earlier.[15] The text of all of these "stone posters," as Bergaigne has called them, is basically the same, differing from one stele to another only in the name of the divinity to which the monastery was dedicated. After a detailed genealogy of Yaśovarman, and a eulogy of this king who, if the panegyrist is to be believed, combined physical power and skill with the highest degree of intelligence, the inscriptions give the rules of the monasteries, uniformly called Yaśodharāśrama, in the form of a royal ordinance (*śāsana*).

In 893, Yaśovarman erected a sanctuary in the middle of the Indrataṭāka, the great artificial lake dug by his father north of the capital. The sanctuary was composed of four brick towers designed, like those of Preah Kô, to shelter the statues of the king's parents and grandparents;[16] it is the monument known today under the name Lolei, which seems to recall, as I have said earlier, the name of Hariha*rālaya*.

Yaśovarman did not reside in this capital for long, and it is possible that from the moment of his accession he had planned to move the sanctuary of the Devarāja and the seat of the temporal power: "Then," says the inscription of Sdok Kak Thom,[17] "the king founded the city of Yaśodharapura and took the Devarāja away from Hariharālaya to establish it in this capital. Then the king erected the Central Mountain. The Lord of Śivāśrama [surname of the teacher Vāmaśiva] erected the sacred linga in the middle."

For a long time it was thought that this text referred to the foundation of Angkor Thom and of the Bayon. But Philippe Stern, in a monograph that has become a classic,[18] has proved that it is impossible that a monument built and decorated the way the Bayon is could date back to the end of the ninth century, and I for my part have shown that Angkor Thom as it appears today was built not earlier than the end of the twelfth century.[19] The city founded by Yaśovarman has been identified by Victor Goloubew with a vast quadrangle bounded on the west and south sides by a still visible double wall of earth and a moat now transformed into rice fields and on the east side by the river of Siem Reap, which was deflected from its original course.[20] The center of the quadrangle is marked by the hill Phnom Bakhèng, crowned by a pyramidical structure built in a style that is certainly of this period; an inscription indicates that it sheltered the linga Yaśodhareśvara.[21]

What reasons provoked this relocation of the capital and determined the choice of the new location?

The site of Hariharālaya, crowded with monuments built during the preceding reigns, undoubtedly did not lend itself to the realization of the urban projects of the young king. Besides, if, as I believe, the temple of the loyal linga had to become the mausoleum of its founder, it had to be rebuilt at each change of reign, at the same time that the linga changed names or was replaced by a new linga.[22] That Yaśovarman might want to surpass his father's Indreśvara by constructing a temple for the linga Yaśodhareśvara on a natural hill would be in no way surprising. Now, of the three hills he had to choose from in the vicinity of Hariharālaya, Phnom Bok was too high and awkward to mark the center of a city, and Phnom Krom was too close to the Great Lake. There remained Phnom Bakhèng. The height and dimensions of Phnom Bakhèng were well suited to the king's purpose, and this is undoubtedly why he chose it. He was satisfied to construct a triple sanctuary dedicated to the Trimūrti on each of the other two hills.[23]

At the same time that Yaśovarman laid out his capital and connected it to the old one by a road which went from its eastern entrance to the northeastern corner of the Indrataṭāka, the artificial lake dug by his father, he constructed another artificial lake, an immense reservoir measuring seven kilometers long and 1800 meters wide, northeast of the new city. This reservoir, named Yaśodharataṭāka, was bordered by a strong earthen levee, in the four corners of which Yaśovarman placed steles with long Sanskrit inscriptions in pre-Nāgarī script reproducing his genealogy, developing his panegyric, and exalting his work.[24] On the southern bank of this immense body of water, now dry and known by the name Eastern Baray, the king had a series of monasteries built for the various sects [25] that his religious eclecticism permitted him to divide his favors among: the Sivaite Brāhmaṇāśrama for the Śaivas, the Pāśupatas, and the Tapasvins; [26] the Vishnuite Vaishṇavāśrama for the Pāncharātras, the Bhāgavatas, and the Sāttvatas; [27] and perhaps also a Buddhist Saugatāśrama, the stele of which, moved from its original site, has been found at Tép Pranam in Angkor Thom.[28]

It was also during the reign of Yaśovarman that construction was begun on the Sivaite temples of Śikharīśvara ("the Siva of the summit") at Preah Vihear and of Bhadreśvara at Śivapura (Phnom Sandak).[29]

The foundation of Yaśodharapura, on the site that was to remain the capital of Cambodia until the fifteenth century, must suffice to illustrate the reign of Yaśovarman, since the political history of his reign is largely unknown. His two-script inscriptions cover a vast area, extending from lower Laos in the north[30] to the coast of the Gulf of Siam between the regions of Čhanthabun[31] and of Hatien in the south.[32] A campaign in Champa that was attributed to him not long ago on the basis of a text of the twelfth century really took place in the twelfth century.[33] The boundaries assigned to Yaśovarman's kingdom by an inscription of his nephew Rājendravarman[34] are the Sūkshma-Kāmrātas (on the coast of Burma), the sea (Gulf of Siam), Champa, and China. The "China" must mean Nanchao, which a Chinese text expressly mentions as bordering Cambodia in the second half of the ninth century.[35] The mention of a naval victory "over thousands of barks with white sails"[36] may refer to the Chams, or perhaps to some new Indonesian raid.

Yaśovarman's reign ended around 900,[37] and he received the posthumous name Paramaśivaloka.[38]

We know very little about his two sons who succeeded him.

The elder, Harshavarman I, who made a donation in 912 in the ancient capital of Funan,[39] was the founder of the little temple-mountain of Baksei Chamkrong at the foot of Phnom Bakhèng.[40] He was undoubtedly still reigning in 922.[41] At his death, which followed shortly afterwards, he received the posthumous name Rudraloka.

About the younger brother, Īśānavarman II, we know scarcely anything except his posthumous name Paramarudraloka. He apparently was reigning in 925,[42] but it is stated that in 921[43] one of his maternal uncles "left the city of Yaśodharapura to reign at Ch'ok Gargyar, taking the Devarāja with him."[44] It seems likely that there was a usurpation on the part of this uncle, who reigned under the name Jayavarman (IV). A later text gives the date of this uncle's accession as 928.[45] This was perhaps the date of the death of Īśānavarman II, thanks to which the uncle was finally able to play the part of a legitimate sovereign.

Jayavarman IV built his new residence on the present-day site of Koh Ker,[46] in the vicinity of a large body of water designed by him. He decorated this site with monuments of colossal dimensions;[47] the most remarkable of these is the great five-stepped pyramid, on the summit of which one still finds the pedestal of the royal linga Tribhuvaneśvara. The inscriptions designate this linga by the name *kamrateng jagat ta rājya,* "the god who is the royalty," and describe the raising of the linga to the height of thirty-five meters as an unparalleled wonder.[48] About twenty years after the construction of this splendid edifice, which undoubtedly constitutes an innovation in the conception of the Devarāja,[49] the new capital was abandoned in its turn in favor of the old.

Jayavarman IV—whose posthumous name was Paramaśivapada—married a sister of Yaśovarman, Jayadevī,[50] by whom he had a son who succeeded him in 941 [51] under the name Harshavarman II. Harshavarman II—whose posthumous name was Brahmaloka—reigned only two or three years.

Another sister of Yaśovarman, an older sister named Mahendradevī, had married a certain Mahendravarman whom the genealogists connect to the remote dynasties of pre-Angkorian Cambodia in a loose and highly suspect fashion.[52] He was chief of Bhavapura, that is, of the nucleus of ancient Chenla,[53] which had continued to lead an independent existence after the death of Jayavarman I. A son, Rājendravarman, was born of this union. Rājendravarman was thus at the same time nephew of Jayavarman IV and of Yaśovarman and the elder cousin (the inscriptions say "brother") of Harshavarman II.

The death of Harshavarman II, from natural causes or otherwise, when he was still a child,[54] brought Rājendravarman to power. Rājendravarman was himself very young, but his claims seem to have been more substantial than those of his uncle and his cousin, for he came into the inheritance of Bhavapura through his father. He applied himself immediately to resuming the Angkorian tradition by returning to establish himself at Yaśodharapura, bringing back the Devarāja.[55] "Just as Kuśa [son of Rāma and Sītā] had done for Ayodhyā, he restored the sacred city of Yaśodharapurī, which had been abandoned for a long time, and made it superb and charming by constructing a palace with a sanctuary of brilliant gold, like the palace of Mahendra on earth." [56] Perhaps this passage refers to a first state of the Phimeanakas, which is situated, as has been noted,[57] at the intersection of the north-south axis of Yaśodharapura (centered at Phnom Bakhèng) and the east-west axis of the Yaśodharataṭāka (Eastern Baray)—therefore, at the intersection of the axes of the two great accomplishments of Yaśovarman.

Following the example of Yaśovarman, who had built the sanctuary of Lolei, consecrated to the memory of his parents deified in the forms of Siva and Umā, in the middle of the Indrataṭāka dug by his father Indravarman,[58] Rājendravarman in 952 built a temple known as the Eastern Mébon in the middle of the Yaśodharataṭāka dug by his uncle Yaśovarman. In its five brick towers, arranged in a quincunx, he placed statues of his parents in the forms of Siva and Umā, statues of Vishnu and Brahma, and, in the center, the royal linga Rājendreśvara (perhaps placed here until it was possible to consecrate a special temple to it in the restored city). This complex was surrounded, as at Bakong, by eight towers sheltering eight lingas of Siva.[59] Nine years later, in 961, perhaps this time in imitation of Preah Kô, built south of the Indrataṭāka, he built, to the south of Yaśodharataṭāka, the temple-mountain of Prè Rup, comprising (1) in the center, the linga Rājendrabhadreśvara, the name of which evokes both that of the king and that of Bhadreśvara, a sort of national divinity venerated in the ancient sanctuary of Vat Ph'u, cradle of the Kambujas; [60] (2) in the four corner towers of the upper terrace, another linga named Rājendravarmeśvara, "erected in view of the prosperity of the king and as if this were his own royal essence," an image of Vishṇu Rājendraviśvarūpa in memory of his early ancestors, a Śiva Rājendravarmadeveśvara in memory of his predecessor Harshavarman II, and an Umā on behalf of his aunt Jayadevī, mother of Harshavarman II; and (3) the eight forms (*mūrti*) of Siva.[61]

The monuments that are associated with the name of Rājendravarman or that date from his reign are numerous.[62] Most of them were sponsored by officials or high-ranking Brahmans who must have taken advantage of the tender age of the sovereign to assure themselves of privileged positions at the court. This sort of tutelage of the king by great dignitaries also continued in the following reign and undoubtedly for the same reason: the extreme youth of the king at the time of his accession. Among the persons of note during Rājendravarman's reign we must cite in first place the Rājakulamahāmantri, "great adviser of the royal family," who seems to have played the role of a regent or prime minister; [63] the Brahman Śivāchārya, who had been in the service of the kings since Īśānavarman II as a *hotar* (royal chaplain); [64] and finally the emissary (*chāra*) Kavīndrārimathana, whom the king charged with the construction of his palace and of the sanctuary known as the Eastern Mébon.[65] Kavīndrārimathana was a Buddhist, and he had Sanskrit inscriptions engraved on the three towers of the monument of Bat Chum founded under his supervision to shelter the images of the

Buddha, Vajrapāṇi, and Prajñā. These inscriptions stand chronologically between the stele of Tép Pranam, which tells of the construction of a Buddhist āśrama by Yaśovarman,[66] and the stele of Vat Sithor.[67] They prove the continuity, in certain quarters, of Mahayanist Buddhism, from whose adherents the Sivaite sovereigns did not disdain to recruit their officials.

All that epigraphy tells us about the political history of Cambodia under Rājendravarman is that "his brilliance burned the enemy kingdoms beginning with Champa"; [68] this is probably an allusion to the expedition that he sent to Champa about 950, in the course of which, as we shall see presently,[69] the Khmer armies removed the gold statue from the temple of Po Nagar at Nhatrang.

Rājendravarman's reign ended in 968, and he received the posthumous name of Śivaloka. In the last year of his reign, 967, the temple of Tribhuvanamaheśvara at Īśvarapura (Banteay Srei) was founded by Yajñavarāha, a grandson of Harshavarman I who, in the Khmer text of the stele of Banteay Srei, is known as "holy teacher," i.e. (*Steng An'*) Vraḥ Guru.[70] It is possible that this was the Brahman scholar who was promoted in the following reign to the dignity of *Kamrateng an'* Vraḥ Guru. In any case, a high dignitary bearing this title appears in numerous inscriptions of Jayavarman V and seems to have played a leading role at the beginning of the reign.

Jayavarman V, son of Rājendravarman, was in fact very young when he came to power in 968, for it was not until six years later, in 974, that he finished his studies under the direction of the Vraḥ Guru.[71] His reign of about thirty years, the political history of which is as little known as that of the preceding reigns, was occupied in part by the construction of a new residence, named Jayendranagarī, work on which was in progress in 978.[72] Its center was distinguished by the "gold mountain" or the "gold horn" (*Hemagiri, Hemaśṛingagiri,* classical designations of Meru). We are tempted to place this "gold mountain" at Ta Kèo, an incomplete temple-mountain situated west of the western bank of the Eastern Baray,[73] but this monument cannot be earlier than the first years of the eleventh century.

Jayavarman V gave his sister Indralakshmī in marriage to the Indian Brahman Divākarabhaṭṭa, who had been born in India on the banks of the Yamunā and who was the builder of various Sivaite structures.[74] During Jayavarman V's reign we see two "foreign" Brahmans (*paradeśa*), undoubtedly Indians, buying land and founding Sivaite sanctuaries on it.[75] The great dignitaries revealed by the inscriptions were, in general, like the king himself, adherents of the official Sivaism. But, as during preceding reigns, Buddhism continued to be practiced by some officials of high rank. The inscriptions[76] give some idea of this Buddhism. From the doctrinal point of view, it presented itself as the heir of the Yogāchāra school[77] and the representative of the "pure doctrines of the void and of subjectivity" restored in Cambodia by the efforts of Kīrtipaṇḍita, but in practice it borrowed part of its terminology from Hinduist rituals and involved above all the worship of the Bodhisattva Lokeśvara.[78]

Jayavarman V died in 1001 and received the posthumous name Paramavīraloka. He was succeeded by his nephew Udayādityavarman I, who reigned only a few months.[79]

The reigns from Indravarman to Jayavarman V, which occupied more than a century, constituted on the whole a period of grandeur that corresponded in part to a period of anarchy in the history of China lasting through the end of the T'ang and throughout the Five Dynasties. During this stable period of its history, Angkorian civilization, which was to play such an important role in the cultural evolution of the central Indochinese Peninsula and the brilliance of which was to exercise such a great influence on the Thai kingdoms of the Mekong and the Menam, assumed a distinctive form and fixed the characteristics that were to remain its own until its decline in the fourteenth century. It is not my intention to describe this civilization in detail here—especially since the work has already been started by Etienne Aymonier with the sources he has at his command.[80] Inscriptions by their very nature are incomplete sources; they tell us nothing directly about the life of the people, their material civilization,[81] their beliefs and customs. We must wait until the end of the thirteenth century, until the eve of Cambodia's decline, to find a living picture of Cambodia and its inhabitants in the account of the Chinese envoy Chou Ta-kuan. The inscriptions from the ninth to eleventh centuries tell us mostly about the high clergy of the official religion and the world of the court insofar as their activity was oriented toward the construction of religious edifices. No archives or documents written on hides or palm leaves are extant, and because all Khmer monuments, except for a few bridges, are religious edifices, the inscriptions engraved on these monuments are above all religious in character and we are obliged to study Angkorian civilization through this distorting mirror.

The king,[82] "master of all from the highest to the lowest," was the pivot of the whole political organization of the state, the source and sum of all authority. But we must not go so far as to represent the sovereign reigning at Angkor as an absolute despot, ruling only to suit his own pleasure. On the contrary, he was bound by the rules of the princely caste and by the maxims of policy and royal conduct; he was the guardian of the law and established order, the final judge of cases litigants wished to submit to his decision.[83] The inscriptions, which by their very nature inform us mostly about the religious side of Khmer civilization, represent the king as the protector of religion, the preserver of religious establishments that were entrusted to his care by donors. He performs the sacrifices and all the ritual ceremonies that are expected to bring divine favor to the country, defends it against foreign enemies, and insures domestic peace by imposing on everyone the obligation to respect the social order, that is, the division between the various castes or corporate bodies. We do not know for certain whether he was considered the ultimate owner of all the land of his kingdom, but we see him distributing unoccupied land and confirming land transactions. The sovereign, for whom reigning consists of "devouring the kingdom" (as a governor "devours" his province), appears less as an administrator than as a god on earth. His capital, with its walls and its moat, represents the universe in miniature, surrounded by the chain of mountains of Chakravāḷa and by the ocean.[84] Its center is marked by a temple-mountain that represents Meru, and on the summit of this temple-mountain is the Devarāja (*kamrateng jagat ta rājya*), the royal linga received from Siva through the intermediary of a Brahman.[85] We do not know whether this linga that contained the "royal essence," the *"moi subtil"* of the king, remained the same linga throughout the successive reigns[86] or whether, on the other hand, each of the various lingas consecrated by the kings upon their accession and bearing their names (Indreśvara, Yaśodhareśvara, Rājendreśvara, etc.) was in its turn the Devarāja. Each king who had the time and means built his temple-mountain in the center of his capital, and we have some reason to think that at his death this personal temple became his mausoleum.[87] When he died, the sovereign received a posthumous name indicating the heaven (*svargata*) to which he had gone and the god in whom he had been absorbed.

The government of the country was in the hands of an aristocratic oligarchy, and the great offices were held by members of the royal family. The offices of chaplain of the king, officiating priest of the Devarāja, and tutor of the young princes were reserved to members of great priestly families, within which offices were transmitted in the female line, the normal heir being the son of the sister or the younger brother. The Brahmanic families were often related to the royal family: the marriages between Brahmans and Kshatriyas seem to have been frequent, these two castes, representing the intellectual element and Indian culture, constituting a class separate from and superior to the masses. We need not conclude, however, that this aristocracy was different racially from the rest of the population; Khmer names were common among the royal family and even among the priests. The inscriptions emanating from this aristocracy, the only literary works that have come down to us, give an idea of the extent of its Sanskrit culture, which must have been renewed from time to time by the arrival of Brahmans from India, already noted.

The inscriptions inform us of a whole hierarchy of officials, which implies a highly developed administration. There were ministers, army leaders, advisers, inspectors, provincial heads, district heads, village chiefs, chiefs of the population, chiefs of warehouses, chiefs of corvée labor, and many other officials whose titles are more or less clear. These officials were divided into four categories, but these categories are not clearly defined.

We know very little about the life of the peasants and the villagers except that they must have been impressed in great numbers as servants in the service of the sanctuaries and monasteries or hermitages with which the piety of the ruling classes continually covered the countryside. The inscriptions give interminable lists of names of these slaves about whom we know nothing but their names, which are often very uncomplimentary epithets ("dog," "cat," "detestable," "stinking") that signify the scorn in which these people were held. These names have weathered the ravages of time and been passed on to posterity.

The religion of the governing classes was never unified.[88] In the ninth and tenth centuries, Sivaism predominated. It was not until the twelfth century that, parallel to what was then occurring in India, Vishnuism became powerful enough to give rise to great establishments of the importance of Angkor Wat. Buddhism always had some adherents, and we shall see great kings like Sūryavarman I and especially Jayavarman VII sponsor it officially in the following centuries. This reciprocal tolerance, moving at times toward a true syncretism, which was expressed in sculpture and epigraphy [89] and was not peculiar to Cambodia,[90] is explained by the very structure of society in Farther India. As Sylvain Lévi has rightly observed: "In the Indochinese Peninsula, in Indonesia, the presence of the Brahmanic religion in no way threatened the existence of Buddhism. Sivaism and Vishnuism, like Buddhism, were imported things, foreign to the land. The kings, the court, the nobility, were able to adopt them as an elegant and refined culture; it was not a civilization that penetrated deeply into the masses. Social life there continued on without regard to Manu and the other Brahmanic codes. But in India it was otherwise: *Brahmanism was responsible for social order;* the two were identical." [91] This explains India's intolerance with regard to Buddhism, a phenomenon of which there is no evidence in Cambodia until the thirteenth century, after the Buddhist fervor of Jayavarman VII.[92]

From the ninth to the end of the twelfth century, an uninterrupted line of evidence shows the existence of worship of images that have the attributes of great figures of the Brahmanic and Buddhist pantheons but bear names that recall the titles and appearance of human beings—dead or even living.

Only a few of the innumerable statues of Vishnu, Siva, Harihara, Lakshmī, and Pārvatī and of the Bodhisattvas that ancient Cambodia has bequeathed us are "impersonal" representations of these great figures of the Indian pantheon. The great majority of these images are of kings, princes, or great dignitaries represented with the traits of the god into which they have been or will be absorbed at the end of their earthly existence. The names borne by the statues, usually composed by fusing the name of the human counterpart with that of the god, indicate strongly that what is involved here is a personal cult.[93]

Most of the great Khmer monuments were consecrated to this aristocratic cult. They did not originate from popular devotion;

they were royal, princely, or mandarin structures which served as mausoleums and in which the worship of deceased parents and ancestors was conducted. They were mausoleums that could be built even during the lifetime and under the direction of the individuals who were to be adored there.[94]

The purpose of these structures explains their architectural symbolism.[95] The gods of India reside on the summits and move about in flying palaces. The use of the pyramid in architecture is evidently an attempt to evoke a mountain. For want of a high pyramid, five sanctuaries arranged in a quincunx recall the five summits of Mount Meru. As for the flying palaces, it is sufficient that a basement be decorated with *garuḍas* or birds forming atlantes for the idea to be suggested immediately.

Such are the essential traits of this civilization that, in the ninth and tenth centuries, with the temples of Kulèn, Rolûos, and Bakhèng and the great monuments of Koh Ker, Eastern Mébon, Prè Rup, Banteay Srei, and the Khleang, marks a high point from the artistic point of view that will be surpassed only by Angkor Wat.

We have no information about what happened in this period in the lower Menam Basin, site of the ancient kingdom of Dvāravatī. The sole document that comes from this area is a Sanskrit and Khmer inscription found on the island of Ayutthaya.[96] Dated the year 937, it tells about a line of princes of Chānāśapura:[97] the first of the line was the king Bhagadatta; then, after an undetermined number of generations, we hear of Sundaraparākrama, his son Sundaravarman, and finally the kings Narapatisiṃhavarman and Mangalavarman, both sons of Sundaravarman. Mangalavarman, the author of the inscription, consecrated a statue of Devī, a likeness of his mother. These names are not found in the epigraphy of Cambodia, but the inscription in the Khmer language, which gives a list of slaves, proves that three-quarters of a century before the area was incorporated into Cambodia the Khmers had replaced the Mon population that had occupied it in the seventh century.[98]

2. THE CHAM DYNASTY OF INDRAPURA

In Champa in 875, after a twenty-year gap in documentation, we are suddenly presented with a new dynasty reigning in the north,[99] at Indrapura in the modern province of Quang-nam, and at the same time the Chinese historians change the name of the country once more—this time to Chan-ch'eng,[100] "the Chan city" (Champāpura).

The founder of the dynasty of Indrapura, who took the name of Indravarman (II) at his accession, was called by his personal name Lakshmīndra Bhūmīśvara Grāmasvāmin. This was done so that he could pass for a descendant of the mythical ancestor Uroja; cloaking his grandfather Rudravarman and his father Bhadravarman with the title of king, he insists in his inscriptions that "the royalty was given to him by neither his grandfather nor his father but he assumed the sovereignty of Champa solely by means of destiny and thanks to the merit he acquired in numerous previous existences." Indravarman II may have been designated king, at the request of the great men of the kingdom, by Vikrāntavarman III, who died without posterity.[101] He seems to have had a peaceful reign. In 877 Indravarman II sent an embassy to China. Two years before, in 875, he had constructed a great Buddhist monument that is the first evidence of the existence of Mahayana Buddhism in Champa: this was the monastery of Lakshmīndralokeśvara, the name of which recalls the personal name of the founder. The Buddhist ruins of Đông-dương southeast of Mi-sơn have been identified with this monastery.[102]

At his death, Indravarman II received the posthumous name of Paramabuddhaloka. He was succeeded by his nephew Jaya Siṃhavarman I, for whom we have only two dates, 898 and 903, given by the inscriptions that deal with the erection of statues of apotheosis made during his reign.[103] Around the same time, a relative of the queen Tribhuvanadevī, Po Klung Pilih Rājadvāra, who was to continue to occupy high offices under the three following kings, went on a pilgrimage (*siddhayātrā*) to Java (Yavadvīpapura).[104] Perhaps this was the beginning of the Javanese influence on Cham art that is found in this period at Khương-my and at Mi-sơn.[105]

The inscription left by this official tells of the successor to Jaya Siṃhavarman I, his son Jayaśaktivarman. We know nothing else about this successor except that he must have had a very short reign. Bhadravarman II, who reigned next but whose family ties with his predecessor are not known, seems to have had a troubled accession. He was reigning in 908 and in 910.[106]

Bhadravarman II's son, Indravarman III, whose literary and philosophic knowledge is praised in epigraphy,[107] consecrated a golden statue of Bhagavatī in 918 at Po Nagar in Nha-trang. During his reign, which lasted more than forty years, he had to repel a Khmer invasion around 950 in the region of Nha-trang;[108] the gold statue was stolen by the invaders "dominated by cupidity and other vices," but the Khmer armies of Rājendravarman finally suffered a bloody defeat.[109] Before his death, which took place around 959, Indravarman III had time to renew relations with China, which had been interrupted during the period of anarchy lasting through the end of the T'ang and throughout the Five Dynasties: in 951, 958,[110] and 959, embassies were sent to the court of the Later Chou.[111]

Indravarman III's successor, Jaya Indravarman I, in 960 sent presents to the first emperor of the Sung, whose accession coincided with his. Five embassies sent at intervals from 962 to 971 prove the regularity of the relations between the two countries.[112] In 965, Jaya Indravarman I restored the sanctuary of Po Nagar that had been pillaged fifteen years previously by the Khmers and installed a stone image of the goddess there.[113]

In 972 a new king appeared on the throne of Champa. We have no inscriptions for him, but his name, judging from the Chinese transcription, must have been Parameśvaravarman.[114] He showed great punctuality in relations with China, to which he sent no less than seven embassies between 972 and 979. He was the first Cham king to have trouble with the newly independent Vietnamese kingdom of Đai Cô Viêt. That state had shortly before liberated itself from Chinese domination, and after the founder of the independent Đinh dynasty had been assassinated in 979, a member of the Ngô dynasty took refuge in Champa and asked Parameśvaravarman to help him reconquer the throne that his family had occupied from 939 to 965. A sea-borne expedition, organized in 979, was approaching Hoa-lư, the Đinh capital,[115] when it was destroyed by a gale that spared only the junk of the Cham king.[116]

In the following year, a palace intrigue brought a high dignitary named Lê Hoan to the throne of Đai Cô Viêt. Lê Hoan, founder of the early Lê dynasty, immediately sent an embassy to Champa. When King Parameśvaravarman made the mistake of holding the envoy of Đai Cô Viêt as a prisoner, Lê Hoan organized a retaliatory expedition that cost the life of the Cham sovereign and led to the destruction of the Cham capital in 982. The new king, whose name in Chinese characters seems to correspond to Indravarman (IV), left Indrapura just in time to take refuge in the southern part of his kingdom, from which in 985 he asked in vain for aid from the emperor of China.

During this time, in the north of the country a Vietnamese named Lưu Kê Tông seized power. In 983 he successfully resisted an attempted invasion by Lê Hoan. On the death of Indravarman IV, he officially proclaimed himself king of Champa, and in 986 he notified the court of China of his accession. This domination by a foreigner led to an exodus of inhabitants, a certain number of whom took refuge at Hainan and Kwangchou.[117]

In 988, the Chams rallied around one of their own. They placed him on the throne at Vijaya, in modern Binh-định, and when the Vietnamese usurper Lưu Kê Tông died in the following year, they proclaimed him king under the name Harivarman II. Scarcely had he been installed when he had to face a new Vietnamese invasion in the north of his kingdom in 990. After a short period of peace, marked by the erection of an Īśānabhadreśvara at Mi-sơn in 991,[118] by an exchange of presents with the emperor of China in 992, and by the liberation in the same year of 360 Cham prisoners detained at Tongking, hostilities with Lê Hoan began again, this time because of the activities of the Chams, who in 995 and 997 multiplied their raids along their northern frontier.

Harivarman II reinstalled himself at Indrapura, but his successor, who reigned from 999 and for whom we have only an incomplete name, Yang Pu Ku Vijaya Śrī—,[119] finally abandoned this extremely vulnerable capital in the year 1000 and established himself at Vijaya, in the region of Binh-dinh.[120] Champa never ceased to be subjected to the increasingly strong pressure of its neighbor to the north, and from the eleventh century, in spite of some revivals, the history of Champa was to be no more than the history of the retreat of Indian civilization before that of China.

3. THE JAVANESE KINGDOM OF MATARĀM

The decline of the power of the Buddhist Śailendras in central Java is indicated, as we have seen,[121] by the presence near Prambanan of a Sivaite inscription of 863 that perhaps relates to the cult of Agastya.[122] The construction of the Hindu monuments of the Prambanan group[123] in the beginning of the tenth century confirms this evidence. But it does not necessarily follow that Buddhism disappeared completely from this region: the Buddhist monuments of the Borobudur,[124] Plaosan, and Sajivan[125] prove the contrary, and there are numerous indications that the reciprocal tolerance between Buddhism and Hinduism, and in some cases the syncretism of the two, was as marked in Java as in Cambodia.[126]

The embassies sent to China by She-p'o in 860 and 873 are the principal sources of the information given by the *New History of the T'ang* on the country and its inhabitants:[127]

> The people make fortifications of wood and even the largest houses are covered with palmleaves. They have couches of ivory and mats of the outer skin of bamboo.
>
> The land produces tortoise-shell, gold and silver, rhinoceros-horns and ivory. . . . They have letters and are acquainted with astronomy. . . .
>
> In this country there are poisonous girls; when one has intercourse with them, he gets painful ulcers and dies, but his body does not decay.[128]
>
> The king lives in the town of Djava (Djapa), but his ancestor Ki-yen had lived more to the east at the town Pa-lu-ka-si.[129] On different sides there are twenty eight small countries, all acknowledging the supremacy of Djava. There are thirty two high ministers and the Da-tso-kan-hiung is the first of them.[130]

From epigraphy we hear of:

in 856–60, Lokapāla, who is sometimes identified with the following;[131]

in 863–82, Rakai Kayuwangi, also known as Sajjanotsavatunga;[132]

in 887, Rakai Gurunwangi, perhaps identical with the preceding;[133]

in 890, Rakai Limus dyaḥ Devendra, reigning perhaps in the east;[134]

in 896, Rakai Watuhumalang.[135]

All these princes left inscriptions in the Keḍu Plain near Prambanan. It was in this region, where the modern city of Jogjakarta is located, that the center of the state of Matarām was located. The name Matarām, applied retrospectively to the kingdom of Sanjaya,[136] was adopted in the tenth century as the official name of the country that reunited the center and east of the island under the same authority in order to indicate that the state was no longer confined to eastern Java. Since all the monuments of this southern region are of a funerary character, it is possible that the *kraton,* or residence of the sovereign, was located farther north.[137]

With the king named Balitung we leave a period that is in general very poorly known and step once more onto firmer ground. Certain indications lead us to think that Balitung was originally from the eastern part of the island, and that he acquired rights to the center by marriage.[138] It is in the inscriptions of his reign, which occur at intervals between 899 and 910,[139] that the name Matarām appears for the first time. It seems that Balitung had plans to resume, by means of real or fictitious dynastic ties, the Sivaite tradition interrupted by the episode of the Buddhist Śailendras.[140]

Balitung was succeeded around 913 [141] by King Daksha, who had appeared in the charters of his predecessor as one of the highest dignitaries (*rakryan ri Hino, mapatih i Hino*).[142] Like Balitung, Daksha joined the center and east of Java under his authority and resided in the region of Jogjakarta. Perhaps it was he who had the monument of Loro Jonggrang built at Prambanan as the funerary temple of his predecessor,[143] whose eastern origin would explain the affinity of the art of this group with that of the eastern part of the island.[144] In any case, it was he who instituted an era of Sanjaya that begins with March 18, 717, and is attested to by two inscriptions, one dated 910 (before his accession) and the other 913.[145]

The reign of Daksha was short, and so were those of his successors Tuloḍong and Wawa.

Tuloḍong, for whom we know the dates 919–21, seems also to have reigned over both the center and the east.[146] In 919 the name Rakai Halu, Lord Siṇḍok,[147] appears in one of his inscriptions. Siṇḍok, probably a grandson of Daksha, was to mount the throne ten years later.

Wawa reigned in 927–28.[148] The highest dignitary during his reign was still Siṇḍok. The original location of the epigraphic documents indicates that during Wawa's reign the administrative center of the kingdom was moved to the east; however, we cannot be sure that the central part of the island had already been abandoned. In any case, his inscriptions come exclusively from the east.

It has been claimed, rightly or wrongly, that around 927 Wawa became a priest under the name of Vāgīśvara.[149] If he did, he may have continued to maintain nominal power, for the first act of his successor Siṇḍok[150] is dated 929.

The accession of Siṇḍok marks the definitive transfer of the capital to the east, between the mountains Smeru and Wilis. This move is evidenced in archaeology by the decline and then abandonment of the center and by the multiplication of structures in the east. The reason for this move is not completely clear.[151] One scholar has thought that an earthquake or epidemic devastated the center of the island.[152] Others have put forth the hypothesis that a viceroy in the east became independent and absorbed the suzerain state,[153] as Chenla or the principality of the Kambujas had done with regard to Funan. And still others have envisioned a return to the offensive on the part of the Śailendras from Sumatra or have seen at least a desire of the Javanese sovereigns to remove themselves from dangerous rivals who were always ready to lay claim to the ancient cradle of their power.[154] One thing is certain: abandonment of the center of Java did not mean a spiritual break; the kings reigning in the east continued to invoke the gods of Matarām.

Although Siṇḍok was probably the grandson of Daksha, as I have said, up to the beginning of the thirteenth century Siṇḍok, under his reign name Śrī Īśāna(vikramadharmottungadeva), was always considered the founder of Javanese power in the east of the island. The result of his move of the capital to the east was a new incursion of Śrivijaya in the west of the island, where we see the Sumatran kingdom re-enthroning a prince of Sunda in 942.[155] The inscriptions of Siṇḍok, which number about twenty and appear at intervals between 929 and 948,[156] constitute one of the most valuable sources for the study of the organization and institutions of Java. They come from the upper Brantas Valley, and we can undoubtedly attribute to Siṇḍok some of the structures in this region (at Belahan, Gunung Gangsir, Sangariti).[157] None of these structures, however, is comparable to the monuments built by his predecessors in the Keḍu Plain.

The Javanese *Rāmāyaṇa* was composed a little later in Siṇḍok's reign,[158] and, in spite of the clearly Hindu character of his inscriptions and structures, we still attribute to his reign the composition, by Sambharasūryāvaraṇa, of the work named *Sang hyang Kamahāyānikan*,[159] a Tantric Buddhist treatise that is infinitely valuable for the understanding of Javanese Buddhism and the interpretation of architecture and iconography.

According to an inscription of Airlanga of 1041,[160] Siṇḍok was succeeded by his daughter Īśānatungavijayā, who was the wife of a certain Lokapāla.

Their son and successor was Makuṭavaṃśavardhana, about whom we know nothing except that his daughter Mahendradattā, as we shall see, married a prince of Bali.

The island of Bali from the eighth or ninth century shows traces of Buddhism that are perhaps of Javanese or Sumatran origin but could also have been brought directly from India. The first dated documents appear in Bali shortly before the accession of Siṇḍok in Java. The inscriptions of 896 and 911 do not bear the name of any king, but that of 914 is in the name of the *adhipati* Śrī Kesarivarma.[161] The first inscriptions of Ugrasena (915–39), who reigned at Siṃhamandava or Siṃhadvālapura, appear in the following year. These inscriptions reveal an Indo-Balinese society that was independent of Java, used a dialect peculiar to the island, and practiced Buddhism and Sivaism at the same time.[162]

In 953, an inscription mentions a sovereign who had among his names that of Agni.

Beginning in 955, Balinese epigraphy emanates from a dynasty whose kings all bear names ending in *-varmadeva:* [163]

955, Tabanendravarmadeva and Subhadrikāvarmadevī;

960, Chandrabhayasiṃhavarmadeva;

975, Janasādhuvarmadeva;

984, Śrī Vijayamahādevī.[164]

Then, from 989 to 1011 the inscriptions are in the name of the king Udāyana (Dharmodāyanavarmadeva) and the queen Mahendradattā (Guṇapriyadharmapatnī), who was, as we have just seen, the daughter of Makuṭavaṃśavardhana, the grandson of Siṇḍok. This Javanese marriage resulted in greater penetration of Hinduism in Bali and the introduction of Javanese culture, particularly of Tantrism. It also resulted in the birth in 1001 [165] of Airlanga, the future Javanese sovereign whose history will be told in the next chapter.

The most ancient information of Chinese origin concerning the island of Borneo (P'o-ni),[166] which, it will be recalled, had been touched by Indian culture very early, is from this period (977).

But let us return to Java.

Around 990 a son or son-in-law of Makuṭavaṃśa, Dharmavaṃśa Tguḥ Anantavikrama,[167] came to power. It was during his reign, in 996, that the poem *Virāṭaparva* was composed. Dharmavaṃśa inaugurated an aggressive policy with regard to Śrīvijaya. At least that is what appears from the information given in 992 to the court of China by the ambassadors from Java and Śrīvijaya, who speak of the invasion of San-fo-ch'i by She-p'o and of continual hostilities between the two countries.[168] We will see in the following chapter that this Javanese aggression around 990[169] probably resulted in a counteroffensive on the part of the Sumatran kingdom. There are good reasons for attributing the Sumatran expedition of 1016–17, the death of the Javanese king, and the destruction of his residence ultimately to this Javanese aggression.

4. SAN-FO-CH'I, OR THE SUMATRAN KINGDOM OF ŚRĪVIJAYA

In a passage of his *Hindoe-Javaansche Geschiedenis*,[170] N. J. Krom has characterized very well the measures which the Sumatran kingdom felt forced to take in order to protect its privileged position. The choice of a port for the seamen in this part of the archipelago was limited. The port had to fulfill the following conditions: it had to be a center possessing a certain degree of civilization; it had to be well located geographically; it had to have a well-protected harbor, for example, at the mouth of a river; and it had to have a safe anchorage. But the possession and defense of such a port of call was not possible without perpetual recourse to force. To preserve his monopoly, the master of this port had to neutralize his rivals or make vassals of them; this was necessary in order to maintain the upper hand over the commerce of the straits and make his influence felt on both shores.

For those astute merchants, the Arabo-Persians,[171] it was clearly possession of both sides of the straits that constituted the power of the maharaja of Zābag. Throughout their accounts, the affirmation that the maharaja reigned simultaneously over Kalah (on the Malay Peninsula north of the Isthmus of Kra)[172] and over Sribuza (Śrīvijaya = Palembang = Sumatra) is repeated like a refrain. Here is what one of them wrote around 916:[173]

> The city of Zābag faces in the direction of China. The distance between the two is a month by sea, and even less if the winds are favorable. The king of this city is known by the name of *mahārāja*. . . . It is said that

the circumference is 900 parasangs.[174] This king is, in addition, the sovereign of a great number of islands that extend for 1,000 parasangs and even more. Among the states over which he rules is the island called Sribuza, whose circumference is 400 parasangs, and the island called Rāmī [Achin, north of Sumatra], the circumference of which is 800 parasangs. . . . Also part of the possessions of the maharaja is the maritime state of Kalah, which is situated halfway between China and Arabia. . . . It is to this port that the ships of Omān come, and it is from this port that the ships leave for Omān. The authority of the maharaja is felt in these islands. The island where he resides is as fertile as land can be, and the inhabited places follow upon one another without interruption. A reliable source reports that when the cocks of this country crow at sunrise, as they do in Arabia, they answer one another over stretches extending up to 100 parasangs and more, because the villages are contiguous and follow on one another without interruption. . . .

In 995, the geographer Mas'ūdī spoke in grandiloquent terms of the "kingdom of the maharaja, king of the islands of Zābag, among which are Kalah and Sribuza and other islands in the China Sea. All their kings are entitled *mahārāja*. This empire of the maharaja has an enormous population and innumerable armies. Even with the fastest vessel, no one can tour these islands, all of which are inhabited, in two years. Their king possesses more kinds of perfume and aromatic substances than are possessed by any other king. His lands produce camphor, aloes, cloves, sandalwood, musk, cardamom, cubeb, etc. . . ." [175]

For the Chinese, Shih-li-fo-shih has become San-fo-ch'i,[176] which from 904–905 on sent numerous embassies to the court of China. All the commerce of China and India is said to have passed through this uncontested master of the straits.[177] After having become a great economic power, however, Śrīvijaya seems to have neglected the spiritual values that attracted the Chinese pilgrim I-ching there in the seventh century. In fact, while the Javanese kings were covering their island with religious buildings, the Śrīvijayan sovereigns were preoccupied with superintending the traffic of the straits rather than with building lasting monuments, and they have left us only insignificant brick towers and a very small number of inscriptions.

Among the Śrīvijayan kings, the *History of the Sung*[178] tells us of Si-li Hu-ta-hsia-li-tan in 960 and of Shih-li Wu-yeh in 962; both these names are probably transcriptions of the same name, Śrī Udayāditya(varman).[179] The accounts of embassies to China in 971, 972, 974, and 975 do not give any king's name; embassies of 980 and 983 are said to come from a King Hsia-ch'ih, in Malay *Haji,* which is simply a royal title. It was during the reign of this king in 983 that "the priest Fa-yü, returning from India where he had been seeking sacred books, arrived at San-fo-ch'i and there met the Indian priest Mi-mo-lo-shih-li [i.e., Vimalaśrī], who after a short conversation entrusted him with a petition in which he expressed the desire to go to the Middle Kingdom and translate sacred books there."[180]

"In 988," says the *History of the Sung,* "an ambassador arrived for the purpose of presenting tribute. During the winter of 992, it was learned from Canton that this ambassador, who had left the capital of China two years before, had learned in the south that his country had been invaded by She-p'o and, as a consequence, had remained in Canton for a year. In the spring of 992, the ambassador went to Champa with his ship, but since he did not hear any good news there, he returned to China and requested that an imperial decree be promulgated placing San-fo-ch'i under the protection of China."

We have seen that the Javanese envoys of the same year, 992, brought corroborative information to China, saying that their country was continually at war with San-fo-ch'i, but what they did not say was that the aggression came from Java.[181] Perhaps it was the more or less effective protection of China, or perhaps only its tacit consent, that encouraged Śrīvijaya to undertake reprisals on Java which will be discussed in the following chapter.

5. BURMA

For the period covered by this chapter, the Burmese chronicles continue to furnish, for Pagan as well as for Pegu, lists of kings[182] that are unverifiable because of the lack of cross-references in epigraphy or Chinese annals. The dependence of these chronicles on legend and folklore is obvious. For example, they place a usurper, Nyaung-u Sô-rahan, on the throne of Pagan in 931. He was an old gardener who supposedly killed the king Theingo (Singho) because the latter had picked cucumbers in his garden.[183] The same story, however, has been used for the origin of the present Cambodian dynasty, and other versions of it are known.[184]

According to the Burmese chronicles,[185] the gardener-usurper was in turn overthrown in 964 by Kunshô Kyaungphyu, a representative of the legitimate line who took over as his wives the three queens of his predecessor. But in 986, the two brothers of the gardener and the two first queens lured this prince into a monastery and forced him to don monk's robes. After a reign of six years, the elder brother, Kyiso, perished in a hunt. The younger brother, Sokkate, who succeeded him in 992, was killed in 1044 by a son of Kunshô Kyaungphyu by his third queen. This son was the famous Anôratha (Aniruddha), whose history will be told in the following chapter.

CHAPTER IX

THREE GREAT KINGS: SŪRYAVARMAN I IN CAMBODIA, AIRLANGA IN JAVA, AND ANÔRATHA IN BURMA

First Three Quarters of the Eleventh Century

1. CAMBODIA: SŪRYAVARMAN I (1002–50) AND THE EXPANSION TO THE WEST; UDAYĀDITYAVARMAN II (1050–66)

Neither Khmer epigraphy nor Chinese documents give a hint about the developments that led to the accession in Cambodia of Sūryavarman I, that sovereign of the sun race whose family ties with his predecessors may have been entirely fabricated by the official genealogists. The late chronicles of the principalities of the upper Menam Valley, written in Chiangmai in the fifteenth to sixteenth centuries, deal only with the expansion of Khmer power in the Menam Basin; it would in any case be unwise to give too much credence to this data.

The Khmer epigraphy of the first ten years of the eleventh century shows three kings reigning simultaneously. The relationship between these kings is not clear, but they seem to have been antagonists.

The nephew of Jayavarman V, Udayādityavarman I, whose only two known inscriptions come from Koh Ker [1] and Mlu Prei,[2] came to the throne in 1001. In that same year, a prince bearing the name Sūryavarman and the title *kaṃtvan,* which apparently denotes royal ancestry in the female line,[3] is mentioned in an inscription from Sambor on the Mekong [4] and another from the vicinity of Kompong Thom.[5] In the following year, 1002, we have two more of his inscriptions from the same region.[6] A King Jayavīravarman appears from 1003 to 1006; according to his inscriptions,[7] he had been established on the throne of Angkor since 1002. After this, Sūryavarman became the uncontested master in the capital, and in 1011 he had the oath of allegiance, followed by long lists of names of dignitaries in the form of signatures,[8] engraved on the inner surface of the entrance pavilion of the Royal Palace.

We can gather from these inscriptions [9] that the accession of Udayādityavarman I in 1001 led to rivalry between Jayavīravarman, who reigned at Angkor at least from 1003 to 1006, and Sūryavarman, who had established himself in the east. The inscriptions indicate that between 1005 and 1007 Sūryavarman led a large-scale expedition in which sacred places were damaged.[10] "He seized the kingdom from a king in the midst of a host of other kings," says one of them.[11] The war lasted nine years,[12] and the installation of Sūryavarman at Angkor must date around 1010; but later, in his inscriptions, he dated his accession in 1002, that is, the time of the death or disappearance of Udayādityavarman I.

Sūryavarman claimed to have descended, on the maternal side, from Indravarman [13] and to be related through his wife Vīralakshmī to the son of Yaśovarman.[14] The first assertion cannot be verified. As for the second, the name of *Vīra*lakshmī seems to indicate that this princess was related in some way to Jaya*vīra*varman, and we may have here an example of the legitimization of power by means of marriage to the wife or daughter [15] of a predecessor.

The favor Sūryavarman accorded to Buddhism earned him the posthumous name Nirvāṇapada. His sponsorship of Buddhism in no way, however, interrupted the continuity of the worship rendered to the Devarāja, thus exemplifying the syncretism we spoke of earlier.[16] "During his reign," says the inscription of Sdok Kak Thom,[17] "the members of the family [of priests of the Devarāja] officated for the Devarāja as before." He even singled out from this family a nephew of the great priest Śivāchārya, named Sadāśiva, had him quit the religious state, gave him one of his sisters-in-law in marriage, and elevated him to the dignity of Kaṃsteng Śrī Jayendrapaṇḍita, the first step in a career that was to become particularly brilliant during the following reign. Continuing the work begun by his uncle, Sadāśiva-Jayendrapaṇḍita "restored the structures that had been destroyed when the king led forth his army." [18]

The installation of Sūryavarman I at Angkor was accompanied, as I have said, by the taking of a solemn oath by certain officials, the formula for which was engraved at the entrance of the palace. It was apparently also marked by the completion of the Phimeanakas, notably its vaulted gallery, and of Ta Kèo [19] and by the construction of the entrance pavilions (*gopuras*) of the Royal Palace.[20] Other important works that can be attributed to him include the temple of Phnom Chisor,[21] the name of which recalls the ancient name of the hill on which it was built (Sūryaparvata, "mountain of the sun or of Sūrya[varman]"), certain parts of Preah Vihear[22] and of Preah Khan of Kompong Svay,[23] and the monuments of Vat Ek and of Baset near Battambang.[24] All these works are associated with the names of Brahman scholars who occupied high positions and who are known to us from epigraphy.[25]

It may be that in 1012 or shortly afterwards, Sūryavarman I, feeling himself threatened, solicited the aid of Rājendrachoḷa I by making him a present of a chariot.[26] According to R. C. Majumdar,[27] the threat undoubtedly came from the king of Śrīvijaya, Māravijayottungavarman, established at Kaṭāha, against whom we see Rājendrachoḷa I launch a first expedition a little later.

The story of the Khmer expansion in the Menam Basin is reported in the following fashion by the various Pali chronicles composed in Chiangmai: the *Chāmadevīvaṃsa* (written at the beginning of the fifteenth century),[28] the *Jinakālamālī* (finished in 1516),[29] and the *Mūlasāsana*.[30] A king of Haripunjaya (Lamphun) named Atrāsataka (var. Trābaka, Baka) went to attack Lavo (Lopburi), where Ucch'iṭṭhachakkavatti (var. Ucch'itta-, Ucchitta-) reigned. At the moment when the two sovereigns were preparing for battle, a king of Siridhammanagara (Ligor) named Sujita (var. Jīvaka, Vararāja) arrived off Lavo with a considerable army and fleet. Confronted by this third depredator, the two adversaries fled in the direction of Haripunjaya. Ucch'iṭṭha arrived first, proclaimed himself king there, and married the wife of his adversary, who withdrew by boat to the south. Sujita, the king of Ligor, established himself as master at Lavo. At the end of three years, his successor, or perhaps his son,[31] Kambojarāja, went to attack Ucch'iṭṭha again at Haripunjaya, but he was defeated and had to return to his capital.

As we have seen, this little drama had three principal actors: two rival kings who disputed the possession of Lavo,[32] and a foreign king from the south, who settled the quarrel by installing himself there and whose successor, "King of the Kambojas," then launched an unsuccessful expedition against the former king of Lavo established in his new state. We are tempted to identify this Kambojarāja with Sūryavarman I, for even if these conflicts between Cambodia and the Mon kingdom of Haripunjaya, related in the chronicles cited above, are imaginary, we nonetheless still have clear manifestations of Cambodian expansion in the era of Sūryavarman I in the region west of the Great Lake, where his inscriptions are particularly numerous. The reclaiming of those lands, until then left fallow or scarcely exploited, was effected by the expedient of setting up religious establishments and making grants of unused land to private persons.[33] This resulted in the creation of villages serving the temples and the cultivation of the soil by means of irrigation works.

Evidence of the Khmer occupation in the lower Menam in the eleventh century is given by a group of inscriptions from Lopburi,[34] at least one of which emanates from Sūryavarman I. How far north did this sovereignty or suzerainty of the king of Angkor extend? The local chronicles speak of a Khmer occupation that embraced the whole Menam Basin and the Mekong Basin up to Chiangsaen or beyond,[35] but the archaeological remains that are attributable to Khmer influence—and these are, moreover, later than the eleventh century—do not go beyond Luang Phrabang[36] on the Mekong and Sukhothai-Sawankhalok on the Menam.[37] For the era of Sūryavarman I, it is prudent to limit ourselves to the particulars given in the epigraphy of Lopburi. An inscription of 1022–25 tells us that during Sūryavarman I's reign monks belonging to two schools of Buddhism (*bhikshu mahāyāna* and *sthavira*) and Brahmans practicing the exercises of Yoga (*tapasvi yogi*) lived side by side in Lavo. Another Khmer inscription, the date of which is lost, but which must date back almost to the same era, is Vishnuite. "In short, epigraphy attests for us that the various religions practiced in the Khmer empire had their priests and sanctuaries at Lavo, but the predominance of Buddhist monuments and images at Lopburi proves that, even under Khmer domination, Buddhism preserved the importance there that it had at the time of the kingdom of Dvāravatī."[38]

At the beginning of the year 1050,[39] Sūryavarman I died and received the posthumous name of Nirvāṇapada. He was succeeded by Udayādityavarman II. The new king conferred the semi-royal title of *Dhūli Jeng* ("dust of the feet") Vraḥ Kamrateng An' Śrī Jayendravarman on the former chief priest of the Devarāja, Sadāśiva-Jayendrapaṇḍita, who had married a sister of the queen Vīralakshmī and become the king's spiritual master.[40]

It was undoubtedly under the inspiration of this high dignitary who belonged to the illustrious family of the priests of the Devarāja that Udayādityavarman II decided to build a new temple-mountain for the royal linga more beautiful than those of his predecessors. "Seeing that in the middle of the Jambudvīpa, the home of the gods, rose the mountain of gold (Meru), he had constructed, as in emulation, a mountain of gold in the center of his city. On the top of this gold mountain, in a gold temple shining with a heavenly light, he erected a Śivalinga in gold." [41] This edifice, "ornament of the three worlds," was none other than the Baphuon,[42] "the sight of which is really impressive" the Chinese Chou Ta-kuan [43] said at the end of the thirteenth century. This monument marked the center of a city whose boundaries coincided approximately with those of Angkor Thom today. The capital did not yet have its permanent walls of laterite, for these walls were a contribution of Jayavarman VII's, but it was furrowed by a great number of canals the network of which has been rediscovered.[44]

At the same time, Udayādityavarman II had a huge artificial lake dug west of the capital. The lake was 8 kilometers by 2.2 kilometers, even larger than the Yaśodharataṭāka of Yaśovarman, or Eastern Baray, which perhaps was already showing signs of drying up. In the center of this Western Baray, he had a temple built on an islet, and beside the temple he placed a colossal bronze statue representing the god Vishnu deep in his cosmic slumbers and resting on the waters of the ocean.[45]

During his sixteen-year reign, Udayādityavarman II had to cope with a series of uprisings. The repression of these uprisings, which was entrusted to a General Sangrāma, is recounted in epic style by a Sanskrit stele [46] placed at the base of the Baphuon, the temple of the royal linga, to which the conquering general made a gift of his booty.

The first revolt took place in 1051. It occurred in the south of the country, and its leader was Aravindahrada, "well instructed in the science of archery, leader of an army of heroes, who forcefully held, in the southern region, the burden of half the land." Vanquished by Sangrāma, the rebel "fled with the greatest haste to the city of Champā."

The year 1065, the last of the reign, saw two other revolts. In the northwest,[47] "a clever man favored by the king, a valiant hero named Kaṃvau whom the king had made general of the army, blinded by the brilliance of his grandeur, and secretly planning the ruin of the very one to whose powerful favor he owed this grandeur, left the city with his troops." He wounded Sangrāma in the jaw before being killed by three arrows.

Shortly afterwards, in the east, a man named Slvat, his younger brother Siddhikāra, and a third warrior named Saśāntibhuvana, fomented new troubles. Sangrāma quickly put them down and celebrated his victories by various pious endowments.

We do not know the posthumous name of Udayādityavarman II. He was succeeded in 1066[48] by his younger brother, Harshavarman III.

2. CHAMPA FROM 1000 TO 1074

In the preceding chapter we saw the first fall of the Cham capital before the Vietnamese thrust from the north. The eleventh century was to see this pressure accentuated to the point of forcing the Chams to abandon their northern provinces. Up to the middle of the century epigraphy is silent, and the historian must rely on Chinese and Vietnamese sources.

The king Yang Pu Ku Vijaya, who came to the throne in the very last years of the tenth century, evacuated Indrapura (Quang-nam) in the year 1000 to establish himself at Vijaya (Binh-đinh).[49] In 1004–1005 he sent to China an embassy that announced this change of capital.[50]

He was succeeded before 1010 by a king whose name in Chinese characters appears to be a transcription of Harivarman (III). This king reigned about ten years.[51]

In 1021, Parameśvaravarman II,[52] who had sent an embassy to China three years before, saw the northern frontier of his states, in modern Quang-binh, attacked by the eldest son of Ly Thai-tô (founder of the Vietnamese dynasty of Ly), Phât-Ma, who later, in 1028, was to succeed his father under the name Ly Thai-tông. The Chams were beaten and suffered a new invasion in 1026.

Between 1030 and 1041, King Vikrāntavarman IV reigned. Details of his reign are obscure, but it was apparently troubled. In 1042 his son Jaya Siṃhavarman II[53] requested investiture from the court of China. The following year, he went to pillage the coast of Đai Viêt. King Ly Thai-tông prepared, in reprisal, a maritime expedition and took command of it himself in 1044. At the first encounter, probably in modern Thưa-thiên, the Chams were routed and their king decapitated on the battlefield. Ly Thai-tông pushed on to Vijaya, seized it, and took the royal harem away with him.[54]

The successor of Jaya Siṃhavarman II was a warrior of noble family who at his accession took the name Jaya Parameśvaravarman I. With his reign, inscriptions appear again in the south. In 1050, when the people of Pāṇḍuranga, "vicious, threatening, always in revolt against their sovereign," refused to recognize him, he ordered his nephew, the Yuvarāja Śrī Devarāja Mahāsenāpati, to go and subdue them.[55] The Yuvarāja did, and to celebrate his victory, he had a linga erected on the hill of Po Klaung Garai and set up a column of victory.[56] For his part, the king proceeded the same year with the restoration of the sanctuary of Po Nagar at Nha-trang and gave it slaves, among whom were Khmers, Chinese, and men of Pukāṃ (Burmese of Pagan) and Syāṃ (Siamese, or Thai).[57] Anxious to remain on good terms with his neighbors to the north, he sent three embassies to China between 1050 and 1056, and five to Đai Viêt from 1047 to 1060.[58]

All we know about the next king, Bhadravarman III, is that he reigned for only a brief time and that he was reigning in 1061.[59] At the end of the same year, his younger brother Rudravarman III succeeded him.

Rudravarman III sent an embassy to China in 1062. He also sent three embassies to Đai Viêt—in 1063, 1065, and 1068. But from the beginning of his reign he had been preparing for a war against Đai Viêt, and he launched his attack at the end of 1068. King Ly Thanh-tông, quick to respond, led his fleet to Śrī Banđi (Qui-nhơn), near the Cham capital. He defeated the Cham army that waited for him in the interior. Since Rudravarman III had left the city during the night, his people surrendered to Ly Thanh-tông, who made his entry there without difficulty. "He immediately sent troops to follow the fleeing king, who was caught and made prisoner in Cambodian territory (in the fourth month of 1069). The following month, he held a great feast for all his ministers in the palace of the king of Champa and, to show positively that he had conquered him and reduced him to nothing, he executed a shield dance and played a shuttlecock game on the steps of the throne room. At the same time he hastened to announce the news of his victory and of the capture of the king to the Chinese emperor, Shen Tsung. After taking a census, which showed more than 2,560 families, he ordered that all the houses in the enclosure and suburbs of Vijaya be set on fire." [60]

King Ly Thanh-tông carried King Rudravarman III and his family off to Tongking as prisoners, but he freed them in 1069 in exchange for Rudravarman III's abandonment of his three northern provinces, corresponding approximately to Quang-binh and Quang-tri. We do not know whether, upon his return from captivity, the Cham king was ever able to re-establish his authority over his greatly troubled and reduced country. It is clear, however, that the dynasty that had reigned since 1044 perished with him in about 1074.

3. ŚRĪVIJAYA AND ITS RELATIONS WITH THE CHOḶAS OF TANJORE (1003–30)

We have seen in the preceding chapter that during the last decade of the tenth century Śrīvijaya was subjected to a Javanese invasion and requested protection from China. In the beginning of the eleventh century the king Chūḷāmaṇivarmadeva, during whose reign the master Dharmakīrti composed a commentary on the *Abhisamayālankara*,[61] continued to maintain the best of relations with China. "In the year 1003, the king Sê-li-chu-la-wu-ni-fu-ma-tiau-hwa sent two envoys to bring tribute; they told that in their country a Buddhist temple had been erected in order to pray for the long life of the emperor and that they wanted a name and bells for it, by which the emperor would show that he appreciated their good intentions. An edict was issued by which the temple got the name of Ch'êng-t'ien-wan-shou ['ten thousand years of receiving from Heaven'] and bells were cast to be given to them." [62] Other embassies were sent to China in 1004, 1008, 1016, 1017, and 1018.[63]

At the same time, around 1005, the king of Śrīvijaya, following the example of his predecessor Bālaputra, who had built a monastery at Nālandā in Bengal,[64] had a Buddhist temple bearing his name, the Chūḷāmaṇivarmavihāra,[65] built at Nāgīpaṭṭana (Negapatam, on the Cormandel coast). The Choḷa Rājarāja I offered the revenues of a large village to this temple.

This friendly attitude of Chūḷāmaṇivarmadeva toward the two great powers of the era—China and the Choḷas of Tanjore [66] (the latter, in spite of their distance, were able, as the future would prove, to become dangerous enemies)—made it possible for his son Māravijayottungavarman to have a free hand against Java. He certainly took striking revenge for the Javanese aggression of 992, if it is true that the catastrophe that befell Java in 1016, and about which we are so poorly informed, was the consequence of reprisals by Śrīvijaya. We know that Māravijayottungavarman was already on the throne in 1008, for in that year he sent tribute to China.[67]

An inscription known as the "great charter of Leyden," [68] made during the reign of Rājendrachoḷa I, which began in 1014,[69] informs us that the new Choḷa king composed an edict for the village offered by his father Rājarāja to the Chūḷāmaṇivarmavihāra. This inscription styles Māravijayottungavarman the "descendant of the Śailendra family, king of Śrīvijaya and Kaṭāha [Kiḍāra in the Tamil inscription]." This combined mention of Śrīvijaya (Palembang) and Kaṭāha (Kedah on the Malay Peninsula) confirms startlingly the evidence of the Arab geographers, for whom the maharaja of Zābag is master of Sribuza and Kalah (Kra).[70] The two poles of the empire, Sumatra and the Malay Peninsula, are the same in the two cases: the maharaja holds the two shores of the straits.

But the expansionist policy and the commercial methods that the kings of Śrīvijaya were obliged to apply to maintain themselves in this privileged position were bound to put them soon in conflict with the thalassocracy of the Choḷas. The conflict occurred shortly after Śrīvijaya had accomplished its aggressive designs against Java, thus bringing to an end the temporary need for conciliating the Choḷas.

As early as 1007, Rājarāja I bragged of having conquered twelve thousand islands.[71] Ten years later, his son Rājendrachoḷa I may have attempted a first raid against Kaṭāha,[72] that is, against the peninsular possessions of the Śailendras of Sumatra.[73] If this expedition did take place, it was only the prelude to the great raid of 1025, details of which are given in an inscription of Rājendrachoḷa at Tanjore dated 1030–31.[74] The inscription states that, after having sent "numerous ships into the midst of the rolling sea and seized Sangrāmavijayottungavarman, King of Kadāram," Rājendrachoḷa I conquered successively: [75]

Śrīvijaya (Palembang),
Paṇṇai (Panai on the east coast of Sumatra, facing Malacca),
Malaiyūr (the Malāyu of the seventh century, that is, Jambi),

Māyiruḍingam (the Jih-lo-t'ing of the Chinese,[76] some part of the Malay Peninsula),
Ilangāśogam (Langkasuka),[77]
Māppappālam (Papphāla, located by the Singhalese chronicle, *Mahāvaṃsa,* on the coast of Pegu),
Mevilimbangam (identified by Sylvain Lévi [78] with Karmaranga, or Kāmalangka, on the isthmus of Ligor),
Vaḷaippandūru (perhaps Pāṇḍur[anga], in Champa,[79] preceded either by the Tamil word *valai* ["fortress"] or the Cham word *palei* ["village"]),
Talaittakkolam (Takkōla of Ptolemy and of the *Milindapaṇha,* on the Isthmus of Kra),
Mādamālingam (Tāmbralinga,[80] or Chinese Tan-ma-ling, whose center was at Ligor),
Ilāmurideśam (Lāmurī of the Arabs and Lambri of Marco Polo,[81] at the northern tip of Sumatra),
Māṇakkavāram (the Nicobar Islands),
Kaḍāram (Kedah).

It is not certain that the order in which these places are listed indicates the chronology of events, but if it does, it shows that, after the attack on the island capital Śrīvijaya, i.e., Palembang, and the capture of King Sangrāmavijayottungavarman, the Choḷa king occupied a few points on the east coast of Sumatra, then the various possessions of the maharaja on the Malay Peninsula,[82] then Achin and the Nicobars, and finally Kedah, the continental capital. Perhaps this raid has left some traces in the memory of the Malays of the peninsula, for their annals tell how the Tamil king Raja Cholan (or Suran) destroyed Ganganagara on the Dinding River, as well as a fort on the Lengiu, a tributary of the Johore River, and finally occupied Tumasik, the site of the future Singapore.[83]

However that may be, the expedition of Rājendrachoḷa I seems not to have had lasting political consequences. At most, the capture of Sangrāmavijayottungavarman resulted in the accession of a new king. In 1028 this new king sent an embassy to China. The *History of the Sung* gives his name as Shih-li Tieh-hua, that is, Śrī Deva (undoubtedly incomplete).[84]

Nevertheless, the shock felt by Śrīvijaya led it to come to terms with its old rival: we will see that the reconciliation with Java was probably even sealed by a matrimonial alliance.

We have seen above that Dharmakīrti lived in Śrīvijaya during the reign of Chūḷāmaṇivarman. He must have continued to reside there under Māravijayottungavarman, since, according to the Tibetan Bu-ston,[85] it was from 1011 to 1023 that Atīśa "went to follow the teaching of Dharmakīrti, head of the Buddhist congregation in the island of Suvarṇadvīpa,[86] during the reign of King Dharmapāla." This name Dharmapāla does not correspond to any of the royal names that the Chinese texts and epigraphy give us for Śrīvijaya. Perhaps it is the title ("Protector of the Law")[87] of Māravijayottungavarman or of his successor.

In any case, the persistence of Mahayana Buddhism in Sumatra is evidenced at Tapanuli, on the west coast, by the casting in 1024 of a statue inscribed to Lokanātha, that is, the Bodhisattva Lokeśvara, represented standing between two figures of Tārā;[88] and a Nepalese iconographic manuscript from the beginning of the eleventh century attests to the popularity enjoyed in the Buddhist world by a certain statue of Lokanātha in Śrīvijayapura.[89]

4. JAVA: AIRLANGA (1016–49)

We have seen[90] that the king of Bali, Udāyana, married the Javanese princess Mahendradattā, great-granddaughter of Siṇḍok. A son of this marriage was born in Bali around 1001; this was Airlanga, who in the prime of his youth was invited[91] to come and conclude his betrothal with one of the daughters of the king reigning in the east of Java at that time.[92] He was at the court of this king at the time of the tragic events of 1016.[93] The causes of the disaster that led to the destruction of the capital and the death of the king have been the subject of as many and various conjectures as the transfer of the capital from the center to the east seventy-five years earlier. The most likely and generally accepted hypothesis is that, since Śrīvijaya was at peace with India and more or less effectively protected by China, it took its revenge in 1016 for the Javanese invasion of 992. The restoration of Java did, indeed, coincide with the temporary weakening of the Sumatran kingdom following the Choḷa raid of 1025.[94] The role of Śrīvijaya in 1016, however, may have been limited to provoking or supporting an internal revolt in the Javanese state. The principal assailant was in fact a prince of Wurawari, who has been regarded as coming from the Malay Peninsula[95] but who may simply have been a local chief.[96]

After the "debacle" (*pralaya*), as it was called by the Javanese inscription that tells about the events of 1016,[97] the young Airlanga, then sixteen years old, took refuge among hermits on Mount

Vanagiri, where he stayed four years. Notables and Brahmans came to plead with him to accept the royal power as successor of his father-in-law, and in 1019 he was officially crowned with the title Śrī Mahārāja Rakai Halu Śrī Lokeśvara Dharmavaṃśa Airlanga Anantavikramottungadeva. His authority at that time did not extend beyond a small territory situated on the northern coast of the island between Surabaya and Pasuruhan. He had to wait another ten or so years before beginning the reconquest of his states, a task that was undoubtedly facilitated by the weakening of Śrīvijaya, victim of the Choḷa aggression of 1025.

It is possible that as early as 1022 Airlanga succeeded his father in Bali, where the catastrophe of 1016 had no repercussions,[98] but this is not certain, and the Dharmavaṃśavardhana Marakaṭapankajasthānottungadeva, whose inscriptions we have in Bali from 1022 to 1026, is undoubtedly an entirely different person from Airlanga, perhaps a viceroy governing in his name.[99]

Airlanga began his campaigns in Java in 1028–29 with the aim of recovering his kingdom, divided among many competitors. He seems first to have attacked Bhīshmaprabhāva, who was the son of a king; then, in 1030, Vijaya, prince of Wengker (on the plain of Madiun), who suffered a temporary defeat. In 1031 he defeated Adhamāpanuda and set fire to his residence. In 1032 he rid the country of a woman "endowed with a formidable power, similar to a *rākshasī*," and devastated the southern region, "which he burned with his tongue like a fiery serpent." Then he may still have had to fight against the prince of Wurawari. As for Vijaya, prince of Wengker, beaten and obliged to flee "abandoning his wife, children, treasures, and royal vehicles," he was seized by his own troops and died in 1035.[100]

In 1037, Airlanga, "having placed his feet on the head of his enemies, took his place on the throne of lions, decorated with jewels." Since his states were considerably enlarged, he established his residence in the east, at Kahuripan, the site of which has still not been identified.

Following his victories, Airlanga founded the monastery of Puchangan (in Sanskrit Pūgavat, "the mountain of the areca palms"), not, as has been believed, on Penanggungan,[101] but on Puchangan in the delta of the Brantas.[102] It was dedicated in 1041,[103] perhaps on the occasion of the death of a princess who from 1030 to around 1041 is mentioned in the edicts of Airlanga as first dignitary of the court (Rakryan mahāmantri i Hino).[104] Her name, Sangrāmavijaya Dharmaprasādottungadevī, closely resembles that of Sangrāmavijayottungavarman, the king of Śrīvijaya who was led away into captivity at the time of the Choḷa raid of 1025. The presence in Java, shortly after these events, of a princess bearing a name that recalls a Sumatran title, and the foundation by Airlanga in 1035 of a monastery named Śrīvijayaśrama,[105] seem to indicate a rapprochement between the two rivals following the weakening of Śrīvijaya and the coming to power of Airlanga. As for the ties that united the princess to her namesake on the one hand and to Airlanga on the other, the most probable theory is that she was the daughter of Sangrāmavijayottungavarman whom Airlanga had married around 1030.[106] From this time a certain balance comes into being between the two states that had been rivals for such a long time, Śrīvijaya maintaining political supremacy in the west of the archipelago[107] and Java in the east. Contemporary documents show, however, that the commercial relations of Java extended also to the west: the inscriptions[108] mention the Kling (Indians of Kalinga), the Ārya (non-Dravidian Indians), the Gola (Gauḍa of Bengal), Singhala (Singhaḷese), Karṇaṭaka (Kanarese), Cholika (Choḷas of Coromandel), Malyala (Malabars), Paṇḍikira (Pāṇḍyas and Keras), Draviḍa (Tamils), Champa (Chams), Remen (Mons or Malays of Rāmnī, i.e., Achin), and Kmir (Khmers), who must have arrived in the states of Airlanga by the ports situated at the mouth of the Brantas in the bay of Surabaya and, farther north, around Tuban.

Inscriptions that mention the three religious sects of Śaiva (Sivaites), Sogata (Buddhists), and Ṛishi (ascetics) or, on the other hand, of Sogata, Maheśvara, and Mahābrāhmaṇa prove the coexistence, the symbiosis, of Buddhism and Sivaite Hinduism in Java, just as in Cambodia in the same era. But, as his successors were to do, Airlanga represented himself as an incarnation of Vishnu.

From 1042 on, he perhaps entered the religious life, although still retaining his power. At his death in 1049,[109] he was buried at a place called "Bath of Belahan," on the eastern slope of Penanggungan. Once to be seen there was a beautiful statue of Vishnu on Garuḍa between two images of Lakshmī, probably representations of the king and two of his wives, as well as a stone bearing a chronogram which gives in a sort of rebus the date *śaka* 971, i.e., 1049.[110]

The reign of Airlanga, which was of such great political importance, was also marked by a certain literary activity,[111] but works have wrongly been attributed to his reign that were really composed during the reign of his predecessor, Dharmavaṃśa Tguḥ Anantavikrama, with whom Airlanga has erroneously been identified.[112] It is almost certain that the *Arjunavivāha* ("Marriage of Arjuna") [113] was written in 1035 by the poet Kaṇva as an epithalamium for the marriage of Airlanga with the Sumatran princess.[114]

Before his death, Airlanga divided his kingdom in two, and this division lasted, theoretically at least, until the end of the Indo-Javanese era. We can only make conjectures about the reasons that inspired such a step in a man whose every other action was directed toward unifying his states. We do not know of any legitimate sons of his,[115] and we may guess that, to avoid a conflict after his death between two children born of concubines and having the same rights, he resolved to settle the question during his lifetime.[116]

The frontier between the two kingdoms of Janggala and Panjalu was marked either by a wall, the ruins of which can still be seen between Mount Kawi and the southern coast of the island,[117] or by the course of the Brantas.[118] Janggala lay to the east and must have included the region of Malang and the Brantas Delta with the ports of Surabaya, Rembang, and Pasuruhan. Its capital was Kahuripan, Airlanga's capital. On the west was Panjalu, better known by the name Kaḍiri, which included the residencies of Kediri and Madiun, with an access to the sea on the bay of Surabaya. Its capital was Daha (present-day Kediri). In fact, although it had precedence and was the theoretical successor of the kingdom of Airlanga, Janggala was soon absorbed by Panjalu.[119]

For the island of Bali, we have inscriptions from 1050 to 1078 [120] emanating from a person who is known as *anak wungśu*, that is, "younger son" (*bālaputra*) or perhaps "son-in-law"—very probably of the parents of Airlanga; he was, therefore, probably the younger brother or brother-in-law of Airlanga.

5. ŚRĪVIJAYA AND THE CHOḶAS (1067–69)

The sources are silent about what happened in Śrīvijaya from 1030 to 1064. In 1064 the name of a certain Dharmavīra, otherwise unknown, is inscribed at Solok, to the west of Jambi, on a *makara* image executed in a style that seems to show the influence of Javanese art.[121]

In 1067, one of the highest dignitaries of San-fo-ch'i, whom the *History of the Sung* calls Ti-hua-ch'ieh-lo,[122] the normal transcription of Divākara, arrived in China. Some authors[123] see here rather a transcription of Devakula. They base their argument on the fact that the Choḷa king Rājendra*devakulo*ttunga (also known as Kulottunga I), who sent an embassy to China ten years later in 1077, is designated in the *History of the Sung* by an almost identical name (Ti-hua-chia-lo).[124] According to them, it was the same person in both cases: born of a daughter of Rājendrachoḷa and of Rājarāja I of Vengī,[125] he is presumed to have held many high offices in Śrīvijaya before coming to the throne of the Choḷas in 1070; he himself seems to allude to such a background in the first inscriptions of his reign.

However that may be, the year that followed the embassy of 1067 saw a new aggression of the Choḷas against the Malay Peninsula. In the seventh year of his reign, in 1068–69, Vīrarājendra, son or grandson of the Rājendrachoḷa who had led the expedition of 1025, "conquered Kaḍāram on behalf of the king who had come to ask for his aid and protection and delivered the conquered country to him."[126] Perhaps it was on the advice of his Choḷa minister Devakula,[127] if this identification is indeed correct, that the king of Śrīvijaya made an appeal for assistance from Vīrarājendra to repress a revolt or an attempt at secession on the peninsula. Was it also the presence of a Choḷa adviser at the court of Śrīvijaya, and the willingness of the Choḷa king to reconquer territory on behalf of this country, that led Chinese historians to believe that during the period 1068–77 "Chou-lien (Choḷa) was a vassal of San-fo-ch'i"?[128]

6. BURMA: ANÔRATHA (1044–77)

"When a standard history of Burma comes to be written," writes G. E. Harvey,[129] "it will be necessary to divide the reigns of such kings as Anawrahta into two parts: the first will be The Evidence, e.g., inscriptions showing him to have actually existed and what he did, and the second part will be The Anawrahta Legend." The time has not yet come to write such a history, and in the lines that follow, the data extracted from an epigraphy that has only recently begun to be utilized[130] are interwoven with the least improbable elements of the legend.[131]

We saw at the end of the preceding chapter that Anôratha[132] was the son of King Kunshô Kyaungphyu and of one of the three princesses who had previously been married to the regicidal gardener. He spent his youth in the monastery in which his father was in compulsory residence. Getting into a quarrel one day with his cousin, King Sokkate, he killed him in single combat at Myinkaba near Pagan. The throne having thus become vacant, he offered it to his father, but his father refused it, preferring to remain in the monastery.

Anôratha, who became king in 1044,[133] increased the territory of the kingdom of Pagan, which at the beginning was still small. In internal affairs, his two most remarkable achievements were the creation of a system of irrigation east of his capital, in the rice plain of Kyaukse, which became the granary of northern Burma,[134] and the conversion of the country to Theravada Buddhism.[135]

The establishment of Theravada Buddhism in Pagan was, according to legend, the result of a campaign in 1057 against Sudhammavatī (Thaton, in Pegu).

Lower Burma, that is, the Mon country, was one of the earliest countries converted to Buddhism.[136] But numerous vestiges of Hinduism have also been found in this country, and they prove that Buddhism was not the only religion known there. It has been suggested,[137] not without some probability, that Buddhism could have been introduced or at least fortified by the mass arrival in the first half of the eleventh century of Mons from Haripunjaya who were fleeing from a cholera epidemic and perhaps also from the Khmer armies of Sūryavarman I.

When Buddhism began to decline in India, the Mons maintained spiritual contact with southern India (Kānchī, i.e., Conjeevaram) and with Ceylon, holy land of Theravada Buddhism. In 1056, the monk Shin Arahan,[138] son of a Brahman of Thaton and undoubtedly a disciple of the Kānchī school, came to Pagan and won the king over to his doctrine.

Desiring to obtain a collection of the sacred writings of the Pali canon, Anôratha sent one of his ministers to Thaton.[139] His request was refused by King Makuṭa.[140] Anôratha then organized an expedition against his uncooperative neighbor, and in 1057, after a three months' siege, he took the city of Thaton.[141] There he found thirty collections of the *Tripiṭaka,* which he took back to Pagan along with King Makuṭa, his ministers, monks, and a great number of artisans.

The political result of the conquest of Thaton was the submission of the whole delta [142] and its Indian principalities,[143] thus opening a window on the sea for the Burmese; the cultural result was the conversion of Pagan to Theravada Buddhism and the decline of Tantric Mahayana,[144] which was undoubtedly obliged to transfer its temples *extra muros*. In sum, the influence of the more refined Mon civilization was brought to bear on the still relatively unrefined Burmese population. The numerous prisoners brought back from Thaton taught the Burmese their literature, their art, and, above all, their script. The first inscription in the Burmese language, written in Mon characters, dates from the year after the conquest, 1058.[145] Two of the most ancient monuments of Pagan, Nan-paya and Manuha, were built by the captive King Makuṭa around 1060.[146]

Anôratha was certainly a great conquerer who, not content with having brought all of the Irrawaddy Basin under his domination, turned his forces against his neighbors. Unfortunately, we have very few details concerning the campaigns that dominate his legend. To the west, he conquered the north of Arakan and seems to have pushed on to Chittagong.[147] In the direction of Cambodia, the chronicles of the Thai principalities of the upper Menam [148] attribute a campaign to him, although there is no hint of such a campaign in contemporary Khmer sources. In the north, he is supposed to have gone beyond Bhamo to Ta-li in Nanchao in an attempt to obtain a tooth-relic of the Buddha, and to have returned with nothing but a jade image.[149] One fact is certain: votive tablets in his name have been found from the mouths of the Irrawaddy River in the south to the town of Mong Mit in the north.[150]

His reputation having spread to Ceylon, King Vijayabāhu I (1055–56—1110–11) [151] at first requested his military aid to repel a Choḷa invasion,[152] then, having succeeded in meeting this threat on his own, contented himself with asking Anôratha in 1071 for monks and canonic texts in order to restore the ravages caused by the war.[153] In exchange, the Burmese envoys brought back to Pagan a copy of the famous tooth-relic of Ceylon. This prize was placed in the great temple of Shwezigon, the construction of which had been started in about 1059[154] but was not completed until the reign of Kyanzittha.

Anôratha died in 1077 in a hunting accident. He left a kingdom that extended from Bhamo to the Gulf of Martaban, embracing northern Arakan and the north of Tenasserim, and was defended by a series of fortified cities;[155] a kingdom that had been won over to Theravada Buddhism and refined from the artistic and cultural point of view by Mon influence; a kingdom that was capable of playing the role of a great power on the Indochinese Peninsula.

This chapter has concentrated on Kings Sūryavarman I, Airlanga, and Anôratha. Their reigns had political consequences of great importance, for it was during their reigns that Javanese power was restored and the power of the Mons in the basins of the Menam and Irrawaddy was replaced by the power of the Khmers and Burmese. Moreover, this period marks the retreat of the Chams before the Vietnamese, to whom they abandoned their northern provinces. It also contains the first signs of weakness on the part of Śrīvijaya, which had been shaken by the Javanese invasion of the preceding century and was further shaken by the Choḷa raids. Burma, Cambodia, and Java, taking advantage of the weakness of Sung China, were henceforth to be the three great protagonists in the history of Farther India.

CHAPTER X

THE MAHĪDHARAPURA DYNASTY OF CAMBODIA, THE PAGAN DYNASTY OF BURMA, AND THE JAVANESE KINGDOM OF KADIRI

End of the Eleventh Century and First Three Quarters of the Twelfth Century

1. CAMBODIA: THE FIRST KINGS OF THE MAHĪDHARAPURA DYNASTY (1080–1112)

Harshavarman III, who came to the throne in Cambodia in 1066, busied himself with repairing the structures ruined in the wars of the preceding reign.[1] Between 1074 and 1080, he himself had reason to quarrel with the Chams, whose King Harivarman IV is said to have "defeated the troops of Cambodia at Someśvara and seized the prince Śrī Nandavarmadeva, who commanded this army and who had been sent with the rank of *senāpati*."[2] Perhaps it was on the occasion of this battle that Prince Pāng, younger brother of the king of Champa, and later king himself under the name of Paramabodhisattva, "went to take [in Cambodia] the city of Śambhupura [Sambor on the Mekong], destroyed all its sanctuaries, and gave the Khmers whom he had seized to the various sanctuaries of Śrī Īśānabhadreśvara [at Mi-sơn]."[3]

"In 1076, the Chinese, having decided on an expedition against Tongking, persuaded the neighbors of this country, Champa and Cambodia, to take part in the battle: while the army of Kuo K'uei moved down on Hanoi by the way of Lang-sơn, the Chams and Cambodians invaded Nghê-an. The defeat of the Chinese led to the retreat of their allies; we have no information about their movements."[4]

Harshavarman III received the posthumous name Sadāśivapada.[5] He was succeeded in 1080 by Jayavarman VI.[6] The genealogy of Jayavarman VI, as it is given in an inscription of his grandnephew Sūryavarman II,[7] indicates no relationship either with the dynasty founded by Sūryavarman I or with preceding dynasties. He was the son of Hiraṇyavarman from Kshitīndragrāma, an otherwise unknown locality, and of Hiraṇyalakshmī. Later, the inscriptions of Jayavarman VII say that he belonged to the nobility of Mahīdharapura,[8] a city whose site remains unidentified. Perhaps he was a high dignitary, a provincial governor, who, taking advantage of the weakening of central authority following the troubled reign of Udayādityavarman II, became more or less independent in the north, where his establishments and those of his successors are particularly numerous. He seems to have been aided in the realization of his plans by the priest Divākarapaṇḍita, who, after having been in the service of Harshavarman III for some time, threw in his lot with the newcomers, conducted the coronation of Jayavarman VI and his two successors, and received quasi-royal titles from them.[9]

It is not certain that Jayavarman VI ever reigned at Angkor, where he is mentioned only in an unfinished inscription [10] and where Harshavarman may have been succeeded by a king named Nṛipatīndravarman [11] who reigned there until around 1113. We shall see, in fact, that Sūryavarman II claimed to have seized power from *two* kings at this date. The first was his uncle Dharaṇīndravarman I, for whom there are no longer any inscriptions remaining in the Angkor group; [12] one is tempted to see in the other king a successor of Harshavarman III who maintained power in the capital through the first decade of the twelfth century.

Little is known about the reign of Jayavarman VI. The inscriptions of his successors, and even more clearly those of the Brahman Divākara, associate his name with some constructions in the Sivaite monuments of Phnom Sandak, Preah Vihear, and Vat Ph'u [13] and at the Buddhist temple of Phimai. At his death he received the posthumous name Paramakaivalyapada.

Of his two brothers, the younger, who had received the title of Yuvarāja, or heir apparent, died prematurely,[14] and it was the elder, Dharaṇīndravarman I, who succeeded Jayavarman VI in 1107; [15] he was crowned, as I have already said, by Divākara. "Without having desired royalty," says an inscription, "when the king, his younger brother, had returned to the heavens, through simple compassion and yielding to the prayers of the human multitudes without a protector, he governed the land with prudence." [16] He continued the building and endowment program of the preceding reign and pursued traditionalism to the point of taking as a wife Queen Vijayendralakshmī, who had first been married to the heir apparent prince who died before reigning, then to Jayavarman VI.[17]

He had reigned for five years when his grandnephew in the female line, "still quite young," says the same inscription, "at the end of his studies, proved to be the answer to the desires of the royal honor of his family, a family now in the dependence of two masters."[18] This was Sūryavarman II, whose brilliant career we shall see presently.

2. CHAMPA FROM 1074 TO 1113

In Champa, Prince Thāng (Vishṇumūrti, Mādhavamūrti, or Devatāmūrti), who was a descendant through his father of the coconut palm family (*narikelavaṃśa*) and through his mother of the areca palm family (*kramukavaṃśa),* was proclaimed king in 1074 under the name of Harivarman (IV).[19] At the very beginning of his reign, he repulsed a Vietnamese attack,[20] and, as we have seen above, he was victorious over the Khmers and carried the war into their country to the Mekong. In 1076, he took part, somewhat reluctantly, in the coalition led by China against Đai Viêt; the following year he sent tribute to Đai Viêt.[21]

Harivarman IV spent a great part of his reign "restoring to Champa its ancient splendor,"[22] restoring Champāpura and Siṃhapura (in Quang-nam) and making numerous endowments at Mi-sơn. In 1080, he had his nine-year-old son, Prince Vāk, crowned under the name Jaya Indravarman (II), and he died in retirement in the following year.[23]

Since the young king "did not know how to govern the kingdom properly and did everything contrary to the rules of the government,"[24] it was necessary to find a regent at the end of a month. The choice fell on an uncle of the king, the Prince Pāng who had conquered Śambhupura from the Khmers during the preceding reign. He was crowned king under the name Paramabodhisattva. Apparently, he held onto the power to the point of true usurpation, for, after six years of a reign during which the uncle sent tribute to Đai Viêt each year[25] and repressed an attempt of the always rebellious Pāṇḍuranga to achieve autonomy,[26] the faction of the nephew again got the upper hand and placed him back on the throne by means of a *coup de force* in 1086.[27]

Upon his re-establishment on the throne, Jaya Indravarman II resumed relations with China. Until 1091 he also sent regular tribute to Đai Viêt. After an interruption of several years, for which he was rebuked, he resumed sending missions to Đai Viêt from

1095 to 1102. In 1103, however, after a Vietnamese refugee had encouraged him to believe he would be able to recover the three Cham provinces in the north that had been lost in 1069, he discontinued the missions again and launched an attack on the provinces. The campaign was successful at first, but he was able to hold the provinces only a few months.[28] He then reigned peacefully until around 1113, continuing the restorations of his predecessors and building structures at Mi-sơn.

3. BURMA: THE KINGS OF PAGAN, SUCCESSORS OF ANÔRATHA (1077–1112)

Concerning the descendants of Anôratha who reigned after him at Pagan, late chronicles report many anecdotes—often romantic, sometimes scandalous—that are outside the domain of history. Epigraphy permits us to fix the dates of their accessions and of the edifices they built that made their capital one of the richest archaeological sites of the Indochinese Peninsula.[29]

Anôratha left two sons when he died in 1077: Sôlu, born of a wife he had married before becoming king,[30] and Kyanzittha, son of the Indian or Arakanese princess[31] Panchakalyāṇī but probably really fathered by a mandarin who had been entrusted with bringing her to Pagan.[32] After having barely escaped death in his early years during a "massacre of the innocents" ordered by Anôratha,[33] Kyanzittha, suspected of being the lover of Queen Maṇichanda, or Chandadevī, daughter of the king of Pegu, was banished from the court.[34]

Sôlu, named Mang Lulang, "the young king," in epigraphy, came to power in 1077.[35] He began his reign by marrying his stepmother, the Peguan queen, whom he gave the title Khin U. He then recalled Kyanzittha, but Kyanzittha was soon sent back into exile for the same reason he had been banished before.[36] Kyanzittha's unequaled bravery got him recalled again to aid in putting down a revolt by a foster-brother of Sôlu's, Ngayaman Kan,[37] to whom the king had entrusted the government of Pegu. In spite of Kyanzittha's aid, Sôlu was unsuccessful in putting down the revolt and, after various romantic incidents, was killed by the rebel.[38]

Kyanzittha, designated in epigraphy by the title Thiluing Mang,[39] or King of T'ilaing (in the northeast of Meiktila), was chosen to succeed Sôlu in 1084.[40] He first had to reconquer his kingdom from the Mons of Pegu. Ngayaman Kan entrenched himself at a site where the city of Ava was later built. Kyanzittha assembled his forces in the rice plain of Kyaukse and marched on Pagan; he had no difficulty in defeating the Peguans. Ngayaman Kan perished in the retreat.[41]

Kyanzittha was then crowned, probably in 1086,[42] by the venerable Shin Arahan. He took the name Tribhuvanāditya Dhammarāja, a title that was borne from then on by all the kings of the dynasty. Following his predecessors, he in his turn married the Peguan Khin U,[43] possession of whom perhaps legitimized the sovereignty of the king of Pagan over the Mon country. His only daughter, Shwe-einthi, born of the queen Abeyadana (Abhayaratanā) whom Kyanzittha had married before his coronation, was married to Sôyun, son of Sôlu.[44] She had a son by this marriage, the future Alaung-sithu (Jayasūra I), whom from his birth Kyanzittha proclaimed king, declaring himself regent in his name.[45] In addition, at the time of his exile during the reign of his father Anôratha, Kyanzittha had had a son by Sambhulā, the niece of a hermit whom he had met in the forest.[46] When she presented herself at court,[47] he accepted her as fourth queen, with the title Trilokavataṃsikā (Burmese U Sauk Pan),[48] and entrusted the government of Dhaññavatī (northern Arakan) to her son Rājakumāra, whom he gave the title of Jayakhettara.[49]

The great achievement of Kyanzittha, which by itself would have been enough to establish his fame, was the construction of the temple of Ananda (*Anantapaññā,* "infinite wisdom") at Pagan in imitation, legend says,[50] of the grotto of Nandamūla on Mount Gandamādana. One scholar has tried to identify this legendary grotto with the temple of Udayagiri in Orissa;[51] the king must have heard about this temple from the Indian monks who came to Burma to escape the persecution Buddhism suffered in their country. But it is also possible that the temple of Paharpur, in northern Bengal, served as a model for the architect of the Ananda.[52] The architect was not allowed to survive the dedication of his masterpiece, which took place in 1090; he and a child were buried alive to serve as guardian spirits of the temple.[53]

Among other works carried out during the reign of Kyanzittha were the completion of the pagoda of Shwezigon, where Kyanzittha's most important inscriptions were placed,[54] and repairs on the temple of Bodhgaya in India.[55] Kyanzittha also undertook irrigation works, built a new palace around 1101–1102,[56] and had numerous inscriptions engraved in the Mon language, still considered at that time the language of civilization.[57]

There is no doubt that the restorer of Bodhgaya and the founder of the Ananda, where he had his statue placed in the attitude of prayer,[58] was a fervent follower of Buddhism. He did some proselytizing himself on occasion: he converted a Choḷa prince, who was passing through Burma, by sending him a text on The Three Jewels that he himself had composed and written on a gold leaf. But we still find numerous traces of Hinduism during his reign,[60] and Brahmans played a dominant role in the royal ceremonies at court.[61] Kyanzittha obviously held the Mons in great esteem, as is shown by his inscriptions in the Mon language and the Mon style of the sculptures and decorations of his monuments.

In 1103, Kyanzittha sent to China the first Burmese embassy that is mentioned in the *History of the Sung*.[62] Three years later, in 1106, "envoys of the kingdom of P'u-kan (Pagan) having come to offer tribute, the emperor at first gave the order to receive them and give them the same treatment accorded the envoys of Chou-lien (Choḷa), but the president of the Council of Rites made the following observations: 'Chou-lien is a vassal of San-fo-ch'i;[63] that is why during the *hsi-ning* years (1068–1077) it was enough to write to the king of this country on heavy paper, with an envelope of plain material. The king of P'u-kan, on the other hand, is a sovereign of the great kingdom of the Fan (the Brahmans; that is, the Indian countries). One must not behave disdainfully toward him. One ought to accord to him the same honors as to the princes of Ta-shih (Arabs) and Chiao-chih (Tongking), by writing to him on silk with flowers of gold, white on the back, a letter which you enclose in a little box ringed with gold, with a silver lock and double envelope of taffeta and satin.' The emperor approved of his observations and decided that it would be thus."[64] I have cited this passage in its entirety because it shows the prestige that the kingdom of Pagan already—only sixty-two years after the accession to power of Anôratha, who was its real founder—enjoyed at the court of China, which was always anxious to maintain an exact hierarchy among foreign sovereigns.

Kyanzittha died in 1112 or shortly afterward, for it was undoubtedly on the occasion of the illness that led to his demise that his son Rājakumāra, son of the queen Trilokavataṃsikā, had a gold statue of the Buddha cast and inscribed in four languages (Pali, Pyu, Mon, Burmese); this is the extremely valuable inscription of the pillar of Myazedi, south of Pagan.[65]

4. INDONESIA FROM 1078 TO 1109; THE KINGDOM OF KAḌIRI

For the period that includes the last quarter of the eleventh century and the first decade of the twelfth, the only record we have of San-fo-ch'i in the histories is the mention in the *History of the Sung* of a series of embassies it sent to China between 1078 and 1097.[66] In addition, the relations between Sumatra and southern India are shown by an inscription in Tamil found near Baros on the west coast of the island. This inscription is dated 1088 and emanates from a powerful corporation of merchants of southern India.[67] In 1089–90, at the request of the king of Kiḍāra, the Choḷa Kulottunga I[68] granted a new charter to the Śrī Śailendra Chūḍāmaṇivarmavihāra,[69] that is, to the sanctuary built at Negapatam at the order of Śailendra Chūḍāmaṇivarman around 1005.[70]

During the same period, information is not much more abundant for Java and Bali.

For Java, Chinese evidence of the eleventh century gives so slight an impression of a division of the ancient kingdom of Airlanga into two states that we can suppose that Kaḍiri, the only one that has left epigraphic traces, occupied all the ports of the coast and was the sole representative of She-p'o for the merchants from the Middle Kingdom. Kaḍiri sent an embassy to China in 1109.[71]

We have a great number of inscriptions from Kaḍiri that tell us the names of kings with their dates but contain very little else of historical substance. The composition by Triguṇa of the *Kṛishṇāyana*,[72] an epic poem dealing with the legend of Krishna depicted in the bas-reliefs of Chandi Jago[73] and Panataran,[74] dates from this period.

In 1098, Sakalendukiraṇa, a princess whose complete title[75] indicates dynastic ties with the family of Airlanga,[76] appears in Bali.

The *History of the Sung* registers an embassy to China in 1082 from King Śrī Mahārāja of P'o-ni, that is, from the west coast of Borneo.[77]

5. CAMBODIA FROM THE ACCESSION OF SŪRYAVARMAN II (1113) TO THE TAKING OF ANGKOR BY THE CHAMS (1177)

In Cambodia, the accession of Sūryavarman II coincided exactly with the death of Jaya Indravarman II in Champa and that of Kyanzittha at Pagan. If the relationships between all these countries were better known, perhaps we could find a cause-and-effect relationship between the disappearance of these two powerful sovereigns and the assumption of power by this ambitious Khmer king who was to lead his troops to the east as well as to the west.

We have seen that Sūryavarman II had "taken the royalty by unifying a double kingdom."[78] We are certain that one of the two kings was Dharaṇīndravarman I: "After a battle that lasted one day, King Śrī Dharaṇīndravarman was stripped of his defenseless kingdom by Śrī Sūryavarman."[79] The struggle must have been violent: "Releasing the ocean of his armies on the field of combat, he [Sūryavarman II] gave terrible battle; leaping on the head of the elephant of the enemy king, he slew him, just as Garuda swooping down from the top of a mountain kills a serpent."[80] Dharaṇīndravarman I received the posthumous name of Paramanishkalapada. We do not know the name of the other king from whom Sūryavarman II took power; as has been said,[81] he was perhaps a descendant of Harshavarman III. The indispensable Brahman Divākara legitimized the *coup de force* of Sūryavarman II by conducting his coronation in 1113.[82]

The new king did not lose any time in renewing relations with the court of China, which had been interrupted, it seems, for several reigns. The *History of the Sung* mentions embassies in 1116 and in 1120.

Sūryavarman II was a great conqueror who led the Khmer armies farther than they had ever been before. "He saw the kings of the other countries that he desired to subjugate coming to bring tribute. He himself went into the countries of his enemies and eclipsed the glory of the victorious Raghu [an ancestor of Rāma]."[83] In his *Royaume de Champa,* Georges Maspero gives very precise details on the battles against Đai Viêt and Champa; I can do no better than to reproduce his account[84] here:

> From the time that he took the crown, Sūryavarman II began harassing Champa. In 1123 and 1124, in fact, Đai Viêt constantly gave

asylum to bands of Cambodians or Chams who sought refuge in its territory from the pursuit of their enemy. In 1128, Sūryavarman led 20,000 men against Đai Viêt. After having been driven from Nghê-an by Ly Công Binh, the following autumn he sent a fleet of more than 700 vessels to pillage the coasts of Thanh-hoa, and from then on he attacked this empire continuously, often dragging Champa along with him, willingly or by force. Thus we see Champa, which in the beginning of 1131 sent tribute to the emperor Ly Thân-tông, invading Nghê-an the following year together with the Khmers.[85] They were soon driven away, however, by the garrisons of Nghê-an and Thanh-hoa reunited under the command of Đương Anh-nhe. Jaya Indravarman III did not wish to carry these exploits further, and in 1136 he performed his duties of vassalage toward Ly Thân-tông. He did not take part in the new campaign that Sūryavarman led against Đai Viêt (1138).[86] The Khmer sovereign, unsuccessful in this undertaking, turned on him with all his conquering ardor. In 1145 he invaded Champa, seized Vijaya, and made himself master of the kingdom. Jaya Indravarman III disappeared during the war, prisoner of the victor or dead on the battlefield.

The Khmer occupation of the northern part of Champa, with its capital at Vijaya (Binh-đinh), lasted until 1149.[87] When a new king, Jaya Harivarman I, established himself in 1147 in the south at Pāṇḍuranga,[88] Sūryavarman II sent an army against him. This army, composed of Khmers and Chams and under the orders of the *senāpati* Śankara, was defeated in 1148 on the plain of Rājapura.[89] An army "a thousand times stronger" met the same fate at Vīrapura.[90] At this point Sūryavarman II proclaimed "a Kshatriya, Prince Harideva, his brother-in-law, younger brother of his first wife,"[91] king of Champa at Vijaya. Jaya Harivarman I marched on Vijaya and on the plain of Mahīśa "defeated and killed Harideva, destroyed this king with all the Cham and Cambodian *senāpati* and the Cham and Cambodian troops; they all perished."[92] The Cham king entered Vijaya and was crowned there in 1149.[93] That was the end of the Khmer occupation.

After this defeat, Sūryavarman II resumed hostilities against Đai Viêt and "in 1150 sent a new expedition. The result was even worse than before. The expedition had been sent on its way in the fall without regard for the season. The rains of September and October were disastrous. Fever swept through the troops while they were crossing the Wu-wen Mountains, that is, the Annamite chain, and they arrived at Nghê-an so weak that they withdrew voluntarily without ever going into action."[94]

We have some indications of the battles in the west in the chronicles of the Thai principalities of the upper Menam. These chronicles tell of struggles between the Kambojas of Lavo (Lopburi) and the Ramaññas (Mons) of Haripunjaya (Lamphun). Haripunjaya was the upper Menam principality, founded in the seventh century by the Mons from Lavo,[95] that had been involved in the troubles marking the accession of Sūryavarman I.[96] Since Lavo had been part of the Khmer kingdom from the preceding century, we must understand the "king of Lavo" to have been either a Cambodian viceroy or governor or the Cambodian sovereign himself. The chronicles, moreover, put a certain number of expressions that are pure Khmer into the mouths of the Kambojas of Lavo.[97] The wars were provoked, according to these texts, by Ādityarāja, the builder of Mahābalachetiya (Vat Kukut) and the discoverer of the Great Relic of Lamphun,[98] who came to power at the latest around 1150 after a series of kings whose histories we do not know.[99] He allegedly came to Lavo to challenge the Khmers but they put his army to flight and pursued it up to the walls of Haripunjaya. The Khmers were unable to take the city and had to turn back, but they returned to the attack on two occasions: the first time, the expedition ended with an agreement with Ādityarāja and with the establishment of the Khmers in a village called Kambojagāma southeast of Haripunjaya; since the pact was not approved by their sovereign, however, the Khmers had to conduct a new expedition, and this one failed completely.[100]

Given the unreliability of the chronology, it is not certain that these events all took place during the reign of Sūryavarman II. We cannot help but notice that the war against the Mons of the upper Menam, like the campaigns against the Chams, had an unfortunate end for the Cambodians. But we know of these events only from sources hostile to Cambodia, sources that may have intentionally distorted the facts. However that may be, a great expansion of Cambodian sovereignty on the Indochinese Peninsula in the middle of the twelfth century is recorded in the *History of the Sung,*[101] which states that Chenla (Cambodia) was bordered by the southern frontiers of Chan-ch'eng (Champa) in the north, by the sea to the east, by P'u-kan (the kingdom of Pagan) in the west, and by Chia-lo-hsi (Grahi, in the region of

Chaiya and of the Bay of Bandọn on the east coast of the Malay Peninsula)[102] in the south.

In 1128, the emperor of China "conferred high dignities on the king of Chenla, named Chin-p'ou-pin-shen,[103] who was recognized as a great vassal of the empire. Some difficulties having to do with affairs of commerce were then examined and settled," between 1131 and 1147.[104]

With regard to internal affairs, the reign of Sūryavarman II, as it appears in epigraphy, was marked by endowments at Phnom Chisor, Phnom Sandak, Vat Ph'u, and Preah Vihear and by a series of buildings including the principal elements of Preah Pithu in Angkor Thom, Chau Say Tévoda and Thommanon east of the city, and finally the masterpiece of Khmer art, Angkor Wat,[105] constructed during the lifetime of the king for whom it was to serve as a funerary temple.[106] It was in Angkor Wat that Sūryavarman II was to be deified in the form of a statue of Vishnu with the posthumous name Paramavishṇuloka.

The name Paramavishṇuloka is an indication of the favor Vishnuism enjoyed at the court, a favor that manifested itself less in the building of temples dedicated to Vishnu than in the decoration of edifices inspired for the most part by the legendary cycle of Vishnu-Krishna.[107] This fervor for a cult that was more capable than Sivaism of inspiring devotion (*bhakti*), the mystic pouring out of the soul toward the divinity, is found in the same period in Java, where the kings of Kaḍiri all represented themselves as incarnations of Vishnu. It is also synchronous with the religious movement that in India, at the beginning of the twelfth century, inspired Rāmānuja, the founder of modern Vishnuism.[108]

The end of the reign of Sūryavarman II is obscure, and the date of his death is still unknown. The last inscription in his name is of 1145,[109] but there is every reason to believe that he was the instigator of the campaign of 1150 against Tongking and, therefore, that he reigned at least until that date.

It is possible that the question of Khmer suzerainty over Lavo (Lopburi) was reopened by the death of Sūryavarman II. This state, which the Chinese called Lo-hu, had already sent a mission to China on its own in 1115, only two years after the accession of Sūryavarman II, at a time when this young king undoubtedly had not yet established his authority over the outlying dependencies of his kingdom. A new embassy in 1155, perhaps following the death of Sūryavarman II, probably corresponded with a new attempt to cut the ties of dependence to Angkor.[110] An inscription of 1167 found in Siam in the region of Nagara Svarga (Nakhọn Sawan) mentions a sovereign king, named Dharmāśoka, who may well have reigned in a kingdom of Lavo that had become independent.[111]

The successor of Sūryavarman II, named Dharaṇīndravarman II, was not his direct descendant, but his cousin.[112] Perhaps he became king as a result of some palace revolution. If he did, this would explain the silence of epigraphy concerning the last days of Sūryavarman II. In addition, the new sovereign was Buddhist,[113] and although the Hindu kings had been tolerant of Buddhism, there had nevertheless been a long tradition of Hindu orthodoxy. This tradition was now broken. All we know about Dharaṇīndravarman II is that he married a daughter of Harshavarman III, Princess Chūḍāmaṇi, by whom in about 1125 he had a son who was to reign much later under the name of Jayavarman VII.[114] We can, with some probability, attribute the major part of the building of the Preah Khan of Kompong Svay to him.

Dharaṇīndravarman II was succeeded at an undetermined date by a Yaśovarman (II) whose genealogy is not known. His reign was marked by a dramatic incident mentioned in an inscription of the temple of Banteay Ch'mar and represented on a bas-relief of the same monument: a mysterious being, to whom the text gives the name—and the sculpture the likeness—of Rāhu (Asura, who devours the sun and the moon at the time of eclipses), attacked the king, who was saved by a young prince, probably a son of the future Jayavarman VII.

Around 1165, Yaśovarman II was overthrown by a mandarin who proclaimed himself king under the name of Tribhuvanādityavarman. The future Jayavarman VII, then in Champa, returned precipitately to defend Yaśovarman, to whom he must have been related, or simply allied, during this troubled period,[115] but he arrived too late.

At the same time that this rebel took possession of the throne of Cambodia, another seized that of Champa in 1166–67 under the name of Jaya Indravarman IV. After coming to an agreement with Đai Viêt in 1170, he turned against Cambodia. "Jaya Indravarman, the king of the Chams, presumptuous as Rāvaṇa, transporting his army in chariots, went to fight the country of Kambu, like to heaven," says an inscription.[116] But the struggle was indecisive. Then, changing his plans, Jaya Indravarman tried to take over Cambodia by sea. The expedition was sent in 1177.[117] Sailing along the coast, the Cham fleet, guided by a Chinese castaway, arrived at the mouth of the Mekong and sailed up to the Great Lake. Angkor was surprised, the usurper Tribhuvanāditya killed, and the city pillaged. Such a catastrophe, coming after twenty years of internal troubles, would seem to have made it inevitable that restoration of the country could be accomplished only with great difficulty.

6. CHAMPA FROM 1113 TO 1177

King Jaya Indravarman II of Champa died around 1113 and was succeeded by his nephew Harivarman V, who reigned peacefully, continuing the establishments at Mi-sơn and remaining on excellent terms with China and Đai Viêt, with which he exchanged numerous embassies between 1116 and 1126.[118] Perhaps for lack of a suitable heir to succeed him, in 1133 Harivarman V seems to have adopted as Yuvarāja a prince of uncertain origin, born in 1106, who succeeded him in 1139 under the name of Jaya Indravarman (III).[119]

The endowments of the new king at Mi-sơn in 1140 [120] and at Po Nagar in Nha-trang in 1143 [121] prove that his authority was recognized in the north as well as in the south. We have seen above [122] how, after having aided the Khmers in an expedition against Nghê-an in 1131, he reconciled his differences with Đai Viêt and then underwent the Khmer invasion of 1145, in which he disappeared.

Since the capital and the greater part of the country were in the hands of the Khmers,[123] the people of Pāṇḍuranga gave asylum to the new king Rudravarman IV, who had been crowned in 1145 and had fled to the south. He never reigned. This king received the posthumous name Brahmaloka.[124] His son Ratnabhūmivijaya, Prince Śivānandana, was a descendant of Paramabodhisattva and had been in exile under Harivarman V and Jaya Indravarman III. "At first he left his country and for a long time he met with fortune and misfortune in foreign countries; then he returned to the land of Champa." He had accompanied his father in the flight to Pāṇḍuranga, where the inhabitants proclaimed him king in 1147 under the name of Jaya Harivarman (I).[125] It was he who in 1148 victoriously withstood the attack of Sūryavarman II and in 1149 reconquered the capital of Vijaya from the Khmer Prince Harideva. Immediately after reconquering Vijaya, he had himself crowned there.

But his task had only begun, for during his seventeen-year reign, he was constantly fighting to maintain his authority. First he had to contend with the Kirāṭas, that is, the hill tribes, "Radê, Mada and other barbarians (Mlecch'a)," grouped under the command of his disloyal brother-in-law, Vaṃśarāja.[126] Vaṃśarāja, beaten in 1150, requested aid from the emperor of Đai Viêt, who gave him five thousand soldiers from Thanh-hoa and Nghê-an.[127] "The king of the Yavanas [Vietnamese]," says an inscription of Mi-sơn, "because he learned that the king of Cambodia created obstacles for Jaya Harivarman, proclaimed Vaṃśarāja, a man of Champa, king; he gave him many Yavana *senāpati,* with many very valorous Yavana troops numbering a hundred thousand men and a thousand. . . . They advanced to the plains of Dalvā [and of Lavang]. Then Jaya Harivarman led all the troops of Vijaya. The two parties engaged in a terrible combat. Jaya Harivarman defeated Vaṃśarāja. The Yavana troops died in great numbers."[128] After he had pacified this area, Jaya Harivarman I subdued Amarāvatī (Quang-nam) in 1151,[129] then Pāṇḍuranga in 1160 after five years of battle.[130]

Victorious all along the line, he multiplied the religious establishments at Mi-sơn and Po Nagar,[131] the two great sacred places of the kingdom. He sent an embassy to China in 1155 and a series of embassies to Đai Viêt between 1152 and 1166.[132]

Jaya Harivarman I had at his court a high dignitary named Jaya Indravarman of Grāmapura, "expert in all weapons; . . . versed in all the *śāstras;* learned in grammar, astrology, etc.; knowing all the philosophic doctrines; learned in the doctrine of the Mahayana, etc.; expert in all the *Dharmaśāstras,* following especially the *Nāradīya* and the *Bhārgavīya;* taking pleasure in the *dharma. . . .*"[133] In 1163–65, we see him making endowments at Mi-sơn.[134]

We do not know exactly what happened at the death of Jaya Harivarman I in 1166–67. It is not certain that his son Jaya Harivarman (II) ever reigned.[135] In any case, Jaya Indravarman of Grāmapura succeeded in supplanting him and requested investiture from the court of China in 1167.[136]

The whole beginning of the reign of Jaya Indravarman (IV) was taken up with hostilities against Cambodia, in anticipation of which he attempted to conciliate the emperor of Đai Viêt in 1170 by sending presents.[137] In 1177, guided by a Chinese castaway,[138] "the king of Chan-ch'eng attacked the capital of Chenla without warning with a powerful fleet, pillaged it, and put the king of Chenla to death without listening to a single peace proposal. These events produced a great hatred that bore fruit in the fifth year of *ch'ing-yüan* [1190]." [139]

7. BURMA FROM 1113 TO 1173

At Pagan, Kyanzittha, who died in 1112 or shortly after, was succeeded by his grandson Alaung-sithu (Chan'sû = Jayasūra), who had been born in 1089. Alaung-sithu was crowned under the name Tribhuvanāditya Pavaradhammarāja. The new sovereign, perhaps of Mon origin on his father's side,[140] was the great-grandson of Anôratha on his mother's side. At the beginning of his long reign of fifty-five years, he had to put down a rebellion in the south of Arakan, and he made his domination felt down to Tenasserim.[141]

On his return from these expeditions, Alaung-sithu saw the old Shin Arahan die at the age of eighty-one [142]—the man who, about sixty years earlier, had converted Anôratha to Theravada Buddhism and indirectly instigated the conquest of Thaton.[143]

In 1118,[144] Alaung-sithu placed Letyaminnan on the throne of Arakan. Letyaminnan was the son of the legitimate sovereign who had been overthrown by a usurper. In gratitude for this restoration,[145] Letyaminnan had repairs made on the sanctuary of Bodhgaya in India.[146]

The *Glass Palace Chronicle* attributes to Alaung-sithu a series of journeys through his states, the construction of various works of public utility, and the erection of a great number of monuments. He supposedly went to Malaya, to the islands of the Arakan coast, to Chittagong and perhaps even Bengal, and to the forests of the Bhamo district. As early as 1115, he is supposed to have sent a mission to Nanchao,[147] and he then went there himself in an unsuccessful attempt to obtain the tooth-relic [148] sought previously by his great-grandfather Anôratha.

The principal constructions of his reign in the capital are the temple of Shwegu of 1131 [149] and the beautiful Thatbyinnyu

(Sabbaññu, "the Omniscient")[150] of 1150. They mark the transition between the period of Mon influence and the typically Burmese period of the following reigns. The composition in 1154 of the famous Pali grammar *Saddanīti* by the Burmese Aggavaṃsa[151] proves that, a century after the introduction of Theravada Buddhism, Pagan had become an important center of Pali scholarship.[152]

The *Glass Palace Chronicle* says that, since the eldest son of the king, Minshinsô, born of the queen Yadanabon, had been exiled because he was violent and insolent,[153] the second son, Narathu (Narasūra), born of the daughter of a minister of King Kyanzittha, was brought to power. In 1167,[154] when the eighty-one-year-old Alaung-sithu fell ill, Narathu did not hesitate to hasten the death of the old man.[155] Then began a whole series of assassinations. After three years of a bloody reign, marked by the murder of his brother Minshinsô, a great number of nobles, officials, and servants, and the princess of Pateikkaya,[156] Narathu himself died as the victim of an emissary of the princess's father.[157] Before dying, and to calm his remorse, he had time to build the Dhammayan (Dhamaraṃsi), the largest monument of Pagan.[158] The son of Narathu, Naratheinkha (Narasingha), reigned no more than three years, from 1170 to 1173, and was killed by his young brother Narapatisithu (Narapatijayasūra, or Jayasūra II), whose wife he had stolen.[159]

This is the *Chronicle*'s very romanticized account of the events following the death of Alaung-sithu. But all we can conclude from epigraphy is that Alaung-sithu died a septuagenarian. His successor Narathu died in 1165, assassinated by foreigners, probably Singhalese who had invaded the country the year before.[160] The *Chronicle* claims that Narathu had a son Naratheinkha who, after a reign of three years, supposedly was assassinated in 1173 by his younger brother. This Naratheinkha does not seem to have ever existed. In fact, we know of no kings of Pagan between 1165 and 1173. In 1173, perhaps with the aid of the Singhalese, the dynasty of Anôratha was restored in the person of Narapatisithu.[161]

8. INDONESIA FROM 1115 TO 1178; THE KINGDOM OF KAḌIRI

Compared with the wars of the Khmers and Chams and the dramas of the Burmese, the history of the states of Indonesia during this whole period is singularly colorless.

For San-fo-ch'i, we have only the mention in the *History of the Sung* of one embassy sent to China in 1156 by the king Śrī Mahārāja and another embassy in 1178.[162] Ma Tuan-lin cites a third embassy in 1176 and adds that the king who sent the embassy of 1178 began his reign in 1169.[163] The Arab geographers continue to speak of Zābag and the maharaja, but they are copying from one another without adding much information to that of their predecessors. Edrīsī, who wrote in 1154, gives, however, an interesting detail: "It is said that when the state of affairs of China became troubled by rebellions and when tyranny and confusion became excessive in India, the inhabitants of China transferred their trade to Zābag and the other islands dependent on it, entered into relations with it, and familiarized themselves with its inhabitants because of their justice, the goodness of their conduct, the pleasantness of their customs, and their facility in business. It is because of this that this island is so heavily populated and so often frequented by foreigners."[164]

For Java, we have only the names of a series of kings of Kaḍiri, mentioned in foundation charters:[165]

Bāmeśvara (1117–30),[166] who received privileges from the emperor of China in 1129 and 1132.[167]

Varmeśvara, also known as Jayabhaya (1135–79),[168] who was perhaps the son of Bāmeśvara. During his reign, in 1157, the poet Sedah began the Javanese version of the *Bhāratayuddha*,[169] a history of the battles of the *Mahābhārata* that was finished by Panuluh, author of the *Harivaṃśa*,[170] a collection of legends about Vishnu.

Sarveśvara,[171] who was reigning in 1159–61.

Aryeśvara,[172] who was reigning in 1171.

Kronchāryadīpa (also known as Gandra),[173] who was reigning in 1181.

For Bali, we have only the names of Śūrādhipa in 1115–19 and of Jayaśakti in 1146–50.[174]

CHAPTER XI

CAMBODIA AT THE HEIGHT OF ITS POWER; THE INTRODUCTION OF SINGHALESE BUDDHISM IN BURMA; AND THE JAVANESE KINGDOM OF SINGHASĀRI

Last Quarter of the Twelfth Century and First Two Thirds of the Thirteenth Century

1. CAMBODIA: JAYAVARMAN VII (1181–*CA.* 1218) AND THE ANNEXATION OF CHAMPA

Jayavarman VII inherited the difficult task of pulling Cambodia from the "sea of misfortune into which it had been plunged"[1] by the Cham invasion of 1177.

Through his father, Dharaṇīndravarman II, he was a second cousin of Sūryavarman II, and through his mother, Chūḍāmaṇi, daughter of Harshavarman III, he was a descendant of the kings of the dynasty that had reigned over the country for almost the whole of the eleventh century and that was related, on the female side, to the ancient kings of pre-Angkorian Cambodia. He was born at the latest in 1125,[2] during the reign of Sūryavarman II, and he married, undoubtedly while still young, Princess Jayarājadevī, who seems to have had great influence over him.

Jayavarman left Cambodia—just when is not known—to conduct a military expedition in Champa, at Vijaya (Binh-đinh), where he learned of the death of his father, the accession of Yaśovarman II, and finally of the usurpation of Tribhuvanāditya. "He returned in great haste to aid King Yaśovarman," says the stele of the Phimeanakas. We may assume that he also wanted to assert his rights to the throne. "But," continues the inscription, "Yaśovarman had been stripped of throne and life by the usurper, and Jayavarman remained in Cambodia waiting for the propitious moment to save the land heavy with crimes." He had to wait fifteen years.

When the Cham invasion had rid the country of the usurper, Jayavarman realized that the hour had come. But before proclaiming himself king, he had to deliver the country from the invaders. He waged a series of battles against the Chams; especially noteworthy was a naval battle—represented in almost identical fashion on the walls of the Bayon and of Banteay Ch'mar—that finally succeeded in liberating the country.[3]

By 1181, four years after the invasion of 1177, Cambodia had become calm again and Jayavarman had himself crowned. He then undertook the restoration of the capital, encircling it with the moats and the wall that constitute the enclosures of present-day Angkor Thom.[4]

At the time of the Cham invasion, Jayavarman, in the words of Ma Tuan-lin,[5] "decided to wreak terrible vengeance on his enemies, which he succeeded in doing after eighteen years of patient dissimulation."

But, before keeping his oath and waging war against the Chams, he had to cope with a revolt in the interior of his states that broke out at Malyang, in the south of the modern province of Battambang.[6] To put it down, he solicited the assistance of a young refugee Cham prince, who is described in a Cham inscription of Mi-sơn [7] in these terms:

> When he was in the prime of youth, in *śaka* 1104 [1182 A.D.], Prince Vidyānandana went to Cambodia. The king of Cambodia, seeing that he had all the thirty-three marks [of the fated man], took an interest in him and taught him, like a prince, all the sciences and military skills. While he was living in Cambodia, a city in this kingdom named Malyang, which was inhabited by a throng of wicked men over whom the Cambodians had established their mastery, revolted against the king of Cambodia. This king, seeing that the prince was well versed in military science, charged him with leading the Cambodian troops to take the city of Malyang. He complied completely with the wishes of the king of Cambodia. This king, seeing his valor, conferred on him the high rank of Yuvarāja and gave him all the possessions and good things that could be found in the kingdom of Cambodia.

This young Cham prince served as an instrument of Jayavarman's revenge against Champa. Jayavarman prepared for this revenge, the fruit of long years of "patient dissimulation," by making sure of the neutrality of the emperor of Đai Viêt, Ly Cao-tông, in 1190.[8] He then had only to wait for a propitious occasion. This was offered him the same year by a new attack of the Cham king Jaya Indravarman ong Vatuv.[9]

Did he himself take part in the battle against Champa? We are not certain, although an inscription of the temple of Po Nagar at Nha-trang says that he "took the capital of Champa and carried off all the lingas." [10] In any case, he entrusted the command of his troops to the young Cham prince Vidyānandana. This prince seized the capital Vijaya (Binh-đinh) and King Jaya Indravarman, whom he brought back as a prisoner to Cambodia. In Jaya Indravarman's place he put Prince In, the brother-in-law of King Jayavarman VII, who took the reign name Sūryajayavarmadeva. Vidyānandana carved out a kingdom for himself to the south, at Pāṇḍuranga, under the name of Sūryavarmadeva. Thus Champa was divided between two kings, one of whom was related to the king of Cambodia and the other enfeoffed to him. This state of affairs did not last long. A revolt at Vijaya drove the brother-in-law of Jayavarman VII back to Cambodia and put in his place the Cham prince Rashupati (Jaya Indravarman V). Vidyānandana, i.e., Sūryavarmadeva, master at Phan-rang, took advantage of this revolt to throw off the yoke of the king of Cambodia and reunify the country in his own interest, killing successively the two Jaya Indravarmans, the one from Vijaya (i.e., Rashupati) and the other the former prisoner of Cambodia, whom Jayavarman VII had probably sent against Vidyānandana.

By 1192, Vidyānandana-Sūryavarmadeva was reigning "without opposition" over the unified country.[11] In 1193 and 1194, Jayavarman VII tried unsuccessfully to bring him back to obedience.[12] It was not until 1203 that the Cham king's paternal uncle, the Yuvarāja ong Dhanapatigrāma, in the pay of Cambodia, succeeded in expelling him.[13] Vidyānandana-Sūryavarmadeva requested asylum from the emperor of Đai Viêt; he was turned down, even though the emperor had granted him investiture in 1199, and he disappeared without a trace. From 1203 to 1220, Champa was a Khmer province, under the government of the Yuvarāja ong Dhanapatigrāma, who was soon joined by a grandson of King Jaya Harivarman I, Prince Angśarāja of Turai-vijaya, who had been raised at the court of Jayavarman VII and promoted by him in 1201 to the rank of Yuvarāja.[14] This prince led the Cambodian troops, with Burmese and Siamese contingents, against Đai Viêt in 1207.[15] We shall see that in 1226 he became king of Champa under the name Jaya Parameśvaravarman II. During this reign Khmer art continued to have some influence on Cham art at Binh-đinh.[16]

Jayavarman VII's quarrels with his neighbors to the east did not prevent him from extending the limits of his empire in the north and west. The northernmost of the Cambodian inscriptions, that of Sai Fọng, on the Mekong across from Wiangčhan, dated 1186, dates from his reign.

The list of the dependencies of Chenla given by Chao Ju-kua in 1225,[17] but borrowed in part from the *Ling-wai Tai-ta* of 1178, shows that Cambodia then exercised at least nominal suzerainty over a part of the Malay Peninsula and even into Burma. Expressing the same general idea, an inscription of Jayavarman dated 1191 [18] tells us that his daily wash-water was furnished by "the Brahmans beginning with Sūryabhaṭṭa, by the king of Java, by the king of the Yavanas, and by the two kings of the Chams." The Brahman Sūryabhaṭṭa was probably the chief court Brahman. The king of the Yavanas was the emperor of Đai Viêt who came to the throne in 1175 under the name of Ly Cao-tông and reigned until 1210. The king of Java was undoubtedly Kāmeśvara. The two kings of Champa were, as we have just seen, Sūryajayavarmadeva, king at Vijaya (Binh-đinh), brother-in-law of Jayavarman VII, and Sūryavarmadeva, king at Pāṇḍuranga (Phan-rang), the former Prince Vidyānandana, protégé of Jayavarman VII. We know that the tribute of water was a sign of allegiance. It is possible that the two kings of Champa actually paid such tribute, but it is infinitely less likely that the two others did.

At the death of Jayarājadevī, the king conferred the title of first queen on her elder sister Indradevī, who "surpassed in her knowledge the knowledge of philosophers" and whom he had named principal teacher at a Buddhist monastery, where she instructed the women. It was she who composed in impeccable Sanskrit the inscription of the Phimeanakas,[19] a panegyric of her sister, from which we draw most of our biographical information concerning the career of Jayavarman VII.

We do not know the exact date of Jayavarman VII's death,[20] but he probably reigned until around 1218.[21] He received the posthumous name Mahāparamasaugata.[22]

In physical appearance, he was a rather corpulent man with heavy features who wore his hair pulled back on top of his head in a small chignon. All these details, which appear clearly on the bas-reliefs,[23] are found on four statues which obviously represent the same person and are almost certainly portraits of Jayavarman VII.[24]

From the exceptionally rich biographical data on Jayavarman VII emerges the image of an energetic, ambitious man who, after long years of waiting and trial, saved his country from ruin and raised it to the height of its power. The inscriptions represent him as a fervent Buddhist who received this faith from his father Dharaṇīndravarman II, who had broken with the tradition of his Hindu predecessors and "found his satisfaction in this nectar that is the religion of Śākyamuni." [25] Theirs was the Buddhism of the Greater Vehicle. Devotion to Lokeśvara was central in their Mahayanist faith; it was in the form of this compassionate Bodhisattva that individuals, dead or even living, were apotheosized.

Although we can scarcely doubt that Jayavarman VII was personally a Buddhist, we nevertheless observe that Brahmans continued to play a more than negligible role at court. An inscription of Angkor Thom [26] tells us about the curious figure of a Brahman scholar who "having learned that Cambodia was full of eminent experts on the Veda, came here to manifest his knowledge." His name was Hṛishīkeśa; he belonged to the Brahmanic clan of the Bhāradvāja and came from Narapatideśa, "which can be identified with some probability with Burma, where King Narapatisithu was reigning at precisely this time." [27] Jayavarman VII made him his chief priest *(purohita)* and conferred on him the title of Jayamahāpradhāna. He continued to serve under the two successors of Jayavarman VII.

The personality of Jayavarman VII, which the inscriptions provide only glimpses of, finds full expression in the architectural work he conceived. This work consists of Angkor Thom with its walls, its moats, its five gateways, and the Bayon in the center; it consists, in the environs of the capital, of Banteay Kdei, Ta Prohm, Preah Khan, Neak Peân, and a whole group of sanctuaries of lesser importance; it consists of Banteay Ch'mar in the northwest, Vat Nokor at Kompong Cham, Ta Prohm at Bati, almost all characterized by towers decorated with large human faces; [28] it consists of the rest houses placed along the long raised highways, many of which may have been laid out by him; and it consists of 102 hospitals widely distributed throughout the kingdom.

In view of the extensiveness of this work, we may ask ourselves whether in certain cases he might not have finished monuments begun by his predecessors and taken full credit for them himself or whether, on the other hand, the edifices begun by him might not have been finished by his successor. One flaw in the first hypothesis is the fact that from the end of the reign of

Sūryavarman II, the creator of Angkor Wat, to the beginning of the reign of Jayavarman VII the country was prey to a series of revolutions, a situation scarcely favorable to the construction of large architectural groups.[29] The second hypothesis would have greater validity if there had not been, as I believe there was,[30] a temporary restoration of Sivaite orthodoxy, which encouraged acts of vandalism from which the monuments of Jayavarman VII suffered, preceding the reign of his second successor, Jayavarman VIII, in the second half of the thirteenth century.

The earliest of these monuments is perhaps Banteay Kdei, which was constructed east of the capital on the ancient site of Kuṭi [31] and directly to the east of which is the magnificent basin, still full of water in all seasons, that is called the Sras Srang, or "Royal Bath." Lacking the stele which would undoubtedly have told us the ancient name, we can suppose that Banteay Kdei corresponded to the Pūrvatathāgata, or "Buddha of the East," of the inscriptions.[32]

Rājavihāra, today Ta Prohm, so close to Banteay Kdei that its southeast corner almost touches the northwest corner of Banteay Kdei, was constructed in 1186 to shelter an image of the queen mother Jayarājachūḍāmaṇi in the form of Prajñāpāramitā (the "Perfection of Insight," mystic mother of the Buddhas) and an image of Jayamangalārtha, guru of the king.[33]

Five years after Ta Prohm, in 1191, the king dedicated north of the capital the temple of Jayaśrī, which today bears the name Preah Khan and which was designed to shelter the statue of his father, King Dharaṇīndravarman II, deified in the form of the Bodhisattva Lokeśvara under the name Jayavarmeśvara.[34]

Among the lesser structures of Preah Khan the foundation stele of the temple mentions the little temple of Rājyaśrī, built in the middle of the great artificial lake dug to the east of the monument. This temple, now known under the name Neak Peân, is described as "an eminent island, deriving its charm from its lake and cleansing the impurity of sin from those who come to it." It is the architectural representation of Lake Anavatāpta, which, according to Indian tradition, is located in the confines of the Himalayas, and its waters gush out of gargoyles in the form of the heads of animals.[35]

From around 1190 on, important alterations, particularly the construction of towers with human faces and of new encircling galleries, were made in earlier monuments. It was also at the end of the reign that work was begun on Banteay Ch'mar and on the Bayon, or central temple of Angkor Thom, which was situated in the geometric center of the restored city. It is important to note that both the Bayon and the twelve-kilometer wall around the city were new. Although the architectural symbolism of the Bayon is obscured by the fact that its plan underwent two, or perhaps three, modifications in the course of its execution,[36] we can state that its central solid mass corresponds to the central mountain of the ancient capitals. Instead of the Devarāja of the preceding reigns represented by a gold linga, however, the central sanctuary sheltered an enormous stone statue[37] of the Buddharāja. This statue was not only a Buddhist substitute for the Sivaite Devarāja but also a statue of apotheosis of the founder king, whose features are undoubtedly also to be seen on the upper parts of the towers in the form of the Bodhisattva Lokeśvara Samantamukha, "who has faces in all directions."[38] The interior and exterior galleries of the Bayon are covered with bas-reliefs which are invaluable for understanding the material life of the Khmers in the twelfth century.[39]

The inscriptions engraved at the entrance of the chapels of the Bayon[40] reveal further that it was a sort of pantheon where the family cults of the king and the provincial cults of the country were centered. Just as the city with its wall and central mountain represents the universe in miniature, the Bayon represents the kingdom in miniature.

Four axial avenues extend in the four directions from the Bayon; these avenues are augmented by a fifth that begins at the entrance of the old Royal Palace, an inheritance from the preceding reigns, and proceeds to the east. These avenues lead to five monumental gates, each of which reproduces the basic motif of the central temple, that is, the tower with human faces looking toward the four cardinal points. Outside the gates the city is approached by causeways flanked by balustrades in the form of *nāgas*. These balustrades symbolize the rainbow, which in Indian tradition is the connecting link between the world of men and the world of the gods, represented on earth by the royal city.

Among the numerous religious monuments of the king enumerated in the stele of Preah Khan[42] are twenty-three statues named Jayabuddhamahānātha that have been preserved in many cities, among which are Lopburi, Suphan, Ratburi, Phetchaburi, and Mưang Sing, all of which are in Thailand today. The name given to these statues recalls that of the king. Perhaps it was in order to shelter these statues that some of the provincial sanctuaries, whose style permits us to attribute them to the reign of Jayavarman VII, were built: for example, Vat Nokor of Kompong Cham and Ta Prohm of Bati.[43] As for Banteay Ch'mar,[44] it was a temple consecrated to the memory of one of the sons of Jayavarman VII, Prince Śrīndrakumāra, and four companions in arms who saved the life of the prince, notably at the time of his combat against the monster Rāhu[45] and in the course of a military expedition in Champa.

The stele of Preah Khan[46] mentions 121 "houses with fire," or rest houses, about fifteen kilometers apart, built by Jayavarman VII along the routes cutting across the kingdom: fifty-seven are on the route from Angkor to the capital of Champa (Phan-rang or Vijaya in Binh-đinh), seventeen (of which eight have been found) on the route from Angkor to Phimai on the Khorat Plateau, forty-four on a circuit marked by cities the locations of which are still uncertain, one at Phnom Chisor, and two others that are still unidentified. A century later, this system still existed and caught the attention of the Chinese envoy Chou Ta-kuan, who wrote in the account of his voyage: "On the major roads there are rest houses comparable to our post houses."[47]

The creation of rest houses was coupled with the construction of 102 hospitals,[48] distributed throughout the entire country. We are sure of the sites of about fifteen of them, thanks to the discovery *in situ* of their foundation steles, the Sanskrit texts of which are almost uniformly identical.[49] If we add seventeen other monuments that are similar in architectural arrangement to the remains in which the steles were found and that seem to date from the same period, we can say that we know the locations of more than thirty of the 102 hospitals of Jayavarman VII, or close to a third.[50]

The foundation steles give us interesting information on the organization[51] of these establishments, which were placed under the protection of the healer Buddha, Bhaishajyaguru Vaidūryaprabhā, "the master of remedies who has the brilliance of beryl," who is still one of the most popular Buddhas today in China and Tibet.[52]

Such, in short, was the work of Jayavarman VII, a very heavy program for a people who were already exhausted by the wars and the constructions of Sūryavarman II and who henceforth would find themselves helpless against the attacks of their neighbors.

2. BURMA: NARAPATISITHU (1173–1210) AND THE INTRODUCTION OF SINGHALESE BUDDHISM

The Glass Palace Chronicle claims that Narapatisithu (Narapatijayasūra, or Jayasūra II), who became king at Pagan in 1173 after the murder of his older brother Naratheinkha (Narasingha), began his reign by ridding himself of the perpetrator of the crime that he himself had ordered as the principal counselor of the late king.[53] But epigraphy says nothing about these events, although this does not mean that they are necessarily entirely imaginary.

At the beginning of his reign, Narapatisithu had a disagreement with the representative of King Parākramabāhu I of Ceylon, a representative who was established in one of the ports of the delta, probably Bassein. The vexation of the king mounted to such a point that he imprisoned Singhalese envoys and tradesmen and seized their merchandise and finally captured a princess of Ceylon who was crossing Burma on her way to Cambodia. The result was a retaliatory raid launched by Parākramabāhu in 1180. Surprised by a storm, the Singhalese boats were scattered. One of them landed at Kākadīpa ("island of the crows"), five others at Kusumi (Bassein); the one carrying the leader of the expedition reached Papphāla. The Singhalese disembarked pillaging, burning, massacring, and taking prisoners.[54]

This raid did not keep the relations between Ceylon and Burma from drawing closer on the spiritual plane. Panthagu, successor of Shin Arahan as the head of the Buddhist clergy, had left Pagan in 1167 after the first crimes of King Narathu and had gone to Ceylon;[55] he returned to Burma shortly after the accession of Narapatisithu. He died in Pagan at the age of ninety, shortly after 1173, apparently not without having praised the excellence of Singhalese Buddhism, which was then being reinvigorated by King Parākramabāhu I (around 1153–86), who recognized the orthodoxy of the sect of Mahāvihāra.[56] The successor of Panthagu, a Mon named Uttarajīva, embarked for Ceylon in 1180[57] with a group of monks, bearers of a message of peace addressed to the sovereign of the island.[58] He left there a young Mon novice, twenty years old, named Chapaṭa, who remained in Ceylon for ten years and returned in 1190 with four other monks who, like him, had received ordination according to the rites of the Mahāvihāra; one of them, Tāmalinda, was a son of the king of Cambodia,[59] undoubtedly Jayavarman VII.

Their return brought about a schism in the Burmese church, which, we remember, had been founded by Shin Arahan, a disciple of the Kānchī school,[60] and marked the beginning of the permanent establishment of Singhalese Buddhism on the Indochinese Peninsula.[61] Chapaṭa, also known as Saddhammajotipāla, was the author of a series of works in Pali, notably the grammatical treatise *Suttaniddesa* and the *Sankhepavaṇṇanā*, a commentary on the compendium of metaphysics named *Abhidhammatthasangaha*.[62]

Another Mon monk of the same sect, Dhammavilāsa, who as a monk was known as Sāriputta, was the author of the first collection of laws composed in the Mon country, the *Dhammavilasa Dhammathat*, written in Pali and known through a Burmese translation of the eighteenth century.[63]

In 1197, Narapatisithu received new relics from Ceylon.[64]

Narapatisithu, whose authority extended to Mergui and to the Shan states, seems to have had quite a peaceful and prosperous reign which permitted him to develop his irrigation works.[65] He enriched his capital with several monuments, of which the two main ones were: Sulamani [66] (1183), which marks the final decline of Mon influence; and Gôdôpalin (before 1230).

Before dying in 1210, he chose as heir apparent his young son Zeyatheinkha (Jayasiṃha), whose mother was a concubine,[67] and succeeded in getting him recognized by his elder brothers of higher rank.[68]

3. INDONESIA AT THE END OF THE TWELFTH CENTURY: THE WEAKENING OF ŚRĪVIJAYA (PALEMBANG) TO THE BENEFIT OF MALĀYU (JAMBI)

We have already mentioned the embassy to China from San-fo-ch'i in 1178, the last registered in the *History of the Sung*. This same year saw the publication of the *Ling-wai Tai-ta* of Chou Ch'ü-fei, the information in which was reproduced for the most part in 1225 in the *Chu-fan-chih* of Chao Ju-kua.[69] In reading

Chao Ju-kua, we get the impression that the Sumatran kingdom was beginning to break apart by the end of the twelfth century: Chan-pei (Jambi), the former Malāyu, is not listed among the dependencies of San-fo-ch'i, and the *Ling-wai Tai-ta* says that as early as 1079, and then in 1082 and 1088, this state had sent embassies to China on its own initiative.[70] Tan-ma-ling, Ling-ya-ssu-chia, Fo-lo-an, Sin-t'o, Chien-t'o, Chien-pi (Kampe), and Lan-wu-li (Achin), although listed among the dependencies of San-fo-ch'i, were the subject of separate notices,[71] and concerning Chien-pi the text explicitly states that "formerly it was a dependency of San-fo-ts'i, but, after a fight, it set up a king of its own." [72]

If it is premature to speak of the decline of Śrīvijaya as early as 1178,[73] it is nevertheless necessary to take into account new factors in the large island, especially concerning Malāyu (Jambi), which perhaps as early as this period became the center of gravity of the empire of the maharaja at the expense of Palembang.[74] In 1183, a king named Trailokyarāja Maulibhūshaṇavarmadeva cast a bronze Buddha called the "Buddha of Grahi" at Chaiya on the Bay of Bandọn.[75] the name of this king recalls in striking fashion the title system in use in Malāyu,[76] and we wonder if the king responsible for this statue on the Malay Peninsula was not a king of Malāyu.

Whether it had its center at Palembang or at Jambi, the Sumatran kingdom known to the Chinese under the name of San-fo-ch'i was still a great power, "an important thoroughfare," says Chou Ch'ü-fei, "on the sea-routes of the Foreigners on their way to and from (China)," [77] and continued to draw its power from the simultaneous possession of the two shores of the straits.

In Java, during the last two decades of the twelfth century, we know the names of two kings of Kaḍiri: Kāmeśvara and Śṛinga.

For Kāmeśvara we have inscriptions of 1182 and 1185.[78] During his reign Tanakung composed the metric treatise named *Vṛittasanchaya.*[79] It was also during his reign that Dharmaja wrote the *Smaradahana,* a poem tracing the history of Love reduced to cinders by Siva [80] but also a poem written for the times, as its name alone clearly shows.[81] Kāmeśvara's wife was a princess of Janggala, and it was perhaps this royal couple who served as the historical basis for the tales of the Raden Panji cycle,[82] which became very popular and, under the name *Inao* (Javanese *Hino*), spread to Thailand [83] and to Cambodia [84] and became very popular there also.

For Śṛinga, who will be discussed later under his name Kṛitajaya, we have inscriptions dated from 1194 to 1205.[85]

The commercial prosperity of Java in this period is apparent from a remark by Chou Ch'ü-fei in his *Ling-wai Tai-ta* (1178): "Of all the wealthy foreign lands which have great store of precious and varied goods, none surpass the realm of the Arabs (Ta-shï). Next to them comes Java (Shö-p'o); the third is Palembang (San-fo-ts'i). . . ." [86]

In Bali, the inscriptions between 1178 and 1181 are in the name of Jayapangus; [87] those of 1204, in the name of Adikuntiketana and his son Parameśvara.[88] The funerary site and the stone cloister of Tampak Siring, one of the archaeological curiosities of the island,[89] date from this period.

4. CAMBODIA IN THE FIRST HALF OF THE THIRTEENTH CENTURY

The circumstances in which the critical succession to the throne vacated by Jayavarman VII took place are very obscure. He had many sons, of whom we know at least four: Sūryakumāra, author of the inscription of Ta Prohm; [90] Vīrakumāra, author of the inscription of Preah Khan [91] and son of the queen Rājendradevī; ———indravarman, governor of Lavo [92] and son of the queen Jayarājadevī; and finally Śrīndrakumāra, whose statue, surrounded by those of four companions in arms, was placed in the central chapel of Banteay Ch'mar.[93] Was it Śrīndrakumāra who succeeded his father under the name of Indravarman (II)? The similarity of the names proves little. Moreover, if, as it appears from the inscription of Banteay Ch'mar,[94] Śrīndrakumāra was old enough to aid King Yaśovarman II against Rāhu before 1165, it is difficult to believe that he was still living in 1243, the date of the death of Indravarman II.[95] The lack of epigraphy for the whole beginning of the thirteenth century condemns us to ignorance.

We are informed by Chinese and Vietnamese sources that in 1216 and in 1218 "for the last time, Cambodian armies descended on Nghê-an; they came through Champa and with a contingent of troops of that country; the allies were nevertheless defeated again and had to withdraw." [96] In 1220, the Cambodians evacuated Champa,[97] restoring the throne of Vijaya to the Cham prince Angśarāja of Turai-vijaya. Angśarāja was the eldest son of Jaya Harivarman II, who, as we have seen, had been raised at the court of Jayavarman VII and had been returned to his country at the beginning of the Khmer occupation.[98] This retreat of Cambodia, contemporaneous with the emancipation of the Thai principalities, was perhaps a consequence of the death of Jayavarman VII.[99]

In his *Chu-fan-chih,* published in 1225, Chao Ju-kua refers to the wars between Cambodia and Champa in the last quarter of the twelfth century and to the annexation of the second by the first.[100] According to Chao Ju-kua, Cambodia touched, on the south, Chia-lo-hsi (Grahi), a vassal of San-fo-ch'i situated, as we have seen, on the Malay Peninsula at the latitude of the Bay of Bandọn.[101] Its dependencies were:

Teng-liu-mei (on the Malay Peninsula),[102]
Po-ssu-lan (on the coast of the Gulf of Siam),
Lo-hu (Lavo, Lopburi),
San-lo (the country of Syāṃ on the upper Menam?),[103]
Chen-li-fu (on the coast of the Gulf of Siam),[104]
Ma-lo-wen (perhaps Malyang, in the south of Battambang),
Lu-yang (?),
T'un-li-fu (?),
P'u-kan (Pagan),
Wa-li (in upper Burma),
Si-p'eng (?),
Tu-huai-sün (?).

This list shows that, on the eve of the Thai expansion, Cambodia was still master of the Menam Basin and of a part of the Malay Peninsula. Its claims over Burma were perhaps based on the fact that Burmese contingents accompanied Cambodian armies in their expedition of 1207 against Đai Viêt.[105]

We know only one date for King Indravarman II, that of his death, 1243.[106]

5. CHAMPA AFTER THE END OF THE KHMER OCCUPATION (1220–57)

That it was impossible for the successor of Jayavarman VII to maintain the unity of the Cambodian empire became clear in Champa as early as 1220. In this year, says an inscription, "the Khmers went to the sacred country and the people of Champa came to Vijaya."[107] This evacuation, voluntary or imposed, was followed six years later by the coronation, under the name of Jaya Parameśvaravarman (II),[108] of Prince Angśarāja of Turai-vijaya, who, we recall, was a grandson of Jaya Harivarman I and had been brought up at the court of Jayavarman VII.[109] "Thus ends," says Georges Maspero,[110] "this Hundred Years' War between the Chams and the Khmers. The latter, henceforth engrossed with a new enemy, Siam, no longer will dream of the conquest of Champa. They will limit themselves, for centuries, merely to following the events that will occur in this kingdom. Adventurers greedy for booty and glory will go to the head of irregular bands, putting their forces at the service of various pretenders and playing a large part in all the civil wars." A great part of the reign of Jaya Parameśvaravarman II was taken up with the restoration of irrigation works and the rebuilding of ruins that had accumulated in the country during the wars. "He reestablished all the lingas of the south save those of Yang Pu Nagara [Po Nagar of Nha-trang] and the lingas of the north save those of Śrīśānabhadreśvara [Mi-sơn]."[111]

Toward the end of his reign, he came into conflict with Đai Viêt, where a new dynasty, the Trân, had been reigning since 1225. The emperor Trân Thai-tông sent to the Cham king protests against the incessant piracy to which the Chams subjected the coasts of Đai Viêt; Jaya Parameśvaravarman responded by demanding the retrocession of the three provinces of the north, a constant source of trouble between the two countries. In 1252, the emperor of Đai Viêt himself led a punitive expedition that brought back many prisoners, among whom were dignitaries and women of the palace.[112]

This conflict may have resulted in the death of the king, for shortly afterward we find on the throne his younger brother, Prince Harideva of Sakañ-vijaya, who as Yuvarāja had in 1249 conducted an expedition against Pāṇḍuranga.[113] This new king, who "knew all the sciences and was versed in the philosophy of the various schools,"[114] took Jaya Indravarman (VI) as his reign name. He reigned for only a short time; in 1257 he was assassinated by his nephew Harideva.[115]

6. BURMA: THE LAST KINGS OF PAGAN (1210–74)

The Glass Palace Chronicle says that, before dying in 1210, Narapatisithu chose as his heir his young son Zeyatheinkha (Jayasiṃha), also known as Nadaungmya, whose mother was a concubine; that his other brothers of higher birth accepted him because "the royal parasol miraculously inclined itself" toward him (hence the name T'i-lo-min-lo by which he is known); and that the new king had the wisdom to relinquish power to his brothers.[116] It seems that in reality things happened differently: Zeyatheinkha resigned only part of his power to his ministers after his accession to the throne in 1211.[117] His reign, which came to an end no later than 1231, was marked by the construction of the last two great monuments of the capital, the Mahabodhi,[118] a replica of the famous temple of Bodhgaya in India, and the T'i-lo-min-lo,[119] built on the spot where "the parasol inclined itself."

If we believe the *Chronicle,* T'i-lo-min-lo was succeeded by his son Kyôzwa, a prince of great piety who abandoned effective power to his son Uzana so that he could spend his days with the Buddhist monks.[120] But, according to epigraphy, Nadaungmya was succeeded first by his eldest son Narasiṃha Uzana,[121] then in 1235 by his younger son Kyôzwa (I).[122] Kyôzwa strengthened internal security and restored finances. His reign was marked by some literary activity, especially grammatical.[123] He died in 1250. Uzana, who was both his nephew and his son-in-law, succeeded him; he reigned only four years and died in a hunting accident.[124]

At Uzana's death in 1256, the legitimate heir, Thingathu (Singhasūra), was supplanted by Narathihapate (Narasīhapati),[125] the sixteen-year-old son of a concubine. He is known by the name Tarukphyi, "he who fled before the Taruks [Mongols]." The *Chronicle* says that the minister Yazathinkyan (Rājasankrama), to whom he owed his elevation, was quickly brushed aside, as one removes the scaffolding once the pagoda is built,[126] but was soon recalled to repress the troubles at Martaban and in Arakan.[127] We have no epigraphic proof of these assertions.

In 1274 the king undertook the construction of the temple of Mingalazedi (Mangalachetiya) as a site for statues of the princes and princesses of the dynasty. Soothsayers predicted that the temple's completion would mark the end of the kingdom.[128] Pagan did in fact soon fall into the hands of the Mongols.

7. ŚRĪVIJAYA ON THE EVE OF ITS DISMEMBERMENT (1225–70)

Despite the portents of its approaching breakup, San-fo-ch'i was still a great power at the beginning of the thirteenth century. Chao Ju-kua attributes to it no less than fifteen vassal states:[129]

P'eng-feng (Pahang),
Teng-ya-nung (Trengganu),
Ling-ya-ssu-chia (Langkasuka),
Chi-lan-tan (Kelantan),
Fo-lo-an (Kuala Berang),[130]
Jih-lo-t'ing (on the eastern coast of the peninsula?),[131]
Ch'ien-mai-pa-t'a (?),[132]
Tan-ma-ling (Tāmbralinga, in the region of Ligor),
Chia-lo-hsi (Grahi, on the Bay of Bandọn),[133]
Pa-lin-feng (Palembang),
Sin-t'o (Sunda, western Java),[134]
Chien-pi (Kampe, on the east coast of Sumatra),
Lan-wu-li (Lāmurī, northern extremity of Sumatra),
Si-lan (Ceylon?).

This list covers all of the Malay Peninsula south of the Bay of Bandọn and all of western Indonesia; the maharaja always drew his strength from the simultaneous possession of the two shores of the strait: Śrīvijaya-Kaṭāha, or Sribuza-Kalah.

This thalassocracy, however, seems to have degenerated into an outright piratical enterprise. "This country," writes Chao Ju-kua,[135] "lying in the ocean and controlling the straits through which foreigners' sea and land traffic, in either direction must pass. . . . If a merchant ship passes by without entering, their boats go forth to make a combined attack, and all are ready to die (in the attempt). This is the reason why this country is a great shipping centre."

We have seen in the preceding chapter that, by the end of the eleventh century, Kampe and Malāyu, on the eastern coast of Sumatra, had broken away from Śrīvijaya. Chao Ju-kua no longer includes Jambi or Malāyu in his list, but he includes Palembang, which, consequently, could no longer have been the capital of the empire.[136] The weakening of the empire's authority is undeniably established in 1230 on the Malay Peninsula. At this date, Dharmarāja Chandrabhānu, King of Tāmbralinga (Ligor), belonging to the "family of the lotus" (*padmavaṃśa*), had an inscription engraved[137] at Chaiya, on the former site of Grahi, which had undoubtedly recently been annexed. This inscription shows every sign of emanating from an independent sovereign.[138] Chandrabhānu is named in the Singhalese *Mahāvaṃsa* with the epithet of the king of the Jāvakas, and it must also have been he who appeared in the epigraphy of the Pāṇḍyas of southernmost India[139] with a title of

Śāvakan. Comparative study of these texts [140] and of the Pali chronicle *Jinakālamālī* [141] permits us to state that in 1247 Chandrabhānu, perhaps with the peaceful intention of obtaining a relic or an image of the Buddha, sent a mission to Ceylon that ended in an armed conflict and the probable establishment of a colony of Jāvakas on the island. Around 1263, Jaṭāvarman Vīra Pāṇḍya was called to Ceylon to put down disturbances that resulted from the establishment of the suzerainty of the Pāṇḍyas on the island in 1258 by his brother Jaṭāvarman Sundara Pāṇḍya. He had to fight against two Singhalese princes and a Jāvaka prince, perhaps a son of Chandrabhānu, who was established at Ceylon and whose submission he obtained. Around 1270 Chandrabhānu sent a second expedition, this time to demand the tooth relic and the bowl of the Buddha; he suffered a new and serious defeat.[142]

The weakening of Tāmbralinga, the most important of the dependencies of Śrīvijaya on the peninsula, which maintained only very loose ties with the Sumatran mother country, was to facilitate the task of the Thai conqueror some twenty years later. Chandrabhānu, moreover, seems to have maintained friendly relations with the Thai,[143] perhaps already indicating a sort of recognition of the suzerainty of Sukhothai.[144] But the first blow was dealt Śrīvijaya by Java, whose history during the first three quarters of the thirteenth century must now be traced.

8. JAVA: THE END OF THE KINGDOM OF KAḌIRI (1222) AND THE BEGINNING OF THE KINGDOM OF SINGHASĀRI (UP TO 1268) [145]

At the beginning of the thirteenth century, the throne of Kaḍiri was occupied by Kṛitajaya (also known as Śṛinga).[146] Near the end of his reign (in 1222), an adventurer named Angrok, who had taken over the government of Tumapel northeast of Malang, brought the former Janggala under his power. He then took advantage of the first occasion that presented itself to revolt against his master, the king of Kaḍiri. The founding of a new dynasty at Tumapel in Janggala has been regarded as marking the reunion of the two kingdoms of Janggala and Panjalu (Kaḍiri), which constituted the two halves of the kingdom of Airlanga. Actually, Janggala, we recall, had from the start been absorbed by Kaḍiri [147] and the merger had in fact taken place long before. But, since Janggala contained the old capital, the usurper, in proclaiming himself sovereign in the more important of the two halves of the kingdom of Airlanga, gave the impression of restoring the traditions of the former Javanese state.

The account of Java in the *Chu-fan-chih* of 1225 reflects the troubled situation in the second decade of the thirteenth century, and the contradictions of Chao Ju-kua are manifestly caused by the rapidity with which events moved, culminating in the final fall of Kaḍiri in 1222.

In his fourteenth chapter,[148] Chao Ju-kua uses the old name She-p'o, which he says is also called P'u-chia-long (Pekalongan), in giving information drawn for the most part from the *Ling-wai Tai-ta* of 1178. He concludes by saying that to prevent the smuggling of copper money outside of China, "Our Court has repeatedly forbidden all trade (with this country), but the foreign traders, for the purpose of deceiving (the government), changed its name and referred to it as Su-chi-tan." And it is under the name Su-chi-tan that Chao Ju-kua describes the Javanese kingdom of his times in his fifteenth chapter.

Su-chi-tan has been identified with several places, the most probable of which seems to be Sukadana, in the immediate vicinity of Surabaya.[149] The territory it covered is very difficult to determine, for the information given by Chao Ju-kua is contradictory. The reason for this is that the information is for various dates and the most recent seems to come after the fall of Kaḍiri. Thus, at the beginning of his chapter, Chao Ju-kua says that Su-chi-tan touches Sin-t'o (Sunda) in the west and Ta-pan (Tuban or Tumapel) in the east, thus giving it an area corresponding roughly to the territory of Kaḍiri without Janggala; this description assumes that Janggala is independent. But in the list of the dependencies of Su-chi-tan,[150] Chao Ju-kua includes Ta-pan and Jong-ya-lu (Janggala or Ujung Galuh, a port in the Brantas Delta), a statement that expresses a former state of affairs. Finally, at the end of his chapter on San-fo-ch'i,[151] Chao Ju-kua writes that this country (which includes Sin-t'o, or Sunda, among its dependencies) touches Jong-ya-lu on the east, which can only mean that Janggala not only became independent but even absorbed Kaḍiri.

Aside from Ta-pan and Jong-ya-lu, Chao Ju-kua mentions among the dependencies of Su-chi-tan: [152]

On the island of Java:
- Po-hua-yuan (?),
- Ma-teng (Medang),

Hsi-ning (?),
Teng-che (the eastern cape).

On the neighboring islands:

Ta-kang (?),
Huang-ma-chu (?),
Ma-li (Bali?),
Niu-lun (?),
Tan-jung-wu-lo (Tanjong Pura, southwest Borneo),
Ti-wu (Timor),
P'ing-ya-i (Bangai, east of Celebes),
Wu-nu-ku (the Moluccas).[153]

With Angrok, the founder of the kingdom of Tumapel, Javanese historiography assumes a new character that it is to retain until the end of the Indian period. It is in fact based to a great extent on two chronicles in Javanese, the *Nāgarakṛitāgama* of Prapancha (1365) [154] and the *Pararaton* (dating from the end of the fifteenth century).[155] These two Javanese chronicles, like the Burmese chronicles, give detailed biographies of the kings and persons of their entourage, details on their private lives, and accounts of the scandals and dramas of the court that epigraphy ignores.

Angrok was the son of peasants, but he had himself represented as a son of Śiva Girīndra ("Siva king of the mountain"),[156] an epithet that recalls, perhaps intentionally, the old title of the Śailendras. After spending his youth as a highway robber, he entered the service of Tungul Ametung, governor of Tumapel, whom he assassinated and whose wife Ḍeḍes he married.[157] He strengthened his position east of Mount Kawi and then took advantage of a conflict between King Kṛitajaya and the clergy, in which the clergy sided with him, to proclaim himself king under the name of Rājasa.[158]

In 1221 he marched on Kaḍiri and waged a decisive battle at Ganter,[159] the site of which is unidentified. Kṛitajaya fled and disappeared without a trace. Kaḍiri consequently became an integral part of the kingdom of Tumapel, which subsequently became better known by the name of its capital, Singhasāri, at first called Kuṭarāja.

After a reign of six years that seems to have been peaceful, Rājasa was assassinated in 1227 at the instigation of Anūshapati, son of Queen Ḍeḍes and the former governor of Tumapel. Anūshapati thus avenged the death of his father.[160]

Anūshapati, also known as Anūshanātha, then succeeded Rājasa and reigned until 1248. In that year, in the course of a cockfight, he in turn was assassinated by Tohjaya, son of Rājasa and a concubine.[161] His funerary temple is Chandi Kidal,[162] southeast of Malang, a monument still completely permeated with the Indo-Javanese classical tradition.

Tohjaya reigned only a few months in 1248 and met his death in a palace revolt fomented by his two nephews, Ranga Wuni, the son of Anūshanātha, and Mahīsha Champaka, the grandson of Rājasa.[163] These two princes reigned together, the first under the name Vishṇuvardhana and the second under that of Narasiṃhamūrti.[164] The main event of the reign of Vishṇuvardhana (1248–68) was the repression of the revolt of a certain Lingapati.[165] By 1254, Vishṇuvardhana had turned over effective power to his son Kṛitanagara, and it was at this time that the capital Kuṭarāja took the name of Singhasāri.[166] At his death, which took place in 1268, Vishṇuvardhana was deified in the form of Siva at Waleri (Meleri, near Blitar) and in the form of Amoghapāśa (one of the forms of the Bodhisattva Avalokiteśvara) at Jajaghu (Chandi Jago).[167] The famous temple of Chandi Jago, decorated with bas-reliefs illustrating episodes from various Indo-Javanese poems—the *Kunjarakarṇa,*[168] the *Pārthayajña,*[169] the *Arjunavivāha,*[170] and the *Kṛishṇāyana*[171]—is more Indonesian in style than preceding funerary monuments.[172] This decline of Indian culture, with the return to ancestral traditions of the autochthonous substratum, is a general phenomenon in Farther India in the thirteenth century.

To the internal causes of this decline that have been mentioned previously,[173] we can add two others here: the Muslim invasions in India, which, after having stimulated an exodus of intellectuals abroad,[174] dried up for a time the source on which the Indian colonies depended to reinvigorate themselves; and the Mongol conquests, which brought about the ruin of the old Indianized kingdoms, as we shall see in the following chapter.

CHAPTER XII

THE REPERCUSSIONS OF THE MONGOL CONQUESTS

Last Third of the Thirteenth Century

The thirteenth century found all of Eurasia under the banner of the Mongols. Farther India did not escape their thrust, for from the time of his accession as Great Khan in 1260, Kublai Khan, grandson of Genghis Khan and conqueror of China (where he founded the new dynasty of Yuan in 1280), sought to obtain oaths of vassalage from the foreign sovereigns who had been offering such oaths to the Chinese Sung dynasty. Although in this area the Sino-Mongol armies met with only defeat or short-lived success, their impact produced deep repercussions, the most important of which was the advent of Thai power in the Menam Basin and Burma[1] with all its consequences for Cambodia and for the principalities of the Mekong and the Malay Peninsula.

1. THE THAI

The Thai, established in Yunnan, where for a long time it was believed they had founded the kingdom of Nanchao in the eighth century (it seems that actually a Tibeto-Burman dialect, Lolo or Min-chia, was spoken there),[2] were to achieve their independence only much later in the valleys of the central Indochinese Peninsula and of Burma. One hears occasionally of the "invasion of the Thai," a consequence of the "Mongol pressure" of the thirteenth century. Actually the Thai "invasion" was instead a gradual infiltration along the rivers and streams that had undoubtedly been going on for a very long time, part of the general drift of population from the north to the south that characterizes the peopling of the Indochinese Peninsula.[3] But it is a fact that around 1220, perhaps following the death of Jayavarman VII, which can be placed shortly before that date, there was a great deal of change and unrest on the southern borders of Yunnan. According to traditional dates, given here with a great deal of reservation, the Thai principality of Mogaung, north of Bhamo, was founded in 1215; that of Moné or Mưang Nai, on a western tributary of the Salween, was founded in 1223; and Assam was conquered by the Thai in 1229.[4] At about the same time, the Thai chiefs of Chiangrung and Ngoen Yang (site of Chiangsaen) on the upper Mekong formed an alliance by means of a marriage between their children.[5] The legendary descent of Khun Bọrom and the mass arrival of the Thai, via Nam U, at the site of Luang Phrabang probably date back to this same period.[6] By the middle of the thirteenth century, the Thai had already "drowned" the Khmer, Mon, and Indianized Burmese communities of the valleys of the south. And when the Thai had acquired some cohesion, their chiefs seem, in the internal organization of their principalities as well as in their policy toward the old Indian civilizations of the valleys and deltas, to have been inspired by the example of the Mongols, whose epic feats captured their imagination. We shall see that the inscription of Rāma Khamhaeng, the great Siamese conqueror of the end of the thirteenth century, even sounds sometimes like an echo of the exploits of Genghis Khan. For their part, the Mongols, after their seizure of Ta-li on January 7, 1253 and their pacification of Yunnan in 1257, did not look with disfavor on the creation of a series of Thai principalities at the expense of the old Indianized kingdoms, for they believed that these principalities would be easier to maintain in submission to the Middle Kingdom. But this combination of political events seems to have resulted not so much from a sudden change in the population stock of the peninsula as from the seizure of power by a governing class of Thai origin. In Burma, the seizure of Pagan by the Mongols in 1287 resulted in the temporary disappearance of the Burmese kingdom and the division of the country into principalities governed by Thai chiefs. In the upper Menam Basin, a Thai chief from Chiangrai drove the Mon dynasty from Haripunjaya and founded a new capital, Chiangmai, a short distance from the old one. At Sukhothai (Sukhodaya) a proclamation of independence was followed by a rapid conquest that resulted in the substitution of the government of the Thai for the Khmer administration in the Menam Basin and on the upper Mekong.

The Thai first enter the history of Farther India in the eleventh century with the mention of Syāṃ slaves or prisoners of war in Cham epigraphy, where they were included along with Chinese, Vietnamese, Cambodians, and Burmese.[7] In the twelfth century, the bas-reliefs of Angkor Wat represent at the head of the great procession of the southern gallery a group of warriors who wear a costume entirely different from that of the Khmers and whom two short inscriptions identify as *Syāṃ*.[8] They were very probably Thai of the middle Menam, for it was to the kingdom of Sukhothai that the Chinese applied the name *Sien,* used for the first time by the *History of the Yuan* in connection with an embassy of 1282 sent by sea and intercepted by the Chams.[9]

These "savages," as the Syāṃ of Angkor Wat are sometimes called, were savages only in their dress. They must have had a social organization of which there are still some traces in the social organization of the Laotian principalities,[10] and of which the feudal regime of the Mường of upper Tongking and of Thanh-hoa undoubtedly gives an approximate idea.[11] Having lived for a long time in Yunnan in the orbit of Chinese civilization, they not only must have had a considerably advanced material culture but also must have had some contact with India and Buddhism by means of the route that joined India and China through Assam and Yunnan.[12] Such contact would explain the very clear evidence of the influence of the art of the Pālas and Senas of Bengal on the Buddhist art of the Thai in the northernmost part of the Menam Basin.[13] Moreover, the Thai have always been remarkable assimilators: they have never hesitated to appropriate for themselves whatever in the civilization of their neighbors and masters might place them in a position to fight victoriously against them.

The rapid success of the Thai in the Menam Basin was, as we shall see, the consequence of the weakening of Cambodia and also of the decline, then fall, of Burmese power under the blows of the Mongols. We are more and more disposed to believe that the Thai success was less the result of a mass migration than the consequence of the gradual engulfing of the sedentary populations (Mon-Khmer- or Tibeto-Burman-speaking peoples) by immigrants who arrived in ever greater numbers and finally imposed themselves as masters over the earlier inhabitants.

2. CAMBODIA: DEFEAT OF A MONGOL INCURSION IN 1282

In Cambodia, Indravarman II was succeeded, perhaps not immediately, by Jayavarman VIII, during whose reign the Mongols made their appearance in Cambodia, although in a rather benign fashion.

In 1268, when the emperor of Đai Viêt complained to Kublai Khan of the attacks by Cambodia and Champa, the Great Khan ordered him to defend himself with the aid of Burmese contingents.[14] But it was only about fifteen years later that Cambodian territory was invaded by a Mongol force dispatched by a General Sogatu, who, as we shall see, was to invade the north and center of Champa in 1283. He sent to Cambodia, probably by the route from Quang-tri to Savannakhet,[15] a chief of a hundred and a chief of a thousand named Sulaymān. They "were captured and never returned."[16] Nevertheless, Cambodia found it prudent to offer tribute to Kublai Khan in 1285.[17] We shall see that Jayavarman VIII was less fortunate with the Thai of the Menam.

3. CHAMPA: THE MONGOL INVASION (1283–85)

In Champa, Harideva,[18] who had "seized the throne," took the royal name Jaya Siṃhavarman, then changed it in 1266 at the time of his coronation to Indravarman (V).[19] Anxious to preserve good-neighbor relations with Đai Viêt, he sent no less than four embassies there from 1266 to 1270. But he soon had to face a Mongol invasion.[20]

In 1278, then again in 1280, Indravarman V was invited to present himself at the court of Peking. He succeeded in avoiding this invitation by sending embassies and presents. But in 1281 Sogatu and Liu Shen were ordered to establish a Mongol administration in Champa. The populace, stirred up by Prince Harijit, son of the king, did not readily accept this protectorateship.

Then Kublai organized an expedition that lasted more than two years (1283–85). The details, which lie outside the scope of this work, are fairly well known. The retreat of the old king into the mountains[21] and the refusal of the Vietnamese to let the Mongol army pass over their territory resulted in a long, drawn-out, difficult battle that was scarcely popular among the assailants. The invasion of Tongking by Toghọn, a son of Kublai, although it resulted in the seizure of the capital in 1285, turned out badly for the Mongols, who were finally defeated by Trân Nhân-tông in Thanh-hoa. Toghon was driven to the north, and Sogatu, who had come from the south to join him, after debarking in Champa was killed and decapitated.

"Thus Champa was rid of the Mongols, who lost many men and officers there without gaining any advantage to speak of. Indravarman V, desiring to prevent their return, sent an ambassador to Kublai, who was presented to him on October 6, 1285, at the same time as an envoy from Cambodia." [22]

Indravarman V, who, according to Marco Polo's account, was then "exceedingly old," [23] must have died shortly afterward.

4. BURMA: FROM 1271 TO THE SEIZURE OF PAGAN BY THE MONGOLS (1287)

The Mongols annexed Yunnan in 1253–57, and in 1271, perhaps at the instigation of Thai intriguers, the governor of this province sent a mission to Burma charged with demanding the tribute of vassalage in the name of Kublai Khan.[24] King Narathihapate (Narasīhapati) did not receive the members of the mission and sent them back with an official bearing a message of friendship for the Great Khan.

In 1273, an embassy from Kublai, which left Peking on March 3, arrived in Pagan with a letter demanding the dispatch of a delegation of princes and ministers to the court of Peking. It is generally believed that King Narathihapate had the ambassadors executed, but it is possible that they were assassinated in Yunnan on their way back to China. The matter was reported to Peking by the governor of Yunnan, but the emperor decided to allow this insult to go unavenged for a little while.

In 1277, the Burmese invaded the State of the Golden Teeth, on the Taping upstream from Bhamo, which had submitted to Kublai. They did it, says Marco Polo,[25] "with such a force that the Great Kaan should never again think of sending another army into that province." The chief asked for the protection of Kublai Khan, who, deciding to act, entrusted the execution of his plans to the local garrisons. The army of Ta-li advanced toward the Burmese and defeated them on the banks of the river, but this was merely a border incident.

"During the winter of 1277–1278, a second Chinese expedition commanded by Nasr-uddin ended in the seizure of Kaungsin, the Burmese stronghold that defended the Bhamo pass. . . . These two expeditions, however, did not succeed in penetrating beyond the thick curtain of the many small Thai principalities that today still separate Yunnan from Burma proper. The final catastrophe did not take place until 1283." [26]

It was in that year, 1283, that a new expedition commanded by Hsiang-wu-t'a-erh (Sangqudar), after a battle at Ngasaungkyam on December 3, took the fort of Kaung-sin again on December 9 and pushed farther south in the Irrawaddy Valley. It did not, however, reach Pagan. King Narathihapate evacuated Pagan before the imminent approach of the Chinese and fled to Prome. Negotiations for the establishment of a Chinese protectorate were begun after Tagaung was seized (January, 1284). In the following year, the king tendered his submission and sent to Peking an embassy that succeeded in persuading the emperor to give orders to withdraw his troops. The north of Burma became the Chinese province of Cheng-mien and remained so until 1303; the south became the province of Mien-chung, which was abolished as early as August 18, 1290.

King Narathihapate was on the verge of regaining his capital in 1287 when he was poisoned at Prome by his own son Thihathu (Sīhasūra). Unrest followed, and the governor of Yunnan ignored the orders of evacuation.

"In 1287, a fourth Chinese expedition commanded by Prince Ye-sin Timour finally reached Pagan at the cost of considerable losses. We do not know if the capital had to admit the presence of Chinese troops." [27]

The fall of Pagan produced effects on the Thai of Burma which we will discuss later; we shall now proceed to examine its repercussions on the Thai of the Menam.

5. THE LIBERATION OF THE THAI OF THE MENAM IN THE SECOND HALF OF THE THIRTEENTH CENTURY: THE BEGINNINGS OF THE KINGDOM OF SUKHOTHAI (FROM AROUND 1220 TO 1292)

It will be recalled that the Menam Basin, originally populated by the Mons, had been the seat of the kingdom of Dvāravatī in the seventh century. In the eleventh the Khmers had established themselves at Lavo, and in the twelfth they had extended their domination to the borders of the kingdom of Haripunjaya, coming into conflict with King Ādityarāja.

At the beginning of the thirteenth century, the kingdom of Haripunjaya was still governed by a Mon dynasty. One of the kings mentioned in the chronicles of Haripunjaya left inscriptions in the Mon language intermingled with passages in Pali at Lamphun, on the site of ancient Haripunjaya. This king was Sabbādhisiddhi, for whom we have two inscriptions containing the dates 1213, 1218, and 1219. They tell of various endowments to Buddhist monuments,[28] one of which, Vat Kukut, corresponds to the Mahābalachetiya built by Ādityarāja.[29] For the period after the reign of Sabbādhisiddhi up to the time of the Thai conquest, the chronicles provide us with only a list of the names of the kings.[30]

These kings had as neighbors to the northeast the Lao princes of Ngoen Yang (Chiangsaen), the last of whom, Mangrai, born in 1239, succeeded his father in 1261. The following year, moving his capital south, he founded Chiangrai. Then, extending his authority toward the northeast and southwest, he took Chiangkhong in 1269 and founded Mưang Fang in 1273.[31] In 1287, says an ancient text, Mangrai, prince of Chiangrai, Ngam Mưang, prince of Mưang Phayao (on the upper Mae Ing), and Rāma Khamhaeng, king of Sukhothai, "met in a propitious place, concluded a strong pact of friendship, and then each returned to his own country." [32]

It is undoubtedly no mere coincidence that this alliance of the three Thai chiefs took place in the same year that Pagan was taken by Sino-Mongol troops. We shall see that, in the decade that followed, Mangrai ended the Mon domination over Haripunjaya and founded, at some distance from this city, Chiangmai, the "new capital" of the Thai. As for Rāma Khamhaeng, who was to have even more brilliant success, the following paragraphs relate the origins of the dynasty to which he belonged.

On the middle Menam, the Thai, known to their neighbors under the name Syāṃ, had undoubtedly gained a foothold quite a long time before.[33] The Khmer remains that are still to be seen at Sukhothai and at Sawankhalok [34] prove that the Khmers were dominant over this region at least from the time of Jayavarman VII and perhaps from the era of Sūryavarman II. But around the middle of the thirteenth century the Syāṃ of Sukhothai became independent under circumstances that are revealed to us by an inscription of about a century later.[35]

A Thai prince, Pha Mưang, chief of Mưang Rat [36] and perhaps son of the former Thai chief of Sukhothai under Khmer suzerainty, had received the title of Kamrateng An' Śrī Indrapatīndrāditya from the Cambodian sovereign and had married the Khmer princess Sikharamahādevī. He had ties of friendship with another Thai prince, Bang Klang Thao, chief of Bang Yang. Following events that are not clear,[37] the two Thai chiefs came into conflict with the Khmer governor of Sukhothai. After the seizure of Si Satchanalai (present-day Sawankhalok), the twin city of Sukhothai, the two allies drove the Cambodian governor out of Sukhothai. Pha Mưang installed his friend Bang Klang Thao there, crowning him king and conferring on him his own title of Kamrateng An' Pha Mưang Śrī Indrapatīndrāditya.

We have no precise dates for any of the events that marked the acquisition of political independence by the Thai of Sukhothai and led to the enthronement of Indrāditya. But since Rāma Khamhaeng, his third son, who was his second successor, reigned in the last two decades of the century, we can date the coronation of Indrāditya around 1220. Later, the country of Lavo seems also to have become detached from Cambodia, for from 1289 to 1299 we see it sending embassies to China.[38] We shall see that in the middle of the following century it was governed by a Thai prince.

All we know about Indrāditya and his immediate successor is what we are told by the stele of Rāma Khamhaeng, composed in 1292.[39] This famous inscription in addition gives interesting details on Rāma Khamhaeng's youth that merit citing:

> My father was named Śrī Indrāditya; my mother was named Nang Sưang; my older brother was named Ban Mưang. We were five children born of the same womb: three boys, two girls. My eldest brother died when he was still little. When I had grown and reached the age of nineteen, Khun Sam Chon, chief of Mưang Chọt, came to attack Mưang Tak.[40] My father went to fight him from the left; Khun Sam Chon came from the right and attacked in force. My father's people fled and dispersed in complete disorder. I did not flee, I climbed on the elephant Anekaphon [Anekabala, "immense power"] and drove it in front of my father. I began a duel of elephants with Khun Sam Chon: I smote his elephant named Mat Mưang ["gold of the country"] and put it out of the battle. Khun Sam Chon fled. Then my father gave me the name Phra Rāma Khamhaeng ["Rama the Strong"] because I had smitten the elephant of Khun Sam Chon.
>
> During the lifetime of my father, I served my father, I served my mother. If I caught some game or fish, I brought it to my father; if I had any fruit, acid or sweet, delicious and tasty, I brought it to my father. If I went on an elephant hunt and caught some, I brought them to my father. If I went to attack a village or city and brought back elephants, boys, girls, silver, gold, I gave them to my father.[41]
>
> When my father died, there remained my elder brother.[42] I continued to serve my elder brother as I had served my father. When my brother died, the whole kingdom passed on to me.

We shall soon see the brilliant career of this king, during whose reign the young Thai kingdom was transformed by Singhalese Buddhism and Khmer civilization. During this process of transformation the social structure of the kingdom did, however, retain some characteristics corresponding to those of the Mongols.

Just as in the "family of gold" at the top of the Mongol social structure the Great Khan was the chief and the princes were the sons of the Great Khan,[43] so Rāma Khamhaeng was the *phọ khun* (the father [of the] *khun*) and the princes and high dignitaries were the *luk khun* (sons [of the] *khun*). Just as the Mongol aristocracy, in defining the various social classes, distinguished its own members, "warriors or faithful persons who are free men par excellence," from "the plebians who comprise the common people and, finally, the serfs who are basically of non-Mongolian race,"[44] so the Thai military aristocracy distinguished itself at this time from the conquered populations: the ethnic term *Thai* took on the meaning of "free man" in Siamese,[45] thus differentiating the Thai from the natives encompassed in Thai society as serfs. Finally, the division of the Mongol population capable of bearing arms into tens, hundreds, thousands, and ten thousands under the orders of commanders furnished by the aristocracy of the *noyan*[46] is duplicated exactly in the military and administrative organization of the Thai.[47]

We do not know the date at which Rāma Khamhaeng, son of the founder of the dynasty of Sukhothai, succeeded his elder brother Ban Mưang. His inscription[48] mentions only three dates:

1283, the date of the invention of Siamese writing, or more exactly of the type of writing used in the inscription. "Heretofore these characters of Thai writing did not exist. In 1205 [i.e., A.D. 1283], the year of the goat, King Rāma Khamhaeng applied all his energy and all his heart to inventing these characters of Thai writing, and these characters exist because the king invented them." We know that these characters constitute an improvement over a proto-Siamese writing, which was itself an adaptation of Khmer cursive writing of the thirteenth century put to use in writing Thai.[49]

1285, the date of the erection in the center of Si Satchanalai (Śrī Sajjanālaya, i.e., Sawankhalok) of a stupa that took six years to build.[50]

1292, the date of the construction at Sukhothai of a stone throne named Manangsilāpātra,[51] "placed here so that all can gaze on the king Rāma Khamhaeng, son of the king Śrī Indrāditya, sovereign of Mưang Si Satchanalai and Mưang Sukhothai as well as of the Ma, Kao, Lao, the Thai who live

> under the canopy of heaven,[52] and the river-dwelling Thai of the Nam U and the Mekong, coming to render him homage."

This chronological data would indicate that Rāma Khamhaeng came to power before 1283.

And if the date of 1281 for the seizure of power of Makatho at Martaban[53] is correct, it is necessary to date the accession of Rāma Khamhaeng even earlier than that date, since by then he was already powerful enough to be able to grant investiture to one of his protégés in a quite distant region.

6. JAVA: THE END OF THE KINGDOM OF SINGHASĀRI (1269–92); THE MONGOL EXPEDITION OF 1293; AND THE FOUNDATION OF THE KINGDOM OF MAJAPAHIT

The Javanese king Kṛitanagara, known later under the name Śivabuddha, was king of reunited Janggala and Panjalu, and the inscriptions he has left, notably those of 1266 and 1269, give us some idea of the administration of his times.[54]

Internally, the king was, once again, confronted by rebels: Bhayarāja in 1270, Mahīsha Rangkah in 1280.[55]

Abroad, the reign of Kṛitanagara was marked by a considerable expansion of Javanese power in all directions. In 1275, taking advantage of the decline of Śrīvijaya, he sent a military expedition to the west which established Javanese suzerainty over Malāyu[56] and probably also over Sunda, Madura, and part of the Malay Peninsula, for Pahang is listed among the dependencies of Kṛitanagara in the *Nāgarakṛitāgama*.[57]

After establishing his authority in Sumatra, Kṛitanagara turned toward Bali, whose king he brought back as a prisoner in 1284.[58] Kṛitanagara must have felt himself strong enough, and above all far enough away from China, to resist the demands of the Mongols, who from 1279 had been insisting that a member of the royal family be sent to the court of Peking. The missions of 1280 and 1281 came to nothing. In 1289 it seems that the envoy of Kublai was mistreated by the Javanese, and to avenge this insult the Great Khan decided in 1292 to send to Java an expedition that will be discussed presently.[59]

King Kṛitanagara, whose portrait-statue in the form of the Buddha Akshobhya can be seen at Surabaya,[60] was a personality who is very differently evaluated by the historical sources, the

Nāgarakṛitāgama and the *Pararaton:* he is represented by one as a fine scholar, by the other as a drunkard. What is certain is that he was a great king, remarkable for his ardor in extending the authority of Java over the neighboring countries and for his zeal for the *kālachakra* form of Tantric Buddhism. This form, coming from Bengal where it had been developed toward the end of the Pāla dynasty, spread to Tibet and Nepal and into the archipelago. It reached its culmination in Java because of syncretism with the worship of Śiva Bhairava. The cult of Siva-Buddha,[61] by applying itself particularly to the redemption of souls of the dead, found receptive ground in Indonesian ancestor worship.

Kṛitanagara met death under dramatic circumstances. He elevated a common man to the rank of Ārya Vīrarāja, but, not feeling sure of him, sent him far from the court and named him governor in the east on the island of Madura.[62] The viceroy of Kaḍiri since 1271 had been a certain Jayakatwang,[63] who very probably was a descendant of the ancient kings and dreamed of supreme power. He joined forces with Vīrarāja and notified him of the propitious moment to attack Kṛitanagara. The battle took place in 1292 and, after various incidents reported by the *Pararaton,*[64] ended in the seizure of the royal residence at Singhasāri and the death of King Kṛitanagara between May 18 and June 15 of that year.

Jayakatwang, master of Java, became in a way the founder of a new kingdom of Kaḍiri. This new kingdom, however, had only a momentary existence, for the Mongol expedition designed to chastise Kṛitanagara actually resulted in restoring the throne to its legitimate possessor.

Jayakatwang, now master of Singhasāri, immediately encountered opposition from Raden Vijaya.[65] This prince, who was a grandson of Mahīsha Champaka and great-grandson of Rājasa and was thus a direct descendant of the founder of the dynasty of Singhasāri, had in addition married Gāyatrī (a *rājapatnī*), a daughter of the King Kṛitanagara who had just been killed in the revolt of Jayakatwang. Together with Ardharāja, a son of Jayakatwang but also a son-in-law of Kṛitanagara, Raden Vijaya commanded in 1292 a corps of troops that Kṛitanagara, before his death, had sent north against the rebels and that Jayakatwang's troops had not yet encountered.

Vijaya attacked Jayakatwang's forces and inflicted three defeats on them. But these successes were only temporary, and the situation at first favorable to Vijaya was reversed both by the arrival of reinforcements from Kaḍiri and by the news of the fall of Singhasāri, which had a demoralizing effect on Vijaya's troops.[66] Forced to flee, Vijaya reached the island of Madura to solicit the aid of Vīrarāja, of whose treason he was not aware. Vīrarāja decided it was in his interest to side with Vijaya from then on.

With Vīrarāja's aid, Vijaya returned accompanied by a group of Madurese to establish himself in the lower Brantas Valley[67] on the site of Majapahit, which was to become the capital of the restored Javanese kingdom.

This restoration took place in the last months of the year 1292, when Kublai Khan had already launched his punitive expedition against Kṛitanagara, of whose death he was unaware. On learning of the arrival of this expedition, Vijaya conceived the ingenious idea of using the Chinese to realize his great plans. We shall see how the Chinese fleet sailed along the coast of Champa without being able to land.[68] It then went on to Java by way of the archipelago of the Karimatas. At the little island of Gelam (southwest of Borneo), at the beginning of 1293, the three chiefs of the expedition—Shih-pi, a Mongol, Yi-k'o-mu-su (or Ye-hei-mi-she),[69] a Uighur experienced in overseas voyages, and Kao-hsing, a Chinese—stopped to hold counsel. Before reassembling in the port of Tuban, on the north coast of Java, they sent a messenger to Singhasāri who, on his return, reported the news of the death of Kṛitanagara and the submission of Vijaya.

The Javanese fleet of Jayakatwang, assembled at the mouth of the river of Surabaya, was captured by the Chinese, who then began to penetrate into the interior. Vijaya sent them messages soliciting their aid against Jayakatwang, who was advancing on Majapahit. The Chinese succeeded in stopping Jayakatwang and rescuing Majapahit on March 3, 1293; they then marched on Kaḍiri, with Vijaya in the rear guard. After a long and bloody battle, the troops of Kaḍiri took flight, and Jayakatwang, besieged in his palace, ended by submitting on April 26, 1293.

Vijaya then requested permission from the Chinese to return to Majapahit with a Chinese escort to seek there the tribute promised to the Great Khan. In reality, he was seeking to rid himself of his allies, who were no longer useful to him after the defeat of his adversary. He began, on May 26, 1293, by massacring his escort; then, with his Javanese, he turned against the Chinese establishtd at Kaḍiri and forced them to get back on their ships. On May 31 they sailed again for China, where they arrived on August 8.

When the Chinese chiefs left Java they took with them about a hundred prisoners, among whom were the children of Jayakatwang. As for Jayakatwang himself, he must have died in Java after a brief captivity. The Mongol expedition designed to chastise Kṛitanagara thus had the unintended result of placing his legitimate heir on the throne.

Vijaya, the founder of the kingdom of Majapahit, took the reign name Kṛitarājasa Jayavardhana. His wives were the four daughters of Kṛitanagara.[70] By the eldest, Queen Parameśvarī Tribhuvanā,[71] he had a son Kāla Gemet, who was crowned in 1295 as Prince of Kadiri, with the title of Jayanagara.[72]

Normal relations seem to have been restored with China, for we find mention of four Javanese embassies during the reign of Kṛitarājasa.[73]

With respect to internal affairs, it is now clear that Kṛitarājasa faced various revolts, for a chronology proposed by C. C. Berg[74] has shown that the revolts that were formerly believed to have occurred during the reign of his son Jayanagara actually took place during Kṛitarājasa's reign. These revolts will be discussed in the following chapter.

7. SUMATRA AND ITS DEPENDENCIES AT THE TIME OF MARCO POLO; THE BEGINNINGS OF ISLAM

Tangible proof of the ascendancy of Java over Sumatra is furnished by an inscription found[75] on the upper Batang Hari, the river of Jambi. This text states that in 1286 an image of the Buddha Amoghapāśalokeśvara (in whose form the father of Kṛitanagara had been deified at Chandi Jago) was brought from Java (*bhūmi Jāva*) to the country of gold (*Suvarṇabhūmi*) by four Javanese officials and erected at Dharmāśraya by order of the Mahārājadhirāja Śrī Kṛitanagara Vikramadharmottungadeva and that this statue was the joy of all the subjects (*prajā*) of the country of Malāyu, beginning with the king Mahārāja Śrīmat Tribhuvanarāja Maulivarmadeva.[76]

The ascendancy of Java over its neighbor to the west was contemporaneous with the conquest of the Malay Peninsula by the Thai. This conquest is alluded to by the Mon chronicles before

1280.[77] In addition, the *History of the Yuan* tells us that in 1295 "the people of Sien [the Syāṃ, or Thai, of Sukhothai] and of Ma-li-yü-erh [Malāyur] have long been killing each other." [78]

The simultaneous, if not combined, action of the Javanese and the Thai stripped Śrīvijaya at once of its island and continental possessions and snatched from it the mastery of the straits of Malacca and Sunda. At the same time, the Sumatranese kingdom began to feel the effects of another cause of the disintegration of Indo-Malaysian culture. By 1281, Islam, propagated by merchants, must already have made great progress there, for the court of China chose to send Muslims, named Sulaymān and Chams'ud-dīn, to Malāyu.[79] Ten years later, in his description of Perlak, in the extreme north of Sumatra, Marco Polo [80] notes "that in the kingdom of Ferlec the people were all idolaters, but, on account of the Saracen traders who frequent the kingdom with their ships, they have been converted to the Law of Mahomet." And the Islamization of the principality of Samudra around the same time has been revealed by the discovery of the tombstone of the Sultan Malik al-Sāleh, who died in 1297.[81]

Immediately following his chapter on Champa, Marco Polo gives a very short paragraph on Java, "the largest island in the world," an island which he had not visited himself. His information on the archipelago dates from before the Mongol expedition, for he says of the Javanese that they "pay tribute to no one" and "that the Great Kaan was never able to take it on account of the great distance, and the dangers of the voyage thither." [82] He would not have said that they "pay tribute to no one"—a phrase he repeats later in connection with the Malay Peninsula and Sumatra—after the expedition of 1293, for we know that in 1293 Yi-k'o-mu-su, who left for the Java campaign, "sent Cheng-kuei to announce the imperial orders in Mu-lai-yu and in other small kingdoms; all [the kings of these countries] sent their sons or their brothers to make their submission." [83]

After mentioning the islands of Sondur and Condur (Poulo Condore), Marco Polo speaks of the kingdom of Lochac, that is, Langkasuka on the Malay Peninsula.[84] "They pay tribute to no one, for their land is so situated that no one can enter it to do any mischief. If it were possible to do so, the Great Kaan would soon make it submit to him." [85]

Coming then to the island of Pentan (Bintang) and the city of Malaiur, Marco Polo says: "The city is very large and noble. There is a great deal of trade in spices and other wares. For there is great abundance in that island of such products."[86]

Marco Polo seems not to have known when he was at Malaiur that he was already on Sumatra, which he calls "Java Minor" and on which he says there were eight kingdoms, each having its own king and language. He stopped at six, all of which, except for the last, were located in the extreme north of the island. The six kingdoms were:

Ferlec (Perlak), where he observed, as we have seen, the presence of Muslims: "... only, however, the inhabitants of the city. The inhabitants of the mountains are like beasts."[87]

Basman (Pasaman, on the southwest coast): "... they are people who have no Law, unless it be that of brute beasts. They call themselves lieges of the Great Kaan, but pay him no tribute, as they are so far away that the Great Kaan's armies could never go there."[88]

Sumatra (Samudra, i.e., Pasai):[89] "Here Marco Polo in person resided five months, because the weather prevented him from continuing his voyage." Here the Venetian drank palm liquor, which was "better than any wine or any other drink that was ever drunk."[90]

Dagroian, where he describes cannibalistic rites;[91]

Lambri (Lāmurī, i.e., Achin), where he mentions men with tails;[92]

Fansur (Baros, on the west coast), the country of camphor and of the tree that yields flour used in making bread. "Messer Marco . . . repeatedly ate this bread" and found it "very good."[93]

Finally Marco Polo speaks of the Nicobars, the Andamans, and Ceylon.

Marco Polo does not appear to have suspected that he was traveling over the ruins of an empire which, three-quarters of a century before, Chao Ju-kua still spoke of as a great commercial center controlling the two shores of the straits. No longer do we hear of the empire of the maharaja, but of eight states, each of which is a "kingdom by itself." It is true that the six states he mentions were minute principalities grouped at the northern tip of the island. Malāyu, which he mentions only briefly and which he undoubtedly did not visit, must still have constituted a state of some importance: it sent embassies to China in 1299 and

1301.[94] But the Javanese expedition of 1275 had snatched mastery of the straits from the heir of Śrīvijaya.[95] The establishment of the Javanese at Tumasik [96] (located at the site of present-day Singapore) perhaps also dates from this period; the Javanese placed here a stele with a Javanese inscription that has, unfortunately, been destroyed.[97]

We can say that at the end of the thirteenth century the empire of the maharaja (Śrīvijaya, Zābag, San-fo-ch'i) had ceased to exist. With it disappeared the only state that had succeeded in dominating the islands and the peninsula simultaneously. The reason for its power and duration was that, possessing simultaneously the maritime routes of the straits and the land routes of the peninsula, it was absolute master of the traffic between the West and the China Sea. Its fall was caused by the simultaneous pressure on its two flanks of Siam and Java: Siam wrested from it its continental possessions; Java, its island possessions and mastery of the straits. One cause of weakness was the harshness of its commercial policy, which gave rise to rivalry and conflicts. And Islam accomplished the ruin of its Indian spiritual patrimony, which in the seventh century had aroused the admiration of the Chinese pilgrim I-ching.

8. THE THAI KINGDOM OF SUKHOTHAI AT THE END OF THE THIRTEENTH CENTURY: RĀMA KHAMHAENG

By 1292, the probable date of his stele and also of his dispatch of a golden letter to the court of the Mongols,[98] Rāma Khamhaeng had already created a sort of hegemony over a great number of Thai tribes. A postscript to the inscription, which seems to have been carved after this date, gives details on his conquests:

> Rāma Khamhaeng is the chief and the sovereign of all the Thai. He is the master who instructs all the Thai so that they know in truth the merits and the Law. Among all the men who live in Thai country, one would search in vain for his equal in science and in knowledge, in courage and in endurance, in strength and in energy. He has defeated the throng of his enemies possessing large cities and numerous elephants. In the east he has conquered the country to Saraluang [Phičhit], Sọng Khwae [Phitsanulok], Lum̩ [Lomsak], Bachai, Sakha as far as the shores of the Mekong, and beyond to Wiangčhan and Wiangkham that mark the border. In the south, he has conquered the country to Khonthi [on the Mae Ping between Kamphaeng Phet and Nakhọn Sawan], Phraek [Paknam Pho], Suphannaphum, Ratburi, Phetchaburi, Si Thammarat [Ligor], up to the sea that marks the border. In the west, he has conquered the country up to

Mư'ang Chọt [Mae Sọt], Hongsawatī [Pegu], and up to the sea that marks the border. In the north, he has conquered the country up to Mư'ang Phlae [Phrae], Mư'ang Man, Mư'ang Phlua [on the Nan River], and from the other side of the Mekong up to Mư'ang Chawa [Luang Phrabang], which marks the border.

He has established and maintained all the inhabitants of these countries in the observance of the Law, without exception.[99]

That this enumeration of conquered countries was not idle boasting is proved by checking against various foreign sources.

The conquest of former Khmer possessions in the Menam and Mekong basins was apparently the result of a war that, in 1296, Chou Ta-kuan, envoy of the Mongols to Cambodia, spoke of in these terms: "In the recent war with the Siamese, all the Khmer people have been obliged to fight, and the country has been entirely destroyed."[100]

The final conquest of the Malay Peninsula, where Thai penetration had begun as early as the era of Chandrabhānu,[101] must have taken place around 1294. The *History of the Yuan,* after recounting that an envoy from Siam was presented at the court of China in 1295, received a gold tablet, and returned with a Chinese mission, goes on to say that "since the people of Sien and of Ma-li-yü-erh have long been killing each other and are all in submission at this moment, an imperial order has been issued telling the people of Sien: do no harm to the Ma-li-yü-erh and hold to your promise."[102] In order to direct this campaign, Rāma Khamhaeng apparently established himself for a while at Phetchaburi, for in 1294, just before the mention of an imperial order of the seventh month enjoining "the king of the kingdom of Sien, Kan-mu-ting [*Kamrateng,* Khmer royal title], to come to the court,"[103] the *History of the Yuan* mentions the arrival in the sixth month of the ambassador from Kan-mu-ting, from the city of Pi-ch'a-pu-li, who came bearing tribute.[104]

The extension of the domination of Rāma Khamhaeng to the west, which will be studied in more detail when speaking of Burma, originated in a romantic adventure. Legend tells of a young merchant from Donwun (near Thaton) of Thai origin and named Makatho who went one day to Sukhothai, where he entered into the service of the king. Very intelligent, he was soon in favor and became governor of the palace. In the absence of the king, he seduced one of the king's daughters and fled with her to Martaban, where he succeeded, after various incidents, in getting the Burmese governor, Aleimma, assassinated and installing himself in his place. These events took place in 1281, before the fall of Pagan. Having become all-powerful in the country, Makatho asked for investiture from Rāma Khamhaeng, who pardoned him for the abduction of his daughter and granted him the Thai title of Chao Fa Rua:[105] this is the Wareru of the Burmese chronicles, who will be discussed later.

The inscription of Rāma Khamhaeng says that Luang Phrabang marks the border in the north of the country, although, strictly speaking, it is located northeast of Sukhothai. Straight north and to the northwest, the region bordering Rāma Khamhaeng's states was under the control of two Thai princes, Ngam Mưang, chief of Phayao, and Mangrai, chief of Chiangrai, who in 1287, the year of the fall of Pagan, concluded an alliance with Rāma Khamhaeng.

Rāma Khamhaeng himself was involved in a romantic adventure: an amorous intrigue with one of the wives of Ngam Mưang.[106] Ngam Mưang, having succeeded in proving him guilty, hesitated to put him to death, fearing lest the spirit of revenge reign from then on between the two countries. He decided to appeal to the prince of Chiangrai, their mutual friend, to arbitrate: this prince succeeded in reconciling the two rivals, at the price of a fine of 990,000 cowries to be paid by the seducer. Then the three princes renewed their oath of alliance by drinking a brew in which each of them had mixed a bit of his blood; thus they showed the feeling of ethnic unity which was the power of the Thai chiefs in the era of their expansion.[107]

The *History of the Yuan,* which dates the first diplomatic relations between China and Siam back to 1282, mentions embassies from Sien in 1292, 1294, 1295, 1297, and 1299[108] and up to 1323. We do not know if the imperial order of 1294, enjoining the king of Sien "to come to the court, or, if he had an excuse, to have his son, his brother, and some envoys come as hostages,"[109] was indeed obeyed.

Siamese tradition claims that Phra Ruang—the name under which the Siamese confuse the first kings of Sukhothai, although it is applied most particularly to Rāma Khamhaeng—himself went to China once, and perhaps twice, and that he brought back the art of ceramics.[110] On this point, tradition perhaps bears some truth, for it is hardly to be doubted that some pottery kilns of Sukhothai and Sawankhalok were established by Chinese.[111]

The inscription of 1292 gives a picture of Rāma Khamhaeng's government that is worth reproducing in its entirety:

> During the lifetime of Rāma Khamhaeng, this city of Sukhotai is prosperous. In the water there is fish, in the fields there is rice; the lord of the country does not levy taxes on his subjects who go along the road together, leading cattle to market, riding horses for sale. Whoever wishes to trade in elephants or in horses, does so; whoever wishes to trade in silver, in gold, does so. If a common man, a noble, or a chief falls ill, dies, or disappears, the house of his ancestors, his clothing, his elephants, his family, his rice granaries, his slaves, the areca and betel plantations of his ancestors are all transmitted to his children. If the common people, the nobles, or the chiefs get into disagreement, the king conducts a thorough inquiry, then settles the matter for his subjects with complete impartiality; he does not connive with the thief and the receiver of stolen goods; if he sees the rice of others, he does not covet it; and if he sees the treasure of others, he is not envious of it. Whoever goes by elephant in search of him and places his own country under his protection, he gives him aid and assistance; if the stranger has neither elephants, nor horses, nor servants, nor wives, nor silver, nor gold, he gives him some and invites him to regard himself as in his own country. If he captures warriors or enemy soldiers, he neither kills nor beats them. There is a bell suspended in the embrasure of the palace doorway: if an inhabitant of the kingdom has any grievance or any matter that is gnawing at his entrails and tormenting his spirit and he wants to reveal it to the king, it is not difficult; he has only to strike the bell hanging there. Every time King Rāma Khamhaeng hears this appeal, he questions the plaintiff about his affair and judges it with complete impartiality.[112]

The inscription then describes the city of Sukhothai with its triple wall and its four gates, the pond that marks its center, the "marvelous pond of clear and delicious water like the water of the Mekong in the dry season," the sanctuaries within the walls; then to the west of the city the Aranyika monastery (Wat Taphan Hin), where there lived a learned Mahāthera from Nagara Śrī Dharmarāja (Ligor); to the east a great lake; to the north the market (*talat pasan,* i.e., bazaar) and a *prasat* which must correspond to the Khmer monument of Wat Phra Phai Luang;[113] to the south, the hill (Khao Luang) on which resided a formidable spirit, Phra Khaphung,[114] "superior to all the spirits of the country. If the prince who is sovereign in Mưang Sukhothai worships this spirit properly and presents it ritual offerings, then this country will be stable and prosperous; but if he does not perform the prescribed worship and does not present ritual offerings, then the spirit of this hill will no longer protect or respect this country, which will fall into decline." These animistic rites did not prevent the king and his people from practicing the Theravada Buddhism using the Pali language, which, during the reign of Rāma Khamhaeng's successors, was to submit more and more to Singhalese orthodoxy. "King Rāma Khamhaeng, sovereign of this Mưang Sukhothai, as well as the princes and princesses, men as well as women, nobles and chiefs, all without exception, without distinction of rank or sex, devoutly practice the religion of the Buddha and observe the precepts during the period of retreat during the rainy season. At the end of the rainy season, the ceremonies of the Kathin [offering of robes to the monks] take place and last a month." The most important of these ceremonies took place west of the city, at the monastery of the Aranyika, from which the population returned forming a joyous and noisy procession. The end of Kathin coincided with the feast of lights, a rite of Indian origin (Dīvalī or Dīpavalī),[115] which the Chinese envoy Chou Ta-kuan describes at Angkor at the same period.[116] "This Mưang Sukhothai has four gates: an immense crowd pushes in through them to see the king light the candles and to enjoy the fire, and this Mưang Sukhothai is full to bursting with people."

9. THE THAI KINGDOM OF LAN NA: FOUNDATION OF CHIANGMAI (1296)

While Rāma Khamhaeng was establishing Thai domination over the populations of the central Indochinese Peninsula from Luang Phrabang to Ligor, with the exception of Lavo (Lopburi), which was not named in the inscription and which sent a series of embassies to China from 1289 to 1299,[117] his ally Mangrai, who founded Chiangrai in 1262, drove the Mons from Haripunjaya (Lamphun).

As early as 1288, the year that followed the fall of Pagan and the conclusion of the alliance with Rāma Khamhaeng and Ngam Mưang, Mangrai sent to Haripunjaya an emissary who was able to win the confidence of the Mon king Yiba and was given the office of preceptor. When he had sufficiently exasperated the inhabitants with his exactions, he notified Mangrai, who in 1291–92 marched on the town and plucked it like a ripe fruit.[118] The Mon king fled to Khelang (the old site of Lampang), where his son lived;

after an unsuccessful attempt at reconquest during which the son was killed, Yiba took refuge at Phitsanulok.[119]

In 1296, Mangrai founded on the Mae Ping, about twenty kilometers north of Haripunjaya, the city of Chiangmai, "the new city." Mangrai and his two allies chose the site as early as 1292 and presided over the construction of the temple of Wat Chiang Man, built to mark the site.[120] The new city had a brilliant destiny not only as a political center but also as a cultural center,[121] and it is even today the second city of Thailand. The state of which it was the capital bore the name of Yonaraṭṭha or Yonakaraṭṭha (kingdom of the Yûon) or of Bingaraṭṭha (kingdom of the Mae Ping) in the Pali chronicles;[122] it is the Lan Na of the Siamese and the Pa-pai-si-fu of the Chinese. Pa-pai-si-fu is mentioned for the first time under the date October 11, 1292, in the *History of the Yuan*.[123]

The chronicle of Chiangmai states that Mangrai went to Pegu and married a princess there and then went to Burma, from which he brought back artisans,[124] but we have no confirmation of these journeys from the Mons or Burmese.

10 THE THAI IN BURMA AT THE END OF THE THIRTEENTH CENTURY

After the fall of Pagan, the Irrawaddy Basin fell into anarchy, and it is impossible to proceed here with a detailed history of the Thai principalities which, under the nominal authority of China, built themselves on the ruins of the Burmese dynasty. Roughly, the country was divided into three parts: in the south, the delta, peopled by the Mons, under the authority of Makatho, also known as Chao Fa Rua or Wareru, who by 1281 had established himself at Martaban; in the north, Upper Burma, the future kingdom of Ava, where the descendants of the kings of Pagan continued to reign under the tutelage of three Thai brothers, Athinkhaya (Asaṃkhyā), Yazathinkyan (Rājasaṃkram), and Thihathu (Sīhasūra), sons of a Thai chief who had become estranged from his family and around 1260 had established himself at Myinsaing, where he got married; and in the southeast on the Sittang River, the principality of Toungoo, founded in 1280.

We have seen that in 1287, Narathihapate, driven from Pagan by the Mongols, had been poisoned at Prome by his son Thihathu (Sīhasūra).[125] Thihathu then rid himself of some of his brothers and tried to seize Haṃsavatī (Pegu), but he lost his life in the attempt and the city remained in the hands of the governor Tarabya, who had become independent there even before the fall of Pagan.[126]

Makatho, or Wareru, the Thai chief of Martaban, made common cause with Tarabya, whose daughter he married and to whom he gave his own daughter. The two allies succeeded in occupying the delta after driving out the Burmese governors, but soon discord arose between them and Wareru had to get rid of his rival. After he became sole king of Pegu he continued to reside at Martaban, where he died in 1313, a victim of assassination by the children of Tarabya, who were also his own grandsons. The name of Wareru is associated with a version of the code of laws[127] known under the name of *Wagaru Dhammathat,* which is undoubtedly one of the first vehicles by which the laws of Manu moved into Siam.[128]

What was happening during this period in the center and the east?

At the death of Thihathu (Sīhasūra), killed at Pegu, the throne of Pagan reverted to his elder brother Kyôzwa (II), who had resisted him and who established the Burmese government again at Pagan; he was crowned there at the end of the month of May of the year 1289.[129] In 1297 he sent his eldest son (Siṃhapati) to China to receive investiture in his place. But the court of Peking was apparently following a policy of "divide and rule," and in consequence it crowned as many local chiefs as possible. Thus in 1297, China gave a silver seal and a title to the king and at the same time gave an honorific tablet to Athinkhaya, the eldest of the three brothers who divided the government of the rice district of Kyaukse and who since 1294 had gradually arrogated royal titles to themselves.

These three brothers had been presented by their father to Narathihapate, who had entrusted them with various missions, and they remained in royal favor under King Kyôzwa (II), who turned over to them the administration of the three provinces of Myinsaing, Mekkaya, and Pinle. They also continued to administer a large portion of the rice district of Kyaukse, which they had taken over during the interregnum from 1284 to 1289. The king was poorly repaid for his favor, for in the same year that Athinkhaya received his honorific tablet, in July 1297, he seized the king and held him captive at Myinsaing.

The country was by this time in full revolt: the Mons of the delta were in rebellion from 1289 on, and in 1298 the northern tribes followed suit. The city of Pagan was destroyed and set on fire by the rebels. Athinkhaya went through the formality of replacing Kyôzwa with his son Zo-nit, who gave his first audience on May 8, 1299; he is known in epigraphy by the name Mang Lulang.[130] On May 10, the three brothers had King Kyôzwa and his son Siṃhapati executed. Another son, Kumārakassapa, rival of Zo-nit, was able to flee to China, where he was proclaimed king on June 22, 1300. At his instigation, a fifth and last expedition came down into the Irrawaddy Valley during the autumn of 1300. It besieged Myinsaing during the winter of 1300–1301. Athinkhaya and his two brothers succeeded in raising the siege by bribing the Mongol general staff. The Chinese troops withdrew with Kumārakassapa, the province of Burma was abolished on April 4, 1303, and Zo-nit and his son Zo-moun-nit continued to reign at least in name at Pagan.

11. CAMBODIA AT THE END OF THE THIRTEENTH CENTURY: ACCOUNT OF CHOU TA-KUAN (1296)

We have seen that, shortly before the Chinese envoy Chou Ta-kuan came to Cambodia in 1296, a disastrous war with the Thai of Sukhothai had ravaged the country. King Jayavarman VIII was elderly at the time of these events: "A land ruled by an old king," says an inscription,[131] "clearly demonstrates the inconvenience of having a superabundance of brambles [enemies]." According to two inscriptions of the following century,[132] he abdicated in 1295 and had the crown bestowed on Prince Śrīndravarman, who had married his eldest daughter Śrīndrabhūpeśvarachūḍā.[133] But, according to the evidence of Chou Ta-kuan, who arrived in Cambodia the following year, the change of reign was more dramatic.

"The new prince," says Chou Ta-kuan, "is the son-in-law of the former; he had pursued a military career. The father-in-law loved his daughter; the daughter stole the golden sword from him and took it to her husband. But then the son deprived of succession plotted to raise troops. The new prince learned of this, cut off the son's toes, and shut him up in a dungeon."[134] An inscription of Śrīndravarman seems in fact to make a discreet allusion to the rivalries that preceded his accession. "The land, once sheltered at the same time and in all parts *under a multitude of white parasols of kings,* suffered the burning of the sun; now, in the shade of a single white parasol [of the new king] it no longer feels it."[135]

The scanty facts we have concerning the successors of Jayavarman VII have been extracted from epigraphic sources. These inscriptions emanate from Brahman scholars who seem to have wanted to renew the tradition of the great priestly families of preceding centuries, a tradition interrupted by the Buddhist fervor of Dharaṇīndravarman II, Jayavarman VII, and their wives. This temporary restoration of Sivaite orthodoxy was undoubtedly responsible both for the iconoclastic violence that was directed toward the monuments of Jayavarman VII's era and resulted in the effacement of innumerable bas-relief images of the Buddha that had decorated the walls and pillars of the temples and for the replacement of these images by lingas or images of ascetics in prayer.

The little that the inscriptions tell us of the reign of Jayavarman VIII, or of him under his posthumous name Parameśvarapada,[136] seems to permit us to impute to him part of the responsibility for these acts of vandalism. One of his wives, Queen Chakravartirājadevī, was the daughter of the Brahman who had come from Burma at the time of Jayavarman VII and had received the title Jayamahāpradhāna.[137] A sister-in-law of this Brahman married a scholar-professor, Jayamangalārtha, by whom she had a son who was awarded the same title. Jayavarman VIII held this son, who was a cousin of the queen, in such favor that in 1295, the same year as his voluntary or forced abdication, he had a temple erected in the capital[138] in which to place a statue of him. (Incidentally, this second Jayamangalārtha must have been over a hundred years old when he died during the reign of the second successor of Jayavarman VIII.)[139] In addition, the last Sanskrit inscription from Cambodia, that is, the one from Angkor Wat, informs us of another Brahman scholar named Vidyeśavid, a descendant of the Brahman Sarvajñamuni who was "born in Āryadeśa [i.e., India] and came through piety to the country of Kambu."[140] It was this Brahman who, at the request of Jayavarman VIII, whose royal chaplain (*hotar*) he was, crowned Jayavarman VIII's son-in-law Śrīndravarman king.[141]

But Singhalese Buddhism, which, as we recall, one of the sons of Jayavarman VII went to study in Ceylon,[142] already had its followers and monks at the time of Chou Ta-kuan's visit. Chou accompanied the ambassador sent to Cambodia in 1295 in order to try to obtain tribute. He left Wen-chou (Che-chiang) on the twentieth day of the second month of the year 1296 and returned on the twelfth day of the eighth month of the year 1297.[143] "The embassy, according to him, was very successful, and homage was rendered; but perhaps he was too interested in the affair for us to accord full credence to what he says. As a matter of fact, there is no trace of regular officical relations following the mission of 1296."[144]

More important for the historian than the obtaining of tribute, the principal result of the voyage of Chou Ta-kuan was the composition of his famous memoirs on the customs of Cambodia, translated as early as 1819 by J. P. Abel Rémusat,[145] and again by Paul Pelliot in 1902.[146]

After giving the geographic position of the country of Chenla or Chanla, also called Kan-pu-che or Kan-p'u-che (Kambuja), Chou Ta-kuan briefly describes his itinerary: from China to the mouths of the Mekong, then the way up the river and the arm of the Great Lake via Ch'anan (Kompong Ch'nang), Fo-ts'un (Pursat), and Kan-p'ang (Kompong), the port of the capital, to the capital itself. He describes a city that corresponds exactly to the city of Jayavarman VII, present-day Angkor Thom, with its walls and moats, its five gates preceded by bridges with balustrades of *nāgas,* the gold tower (the Bayon) in the center of the city, the copper tower (the Baphuon) one *li* to the north, the Royal Palace another *li* farther north. Outside the city he mentions: to the south, the tower of Lu Pan (Phnom Bakhèng) and the tomb of Lu Pan (Angkor Wat); to the east, the eastern lake (Eastern Baray); to the north, the northern lake (Veal Reachdak, or the Baray of Preah Khan) with the temple of Neak Peân in the middle.

Chou Ta-kuan then describes the various kinds of dwellings, beginning with the Royal Palace in which "there is a gold tower [the Phimeanakas] at the top of which the king sleeps. All the natives claim that there is a spirit in the tower, a serpent with nine heads, which is the master of the soil of the whole kingdom. It appears every night in the form of a woman. It is with this spirit that the king first sleeps and unites himself."

With regard to dress, he notes the fashion for Western materials, and describes the royal costume in this manner: "Only the prince is allowed to wear closely woven floral materials. He wears a gold diadem, similar to those that are on the head of the Vajradharas. When he does not wear the diadem, he simply winds a garland of fragrant flowers into his chignon. The flowers remind one of jasmine. Around his neck he has nearly three pounds of large pearls. On his wrists, ankles, and fingers, he wears bracelets and gold rings set with cat's-eyes. He goes barefoot, and the soles of his feet and the palms of his hands are tinted red with a red dye. When he goes out, he holds a gold sword in his hand."

With regard to the officials, "ministers, generals, astronomers," and lesser employees, Chou Ta-kuan notes very accurately the character of the aristocratic oligarchy that was Cambodian administration. "Most of the time, those chosen for offices are princes; if they are not, they offer their daughters as royal concubines." He confirms the evidence of epigraphy on the insignia of office: palanquins with shafts of gold or silver, parasols with gold or silver handles. "Officials having the right of a gold parasol are called *pa-ting* or *an-ting* (*mrateng, amteng*); those that have silver parasols are called *ssu-la-ti* (*śresṭhin*)."

The Chinese visitor recognized the existence of three religious sects: the *Pan-k'i* (*paṇḍita*), that is, the Brahmans, "whom we see dressed like other men, except for a strand of white thread that they wear around the neck and that is the distinctive mark of the educated"; the *Chu-ku* (Siamese *chao ku,* "lord," term of address for Buddhist monks), who "shave their heads, wear yellow garments, uncover the right shoulder, fasten a skirt of material around the lower part of the body, go barefoot," worship an image "altogether similar to Buddha Śākyamuni, and which they call Po-lai [Preah]," take only one meal a day, and recite numerous texts written on palm leaves; the *Pa-ssu-wei* ([*ta*]*pasvin,* ascetics), worshippers of the linga, "a block of stone very similar to the stone of the altar of the god of the soil in China."

Chou Ta-kuan professed some scorn for the morals of the "large and very black" inhabitants, but he saw women of the aristocracy "white as jade." According to him, "the sovereign has five wives, one of the private apartment properly speaking, and four of the four cardinal points," not to mention thousands of concubines.

In a long paragraph based on information whose accuracy he does not guarantee ("as Chinese are not allowed to witness these things, we cannot know the exact truth"), he describes under the obscure name *chen-t'an* a rite of defloration of nubile girls.

Slaves appear to have been recruited almost exclusively among savages, "men of mountain solitudes," who understood the common language; other savages, "who do not submit to civilization, wander in the mountains."

Chou Ta-kuan very exactly characterizes the Khmer language, in comparison with Chinese, by the order of words in a phrase, the modifier following the word modified in reverse of Chinese. The words Chou Ta-kuan cites, numerals and kinship terms, are easily recognizable. No specimens have come down to us of the writings in chalk on blackened skin mentioned by Chou Ta-kuan, but undoubtedly the *krang* on black paper are modern counterparts.

The festivals of the twelve months are the subject of an interesting chapter in which there seems to be some confusion between the numbers of the Chinese months and the Cambodian months. Among these festivals, Chou Ta-kuan mentions a feast of lights, which must have been connected with the feast of the dead; a "throwing of the ball," which in modern times accompanies the alternate chants of boys and girls at the time of the new year; the washing of Buddha images, which also took place at new year's; the survey of the population, a sort of census that was also at one time conducted in Siam; and the burning of rice, an agricultural celebration marking the end of the harvest.

As far as justice was concerned, Chou Ta-kuan notes that "disputes of the people, however insignificant, always go to the sovereign." Beyond this, he speaks only of tortures and ordeals.

Among the illnesses, he cites leprosy, "a malady caused by the climatic conditions of the country. There was a sovereign who contracted this malady; perhaps that is why the people do not consider it with scorn."

On the matter of funeral rites, he mentions hardly anything but the exposure of the body to wild animals. "Now, there are also a few people who burn their dead; these are for the most part descendants of the Chinese. . . . The sovereign is interred in a tower, but I do not know if his body is buried or only his bones."

Chou Ta-kuan then speaks of agriculture, mentioning in this regard floating rice; he then describes the physical configuration of the country, its products, the commerce that took place there, the Chinese goods in demand there, the plants and animals. He describes the furniture and tableware of the Cambodians, which have always been and still are rudimentary, the vehicles and palanquins, and the boats (junks and canoes).

Among the ninety provinces, he names Chen-p'u, Ch'a-nan, Pa-chien, Mu-liang, Pa-hsie, P'u-mai, Che-kun, Mu-tsin-po, Lai Kan-k'eng, and Pa-ssu-li, very few of which it is possible to identify.[147]

"Each village has a temple or a stupa. Even villages with very few inhabitants have a police officer called *mai-tsieh* (*mé srok?*). On the major roads there are rest houses comparable to our post houses; they are called *senmu* (*saṃnak*)."

After some details on the collection of human bile (which was still practiced at the time when the French protectorate was established), on baths, and on armaments,[148] Chou Ta-kuan concludes his account with a description of an outing of the king that is worth citing in its entirety:

> I have spent more than a year in the country, and I have seen him go out four or five times. When the prince goes out, troops head the escort; then come the standards, the pennants, and the music.
>
> Young girls of the palace, three to five hundred in number, who wear floral materials and flowers in their hair and hold candles in their hands, form one troop; even in broad daylight their candles are lit. Then come girls of the palace carrying gold and silver royal utensils and a whole series of ornaments, all of a very peculiar shape and the uses of which are unknown to me. Then there are the girls of the palace carrying lances and shields, who comprise the private guard of the prince; they also form a troop. Following are goat-carts and horse-carts, all decorated with gold. The ministers and princes are mounted on elephants; in front of them one can see from afar their red parasols, which are innumerable. After them come the wives and concubines of the king, in palanquins, in carts, on horses and elephants. They have, certainly, more than a hundred parasols flecked with gold. After them is the sovereign, standing on an elephant and holding the precious sword in his hand. The tusks of the elephant are also sheathed in gold. There are more than twenty white parasols flecked with gold, with handles of gold.
>
> Numerous elephants crowd around him, and there are more troops to protect him. If the king goes to a nearby place, he uses only gold palanquins carried by ten girls of the palace. Most frequently the king, on his outings, goes to see a small gold tower in front of which is a gold Buddha. Those who see the king must prostrate themselves and touch the ground in front of them. This is what is called *san-pa* (*sampeaḥ*). If they do not, they are seized by those in charge of the ceremonies, who do not let them go until they have paid for their transgres-

sion. Twice each day the king holds audience for the affairs of government. There is no fixed agenda. Those officials or commoners who wish to see the sovereign, sit on the ground to wait for him. After some time, one hears distant music in the palace, and, outside, conches are blown in welcome to the king.

I have heard it said that he uses only a gold palanquin. He does not have to go far. An instant later you see two girls of the palace raise the curtain with their tiny fingers, and the king, holding the sword in his hand, appears at the golden window. Ministers and common people clasp their hands and strike the ground in front of them; when the sound of the conches stops, they can raise their heads again. Immediately thereafter the king sits down. In the place where he sits there is a lion skin, which is a hereditary royal treasure.

When business is concluded, the prince returns; the two girls let the curtain fall, and everyone rises.

We see from this that, even though this is a barbarous kingdom, these people know what a prince is.

12. CHAMPA AT THE END OF THE THIRTEENTH CENTURY

In Champa, Indravarman V, already quite old at the time of the visit of Marco Polo in 1285, must have died shortly afterward. He was succeeded by his son, Prince Harijit, who took as his reign name Jaya Siṃhavarman (III). This is the Chê Mân of the Vietnamese.[149]

Jaya Siṃhavarman III, by his firm stance in 1292, when the Mongol fleet passed by on the way to the archipelago to avenge the Javanese insult to the envoys of Kublai and to obtain the submission of the small states of Sumatra, was able to prevent the Mongols from landing on the coasts of Champa.[150]

After marrying a Javanese princess, Queen Tapasī, he sought the hand of a Vietnamese princess, and in 1306 he obtained from the Emperor Trân Anh-tông—in exchange for two Cham provinces situated north of the Col des Nuages [151]—the hand of the Emperor's sister, Princess Huyên Trân, who received the title Parameśvarī.[152]

He died the following year, after having erected at Phanrang the temple of Po Klaung Garai [153] and at Darlac the temple of Yang Prong.[154]

CHAPTER XIII

THE DECLINE OF THE INDIAN KINGDOMS

First Half of the Fourteenth Century

We have seen in the preceding chapter the political repercussions of the coming to power of the Mongols in China. These political changes were accompanied by great changes in the spiritual realm. At the beginning of the fourteenth century, Sanskrit culture was in full decline; the last Sanskrit inscriptions date from 1253 in Champa, from around 1330 in Cambodia, from 1378 in Sumatra. In the Menam and Mekong basins, what remained of Hinduism and Mahayana Buddhism gave way to the orthodoxy of Singhalese Buddhism, which had been introduced on the Indochinese Peninsula by the Mons of Burma and was disseminated further by the Thai. In Sumatra, Islam began to make its appearance. In Java and Bali, Indian Tantrism was strongly influenced by the native Indonesian substratum, at least in its literary and artistic expression.

The Indian period in the history of Farther India was beginning to close following the decrease in cultural exchanges with India proper that resulted from the Muslim invasions that took place there.

1. THE END OF THE THAI KINGDOM OF SUKHOTHAI AND THE FOUNDING OF AYUTTHAYA (1350)

We do not know the exact date of the death of Rāma Khamhaeng. A passage of the *History of the Yuan* [1] seems to indicate that it took place sometime between the embassy of 1295 and that of 1299. In 1299, this history says, "the king of Sien presented a petition to the throne stating that, *when his father was on the throne,* the court had granted him a gift of white horses with saddles and bridles and vestments of gold thread, and he requested that the same be granted to him in conformity with this precedent." This petition, which met with a partial refusal, would seem to have emanated from a new king. However, accession of the successor of Rāma Khamhaeng before 1299 seems difficult to reconcile with the statement in the *Rājādhirāja,* or *History of Martaban,* that, at the death of Wareru in 1313, his successor received from "Phra Ruang" the title of Rāmapraṭishtha, i.e., "established by Rama"; this title could scarcely have been conferred by anyone but Rāma Khamhaeng.[2] Moreover, if the son of Rāma Khamhaeng had succeeded his father before 1299, he must have reigned about fifty years, which seems very long for a king about whom we know so little. It is more probable that Rāma Khamhaeng ceased to reign shortly before 1318, the date at which the king of Martaban invaded Tavoy and Tenasserim.[3]

If this conjecture is accurate, it was still Rāma Khamhaeng who in 1313 organized the raids on Champa that are mentioned by the annals of Vietnam.[4] To conduct these raids, his troops had to cross territories that had belonged to Cambodia and that Cambodia had either lost or was no longer able to defend against its formidable neighbor.

Legend claims that Phra Ruang disappeared in the rapids of the rivers of Sawankhalok.[5] It is difficult to say whether this legend rests on historical fact or even whether it applies to Rāma Khamhaeng or to some other king of his dynasty.

Rāma Khamhaeng was succeeded by his son Loe Thai. Scholars, following an incorrect reading,[6] for a long time called him Sưa Thai, or "the Tiger of the Thai"; this *idolum libri* still appears from time to time in books.

The name of Loe Thai can be associated with only a few historical events.

With respect to Burma, he seems to have taken advantage of the troubles that arose in Martaban to recapture Tavoy and Tenasserim.[7] But he was less fortunate when he tried to revenge the death of his grandson who had tried to seize power at Martaban: his army was defeated and Martaban ceased to recognize his suzerainty.[8]

It was still Loe Thai, judging from the date, who in 1335 sent a delegation to the Cưa Rao Pass in the Indochinese cordillera to greet the Emperor of Đai Viêt, Trân Hiên-tông, who was then conducting a campaign against the Thai kingdom of Ai-lao (southwest of Yunnan).[9]

Loe Thai designated his son Lư Thai as viceroy at Satchanalai (Sawankhalok) around 1340, and he very probably died in 1347.[10] Loe Thai's devotion to Buddhism and his religious works earned him the title Dharmarāja or Dharmikarāja, "pious king,"[11] which his successors bore after him. We owe to him particularly the construction of many *Buddhapāda,* or imprints of the foot of the Buddha, made in imitation of the one worshipped in Ceylon on the summit of Sumanakūṭa,[12] or Adam's Peak.

The relations between Sukhothai and Ceylon, the main center of Buddhism, became closer during the reign of Loe Thai, in part thanks to the activities of a Thai prince who assumed the yellow robe and made a journey to India and Ceylon, from which he brought back miraculous relics. This prince, who after his journey received the title of Mahāthera Śrī Sradhārājachūlāmuni Śrī Ratanalankādipa Mahāsāmi, was a grandson of the Pha Mưang who had placed the father of Rāma Khamhaeng on the throne of Sukhothai. After a worldly youth, "now doing good, now doing evil, now laughing, now crying, now winning, now losing, now happy, now unhappy, turning, going and coming, the unquiet heart in the midst of this world of transmigrations," it seems that around the age of thirty he lost a son and this bereavement made him understand that "this world of transmigrations is unstable, ephemeral, illusory." After having "practiced the perfection of liberality," in imitation of the Buddha in his last earthly existence, "he put on the robes and quit the world, carrying the beggar's bowl in a sash slung over his shoulder." Siam has seen many such curious figures of "prince monks" even well into the twentieth century. A long inscription that comes from Sukhothai, and from which the above passages are extracted, gives a detailed account of this prince's career.[13] He is undoubtedly the same person spoken of in an inscription[14] that tells of a prince's travels in the north to Mưang Fang, Phrae, Lamphun, and Tak, then to India "to the Kingdom of Kalinga, to Pātaliputra, to Choḷamaṇdala, to the kingdom of the Mallas, and to the island of Lankā [Ceylon] to try to find precious relics."

The religious buildings attributed to this prince by these two inscriptions are designated in too vague a way to be identified with certainty. He was responsible for important works of enlargement and restoration in a monument that corresponds to, and must be, Wat Mahathat of Sukhothai.[15] These labors were executed in part by workers brought back from Ceylon; here is a valuable indication of the possible origins of the Singhalese influence that has been detected in the art of Sukhothai.[16]

Loe Thai was succeeded by his son Lử Thai, viceroy at Si Satchanalai (Sawankhalok).[17] This prince was a scholar who in 1345 composed a massive treatise on Buddhist cosmology, the *Traibhūmikathā,* which has come down to us in a little-altered old Siamese translation known as the *Traiphum Phra Ruang.* Modern versions of it today still constitute the basis of popular concepts of Buddhism in Siam and Cambodia.

In 1347, Lử Thai went to Sukhothai, where troubles seem to have broken out, undoubtedly at the death of his father. He seized the city and had himself crowned king there with the title Śrī Sūryavaṃśa Rāma Mahādharmarājādhirāja.[19]

Once on the throne of Sukhothai, Lử Thai seems to have been more concerned with the morals and religion of his subjects than with military conquests.

"His Majesty," says one of his inscriptions, "has thoroughly studied the sacred scriptures. He has studied the Vinaya and the Abhidharma according to the system of the traditional masters, beginning with the Brahmans and the ascetics. The king knows the Veda, the treatises and traditions, the law and the maxims, beginning with the treatises on astronomy. . . . His knowledge is unequaled. . . . He knows the short years and the years with intercalary months, the days, the lunar mansions. Using his authority, he has reformed the calendar." [20]

"This king," says another inscription, "reigned by observing the ten royal precepts. He knows how to take pity on all his subjects. If he sees the rice of others, he does not covet it; if he sees the wealth of others, he is not annoyed by it. . . . If he catches people guilty of deceit and insolence, people who put poison in his rice in order to cause him sickness and death, he never kills or beats them, but he pardons all who behave wickedly toward him. The reason why he represses his heart and quells his spirit and does not become angry when it would be proper for him to do so, is that he has the desire to become a Buddha and the desire to lead all creatures beyond the ocean of sorrows of transmigration." [21]

Unfortunately for him, this wise and pious monarch who reformed the calendar and pardoned offenses had a more ambitious neighbor to the south, the kingdom of Lavo. We have only one historical fact about the kingdom of Lavo in the thirteenth century: according to the *History of the Yuan,* which mentions it by the name Lo-hu, it sent several embassies to China between 1289 and 1299.[22] According to tradition without known historical basis,[23] a Thai chief named Jayaśrī, a descendant of a prince of Chiangsaen, had settled in Phra Pathom and had taken as his son-in-law the chief of Mưang U Thọng, an ancient city the remains of which can still be seen in the Suphan region.[24] Around 1347, following a cholera epidemic, this prince of U Thọng, who meanwhile had succeeded his father-in-law, abandoned his residence and went to found a new capital[25] fifty kilometers south of Lavo (Lopburi) on an island of the Menam, at a crossroads of major river routes. He gave it the name of Dvāravatī Srī Ayudhyā[26] at the time of his coronation in 1350 under the name Rāmādhipati. The preceding year, in 1349,[27] he had launched an expedition to the north which, without striking a blow, brought about the submission of Sukhothai and its pious king, whose peaceful inclinations perhaps had some influence on the decision of the founder of Ayutthaya. Deprived of his independence, King Lư Thai turned more and more to religion, building temples and monasteries, welcoming monks from Ceylon, and finally entering into the order himself in 1361.

At Sukhothai, between 1250 and 1350, the Siamese were able to develop their own characteristic civilization, institutions, and art. The city was situated on the border between the zone of Khmer influence and the zone of Mon and Burmese influence. Via the Mae Yom River, it was in close relations with Lopburi and the former Khmer provinces of the lower Menam. It was, moreover, situated at the end of the route coming from Lower Burma, which assured its relations with the west, and especially with Ceylon.

During the Sukhothai era, then, the Siamese showed a marked and perhaps deliberate contrast with Khmer civilization in some areas, notably in politics and art.[28] On the other hand, from the beginning of the foundation of Ayutthaya, they borrowed from Cambodia its political organization, material civilization, system of writing, and a considerable number of words. The Siamese artists were beholden to the school of the Khmer artists and transformed Khmer art not only according to their own genius but also as a result of the strong influences of their contact with their neighbors to the west, the Mons and the Burmese. From the Mons and the Burmese the Siamese received their legal traditions, of Indian origin, and above all their Singhalese Buddhism with its artistic traditions.

2. THE FOUNDING OF THE LAOTIAN KINGDOM OF LAN CHANG (1353)

We have seen that, by the beginning of the fourteenth century, the Thai of Sukhothai had consolidated their authority over all the territory of present-day Thailand with the exception of the eastern provinces, which were still Cambodian. But these in their turn soon fell in part under the domination of another branch of the Thai family, that which we call Laotian.

It will be recalled that at the end of the twelfth century Khmer domination extended up the Mekong to Wiangčhan, a fact that was proved by the discovery at Sai Fọng of a stele of one of the hospitals of Jayavarman VII. "We know, moreover," writes Henri Maspero,[29] "that Wiangčhan came under Siamese domination in the last years of the thirteenth century, conquered by Rāma Khamhaeng who probably seized it from the Cambodians; unfortunately, the silence of Vietnamese and Chinese documents in the thirteenth century prevents us from establishing the fact precisely. What is certain is that after the loss of Wiangčhan the Cambodians still remained for a long time masters of the country situated downstream from the great bend of the Mekong, and that they still occupied it during the first half of the fourteenth century. It took the formation of a powerful enough Laotian state, formed from the union of the principalities of Mư̛ang Chawa, modern Luang Phrabang, and of Wiangčhan, to drive the Cambodians to the south and to gradually confine them to territories that were Cambodian in population."

The formation of this Laotian state was favored by the weakening of Sukhothai; it is undoubtedly significant that the founding of the kingdom of Wiangčhan by Fa Ngum took place in 1353,[30] four years after the submission of Sukhothai to the young kingdom of Ayutthaya.

"Native tradition," writes Louis Finot,[31] "knows nothing about the period between the mythical Khun Lọ (son of the legendary Khun Bọrom) and the fourteenth century. It only preserves a list of names of chiefs designated first by the title *khun*, then by that of *thao*, finally by that of *phraya*. There were fifteen *khun* and six *thao*. The last of the *thao*, Thao Tavang, had a son,

Phraya Lang, the first of the *phrayas;* it is to him that the memories of Laotians about their history go back."

Phraya Lang, having governed his kingdom badly, was exiled to the mountains (or put in a cage at Pak U, according to another tradition) and replaced by his son Phraya Khamphong. When the latter had a son, he sent a message to the dethroned king to ask him what name he wanted his grandson to be given. The angry old man only answered: *"Phi fa pha!"* ("May Heaven strike you down!") Upon receiving this answer, Phraya Khamphong, without further ado, called his son Phi Fa, Spirit of Heaven. This pompous name was hardly justified. Phi Fa had nothing in common with the god whose name he bore except a lively taste for women, which did not stop even at the doors of his father's harem. He was driven out and did not reign. Before his expulsion, he had a son, the future Phraya Fa Ngum, in 1316.

The exiled prince and his son found refuge at the court of the king of Cambodia, who must have then been Jayavarmadi-parameśvara, the king who came to the throne of Angkor in 1327.[32] The young Fa Ngum was raised by a religious scholar of the capital whom the Laotian chronicles call Maha Pasaman Čhao (Phra Mahāsamana). When he was sixteen years old, the king of Cambodia gave him in marriage his daughter, Princess Kaeo or Yǫt Kaeo, also known as Kaeo Lǫt Fa. Then at a date that is unknown, but must have been between 1340 and 1350, the king gave Fa Ngum an army so that he could reconquer the kingdom of his fathers.

The Laotian chronicle *Nithan Khun Bǫrom*[33] tells—with a great deal of detail, the historicity of which needs to be confirmed by other evidence—the story of the victorious advance of this expedition along the Mekong Valley through Bassac, Kham-muan, Trân-ninh, the Hua Phan (where Fa Ngum negotiated with Đai Viêt and fixed the border at the watershed separating the Red River and the Mekong), and the Sip Sǫng Phan Na and then the descent on Chiangdong-Chiangthǫng (Luang Phrabang), where Fa Ngum was proclaimed king. According to the chronicle, Fa Ngum then went back up the Mekong and conducted a victorious campaign against Lan Na, whose king Sam Phaya, after having tried to resist at Chiangsaen, fled to Chiangrai and there negotiated a treaty with Fa Ngum. On his return, Fa Ngum conquered the Kha populations. Thus far Fa Ngum had avoided Wiangčhan. He now seized it by using a classic ruse: he left a stock of gold and silver arrows, feigned retreat, then pounced on his adversaries when they left their ranks to gather up the precious metal. After taking Wiangčhan, Fa Ngum advanced on the Khorat Plateau to Rǫi-et; then, having organized all his conquests, he returned by Wiangčhan to Chiangdong-Chiangthǫng, where his solemn coronation took place. The *Nithan Khun Bǫrom*, in its account of all these events, attributes the facility with which Fa Ngum obtained the submission of the chiefs in the conquered countries and the friendship of the neighboring kings to a feeling of a common origin. "Like you, we are descendants of Khun Bǫrom," the envoys of Trân-ninh told him. "We are brothers through Khun Bǫrom and must not fight with armies between us," affirms a Lü chief of the Sip Sǫng Phan Na. The king of Ayutthaya himself, to stop the march of Fa Ngum on the Khorat Plateau, reminded him that they were "brothers since Bǫrom," offered him territories, and promised him one of his daughters in marriage. Here is a new example among the Thai chiefs of this feeling of a common ethnic origin that has already been noted in connection with Rāma Kham-haeng.[34]

Another source, the *Phongsawadan*,[35] gives a shorter itinerary for the expedition of Fa Ngum, having him go directly from Trân-ninh to Chiangdong-Chiangthǫng. The *Phongsawadan* also gives a somewhat different chronological sequence of events: it places after his coronation, rather than before it, Fa Ngum's negotiations with Đai Viêt for the delimitation of the border and his campaign on the Khorat Plateau.

However that may be, various texts agree that the solemn coronation of Fa Ngum, which marks the founding of the kingdom of Lan Chang,[36] took place in 1353; this date has most probably been transmitted correctly. To my knowledge, the only mention of Fa Ngum in epigraphy is found in an inscription of Sukhothai dating after 1359; this inscription says that Sukhothai had for a neighbor to the east, on the Mekong, Čhao Phraya Fa Ngǫm.[37]

The accession of Fa Ngum is important not only because it marks the establishment of a state destined to play a major political role in the central Indochinese Peninsula but also because it resulted in the introduction into the upper Mekong of Khmer culture and of Singhalese Buddhism through the intermediary of Cambodia. Shortly after his accession, in fact, Fa Ngum sent to Cambodia a mission led by his old religious tutor, Maha Pasaman, and made up of monks and artisans. In addition to a number of sacred texts, they brought back the famous statue of Phra Bang that was to give its name to the capital of Lan Chang. This mission had all the more success because its efforts were brought to bear on a terrain already marked by the imprint of Cambodian Buddhism.[38]

3. THE THAI KINGDOM OF LAN NA

We have seen that, in the course of his campaign against Lan Na, Fa Ngum advanced to Chiangrai, where the king of Lan Na, Sam Phaya, had taken refuge. In view of the date, this must have been King Pha Yu, great-grandson of Mangrai.

The death of Mangrai around 1315,[39] after a reign of about fifty years, was the signal for competition between his heirs. Of his three sons mentioned in the chronicles, he had passed over the eldest[40] and had removed the youngest by sending him to the Thai of the upper Salween, where he founded the principality of Mưang Nai (Moné).[41] There remained the second son, Grāma (Khun Kham), or Jayasangrāma, who had taken part in the battle against Yiba, the last king of Haripunjaya.[42] It was he who succeeded Mangrai. After a few months, however, he had himself replaced at Chiangmai by his son Saen Phu, established two other sons at Mưang Fang and at Chiangkhọng, and himself retired to Chiangrai.[43]

But, when the prince of Mưang Nai received the news of the death of his father, Mangrai, he came to claim the throne, or at least his part of the inheritance. Saen Phu and his brother Nam Thuem, prince of Chiangkhọng, took refuge near their father at Chiangrai, while their uncle, the prince of Mưang Nai, occupied Haripunjaya.[44]

What happened afterwards is very confused, and it suffices to note here that Nam Thuem succeeded in driving out the invader and retaking Haripunjaya. But his father did not leave him there; he sent him to Chiangtung[45] and put Saen Phu back on the throne of Chiangmai in 1322 or 1324.[46]

Saen Phu in his turn soon established his son Kham Fu at Chiangmai so he could go to Chiangrai to care for his father (Jayasangrāma), who died in 1325 or 1327.[47]

Then Saen Phu regained power over the whole territory. In 1325 or 1328[48] he founded the city of Chiangsaen, which bears his name, on an already ancient site. He died in 1334[49] and was replaced by his son Kham Fu, who reigned only a few years and died at Chiangrai.[50]

Kham Fu was succeeded by his son Pha Yu, who was crowned at Chiangrai but at the end of three years established the capital at Chiangmai again. He enlarged and fortified the city of Chiangmai.[51] At its center he built a temple in which to place the ashes of his father;[52] this temple later took the name of Wat Phra Sing when the statue of Phra Sing, or Phra Sihing, "the Singhalese Buddha," was installed there.[53] The date of Pha Yu's death is uncertain.[54]

4. BURMA UNDER THE DOMINATION OF THE THAI

The events that took place in Burma in the Thai principalities during the first half of the fourteenth century are complex; it will suffice to give the following facts.

In the south, the assassination of Wareru was the signal for a series of conflicts with the kingdom of Sukhothai to which we have already alluded.[55] The descendants of the Thai chief, beginning with Binnya U (1353–85), established themselves at Haṃsavatī (Pegu),[56] where they reigned until the conquest of the city in 1539 by the Burmese king of Toungoo.

In the central region, the three Thai brothers, after suceeding in getting rid of the Mongols, made every effort to win their favor and succeeded in getting the Chinese province of Burma abolished in 1303. The youngest brother, Thihathu, who had affirmed his supremacy in 1306,[57] was crowned king on April 20, 1309.[58] At the death of the eldest brother Athinkhaya in 1310, he and his other brother were left masters of the situation. In 1312, he chose Pinya, also known as Vijayapura, as his residence.[59] His descendants continued to reign there until 1364.

One of Thihathu's sons, Athinkhaya,[60] established himself in 1315 at Sagaing, from which he dominated the north and west. It was an offshoot of this branch from Sagaing, Thadôminbya, who in 1364 founded the city of Ava[61] on the Irrawaddy, at the entrance to the Kyaukse plain, a city that was to remain the capital for five centuries.

Finally, in the east, the powerful city of Toungoo, which had been founded in 1280 and remained the place of refuge for Burmese desiring to escape Thai domination, became the capital of a new Burmese state in 1347 when Thinkhaba took the title of king there.[62] It was one of his descendants who in 1539 was to conquer Haṃsavatī (Pegu) and found a powerful Burmese state there.

5. CAMBODIA: THE LAST KINGS MENTIONED IN EPIGRAPHY

At Angkor, King Śrīndravarman, who was reigning at the time of the visit of Chou Ta-kuan, remained in power until 1307, at which date "he abdicated in favor of the prince heir apparent (Yuvarāja) and retired into the forest."[63] We owe to him the oldest Cambodian inscription in the Pali language,[64] an inscription commemorating the construction of a *vihāra* and of an image of the Buddha in 1309, two years after the abdication of the king.

We do not know the relationship of the new king to Śrīndravarman; an inscription tells us that he was a relative (*vaṃśa*) without being more specific. On coming to the throne, he took the name of Śrīndrajayavarman. He reigned twenty years. He embellished the temple built in the capital by Jayavarman VIII in honor of the Brahman Jayamangalārtha who died during his reign at the age of 104.[65] Aside from the coming of a Chinese mission in 1320 charged with buying tame elephants in Cambodia,[66] we know no other events which we can attribute to his reign.

In 1327, Śrīndrajayavarman was replaced by Jayavarmādiparameśvara,[67] whose relationship to him is not known. We know this king only through a Khmer inscription from the Bayon[68] and through a Sanskrit inscription that is called the Angkor Wat inscription[69] but was actually found at a site formerly called Kapilapura, to the northeast of the temple.[70] This Sanskrit inscription, which was composed by the Brahman scholar Vidyeśadhīmant, servant of Kings Śrīndravarman, Śrīndrajayavarman, and Jayavarmādiparameśvara,[71] is the last Sanskrit inscription of Cambodia. Completely impregnated with Sivaite mysticism, it proves that, in a country where Singhalese Buddhism must already have made very great progress, Hinduism found a last refuge at the court of the successors of Jayavarman VII. Indeed, even today, six centuries later, it has still not been driven out; the Bakō, or court Brahmans, still officiate in the royal ceremonies of modern Cambodia.[72]

We do not know how long Jayavarmādiparameśvara reigned. It was undoubtedly he who sent an embassy to China in 1330[73] and in 1335 dispatched a delegation to the Cửa Rao Pass to greet the Emperor of Đai Viêt, Trân Hiên-tông, a delegation that must have met there the delegation from Sukhothai.[74] It is impossible for the moment to establish the connection between Jayavarmādiparameśvara, the last king mentioned in the great inscription of Angkor Wat, and the first kings of the Cambodian chronicle, which begins around 1350 with a king bearing the posthumous name Mahānippean or Nippeanbat, i.e., Nirvāṇapada.[75] The break between the kings of ancient epigraphy and those of the chronicle is for the moment complete.

It is interesting to note that in the middle of the fourteenth century, on the eve of the founding of Ayutthaya and the coronation of the first king of the Siamese dynasty that would bring about the ruin of Angkor, Wang Ta-yüan could still write in his *Tao-i Chih-lioh* that the country of Cambodia was commonly called "Chenla the rich."[76]

6. CHAMPA

In Champa, the "son of Śrī Harijit," that is, of Jayasiṃhavarman III and Queen Bhāskaradevī, came to the throne in 1307 at the age of twenty-three. Georges Maspero[77] somewhat arbitrarily gives him the name of Jayasiṃhavarman IV. The annals of Vietnam call him Chê Chi. Persistent rebellions in the old Cham provinces north of the Col des Nuages that had been ceded to Đai Viêt in exchange for the Vietnamese princess[78] obliged the Emperor Trân Ahn-tông to lead an expedition there in 1312. The expedition resulted in the capture of the Cham king, who was brought back a prisoner and died in Tongking in 1313.[79] His brother was entrusted with the administration of the country as "feudatory prince of the second rank." It was thus as suzerain protector of Champa that the emperor of Đai Viêt defended it in this same year 1313 against the Siamese raid that has been mentioned.[80]

In 1314, Emperor Trân Ahn-tông abdicated in favor of his son Trân Minh-tông, and this provided the "feudatory prince," whom the Vietnamese annals call Chê Nang, the opportunity to try to reconquer the provinces of the north and to make himself independent. He was defeated in 1318 and took refuge in Java.[81]

The emperor of Đai Viêt then placed a military chief, called Chê A-nan in the Vietnamese sources, on the throne of Champa.

This chief soon attempted in his turn to liberate himself by relying on the Mongols. His victory over Vietnamese troops in 1326 allowed him to cease performing acts of vassalage.[82] Thereafter he had a peaceful reign. During his reign the Franciscan priest Odoric of Pordenone visited the country; in his account of his journey,[83] Odoric devotes a paragraph to the kingdom "which is called Zampa,[84] and 'tis a very fine country, having great store of victuals and of all good things." He attributes to the king the procreation of two hundred children, "for he hath many wives and other women whom he keepeth." He notes the abundance of the schools of fish that frequent the coast, fish that come "in order to pay homage to their emperor." The most interesting statement in his account is his allusion to the Indian practice called *sati:* "When a man dies in this country, they bury his wife with him, for they say that she should live with him in the other world also."[85]

At the death of Chê A-nan in 1342, his son-in-law, called Tra-hoa Bô-dê in the Vietnamese sources, succeeded in supplanting the legitimate heir Chê Mô, although he had to fight against him for some ten years before he finally eliminated him. The success he achieved over Vietnamese troops brought in by Chê Mô stimulated him to attempt to reconquer the Hué region in 1353, but in this enterprise he failed. His reign was marked by the visit of the Berber traveler Ibn Baṭūṭa, if, as has been suggested,[86] the country of Ṭawālisī mentioned by this author in his account really refers to Champa. We do not know when Tra-hoa Bô-dê's reign came to an end.[87]

7. THE MALAY PENINSULA AND SUMATRA: THE SPREAD OF ISLAM

On the Malay Peninsula, the recommendation made by the court of Peking in 1295 to the Thai of Sukhothai to "do no harm to the Ma-li-yü-erh and hold to your promise"[88] seems not to have been observed for very long if we are to believe Wang Ta-yüan, who writes in the middle of the fourteenth century in his *Tao-i Chih-lioh:*[89] "The people [of Sien] are much given to piracy. . . . in recent years they came with seventy odd junks and raided Tan-ma-hsi[90] and attacked the city moat. (The town) resisted for a month, the place having closed its gates and defending itself, and they not daring to assault it." The same author also mentions, among others, the states of Ting-chia-lu,[91] P'eng-heng (Pahang),[92]

Chi-lan-tan (Kelantan), [93] Tan-ma-ling (Tāmbralinga),[94] and Lung-ya-hsi-chiao (Langkasuka) [95] and various islands; he enumerates their products but does not give any historical details.

At Trengganu, on the east coast of the peninsula, a Malay inscription which is presumed to date from 1326–27, but which could have been later, is the oldest document relating to the Islamization of the peninsula.[96] On the other hand, around 1345–46 Ibn Baṭūṭa, the envoy of the Sultan of Delhi, Muhammed Ibn Toghluk, who visited Kāḳula [97] on his way to China, speaks of the Sultan of Mul Djāwa (the name by which he designates the Malay Peninsula) as being an infidel.[98] We have seen in the preceding chapter that for Sumatra the evidence concerning the introduction of Islam begins about 1281. Ibn Baṭūṭa claims to have been received in the sultanate of Sumuṭra by Malik az-Zāhir, a claim that has been placed in doubt.[99] However that may be, the account of Ibn Baṭūṭa contains some interesting details. It says that the sultan is a devotee of the sect of the Shafi'ites and that his country is surrounded by infidels. "He makes war often, especially against the infidels. . . . His subjects also follow the Shafi'ite rite; they love to fight the heathens, and march willingly with their sovereign. They have been victorious over the neighboring infidels, who pay them tribute in order to obtain peace." [100] The oldest tombstone inscription found at Samudra-Pasai dates from 1320.[101]

Islam, which seems to have been imported to Sumatra principally by people from Gujarat and the Gulf of Cambay,[102] was still far from having conquered all the small principalities of the north of the island by the middle of the fourteenth century. Odoric of Pordenone in 1321 mentions some of these principalities: [103] Lamori (Achin), where "all the women be in common" and where the people "eat man's flesh"; Sumoltra, whose inhabitants "brand themselves on the face with a little hot iron in some twelve places; and this is done by men and women both." [104] As for Wang Ta-yüan, he lists the same states under the names of Nan-wu-li [105] and Su-wen-ta-la,[106] and he adds Tan-yang [107] (Tamiang, the Dagroian of Marco Polo?); again he is content to enumerate products without describing the political situation. In the center and south of the island, we know of only two states: San-fo-ch'i,[108] which for Wang Ta-yüan corresponded to the Jambi River Valley,[109] that is, the ancient Malāyu, which, as we have seen, had become in the thirteenth century the center of gravity of the old empire of the maharaja; and Ch'iu-chiang, "the old estuary," [110] which is undoubtedly Palembang.

For its part, epigraphy shows that Malāyu remained the only Sumatranese state of some political importance and that it had become the refuge of Indian culture in opposition to the sultanates of the north that were already Islamized or in the process of becoming so. But Malāyu's center tended gradually to become more and more distant from the eastern coast of the island, to sequester itself in the interior near what was to be Minangkabau.

Many inscriptions tell us that in this region in the middle of the fourteenth century there was a "sovereign of the Land of Gold" (*kanakamedinīndra*) [111] named Ādityavarman, son of Advayavarman. His name appears in Java as early as 1343 on an image of the Bodhisattva Manjuśrī that was originally in Chandi Jago.[112] Its presence there seems to indicate that at this date the future king, who was somehow related to Queen Rājapatnī, wife of Kṛitarājasa, lived at the court of Majapahit.[113]

In 1347 he was at Malāyupura, where he had a Sanskrit text engraved [114] on the back of an image of Amoghapāśa. This image, found at Rambahan, was, according to the inscription of Padang Rocho, brought from Java in 1286.[115] At Malāyupura, Ādityavarman bore the royal title of Udayādityavarman (or Ādityavarmodaya) Pratāpaparākramarājendra Maulimālivarmadeva, a title in which one scholar believes he can detect an attempt at synthesis of the royal titles traditionally in use in Śrīvijaya and Malāyu.[116]

This inscription gives, moreover, interesting indications about the Tantric rites that were practiced in Indonesia in the fourteenth century, many of which are perpetuated in Bali to this day.[117] The Buddhism of King Ādityavarman, who represented himself as an incarnation of Lokeśvara, like that of the kings of Majapahit, stemmed from the *kālachakra* system.[118]

Another inscription of the same date, but without historic interest, has been found at Pagar Ruyung, in the heart of Minangkabau.[119] This region has furnished many other inscriptions from this long reign that lasted at least until 1375.

8. JAVA: THE KINGDOM OF MAJAPAHIT TO THE ACCESSION OF HAYAM WURUK (1350)

We have seen above that, according to a new chronology,[120] the reign of Kṛitarājasa, which we had once thought peaceful, was on the contrary troubled by a series of rebellions, rebellions that were once assumed to have taken place during the reign of his successor Jayanagara. In 1295 there was an abortive revolt in the Tuban region of one of Kṛitarājasa's former companions in arms, Ranga Lawe, who had become one of the highest dignitaries of the kingdom.[121] Then the old Vīrarāja declared himself independent at Lumajang,[122] situated in the eastern part of Java, immediately south of the island of Madura. The years 1298 to 1300 were taken up with a battle against Sora, another of the king's former companions in arms, who was finally defeated and killed. Then Nambi, a son of Vīrarāja, withdrew to Lembah and fortified himself there. Finally, in 1302, there was a revolt of Juru Demung, one of the accomplices of Sora.[123]

Kṛitarājasa died in 1309. From his Sivaite funerary temple situated at Simping[124] comes the beautiful statue, now in the Museum of Batavia, representing him in the form of Harihara.[125] His son Jayanagara (the Kāla Gemet of the *Pararaton*) took the reign name Śrī Sundarapāṇḍyadevādhīśvara Vikramottungadeva, a name which emphasized the spiritual relations between Java and the Pāṇḍya country at the extreme south of India, witnessed as early as the era of Sanjaya.[126] Two years after his accession the elderly Vīrarāja, who had given so much trouble to his predecessors, died. In 1312, the king proceeded with the burial, at Pūrva Patapan,[127] of Kṛitanagara, who had been dead for twenty years. In the following year Juru Demung, who had revolted in 1302, died, thus ridding Jayanagara of another adversary of his father. But in 1314 a new rebellion broke out, that of Gajah Biru, another of the accomplices of Sora.[128]

After the death of Nambi in 1316 and the submission of the district of Lumajang,[129] one would think that tranquillity would return, but in 1319 Kuṭi revolted, and this revolt forced the king to abandon his capital temporarily. He was escorted by twenty-five palace guards under the command of Gajah Mada,[130] whom we will hear more about when we come to the regency period (1328–50).

In spite of these troubles, which are stressed in the chronicle, the power of Majapahit was evident. Odoric of Pordenone, who visited Java in 1321, gives an interesting description of this island, "which hath a compass of a good three thousand miles. And the king of it hath subject to himself seven crowned kings. Now this island is populous exceedingly, and is the second best of all islands that exist. . . . The king of this island hath a palace which is truly marvelous. For it is very great. . . . Now the Great Khan of Cathay many a time engaged in war with this king; but this king always vanquished and got the better of him."[131]

From 1325 to 1328, Jayanagara sent annual embassies without fail to the court of China.[132] One of the ambassadors of 1325, Seng-chia-li-yeh, must have been identical to the Seng-ch'ia-lieh-yu-lan whom we meet in 1375 as king of Sumatra.[133] In 1328 Jayanagara died, assassinated by a noble whose wife he had seduced.[134] A great part of the Panataran group dates from his reign.[135]

Since Jayanagara had no sons, the crown reverted to the daughter of Kṛitanagara, the Rājapatnī Gāyatrī, first wife of Kṛitarājasa. But she had entered religious orders as a *bhikshuṇī*[136] and her daughter Tribhuvanā therefore assumed the regency in her name.[137] In 1329 or 1330, Tribhuvanā married a noble, Chakradhara[138] or Chakreśvara, who received the name Kṛitavardhana with the title of Prince of Singhasāri.[139] She had a son by him in 1334, and this son, Hayam Wuruk,[140] became king at the death of his grandmother in 1350.

The great figure of the regency period was Gajah Mada, whom we have seen above sharing the fortunes of King Jayanagara when he fled before the rebel Kuṭi. At first *pati,* that is, prime minister, of Kahuripan, then of Daha, he became *pati* of Majapahit in 1331.[141] His unceasing efforts were devoted to the extension of Javanese supremacy in the archipelago.[142] On Bali, for example, where the accomplishments of the campaign of Kṛitanagara in 1284 had been lost so completely that the island had become independent again, an expedition of 1343 led to the destruction of the local princely family[143] and a Javanization of the island that was to be intensified during the reign of Hayam Wuruk.

The *History of the Yuan*[144] mentions a Javanese embassy to China in 1332 led by Seng-chia-la, apparently the same person who led the embassy of 1325. Wang Ta-yüan[145] in 1350 describes Java (Chao-wa) as a prosperous, fertile country whose numerous and peaceable people are "foremost of the barbarians of the eastern seas."

The death of the old Rājapatnī in 1350 ended the regency of her daughter, and she made way for her son, Hayam Wuruk, who reigned under the name Rājasanagara.

CHAPTER XIV

THE END OF THE INDIAN KINGDOMS

From the Middle of the Fourteenth Century to the Seizure of Malacca by the Portuguese in 1511

The middle of the fourteenth century may be considered a turning point in the history of Farther India. The year 1347 was marked by both the founding of the Burmese kingdom of Toungoo, from which the creator of the powerful Burmese state of Pegu was to arise in the sixteenth century, and the founding of the Sumatran kingdom of Ādityavarman, a kingdom that still bore the name of Malāyu but already corresponded to the future Minangkabau. The year 1353 saw both the founding of the Laotian kingdom of Lan Chang by Fa Ngum and the restoration of Haṃsavatī (Pegu) by Binnya U.

By an unusual coincidence, 1350 saw both the accession of Hayam Wuruk (Rājasanagara), the greatest king of Majapahit, the king who extended its suzerainty to its farthest limits, and the accession of Rāmādhipati, the founder of Ayutthaya, the unifier of the countries of Syāṃ (Sukhothai) and Lavo (Lopburi). Ayutthaya and Majapahit, the first continental, the second insular, became the two poles of Farther India, the greatest part of which was thus divided into two zones of influence. The lists of the dependencies of Ayutthaya and Majapahit even overlap to some extent in the southern part of the Malay Peninsula.

It is significant that the regrouping of the small states within the spheres of influence of these two great powers took place just at the time of the beginning of the decline of the Mongol dynasty, which had followed the opposite policy of encouraging the creation of numerous small principalities whose obedience was easier to maintain.

The history of the states that arose around 1350—the Thai kingdoms of Ayutthaya and Lan Chang, the Burmese kingdoms of Toungoo and Ava—lies outside the scope of the present work, devoted as it is to the ancient period of Farther India. It will suffice here to follow the Indian kingdoms of Southeast Asia up to their decline, relating very briefly what happened in Cambodia up to the abandonment of Angkor around 1430, in Champa up to the conquest of Vijaya by the Vietnamese in 1470, in Malaysia and the archipelago up to the seizure of Malacca by the Portuguese in 1511.

1. CAMBODIA: FROM 1350 TO THE ABANDONMENT OF ANGKOR IN THE MIDDLE OF THE FIFTEENTH CENTURY

Cambodia in the middle of the fourteenth century [1] was the only one of these old kingdoms whose kings still resided in their ancient capital; the Khmer kings still occupied Yaśodharapura (Angkor). But they were hardly secure there. As early as 1352, Rāmādhipati, founder and first king of Ayutthaya, went to lay siege to the city,[2] where Lampong-rājā, son of Nirvāṇapada (1346–51), was then reigning. If we believe the *Annals of Ayutthaya,* Angkor was seized the following year and the king of Siam placed one of his sons on the throne. This prince died almost immediately. Two other Siamese princes, one succeeding the other, reigned until 1357, when a brother of Lampong-rājā who had taken refuge in Laos reconquered the city and was crowned there under the name of Sūryavaṃśa Rājādhirāja.[3]

Sūryavaṃśa Rājādhirāja defended his country from new Siamese attacks and seems to have maintained his border at Khorat in the north and at Pračhin in the west. It may have been he who in 1370 received an order from the first Ming emperor to submit and send tribute immediately; the *History of the Ming* calls this king Hu-erh-na.[4] He reigned about twenty years and was succeeded by one of his nephews, a son of Lampong-rājā, known under the name of Paramarāma.

In 1379, the *History of the Ming* [5] mentions for the first time King Ts'an-ta Kan-wu-che-ch'e-ta-che (Samdach Kambujādhirāja). This king must undoubtedly be identified with Paramarāma, but we know nothing else about him.

Around 1380, Paramarāma was succeeded by his brother Dhammāsokarājādhirāja,[6] who appears in 1387 in the *History of the Ming* [7] under the name of Ts'an-lie Pao-p'i-sie Kan-p'u-che (Samdach Chao Ponhea Kambuja).

In 1393, the King of Siam, Ramesuan (Rāmeśvara), invaded Cambodia and besieged its capital. According to the Siamese annals, Angkor was taken the following year.[8] King Dhammāsoka was killed and replaced by a son of the king of Siam, Indarāja, but Indarāja was soon assassinated.[9]

The History of the Ming[10] mentions under the date 1404 a King Ts'an-lie P'o-p'i-ya (Samdach Chao Ponhea), whose identity is not known.[11] His death was announced at the court of China in 1405, and he was succeeded by his son Ts'an-lie Chao-p'ing-ya,[12] who certainly corresponds to the Chao Ponhea Yat of Cambodian sources.[13] Chao Ponhea Yat took the glorious name Sūryavarman upon his accession. It was during the course of his long reign of almost fifty years, in 1431, that the decision was taken to abandon the capital because it was too exposed and too difficult to defend. After a short stay at Basan (Srei Santhor), from which he was driven by floods, Chao Ponhea Yat proceeded to establish himself at the Quatre-Bras (Four Branches), on the site of the present-day city of Phnom Penh.[14]

2. CHAMPA: FROM THE ACCESSION OF CHÊ BÔNG NGA (1360) TO THE FINAL ABANDONMENT OF VIJAYA (1471)

In chapter nine of his *Royaume de Champa,* Georges Maspero gives an account of the reign of Chê Bông Nga under the title "L'apogée." This term runs the risk of giving a completely inaccurate idea of the importance of this reign. It is true that the reign was rich in military glory, but this glory can be compared to the last rays of a setting sun. In view of the dynamism of the Vietnamese and their centuries-long demographic pressure, the attempts at reconquest by Chê Bông Nga were something of an anachronism and his hold over reconquered areas was doomed in advance to be short-lived.

We do not know the origins of Chê Bông Nga, whom the *History of the Ming* calls Ngo-ta Ngo-che and who seems to have survived in the historic legend of the Chams under the name of Binasuor.[15] His reign must have begun around 1360. By taking advantage first of all of the decline of the Mongols and later coming to an agreement with the first Ming emperor, who recognized him as king of Champa in 1369,[16] he was able to lead a series of victorious campaigns against Đai Viêt from 1361 to 1390. These campaigns were almost continuous: in 1361, the pillage of the port of Đa-li;[17] in 1368, the defeat of the Vietnamese in a place called "Cham Cavern" in present-day Quang-nam;[18] in 1371, the invasion of the Tongking Delta and the sack of

Hanoi;[19] in 1377, the defeat of the Vietnamese before Vijaya (Cha-ban) in Binh-đinh and the killing of King Trân Duê-tông, followed by a new invasion of Tongking and a new pillage of Hanoi;[20] in 1380, the pillage of Nghê-an and Thanh-hoa;[21] in 1384, an attack on Tongking by land;[22] in 1389, a new victorious campaign in Tongking which brought the Chams to the present-day province of Hưng-yên.[23] "At this point the treason of a low-ranking officer stopped the victorious march of the Chams and saved Annam from an invasion in which its independence might have been destroyed."[24] Chê Bông Nga, whose ship was surrounded, was killed (February, 1390), and his troops withdrew.

One of Chê Bông Nga's generals, whom the Vietnamese sources call La Khai and a Cham inscription of Binh-đinh calls Jaya Siṃhavarman,[25] succeeded him after driving out his sons. Jaya Siṃhavarman had to abandon to Đai Viêt all the territory situated north of the Col des Nuages (an area corresponding to the present-day provinces of Quang-binh, Quang-tri, and Thưa-thiên), which had been recovered by his predecessor.[26]

He died in 1400 and was replaced by his son Ngauk Klaung Vijaya, who first took the name Vīrabhadravarman and in 1432 was crowned under the name of Indravarman.[27] The *History of the Ming* calls him Chang-pa-ti-lai (Champādhirāja); the Vietnamese annals call him Ba Đich-lai.

His reign began badly, for in 1402, in order to avoid a new war with Đai Viêt, he had to cede the province of Indrapura, corresponding to present-day Quang-nam, in the northern part of the territory of Amarāvatī.[28] This is the region where the heart of ancient Champa beat in the sanctuary of Bhadreśvara (Mi-sơn). He regained it in 1407[29] thanks to the support of China, which had just annexed Đai Viêt outright in suppressing the usurping dynasty of the Hô (1400–1407).

Now safe in the north, the Cham king took vengeance on Cambodia, where Chao Ponhea Yat, the last king of Angkor, was reigning. In 1421 he commemorated his victories over the Khmers by the inscription of Vishnu of Biên-hoa.[30]

Peaceful relations between Champa and its neighbor to the north were re-established in 1428 with the accession of Lê Lơi, the liberator of Vietnam.[31]

A Javanese tradition that is difficult to reconcile with the last evidence of Cham epigraphy, still completely Hindu, claims that at the beginning of the fifteenth century Islam was introduced to Java by a Cham princess, a sister of the king, who was married to one of the sovereigns of Majapahit.[32] We have, however, no real proof that Islam had penetrated into Champa before the Chams were driven out of Vijaya in 1471.

After the long and relatively successful reign of Ngauk Klaung Vijaya, or Indravarman VI, which came to an end in 1441, the country fell into a rapid decline. In thirty years, five kings succeeded to the throne in the midst of civil wars and Vietnamese invasions of the Lê kings Nhân-tông and Thanh-tông.[33] The Cham capital, Vijaya, in Binh-đinh (Cha-ban) was taken by the Vietnamese in 1446,[34] then reconquered by the Chams. In 1471, it fell permanently into the hands of the Vietnamese, who killed 60,000 people there and took away 30,000 prisoners, among whom were the king and 50 members of the royal family.[35] From then on, Champa continued to exist for a while, but it was reduced to the territories situated south of Cape Varella, where today are located the last remnants of the Cham people.[36]

3. JAVA: FROM THE ACCESSION OF HAYAM WURUK (RĀJASANAGARA) IN 1350 TO THE END OF THE KINGDOM OF MAJAPAHIT AROUND 1520

In Java the long reign of Rājasanagara (1350–89) marks the apogee of the kingdom of Majapahit. The reign opened with a bloody drama, the victim of which was a certain King Mahārāja whom an inscription of 1333[37] presents as the founder of the kingdom of Pajajaran, a Sundanese kingdom that still occupied the western part of the island of Java at the beginning of the sixteenth century.[38] In 1357 he came to Majapahit, bringing his daughter who was to marry Rājasanagara, and established himself with his followers at Bubat, north of the capital. He thought the marriage was to be a union between equals, but the prime minister, Gajah Mada, insisted on treating the fiancée as a vassal princess brought in tribute. The discussion degenerated into an armed conflict in which the Sundanese king and his followers met their death.[39]

The expansion of Javanese suzerainty in the time of Rājasanagara is evident from the list of dependencies of Majapahit transmitted by the *Nāgarakṛitāgama*.[40] Roughly, the kingdom comprised all of what was to become the Dutch East Indies (with perhaps the exception of the north of Celebes) and a great part of the Malay Peninsula,[41] but it did not extend to the Philippines.

In Bali, the charters of 1384–86 in the name of Vijayarājasa, or Bhre Wengker,[42] seem to indicate that this uncle of Rājasanagara exercised a sort of viceroyalty, if not true sovereignty, there. The intensive Javanization of Bali in the fourteenth century, the initial cause of which was the conquest of 1343, was more important for the ultimate destiny of the island than the mass Javanese emigration of the following century.[43]

A Javanese inscription of this period found on the island of Sumbawa[44] constitutes tangible evidence of the expansion of Majapahit in the east of the archipelago. According to the *Nāgarakṛitāgama,*[45] the countries maintaining friendly relations with Majapahit were Syangkāyodhyapura ("Siam with Ayutthaya"), Dharmanagarī (Ligor), Marutma (Martaban), Rājapura (?), Singhanagarī (?), Champā, Kamboja, and Yavana (Đai Viêt).

Information on the relations of Rājasanagara with China is provided by the *History of the Ming,*[46] which mentions between 1370 and 1381 many embassies from King Pa-ta-na-pa-na-wu, or Bhatara Prabhu, which is simply a royal title. Between the entries concerning the embassies of 1377 and 1379 the Chinese text notes that there was on the island of Java a king in the west and a king in the east: the first was named Wu-lao-po-wu, another transcription of Bhatara (or, rather, Bhra) Prabhu; the second was named Wu-yüan-lao-wang-chieh,[47] which in my opinion represents Bhre Wengker, or Vijayarājasa, whose decrees in Bali in 1384–86 have been mentioned above. If the information given by the *History of the Ming* for 1377–79 is accurate for this period, it seems clear that the division of the kingdom in two, which must have had fatal consequences for the following reign, dates from the reign of Rājasanagara, who entrusted to his uncle the government of one part of his domain.

The *Nāgarakṛitāgama,* a historical poem composed during this reign by Prapancha,[48] gives some idea of the internal administration of the country at the beginning of the reign.[49] At the center was the king, assisted by his father, Kṛitavardhana, and his uncle, Vijayarājasa. Below them was a hierarchy of officials headed by a council of five ministers. The most important of these ministers, the *mapatih* (*mahāpati*), was the old Gajah Mada. He disappeared from the scene in 1364, after a half-century devoted to service of the dynasty. His name is connected with the drafting of a law code of which we have only a later version.[50]

Aside from Prapancha, the author of the *Nāgarakṛitāgama* already mentioned, the reign of Rājasanagara was, from the literary point of view, given luster by the poet Tantular, the author of the *Arjunavijaya* and of the *Purushādaśānta* (or *Sutasoma*). The *Purushādaśānta* is particularly valuable for the information it gives on Siva-Buddha syncretism.[51]

The religious monuments of the reign are numerous. The only one worth mentioning here is the central temple of Panataran,[52] with its famous bas-reliefs representing scenes of the *Rāmāyaṇa* and of the *Kṛishṇāyana*. It was begun in 1347 during the regency period, but it was completed by Rājasanagara and it was his favorite sanctuary.

Rājasanagara died in 1389. He was succeeded by Vikramavardhana, who was both his nephew and his son-in-law. Vikramavardhana's reign marks the beginning of the decline of Majapahit, a decline that accelerated greatly during the reigns of his successors. The main cause of the decline was the development of Malacca as a commercial center and a nucleus for the diffusion of Islam. Islam, introduced at first on the coast,[53] soon penetrated to the interior. The oldest evidence of the presence of Islam in the island is the inscription of Leran, dated either 1082 or 1102,[54] but it is a completely isolated document. Then comes the inscription of 1419 at Gresik [55] on the tomb of Malik Ibrahim, who was perhaps a propagator of the new religion.

Another cause of Majapahit's decline was the war of succession between Vikramavardhana and his brother-in-law Vīrabhūmi, a son of Rājasanagara by a concubine. Vīrabhūmi was established in the east as his great-uncle Vijayarājasa (Bhre Wengker) had been. Hostilities began in 1401 and ended in 1406 with the death of Vīrabhūmi.[56]. This war of succession resulted not only in the weakening of the kingdom of Majapahit but also, indirectly, in the founding of Malacca in 1403 if it is true that the creator of this new political and commercial center, Parameśvara, was one of the protagonists who later fled from Java to take refuge at Tumasik (Singapore).[57]

Still another reason for the decline of Majapahit was the effort China made, under the emperor Yung Lo, to supplant Java as suzerain over the archipelago and on the peninsula: to effect this was one of the aims of the famous missions of the eunuch Cheng Ho,[58] which resulted in the sending of various embassies to China from the former tributaries of Majapahit.[59]

Suhitā, the daughter of Vikramavardhana, reigned until 1447 and was succeeded by her brother Bhre Tumapel, or Kṛitavijaya (1447–51).[60] From this period it seems that the Indian cults, already contaminated by native rites, withdrew before the advance of Islam. They withdrew to the mountains, which were generally the ancient places of the pre-Indian Indonesian cults. There are records of the building of religious edifices connected with Indian cults on the Penangungan in 1434–42, on the Wilis in 1449, on the Merbabu in 1438 and 1449, and on the Lawu in 1437–57.[61]

The genealogical relationships among the last kings, Rājasavardhana (1451–53), Pūrvaviśesha (1456–66), Singhavikramavardhana (1466–78),[62] are obscure, and the dates given for them are subject to revision.

In 1478, Majapahit put down an invasion (the origin of this invasion is disputed),[63] and in 1486 there appeared a new dynasty, that of the Girīndravardhana. This dynasty was still Indian in culture, as its charters show.[64] The last embassy from Java to China was in 1499.[65] Islam made rapid progress; the last positive evidence of Hinduism in Java dates from 1513–15,[66] not long after the seizure of Malacca by the Portuguese.

Evidence of the existence of the kingdom of Majapahit ends between 1513 and 1528, but what remained of the kingdom cannot be said to have fallen suddenly under the blows of the Muslims. There was rather a progressive weakening of the capital at the same time that the port establishments in Muslim hands increased in prosperity and power.[67]

Indian culture took refuge in certain districts of the east, and especially on Bali. Thus, this island became, and to the present has remained, an intellectual center preserving the essentials of Indo-Javanese literature and religion which Islam rapidly caused to disappear in Java. Bali played the same role of preserver for Java as Tibet did for Buddhist India.

4. SUMATRA: THE HEIRS OF THE OLD KINGDOM OF THE MAHARAJA IN THE FOURTEENTH CENTURY

In Sumatra, in the region of Minangkabau, Ādityavarman continued to reign at least until 1375, the date of the last inscription we have from him.[68] It is undoubtedly this king, whose fervor for Tantric Buddhism of the *kālachakra* we have seen, who is represented in the form of Śiva Bhairava in the beautiful statue of Sungei Langsat.[69]

His Yuvarāja, or heir apparent, was his son Anangavarman; we do not know if he actually succeeded him.[70]

For the east coast of the island we lack information on the period between 1350, the date of the *Tao-i Chih-lioh,* and 1370, the date when the first Ming emperor sent ambassadors to foreign countries to obtain the tribute of vassalage.

In 1371 the *History of the Ming* mentions a King Ma-ha-la-cha Pa-la-pu (Maharaja Prabhu) [71] of San-fo-ch'i, whose center was then Jambi; in 1373, a King Ta-ma-sha-na-a-che; [72] in 1376, the replacement of the latter by his son Ma-na-che Wu-li (Maharaja Mauli . . .).[73]

But at this time the country was divided among three kings; [74] the two others were Ma-na-ha Pao-lin-pang (Maharaja Palembang), who sent an embassy to China in 1374, and Seng-ch'ia-lieh-yu-lan,[75] who sent one in 1375. We have seen that the latter was perhaps the former Javanese ambassador who had been sent to China in 1325 and 1332 by the court of Majapahit.[76]

We do not know how the three kings divided the ancient territory of Śrīvijaya. But the title of Maharaja Palembang in itself gives his location, and that of Maharaja Mauli . . . indicates an heir of the Maulivarmadeva of Malāyu and therefore a king reigning in the Jambi region and in the valley of the Batang Hari. In 1376, the latter obtained from the emperor of China the restored title of "King of San-fo-ch'i," but according to the *History of the Ming:* [77] "At that time however San-bo-tsai [San-fo-ch'i] had already been conquered by Java, and the king of this country, hearing that the Emperor had appointed a king over San-bo-tsai, became very angry and sent men who waylaid and killed the imperial envoys."

The Javanese conquest mentioned here was apparently a punitive expedition against a vassal that was displaying a distressing tendency toward independence.[78] "After this occurrence," adds the *History of the Ming,* San-fo-ch'i "became gradually poorer and no tribute was brought from this country any more." [79] And further on: "At that time Java had completely conquered San-bo-tsai and changed its name to Ku-kang [the old estuary (of the

Musi), or Palembang].[80] When San-bo-tsai went down, the whole country was disturbed and the Javanese could not keep all the land; for this reason the Chinese, who were established there, stood up for themselves, and a man from Nan-hai (Namhoi) in Canton, called Liang Tau-ming, who had lived there a long time and roamed over the sea, followed by several thousand men from Fukien and Canton, was taken by them as their chief." [81]

I shall leave off here with the history of the old impoverished Sumatran kingdom, in full decline, fallen into the hands of Chinese pirates. We have seen that the inheritance of its former dependencies had been divided between the suzerainties of Siam and Java. A Siamese law that is dated 1358, but must actually be from the fifteenth century,[82] cites Uyong Tanah (Johore), Malākā, Malāyu, and Varavāri [83] as southern dependencies of Ayutthaya. For its part, the *Nāgarakṛitāgama,* in 1365, enumerates the following as possessions of Majapahit: [84]

On the Malay Peninsula:

> Pahang, Hujung Tanah (Johore), Lengkasuka, Sai (Saiburi), Kalanten, Tringgano, Naśor (Pattani??), Paka (south of Dungun), Muwar (northwest of Johore), Dungun (south of Trengganu), Tumasik (Singapore), Sang Hyang Hujung (Cape Rachado), Kelang (Trang), Keḍa, Jere (Gunung Jerai, near Kedah), Kanjap (?), and Nirān (?);

On Sumatra:

> Jambi, Palembang, Karitang (south of Indragiri), Teba (i.e., Toba, upper Jambi), Dharmāśraya (upper Batang Hari), Kaṇḍis (north of Dharmāśraya), Kahwas (west of Kaṇḍis), Manangkabo, Siyak, Rekan (Rokan, south of Panai), Kāmpar, Panai, Kampe, Haru (south of Kampe), Maṇḍahiling, Tumihang, Parlāk, Barat (western coast of Achin), Lawas (south of Perlak), Samudra, Lāmurī, Batan (?), Lampung, and Barus.[85]

But the true heirs of the commercial prosperity of Śrīvijaya were the Arabs, who monopolized the spice trade and made themselves the allies and protectors of the little Malay states. China, after the great maritime voyages of the reign of Yung Lo, retreated into itself and from then on was content with a nominal political suzerainty over the countries of the south.

With the Arabs masters of commerce, Islam, which had already obtained a foothold in Sumatra in the state of Perlak (Marco Polo), then in that of Samudra (Ibn Baṭūṭa), spread rapidly over the island. At the beginning of the fifteenth century Ma Huan, the

Chinese Muslim who accompanied the eunuch Cheng Ho on the mission of 1413, noted in his *Ying-yai Sheng-lan* the existence of Islam in the states of A-lu (Haru) and Nan-po-li (Lambri).[86] The importance of the northern part of Sumatra as a center for the diffusion of Islam stems from the fact that in the thirteenth century Pasai, neighbor of Samudra, had replaced Kedah (on the peninsula) as the commercial center of the area.[87] In the fifteenth century, Malacca supplanted Pasai, but after the fall of Malacca, Sumatra became, with the rise of Achin, once more the principal Muslim commercial center.[88]

5. MALACCA: FROM ITS FOUNDATION IN 1403 TO ITS SEIZURE BY THE PORTUGUESE IN 1511

Malacca is not mentioned by Marco Polo or Odoric of Pordenone or Ibn Baṭūṭa or even the *Nāgarakṛitāgama* (1365).[89] It is possible that there may already have been an establishment of Sumatran origin on this site and that the stone *makara* of St. Paul's Hill is what remains of such an establishment.[90] But as a political and commercial center, Malacca really dates only from the first years of the fifteenth century.

The founder of Malacca was a certain Parameśvara, who was, according to Albuquerque, a native of Palembang and who was, in any case, the husband of a princess of Majapahit.[91] He revolted, probably following the death of Hayam Wuruk (1389), taking advantage of the decline of the power of Majapahit which followed that event. He then took refuge at Tumasik (Singapore), which, of all the peninsular possessions of the kingdom of Palembang, was the most distant from the kingdom of Ayutthaya. He slew its Malay chief, who governed in the name of Siam or, more probably, of a vassal of Siam (Pahang or Pattani). After reigning a few years at Tumasik, he was driven out by Ayutthaya and fled first to Muar, then to Bertam, and finally to Malacca, where the eunuch Yin-ch'ing found him established in 1403.[92] His policy consisted of relying on China. In 1405, he sent an embassy to China, after which the emperor conferred the title "King of Malacca" on him. After the visit of the eunuch Cheng Ho in 1409, he himself visited China with his family in 1411.[93] He founded at Malacca the basis of a prosperous settlement[94] and returned to China for another visit in 1414. He and his family went to China again in 1419[95] to request support against Siam, with which Malacca was in a chronic state of hostility, for the kingdom of Ayutthaya was seeking to substitute its suzerainty for that of weakening Majapahit. He married a daughter of the king of Pasai, whose dynasty may have maintained claims over the former peninsular possessions of Palembang, and was converted to Islam at the age of seventy-two.[96] From then on he took the name Megat Iskandar Shah.[97]

He was succeeded in 1424 by his son, Śrī Mahārāja, who went to China in the year of his accession. He returned there in 1433 with his family and sent embassies there until 1435.[98] At his death in 1444, he was replaced by his son Raja Ibrahim,[99] whom the *History of the Ming* calls Si-li Pa-mi-si-wa-erh-ch'ü-pa Sha [100] (Śrī Parameśvaradeva Shah).[101]

Raja Ibrahim was killed after two years in the course of a palace revolution that placed his half-brother, Raja Kasim, on the throne. Raja Kasim was the son of a concubine who was the daughter of a Tamil Muslim merchant of Pasai.[102] He took the title of Muzaffar Shah [103] and reigned thirteen years, until 1459.

Raja Kasim's son Sultan Mansur Shah [104] enlarged his state, incorporating into it notably the tin-bearing districts of the kingdom of Kedah,[105] but he was the victim of harem intrigues.[106] At his death in October 1477,[107] he was succeeded by his son Ala'ud-din Riayat Shah, who died mysteriously in 1488 and was replaced by his younger brother Mahmud, the last sultan of Malacca.[108]

Malacca became a first-rate political power that was capable of resisting the pressure of Siam; a great commercial center; and a powerful nucleus of Islamic expansion. This was the era when Vasco da Gama, after rounding the Cape of Good Hope, arrived at Calicut (1498), opening a new route to the spice trade which had made the fortune of the Arabs and Venetians. The Portuguese soon pushed farther to the east, in search of the sources of production of these luxuries so much sought after in Europe. On August 1, 1509, the first Portuguese vessels, under the command of Admiral Diogo Lopes de Sequeira, entered Malacca. On land some members of the expedition were badly treated, and in revenge for this two years later Affonso de Albuquerque, the conqueror of Goa (November 25, 1510), appeared at Malacca. Taking advantage of the unrest that reigned in the city, he seized it on August 10, 1511, a date that marks the beginning of a new period in the history of the countries of the Far East.

CONCLUSION

A review of the fourteen centuries of history treated in this work will help to clarify the sequence of the main events and the relationship between them. And, as I have indicated in the "Introduction," it can be seen at a glance that the twelve chapters devoted to this history (Chapters III to XIV) correspond roughly to as many epochs, each set off by critical dates that are related to developments in India and, even more closely, to developments in China.

The history of the first Indian kingdoms in Southeast Asia begins in the second century A.D. The oldest and best known of these kingdoms, thanks to the Chinese historians, are Funan and Lin-yi. Funan, predecessor of Cambodia in the lower Mekong Basin, extended its conquests to the Malay Peninsula in the second century and seems to have been a sort of empire or federation of small Indianized states whose sovereigns bore the title "King of the Mountain." Lin-yi, or ancient Champa, which had its cradle in the Hué region, sought to expand to the north only to run into the expansive drive of the Vietnamese toward the south and into the political opposition of the Chinese Empire. This was the prologue of a drama that for centuries set the Indianized Chams in opposition to the Sinicized Vietnamese. (Chapter III)

In the middle of the fourth century, the conquests of the emperor Samudragupta in the Ganges Valley and southern India provoked a new exodus to the east that resulted not only in the coming to power of an Indo-Scythian in Funan but also in a general resurgence of Indianization abroad in which southern India, especially the region dominated by the Pallavas of Kānchī, seems to have played a preponderant role. Inscriptions, almost nonexistent before the fourth century, reveal the presence in the fifth century of small Indian kingdoms on Borneo and Java. Such epigraphic evidence permits us to cross-check the data relating to Funan and Lin-yi contained in the Chinese annals from the fourth to sixth centuries. (Chapter IV)

This whole period is characterized by the supremacy of Funan. It is significant that the period corresponds roughly to a troubled era in the history of China: that of the Three Kingdoms and the Six Dynasties.

In the second half of the sixth century the empire of Funan in the lower Mekong Valley collapsed. The kingdom of the Khmers, or Kambujas, was built on its ruins. At the same time, two new powers appeared in the western part of the Indochinese Peninsula: the Mons in the Menam Basin, cradle of the kingdom of Dvāravatī, and the Pyus in the Irrawaddy Basin. The weakness of the Chinese Chin and Ch'en dynasties facilitated the strengthening of the authority of the Cham kings on the coasts both above and below the Col des Nuages. Java began to enter into history with the appearance of a state called Ho-ling in the Chinese histories. (Chapter V)

The birth and rapid expansion of the Sumatran kingdom of Śrīvijaya (Palembang) at the end of the seventh century, an indirect consequence of the dismemberment of Funan, marks the beginning of a new era. In Cambodia, during the whole of the eighth century, there was virtual anarchy, and the country was divided into upper and lower regions; in Champa, the central power withdrew to the south of the country. In central Java during the second half of the eighth century, a Buddhist dynasty abruptly succeeded a Sivaite sovereign. This new dynasty revived the imperial title "King of the Mountain" (*śailendra*), covered the country with great Buddhist monuments, and seems to have exercised a sort of hegemony in the southern seas that extended even to Cambodia. At the same time, a series of maritime raids, conducted from the Sunda Islands, ravaged the coasts of the Indochinese Peninsula from north to south. This agitated period, which followed the accession of the T'ang emperors in China and coincided with the apogee of the Buddhist dynasty of Java, also saw the expansion of Mahayana Buddhism in Farther India under the influence of the Indian Pāla dynasty and the university of Nālandā in Bengal. (Chapter VI)

In the ninth century, the power of the Buddhist Śailendras in Java progressively declined. This decline facilitated the revival of the Khmer kingdom in 802, its liberation from Javanese suzerainty, and the foundation of the Angkorian royal house, which was to be one of the dominant powers of Farther India for four centuries. The decline of the Buddhist dynasty of Java was accompanied by a Sivaite renaissance in the center of the island, a renaissance that had its origin in the east, to which the princes of the former Sivaite dynasty had retired. The Śailendras did not disappear, however; they established a new center of power in Sumatra at Śrīvijaya, which they had governed in the middle of the ninth century as a dependency, and their power there was to last for many centuries. The two future protagonists of Burmese history, the Mon kingdom of Pegu and the Burmese kingdom of Pagan, founded their respective capitals within the space of a few years during the first quarter of the ninth century. (Chapter VII)

At the end of the ninth century and during the tenth, Angkorian civilization flowered, the center of the Cham kingdom was re-established in the Quang-nam region by the Indrapura dynasty, and the maritime power of Śrīvijaya was built up as a result of its complete mastery of the straits. These developments coincided with the weakening of the authority of China toward the end of the T'ang and during the Five Dynasties. Near the end of the tenth century, China, restored by the accession of the Sung, was once more in a position to interfere in the southern seas and it played a part in the quarrels between the Śailendras of Sumatra and the Javanese sovereigns of the kingdom of Matarām that had been established in the east of the island. (Chapter VIII)

The first three-quarters of the eleventh century was a period rich in strong personalities and events of great consequence. In Cambodia, Sūryavarman I, the founder of a new dynasty in 1002, extended his sovereignty to the Menam at the expense of the Mons who had previously occupied the valley. His reign corresponds almost exactly with that of Airlanga, who drew Java out of the anarchy into which the aggressive policy of Śrīvijaya had plunged it, enlarged the territory of his reconquered states, and took advantage of the temporary weakness of Śrīvijaya following a Choḷa raid around 1025 to confine his old rival to Sumatra and force it to accede to an alliance. Just at the time when Sūryavarman I and Airlanga disappeared from the scene in the middle of the eleventh century, Anôratha, the king of

Pagan, pushed his conquests into the Irrawaddy Delta and brought back to Pagan Mon civilization, including its Theravada Buddhism, which he firmly established in his country. (Chapter IX)

The weakening of the Chinese Sung dynasty at the end of the eleventh century favored the ambitions of the Khmer, Cham, and Burmese sovereigns. In Cambodia, a new dynasty founded in 1080 by the conquering king Sūryavarman II, the builder of Angkor Wat, brought the country to a peak of power for the first time, but the troubles that followed Sūryavarman's death led the country to the brink of ruin and resulted in the seizure of Angkor by the Chams in 1177. In Burma, the successors of Anôratha enlarged their state and covered the capital with monuments. In Indonesia, the Sumatran kingdom continued to play the role of a great maritime power, while the kingdom of Kaḍiri in Java, heir of the states of Airlanga, pursued a relatively peaceful policy. (Chapter X)

At the end of the twelfth century, Cambodia, in an almost miraculous recovery, reached a second peak under the Buddhist king Jayavarman VII, the great builder of temples; it annexed Champa for about twenty years and then, after the exertion of this immense effort, began to decline. In Burma, the cultural influence was felt through the intermediary of Ceylon: Singhalese Buddhism, revived in the island by King Parākramabāhu in the twelfth century, penetrated to Burma, a center from which it was to radiate over the Indochinese Peninsula. In Indonesia, Malāyu (Jambi) prepared to assume the inheritance of Śrīvijaya (Palembang), which was beginning to show signs of age and disintegration. On Java, the advent of the kingdom of Singhasāri, which succeeded Kaḍiri in 1222, marked the beginning of the retreat of Indian culture before the resurgence of the Indonesian substratum. (Chapter XI)

The Mongol conquests of the thirteenth century and the attempts of Kublai Khan, successor of the Sung emperors, to establish hegemony over the countries of the southern seas beginning in 1260 had severe repercussions in these countries.[1] The campaigns of the Mongol military chiefs in Champa, Burma, and Java, and the policy of the court of Peking favoring the splitting-up of the old Indian states into small principalities, led in the first half of the thirteenth century to the liberation of the Thai of the middle Menam, who had previously been under the

Khmers, and to the foundation of the Thai kingdom of Sukhothai. The last fifteen years of the thirteenth century saw the fall of the kingdom of Pagan, which was destroyed in 1287 by the Mongols, and the expansion of the Thai into Burma. These years also saw the expansion of the Thai in the valleys of the Menam's upper tributaries at the expense of the Mons and in the lower basin of this river and on the Mekong at the expense of the Khmers. At the same time, the Chams abandoned the provinces north of the Col des Nuages to the Vietnamese. And on Java the Javanese kingdom of Majapahit, founded in 1292, exerted a pressure on the Sumatran kingdom that, combined with the expansion of the Thai of Sukhothai in the Malay Peninsula, led to the dismemberment of the old empire of the maharajas. The Muslim invasions in India proper and the spread of Islam in Indonesia sounded the death knell for Indian culture in Farther India. At the same time, Singhalese Buddhism, introduced from Burma to Siam, made rapid progress in the riverine lands of the Menam and the Mekong. (Chapter XII)

In the first half of the fourteenth century, the Thai consolidated their hold on the Indochinese Peninsula. Already masters of Burma and the upper Menam Valley (kingdoms of Sukhothai and Lan Na), they founded at the same time the Laotian kingdom of Lan Chang on the Mekong and the kingdom of Ayutthaya in the basin of the lower Menam. The Ayutthayan kingdom soon absorbed its neighbor to the north, the kingdom of Sukhothai. Cambodia, threatened by its former vassals, was able, thanks to the prestige of its former glory, to transmit to the Thai what it had preserved of Indian culture. Champa submitted more and more to Vietnamese pressure from the north. In the south, Majapahit exercised an unchallenged suzerainty, for Śrīvijaya had perished. The Indian period in Farther India was coming to an end. (Chapter XIII)

The decline of the Mongol dynasty in the second half of the fourteenth century facilitated the regrouping of the small states under the spheres of influence of the two great powers: Ayutthaya and Majapahit. The abandonment of Angkor by the Khmer kings in the middle of the fifteenth century and the abandonment of Vijaya by the Chams in 1471 marked the final withdrawal of the two old Indianized kingdoms before the "push to the south" of the Thai and Vietnamese. In Indonesia, Islam triumphed in Java around 1520, and Indian culture took refuge in the island of Bali. Malacca, heir of the commercial power of the Sumatran kingdoms from the beginning of the fifteenth century, fell into the hands of the Europeans in 1511. (Chapter XIV)

It is apparent from this résumé that Farther India felt the repercussions of political events in India and, even more so, those in China and that it received over the centuries contributions from the great spiritual currents of India.

Although Farther India was the theater of revolutionary changes, these changes had no notable effects on the history of the world, and, except in the realm of the arts, the area did not enrich the intellectual patrimony of humanity with any masterpieces.

It is because of this purely receptive character that Farther India was so long ignored. It has not entered history except to the extent that it was civilized by India. Without India, its past would be almost unknown; we would know scarcely more about it than we know about the past of New Guinea or Australia.

Even though the countries whose history is outlined in this work owe everything from their titles of nobility to their privilege of possessing a history to India, it would be unjust to pass silently over what Farther India contributed indirectly in exchange. First of all, the region gave the Indians the feeling of having been, in the noblest sense of the term, a great colonizing people, in spite of all the ritual obstacles and racial prejudices that would seem to have prohibited them from playing such a role. The expansive power of their culture and the dynamism of their civilization, of which the Indians seem never to have been completely conscious, manifested themselves in all the countries to which they emigrated.

Study of Farther India, then, provides very valuable documentation that cannot help but further our knowledge of ancient India. General observation shows us that colonies preserve in their customs, beliefs, and language many archaic traits that date back to the origin of colonization and fall into disuse in the mother country. Farther India has been no exception to this rule, and the study of ancient India "viewed from the East,"[2] which has scarcely begun,[3] seems to promise rich results.

But the importance of studying the Indianized countries of Southeast Asia—which, let us repeat, were never political dependencies of India, but rather cultural colonies—lies above all in the observation of the impact of Indian civilization on the primitive civilizations. The present work has no other object than to provide the historical and chronological framework of the implantation of Indian culture and its continued transformation on contact with the native societies. We can measure the power of penetration of this culture by the importance of that which remains of it in these countries even though all of them except Siam passed sooner or later under European domination and a great part of the area was converted to Islam.

Except on the island of Bali[4] and among some Cham groups,[5] the Indian cults in their old form—Sivaism, Vishnuism, the Theravada Buddhism that used the Sanskrit language, and Mahayana Buddhism—have disappeared, but not without leaving traces. In Phnom Penh and Bangkok, Brahmans of very mixed blood, Brahmans who follow Buddhism but wear chignons and the Brahman thread, officiate at all the great royal ceremonies, the ritual of which is an inheritance from the Indian epoch.[6] But these ceremonies are holdovers that interest only the court and do not affect the general population.

In the twelfth and thirteenth centuries the common people received a new contribution from India in the form of Singhalese Buddhism. The penetration of this new faith to the masses cannot be doubted: in Cambodia, Siam, Laos, and Burma, Buddhist cosmogony and cosmology and the doctrines of retribution for one's acts and of transmigration have been deeply implanted in the humblest classes by the teaching of the Buddhist monks.

It is difficult to say what would have happened in Indonesia if Islam had not come to cut the spiritual ties with Brahmanic India. The mildness and tolerance of Islam in Java are often attributed to the character of the Javanese population. But Javanese peoples are not fundamentally different in origin from the other Indonesian peoples, the Bataks of Sumatra, the Dayaks of Borneo, and the mountain people of the Indochinese cordillera, none of whom are known for the gentleness of their ways. So we may ask ourselves if the particular aspect assumed by Islam in Java was not due rather to the influence that Indian religions exercised over the character of the inhabitants of the island for more than ten centuries.

The literary heritage from ancient India is even more apparent than the religious heritage. Throughout the entire Indian period, the *Rāmāyaṇa*[7] and the *Mahābhārata,* the *Harivaṃśa,* and the *Purāṇas* were the principal, if not the only, sources of inspiration for local literature. In all of the Indianized mainland, in Malaysia, and on Java, this epic and legendary literature, to which was added the Buddhist folklore of the *Jātakas,* still makes up the substance of the classical theater, of the dances, and of the shadow-plays and puppet theater. From one end of Farther India to the other, spectators continue to weep over the misfortunes of Rāma and Sītā and to be moved by the virtues of the Bodhisattva, and the theatrical performances they attend have retained their original character of pantomime: the positions and the movements of the arms and legs and the gestures of the hands constitute a silent language capable of suggesting a subject, evoking an action, or expressing a sentiment, exactly as in Indian choreography.

The influence of Indian law has been no less profound. The *dharmaśāstras,* and especially the most famous of them known as the "laws of Manu," have formed the framework for the ordering of local customs of the Indianized countries in somewhat the same fashion that Latin law served the barbarian societies that were constructed on the ruins of the Roman Empire.[8]

The *arthaśāstras,* or political treatises, have also had an influence. They have contributed to the fashioning of the hierarchical administration of the states of Farther India, an administration that is dominated by the person of the king, whose conduct is still theoretically guided by the precepts of the *rājanīti,* or "royal conduct."

Although the Indian colonists undoubtedly spoke Prakrit dialects or Dravidian languages, it was the scholarly language, Sanskrit, that served and still serves to enrich the vocabulary of the native languages with a considerable number of words. And, Christian Era to the first known monuments, which do not date and abstract terms that were borrowed. Technical terms referring to the material world were also borrowed. And so were grammatical particles, which had the important effect of making the native isolating languages more flexible, enabling them to express thoughts natural to the vehicle of flexible languages.

The native languages have not only been enriched and made more flexible by India; they have above all been stabilized, thanks to the use of Indian script. The common origin of the Mon, Burmese, Thai, Khmer, Cham, Javanese, and Balinese systems of writing is still recognizable.

To turn to another area of knowledge: in spite of the virtually universal adoption of the Gregorian calendar for official purposes, the Indian lunar-solar year is still in popular use; and the dating systems in use, including both the Buddhist era system based on 543 B.C. and the "little era" system based on A.D. 638, are also of Indian origin.

Finally, the beneficial influence of a superior civilization freely accepted was strikingly felt in the realm of the arts. In fact, as Sylvain Lévi has said,[9] India "produced its definitive masterworks only through the activity of the foreigner or on foreign soil. . . . In architecture, it is in distant Cambodia and Java that we must seek the two marvels born of the Indian genius: Angkor and the Borobudur."

How did the Indian aesthetic, transplanted to Cambodia, Java, and the other countries of Farther India, give birth to Khmer art, Javanese art, and the other Indian arts of the Far East? This is one of the most delicate problems facing archaeologists.[10] In the study of the common Indian origin of these arts, we must not forget that there is an enormous gap in documentation for the period from the start of Indianization around the beginning of the Christian Era to the first known monuments, which do not date back any farther than the sixth century. The very remarkable differences that clearly distinguish the oldest architectural and sculptural monuments of Champa, Cambodia, and Java from those of India proper would undoubtedly surprise us much less if we had the intermediaries we lack, intermediaries that in architecture were undoubtedly made of perishable materials.

The influence of the native substratum on Indian art was mostly formal, external; that is why, from the very first, it is more striking than the internal ties that unite the plastic arts of Farther India to India. We know no monument in India resembling even remotely the Bayon of Angkor Thom or the Borobudur. And yet these monuments are pure productions of the Indian genius, the deep meaning of which is apparent only to the eyes of the Indianist.[11]

Much the same thing is true in the other domains: religious, literary, and legal. Underneath the diversity of the civilizations of

Farther India, underneath their apparent uniqueness, the cause of which has been defined in Chapter II,[12] lies the imprint of the Indian genius, which gives the countries studied in this volume a family likeness and produces a clear contrast between these countries and the lands that have been civilized by China.

ABBREVIATIONS USED IN NOTES

AA	*Artibus Asiae*
ABIA	*Annual Bibliography of Indian Archaeology*
ARASB	*Annual Report, Archaeological Survey of Burma*
ARASI	*Annual Report, Archaeological Survey of India*
BCAI	*Bulletin de la Commission Archéologique Indochinoise*
BEFEO	*Bulletin de l'Ecole Française d'Extrême-Orient*
BKI	*Bijdragen tot de Taal-, Land-, en Volkenkunde van Nederlandsch-Indië, uitgegeven door het Koninklijk Instituut voor Taal-, Land-, en Volkenkunde van Nederlandsch-Indië*
BMFEA	*Bulletin of the Museum of Far Eastern Antiquities*
BRM	*Bulletin of the Raffles Museum*
BSEI	*Bulletin de la Société des Etudes Indochinoises de Saigon*
BSOAS	*Bulletin of the School of Oriental and African Studies*
Cahiers EFEO	*Cahiers de l'Ecole Française d'Extrême-Orient*
CRAIBL	*Comptes-Rendus de l'Académie des Inscriptions et Belles-Lettres*
Et. Asiat. EFEO	*Etudes asiatiques.* Publications de l'Ecole Française d'Extrême-Orient (Paris, 1925), 2 vols.
FEQ	*Far Eastern Quarterly*
IAL	*Indian Art and Letters*
IHQ	*Indian Historical Quarterly*
ISC	Auguste Barth, *Inscriptions sanscrites du Cambodge* (in Académie des Inscriptions et Belles-Lettres, Notices et extraits des manuscrits de la Bibliothéque du roi et autres bibliothéques, v. 27, no. 1, Paris, 1885), pp. 1–180. Abel Bergaigne, *Inscriptions sanscrites de Campa* (in *ibid.*, 1893), pp. 181–292; *Inscriptions sanscrites du Cambodge* (in *ibid.*, 1893), pp. 293–588.
JA	*Journal Asiatique*
JAOS	*Journal of the American Oriental Society*

JAS	*Journal of Asian Studies*
JASB	*Journal of the Asiatic Society of Bengal*
JBRS	*Journal of the Burma Research Society*
JFMSM	*Journal of the Federated Malay States Museum*
JGIS	*Journal of the Greater India Society*
JRAI	*Journal of the Royal Anthropological Institute*
JRAS	*Journal of the Royal Asiatic Society*
JRASCB	*Journal of the Ceylon Branch of the Royal Asiatic Society*
JRASMB	*Journal of the Malayan Branch of the Royal Asiatic Society*
JRASSB	*Journal of the Straits Branch of the Royal Asiatic Society*
JSEAH	*Journal of Southeast Asian History*
JSS	*Journal of the Siam Society*
JSSS	*Journal of the South Seas Society*
MKAWAL	*Mededeelingen der Koninklijke Akademie van Wetenschappen, Afdeeling Letterkunde*
Publ. EFEO	Publications de l'Ecole Française d'Extrême-Orient
RA	*Revue archéologique*
RAA	*Revue des Arts Asiatiques*
TBG	*Tijdschrift voor Indische Taal-, Land-, en Volkenkunde uitgegeven door het Bataviaasch Genootschap van Kunsten en Wetenschappen*
TKNAG	*Tijdschrift van het Koninklijk Nederlandsch Aardrijkskundig Genootschap*
TP	*T'oung Pao*
VBG	*Verhandelingen van het Bataviaasch Genootschap van Kunsten en Wetenschappen*
VKI	Verhandlingen van het Koninklijk Instituut voor Taal-, Land-, en Volkenkunde van Nederlandsch-Indië
VMKAWAL	*Verslagen en Mededeelingen der Koninklijke Akademie van Wetenschappen, Afdeeling Letterkunde*
VKNAWAL	Verhandlingen der Koninklijke Nederlandse Akademie van Wetenschappen, Afdeeling Letterkunde

NOTES

Note on Third Edition

1. I have been happy to note that my example was soon followed in the following works: André Masson, *Histoire de l'Indochine,* Que sais-je?, no. 398 (Paris, 1950); Reginald le May, *The Culture of South-East Asia* (London, 1954; 2nd ed., 1956); Brian Harrison, *South-East Asia: A Short History* (London, 1955); D. G. E. Hall, *History of South-East Asia* (London, 1955); Lê Thanh Khôi, *Histoire de l'Asie du Sud-Est,* Que sais-je?, no. 804 (Paris, 1959). See D. G. E. Hall, ed., *Historians of South-East Asia* (London, 1961).

Introduction

1. The principal general bibliographies to consult are: Henri Cordier, *Bibliotheca Indosinica,* Publ. EFEO, XV–XVIII, 4 vols. and index (Paris, 1912–32); John F. Embree and Lillian O. Dotson, *A Bibliography of the Peoples and Cultures of Mainland Southeast Asia* (New Haven, 1950); Cecil C. Hobbs, *Southeast Asia: An Annotated Bibliography of Selected References* (Washington, D.C., 1952); American Institute of Pacific Relations, *Southeast Asia: A Selected Bibliography* (New York, 1955).
2. Sylvain Lévi, *L'Inde civilisatrice: Aperçu historique* (Paris, 1938), p. 136.
3. *Ibid.*, p. 30.
4. Compare Richard O. Winstedt, "Indian Influence in the Malay World," *JRAS* (1944), p. 195.
5. Upendra N. Ghoshal, *Progress of Greater Indian Research* (Calcutta, 1943).
6. Further details on these questions can be found in Coedès, *Les Peuples de la péninsule indochinoise* (Paris, 1962), "Ire partie, Le peuplement de l'Indochine," pp. 8–40 (translated under the title *The Making of South East Asia,* by H. M. Wright [London, 1966]).
7. *Histoire de l'Asie* (Paris, 1922); *Histoire de l'Extrême-Orient* (Paris, 1929); *Les Civilisations de l'Orient* (Paris, 1929–30); *L'Asie orientale jusqu'au XVe siècle* (Paris, 1941).
8. *Le Cambodge* (Paris, 1900–1904), Vol. III: *Le Groupe d'Angkor et l'histoire* (Paris, 1904).

9. "Le Fou-nan," *BEFEO*, III, pp. 248–303.
10. *L'Empire khmer, histoire et documents* (Phnom Penh, 1904).
11. *Indian Cultural Influence in Cambodia* (Calcutta, 1928).
12. *Kambuja-Desa, or an Ancient Hindu Colony in Cambodia* (Madras, 1944).
13. *The Ancient Khmer Empire* (Philadelphia, 1951).
14. *Le Royaume de Champa* (Paris, 1928).
15. *Ancient Indian Colonies in the Far East,* I: Champa (Lahore, 1927).
16. *History of Burma* (London, 1883).
17. *History of Burma* (London, 1925).
18. *A History of Siam* (London, 1926).
19. *The Indian Colony of Siam,* Punjab Oriental (Sanskrit) Series, XIII (Lahore, 1927).
20. *Histoire du Laos français* (Paris, 1930).
21. "L'empire sumatranais de Çrīvijaya," *JA* (1922).
22. *Ancient Indian Colonies in the Far East,* II: Suvarṇadvīpa (Dacca, 1937–38).
23. "Śrī Vijaya," *BEFEO,* XL, pp. 239–313; *History of Śrīvijaya* (Madras, 1949).
24. "A History of Malaya," *JRASMB,* XIII (1935), pp. 1–210 (2nd ed., Singapore, 1962); *Malaya and Its History* (London, 1948).
25. "An Introduction to the Study of Ancient Times in the Malay Peninsula and the Straits of Malacca," *JRASMB,* XIII–XIX (1935–41); "Notes on Ancient Times in Malaya," *JRASMB,* XX–XXIV (1947–51).
26. "The Khmer Empire and the Malay Peninsula," *FEQ,* IX (1950), pp. 254–305.
27. *The Golden Khersonese* (Kuala Lumpur, 1961).
28. *Hindoe-Javaansche Geschiedenis* (The Hague, 1926; 2nd ed., 1931).
29. *Geschiedenis van Nederlandsch-Indië,* 2nd ed. (Amsterdam, 1943).
30. *Nusantara, A History of the East Indian Archipelago* (Cambridge, Massachusetts, 1943); *Geschiedenis van den Indische Archipel* (Roermond, 1947); *Nusantara: A History of Indonesia* (Chicago, 1960).
31. *Geschiedenis van Indonesië* (The Hague, 1949).
32. On this subject, see Coedès, "L'avenir des études khmères," paper read at public session of Académie des Inscriptions et Belles-Lettres on November 26, 1960.
33. It should be noted, however, that the University of Rangoon has published during recent years, under the editorship of Gordon H. Luce and Pe Maung Tin, five magnificent albums of reproductions entitled *Inscriptions of Burma,* Oriental Studies Publications, Nos. 2–6 (Rangoon, 1933–39), which cover the period from 1131 to 1364.
34. Aside from the work of Lawrence P. Briggs cited above, n. 13, as well as two brief popular works: Madeleine Giteau, *His-*

toire du Cambodge (Paris, 1958) and Achille Dauphin-Meunier, *Histoire du Cambodge;* Que sais-je?, no. 916 (Paris, 1961).

35. The bibliography given in the notes of the text does not pretend to be exhaustive. It cites only the basic works, where the reader will find the elements of a more complete bibliography.

Chapter I

1. Paris, 1929. See also Pierre Gourou, *Les Pays tropicaux* (Paris, 1947); *L'Asie,* IVe partie (Paris, 1953), chaps. XVII–XIX. For eastern Indochina, see Charles Robequain, *L'Indochine française* (Paris, 1935); for the Malay Peninsula and Indonesia, Charles Robequain, *Le Monde malais* (Paris, 1946).
2. "Pour l'histoire du Rāmāyaṇa," *JA* (January-February, 1918), p. 147.
3. *L'Asie des moussons* (Paris, 1928–29), II, p. 513.
4. Exposition coloniale internationale: Indochine française, Section des Sciences, *La Préhistoire en Indochine* (Paris, 1931), which contains a bibliography of his works; "Préhistoire et protohistoire," in *Un Empire colonial français: l'Indochine,* ed. Georges Maspero (Paris, 1929), I, pp. 83–92.
5. In addition to studies cited in Mansuy's "Préhistoire et protohistoire," see "Recherches sur le préhistorique indochinois," *BEFEO, XXX,* pp. 299–422; *Mégalithes du Haut-Laos,* Publ. EFEO, XXV–XXVI (Paris, 1935); *Emploi de la pierre en des temps reculés,* Publications des Amis du Vieux Hué (Hanoi, 1940).
6. "Notes sur le préhistorique indochinois," *Bulletin du Service Géologique de l'Indochine* (1923–32); "L'Indochine préhistorique," *Revue anthropologique* (1936), pp. 277–314.
7. "Note préliminaire sur les formations cénozoïques et plus récentes de la chaîne annamatique septentrionale et du Haut-Laos (Stratigraphie, Préhistoire, Anthropologie)," *Bulletin du Service Geólogique de l'Indochine,* XXII, 3 (1936). For discoveries since that date, see the works of the same authors in *Proceedings of the Third Congress of Prehistorians of the Far East* (Singapore, 1938), pp. 51–90.
8. *Recherches préhistoriques dans la région de Mlu Prei, accompagnées de comparaisons archéologiques,* Publ. EFEO, XXX (Hanoi, 1943).
9. *Papers on the Ethnology and Archaeology of the Malay Peninsula* (Cambridge, England, 1927); numerous articles in the *Journal of the Federated States Museum,* VII, IX, XII, XV.
10. "Pleistocene Site in the Malay Peninsula," *Nature,* 142 (September 24, 1938), p. 575; and his articles in the *BRM,* Singapore, Ser. B.
11. "Prehistory in Malaya," *JRAS* (1942), pp. 1–13, and "The Stone Age in Malaya," *JRASMB,* XXVI, No. 2 (1953), which contains a good bibliography.

12. "Report on Cave Éxcavations in Perak," *Oudheidkundig Verslag* (1926), pp. 184–93; "Report on Cave Excavations in Perak," *JFMSM,* XII (1928); *Note préliminaire sur les fouilles dans l'abri sous roche de Sampung* (Batavia, 1932); "Bijdrage tot de chronologie van het Neolithicum in Zuid-Oost Azië," *Oudheidkundig Verslag* (1926), pp. 174–80; "Korte Gids voor de prehistorische verzameling," *Koninklijk Bataviaasch Genootschap van Kunsten en Wetenschappen, Jaarboek,* II (1934), pp. 69–106; and his articles in the *BRM,* Singapore, Ser. B.
13. *Megalithic Remains in South-Sumatra* (Zutphen, 1932); and the chapter on prehistory in Frederik W. Stapel, ed., *Geschiedenis van Nederlandsch-Indië* (Amsterdam, 1938–40), I, pp. 8–111.
14. "Uber altpaleolithische Artefakte von Java," *TKNAG* (1936), pp. 41–44; "Das Neolithicum der Umgebung von Bandoeng," *TBG,* LXXV (1935), pp. 324–419; "Das Pleistocän Javas," *Quartär* (Berlin, 1939), pp. 28–53.
15. *The Stone Age of Indonesia,* VKI, XXI (The Hague, 1957); *The Bronze-Iron Age of Indonesia,* VKI, XXII (The Hague, 1958).
16. "Prehistorical Researches in Siam," *JSS,* XXVI (1933), pp. 171–202; "Recherches préhistoriques au Siam," *L'Anthropologie,* XLIII (1933), pp. 1–40. Wilhelm G. Solheim, II, "Thailand and Prehistory," *Silapakara,* VIII, No. 3 (September, 1966), pp. 42–77.
17. "Le paléolithisme du Siam," *L'Anthropologie,* LIV, p. 547.
18. "Prehistoric Discoveries in Siam," *Proceedings of the Prehistoric Society,* n.s. 14 (1948), 2, p. 24; "A Preliminary Note on the Excavation of the Sai-Yok Rock Shelter," *JSS,* XLIX (1961), p. 99; "A Brief Survey of the Sai-Yok Excavations, 1961–62," *JSS,* L (1962), p. 15.
19. "Relics of the Stone Age in Burma," *JBRS,* XXI (1931), pp. 33–51.
20. "The Prehistoric Stone Implements of Burma," *JBRS,* XXV (1935), pp. 1–39; "Copper and Bronze Antiquities from Burma," *JBRS,* XXVIII (1938), pp. 95–99.
21. "The Stone Age of Burma," *Transactions of the American Philosophical Society,* 32 (1943), pp. 341–93; "The Lower Paleolithic Cultures of South and East Asia," *Transactions of the American Philosophical Society,* 38 (1948); "Paleolithic Archaeology in South and East Asia," *Cahiers d'histoire mondiale,* II (Paris, 1954).
22. "Urheimat und früheste Wanderungen der Austronesier," *Anthropos,* XXVII (1932); "Ein Beitrag zur Chronologie des Neolithicums in Şüdost-Asien," in *Festschrift . . . P. W. Schmidt* (Vienna, 1928); "Prehistoric Research in Indonesia," *ABIA,* IX (1934), pp. 26–38; "Vorgeschichtliche Grundlagen der

kolonialindischen Kunst," *Wiener Beiträge zur Kunst- und Kulturgeschichte Asiens,* VIII (1934); *Prehistoric Research in the Netherlands Indies* (New York, 1945); introduction to *Indonesian Art,* Asia Institute (New York, 1948).

23. In *L'Homme avant l'écriture,* ed. André Varagnac (Paris, 1959), pp. 153, 315.
24. Pierre Huard and Edmond Saurin, "Etat actuel de la craniologie indochinoise," *Bulletin du Service Géologique de l'Indochine,* XXV, I (1938).
25. Pieter V. van Stein Callenfels, "The Melanesoid Civilizations of Eastern Asia," *BRM,* Ser. B, I (1936), pp. 41–51.
26. Per Sorensen, "North-South Indication of a Prehistoric Migration into Thailand," *East and West,* n.s. XIV, Nos. 3–4 (September-December, 1963), p. 211.
27. Louis Finot, "L'Indochine préhistorique," *Asie française* (February-July, 1919). See below, p. 8.
28. Richard O. Winstedt, "Slab-Graves and Iron Implements," *JRASMB,* XIX, 1 (1941), pp. 93–100. J. Lowenstein and G. Sieveking, "Papers on the Malayan Metal Age," *JRASMB,* XXIX, 2 (1956).
29. William J. Perry, *The Megalithic Culture of Indonesia* (Manchester, 1918); *The Children of the Sun,* 2nd ed. (London, 1927). H. G. Quaritch Wales, *The Making of Greater India* (London, 1951, 1961); "The Pre-Indian Basis of Khmer Culture," *JRAS* (1952), pp. 117–23; *The Mountain of God* (London, 1953); *Prehistory and Religion in South-East Asia* (London, 1957).
30. C. B. Seligman and H. C. Beck, "Far Eastern Glass: Some Western Origins," *BMFEA,* 10 (1938), pp. 49–50.
31. Victor Goloubew, "L'Âge du bronze au Tonkin et dans Nord-Annam," *BEFEO,* XXIX, pp. 1–46. Olov Janse, *Archaeological Research in Indo-China* (Cambridge, Massachusetts, 1947, 1951, Bruges, 1958), 3 vols.
32. "The Age of Bronze Kettledrums," *BRM,* Ser. B, I, No. 3, p. 150. These dates seemed too early to Victor Goloubew, "Le tambour métallique de Hoang-ha," *BEFEO,* XL, No. 1, p. 396, but they agree very well with the results of the researches of Bernard Karlgren, who tends to place the beginning of Dongson culture in the fourth or third centuries B.C. See Karlgren's "The Date of the Early Dong-son Culture," *BMFEA,* 14 (1942), p. 128. See also Basil Gray, "China or Dong-son," *Oriental Art,* II (1949–50), pp. 99–104.
33. Henri Parmentier, "Dépôts de jarres à Sa-huynh (Quang-ngai, Annam)," *BEFEO,* XXIV, pp. 321–43. Madeleine Colani, *Mégalithes du Haut-Laos,* II, pp. 237 ff.
34. Henri Mansuy, *Stations préhistoriques de Somrong-seng et de Longprao (Cambodge)* (Hanoi, 1902); "Résultats de nouvelles recherches effectuées dans le gisement préhistorique de

Somrong-Sen (Cambodge)," *Mémoires du Service Géologique de l'Indochine,* X, 1.

35. Henri Parmentier, "Vestiges mégalithiques à Xuân-lôc," *BEFEO,* XXVIII, pp. 479–85. Emile Gaspardone, "The Tomb of Xuân-lôc," *JGIS,* IV (1937), pp. 26–35.
36. Below, p. 17.
37. Ivor H. N. Evans has published many notes on this site in the *JFMSM,* XII and XV. Alastair Lamb, "Miscellaneous Archaeological Discoveries," *JRASMB,* XXXVII, 1 (July, 1962), p. 166.
38. Frederik D. K. Bosch, "Het bronzen Buddha-beeld van Celebes' Westkust," *TBG,* LXXIII (1933), pp. 495–513. See also F. D. K. Bosch, "Summary of Archaeological Work in Netherlands India in 1933," *ABIA,* VIII (1933), p. 35.
39. *Kingship* (London, 1927); "India and the Pacific," *Ceylon Journal of Science,* I, 2, pp. 61–84.
40. "L'Inde vue de l'Est: Cultes indiens et indigènes au Champa," *BEFEO,* XXXIII, pp. 367–410.
41. See above, p. 6.
42. Wilhelm Schmidt, "Les peuples Mon-Khmer, trait d'union entre les peuples de l'Asie centrale et de l'Austronésie," *BEFEO,* VII, pp. 213–63; VIII, p. 35. The critics of Guillaume de Hevesy (*Finnisch-Ugrisches aux Indien* [Vienna, 1932] and numerous articles in linguistic journals) have not been able to explain away the undeniable lexicographical relationship between the Mon-Khmer languages and the Munda languages of India (cf. Lawrence P. Briggs, "How Obsolete Are the Theories of Professor Dixon and Pater Schmidt," *JAOS,* 65 [1945], pp. 56 ff.).
43. The works of Sylvain Lévi, Jean Przyluski, and J. Bloch on the pre-Aryan and pre-Dravidian civilizations of India have been brought together by Prabodh C. Bagchi in one volume: *Pre-Aryan and Pre-Dravidian in India* (Calcutta, 1929). See also C. Régamey, "Bibliographie analytique des travaux relatifs aux éléments anaryens dans la civilisation et les langues de l'Inde," *BEFEO,* XXXIV, pp. 429–566.
44. James Hornell, "The Origins and Ethnological Significance of Indian Boat Designs," *Memoirs of the Asiatic Society of Bengal,* VII (1920). Stein Callenfels and Heine-Geldern in their articles cited above. Nicholaas J. Krom, *Hindoe-Javaansche Geschiedenis* (The Hague, 1931), pp. 38 ff.
45. Sylvain Lévi, "Pré-aryen et pré-dravidien dans l'Inde," *JA* (July-September, 1923), pp. 55–57. Hendrik Kern, *Verspreide Geschriften* (The Hague, 1913–29), XV, p. 180. Jean Przyluski, "Les Udumbara," *JA* (January-March, 1926), pp. 1–59; "Les Salva," *JA* (April-June, 1929), pp. 311–54. Hocart, *Kingship;* R. C. Majumdar, "The Malay," *JGIS,* III (1936), pp. 86–96.
46. Kern, "Taalkundige gegevens ter bepaling van het stamland der Maleisch-Polynesische Talen," *Verspreide Geschriften,* VI, p. 105.

47. In *Indochine,* ed. S. Lévi (Paris, 1931), I, p. 54.
48. This is the thesis of Krom, *Hindoe-Javaansche Geschiedenis.*
49. Gabriel Ferrand, "Le K'ouen-louen, et les anciennes navigations inter-océaniques dans les mers du Sud," *JA,* 1919, March-April, pp. 239–333; May-June, pp. 431–92; July-August, pp. 5–68; September-October, pp. 201–41, places this event in the second to fourth centuries A.D. James Hornell, "Indonesian Influence on East African Culture," *JRAI* (1934), p. 315, would place it a little later. See also C. Nooteboom, "De betrekkingen tussen Madagascar en Indonesie," *Zaïre,* III (1949), pp. 881–94.
50. P. V. van Stein Callenfels, "Die Aufgaben der japanischen Prähistorie im Rahmen der internationalen Forschung," *Shizengaku-Zasshi,* IV (1932), p. 6.
51. Nobuhiro Matsumoto, *Le Japonais et les langues austro-asiatiques,* Austro-Asiatica, I (Paris, 1928). O. Gjerdman, "Word-Parallels between Ainu and Other Languages," *Le Monde oriental,* XX (1926), p. 29.
52. Nobuhiro Matsumoto, *Essai sur la mythologie japonaise,* Austro-Asiatica, II (Paris, 1928).
53. G. Montandon, *Traité d'ethnologie culturelle* (Paris, 1934).
54. It would be imprudent to attempt to delineate too precisely the composition of a civilization on which ancient documents are sporadic and about which ideas must be based solely on folklore and ethnology. In his *Hindoe-Javaansche Geschiedenis,* pp. 47 ff., Krom sketches a picture of the Indonesian civilization of Java before the arrival of the Hindus and mentions the *wayang,* or shadow theater, among its characteristics. But the shadow theater (*chāyānaṭaka*) was known to theorists of the Indian theater in the Sanskrit language. (R. Pischel, "Das alt indische Schattenspiel," *Sitzungsberichte der königlich Preussischen Akademie der Wissenschaften* [Berlin], XXIII [1906], pp. 482–502; G. Jacob, *Geschichte des Schattentheaters* [1925].) Compare Ananda K. Coomaraswamy, "The Shadow-Play in Ceylon," *JRAS* (1930), p. 627, and *History of Indian and Indonesian Art* (New York, 1927), p. 89. Was the *wayang* imported into Java by the Hindus or was it part of a common substratum? Anker Rentse, "The Origin of the Wayang Theatre (Shadow Play)," *JRASMB,* XX (1947), pp. 12–15, repudiates an Indian origin. The same question can just as well be put for other cultural elements.
55. Przyluski in *Indochine,* p. 54.
56. Coedès, "Les langues de l'Indochine," *Conférences de l'Institut de Linguistique de l'Université de Paris,* 8 (1940–48), pp. 63–81.
57. Ferrand, "Le K'ouen-louen et les anciennes navigations inter-océaniques."
58. On this question see R. Stein, "Le Lin-yi," *Han-hiue,* II (1947), pp. 211 ff. A. H. Christie, "The Name K'un-lun as an Ethnic Term," *Comptes Rendus du XXIIIe Congrès International des*

Orientalistes (Cambridge, 1954), p. 297. Gordon H. Luce, "The Early Syām in Burma's History," *JSS*, XLVI (1958), p. 191.

59. "K'ouen-louen et Dvīpāntara," *BKI*, 88 (1931), pp. 621–27.
60. *Hindoe-Javaansche Geschiedenis*, p. 110.
61. "The Malay," *JGIS*, III (1936), p. 86. A similar opinion is expressed by K. A. Nilakanta Sastri, "Dvīpāntara," *JGIS*, IX (1942), pp. 1–4.
62. We know that bronze drums of the earliest type and comparable bronze objects have been found in southern Indochina, in the Malay Peninsula, and in the Indonesian islands. See particularly L. Malleret, "Objets de bronze communs au Cambodge, à la Malaise et à l'Indonésie," *AA*, XIX (1956), p. 308; W. Linehan, "Traces of a Bronze Age Culture Associated with Iron Age Implements in the Regions of Klang and the Tembeling, Malaya," *JRASMB*, XXIV, 3 (1951); H. Deydier, "Note sur un tambour de bronze conservé au Musée de Batavia," *BSEI*, XXIV (1949), p. 53; H. R. van Heekeren, "Tambours de bronze," *Amerta*, II (1954), p. 37 (summarized by L. C. Damais, "Bibliographie indonésienne," *BEFEO*, LI [1963], p. 544). On the late Neolithic finds recently discovered in Cochin China, see E. Saurin, "Station préhistorique à Hang-gon près de Xuan-loc," *BEFEO*, LI (1963), p. 433.
63. "Le groupe océanien," *Bulletin de la Société de Linguistique de Paris*, 27 (1927), p. 152. "It is clearly evident that the language community of peoples so different [as the Australians and the Melanesians, the Indonesians and the Polynesians] is a secondary phenomenon and that the language of one of them must have been imposed on all for reasons and under circumstances which now escape us."
64. It must be clearly understood that the ethnic terms used in what follows always designate linguistic or ethno-linguistic groups and never races in the physical sense of the word. In the absence of precise anthropological data, it is necessary to define an ethnic group provisionally on the basis of its customs and beliefs and the language it speaks.
65. Sion's wording in *L'Asie des moussons*, II, p. 403.
66. J. P. Kleiweg de Zwaan, *De rassen van den Indischen Archipel* (Amsterdam, 1925); *Physical Anthropology in the Indian Archipelago and Adjacent Regions* (Amsterdam, 1923). J. H. Nyèssen, *The Races of Java* (Weltevreden, 1929). Jaap Kunst, *The Peoples of the Indian Archipelago* (Leyden, 1946).
67. *L'Asie des moussons*, II, p. 483.
68. *Hindoe-Javaansche Geschiedenis*, chap. 2.
69. On the *wayang*, see above, n. 54.
70. Published under the title *Adatrechtbundel* (The Hague, 1911–).
71. W. W. Skeat and C. O. Blagden, *Pagan Races of the Malay Peninsula* (London, 1906).

72. On the ethnography of French Indochina, see Bonifacy, *Cours d'ethnographie indochinoise* (Hanoi, 1919). Georges Maspero, *L'Indochine,* Vol. I (Paris, 1929). Jean Przyluski, "Les populations de l'Indochine française" in *Indochine,* ed. Lévi, I, pp. 47–60. A. Bigot, "Ethnologie sommaire de l'Indochine française," in *Indochine française* (Hanoi, 1938), pp. 33–58. L. Malleret, *Groupes ethniques de l'Indochine française* (Saigon, 1937).
73. C. C. Lowis, *Tribes of Burma* (Rangoon, 1910). R. Halliday, *The Talaings* (Rangoon, 1917).

Chapter II

1. *L'Art gréco-bouddhique du Gandhāra, étude sur les origines de l'influence classique dans l'art bouddhique de l'Inde et de l'Extrême-Orient* (Paris, 1922), II, p. 618.
2. Louis de La Vallée-Poussin, *Dynasties et histoire de l'Inde depuis Kanishka jusqu'aux invasions musulmanes* (Paris, 1935), p. 360. See also M. N. Srinivas, "A Note on Sanskritization and Westernization," *FEQ,* XV (1956), p. 481. V. Raghavan, "Variety and Integration in the Pattern of Indian Culture," *FEQ,* XV (1956), p. 497. J. F. Staal, "Sanskrit and Sanskritization," *JAS* XXII (1963), pp. 261–75.
3. On these discussions between sociologists and Indianists, see F. D. K. Bosch, *"Local Genius" en oud-javaansche Kunst* (Amsterdam, 1952). Coedès, "Le substrat autochthone et la superstructure indienne au Cambodge et à Java," *Cahiers d'histoire mondiale,* I, 2 (Oct., 1953).
4. "Les origines de la colonisation indienne en Indochine," *BEFEO,* XII, 8, pp. 1–4.
5. Sylvain Lévi, "Pour l'histoire du Rāmāyaṇa," *JA* (January-February, 1918), pp. 80 ff.
6. "Ptolémée, le Niddesa et la Bṛihatkathā," *Et. Asiat. EFEO,* II, pp. 1–55.
7. See below, pp. 62–63.
8. See below, p. 63.
9. The Gupta period began in India in the fourth century A.D. At Phra Pathom have been found many stone "Wheels of the Law" that represent the old aniconic tradition of Buddhism but that, to judge by their decoration, did not precede the sixth century. See Coedès, "Une roue de la Loi avec inscription en pāli provenent du site de P'ra Pathom," *AA,* XIX (1956), p. 221.
10. "Amarāvatī, situated not far from the mouth of the Krishnā," writes Foucher (*Art gréco-bouddhique,* II, p. 617), "seems to have been one of the great ports of embarkation from which Graeco-Buddhist influence was exported to Indochina and Indonesia."

The Amarāvatī school flourished in India from the second to the fourth centuries A.D. The images of the Buddha, generally standing and dressed in pleated monastic robes, which in many cases constitute the oldest tangible evidence of the coming of the Indians to Farther India, belong to this school. These images represent the Buddha Dīpankara, whose name evokes the islands (*dīpa, dvīpa*), and who seems to have been the protector of seamen (Alfred Foucher, *Etude sur l'iconographie bouddhique de l'Inde, d'après des documents nouveaux* [Paris, 1900–1905], I, pp. 77–84). On the dating and the Indian or Singhalese origin of the images of the Buddha called Amarāvatī in Southeast Asia, see Mirella Levi d'Ancona, "Amarāvatī, Ceylon and the Three 'Imported Bronzes,' " *Art Bulletin* XXXIV (1952). Pierre Dupont, "Les Buddhas dits d'Amarāvatī en Asie du Sud-est," *Proceedings, XXIIIe Congrès International des Orientalistes* (Cambridge, 1954), p. 269.

11. Not to mention a bronze Alexandrine lamp (Charles Picard, "La lampe alexandrine de P'ong Tuk [Siam]," *AA,* XVIII [1955], pp. 137–49), evidence of relations with the West that may date back to the period when the Chinese mention the voyage of Roman musicians and acrobats from Burma to China (A.D. 120) and the so-called "embassy" of Marcus Aurelius (A.D. 166).
12. *Etudes d'orientalisme* (Mélanges Linossier), pp. 159–64. See on this subject, Pierre Dupont, "Vishṇu mitrés de l'Indochine occidentale," *BEFEO,* XLI, pp. 233–54.
13. H. G. Quaritch Wales, "The Exploration of Sri Deva, An Ancient City in Indochina," *IAL,* X (1936), pp. 66, 85. See B. Ch. Chhabra, "Expansion of Indo-Aryan Culture," *JASB,* Letters, I (1935), pp. 54–55.
14. Coedès, "The Excavations at P'ong Tük and Their Importance for the Ancient History of Siam," *JSS,* XXI (1928), pl. 18.
15. For Funan, Champa, Malaysia, and Indonesia, see the references in the following chapter.
16. Charles Picard, "A Figurine of the Lysippan Type from the Far East: The Tra Vinh Bronze 'Dancer,' " *AA,* XIX (1956), pp. 342–52.
17. Louis Malleret, *L'Archéologie du delta du Mékong* (Paris, 1959–63), III, p. 115.
18. On the discoveries made at Oc Eo, see Coedès, "Fouilles en Cochinchine: Le Site de Go Oc Eo," *AA,* X (1947), pp. 193–99. Louis Malleret, "La trace de Rome en Indochine," *Actes du XXIIe Congrès International des Orientalistes* (Istanbul, 1951), p. 332 (with a very complete bibliography); *L'Archéologie du delta du Mékong.*
19. Virgile Rougier, "Nouvelles découvertes chames au Quangnam," *BCAI* (1912), pp. 212–13. "Chronique," *BEFEO,* XI, p. 471. "L'Ecole Française d'Extrême-Orient depuis son origine

jusqu'en 1920," *BEFEO,* XXI, p. 72. Ananda K. Coomaraswamy, *History of Indian and Indonesian Art* (New York, 1927), p. 197.

20. Recalling to our minds that fragments of Attic vases dating back to the fourth and fifth centuries before the Christian Era have been found at Tenku Lembu (Perlis). See P. D. R. Williams-Hunt, "Recent Archaeological Discoveries in Malaya," *JRASMB,* XXV (1952), p. 187.
21. See above, p. 7.
22. William Cohn, *Buddha in der Kunst des Ostens* (Leipzig, 1925), p. 28.
23. F. M. Schnitger, *The Archaeology of Hindoo Sumatra* (Leyden, 1937), pl. I.
24. The text to consult for India and the Far East is that of Louis Renou, *La Géographie de Ptolémée, l'Inde,* VII, 1–4 (Paris, 1925). For the attempts at "redressing" the map of Ptolemy and the identification of geographic names of trans-Gangetic India, see especially: G. E. Gerini, *Researches on Ptolemy's Geography of Eastern Asia* (London, 1909); André Berthelot, *L'Asie ancienne centrale et sud-orientale d'après Ptolémée* (Paris, 1930); Albert Herrmann, *Das Land der Seide und Tibet im Lichte der Antike* (Leipzig, 1938). Results based on mathematical calculations are very deceiving, and up to now only philology has permitted us to obtain satisfying identifications.
25. According to J. Pirenne, "La date du Périple de la Mer Erythrée," *JA,* CCXLIX (1961), p. 441, this text dates from around the year A.D. 230 and was consequently later than Ptolemy.
26. "Le K'ouen-louen," *JA* (July-August, 1919), p. 21. The identification of Ye-tiao as Yavadvīpa (Java), accepted by Gabriel Ferrand ("Ye-tiao, Sseu-tiao et Java," *JA* [November-December, 1916], p. 520), has been challenged by R. Stein ("Le Linyi," *Han-hiue,* II [1947], pp. 211 ff). See below, p. 283, n. 63.
27. At least this is widely believed. But, on this subject, Jean Filliozat has brought to my attention a passage of the *Mṛigendrāgama* "which considers sea voyages for conquest or profit permissible and prescribes the use of a bright flame for rites involved." (N. R. Bhatt, *Mṛgendrāgama,* Publications de l'Institut Français d'Indologie, 23 [Pondicherry, 1962], p. 76.)
28. Louis de La Vallée-Poussin, *L'Inde aux temps des Mauryas et des barbares, Grecs, Scythes, Parthes et Yue-tchi,* Histoire du Monde, VI, 1 (Paris, 1930). Compare Sylvain Lévi, "Kanishka et S'ātavāhana," *JA* (January-March, 1936), p. 94.
29. Cornelis C. Berg, *Hoofdlijnen der Javaansche Litteratuur-Geschiedenis* (Groningen, 1929).
30. Eric H. Warmington, *The Commerce between the Roman Empire and India* (Cambridge, 1928). Gabriel Jouveau-Dubreuil, *L'Inde et les Romaines* (Paris, 1921). H. G. Rawlinson, *Intercourse between India and the Western World* (Cambridge, 1916). M. P. Charlesworth, *Trade-Routes and Commerce of*

the Roman Empire (Cambridge, 1926). Jean Filliozat, "Les échanges de l'Inde et de L'Empire romain aux premiers siècles de l'ère chrétienne," *Revue historique* (January-March, 1949). In his review of the present work (*JA*, CCXXXVII [1949], p. 368), Filliozat gives interesting details on the cinnamon or canelle trade. See also, on the trade in camphor and other luxuries, O. W. Wolters, "The *'Po-ssŭ* Pine Trees,'" *BSOAS*, XXIII (1960), pp. 323–50, and Buddha Prakash, "Pārasīkadvīpa," *AA*, XXIV (1961), pp. 399–402.

31. "K'ouen-louen et Dvīpāntara," *BKI*, 88 (1931), p. 627.
32. La Vallée-Poussin, *L'Inde aux temps des Mauryas.*
33. Robert Sewell, "Roman Coins Found in India," *JRAS* (1904), pp. 591–638. William W. Tarn, *The Greeks in Bactria and India*, 2nd ed. (Cambridge, England, 1951), pp. 106–109. Pierre Meile, "Les Yuvanas dans l'Inde tamoule," *JA* (1940–41), pp. 86–87. The most recent and complete list has been given by R. E. M. Wheeler, "Arikamedu," *Ancient India*, 2 (1946), pp. 116–21.
34. On the first relations between India and China by sea, see Paul Pelliot, "L'origine du nom de 'Chine'," *TP*, XIII (1912), pp. 457–61, and K. A. Nilakanta Sastri, "The Beginnings of Intercourse between India and China," *IHQ*, XIV (1938), pp. 380–87. Sastri's conclusions are perhaps debatable, but he gives references. See also the important article of Wang Gungwu, "The Nanhai Trade: A Study of the Early History of Chinese Trade in the South China Sea," *JRASMB*, XXXI, 2 (1958).
35. Paul Pelliot, "Textes chinois concernant l'Indochine hindouisée," *Et. Asiat. EFEO*, II, p. 261.
36. *Ibid.*, p. 255.
37. *L'Inde civilisatrice: Aperçu historique* (Paris, 1939), p. 156.
38. Sylvain Lévi, "Les 'marchands de mer' et leur rôle dans le bouddhisme primitif," *Bulletin de l'Association Française des Amis de l'Orient* (October, 1929), pp. 19–39.
39. "Maṇimekhalā, divinité de la mer," *Bull. Lettres Acad. Belgique* (1930), p. 282. See *IHQ*, VII (1931), pp. 173, 371.
40. "Le K'ouen-louen," pp. 15 ff.
41. On the mixed marriages, substantiated by various texts, see below, p. 24.
42. "History of Malaya," *JRASMB*, XIII (1935), p. 18; "Indian Influence in the Malay World," *JRAS* (1944), p. 186.
43. Nicholaas J. Krom, *Hindoe-Javaansche Geschiedenis* (The Hague, 1931).
44. F. H. van Naerssen, *Culture Contacts and Social Conflicts in Indonesia* (New York, 1947); "De aanvang van het Hindu-indonesische acculturatie process," *Orientalia Neerlandica* (1948), pp. 414–22; "Het sociaal aspect van acculturatie in Indonesia," *Zaïre* (June, 1948).

45. Jacob C. Van Leur, *Indonesian Trade and Society* (The Hague, 1955).
46. Abbreviation of T'ien-chu, i.e., India. See Paul Pelliot, "Le Fou-nan," *BEFEO,* III, p. 252, n. 4.
47. Frederik D. K. Bosch, "Het Lingga-Heiligdom van Dinaja," *TBG,* 64 (1924), pp. 227–91. Robert von Heine-Geldern, "Conceptions of State and Kingship in Southeast Asia," *FEQ,* II (1942), pp. 15–30.
48. "Agastya," *TBG,* 76 (1936), p. 503.
49. Louis de La Vallée-Poussin, *Indo-européens et Indo-iraniens jusque vers 300 av. J.C.,* Histoire du Monde, III (Paris, 1924), pp. 168, 169, 174, 178; *Dynasties et histoire de l'Inde,* p. 361. Sylvain Lévi, *Le Nepal* (Paris, 1905–1908), I, p. 220. L. Renou, *Bibliographie védique* (Paris, 1931), pp. 143, 334.
50. Above, p. 18, and below, p. 52.
51. See below, pp. 87–88.
52. ISC, p. 159, n. 10. Barth's remark is prompted by a text of the eleventh century, but these mixtures of names are observed much earlier.
53. Van Leur, *Indonesian Trade and Society,* p. 100.
54. Pelliot, "Le Fou-nan," p. 279.
55. Tun-sun was a dependency of Funan, probably on the Malay Peninsula; see below, pp. 38–39. This text remains interesting, even if the *p'o-lo-men* of the Chinese text were not all of Brahmanic caste.
56. *Dynasties et histoire de l'Inde,* p. 361.
57. *L'Inde civilisatrice,* p. 23.
58. Coedès, *Les Peuples de la péninsule indochinoise* (Paris, 1962), p. 55.
59. And in Ceylon. See Filliozat's review of the present work, *JA,* CCXXXVII (1949), p. 369.
60. *Indian Influences in Old Balinese Art* (London, 1935), p. 6.
61. W. F. Stutterheim, *Indian Influences in the Lands of the Pacific* (Weltevreden, 1929), pp. 4–5. F. D. K. Bosch, *Het vragstuk van de Hindoe-Kolonisatie van den Archipel* (Leyden, 1946).
62. *Les Peuples de la péninsule indochinoise,* p. 57.
63. Albert Herrmann, "Die Alten Verkehrswege zwischen Indien und Südchina nach Ptolemäus," *Zeitschrift der Gesellschaft für Erdkunde* (1913), p. 771. Paul Wheatley, *The Golden Khersonese* (Kuala Lumpur, 1961).
64. *Pour la compréhension de l'Indochine et de l'Occident* (Hanoi, 1939), p. 51.
65. See below, pp. 130, 142, 184.
66. E. Lunet de Lajonquière, "Le domaine archéologique du Siam," *BCAI* (1909), p. 259; cf. p. 256.
67. *Ibid.* H. G. Quaritch Wales, "A Newly Explored Route of Ancient Indian Cultural Expansion," *IAL,* IX (1935), pp. 1–35; *Towards Angkor* (London, 1937); "Archaeological Researches

on Ancient Indian Colonization in Malaya," *JRASMB,* XVIII, 1 (1940).

68. Jean Y. Claeys, "L'archéologie du Siam," *BEFEO,* XXXI, p. 378. Quaritch Wales, "A Newly Explored Route." Wheatley, *The Golden Khersonese,* p. 190, gives a map of the maritime routes of the Indians and of trans-peninsular routes used by travelers. The same author in "Panarikan," *JSSS* (1954), pp. 1–16, retraces the two routes from Malacca to Pahang following two rivers, with short portages.
69. Quaritch Wales, *Towards Angkor,* p. 111.
70. See below, p. 66.
71. Paul Pelliot, "Deux itinéraires de Chine en Inde, à la fin du VIIIe siècle," *BEFEO,* IV, pp. 142–43. Gordon H. Luce and Pe Maung Tin, "Burma down to the Fall of Pagan," *JBRS,* XXIX (1939), p. 264. The use of this route has been placed in doubt by Walter Liebenthal, "The Ancient Burma Route: A Legend?" *JGIS,* XV (1956), p. 6, but is accepted by Buddha Prakash, "Pūrvavideha," *JGIS,* XV (1956), p. 93.
72. Pelliot, "Deux itinéraires," pp. 154 ff.; "L'origine du nom de 'Chine,'" pp. 733–34. Walter Liebenthal, "Sanskrit Inscriptions from Yunnan," *Monumenta Serica,* XII (1947), pp. 1–40.
73. Inscription from Labu Tuwa near Baros, of 1088. See Krom, *Hindoe-Javaansche Geschiedenis,* p. 304, and below, p. 107.
74. Inscriptions from Khao Phra Narai at Takuapa of the seventh to ninth centuries and from Wat Mahathat of Ligor from the tenth to eleventh centuries. See Coedès, *Recueil des inscriptions du Siam* (Bangkok, 1924–29), II, pp. 49, 57.
75. *Dynasties et histoire de l'Inde,* p. 293.
76. *Cambridge History of India* (Cambridge, 1922), I, p. 212. For a description of this port at its height, drawn from the literature of Sangam, see K. A. Nilakanta Sastri, *The Cōḷas,* 2nd ed. (Madras, 1955), pp. 96, 99. See also Pierre Meile, "Les Yavanas dans l'Inde tamoule," *JA* (1940–41), p. 98.
77. Excavations by Gabriel Jouveau-Dubreil ("Padoukê-Pondichéry," *Le Semeur,* no. 10 [Pondicherry, 1938]; "Les ruines romaines de Pondichéry," *BEFEO,* XL, pp. 448–50) and by Brother L. Faucheux (*Une Vielle cité indienne près de Pondichéry, Virapatnam* [Pondicherry, 1946]) on the site named Arikamedu have shown that there was an emporium there in commercial contact with the Mediterranean West in the first centuries of the Christian Era (P. Z. Pattabiramin, *Les Fouilles d'Arikamedou* [*Podoukè*] [Pondicherry, 1946]). Other excavations carried out more recently by R. E. M. Wheeler have been the subject of an important report in *Ancient India,* No. 2 (1946). See also Jean Filliozat, "Les échanges de l'Inde et de l'Empire romain," *Revue historique* (1949), p. 15.
78. The word *kalam* in the Tamil texts of Sangam, and the word *kola* in the Sanskrit Buddhist texts, have the meaning of

"boat." (See Meile, "Les Yavanas dans l'Inde tamoule," pp. 90–92.) The Chinese used an expression *K'un-lun-tan,* which could be an equivalent of the Greek *kolandia* (information from R. Stein). For his part, Anthony H. Christie, "The Name K'un-lun as an Ethnic Term," *Proceedings, XXIII*e *Congrès International des Orientalistes* (Cambridge, 1954), p. 29, explains the expression *kolandiaphonta megista* (Periplus, §60) as a distortion of *kolandiapha onta* (*ta*) *megista,* and considers *kolandiapha* as a Greek transcription of the Chinese *k'un-lun-po,* the character representing the name for "boat" in various dialects of Southeast Asia. This thesis is developed in Christie's "An Obscure Passage from the Periplus," *BSOAS,* XIX (1957), pp. 345–53.

79. Sylvain Lévi, "Notes sur la géographie ancienne de l'Inde," *JA* (January-March, 1925), pp. 46–57.
80. *Saṃkha Jātaka,* No. 442; *Mahājanaka Jātaka,* No. 539.
81. An old Gujarati proverb alludes to the riches of the seamen returned from Java (*Rās Mālā,* II, 82, cited in Henry Yule and Arthur Burnell, *Hobson-Jobson: A Glossary of Colloquial Anglo-Indian Words and Phrases* [London, 1903], p. 456).
82. Below, p. 53. But K. A. Nilakanta Sastri, *History of Śrīvijaya* (Madras, 1949), p. 16, is inclined to adopt the opinion of Krom, *Hindoe-Javaansche Geschiedenis,* p. 78, who sees in *tārumā* an Indonesian word meaning indigo.
83. Below, p. 77.
84. But see L. C. Damais, "Études sino-indonésiennes," *BEFEO,* LII, No. 1 (1964), p. 97.
85. Hendrik Kern, "Dravidische volksnamen op Sumatra," *Verspreide Geschriften* (The Hague, 1913–29), III, pp. 67–72.
86. Ramesch C. Majumdar, *Ancient Indian Colonies in the Far East,* II: Suvarṇadvīpa, 1 (Dacca, 1937), pp. 226–27.
87. Coedès, "La légende de la Nāgī," *BEFEO,* XI, p. 391.
88. Kashi P. Jayaswal, "History of India c. 150 A.D. to 350 A.D.," *Journal of the Bihar and Orissa Research Society,* XIX (1933), p. 169. Bijan R. Chatterjee, "Recent Advances in Kambuja Studies," *JGIS,* VI (1939), p. 139. K. A. Nilakanta Sastri, "A Note on the Kauṇḍinyas in India," *AA,* XXIV (1961), p. 403.
89. Nilakanta Sastri, "Agastya," pp. 503–504.
90. F. D. K. Bosch, "De inscriptie van Keloerak," *TBG,* 68 (1929), pp. 3–16.
91. "La paléographie des inscriptions du Champa," *BEFEO,* XXXII, pp. 127–39.
92. Below, p. 40.
93. "L'origine de l'alphabet du Champa," *BEFEO,* XXXV, pp. 233–41.
94. Jean Philippe Vogel, "The Yūpa Inscriptions of King Mūlavarman from Koetei (East Borneo)," *BKI,* 74 (1918), pp. 222–32. With regard to these inscriptions Nilakanta Sastri, *History of*

Śrīvijaya, p. 17, has made it clear that it is better to speak of "writing of the eastern coast of Madras" than of "Pallava writing," for the Telugu country has furnished ancient specimens of this type of writing which is not specifically "Pallava" but was used by the Śālankāyanas.

95. Ananda K. Coomaraswamy, *History of Indian and Indonesian Art* (London, 1927); *The Influences of Indian Art* (London, 1927). René Grousset, "L'art Pāla et Sena dans l'Inde extérieure," *Etudes d'orientalisme* (Mél. Linossier), I, pp. 277–85. A. J. Bernet Kempers, *The Bronzes of Nālandā and Hindu-Javanese Art* (Leyden, 1933).
96. Devaprasad Ghosh, "Migration of Indian Decorative Motifs," *JGIS,* II (1935), pp. 37–46; "Relation Between Buddha of Orissa and Java," *Modern Review* (November, 1933).
97. Henri Parmentier, "Origine commune des architectures hindoues dans l'Inde et en Extrême-Orient," *Et. Asiat. EFEO,* II, p. 200.
98. The comparison is proposed by Reginald S. le May, *A Concise History of Buddhist Art in Siam* (Cambridge, 1938), pp. 63–65.
99. Alexander Cunningham, *Archaeological Survey of India, Annual Reports,* XI (1875–78), pp. 40–46. On the possible influence of northern India, see also Gilberte de Coral Rémusat, "De l'origine commune des linteaux de l'Inde Pallava et des linteaux khmers préangkoriens," *RAA,* VIII (1934), p. 249.
100. B. Ch. Chhabra, "Expansion of Indo-Aryan Culture during Pallava Rule, as Evidenced by Inscriptions," *JASB,* Letters, I (1935).
101. However, see Stutterheim, *Indian Influences in the Lands of the Pacific.* Moreover, Robert Lingat has brought to my attention a passage of the *Dharmaśāstra* of Baudhāyana which cites the practice of traveling by sea (I, I, II, 4) as among the customs peculiar to the Brahmans of the north. This practice everywhere else is regarded as bringing contamination (although this idea of contamination seems to be exaggerated [see above, p. 269, n. 27]).
102. Dupont, "Les Buddhas dits d'Amarāvatī en Asie du Sud-est," p. 631; *L'Archéologie mône de Dvāravatī* (Paris, 1959–63), I, pp. 164–67. J. G. de Casparis, "New Evidence on Cultural Relations between Java and Ceylon in Ancient Times," *AA,* XXIV (1961), p. 241.
103. See below, p. 52.
104. See below, p. 81. On the penetration of Indian civilization into Java, see J. G. de Casparis, "Quelques mots sur les groupes sociaux dans l'ancienne Java," *Amerta,* II (1954), p. 44 (summarized by L. C. Damais, "Bibliographie indonésienne," *BEFEO,* LI [1963], p. 546).
105. *Indian Influences in Old-Balinese Art,* p. 7. F. D. K. Bosch, "Uit de grensgebieden tussen Indische invloedsfer en oudinheems volks-geloof op Java," *BKI,* 110 (1954), pp. 1–19,

repudiates at the same time the Indian exaggeration of Ordhendra C. Gangoly ("Relation between Indian and Indonesian Culture," *JGIS,* VII [1940], pp. 51–69, and see my review in *BEFEO,* XL, p. 452) and the Indonesian exaggeration of Stutterheim in order to analyze the various forms of "Javanization" of the Indian elements, which for him is fundamental.

106. Stele of Nagara Jum of 1357. See Coedès, *Recueil des inscriptions du Siam,* I, p. 85; "L'année du lièvre 1219 A.D.," *India Antiqua* (Leyden, 1947), p. 83.
107. Above, p. 24, and below, p. 119.
108. This point has been well clarified by Suniti K. Chatterji, "Hindu Culture and Greater India," in *The Cultural Heritage of India* (Calcutta, 1936), III, p. 87–96, and by K. A. Nilakanta Sastri, *Indian History Congress, 9th Session* (Patna, 1946), Presidential Address, p. 18.

Chapter III

1. See above, p. 16. Since this work is not a treatise on geography but an attempt at historical synthesis, I will mention in this and the following chapters only those names that are of some significance in the history of events or dynasties. A discussion of the various opinions put forth on the location of the geographic names of Ptolemy can be found in Roland Braddell, "Study of Ancient Times in the Malay Peninsula," *JRASMB,* XIII (1935).
2. This is the T'ang period pronounciation, according to Bernhard Karlgren, *Analytic Dictionary of Chinese and Sino-Japanese* (n.p., n.d.), Nos. 41 and 650.
3. Louis Finot, "Sur quelques traditions indochinoises," *Mélanges d'indianisme offerts par ses élèves à M. Sylvain Lévi* (Paris, 1911), p. 203, and "Seance du 14 Janvier 1927," *JA* (January-March, 1927), p. 186. Coedès, "On the Origin of the Śailendras of Indonesia," *JGIS,* I (1934), p. 67. This mountain was apparently one of those mountains on which, as has been said above (pp. 26–27), the founder of a kingdom of the Indian type instituted the worship of a national god, generally that of a linga or of another manifestation of Siva.
4. Coedès, "Les traditions généalogiques des premiers rois d'Angkor," *BEFEO,* XXVIII (1956), p. 127.
5. Coedès, *Inscriptions du Cambodge* (Paris, 1937–), II, p. 110, n. 5. Perhaps Vyādhapura means "the city of the hunter (king)." O. W. Wolters, in fact, has kindly informed me (letter of November 6, 1960) that the T'ai-p'ing Yü-lan, citing the account of K'ang T'ai (below), mentions a king of Funan named P'an-huang-chao (identical ? to Hun P'an-huang, below, p. 38) who captured large elephants in the jungle and domesticated them, bringing about the submission of many countries in this way.
6. Paul Pelliot, "Le Fou-nan," *BEFEO,* III, p. 263.

7. Above, p. 17. Pierre Gourou, "Civilisations et géographie humaine en Asie des moussons," *BEFEO,* XLIV (1954), p. 469, after showing that "the birthplaces of superior civilizations seem to correspond to crossroads of traffic," adds: "The nucleus of the civilization of Funan, out of which the whole of Khmer history was to develop, originated on the western coast of Indochina, at the landing point of Indian cultural influences."
8. Pelliot, "Le Fou-nan," p. 303; "Quelques textes chinois concernant l'Indochine hindouisée," *Et. Asiat. EFEO,* II, p. 243.
9. Pelliot, "Quelques textes," pp. 246–49. On the preponderant role of the Kauṇḍinya clan in southern India, see Bijan R. Chatterjee, "Recent Advances in Kambuja Studies," *JGIS,* VI (1939), p. 139, and above, p. 30.
10. Louis Finot, "Les inscriptions de Mi-sơn (No. III)," *BEFEO,* IV, p. 923. See Coedès, "L'inscription de Baksei Chamkrong," *JA* (May-June, 1909), pp. 476–78, and *Inscriptions du Cambodge,* IV, p. 88.
11. Eveline Porée-Maspero, "Nouvelle étude sur la Nāgī Somā," *JA,* CCXXXVIII (1950), pp. 237–67.
12. Paul Pelliot, trans. and ed., "Mémoires sur les coutumes du Cambodge," *BEFEO,* II, p. 145.
13. Finot, "Sur quelques traditions indochinoises," p. 205.
14. Coedès, "La légende de la Nāgī," *BEFEO,* XI, p. 391.
15. Victor Goloubew ("Les légendes de la Nāgī et de l'Apsaras," *BEFEO,* XXIV, pp. 501–10) has it come from the west, while Jean Przyluski ("La princesse à l'odeur de poisson et la Nāgī dans les traditions de l'Asie orientale," *Et. Asiat. EFEO,* II, pp. 265–84) thinks it was born in the maritime regions of Southeast Asia. On a Malaysian version of this legend, see R. O. Winstedt, "Indra and Saktimuna," *JRASMB,* XXIII (1950), p. 151.
16. Pelliot, "Le Fou-nan," p. 265. According to R. Stein, "Le Lin-yi," *Han-hiue,* II (1947), pp. 251 ff., the "Fan" that the Chinese prefix to the names of most of the kings of Funan as well as those of Champa was not an equivalent of the ending *varman* taken as a family name, as was believed by Georges Maspero, *Le Royaume de Champa* (Paris, 1928), p. 53, n. 7, and Gabriel Ferrand, "Ye-tiao, Sseu-tiao et Java," *JA* (November-December, 1916), pp. 524–30. Stein believes that it is a clan name, of ethnic origin, designating the indigenous element of the royal family. The *Fan,* as in Champa, are opposed to the Indian elements and seem to be maintained in power by the people. But Paul Demiéville (review of Stein's "Lin-yi," *TP,* XL [1951], p. 344) expresses doubts over the firmness of the foundation of this hypothesis.
17. Pelliot, "Le Fou-nan," p. 257.
18. *Ibid.,* pp. 265–66. The *li* equals about 576 meters. On the

reading "Ch'ü-tu, Tu-k'un" instead of "Ch'ü-tu-k'un" (Pelliot), see Stein, "Le Lin-yi."

19. "Le Lin-yi," p. 119. But Demiéville, review of Stein's "Lin-yi," p. 341, contests this identification.
20. As early as 1938, Kattigara was located in the region of Saigon by Albert Herrmann, "Der Magnus Sinus und Cattigara nach Ptolemäus," *Compte-rendu du Congrès international de géographie* (Amsterdam), pp. 123–28. The most recent research is that of Louis Malleret, who, following his discoveries at Oc Eo (above, p. 17), was led to seek Kattigara in this region. His views are set forth in detail in *L'Archéologie du delta du Mékong* (Paris, 1959–63), III, pp. 421–54.
21. On this rather involved question, and on the location of Chiu-chih or Chü-li, see Paul Wheatley, *The Golden Khersonese*, pp. 21–25.
22. Pelliot, "Le Fou-nan," p. 279.
23. *Ibid.*, p. 263, n. 1. Wheatley, *The Golden Khersonese*, pp. 15–21.
24. Pelliot, "Le Fou-nan," p. 266, n. 2 and 3. Gordon H. Luce, "Countries Neighbouring Burma," *JBRS*, XIV (1924), pp. 147, 151.
25. Paul Pelliot, "Deux itinéraires de Chine en Inde, à la fin du VIIIe siècle," *BEFEO*, IV, p. 320, n. 7. Gabriel Ferrand, "Malaka, le Malāyu et Malāyur," App. III, *JA* (July-August, 1918), p. 139. Luce, "Countries Neighbouring Burma," pp. 161–69.
26. Ferrand, "Malaka," p. 143. See Sylvain Lévi, "Pré-aryen et pré-dravidien dans l'Inde," *JA* (July-September, 1923), p. 37.
27. R. O. Winstedt, "A History of Malaya," *JRASMB*, XIII (1935), p. 21.
28. Wheatley, *The Golden Khersonese*, pp. 252–67, discusses the location of Langkasuka in detail.
29. Coedès, "Le royaume de Çrīvijaya," *BEFEO*, XVIII, 6, p. 17. Lévi, "Pré-aryen," p. 45.
30. Coedès, *Recueil des inscriptions du Siam* (Bangkok, 1924–29), II, p. 51, no. XXVII. The date seventh to ninth centuries indicated by Barth is too early. The script is similar to that of the last inscriptions of Funan. See K. A. Nilakanta Sastri, "Agastya," *TBG*, LXXXVI (1936), pp. 508–09. On Tāmbralinga, see O. W. Wolters, "Tāmbralinga," *BSOAS* (1958), pp. 587–607.
31. Sylvain Lévi, "Ptolémée, le Niddesa et la Bṛihatkathā," *Et. Asiat. EFEO*, II, p. 26.
32. *Ibid.*, pp. 3 ff.
33. Roland Braddell, "Ancient Times in the Malay Peninsula," *JRASMB*, XVII (1939), I, pp. 204–206, and XXII (1949), p. 1. Wheatley, *The Golden Khersonese*, pp. 268–72, has furnished good arguments for locating Takkola in the region of Trang.
34. *Transactions and Papers of the Institute of British Geographers*, 21 (1955), p. 69. On this point see Wang Gungwu, "The

Nanhai Trade: A Study of the Early History of Chinese Trade in the South China Sea," *JRASMB,* XXXI, 2 (1958), p. 41, n. 53.

35. On these sites, see Braddell, "Ancient Times," *passim.* H. G. Quaritch Wales, "Archaeological Researches on Ancient Indian Colonization in Malaya," *JRASMB,* XVIII (1940), I, pp. 56–73; "Further Work on Indian Sites in Malaya," *JRASMB,* XX (1947), pp. 1–11. R. O. Winstedt, "Slab-Graves and Iron Implements," *JRASMB,* XIX (1941), I, pp. 93–98.
36. For example, the bronzes of Gupta style described in the state of Perak and on the Bujang River in Kedah (H. G. Quaritch Wales, "Recent Malayan Excavations and Some Wider Implications," *JRAS* [1946], p. 142). These archaeological discoveries are analyzed by Wheatley, *The Golden Khersonese,* pp. 273 ff.
37. On other Indian textual sources, see Vasudeva S. Agrawala, "Some References to Kaṭāhadvīpa in Ancient Indian Literature," *JGIS,* XI (1944), p. 96, and K. A. Nilakanta Sastri, *History of Śrīvijaya* (Madras, 1949), pp. 25–26.
38. On the date of this inscription, see D. C. Sircar, "Date of the Earliest Sanskrit Inscription of Campā," *JGIS,* VI (1939), pp. 53–55. Coedès, "La date de l'inscription sanskrite de Vo-canh," *IHQ,* XVI, 3 (1940), pp. 72, 484. Sircar, "Date of the Earliest Sanskrit Inscription of Campā," *IHQ,* XVII (1941), pp. 107–10. Emile Gaspardone, "La plus ancienne inscription d'Indochine," *JA,* CCXLI (1953), pp. 477–85. K. Kumar Sarkar, "The Earliest Inscription of Indochina," *Sino-Indian Studies,* V, 2 (1956), pp. 77–87. Kamalesvar Bhattacharya, "Précisions sur la paléographie de l'inscription dite de Vo-canh," *AA,* XXIV (1961), pp. 219–24. E. Gaspardone, "L'inscription de Vo-canh et les débuts du sanskrit en Indochine," *Sinologica,* VIII, No. 3 (1965), pp. 129–36.
39. Auguste Barth and Abel Bergaigne, ISC, No. XX, p. 191. Louis Finot, "Les inscriptions du musée de Hanoi," *BEFEO,* XV, 2, p. 3.
40. "Séance du 14 Janvier 1927," *JA* (January-March, 1927), p. 186. See Louis Finot, review of Maspero's *Le Royaume de Champa, BEFEO,* XXVIII, pp. 286–87.
41. Jean Filliozat has kindly informed me that *Māran* "is a frequent designation of the king Pāṇḍya, substantiated from one of the most ancient Tamil texts of Sangam, dating around the beginning of the Christian Era."
42. Lévi, "Ptolémée," pp. 29 ff. Luce, "Countries Neighbouring Burma," pp. 151–58.
43. Pelliot, "Le Fou-nan," p. 303.
44. *Les Peuples de la péninsule indochinoise* (Paris, 1962), p. 62.
45. Wang Gungwu, "The Nan-hai Trade," pp. 31–45.
46. "Le Fou-nan," p. 292.

47. But, see above, p. 39.
48. Pelliot, "Le Fou-nan," p. 303.
49. Above, p. 40. See Robert von Heine-Geldern, "The Drum Named Makalamau," *India Antiqua* (Leyden, 1947), p. 176.
50. Pelliot, "Le Fou-nan," p. 252.
51. *Ibid.*, p. 254.
52. *Ibid.*, p. 255.
53. For this whole section, in addition to other indicated sources, see Maspero, *Le Royaume de Champa,* pp. 43–59 (reviews by L. Aurousseau, *BEFEO,* XIV, 9, pp. 8–43, and Louis Finot, *BEFEO,* XXVIII, pp. 285–92). Stein, "Le Lin-yi," pp. 1–123.
54. Aurousseau, review of Maspero's *Le Royaume de Champa,* p. 27.
55. Stein, "Le Lin-yi," pp. 209–41. But Demiéville, review of Stein's "Lin-yi," p. 346, seems to prefer the first interpretation.
56. Up to now we have always understood that they came from the south, that is, from present-day Quang-nam. But Stein ("Le Lin-yi") has shown that they may also have come from the west, and even from the regions of Siang-lin, away from Chinese domination. The crystallization of the barbarians in a principality Lin-yi took place inside the limits of Jih-nan.
57. On the ethnic Ch'ü, see Stein, "Le Lin-yi," Appendix VI, pp. 209 ff.
58. Henri Parmentier, *Inventaire descriptif des monuments čams de l'Annam* (Paris, 1909–18), I, pp. 241–505. Jean Y. Claeys, "Introduction à l'étude de l'Annam et du Champa," *Bulletin des Amis du Vieux Hué,* 21 (1934), pp. 46–48.
59. Pelliot, "Le Fou-nan," p. 251.
60. Stein, "Le Lin-yi," pp. 1–54.
61. Perhaps through wives of Funanese birth, which, according to Stein, "Le Lin-yi," would explain his clan name *Fan,* on which see above, p. 276, n. 16. Eveline Porée-Maspero remarks that the Fan kings made their appearance in Champa at the moment when they disappeared in Funan after Fan Hsün. On the "historical parallels between Cambodia and Champa" that she establishes from this period, see *Etude sur les rites agraires des Cambodgiens* (Paris, 1962), pp. 144 ff.
62. Stein, "Le Lin-yi," p. 243.

Chapter IV

1. Paul Pelliot, "Le Fou-nan," *BEFEO,* III, pp. 252, 255, 269.
2. R. Stein, "Le Lin-yi," *Han-hiue,* II (1947), pp. 257–58, n. 277, is of the opinion that T'ien-chou means only that his family once came from India.
3. "Kanishka et S'ātavāhana," *JA* (January-March, 1936), pp. 61–121.
4. *Ibid.*, p. 82.

5. Kashi P. Jayaswal, "History of India c. 150 A.D. to 350 A.D.," *Journal of the Bihar and Orissa Research Society,* XIX (1933), pp. 287–89, 301–303.
6. Below, p. 58.
7. Coedès, *Inscriptions du Cambodge* (Paris, 1937–), IV, p. 27.
8. Victor Goloubew, "Les Images de Sūrya au Cambodge," *Cahiers EFEO,* no. 22 (1940), pp. 38–42. Kamaleswar Bhattacharya, *Les Religions brahmaniques dans l'ancien Cambodge* (Paris, 1961), pp. 128–31. See Louis de La Vallée-Poussin, *Dynasties et histoire de l'Inde* (Paris, 1935), p. 350.
9. Coedès, "La date du Bayon," *BEFEO,* XXVIII, p. 105; "Les capitales de Jayavarman II," *BEFEO,* XXVIII, p. 116, n. 1; "Quelques suggestions sur la méthode à suivre pour interpréter les bas-reliefs de Bantay Chmar et de la galerie extérieure du Bayon," *BEFEO,* XXXII, p. 73; *Inscriptions du Cambodge,* I, p. 195. In the *Mahābhārata,* VI, 436, a Brahman from Śakadvīpa bears the name of Maga, i.e., Magus, sun worshiper. See La Vallée-Poussin, *Dynasties et histoire de l'Inde,* p. 350, and Bhattacharya, *Les Religions brahmaniques,* pp. 128–31.
10. Pierre Dupont, "Vishṇu mitrés de l'Indochine occidentale," *BEFEO,* XLI, p. 249.
11. References in R. Gopalan, *History of the Pallavas of Kanchi* (Madras, 1928), Chap. II. Cadambi Minakshi, *Administration and Social Life under the Pallavas* (Madras, 1938)—reviewed in *BEFEO,* XXXVIII, pp. 331–32.
12. Sylvain Lévi, "Pré-aryen et pré-dravidien dans l'Inde," *JA* (January-March, 1926), p. 53. On the Kambojas, see B. C. Law, "Some Ancient Indian Tribes," *Indian Culture,* I, p. 386; Sten Konow, "Notes on the Sakas," *Indian Culture,* II, p. 189; B. R. Chatterjee, "A Current Tradition among the Kambojas of North-India Relating to the Khmers of Cambodia," *AA,* XXIV (1961), p. 253.
13. Above, pp. 17, 37.
14. Louis Malleret, *L'Archéologie du delta du Mékong* (Paris, 1959–63), III, pp. 294 and 304.
15. Georges Maspero, *Le Royaume de Champa* (Paris, 1928), pp. 58–61.
16. Louis Finot, "Deux nouvelles inscriptions de Bhadravarman I," *BEFEO,* II, p. 187. R. C. Majumdar, *Ancient Indian Colonies in the Far East,* I: Champa (Lahore, 1927), Inscription No. 4. B. C. Chhabra, "Expansion of Indo-Aryan Culture during Pallava Rule," *JASB,* Letters, I (1935), p. 50.
17. Auguste Barth and Abel Bergaigne, ISC, XXI, p. 199. Finot, "Deux nouvelles inscriptions," p. 186. Majumdar, *Ancient Indian Colonies,* I, Inscription No. 2. Chhabra, "Expansion of Indo-Aryan Culture," p. 47.
18. Maspero, *Le Royaume de Champa,* p. 63.

19. Barth and Bergaigne, ISC, pp. 203–205.
20. "Deux nouvelles inscriptions," p. 186.
21. Jean Philippe Vogel, "The Yūpa Inscriptions of King Mūlavarman from Kotei (East Borneo)," *BKI*, 74 (1918), p. 232.
22. The old pronunciation of the character *fo,* which commonly was used to transcribe the word *buddha,* is *b'iuat,* which is an acceptable way of rendering *bhadra.* On the other hand *hu ta* is pronounced *huo d'āt,* which would be a much less satisfactory transcription. The equation of Fan Fo with Bhadravarman resolves the difficulty.
23. "Le Lin-yi," pp. 71, 111.
24. Those of Hon Cuc (Finot, "Deux nouvelles inscriptions," p. 186; Majumdar, *Ancient Indian Colonies,* I, Inscription No. 6, p. 9) and Chiêm-sơn (Louis Finot, "Deux nouvelles inscriptions indochinoises," *BEFEO,* XVIII, 10, p. 13; Majumdar, *Ancient Indian Colonies,* I, Inscription No. 5, p. 8).
25. Inscription of Đông-yên-châu (Coedès, "La plus ancienne inscription en langue chame," Mélanges F. W. Thomas, *New Indian Antiquary,* extra ser. I [1939], pp. 46–49).
26. This paragraph and the two preceding ones are taken from Coedès, *Les Peuples de la péninsule indochinoise* (Paris, 1962), p. 70.
27. Finot, "Deux nouvelles inscriptions," p. 190.
28. See above, p. 23.
29. *Ethnographie des peuples étrangers à la Chine, ouvrage composé au XIIIe siècle de notre ère,* trans. Marquis d'Hervey de Saint-Denys, II: Méridionaux (Geneva, 1883), pp. 422–25.
30. In Cham *kalan.*
31. On this word, see Paul Pelliot, trans. and ed., *Mémoires sur les coutumes du Cambodge de Tcheou Ta-kouan,* Posthumous Works of Paul Pelliot, v. III (Paris, 1951), pp. 160–62.
32. The month of harvest.
33. On the other hand, the *History of the Liang,* cited by Maspero, *Le Royaume de Champa,* p. 31, explains this custom in a way that seems more accurate. It says: "The man is of little importance; only the woman is important."
34. Majumdar, *Ancient Indian Colonies,* II: Suvarṇadvīpa (Dacca, 1937), pp. 88–89. See a reproduction in R. O. Winstedt, "History of Malaya," *JRASMB,* XIII (1935), pl. IV, p. 18.
35. Majumdar, *Ancient Indian Colonies,* II, p. 90. Chhabra, "Expansion of Indo-Aryan Culture," p. 15.
36. H. G. Quaritch Wales, "Archaeological Researches on Ancient Indian Colonization," *JRASMB,* XVIII (1940), pp. 8–10. These stanzas seem to be drawn from a sutra of the Mādhyamika school, a school of Mahayana Buddhism founded by Nāgārjuna (René Grousset, *Philosophies indiennes* [Paris, 1931], I, pp. 200–344). On the archaeology of Kedah in general, see Roland Braddell, "Most Ancient Kedah," *Malaya in History,*

vol. 4, no. 2 (1958), pp. 18–40, and especially Alastair Lamb, "Miscellaneous Papers on Early Hindu and Buddhist Settlements in Northern Malaya and Southern Thailand," *JFMSM,* VI, n.s. (1961), pp. 1–47.

37. R. O. Winstedt, "Indian Influence in the Malay World," *JRAS* (1944), p. 187. On the Buddhist images in Gupta style found in Malaysia, see above, p. 278, n. 36, and R. O. Winstedt, "Buddhist Images from Malaya and Sumatra," *IAL,* XVI (1942), p. 41.
38. Chhabra, "Expansion of Indo-Aryan Culture," pp. 16–20 (inscription preserved in the Indian Museum of Calcutta).
39. Gabriel Ferrand, "Le K'ouen-louen et les anciennes navigations inter-océaniques dans les mers du Sud," *JA* (March-April, 1919), p. 256. Gordon H. Luce, "Countries Neighbouring Burma," *JBRS,* XIV (1924), pp. 173–78.
40. J. L. Moens, "Srīvijaya, Yāva en Katāha," *TBG,* LXXVII (1937), pp. 343–44. This article (pp. 317–487 of the *TBG* volume) was translated into English in *JRASMB,* XVII (January, 1940).
41. Paul Wheatley, *The Golden Khersonese* (Kuala Lumpur, 1961), p. 36. On Chih-t'u, see below, p. 78.
42. Paul Pelliot, "Deux intinéraires de Chine en Inde, à la fin du VIIIe siècle," *BEFEO,* IV, p. 276, n. 4, and p. 281.
43. Summary of the discussion in Roland Braddell, "An Introduction to the Study of Ancient Times in the Malay Peninsula and the Straits of Malacca," *JRASMB,* XVII, pt. 1 (1939), pp. 168–69.
44. Above, p. 17.
45. Pelliot, "Le Fou-nan," p. 279.
46. Gabriel Ferrand, "Malaka, le Malāyu et Malāyur," *JA* (July-August, 1918), p. 140.
47. W. P. Groeneveldt, *Notes on the Malay Archipelago and Malacca* (Batavia, 1876), p. 10. I reproduce here the text incorporated by Ma Tuan-lin in his *Ethnographie,* pp. 455–56.
48. On this word, see Pelliot, *Mémoires . . . de Tcheou Ta-kouan,* p. 162.
49. Pelliot, "Deux intinéraires," p. 229. Wheatley, *The Golden Khersonese,* pp. 47–51. Luce, "Countries Neighbouring Burma," pp. 169–72, believes the country was conquered by the king of Funan, Fan Shih-man, and named after his predecessor, P'an-p'an. Stein, "Le Lin-yi," p. 258, seems to share this point of view (see below, p. 284, n. 81).
50. Pelliot, "Le Fou-nan," p. 269, n. 2.
51. See below, p. 56.
52. *Ethnographie,* pp. 463–64.
53. *The Golden Khersonese,* pp. 51–55. See also Hsü Yün-ts'iao, "Notes on Tan-tan," *JRASMB,* XX (1947), pp. 47–63.
54. Vogel, "The Yūpa Inscriptions," pp. 167–232. B. R. Chatterjee, *India and Java* (Calcutta, 1933), II, Inscription, pp. 8–19. B. C. Chhabra, "Three More Yūpa Inscriptions of King Mūlavarman

from Kotei (E. Borneo)," *JGIS,* XII (1945), pp. 14–17 (reprinted in *TBG,* LXXXIII [1949], pp. 370–74, with an additional note by J. G. de Casparis); "Yūpa Inscriptions," *India Antiqua* (Leyden, 1947), pp. 77–82.

55. Chhabra, "Three More Yūpa Inscriptions," p. 39, and Braddell, "An Introduction to the Study of Ancient Times," *JRASMB,* XV, 3 (1937), pp. 118–19.
56. R. Ng. Poerbatjaraka, *Agastya in den Archipel* (Leyden, 1926). K. A. Nilakanta Sastri, "Agastya," *TBG,* LXXVI (1936), pp. 515 ff. Nicholaas J. Krom, *Hindoe-Javaansche Geschiedenis* (The Hague, 1931), p. 72. W. F. Stutterheim, "Waprakeçwara," *BKI,* 92 (1934), p. 203.
57. F. D. K. Bosch, "Ouheden en Koetei," *Oudheidkundig Verslag* (1925), p. 142.
58. *Ibid.,* p. 132. On the Indianization of Borneo, see Ordhendra Coomar Gangoly, "On Some Hindu Relics in Borneo," *JGIS,* III (1936), p. 97. E. Banks, "Ancient Times in Borneo," *JRASMB,* XX (December, 1947), pp. 26–34, and especially the special number of the same periodical, XXII (September 4, 1949), which gives information on the important discovery of Indian statuettes of Gupta and Pāla style at Sambas, in the west of the island, previously announced by Y. S. Tan in *JSSS,* V (1948), pp. 31–42. See also A. B. Griswold, "The Santubon Buddha and Its Context," *Sarawak Museum Journal,* X (1962), p. 363.
59. "Notes," *Rūpam,* 7 (1926), p. 114.
60. Pelliot, "Deux itinéraires," p. 296, n. 2.
61. *Ibid.,* p. 283.
62. Sylvain Lévi, "Pour l'histoire du Rāmāyaṇa," *JA* (January-February, 1918), p. 80.
63. The *History of the Han,* under the date 132, mentions a country, Yeh-t'iao, which has been identified with Java (Pelliot, "Deux itinéraires," p. 266, and Gabriel Ferrand, "Ye-tiao, Sseu-tiao et Java," *JA* [November-December, 1916], p. 520). Stein, "Le Lin-yi," p. 138, disputes this comparison, but Paul Demiéville, review of Stein's "Lin-yi," *TP,* XL (1951), p. 346, defends the identification of *Yeh-t'iao* with *Yavadvīpa* (Greek *Iabadiou*).
64. Above, p. 18.
65. Jean Philippe Vogel, "The Earliest Sanskrit Inscriptions of Java," in *Publicaties van den Oudheidkundigen dienst in Nederlandsch-Indië,* I (Batavia, 1925), pp. 15–35. Chatterjee, *India and Java,* II, Inscription, pp. 20–27. Joseph Minattur, "A Note on the King Kundungga of the East Borneo Inscriptions," *JSEAH,* V, No. 2 (September, 1964), p. 181.
66. F. M. Schnitger, "Tārumānagara," *TBG,* LXXIV (1934), p. 187. See W. F. Stutterheim, "Note on Cultural Relations between South-India and Java," *TBG,* LXXIX (1939), p. 83.

67. W. F. Stutterheim, "De voetafdrukken van Pūrṇawarman," *BKI,* 89 (1932), p. 288.
68. Pelliot, "Deux itinéraires," p. 284. L. C. Damais (review of Poerbatjaraka's *Riwajat Indonesia* in *BEFEO,* XLVIII [1957], p. 611) regards this equivalence as imperfect, since the Chinese characters call forth a restitution such as Tarama or Talama, but perhaps this is being too scrupulous.
69. Above, pp. 7, 18.
70. *Oudheidkundig Verslag,* 1928. F. M. Schnitger, *The Archaeology of Hindoo Sumatra* (Leyden, 1937), pp. 2–3. Nicholaas J. Krom, "Antiquities of Palembang," *ABIA* (1931), pp. 29–33. Devaprasad Ghosh, *JGIS,* III (1936), p. 36 (which gives references to the literature produced by the discovery of this statue).
71. Sylvain Lévi, "Ptolémée, le Niddesa et la Bṛihatkathā," in *Et. Asiat. EFEO,* II, p. 27. Baros, on the western coast of Sumatra, is mentioned in Ptolemy under the form *Barousai.*
72. Hsüan-tsang, *Si-yu-ki: Buddhist Records of the Western World,* trans. by Samuel Beal (London, 1884), I, p. lxxxi.
73. Pelliot, "Deux itinéraires," pp. 274–75. On Guṇavarman, see W. Pachow, "The Voyage of Buddhist Missions to South-East Asia and the Far East," *JGIS,* XVII (1958), p. 9; on the identification of She-p'o with Java, see Damais, review of Poerbatjaraka, p. 641. L. C. Damais, *BEFEO,* LII (1964), p. 126.
74. Pelliot, "Deux itinéraires," pp. 271–72. L. C. Damais, *BEFEO,* LII (1964), p. 96, n. 1.
75. Moens, "Srīvijaya, Yāva en Katāha." See the critique of K. A. Nilakanta Sastri, "Notes on the Historical Geography of the Malay Peninsula and Archipelago," *JGIS,* VII (1940), pp. 15–42.
76. A. Grimes, "The Journey of Fa-hsien from Ceylon to Canton," *JRASMB,* XIX (1941), p. 76. Roland Braddell, "An Introduction to the Study of Ancient Times," *JRASMB,* XIX (1941), pp. 46 ff.; A Note on Sambas and Borneo," *JRASMB,* XXII, 4 (1949), p. 3. Wheatley, *The Golden Khersonese,* p. 39.
77. W. T. Kao, "A Primary Chinese Record Relating to Ho-lo-tan, and Miscellaneous Notes on Srivijaya and Fo-che," *JRASMB,* XXIX (1956), p. 163.
78. Gabriel Ferrand, "Le Kan-t'o-li" (App. III of "Le K'ouen-louen," *JA* [September-October, 1919], pp. 238–41). Jean Przyluski, "Indian Colonization in Sumatra before the Seventh Century," *JGIS,* I (1934), pp. 92–101.
79. Moens, "Srīvijaya, Yāva en Katāha."
80. La Vallée-Poussin, *Dynasties et histoire de l'Inde,* p. 40.
81. Perhaps this name is a corruption of that of the first Kauṇḍinya. It would then refer to a legitimate representative of the Indian element of the royal family, opposed to the indigenous Fan clan (above, p. 279, n. 61). Stein, "Le Lin-yi," p. 258, thinks that this was simply a king descending from Kauṇḍinya

through king P'an-p'an, and that there is no question here of the country of P'an-p'an, about which see above, p. 52.

82. Pelliot, "Le Fou-nan," p. 269.
83. *Ibid.*, p. 255.
84. Louis Finot, "Les inscriptions de Mi-sơn," *BEFEO,* IV, p. 922.
85. See below, p. 70.
86. Maspero, *Le Royaume de Champa,* p. 65. See Louis Finot's review of Maspero's *Le Royaume de Champa* in *BEFEO,* XXVIII, p. 288.
87. On the location of Chü-su and of the capital, see Stein, "Le Lin-yi," pp. 1 ff.
88. See below, p. 65.
89. Pelliot, "Le Fou-nan," p. 257.
90. *Ibid.*, p. 294.
91. Maspero, *Le Royaume de Champa,* p. 75, n. 2, gives sufficient reasons for regarding these two persons as one. But see Stein, "Le Lin-yi," p. 257. We may wonder if this name is not the title *kujula,* in use among the Kushans. See above, p. 47.
92. The monks in question were Sanghapāla and Mandrasena, whose translations appear in the Chinese *Tripitaka* (Bunyin Najio, *A Catalogue of the Chinese Translations of the Buddhist Tripitaka, the Sacred Canon of the Buddhists in China and Japan* [Oxford, 1883], Appendix II, Nos. 101 and 102). See Pelliot, "Le Fou-nan," pp. 284–85. On these two monks, see W. Pachow, "The Voyage of Buddhist Missions to South-East Asia and the Far East," *JGIS,* XVII (1958), p. 13.
93. The *chang* equals ten feet. This passage of the *History of the Southern Ch'i* on the boats is based on a more detailed section from the account of K'ang T'ai in the *T'ai-p'ing Yü-lan* encyclopedia—a section reproduced in Paul Pelliot, "Textes chinois concernant l'Indochine hindouisée," *Et. Asiat. EFEO,* II, pp. 252–53.
94. Pelliot, "Le Fou-nan," pp. 261–62.
95. *Ibid.*, pp. 269–70.
96. This is the system of *trapeang* still in use in Cambodia.
97. It is the pose of "royal ease" often represented in iconography.
98. See Coedès, "La destination funéraire des grands monuments Khmèrs," *BEFEO,* XL, p. 320. These four customs are Indian and date back to the Vedic period (*Atharvaveda,* XVIII, 2, 34).
99. Pelliot, "Le Fou-nan," p. 269.
100. Above, p. 58.
101. Coedès, "A New Inscription from Fu-nan," *JGIS,* IV (1937), pp. 117–21.
102. Coedès, "Deux inscriptions sanskrits du Fou-nan," *BEFEO,* XXXI, pp. 1–12.
103. On this site, see Etienne F. Aymonier, *Le Cambodge* (Paris, 1900–1904), I, pp. 138–39.
104. It seems increasingly probable to me that the reigning king

of the inscription of Thap-mười (stanza II), whose incomplete name begins with the letter *ja* followed by a letter that is partly obliterated but resembles a *ya,* is no other than Jayavarman.

105. This hypothesis, which I have already formulated ("A New Inscription from Fu-nan," p. 119), can be reconciled with the apparently contradictory fact that the inscription of Guṇavarman is paleographically earlier than that of Queen Kulaprabhāvatī. The inscription of Thap-mười had in fact been composed when Guṇavarman was still very young (stanza VII), while the other inscription was composed when the queen planned to retire from the world; her withdrawal was perhaps the result of the murder of her son and the usurpation of the throne by his rival.
106. Pelliot, "Le Fou-nan," p. 270.
107. Coedès, "Deux inscriptions sanskrits du Fou-nan," pp. 8–12.
108. Pachow, "Voyage of Buddhist Missions," p. 14.
109. Barth and Bergaigne, ISC, no. XI, p. 66.
110. Coedès, "L'inscription de Baksei Chamkrong," *JA* (May-June, 1909), pp. 479 ff. See also Coedès, "La tradition généalogique des premiers rois d'Angkor," *BEFEO,* XXVIII, pp. 131 and 139, and Coedès, *Inscriptions du Cambodge,* II, pp. 10 and 155.
111. Coedès, "La tradition généalogique," pp. 127–31.
112. Pelliot, "Le Fou-nan," p. 260. Kalyan Sarkar, "Mahāyāna Buddhism in Fu-nan," *Sino-Indian Studies,* V (1955), expresses the opinion that Maheśvara designates the Bodhisattva and that everything in the petition of the monk Nāgasena relates to Mahayana Buddhism, but this is not very likely at such an early date.
113. Coedès, "La tradition généalogique," pp. 128–30.
114. Henri Parmentier, "L'art présumé du Fou-nan," *BEFEO,* XXXII, pp. 183–89.
115. Georges Groslier, "Note sur la sculpture khmèr ancienne," *Et. Asiat. EFEO,* I, pp. 297–314.
116. Dupont, "Vishṇu mitrés," pp. 233–54; "Les premières images brahmaniques d'Indochine," *BSEI, n.s.,* XXVI (1951), pp. 131–40.
117. Louis Malleret, *Catalogue . . . Musée Blanchard de la Brosse,* I (Hanoi, 1937), Nos. 68–70, pl. XIII–XV. See Goloubew, "Les images de Sūrya au Cambodge," pp. 38–42.
118. It is necessary to make an exception for the enigmatic kingdoms of Huang-chih and Fu-kan-tu-lu (Paul Pelliot's review of F. Hirth and W. W. Rockhill's *Chau Ju-kua* in *TP,* XIII [1912], pp. 457–61). It has been thought possible to identify *Fu-kan* (*tu-lu*) with *Pagan* in Burma (see the discussion in G. H. Luce, "Fu-kan-tu-lu," *JBRS,* XIV [1924], pp. 91–99).
119. Pelliot, "Deux itinéraires," pp. 172–73.
120. G. H. Luce, "Names of the Pyu," *JBRS,* XXII (1932), p. 90, and

XXVIII (1937), p. 241; "Burma down to the Fall of Pagan," *JBRS,* XXIX (1939), p. 269.

121. Gold plaques of Maungun containing the formulas *ye dhamma* and *iti pi so* and the enumeration of nineteen categories, described in Tun Nyein, *Epigraphia Indica,* V, p. 101, and Louis Finot, "Un nouveau document sur le bouddhisme birman," *JA* (July-August, 1912), p. 131; three fragments of an inscription on stone (or baked earth) from Bôbôgyi near Môza, containing a fragment of the *Vibhanga,* described in the same Finot article, p. 135, and the sequel in *JA* (July-August, 1913), p. 193; a reliquary from Môza bearing the inscribed names of four Buddhas and four disciples, described in *ARASI* (1926–27), p. 175; one gold leaf found at Kyundôzu giving the formula *iti pi so,* described in *ARASI* (1928–29), pp. 108–109; twenty gold leaves found at Môza containing extracts from various passages of the Pali canon, described in *ARASB* (1938–39), pp. 12–22. See Nihar-Ranjan Ray, *Sanskrit Buddhism in Burma* (Calcutta, 1936), pp. 3–4.

122. A. P. Phayre, *History of Burma* (London, 1883).

123. Finot, "Un nouveau document," pp. 121–30. Charles Duroiselle, "The Ari of Burma and Tantric Buddhism," *ARASB* (1915–16), p. 80.

124. C. O. Blagden, "Thaton," *JBRS,* V (1915), pp. 26–27.

125. On the meaning of this legend, see Louis Finot, "La légende de Buddhaghosa," *Cinquantenaire Ecole Hautes Etudes* (1921), pp. 101–19.

126. H. G. Quaritch Wales, "The Exploration of Śrī Deva, an Ancient Indian City in Indochina," *IAL,* X (1935), pp. 61–99; "Early Indian Art from the Siamese Jungle," *Illustrated London News* (Jan. 30, 1937), pp. 174–76; *Towards Angkor* (London, 1937), Chap. VII. See above, p. 17.

127. References in Reginald le May, *A Concise History of Buddhist Art in Siam* (Cambridge, 1938). On the recent excavations of the Pierre Dupont mission, see Dupont's accounts in *BEFEO,* XXXVII, pp. 688–89; XXXIX, pp. 351–65; XL, pp. 503–504; and especially his *L'Archéologie mône de Dvāravatī* (Paris, 1959), 2 vols.

128. Coedès, "The Excavations at P'ong Tük," *JSS,* XXI, pt. 3 (1928), pp. 195–209; "Excavations at P'ong Tük in Siam," *ABIA* (1927), pp. 16–20. H. G. Quaritch Wales, "Further Excavations at P'ong Tük," *IAL,* X (1936), pp. 42–48.

Chapter V

1. Paul Pelliot, "Le Fou-nan," *BEFEO,* III, p. 274.
2. See above, pp. 36–37.
3. Paul Pelliot, trans. and ed., "Mémoires sur les coutumes du Cambodge," *BEFEO,* II, p. 123; "Le Fou-nan," p. 272. Instead

of *kshatriya,* it might be better to read *Ch'a-li* as *śrī,* which is prefixed to all names of kings and may have been taken by the Chinese as a family name.

4. Coedès, "Le site primitif du Tchen-la," *BEFEO,* XVIII, 9, pp. 1–3. Also see Coedès, "La tradition généalogique des premiers rois d'Angkor," *BEFEO,* XXVIII, p. 124; "Nouvelles données sur les origines du royaume khmèr," *BEFEO,* XLVIII (1956), pp. 209–20.
5. Quoted from Ma Tuan-lin, *Ethnographie des peuples étrangers à la Chine,* trans. Marquis d'Hervey de Saint-Denis, II: Méridionaux (Geneva, 1883), p. 483.
6. Paul Pelliot, "Deux itinéraires de Chine en Inde, à la fin du VIIIe siècle," *BEFEO,* IV, p. 217.
7. Sir Henry Yule and Arthur C. Burnell, *Hobson-Jobson* (London, 1903), under the entry "Varella."
8. Coedès, "La tradition généalogique," p. 124. This name, which, as we have seen, was that of the royal linga erected in the fourth century by the Cham king Bhadravarman, may have been chosen by Chenla to mark its victory over Champa.
9. Inscription of Baksei Chamkrong, st. XI–XII, in Coedès, *Inscriptions du Cambodge* (Paris, 1937–), IV, p. 95.
10. Victor Goloubew, "Les légendes de la Nāgī et de l'Apsaras," *BEFEO,* XXIV, p. 508.
11. Stele of Ta Prohm, st. VI–VII, in Coedès, "La stèle de Ta Prohm," *BEFEO,* VI, p. 71.
12. Eveline Porée-Maspero, "Nouvelle étude sur la Nāgī Somā," *JA* (1950), pp. 237 ff.
13. Baksei Chamkrong, st. XIII, in Coedès, *Inscriptions du Cambodge,* IV, p. 96.
14. Inscription from the mouth of the Mun, in Erik Seidenfaden, "Complément à *L'Inventaire descriptif des monuments du Cambodge* pour les quatre provinces du Siam oriental," *BEFEO,* XXII, pp. 57–58. See also "Chronique," *BEFEO,* XXII, p. 385.
15. Stele of Ta Prohm, st. IX, in Coedès, "La stèle de Ta Prohm," p. 71.
16. Coedès, *Inscriptions du Cambodge,* VI, p. 102.
17. Louis Finot, "Sur quelques traditions indochinoises," *Mélanges d'Indianisme offerts par ses élèves à M. Sylvain Lévi* (Paris, 1911), pp. 209–11.
18. In *ibid.,* p. 211, Finot seems already to have foreseen this solution.
19. Coedès, *Les Peuples de la péninsule indochinoise* (Paris, 1962), p. 90.
20. And not his brother as has been believed. See the inscription of Si Thep (K. 978) in Coedès, *Inscriptions du Cambodge,* VII.

21. Coedès, "Quelques précisions sur la fin du Fou-nan," *BEFEO,* XLIII, pp. 3–4.
22. Considered as that of Funan before its fall (Finot, "Sur quelques traditions indochinoises," pp. 211–12). But see above, pp. 36–37.
23. See above, p. 10.
24. Auguste Barth and Abel Bergaigne, ISC, No. XI, p. 69.
25. Inscription of Phnom Banteay Neang, in Barth and Bergaigne, ISC, No. III, pp. 26–28.
26. Unfortunately, the date is incomplete. This inscription (K. 978) is published in Coedès, *Inscriptions du Cambodge,* VII.
27. Pierre Dupont, "La dislocation du Tchen-la," *BEFEO,* XLIII, p. 44.
28. Coedès, *Inscriptions du Cambodge,* VI, p. 102.
29. Coedès, "Quelques précisions sur la fin du Fou-nan," p. 2.
30. Louis Finot, "Inscription de Thma Krê," *BEFEO,* III, p. 212. Adhémard Leclère, "Une campagne archéologique au Cambodge," *BEFEO,* IV, p. 739.
31. Seidenfaden, "Complément," p. 92.
32. Auguste Barth, "Inscription sanscrite du Phou Lokhon," *BEFEO,* III, p. 442. Seidenfaden, "Complément," pp. 57–58. "Chronique," *BEFEO,* XXII, p. 385.
33. Seidenfaden, "Complément," p. 59.
34. Barth and Bergaigne, ISC, p. 69.
35. Pelliot, "Le Fou-nan," p. 275.
36. Barth and Bergaigne, ISC, Nos. VI (p. 38) and IX (p. 51).
37. *Ibid.,* no. VII, p. 44.
38. *Ibid.,* no. VIII, p. 47.
39. Coedès, "L'extension du Cambodge vers la sudouest au VIIe siècle," *BEFEO,* XXIV, p. 357.
40. Pelliot, "Mémoires . . . du Cambodge," p. 124; "Le Fou-nan," p. 272.
41. Barth and Bergaigne, ISC, p. 38.
42. Pelliot, "Le Fou-nan," p. 275.
43. *Mémoires sur les contrées occidentales,* trans. S. Julien (Paris, 1857–58), II, p. 82.
44. Henri Parmentier, *L'Art khmèr primitif* (Paris, 1927), I, pp. 44–92.
45. Louis Finot, "Nouvelles inscriptions cambodgiennes," *BCAI* (1912), pp. 184–89.
46. Coedès, *Inscriptions du Cambodge,* IV, pp. 20–23.
47. Barth and Bergaigne, ISC, no. V, p. 31. Coedès, *Inscriptions du Cambodge,* I, p. 252. Henri Mauger, "Le Phnom Bayang," *BEFEO,* XXXVII, pp. 239–62.
48. Louis Finot, "Les inscriptions de Mi-sơn," *BEFEO,* IV, p. 922. See also Coedès, "Note sur deux inscriptions du Champa," *BEFEO,* XII, 8, p. 16.

49. Louis Finot, "Stèle du Çambhuvarman à Mi-sơn," *BEFEO*, III, p. 207.
50. Georges Maspero, *Le Royaume de Champa* (Paris, 1928), p. 81, n. 4.
51. *Ibid.*, p. 82.
52. R. Stein, "Le Lin-yi," *Han-hiue*, 2 (1947), p. 129, shows that it is the itinerary of the expedition of Liu Fang in 605 that enables us to locate the capital of Lin-yi for the first time with any certitude south of the Col des Nuages, in Quang-nam, undoubtedly on the present site of Tra-kiêu, where excavations have revealed an important center. It was around the same period that the term Champa, applied to this region, appeared in the Sanskrit inscriptions of Cambodia and South Vietnam; the Chinese transcription Chan-ch'eng did not come until more than a century later.
53. Finot, "Stèle du Çambhuvarman," p. 207.
54. Finot, "Les inscriptions de Mi-sơn," p. 910.
55. The beginning of the tenth century. See Philippe Stern, "*L'Art du Champa (ancien Annam) et son évolution* (Paris, 1942), p. 70. The monument of Mi-sơn numbered E_1 is the oldest (middle of the seventh century). See Jean Boisselier, *La Statuaire du Champa* (Paris, 1963), chap. III.
56. Maspero, *Le Royaume de Champa*, p. 89, n. 1. I cannot understand why this author affirms twice (pp. 89 and 91) that this princess was married to Prakāśadharma, since it is known that she was the great-grandaunt of the latter. No source, to my knowledge, alludes to such a marriage, which Maspero seems to have invented to justify the accession of Prakāśadharma to power. A comparison of Chinese sources with the inscriptions yields disconcerting results (see *ibid.*). To reconcile these sources, irreconcilable at first glance, they ought to be subjected to a new critical examination.
57. "Because of an offense," says the *New History of the T'ang*; "because of certain circumstances," says the inscription with more reserve.
58. Finot, "Les inscriptions de Mi-sơn," pp. 923–24. Edouard Huber, "L'inscription de Tra-Kiêu," *BEFEO*, XI, p. 263.
59. The sculptures of Tra-kiêu that have been discovered to date are later and in a style corresponding to that of Mi-sơn at the beginning of the tenth century (Stern, *L'Art du Champa*). On the date of the oldest monument of Mi-sơn (E_1), see Jean Boisselier, "Arts du Champa et du Cambodge préangkorien: La date de Mi-sön E_1," *AA*, XIX (1956), p. 197, and above, n. 55.
60. Paul Mus, "L'inscription à Vālmīki de Prakāśadharma," *BEFEO*, XXVIII, p. 152.
61. Inscription of Lai Cam, in Louis Finot, "Une nouvelle inscription de Prakāçadharma," *BEFEO*, XV, 2, p. 112.

62. Maspero, *Le Royaume de Champa*, p. 92.
63. Coedès, "Inscription de Bhavavarman II," *BEFEO*, IV, pp. 691–97.
64. Coedès, *Inscriptions du Cambodge*, I, p. 252.
65. *Ibid.*, p. 3. On Bhavavarman II, see Pierre Dupont, "Tchen-la et Pāṇḍuranga," *BSEI*, XXIV (1949), pp. 10–18.
66. Louis Finot, "L'inscription de Kompong Rŭsei," *BEFEO*, XVIII, 10, p. 15.
67. Coedès, *Inscriptions du Cambodge*, II, p. 193.
68. Barth and Bergaigne, ISC, no. IX, p. 59.
69. Auguste Barth, "Stèle de Vat Phou," *BEFEO*, II, pp. 235–40.
70. Coedès, *Inscriptions du Cambodge*, II, p. 40. (Ed. note: Date corrected by Coedès; Third Edition had 681.)
71. "Chronique," *BEFEO*, XXXIX, p. 341. On this difficult question, see Coedès, *Inscriptions du Cambodge*, IV, pp. 56–57.
72. Below, p. 85.
73. Dupont, "La dislocation du Tchen-la," pp. 17 ff.
74. One of the most remarkable exceptions is Asram Maharosei. See Henri Mauger, "L'Ásram Mahā Rosei," *BEFEO*, XXXVI, pp. 65–95.
75. See also Henri Parmentier, "Complément à l'art khmèr primitif," *BEFEO*, XXXV, pp. 1–115.
76. Philippe Stern, "Motifs indiennes au début de l'art khmèr," *Compte rendu, XXIe, Congrès International des Orientalistes* (Paris, 1948), p. 232, attributes these elements to an extensive contribution around the end of the sixth century or the beginning of the seventh from the Pallava country in southern India.
77. Pierre Dupont, "Les linteaux khmèrs du VIIe siècle," *AA*, XV (1952), pp. 31–83; *La Statuaire préangkorienne* (Ascona, 1955).
78. Coedès, *Inscriptions du Cambodge*, I, p. 5; II, p. 193. On these sects, see below, p. 113. See also Kamaleswar Bhattacharya, "The Pāncarātra Sect in Ancient Cambodia," *JGIS*, XIV (1955), pp. 107–16; *Les Religions brahmaniqûes dans l'ancien Cambodge*, Publ. EFEO, XLIX (Paris, 1961).
79. Dupont, *La Statuaire préangkorienne.*
80. Above, p. 62.
81. Barth and Bergaigne, ISC, No. X, p. 63.
82. Pelliot, "Le Fou-nan," p. 284. See above, p. 67.
83. Manuscripts of these texts are mentioned in the inscriptions of the period. See Barth and Bergaigne, ISC, No. IV, p. 30, and Coedès, "Une inscription du sixième siècle çaka," *BEFEO*, XI, p. 393.
84. Barth and Bergaigne, ISC, No. IV, p. 29 (contrary to Indian usage, the son of a Brahman and a princess of royal blood is born a Kshatriya); No. X, p. 63.
85. *Ibid.*, pp. 124–26.

86. *Ibid.*, p. 360, n. 1.
87. Marcel Ner, "L'organisation familiale en pays moï," *Cahiers de la Société de Géographie de Hanoi,* No. 15 (1928); "Au pays du droit maternel," *BEFEO,* XXX, p. 533. J. S. Furnivall, "Matriarchal Vestiges in Burma," *JBRS,* I (1912), pp. 15–30.
88. Edgar Thurston, *Castes and Tribes of Southern India* (Madras, 1909), vol. V. Govind S. Ghurye, "Dual Organization in India," *JRAI,* LIII (1923), pp. 79–91.
89. Pp. 477–81. In Paul Pelliot, trans. and ed., *Mémoires sur les coutumes du Cambodge de Tcheou Ta-kouan,* Posthumous Works of Paul Pelliot, Vol. III (Paris, 1951), p. 152, we find a translation of the passage of the *History of the Sui* pertaining to the audience hall.
90. *Mémoires sur les contrées occidentales,* II, p. 83. See G. H. Luce, "Countries Neighbouring Burma," *JBRS,* XIV (1924), pp. 178–82.
91. Chuan-lo-p'o-t'i and T'o-lo-po-ti (*New History of the T'ang*); She-ho-po-ti, To-ho-lo-po-ti, and To-ho-lo (I-ching). See also Pelliot, "Deux itinéraires," pp. 223, 232, 360, n. 1.
92. Krung Devamahānagara Pavara *Dvāravatī* Śrī Ayudhyā Mahātilaka Bhavanavaratna Rājadhānī Purīramya. See Prince Dhani Nivat, "The City of Thawarawadi Sri Ayudhya," *JSS,* XXXI (1939), p. 147.
93. Below, p. 222.
94. H. G. Quaritch Wales, "Some Notes on the Kingdom of Dvāravatī," *JGIS,* V (1938), pp. 24–30; *Towards Angkor* (London, 1937), pp. 132–46. During the printing of the present work, the discovery near Phra Pathom of two pieces of silver bearing the name of a King Śrīdvāravatīśvara of Dvāravatī has been announced. Descriptions of these pieces will be published in the *Comptes-rendus de l'Académie des Inscriptions et Belles-Lettres* and in the *Journal of the Siam Society*. See also *Archeologia,* No. 1 (November-December, 1964), p. 58.
95. As far as architecture is concerned, we have at Phra Pathom the lower part of a Buddhist monument resting on a double substructure with steps; on each face, five images of the seated Buddha are placed in niches flanked by colonnettes and pilasters. Other substructures, perhaps older, have been found farther west, at Phong Tǔk on the Kanburi River, associated with a bronze lamp of Hellenistic origin and with statuettes of the Buddha in post-Gupta style. See Pierre Dupont, *L'Archéologie mône de Dvāravatī* (Paris, 1959).
96. E. Lunet de Lajonquière, "Le domaine archéologique du Siam," *BCAI* (1909), pp. 200–37; "Essai d'inventaire archéologique du Siam," *BCAI* (1912), pp. 100–27. Coedès, "Tablettes votives bouddhiques du Siam," *Et. Asiat. EFEO,* I, p. 152, n. 1.; "Les collections archéologiques du Musée National

de Bangkok," *Ars Asiatica,* XII (1928), pp. 20–24; *Recueil des inscriptions du Siam* (Bangkok, 1924–29), II, pp. 1–4. Pierre Dupont, "Musée Guimet, Catalogue des collections indochinoises," *BCAI* (1931–34), pp. 45–53; "Vishṇu mitrés de l'Indochine occidentale," *BEFEO,* XLI, pp. 233–54; "Mission au Siam," *BEFEO,* XXXVII, pp. 686–93; *L'Archéologie môme de Dvāravatī.* Reginald le May, *A Concise History of Buddhist Art in Siam* (Cambridge, Eng., 1938), pp. 21–34. L. P. Briggs, "Dvāravatī, the Most Ancient Kingdom of Siam," *JAOS,* 65 (1945), pp. 98–107.

97. Coedès, "Documents sur l'histoire politique et religieuse du Laos occidental," *BEFEO,* XXV, p. 186; *Recueil des inscriptions du Siam,* II, pp. 17–19; "A propos de deux fragments d'inscription récemment découverts à P'ra Pathom," *CRAIBL* (1952), p. 146. Robert Halliday, "Les inscriptions mons du Siam," *BEFEO,* XXX, pp. 82–85.
98. Pelliot already had intimations of this; see "Deux itinéraires," p. 231. Basing his conclusions on the study of skeletons of doubtful age exhumed at Phong Tŭk, H. G. Quaritch Wales claims that Thai were already in the region at an early period ("Some Ancient Human Skeletons Excavated in Siam," *Man* [June, 1937], pp. 89–90), but this opinion is contested by Erik Seidenfaden, "Recent Archaeological Research Work in Siam," *JSS,* XXX (1938), p. 245.
99. Coedès, "Documents . . . Laos," pp. 16–17. Camille Notton, *Annales du Siam* (Paris, 1926–32), II, pp. 7–33.
100. Coedès, "Documents . . . Laos," pp. 189–200, and Halliday, "Les inscriptions mons du Siam," pp. 86–105.
101. *Mémoires sur les contrées occidentales,* II, p. 82.
102. Junjiro Takakusu, trans., *A Record of the Buddhist Religion as Practised in India and the Malay Archipelago* (*A.D. 671–695*) *by I-Tsing* (Oxford, 1896), p. 9.
103. Pelliot, "Deux itinéraires," pp. 174, 223. Luce, "Countries Neighbouring Burma," pp. 160–61.
104. Léon de Beylié, *L'Architecture hindoue en Extrême-Orient* (Paris, 1907), p. 238. On the excavations of Prome, see the excellent bibliography of G. H. Luce in *JBRS,* XXIX (1939), p. 278, n. 19.
105. Nihar-Ranjan Ray, *Sanskrit Buddhism in Burma* (Calcutta, 1936), pp. 19–30.
106. G. H. Luce, "The Ancient Pyu," *JBRS,* XXVII (1937), p. 247.
107. *Mémoires sur les contrées occidentales,* II, p. 82.
108. See above, p. 51. Pelliot, "Deux itinéraires," p. 406. Gabriel Ferrand, "Malaka, le Malāyu et Malāyur," *JA* (July-August, 1918), pp. 134–45. Sylvain Lévi, "Pré-aryen et pré-dravidien dans l'Inde," *JA* (July-September, 1923), pp. 37 ff. Luce, "Countries Neighbouring Burma," pp. 161–69.
109. *Ethnographie,* pp. 467–70. In Pelliot, *Mémoires . . . de Tcheou*

Ta-kouan, pp. 150–52, we find the passage of the *History of the Sui* used by Ma Tuan-lin. See also in Paul Wheatley, *The Golden Khersonese* (Kuala Lumpur, 1961), pp. 26 ff., the other probable sources of Ma Tuan-lin.

110. Gautama.

111. This information is probably from 609, the date at which a Chinese mission went to the country.

112. *Sādhukāra,* "doer of good," or, more likely, *sārdhakāra,* "fellow-worker."

113. *Dhanada,* "dispenser of good things," a title found engraved on a seal found at Oc Eo.

114. *Karmika,* "agent."

115. *Kulapati,* "head of the family," a title seen in Cambodian epigraphy, where it designates the head of a religious establishment.

116. *Nāyaka,* "guide," seen in an inscription of Lopburi (Coedès, *Recueil des inscriptions du Siam,* II, p. 14).

117. *Pati,* "chief," still in use as a Javanese title.

118. The "taking of the hand" (*pāṇigrahaṇa*) constitutes the basic rite of Hindu marriages.

119. All this ritual is strictly Hindu. On the construction of a funerary monument for the kings, see below, pp. 119–22; Coedès, "La destination funéraire des grands monuments khmèrs," *BEFEO,* XL, pp. 315–43.

120. Above, p. 54.

121. Pelliot, "Deux itinéraires," p. 286. We will notice that they occur during the period of the final fall of Funan.

122. J. L. Moens, "Srivijaya, Yāva en Katāha," *TBG,* LXXVII (1948), pp. 350 ff. R. A. Kern, "Ho-ling," in *Orientalia Neerlandica* (Leyden, 1948), pp. 402–13, distinguishes *two* Ho-lings, one in Kedah, the other in Java. Roland Braddell, "Notes on Ancient Times in Malaya," *JRASMB,* XXIV (1951), pp. 3 ff., places Ho-ling on Borneo. See Hsü Yün-ts'iao, "A Study of Gnomon Recorded in Ancient Chinese Accounts," *JSSS,* VI (1950), pp. 7–12.

123. Pelliot, "Deux itinéraires," p. 265. This was already the opinion of Edouard Chavannes, trans., *Voyages des pèlerins bouddhistes: Les religieux éminents qui allerent chercher la loi dans les pays de l'Occident, mémoire composé à l'époque de la grand dynastie T'ang par I-tsing* (Paris, 1894), p. 42, n. 2.

124. Review of Poerbatjaraka's *Riwajat Indonesia, BEFEO,* XLVIII (1957), pp. 612 and 644. See also *BEFEO,* LII (1964), p. 93.

125. H. Kern, *Verspreide Geschriften* (The Hague, 1913–29), VII, pp. 199–204. B. Ch. Chhabra, "Expansion of Indo-Aryan Culture," *JASB,* Letters (1935), pp. 33–34. B. R. Chatterjee, *India and Java* (Calcutta, 1933), II, Inscr., p. 28.

126. Nicholaas J. Krom, *Hindoe-Javaansche Geschiedenis* (The Hague, 1931), p. 127. According to L. C. Damais (review of

Poerbatjaraka, p. 627), Dieng, the original form of which was Di Hyang, represents the Sanskrit *Devālaya,* "residence of the gods."

127. W. P. Groeneveldt, *Notes on the Malay Archipelago and Malacca* (Batavia, 1876), p. 13.
128. Chavannes, *Voyages des pèlerins bouddhistes,* p. 60.
129. Pelliot, "Deux itinéraires," p. 324.
130. Chavannes, *Voyages des pèlerins bouddhistes,* pp. 116–20.
131. Pelliot, "Deux itinéraires," p. 342.
132. *Ibid.*, p. 324 and n. 5.

Chapter VI

1. They had a factory at Canton from the fourth century (James Hornell, "The Origins and Ethnological Significance of Indian Boat Designs," *Memoirs of the Asiatic Society of Bengal,* VII [1920], p. 199). The Chinese designated them by the term *Ta-shih,* which corresponds to the name *Tājika,* by which they were known in India. See J. A. E. Morley, "The Arabs and the Eastern Trade," *JRASMB,* XII (1949), pp. 143–75. G. R. Tibbetts, "Pre-Islamic Arabia and South-East Asia," *JRASMB,* XXIX (1956), p. 182.
2. Gabriel Ferrand, "Le K'ouen-louen et les anciennes navigations inter-océaniques dans les mers du sud," *JA* (1915); see especially May-June, pp. 450–92, and July-August, pp. 5–68.
3. V. Obdeijn, "De oude Zeehandelsweg door de straat Malakka," *TKNAG,* LXX (1942). R. Soekmono, "Early Civilization of Southeast Asia," *JSS,* XLVI (1958), pp. 17–20. On the historical geography of the southern coastal region of Sumatra, see "La ligne côtière de Çrīvijaya," *Amerta,* III (1955), p. 3. This article is summarized by L. C. Damais, "Bibliographie indonésienne," *BEFEO,* LI (1963), p. 550.
4. Edouard Chavannes, trans., *Voyages des pèlerins bouddhistes: Les religieux éminents qui allerent chercher la loi dans les pays d'Occident, mémoire composé à l'époque de la grand dynastie T'ang par I-tsing* (Paris, 1894), p. 119.
5. Junjiro Takakusu, trans., *A Record of the Buddhist Religion as Practised in India and the Malay Archipelago (A.D. 671–695) by I-Tsing* (Oxford, 1896), p. xxxiv.
6. *Ibid.*, p. 10. O. W. Wolters, "Śrivijayan Expansion in the Seventh Century," *AA,* XXIV (1961), p. 418.
7. Coedès, "Les inscriptions malaises de Çrīvijaya," *BEFEO,* XXX, pp. 29–80. Gabriel Ferrand, "Quatre textes épigraphiques malayo-sanskrits de Sumatra et de Banka," *JA* (October-December, 1932), pp. 271–326.
8. The placing of Shih-li-fo-shih at Palembang was proposed in 1886 by Samuel Beal, "Some Remarks respecting a Place Called Shi-li-fo-tsai," in *Livre des merveilles de l'Inde,* edited by P. A. van der Lith and Marcel Devic (Leyden, 1883–86),

pp. 251–53. More recently, H. G. Quaritch Wales has attempted to place Śrīvijaya at Chaiya on the Bay of Bandọn, in the Siamese part of the Malay Peninsula ("A Newly Explored Route of Ancient Indian Cultural Expansion," *IAL,* IX [1935], pp. 1–31), but this hypothesis is improbable. See Coedès, "A propos d'une nouvelle théorie sur le site de Crīvijaya," *JRASMB,* XIV (1936), pp. 1–9.

9. This date and the following were calculated by W. E. van Wijk (see W. J. Wellan, "Çrīwijaya," *TKNAG,* LI [1934], p. 363) as corresponding respectively to the 13th of April and the 3rd of May, 683. But I have adopted the results of a new calculation by L. C. Damais, "Liste des principales inscriptions datées de l'Indonésie," *BEFEO,* XLVI (1952), p. 98.
10. This delay of a month is established by the inscription of Telaga Batu published in J. G. de Casparis, *Prasasti Indonesia* (Bandung, 1950, 1956), II, pp. 12 ff.
11. Ph. S. van Ronkel, "A Preliminary Note concerning Two Old Malay Inscriptions in Palembang," *Acta Orientalia,* II (1924), p. 21. N. J. Krom, *Hindoe-Javaansche Geschiedenis* (The Hague, 1931), p. 121.
12. J. L. Moens, "Srīvijaya, Yāva en Katāha," *TBG,* LXXVII (1937), pp. 333–35.
13. N. J. Krom, "De Heiligdommen van Palembang," *MKAWAL,* N. R., I, No. 7 (1938), pp. 25–26. See K. A. Nilakanta Sastri, "Śrī Vijaya," *BEFEO,* XL, p. 249; *History of Śrīvijaya* (Madras, 1949), p. 30.
14. F. M. Schnitger, *Oudheidkundige vondsten in Palembang,* Bijlage A: Verslag over de gevonden inscripties door Dr. W. F. Stutterheim (Palembang, 1935). See Krom, "De Heiligdommen," p. 8.
15. B. Ch. Chhabra, "Expansion of Indo-Aryan Culture," *JASB,* Letters, I (1935), p. 31.
16. Coedès, review of Wellan's *Çrīwijaya,* in *BEFEO,* XXXIII, pp. 1003–1004. K. A. Nilakanta Sastri, "Siddhayātrā," *JGIS,* IV (1937), pp. 128–36. On the nature of this expedition, the date of which coincides with the end of the reign of Jayavarman I in Cambodia, I have risked a hypothesis that I do not think it necessary to elaborate on here but that can be found on pages 23–32 of the volume of miscellany offered in homage to Sir Richard Winstedt (John Bastin, ed., *Malayan and Indonesian Studies* [Oxford, 1964]).
17. The date calculated by Damais, "Liste des principales inscriptions," p. 98.
18. The inscription of Telaga Batu (de Casparis, *Prasasti Indonesia,* II, pp. 15 ff.) gives a more detailed text.
19. Showing once more the reluctance to accept the first meaning of "Java" that presents itself naturally to the mind. P. V.

van Stein Callenfels has proposed that this word be considered not as a proper name but as an adjective meaning "exterior"; the inscription would then refer to an expedition "abroad" (see "Correspondance," *BEFEO,* XXX, p. 656).

20. Moens, "Srīvijaya, Yāva en Katāha," p. 363.
21. Paul Pelliot, "Deux itinéraires de Chine en Inde, à la fin du VIIIe siècle," *BEFEO,* IV, p. 284.
22. F. D. K. Bosch, "Een Maleische inscriptie in het Buitenzorgsche," *BKI,* 100 (1941), p. 51.
23. Pelliot, "Deux itinéraires," p. 334.
24. *Ibid.*
25. *Ibid.,* p. 335. On this name, see L. C. Damais, review of Poerbatjaraka's *Riwajat Indonesia, BEFEO,* XLVIII (1957), pp. 624 ff.
26. This question has been studied by Wolters in "Śrīvijayan Expansion"; he places the conquest of Kedah on the Malay Peninsula between 685 and 689, basing his conclusions on a passage in a work by I-ching.
27. One of the teachers of I-ching, Śākyakīrti, lived there (Takakusu, *A Record,* pp. lviii, lix, 184). On the other pilgrims who lived or stopped there, see Chavannes, *Voyages des pèlerins bouddhistes,* pp. 63–64, 126, 144, 159.
28. Takakusu, *A Record,* p. 10.
29. *Ibid.,* p. 11.
30. Chavannes, *Voyages des pèlerins bouddhistes,* pp. 76–77.
31. René Grousset, *Philosophies indiennes* (Paris, 1931), II, pp. 7–149.
32. "Correspondance," *BEFEO,* XXX, p. 656.
33. Coedès, "Les inscriptions malaises de Çrīvijaya," pp. 55–57. The presence of Tantrism in Sumatra toward the end of the seventh century is not surprising. Its introduction may date back to Dharmapāla of Kānchī, a contemporary of the pilgrim Hsüan-tsang, if it is true that this spiritual descendant of the logician Dignāga, a pupil of Asanga, left the university of Nālandā after thirty years of study to go to Suvarṇadvīpa (Sumatra or Malaya). See Anton Schiefner, trans., *Tāranātha's Geschichte des Buddhismus in Indien* (St. Petersburg, 1869), p. 160. F. D. K. Bosch throws doubt on this evidence ("Een Oorkonde van het Groote Klooster te Nālandā," *TBG,* LXV [1925], p. 559, n. 80). But if Tantrism had not yet reached Śrīvijaya in 684, it must have reached Śrīvijaya about thirty years later, for the Indian Vajrabodhi, the introducer of the doctrine in China, stopped at Śrīvijaya in 717 (Pelliot, "Deux itinéraires," p. 336).
34. N. J. Krom, "Antiquities of Palembang," *ABIA* (1931), pp. 29–33. F. M. Schnitger, *The Archaeology of Hindoo Sumatra* (Leyden, 1937). Devaprasad Ghosh, "Early Art of Śrīvijaya,"

JGIS, I (1934), pp. 31–38; "Sources of the Art of Śrīvijaya," *JGIS, III* (1936), pp. 50–56; "Two Bodhisattva Images from Ceylon and Śrīvijaya," *JGIS,* IV (1937), pp. 125–27. W. F. Stutterheim, "Note on a Newly Found Fragment of a Four-Armed Figure from Kota Kapur (Bangka)," *IAL,* XI (1937), pp. 105–109.

35. Pelliot, "Deux itinéraires," p. 335.
36. Coedès, "Le royaume de Çrīvijaya," *BEFEO,* XVIII, 5, pp. 29–31; *Recueil des inscriptions du Siam* (Bangkok, 1924–29), II, No. XXIII, pp. 35–39; "Origin of the Śailendras of Indonesia," *JGIS,* I (1934), pp. 64–68. B. R. Chatterjee, *India and Java* (Calcutta, 1933), II, Inscription, pp. 40–44. Chhabra, "Expansion of Indo-Aryan Culture," pp. 20–27. Nilakanta Sastri, Śrī Vijaya," pp. 252–54. The statuette of Lokeśvara, found in a tin mine in the Perak region, which exhibits undeniable similarities with the art of Śrīvijaya, may date from this period (H. G. Quaritch Wales, "Archaeological Researches in Malaya," *ABIA,* XII (1937), p. 41, n. 1, and pl. XII). On the stele of Wat Sema Mưang, see below, pp. 91–92.
37. A hypothesis first formulated by N. J. Krom, in Frederik W. Stapel, ed., *Geschiedenis van Nederlandsch-Indië* (Amsterdam, 1938–40), I, p. 162, and then accepted by F. D. K. Bosch, "Çrīvijaya, de Çailendra-en de Sañjayavaṃça," *BKI,* 108 (1952). I have brought forth various arguments in favor of this hypothesis; see my "L'Inscription de la stèle de Ligor: Etat présent de son interprétation," *Oriens Extremus,* VI, 1 (1959), p. 44.
38. Pelliot, "Deux itinéraires," p. 211.
39. This period has been studied by Pierre Dupont in "La dislocation du Tchen-la," *BEFEO,* XLIII, pp. 17 ff.; "Tchen-la et Pāṇḍuranga," *BSEI,* XXIV (1949), pp. 1–19.
40. Ma Tuan-lin, *Ethnographie des peuples étrangers à la Chine,* trans. Marquis d' Hervey de Saint-Denys, II: Méridionaux (Geneva, 1883), p. 483.
41. In the Western Baray. "Chronique," *BEFEO,* XXXIX, p. 341. Coedès, *Les Inscriptions du Cambodge* (Paris, 1937–), IV, p. 54.
42. Inscription of Vat Khnat, in Coedès, *Inscriptions du Cambodge,* VII.
43. Auguste Barth and Abel Bergaigne, ISC, p. 369. If there is some relationship between the name of Śambhupura and that of the king Śambhuvarman who left an inscription at Thap-mười concerning the construction of a sanctuary of Pushkarāksha (Coedès, "A propos du Tchen-la d'eau," *BEFEO,* XXXVI, p. 4) and if, moreover, this Pushkarāksha, which might simply be a statue of Vishnu, has some connection with the king Pushkarāksha of the inscription of 716, it is necessary to admit that the city of Śambhupura received this name only

after the reign of Pushkarāksha, of whom Śambhuvarman was a successor. But all this is as hypothetical as the identification of this Śambhuvarman with the Cham king of the same name.

44. Etienne F. Aymonier, *Le Cambodge* (Paris, 1900–1904), I, pp. 299–310. Adhémard Leclère, "Une campagne archéologique au Cambodge," *BEFEO,* IV, pp. 737–49. Henri Parmentier, *L'Art khmèr primitif* (Paris, 1927), I, p. 213.
45. Louis Finot, "Inscription de Práḥ Thāt Kvan Pir," *BEFEO,* IV, p. 675.
46. Barth and Bergaigne, ISC, p. 356.
47. Below, p. 94. Indraloka is also mentioned in the stele of Bakong (Coedès, *Inscriptions du Cambodge,* I, p. 35).
48. Pelliot, "Deux itinéraires," p. 212.
49. Henri Maspero, "La frontière de l'Annam et du Cambodge du VIIIe au XIVe siècle," *BEFEO,* XVIII, 3, p. 29.
50. Coedès, "A propos du Tchen-la d'eau," pp. 3, 11.
51. *Ibid.,* p. 11. R. C. Majumdar, "Les Rois Śailendra de Suvarṇadvīpa," *BEFEO,* XXXIII, pp. 137–38. Coedès, *Inscriptions du Cambodge,* I, p. 74.
52. Inscription of Phnom Bathé. Coedès, "A propos du Tchen-la d'eau," p. 7.
53. Pierre Dupont, "Vishṇu mitrés de l'Indochine occidentale," *BEFEO,* XLI, pp. 233–54. M. C. Subhadradis Diskul, "Mueng Fa Daed, an Ancient Town in North-East Thailand," *AA,* XIX (1956), p. 362.
54. C. O. Blagden, "The Pyu Inscriptions," *Epigraphia Indica,* XII, pp. 127–32; "The Pyu Inscriptions," *JBRS,* VII (1917), pp. 37–44. Louis Finot, "L'épigraphie indochinoise," *BEFEO,* XV, 2, pp. 132–34. See *ARASB* (1924), p. 23.
55. Charles Duroiselle, *ARASI* (1926–27), p. 176, n. 2.
56. *Ibid.* (1927–28), pp. 128, 145.
57. Nihar-Ranjan Ray, *Sanskrit Buddhism in Burma* (Calcutta, 1936), pp. 19–20. Gordon H. Luce, "The Ancient Pyu," *JBRS,* XXVII (1937), p. 243.
58. Above, p. 30.
59. Above, pp. 62–63.
60. Ray, *Sanskrit Buddhism in Burma,* pp. 19–30.
61. Below, p. 106.
62. Above, p. 79.
63. Above, pp. 53–54. According to R. Ng. Poerbatjaraka, Java was under the domination of Śrīvijaya from 697 to 708; then from 708 to 719 it tried to liberate itself; and, finally, from 719 to 730 Sanjaya brought about the conquests mentioned in the third paragraph below. (See Damais's review of Poerbatjaraka's *Riwajat Indonesia, BEFEO,* XLVIII [1957], p. 639.)
64. H. Kern, *Verspreide Geschriften* (The Hague, 1913–29), VII, pp. 115–28. Chatterjee, *India and Java,* II, Inscription, pp. 29–34.

65. Chhabra, "Expansion of Indo-Aryan Culture," p. 37. J. Ph. Vogel, "Aanteekeningen op de inscriptie van Tjanggal," *BKI*, 100 (1941), p. 446.
66. On the name of this country, see Damais's review of Poerbatjaraka, pp. 628–31.
67. Moens, "Srīvijaya, Yāva en Katāha," pp. 426–35 and *passim*.
68. K. A. Nilakanta Sastri, "Kaṭāha," *JGIS*, V (1938), pp. 128–46.
69. K. A. Nilakanta Sastri, "Origin of the Śailendras," *TBG*, LXXV (1935), p. 611; "Agastya," *TBG*, LXXVI (1936), pp. 500–502.
70. W. F. Stutterheim, "Note on Cultural Relations between South-India and Java," *TBG*, LXXIX (1939), pp. 73–84. Vogel, "Aanteekeningen," p. 445.
71. R. Ng. Poerbatjararaka, "De Tjarita Parahijangan," *TBG*, LIX (1920), pp. 403–16. Damais's review of Poerbatjaraka, pp. 633–37.
72. W. F. Stutterheim, "Een belangrijka oorkonde uit de Kedoe," *TBG*, LXVII (1927), pp. 172–215. R. Goris, "De eenheit der Matarāmsche Dynastie," *Feestbundel uitgegeven door het Koninklijk Bataviaasch Genootschap van Kunsten en Wetenschappen* (Weltevreden, 1929), I, pp. 202–206.
73. Jean Przyluski, "The Śailendravamśa," *JGIS*, II (1935), pp. 25–36.
74. R. C. Majumdar, *Ancient Indian Colonies of the Far East*, II: Suvarṇadvīpa (Dacca, 1937), pp. 225–27.
75. Nilakanta Sastri, "Origin of the Śailendras," p. 610; *History of Śrīvijaya* (Madras, 1949), pp. 46–50.
76. Majumdar, *Ancient Indian Colonies*, II, p. 159. L. P. Briggs, "The Origin of the Śailendra Dynasty," *JAOS*, LXX (1950), pp. 76–89.
77. Coedès, "On the Origin of the Śailendras of Indonesia," *JGIS*, I (1934), pp. 66–70. We can reasonably ask ourselves if the breakup of Cambodia does not mark a last gasp of Funan, whose heritage Water Chenla perhaps claimed that it acquired.
78. See above, p. 68.
79. De Casparis, *Prasasti Indonesia*, II, pp. 184–85. *Naravara* also appears in the inscription of Kelurak (*Ibid.*, I, p. 191).
80. "The Çailendra Interregnum," *India Antiqua* (Leyden, 1947), pp. 249–53.
81. L. C. Damais, "Epigrafische aantekeningen," *TBG*, LXXXIII (1949), pp. 21–25. *BEFEO*, LII (1964), p. 128.
82. The Sanskrit inscription of Kalasan in pre-Nāgari letters was published by J. L. A. Brandes, *TBG*, XXXI (1886), pp. 240–60; R. G. Bhandarkar, *JRAS Bombay*, XVII (1887–89), II, pp. 1–10; F. D. K. Bosch, *TBG*, LXVIII (1928), pp. 57–62; B. R. Chatterjee, *India and Java*, II, Inscription, pp. 44–48.
83. Description in N. J. Krom, *Inleiding tot de Hindoe-Javaansche*

Kunst (The Hague, 1923), pp. 257–64. Moens, "Srīvijaya, Yāva en Katāha," p. 434, has given an overly ingenious explanation for this iconography, an explanation inspired by his highly debatable theory of the Indian origin of Sanjaya. See also F. B. Vogler, "Ontwikkeling van de gewijde boukunst in het Hindoeistische Midden-Java," *BKI,* 109 (1953), p. 249.

84. Coedès, "Le Çailendra, 'tuer des héros ennemis,' " *Bingkisan Budi: A Volume of Oriental Studies Presented to Professor Ph. S. van Ronkel* (Leyden, 1950), pp. 58–70.
85. De Casparis, *Prasasti Indonesia,* p. 102.
86. F. D. K. Bosch, "De Inscriptie van Keloerak," *TBG,* LXVIII (1928), pp. 1–56.
87. *Ibid.,* p. 26.
88. An inscription of A.D. 792 in Old Malay was found in 1960 at Chandi Sewu. See L. C. Damais, "Bibliographie indonésienne," *BEFEO,* LI (1963), p. 580.
89. J. L. Moens, "Barabudur, Mendut en Pawon en hun onderlinge samenhang," *TBG,* LXXXIV (1951), p. 326.
90. Notably *Jātakamālā, Lalitavistara, Gaṇḍavyūha, Karmavibhanga.*
91. De Casparis, *Prasasti Indonesia,* I, p. 204.
92. Krom, *Hindoe-Javaansche Geschiedenis,* p. 152. For the description and the bibliography of these monuments, see N. J. Krom, *Inleiding tot de Hindoe-Javaansche Kunst.* For a description of the Borobudur, see the beautiful monograph of N. J. Krom and T. van Erp, *Beschrijving van Borobudur* (The Hague, 1920). For interpretations, see especially the basic work of Paul Mus, "Barabuḍur," *BEFEO,* XXXII–XXXV; see also W. F. Stutterheim, *Tjandi Bara-Boedoer, Naam, Vorm, Beteekenis* (Weltevreden, 1929), and P. H. Pott, *Yoga en Yantra in hunne beteekenis voor de Indische Archaeologie* (Leyden, 1946), and two works by A. J. Bernet Kempers: "Borobudur's Verborgen Voet," *BKI,* 111 (1955), pp. 225–35, and *Ancient Indonesian Art* (Amsterdam, 1959). The hypotheses of J. G. de Casparis presented in *Prasasti Indonesia,* I, particularly on the old name of the monument (p. 164), apparently need not be retained.
93. Below, pp. 128–29. The Sanskrit lexicon *Amaramālā* was translated into Javanese during the reign of Jitendra, an unidentified Śailendra.
94. Pelliot, "Deux itinéraires," p. 225. Ferrand, "Le K'ouen-louen," p. 304, n. 3, has recognized in *P'o-lu-chia-ssu* a Javanese expression *waruh gresik,* "beach of sand." It still survives in the name of the port of the residency of Surabaya, commonly called *Grise,* but P'o-lu-chia-ssu was not necessarily in the same place, since the same name may have been brought from another site to eastern Java. Moens, "Srīvijaya, Yāva en Katāha," pp. 382–86, proposes to identify *P'o-lu-chia-ssu*

with *Baruas,* which is southeast of Kedah, the presumed old capital. This relationship is less acceptable phonetically, and it implies that Ho-ling was located on the peninsula, which raises serious difficulties.

95. F. D. K. Bosch, "De sanskrit inscriptie op den steen van Dinaja (682 çaka)," *TBG,* LVII (1916), pp. 410–44; "Het Lingga-Heiligdom van Dinaja," *TBG,* LXIV (1924), pp. 227–86.
96. W. F. Stutterheim has called attention to a short undated, but paleographically older, inscription from eastern Java: "De oudste inscriptie van Oost-Java?" *BKI,* 95 (1937), pp. 397–401.
97. R. Ng. Poerbatjaraka, *Agastya in den Archipel* (Leyden, 1926), pp. 109–10, considered Chi-yen of the Chinese sources as a transcription of Gajayāna, but R. A. Kern, "Joartan Wedergevonden?" *BKI,* 102 (1943), p. 545, followed by L. C. Damais, in his review of Poerbatjaraka's *Riwajat Indonesia,* prefers to see here a transcription of the Javanese title (*ra*)*kryan,* although this word is more often and more exactly rendered in Chinese as *lo-chi-lien* (see Krom, *Hindoe-Javaansche Geschiedenis,* p. 283).
98. J. G. de Casparis, "Nogmaals de Sanskrit-inscriptie op den steen van Dinojo," *TKNAG,* LXXXI (1941), p. 499, proposes identifying this country with the Kanuruhan of the inscriptions of Siṇḍok (see below, p. 128) and also recognizes the name Kanjuruhan in the name of the village of Kejuron, west of Malang.
99. The Chinese sources mention only the embassies of Ho-ling in 767 and 768 (Pelliot, "Deux itinéraires," p. 286).
100. Georges Maspero, *Le Royaume de Champa* (Paris, 1928), pp. 97–98.
101. Barth and Bergaigne, ISC, p. 252.
102. *Ibid.,* p. 217.
103. Above, p. 84.
104. On this second inscription and the numerous discussions to which it has given rise, see Coedès, "L'inscription de la stèle de Ligor," pp. 42–48.
105. N. J. Krom, *De Sumatraansche periode der Javaansche Geschiedenis* (Leyden, 1919), part of which was translated into French in *BEFEO,* XIX, 5, pp. 127–35.
106. Below, pp. 109 and 142.
107. Coedès, "Origin of the Śailendras of Indonesia," p. 65. Nevertheless, Nilakanta Sastri, *History of Śrīvijaya,* pp. 46 and 56, arguing from the presence in Sumatra of inscriptions in pre-Nāgarī writing and from the resemblances between the stupas of Ligor and those of Padang Lawas, accepts the possibility of the establishment of the Śailendras in Sumatra from the end of the eighth century.
108. "Les rois Śailendra de Suvarṇadvīpa," *BEFEO,* XXXIII, pp. 126–27.

109. *Ibid.*
110. The itinerary of Chia Tan (Pelliot, "Deux itinéraires," pp. 231–33, 349–64, 373) mentions only Lo-yüeh and Ko-lo. *Lo-yüeh* undoubtedly represents (Se)*luyut* on the river of Johore, as proposed by Moens, "Srīvijaya, Yāva en Katāha," p. 337, and N. J. Krom, "De Naam Sumatra," *BKI,* 100 (1941), p. 10. As for Ko-lo (-fu-sha-lo), Paul Wheatley discusses the relation of this place name with Ko-lo-she-fen, Ko-ku-lo, and others and concludes that this country was situated west of Dvāravatī, on the western coast of the Malay Peninsula, in the region of Phuket (*The Golden Khersonese* [Kuala Lumpur, 1961], p. 270).
111. Notably the beautiful bronze Lokeśvaras of the Museum of Bangkok related to statues of Mendut in Java (Coedès, "Les collections archéologiques du Musée National de Bangkok," *Ars Asiatica* [1918], XII, pls. 15–17). See above, p. 296, n. 8, for the theory of H. G. Quaritch Wales on the identification of Śrīvijaya with Chaiya.
112. This is also the view of O. W. Wolters, "Śrīvijayan Expansion in the Seventh Century," *AA,* XXIV (1961), pp. 417–18.
113. W. F. Stutterheim, *A Javanese Period in Sumatran History* (Surakarta, 1929). See the review by F. D. K. Bosch in *TBG,* LXIX (1929), pp. 135–56.
114. Below, p. 108.
115. Below, p. 108.
116. Below, p. 147.
117. Abû Zayd Hasan, *Voyage du marchand arabe Sulaymân en Inde et en Chine, rédigé en 851, suivi de remarques par Abû Zayd Hasan (vers 916)*, trans. and ed. by Gabriel Ferrand (Paris, 1922). On the author of this text, who may not have been the merchant Sulaymān, see Jean Sauvaget, ed. and trans., *'Ahbār as-sīn wa l-hind: Relation de la Chine et de l'Inde, rédigée en* 851 (Paris, 1948), pp. xix ff. It is Abû Zayd's addition to the *'Ahbār as-sīn wa l-hind* that contains the story of the Khmer king.
118. See above, p. 83.
119. G. H. Luce, "The Early Syām in Burma's History," *JSS,* XLVI, pp. 143–44.
120. Pelliot, "Deux itinéraires," p. 212.
121. *Ibid.,* pp. 213–15, 372.
122. Henri Maspero, "La frontière de l'Annam et du Cambodge du VIIe au XIVe siècle," *BEFEO,* XVIII, 3, pp. 30–32.
123. R. Stein, "Le Lin-yi," *Han-hiue,* II (1947), p. 41. Pierre Dupont, "La dislocation du Tchen-la," pp. 41–44.
124. Erik Seidenfaden, "Complément à *L'Inventaire descriptif des monuments du Cambodge* pour les quatre provinces du Siam oriental," *BEFEO,* XXII, p. 90.
125. The inscription of 770 comes from Preah Theat Preah Srei in Thbong Khmum (Coedès, *Inscriptions du Cambodge,* V, p.

33). That of 781 was found at Lobök Srot, in the region of Kratié (Coedès, "Note sur une inscription récemment découverte au Cambodge," *BEFEO,* V, p. 419).

126. Which I have numbered 1 *bis,* in order not to change the numbers of the kings of Angkor from Jayavarman II to VIII.
127. Louis Finot, "Lokeçvara en Indochine," *Et. Asiat. EFEO,* I, p. 235.
128. See Coedès, "A propos du Tchen-la d'eau," p. 12, n. 1. See below, pp. 98, 110. Dupont ("La dislocation du Tchen-la," pp. 17 ff.) has attempted a genealogical and chronological classification of these princes.
129. Above, p. 85.
130. Etienne Aymonier, *Le Cambodge,* I, p. 305. Coedès, *Inscriptions du Cambodge,* III, p. 170.
131. Gilberte de Coral Rémusat, *L'Art khmer* (Paris, 1940), p. 117. Pierre Dupont, "Vishṇu mitrés de l'Indochine occidentale," *BEFEO,* XLI, pp. 233–54; "Les linteaux khmèrs du VIIe siècle," *AA,* XV (1952), pp. 31–83; *La Statuaire préangkorienne* (Ascona, 1955).
132. Maspero, *Le Royaume de Champa,* p. 95.
133. *Ibid.* Pierre Dupont, "Tchen-la et Pāṇḍuranga," *BSEI,* XXIV (1949), pp. 1–19.
134. Barth and Bergaigne, *IŚC,* p. 224.
135. *Ibid.,* pp. 252, 256.
136. *Ibid.,* p. 253.
137. *Ibid.,* p. 217.
138. Maspero, *Le Royaume de Champa,* p. 104.
139. Barth and Bergaigne, *ISC,* p. 226.
140. Pelliot, "Deux itinéraires," p. 152.
141. *Ibid.,* pp. 155–56. The pages that follow give important information on the Indian penetration into Yunnan by the Burma route. On the expansion of Nanchao, see Wilfrid Stott, "The Expansion of the Nan-Chao Kingdom between the Years A.D. 750–860," *TP,* L (1963), p. 190.
142. G. H. Luce, "The Ancient Pyu," *JBRS,* XXVII (1937), p. 249.
143. Nihar-Ranjan Ray, *Sanskrit Buddhism in Burma,* p. 41.
144. La Vallée-Poussin, *Dynasties et histoire de l'Inde,* p. 95.
145. Above, p. 84.
146. Above, pp. 89–91, 94.
147. See H. B. Sarkar, "The Cultural Contact between Java and Bengal," *IHQ,* XIII (1937), pp. 593–94. On Nālandā, see H. D. Sankalia, *The University of Nalanda* (Madras, 1934).
148. On Mahayana Buddhism in Champa in this period, see the images of Buddha enumerated by Jean Boisselier, *La Statuaire de Champa* (Paris, 1963), pp. 75 ff.
149. F. D. K. Bosch, "Buddhistische Gegevens uit Balische Handschriften," *MKAWAL,* LXVIII, Ser. B, No. 3, pp. 43–77. J.

Przyluski, "Le bouddhisme tantrique à Bali," *JA* (January-March, 1931), pp. 159–67. P. H. Pott, *Yoga en Yantra.*

Chapter VII

1. See the basic article on this subject: Pierre Dupont, "Le début de la royauté angkorienne," *BEFEO,* XLVI (1952), pp. 119–76.
2. See the genealogical tables of the inscriptions of Yaśovarman in Auguste Barth and Abel Bergaigne, ISC, I, p. 361. On the stele of Prè Rup, see Coedès, *Inscriptions du Cambodge* Paris, 1937–), I, p. 74; on the reign of Jayavarman II, see also Coedès, *Pour mieux comprendre Angkor* (Paris, 1947), pp. 151–75, certain passages of which are reproduced here.
3. Above, p. 85.
4. Coedès, *Inscriptions du Cambodge,* I, pp. 37–44.
5. Barth and Bergaigne, ISC, pp. 344–45.
6. Louis Finot, "L'inscription de Sdok Kak Thom," *BEFEO,* XV, 2, pp. 53–106. Coedès and Pierre Dupont, "Les stèles de Sdok Kak Thom, Phnom Sandak et Prah Vihar," *BEFEO,* XLIII, pp. 56 ff.
7. R. C. Majumdar, "The Date of Accession of Jayavarman II," *JGIS,* X (1943), p. 52.
8. An inscription of 803 mentions the foundations of an "elder" queen, Jayeshṭhāryā, who reigned at Sambor. See above, p. 94.
9. Coedès, "Les capitales de Jayavarman II," *BEFEO,* XXVIII, pp. 117–19.
10. Henri Parmentier, *L'Art khmèr primitif* (Paris, 1927), I, p. 206.
11. Above, p. 67.
12. Coedès, "Les capitales," pp. 119–20; "Discovery of a Pre-Angkor Monument in the Group of Angkor," *ABIA* (1930), pp. 14–16. Henri Marchal, "Kuṭīçvara," *BEFEO,* XXXVII, pp. 333–47.
13. Coedès, "Les capitales," p. 121; *Inscriptions du Cambodge,* I, p. 187.
14. Philippe Stern, "Hariharālaya et Indrapura," *BEFEO,* XXXVIII, pp. 180–86 (first and second periods).
15. "Amarendrapura dans Amoghapura," *BEFEO,* XXIV, pp. 359–72.
16. *Le Cambodge* (Paris, 1900–1904), III, p. 470.
17. Stern, "Hariharālaya et Indrapura," p. 180, rejects this identification because in this group that is comprised notably of Vat Khnat, the ruins submerged in the Western Baray (which was dug in the eleventh century), and the old parts of Prasat Kôk Pô "there is uniform reuse of materials from the preceding era" while Amarendrapura is supposed to have been "founded" by Jayavarman II. This argument does not seem very convincing to me. The "founding" of a city, especially by a nomad king like Jayavarman II, does not preclude the use of materials appropriated from older nearby monuments.

18. Probably Prasat Khna in Mlu Prei (Coedès, "Le Site de Janapada," *BEFEO,* XLIII, p. 8).
19. Aymonier, *Le Cambodge,* I, p. 428. See Coedès, "Les capitales," p. 122.
20. Philippe Stern, "Travaux exécutés au Phnom Kulèn," *BEFEO,* XXXVIII, pp. 151–73.
21. Philippe Stern, "Le style du Kulèn," *BEFEO,* XXXVIII, pp. 111–49.
22. Henri Parmentier, "L'Art d'Indravarman," *BEFEO,* XIX, 1, pp. 1–91.
23. In a communication to the Société Asiatique, February 8, 1963, entitled "Çivaism tamoule et çivaism khmèr."
24. A good argument in favor of the identification of *Javā* in the inscription of Sdok Kak Thom with the island of Java has been furnished by Gilberte de Coral Rémusat, who draws attention to "Influences javanaises dans l'art de Rolûoh," *JA* (July-September, 1933), p. 190. See also Coral Rémusat, "Concerning Some Indian Influences in Khmer Art," *IAL,* VII (1933), p. 114. These influences have also been studied by Stern, "Le style du Kulèn," pp. 127–28.
25. Coedès, "On the Origin of the Śailendras of Indonesia," *JGIS,* I (1934), p. 70.
26. Coedès, "Note sur l'apothéose au Cambodge," *BCAI* (1911), p. 46.
27. Robert von Heine-Geldern, "Weltbild und Bauform in Südostasien," *Wiener Beiträge zur Kunst und Kultur Asiens,* IV (1930), pp. 28–78.
28. F. D. K. Bosch, "Het Lingga-Heiligdom van Dinaja," *TBG,* LXIV (1924), pp. 227–86.
29. Philippe Stern, "Le temple-montagne khmèr, le culte du linga et le Devarāja," *BEFEO,* XXXIV, pp. 612–16.
30. "L'inscription de Sdok Kak Thom," p. 57.
31. B. R. Chatterjee, *Indian Cultural Influence in Cambodia* (Calcutta, 1928), p. 273; "Tantrism in Cambodia, Sumatra and Java," *Modern Review* (January, 1930), p. 80. P. C. Bagchi, "On Some Tantrik Texts Studied in Ancient Kambuja," *IHQ,* V (1929), pp. 754–69; VI (1930), pp. 97–107.
32. Above, p. 93. See Coedès, review of Bagchi's "On Some Tantrik Texts" in *BEFEO,* XXIX, pp. 356–57.
33. Jean Philippe Vogel, "The Head-Offering to the Goddess in Pallava Sculpture," *BSOAS,* VI, 2 (1931), pp. 539–43.
34. Coedès, "Statuettes décapitées de Savankalok," Institut Indochinois pour l'Etude de l'Homme, *Bulletins et Travaux,* II (1939), p. 190.
35. The *New History of the T'ang* still attributes an embassy of 813 to "Water Chenla." Paul Pelliot, "Deux itinéraires de Chine en Inde, à la fin du VIIIe siècle," *BEFEO,* IV, p. 215, n. 1. See Coedès, "A propos du Tchen-la d'eau," *BEFEO,* XXXVI, p. 13.

36. See below, p. 104.
37. Coedès, "La stèle de Palhal," *BEFEO,* XIII, 6, p. 33.
38. "Chronique," *BEFEO,* XXXI, p. 621. Coedès, "Quelques suggestions sur le méthode à suivre pour interpréter les bas-reliefs de Bantay Chmar . . . ," *BEFEO,* XXXII, p. 80, n. 1.
39. Stern, "Hariharālaya et Indrapura," pp. 186–89 (third period).
40. Coedès, "Nouvelles précisions sur les dates d'avènement de quelques rois des dynasties angkoriennes," *BEFEO,* XLIII, p. 12.
41. A stele from Sambor of the Mekong, dated 803 (Aymonier, *Le Cambodge,* I, p. 305), published in Coedès, *Inscriptions du Cambodge,* III, p. 170, mentions an Indraloka, who was the great-grandfather of the author of the inscription. This seems to be a posthumous name, but we do not know to whom it was applied. I have already indicated that the appearance of a posthumous name at Saṃbor and the mention of the God-King in another inscription of the same locality tend to place the origin of these rites in the kingdom of Śambhupura, homeland of the ancestors of Jayavarman II. See Coedès, "Note sur l'apothéose au Cambodge," p. 48.
42. Coedès, "Le culte de la royauté divinisée, source d'inspiration des grands monuments du Cambodge ancien," *Conferenze,* Serie Orientale Roma V (Rome, 1952), pp. 1–23.
43. Stern, "Le style du Kulèn." Gilberte de Coral Rémusat, *L'Art khmèr, les grandes étapes de son évolution* (Paris, 1940), pp. 117–18.
44. Barth and Bergaigne, ISC, p. 370.
45. Aymonier, *Le Cambodge,* I, p. 422. Coedès, "La stèle de Palhal," p. 34; "Les capitales de Jayavarman II," p. 116.
46. Coedès and Pierre Dupont, "Les inscriptions du Pràsàt Kôk Pô," *BEFEO,* XXXVII, p. 381. Stern, "Hariharālaya et Indrapura," pp. 186–89.
47. Georges Maspero, *Le Royaume de Champa* (Paris, 1928), p. 105, n. 3.
48. Barth and Bergaigne, ISC, p. 269.
49. Etienne Aymonier, "Première étude sur les inscriptions tchames," *JA* (January-February, 1891), p. 24.
50. Barth and Bergaigne, ISC, p. 269.
51. *Ibid.,* pp. 231–37.
52. Pelliot, "Deux itinéraires," p. 153.
53. G. H. Luce, "The Ancient Pyu," *JBRS,* XXVII (1937), p. 249.
54. *Ibid.,* p. 250, n. 3.
55. Ma Tuan-lin, *Ethnographie des peuples étrangers à la Chine,* trans. Marquis d'Hervey de Saint-Denys, II: Meridionaux (Geneva, 1883), pp. 228–35. E. H. Parker, *Burma, with Special Reference to Her Relations with China* (Rangoon, 1893), p. 12. G. H. Luce, "The Ancient Pyu," pp. 250–52.
56. J. S. Furnivall, "The Foundation of Pagan," *JBRS,* I, 2 (1911), pp. 6–9.

57. R. Grant Brown, "The Origin of the Burmese," *JBRS,* II (1912), pp. 1–7. G. H. Luce, "Economic Life of the Early Burman," *JBRS,* XXX (1940), pp. 286–87; "Old Kyaukse and the Coming of the Burmans," *JBRS,* XLII (1959), pp. 75–112; "The Early Syām in Burma's History," *JSS,* XLVI (1952), p. 127.
58. See above, p. 86.
59. "The Ari of Burma and Tantric Buddhism," *ARASI* (1915–16), pp. 79–93. On the etymology of the word *Arī,* see Edouard Huber, Review of the Superintendent, Archaeological Service Burma, in *BEFEO,* IX, p. 584; Louis Finot, "Un nouveau document sur le bouddhisme birman," *JA* (July-August, 1912), pp. 123–28; Maung Tin, "Derivation of Arī," *JBRS,* IX (1919), p. 155 (and the discussion that follows this note in *JBRS,* X [1920], pp. 28, 82, 158, 160).
60. Than Tun, "Religion in Burma, A.D. 1000–1300," *JBRS,* XLII, 2 (1959), p. 59.
61. Coedès, *Les Peuples de la péninsule indochinoise* (Paris, 1962), p. 110. See Htin Aung, "The Lord of the Great Mountain," *JBRS,* XXXVIII (1955), p. 82, and above, pp. 26–27.
62. Pelliot, "Deux itinéraires," p. 172, n. 1.
63. *Ibid.,* p. 156, n. 4.
64. *Ibid.,* pp. 223–24. G. H. Luce, "Burma down to the Fall of Pagan," *JBRS,* XXIX (1939), p. 272.
65. Luce, "The Early Syām in Burma's History," p. 192.
66. C. O. Blagden, "Mon and Rāmaññadesa," *JBRS,* IV (1914), pp. 59–60; "Mon, Rman, Ramañña," *JBRS,* V (1915), p. 27. Some Arabic scholars have thought they could recognize this name in the form of *Rahmā* in various accounts of voyages, but Jean Sauvaget, *Relation de la Chine et de l'Inde* (Paris, 1948), p. 52, has shown the impossibility of this relationship.
67. They were sons of Tissa Dhammarāja Sīharāja, who, according to the legend, descended from a dragon, as did his wife (J. S. Furnivall, "Notes on the History of Hanthawaddy," *JBRS,* III [1913], p. 167).
68. May Oung, "The Chronology of Burma," *JBRS,* II (1912), pp. 15–16. See R. Halliday, "Lik Sming Asah," *JBRS,* VII (1917), p. 205; "Slapat Rājāwang Datow Sming Rong, A History of Kings," *JBRS,* XIII (1923), p. 48, n. 81.
69. A. P. Phayre, *History of Burma* (London, 1883), p. 289. G. E. Harvey, *History of Burma* (London, 1925), p. 368. Maung Hla, "The Chronological Tables of the Kings of Burma Who Reigned at Thayekhittaya (Ancient Prome) and at Pagan," *JBRS,* XIII (1923), pp. 82–94.
70. G. H. Luce, *Mons of the Pagan Dynasty* (Rangoon, 1950).
71. Alastair Lamb, "Miscellaneous Papers on Early Hindu and Buddhist Settlement in Northern Malaya and Southern Thailand," *JFMSM,* n.s. VI (1961), p. 67, n. 2.
72. The translation by E. Hultzsch, published in *JRAS* (1913), p. 337, and *JRAS* (1914), p. 397, is reproduced in Coedès, *Recueil*

des inscriptions du Siam (Bangkok, 1924–29), II, p. 50. K. A. Nilakanta Sastri, "Mahīpāla of the Caṇḍakauśikām," *Journal of Oriental Research,* VI (1932); "Takuapa and Its Tamil Inscription," *JRASMB,* XXII (1949), pp. 25–30.

73. R. Gopalan, *History of the Pallavas of Kanchi* (Madras, 1928), p. 138.
74. See below, p. 158. A third Tamil inscription at Ligor (above, p. 29) is too mutilated to be useful.
75. Pelliot, "Deux itinéraires," p. 286.
76. *Ibid.,* pp. 286–87.
77. Above, p. 54.
78. Above, p. 90.
79. Above, p. 88.
80. L. C. Damais, "Liste des principales inscriptions datées de l'Indonésie," *BEFEO,* XLVI (1952), p. 27.
81. J. G. de Casparis, *Prasasti Indonesia* (Bandung, 1950, 1956), II, p. 219.
82. Damais, "Liste des principales inscriptions," p. 27.
83. Above, p. 92, and below, p. 109.
84. Damais, "Liste des principales inscriptions," p. 31.
85. De Casparis, *Prasasti Indonesia,* II, pp. 289–90.
86. *Ibid.,* pp. 294–97, and I, pp. 107–109 and 133.
87. Above, p. 92. Since Bālaputra's mother was a princess of Śrīvijaya, he was returning to her native land.
88. This author, whose work dates from 844–48, says simply that "the king of Zābag, king of the islands of the southern sea, is called the maharaja." Gabriel Ferrand, *Relations de voyages et textes géographiques arabes, persans et turks relatifs à l'Extrême-Orient du VIIIe au XVIIIe siècles* (Paris, 1913), pp. 23–24, 29–30; "L'empire sumatranais de Çrīvijaya," *JA* (July-September, 1922), pp. 52–53. K. A. Nilakanta Sastri, *History of Śrīvijaya* (Madras, 1949), p. 62.
89. Inscription of Pereng. N. J. Krom, *Hindoe-Javaansche Geschiedenis* (The Hague, 1931), p. 165.
90. Thanks to the Charter of Nālandā published in Hirananda Shastri, "The Nālandā Copper Plate of Devapāladeva," *Epigraphia Indica,* XVII (1924), pp. 310–27.
91. W. F. Stutterheim, *A Javanese Period in Sumatran History* (Surakarta, 1929), pp. 9–12.
92. K. A. Nilakanta Sastri, "Śrī Vijaya," *BEFEO,* XL, p. 267.
93. For the location of this *vihāra* among the ruins of Nālandā, see F. D. K. Bosch, "Een oorkonde van het Groote Klooster te Nālandā," *TBG,* LXV (1925), pp. 509–88.
94. De Casparis, *Prasasti Indonesia,* II, p. 297.

Chapter VIII

1. He was the grandson of King Jayendrādhipativarman, maternal uncle of Jayavarman II. See above, p. 97.

2. Coedès, *Inscriptions du Cambodge* (Paris, 1937–), I, p. 37. See K. A. Nilakanta Sastri, "A Note on the Date of Śankara," *Journal Asiat. Res.*, Madras, XI, p. 285.
3. Auguste Barth and Abel Bergaigne, ISC, p. 361. Coedès, "L'inscription de Baksei Chamkrong," *JA* (May-June, 1909), p. 485; *Inscriptions du Cambodge*, IV, p. 88.
4. Barth and Bergaigne, ISC, p. 361. Coedès, *Inscriptions du Cambodge*, I, p. 24. Pierre Dupont, "La dislocation du Tchen-la et la formation du Cambodge angkorien," *BEFEO*, XLIII, p. 17.
5. Victor Goloubew, "L'hydraulique urbaine et agricole à l'époque des rois d'Angkor," *Bulletin Economique de l'Indochine* (1941). B. P. Groslier, *Angkor: Hommes et pierres* (Paris, 1956); *Indochine, carrefour des arts* (Paris, 1961), pp. 94 ff.
6. The old name of the monument is Parameśvara, posthumous name of Jayavarman II. The towers were built in the eastern part of a large quadrangle, situated to the south of the Indrataṭāka, that perhaps corresponds to the *purī* of Jayavarman II (above, p. 102). The Sanskrit inscriptions of this monument have been published by Barth and Bergaigne, ISC, p. 18. The Khmer inscriptions, which give long lists of servants, have been analyzed by Etienne Aymonier, *Le Cambodge* (Paris, 1900–1904), II, p. 439, and reproduced in volume IV of *Corpus*.
7. Coedès, "Note sur l'apothéose au Cambodge," *BCAI* (1911), p. 40.
8. The excavations at Bakong have revealed that on the site of the sanctuary (unfinished or destroyed) of the linga Indreśvara, on the top of the pyramid, a new tower was constructed in the twelfth century. The eight towers of stuccoed brick at the base of the pyramid and the adjoining structures are contemporaneous with the founding of the temple. The inscriptions of Bakong have been published in Barth and Bergaigne, ISC, p. 310, and in Coedès, *Inscriptions du Cambodge*, I, p. 31.
9. Barth and Bergaigne, ISC, p. 313.
10. Erik Seidenfaden, "Complément à *L'Inventaire descriptif des monuments du Cambodge* pour les quatre provinces du Siam oriental," *BEFEO*, XXII, p. 63.
11. Coedès, *Inscriptions du Cambodge*, I, p. 43.
12. Coedès, "La tradition généalogique des premiers rois d'Angkor," *BEFEO*, XXVIII, p. 124 ff.; "A propos du Tchen-la d'eau," *BEFEO*, XXXVI, pp. 1 ff.
13. He was the grandnephew in the female line of Śivakaivalya, the chief priest of Jayavarman II. Louis Finot, "L'inscription de Sdok Kak Thom," *BEFEO*, XV, 2, pp. 80, 89. See Coedès and Pierre Dupont, "Les stèles de Sdok Kak Thom, Phnom Sandak et Prah Vihar," *BEFEO*, XLIII, p. 62.
14. Coedès, "A la recherche du Yaçodharāçrama," *BEFEO*, XXXII, pp. 84 ff.

15. Above, p. 89. On the characteristics of this script, see the note by Auguste Barth in Barth and Bergaigne, ISC, p. 346.
16. Barth and Bergaigne, ISC, p. 319. The Khmer inscriptions are analyzed by Aymonier, *Le Cambodge,* II, p. 450, and reproduced in volume IV of *Corpus.*
17. Finot, "L'inscription de Sdok Kak Thom," p. 89; Coedès and Dupont, "Les stèles de Sdok Kak Thom," p. 113.
18. *Le Bayon d'Angkor et l'évolution de l'art khmèr* (Paris, 1927).
19. "La date du Bayon," *BEFEO,* XXVIII, p. 81.
20. "Le Phnom Bakheng et la ville de Yaçovarman," *BEFEO,* XXXIII, p. 319; "Nouvelles recherches autour du Phnom Bakhèng," *BEFEO,* XXXIV, p. 576. Since this river flows down from Phnom Kulèn, one scholar has wondered whether this sacred hill did not play a role in regard to Angkor analogous to that played by the religious city of Mi-sởn with regard to Trakiêu, whose river flowed down from the cirque of Mi-sởn (Séance du 10 Février, 1939, *JA* [April-June, 1939], p. 281).
21. Coedès, "Une nouvelle inscription du Phnom Bakhèng," *BEFEO,* XI, p. 396. On the symbolism of Phnom Bakhèng, see Jean Filliozat, "Les mythes cosmiques dans les religions indiennes," *Proceedings of the 7th Congress for the History of Religions* (Amsterdam, 1950), p. 135; *"Le symbolisme du monument du Phnom Bakhèng,"* *BEFEO,* XLIV (1954), pp. 527–54.
22. Philippe Stern, "Le temple-montagne khmèr, le culte du linga et le Devarāja," *BEFEO,* XXXIV, p. 611. See below, p. 119.
23. Maurice Glaize, "Le dégagement du Phnom Krom," *BEFEO,* XL, p. 371.
24. Published in Barth and Bergaigne, ISC, pp. 413 ff.
25. On these sects, see Sir Charles Eliot, *Hinduism and Buddhism: An Historical Sketch* (London, 1921), vol. II.
26. Represented by the ruins of Prei Prasat excavated by G. Trouvé. See his "Etude sur le Prei Prasat," *BEFEO,* XXXII, p. 113. The stele has been published in Barth and Bergaigne, ISC, p. 418. See Coedès, "A la recherche du Yaçodharāçrama," p. 85.
27. Represented by the ruins of Prasat Komnap. See G. Trouvé, "Etude sur le Prei Prasat," p. 113. I have published the stele in "A la recherche du Yaçodharāçrama," p. 89.
28. Coedès, "La stèle de Tép Pranam," *JA* (March-April, 1908), p. 203.
29. These monuments are described in Henri Parmentier, *L'Art khmèr classique* (Paris, 1939), pp. 136, 270.
30. Stele of Huei Thamo. Barth and Bergaigne, ISC, p. 389.
31. Stele of P'aniet (K. 479).
32. Stele of Kuhea Preah. Barth and Bergaigne, ISC, p. 388 (under the name of Phnom Trotoung).
33. Coedès, "Nouvelles données chronologiques et généalogiques sur la dynastie de Mahīdharapura," *BEFEO,* XXIX, p. 316.

34. Coedès, "Inscription de Baksei Chamkrong," p. 499; *Inscriptions du Cambodge,* IV, p. 88.
35. Henri Maspero, "La frontière de l'Annam et du Cambodge du VIIIe au XIVe siècle," *BEFEO,* XVIII, 3, p. 32. See Georges Maspero, "La géographie politique de l'Indochine aux environs de 960 A.D.," *Et. Asiat. EFEO,* II, pp. 94–95.
36. Barth and Bergaigne, ISC, p. 492, n. 3.
37. Coedès, "Nouvelles précisions sur les dates d'avenement de quelques rois des dynasties angkoriennes," *BEFEO,* XLIII, p. 13. One inscription mentions Paramaśivaloka as having issued a decree dated 902 (Coedès, *Inscriptions du Cambodge,* V, pp. 151–52).
38. Aymonier, *Le Cambodge,* III, p. 139.
39. Barth and Bergaigne, ISC, p. 551. See also Coedès, "La tradition généalogique," pp. 127–28.
40. Coedès, "L'inscription de Baksei Chamkrong," p. 500.
41. Coedès, "La date de Koh Ker," *BEFEO,* XXXI, p. 17.
42. Coedès, "A Date of Īśānavarman II," *JGIS,* III (1936), p. 65.
43. Coedès, "La date de Koh Ker," p. 12. It is from the same year as the Vishnuite monument of Prasat Kravan, erected east of Angkor by various high dignitaries.
44. Finot, "L'inscription de Sdok Kak Thom," p. 90; Coedès and Dupont, "Les stèles de Sdok Kak Thom," p. 119.
45. Inscription of Prasat Neang Khmau, in Coedès, *Inscriptions du Cambodge,* II, p. 32. See Coedès, "La date de Koh Ker," p. 17.
46. "Island of glory," a distortion of the word *gargyar* (modern *kokī*), name of the *Hopea* tree of the Dipterocarp family, generally known under its Vietnamese name of *sao.*
47. Parmentier, *L'Art khmèr classique,* pp. 15 ff. On the epigraphy of Koh Ker, see Coedès, *Inscriptions du Cambodge,* I, pp. 47–71.
48. Coedès, *Inscriptions du Cambodge,* I, pp. 68–71.
49. Coedès, "The Real Founder of the Cult of Divine Royalty in Cambodia," *Swami Vivekananda Centenary Memorial Volume, 1963,* ed. R. C. Majumdar (Calcutta, 1964); "Le rôle de la pyramide de Koh Ker dans l'évolution du temple-montagne khmèr," *Paranavitana Felicitation Volume* (Peradinya, to be published).
50. Coedès, *Inscriptions du Cambodge,* I, p. 75.
51. *Ibid.,* pp. 260–61.
52. *Ibid.,* p. 74.
53. Above, p. 67.
54. He was in fact the younger brother of Rājendravarman, whom the stele of Prè Rup represents as very young himself at the time of his accession. Coedès, *Inscriptions du Cambodge,* I, p. 75.
55. Finot, "L'inscription de Sdok Kak Thom," p. 91. Coedès and Dupont, "Les stèles de Sdok Kak Thom," p. 120.

56. Coedès, "Les inscriptions de Bat Chum," *JA* (September-October, 1908), p. 239 (revised translation).
57. Stern, *Le Bayon d'Angkor,* p. 55.
58. Above, p. 110.
59. Stele of Mébon, published in Louis Finot, "Inscriptions d'Aṅkor," *BEFEO,* XXV, p. 351. See Coedès, "La tradition généalogique," p. 137, n. 1.
60. Above, p. 66.
61. Coedès, *Inscriptions du Cambodge,* I, pp. 73 ff.
62. Aymonier, *Le Cambodge,* III, pp. 490–91.
63. His name continues to appear in the inscriptions of Jayavarman V.
64. Finot, "Inscriptions d'Aṅkor," p. 362. He was related to a priestly family made known to us by the inscription of Vat Thipdei. When I published this inscription in *Mélanges d'Indianisme offerts par ses élèves à M. Sylvain Lévi* (Paris, 1911), p. 213, I thought I could identify this Śivāchārya with another Brahman of the same name mentioned in the inscription of Sdok Kak Thom as officiating priest of the Devarāja (Finot, "L'inscription de Sdok Kak Thom," p. 91). But Louis Finot has shown the difficulty of such an identification ("Inscriptions d'Aṅkor," p. 365). On this question, see L. P. Briggs, "The Genealogy and Successors of Śivāchārya," *BEFEO,* XLVI, p. 177.
65. Coedès, "Les inscriptions de Bat Chum," p. 251.
66. Above, p. 113.
67. Below, n. 76.
68. Coedès, "Les inscriptions de Bat Chum," p. 245.
69. Below, p. 124.
70. Coedès, *Inscriptions du Cambodge,* I, p. 148. On Banteay Srei, see Ecole Française d'Extrême-Orient, *Mémoires archéologiques,* I: Le temple d'Īçvarapura (Paris, 1926). Coedès, "La date de Banteay Srei," *BEFEO,* XXIX, p. 289.
71. Coedès, *Inscriptions du Cambodge,* II, 65.
72. Coedès and Pierre Dupont, "Les inscriptions du Pràsàt Kôk Pô," *BEFEO,* XXXVII, pp. 383, 386.
73. Gilberte de Coral Rémusat, Victor Goloubew, and Coedès, "La date du Tà Kèv," *BEFEO,* XXXIV, p. 401. See also Coedès, "La date de Baphuon," *BEFEO,* XXXI, pp. 18–22; Coedès and Dupont, "Les inscriptions du Pràsàt Kôk Pô," pp. 383–84, 411.
74. Preah Einkosei in Siem Reap (Barth and Bergaigne, ISC, p. 77), and Prasat Komphüs in Mlu Prei (Coedès, *Inscriptions du Cambodge,* I, p. 159).
75. Finot, "L'inscription de Sdok Kak Thom," p. 94. Coedès and Dupont, "Les stèles de Sdok Kak Thom," p. 131.
76. E. Senart, "Une inscription bouddhique du Cambodge," *RA* (1883), p. 82. Coedès, "Un document capital sur le bouddhisme en Indochine: le stèle de Vat Sithor," *Studies on Buddhism in Japan,* IV (1942), p. 110; *Inscriptions du Cambodge,* VI, p. 195. H. Kern, "Over den aanhef eener buddhis-

tische inscriptie uit Battambang," *VMKAWAL* (1899), p. 66 (translated by Louis de La Vallée-Poussin in *Muséon,* n.s. 7 [1906], p. 46). Coedès, *Inscriptions du Cambodge,* II, p. 202.

77. Above, p. 84.
78. Louis Finot, "Lokeçvara en Indochine," *Et. Asiat. EFEO,* I, p. 227.
79. Coedès, "Une inscription d'Udayādityavarman I," *BEFEO,* XI, p. 400. F. D. K. Bosch, "De Laatste der Pāṇḍawa's" *BKI,* 104 (1948), pp. 541–71, would identify him with Udāyana, king of Bali (below, p. 129).
80. *Le Cambodge,* III, pp. 530–98.
81. On this subject, see Georges Groslier, *Recherches sur les Cambodgiens* (Paris, 1921).
82. Robert von Heine-Geldern, "Conceptions of State and Kingship in Southeast Asia," *FEQ,* II (1942), pp. 15–30. Jean Imbert, *Histoire des institutions khmères* (Phnom Penh, 1961).
83. R. Lingat, "L'influence juridique de l'Inde au Champa et au Cambodge d'après l'épigraphie," *JA,* CCXXXVII (1949), pp. 273–90.
84. Robert von Heine-Geldern, "Weltbild und Bauform in Südostasien," *Wiener Beiträge zur Kunst und Kultur Asiens,* IV (1930), p. 28.
85. See above, p. 101.
86. It seems improbable, if not impossible, that the large linga erected on the pyramid of Koh Ker, and called *kamrateng jagat ta rājya* in the inscriptions, was taken from Angkor by Jayavarman IV and brought back by Rājendravarman. In the eleventh century, the inscriptions speak of a linga of gold (below, p. 138).
87. Coedès, "Le culte de la royauté divinisée, source d'inspiration des grands monuments du Cambodge ancien," *Conferenze,* Serie Orientale Roma V (Rome, 1952), p. 1. Opinions vary concerning the principles governing royal succession. See Eveline Porée-Maspero, "Nouvelle étude sur la Nāgī Somā," *JA,* CCXXXVIII (1950), p. 237; *Etude sur les rites agraires des Cambodgiens,* I (Paris, 1962), pp. 152–82. Coedès, "Les règles de la succession royale dans l'ancien Cambodge," *BSEI,* n.s. XXVI (1951), pp. 117–30.
88. K. Bhattacharya, *Les religions brahmaniques dans l'ancien Cambodge* (Paris, 1961).
89. Coedès, "La stèle de Tép Pranam," p. 205; "Les inscriptions de Bat Chum," pp. 223–25. And for the following centuries: inscription of Tuol Prasat in Coedès, *Inscriptions du Cambodge,* II, p. 97; Louis Finot, "L'inscription de Prah Khan," *BEFEO,* IV, p. 673; Coedès, "La stèle de Ta Prohm," *BEFEO,* VI, p. 70, n. 4.
90. We shall see the cult of Siva-Buddha in Java, below, p. 199.
91. *L'Inde et le Monde* (Paris, 1928), p. 121.
92. Below, p. 212. "Actually," writes Louis de La Vallée-Poussin in

Dynasties et histoire de l'Inde (Paris, 1935), p. 334, "it is a misinterpretation to speak of Indian 'tolerance' in the sense of 'respect for the beliefs of others,' 'freedom accorded beliefs and practices of which one does not approve.' No Indian sovereign could, without seriously neglecting his duties, fail to establish Dharma ('Good') and exterminate Adharma ('Evil'), for in India, just as in China, even the changing of the seasons depends on the virtue of men. What gives this impression is the fact that, as a general rule, the rulers, like their subjects (and like the educated Brahmans, who, in all truth, do not believe in any god), worship all the gods, believe in the utility of all the liturgies: the kings make donations to the Buddhists, to the Brahmans . . . , as our sovereigns of the Middle Ages gave to various religious orders, each having their chosen god."

93. Coedès, "Note sur l'apothéose au Cambodge," p. 28; *Pour mieux comprendre Angkor* (Paris, 1947), pp. 44–67.
94. Coedès, "La destination funéraire des grands monuments khmèrs," *BEFEO,* XL, p. 315.
95. Coedès, *Pour mieux comprendre Angkor,* pp. 86–120.
96. Coedès, "Une nouvelle inscription d'Ayuthya," *JSS,* XXXV (1944), p. 73.
97. Also mentioned in the inscriptions. Coedès, "Nouvelles données épigraphiques sur l'histoire de l'Indochine centrale," *JA,* CCXLVI (1958), pp. 127–28.
98. Above, pp. 76–77.
99. Louis Finot, "Première stèle de Dong-duong," *BEFEO,* IV, p. 84.
100. Georges Maspero, *Le Royaume de Champa* (Paris, 1928), p. 6, writes incorrectly *Tch'eng-cheng.*
101. The question about whether the grandfather and father of Indravarman actually reigned, or whether he himself was the founder of the dynasty, has been the subject of a discussion between Louis Finot ("Inscriptions de Quang-nam," *BEFEO,* IV, p. 96; "L'épigraphie indochinoise," *BEFEO,* XV, 2, p. 126; review of Maspero's *Le Royaume de Champa, BEFEO,* XXVIII, p. 288) and Georges Maspero (*Le Royaume de Champa,* p. 110, n. 5) which, it seems to me, must be settled in favor of the latter; the terms in which the king relates the circumstances of his accession appear to me explicit.
102. Description in Henri Parmentier, *Inventaire descriptif des monuments čams de l'Annam* (Paris, 1909–18), I, p. 439. On the particular form of the Mahayana at Đông-dương, see Finot, "Lokeçvara en Indochine," p. 232.
103. Inscriptions of Ban-lanh (edited by Finot, "Inscriptions de Quang-nam," p. 99) and of Châu-sa (edited by Edouard Huber, "L'épigraphie de la dynastie de Đong-dương," *BEFEO,* XI, p. 282).
104. Edouard Huber, in translating the stele of Nhan-biêu ("L'épi-

graphie de la dynastie de Đong-dương," p. 299) has rendered this expression as "to acquire the magical science." On this word *siddha-*(or *siddhi-*)*yātrā,* which designates a pilgrimage to a particularly sacred territory charged with magical power, see above, p. 82.

105. Philippe Stern, *L'Art du Champa* (*ancien Annam*) *et son évolution* (Paris, 1942), pp. 66–68, 109. On a possible Chinese influence, see Pierre Dupont, "Les apports chinois dans le style bouddhique de Đong-dương," *BEFEO,* XLIV (1951), pp. 267–74.
106. Inscriptions of Phu-lương and of Lac-thanh published in Edouard Huber, "L'épigraphie de la dynastie de Đong-dương," pp. 283, 285.
107. Barth and Bergaigne, ISC, p. 247.
108. The earliest mention of this battle is found in the stele of the Mébon of 952 (st. CXLVI, Finot, "Inscriptions d'Aṅkor," p. 346).
109. Barth and Bergaigne, ISC, p. 260.
110. According to Kodo Tasaka, "Islam in Champa," *Tohogaku,* IV (1952), p. 52, the envoy P'u Ho San was a Moslem named Abû Hasan and what we have here is the earliest evidence of the existence of Islam in Champa. The Arabic inscriptions discovered in 1902–1907 and deciphered by Paul Ravaisse, "Deux inscriptions coufiques du Champa," *JA,* XX (1922), p. 247, prove that a Moslem colony, enjoying a certain autonomy, existed in Champa in the middle of the tenth century.
111. Maspero, *Le Royaume de Champa,* p. 119.
112. *Ibid.,* p. 120.
113. Barth and Bergaigne, ISC, p. 260.
114. Maspero, *Le Royaume de Champa,* p. 121, n. 1.
115. In the present-day province of Ninh-binh.
116. Henri Maspero, "Le protectorat général d'Annam sous les T'ang," *BEFEO,* X, p. 678.
117. For this whole period, on which the epigraphic sources are silent and which is known only through Chinese texts, see Maspero, *Le Royaume de Champa,* pp. 121 ff.
118. Inscription of Mi-sơn published in Finot, "Inscriptions de Quang-nam," p. 113. On the date of this inscription, see Louis Finot, "Les inscriptions de Jaya Parameçvaravarman I," *BEFEO,* XV, 2, p. 49, and Maspero, *Le Royaume de Champa,* p. 126, n. 3.
119. Maspero, *Le Royaume de Champa,* p. 129.
120. Perhaps on a site marked by the tower of Binh-lâm, which seems to date from the eleventh century. The citadel of Chaban possibly marks the location of Vijaya at a later date, for the Tower of Copper that marks its center dates from the thirteenth century (Stern, *L'Art du Champa,* pp. 71–72).
121. Above, p. 108.

122. Hendrik Kern, *Verspreide Geschriften* (The Hague, 1913–29), VI, p. 277. N. J. Krom, "De inscriptie van Pereng," *BKI,* 75 (1919), p. 16. R. Ng. Poerbatjaraka, *Agastya in den Archipel* (Leyden, 1926), p. 45.
123. N. J. Krom, *Inleiding tot de Hindoe-Javaansche Kunst* (The Hague, 1923), I, p. 440; *Hindoe-Javaansche Geschiedenis* (The Hague, 1931), p. 172.
124. See above, p. 90.
125. Krom, *Inleiding tot de Hindoe-Javaansche Kunst,* II, p. 4; *Hindoe-Javaansche Geschiedenis,* p. 171.
126. *Ibid.* See above, pp. 113, 118, 120–21.
127. W. P. Groeneveldt, *Notes on the Malay Archipelago and Malacca* (Batavia, 1876), p. 13.
128. On the *vishakanyakā* in India, see C. H. Tawney, *The Ocean of Story,* ed. N. M. Penzer (London, 1924–28), II, p. 275.
129. See above, p. 90.
130. Perhaps a transcription of the name of Daksha-, who before succeeding Balitung in 915, appeared in the charters of this country around 901 as the highest dignitary of the court. See Poerbatjaraka, *Agastya,* p. 110, and below, p. 127.
131. L. C. Damais, "Epigrafische Aantekeningen," *TBG,* LXXXIII (1949), pp. 1–6; "Méthode de réduction des dates javanaises en date européenes," *BEFEO,* XLV (1951), pp. 21–23.
132. L. C. Damais, "Liste des principales inscriptions datées d'Indonésie," *BEFEO,* XLVI (1952), pp. 34–43.
133. The identification proposed by N. J. Krom (in F. W. Stapel, ed., *Geschiedenis van Nederlandsch Indië* [Amsterdam, 1938–40], I, p. 168), contested by Damais ("Epigrafische Aantekeningen," p. 22; "Liste des principales inscriptions," p. 42), but confirmed by J. G. de Casparis ("Short Inscriptions from Tjandi Plaosan-Lor," *Berita Dinas Purbakala: Bulletin of the Archeological Service of the Republic of Indonesia,* 4 [1958], p. 22).
134. W. F. Stutterheim, "Oudheidkundige Aanteekeningen," *BKI,* 90 (1933), p. 269. Damais, "Liste des principales inscriptions," p. 43.
135. Damais, "Liste des principales inscriptions," p. 43.
136. Above, p. 88.
137. W. F. Stutterheim, "Oudheidkundige Aanteekeningen," *BKI,* 89 (1932), p. 278; 90 (1933), p. 287.
138. Krom, *Hindoe-Javaansche Geschiedenis,* p. 187.
139. They name him Rakai Watukura, lord Balitung in the East, and Śrī Īśvarakeśava Utsavatunga (or Samarottunga Dharmodaya Mahāśambhu in the center). For the list and the dates of these inscriptions, see Damais, "Liste des principales inscriptions," pp. 42–51.
140. Krom, *Hindoe-Javaansche Geschiedenis,* p. 191, n. 1. R. Goris, "De eenheid der Matarāmsche dynastie, *Feestbundel door het*

Koninklijk Bataviaasch Genootschap van Kunsten en Wetenschappen (Weltevreden, 1929), I, p. 202.

141. On this date, see Damais, "Epigrafische Aantekeningen," p. 25; "La date des inscriptions en ère de Sanjaya," *BEFEO,* XLV (1951), pp. 42 ff.
142. Krom, *Hindoe-Javaansche Geschiedenis,* p. 188. His complete name is Dakshottama Bāhuvajratipakshakshaya.
143. Goris, "De eenheid der Matarāmsche dynastie," p. 206.
144. *Ibid.* W. F. Stutterheim, "Oudheidkundige Aanteekeningen," *BKI,* 90 (1933), p. 267.
145. "The establishment of this new era in the name of a great sovereign of the past makes plausible the hypothesis of a special tie—of kinship?—between Daksha and Sanjaya." Damais, "La date des inscriptions en ère de Sanjaya," p. 62.
146. Krom, *Hindoe-Javaansche Geschiedenis,* p. 194 (Rakai Layang, lord Tuloḍong, Śrī Sajjanasanmatānuragatungadeva). See Himansu Bhusan Sarkar, "A Geographical Introduction to the Study of Kawi Oorkomden," *BKI,* 105 (1949), pp. 107–10. Damais, "Liste des principales inscriptions," pp. 52–55.
147. Krom, *Hindoe-Javaansche Geschiedenis,* p. 196.
148. On this date, see Damais, "Liste des principales inscriptions," pp. 54–57. His complete name is Rakai Pankaja, lord Wawa, Śrī Vijayalokanāmottunga.
149. W. F. Stutterheim, "Een Oorkunde van Koning Pu Wāgiçwara uit 927 A.D.," *TBG,* 75 (1935), p. 420.
150. Śrī Īśānavikrama Dharmottungadeva.
151. See the discussion in *News Letter from the South East Asia Institute,* no. 6 (March, 1948), which cites a study by Bertram Schrieke, "Het einde van de klassieke Hindoe-Javaansche cultuur op Midden Java," *22 Koloniale Vacantiecursus voor Geografen* (Amsterdam, 1941).
152. J. W. Ijzerman, *Beschrijving der oudheden nabij de grens der residentie's Soerakarta en Djogdjakarta* (Batavia, 1891).
153. Pieter Jan Veth, *Java, geographisch, ethnologisch, historisch* (Haarlem, 1896), I, p. 45. J. L. A. Brandes, in *Encyclopaedie van Nederlandsch-Indië* (The Hague, 1895–1905), III, p. 132.
154. Krom, *Hindoe-Javaansche Geschiedenis,* p. 208. J. L. Moens, "Srīvijaya, Yāva en Katāha," *TBG,* 77 (1937), pp. 411, 442.
155. F. D. K. Bosch, "Een Maleische inscriptie in het Buitenzorgsche," *BKI,* 100 (1941), pp. 49–53.
156. For these dates, see Damais, "Epigrafische Aantekeningen," p. 26; "Liste des principales inscriptions," pp. 56–63. In spite of this rich epigraphy, the historicity and the very existence of Sinḍok have been challenged by C. C. Berg (see "Javanese Historiography," in D. G. E. Hall, *Historians of South-East Asia* [London, 1961], p. 18). On the theories of C. C. Berg, see below, p. 344, n. 145.

157. Krom, *Inleiding tot de Hindoe-Javaansche Kunst,* II, pp. 27–35, 307–309.
158. R. Ng. Poerbatjaraka, "Dateering van het Oud-Javaansche Rāmāyaṇa," in *Gedenkschrift van het Koninklijk Instituut voor de Taal-, Land- en Volkenkunde van Nederlandsch-Indië* (The Hague, 1926), p. 265; "Het Oud-Javaansche Rāmāyaṇa," *TBG,* 72 (1932), p. 151. Christiaan Hooykaas at first believed he could attribute the Javanese *Rāmāyaṇa* to a poet named Yogīśvara (*The Old-Javanese Rāmāyaṇa Kakawin* [The Hague, 1955], VKI, XVI), but he has renounced this hypothesis in an article showing that this poem was directly inspired by the Sanskrit *Bhaṭṭikāvya* (*The Old-Javanese Rāmāyaṇa; an Exemplary Kakawin as to Form and Content* [Amsterdam, 1957], VKNAWAL, 65, no. 1).
159. Edited by J. Kats (The Hague, 1910). Translated into German by Kurt Wulff (Copenhagen, 1935) in *Historisk-filologiske Meddelelser,* XXI, 4. See Krom, *Hindoe-Javaansche Geschiedenis,* p. 219.
160. Damais, "Liste des principales inscriptions," p. 62, n. 8.
161. L. C. Damais, "La colonnette de Sanur," *BEFEO,* XLIV (1947–50), pp. 121–28; "Liste des principales inscriptions," pp. 82–83.
162. W. F. Stutterheim, *Oudheden van Bali* (Singaradja, 1929), I; *Indian Influence in Old-Balinese Art* (London, 1935). R. Goris, "Enkele medeelingen nopens de oorkonden gesteld in het Oud-balisch," *Djawa,* XVI (1936), pp. 88–101.
163. See the résumé by L. C. Damais of an article by R. Goris on this dynasty in *BEFEO,* L (1962), pp. 482–83.
164. Damais, "Liste des principales inscriptions," p. 85, n. 5, proposes to identify this princess with the daughter of Siṇḍok, named above Śrī Iśānatungavijayā.
165. *Ibid.,* p. 62, n. 5.
166. Groeneveldt, *Notes on the Malay Archipelago,* p. 108.
167. Damais, "Liste des principales inscriptions," p. 63.
168. Groeneveldt, *Notes on the Malay Archipelago,* pp. 18, 65. Gabriel Ferrand, "L'empire sumatranais de Çrīvijaya," *JA* (July-September, 1922), pp. 18–19.
169. L. C. Damais, "Une trace de l'expédition de Dharmavaṃça à San-fo-ts'i," *Actes, XXII*[e] *Congrès International des Orientalistes* (Istanbul, 1951), p. 323.
170. Pp. 113–14.
171. On all these texts, see Gabriel Ferrand, *Relations de voyages et textes géographiques arabes, persans et turks relatifs à l'Extrême-Orient du VIII*[e] *au XVII*[e] *siècles* (Paris, 1913–14). See also Ferrand, "L'empire sumatranais," pp. 56–57.
172. On Kalah, see Jean Sauvaget, ed. and trans. *'Ahbār as-sīn wa l-hind, Relation de la Chine et de l'Inde, rédigée en 851* (Paris, 1948), p. 43; O. W. Wolters, "Tāmbralinga," *BSOAS.*

XXI (1958), p. 602; Paul Wheatley, *The Golden Khersonese* (Kuala Lumpur, 1961), pp. 224 ff. On the location of Kalah, see S. Q. Fatimi, "In Quest of Kalah," *JSEAH,* I, 2 (1960), p. 65.

173. In part according to the documentation of Abû Zayd Hasan, in his addition to the *'Ahbār as-sīn wa l-hind.* Before his premature death, Jean Sauvaget, the eminent Arabic scholar who edited and translated the *'Ahbār as-sīn wa l-hind,* kindly called to my attention that "the name by which the Arabs supposedly knew the empire of Śrīvijaya, *Sribuza,* does not exist: the Arabic transcription *Srbza* should be interpreted, according to the oldest Arabic system of transcription (in which the foreign *v* is rendered as *b,* and *j* as *z;* there are many other examples of this), as *Srvja.* Thus it transcribes exactly, but naturally without the notation of the vowels, *Śrīvija(ya)*; the omission of the last syllable could be accidental, but it may also have been intentional, for the syllable *-ya* may have been taken for the Arabic ending *-ya* that had no place there."

174. The parasang equals around 6¼ kilometers.

175. Ferrand, *Relations de voyages,* pp. 109–10; "L'empire sumatranais," p. 63.

176. This transcription has not yet been explained in a completely satisfactory manner. The attempt of L. Aurousseau to interpret *san* as a faulty transcription of a character formerly read *che* = *śrī* ("Chronique," *BEFEO,* XXIII, p. 477) apparently has not convinced the Sinologists. In any case, *fo-ch'i* certainly corresponds to *vijaya.*

177. The factory for commercial navigation opened at Canton in 971 received, among other foreigners, persons from San-fo-ch'i (W. W. Rockhill, "Notes on the Relations and Trade of China with the Eastern Archipelago and the Coast of the Indian Ocean during the Fourteenth Century," *TP,* XV [1914], p. 420, n. 1). In 980, the *History of the Sung* mentions the arrival of a merchant of San-fo-ch'i at Ch'ao-chou (Swatow). In 985, the same history cites a purely commercial embassy from San-fo-ch'i. Groeneveldt, *Notes on the Malay Archipelago,* p. 64.

178. Groeneveldt, *Notes on the Malay Archipelago,* pp. 62–68. Ferrand, "L'empire sumatranais," pp. 15–22.

179. Moens, "Srīvijaya, Yāva en Katāha," p. 457.

180. Edouard Chavannes, "Les inscriptions chinoises de Bodh-Gayā," *Revue de l'histoire des religions,* XXXIV (1896), p. 52 (relying on the *History of the Sung,* CCCCXC).

181. According to L. C. Damais, "La date de l'inscription de Hujung Langit," *BEFEO,* L (1962), p. 284, the discernible Javanese influence in an inscription of southern Sumatra in Old-Malay dated 997 was an indirect consequence of this campaign.

182. Arthur P. Phayre, *History of Burma* (London, 1883), p. 280. G. E. Harvey, *History of Burma* (London, 1925), pp. 364, 368.

Maung Hla, "The Chronological Dates of the Kings of Burma Who Reigned at Thayekhittagu (Ancient Prome) and at Pagan," *JBRS,* XIII (1923), p. 93.

183. Harvey, *History of Burma,* p. 18.
184. *Ibid.,* p. 315. See Edouard Huber, "Le jardinier régicide qui devint roi," *BEFEO,* V, p. 176; R. Baradat, "Les Samré ou Pear, population primitive de l'ouest du Cambodge," *BEFEO,* XLI, p. 11.
185. Harvey, *History of Burma,* p. 19. The dates given by this author seem too early, for they tend to ascribe too long a reign to Sokkate and have Anôratha dying at almost one hundred years of age.

Chapter IX

1. Coedès, "La date de Koh Ker," *BEFEO,* XXXI, p. 15, n. 2.
2. Inscription of Prasat Khna. Coedès, "Une inscription d'Udayādityavarman I," *BEFEO,* XI, p. 400.
3. Coedès, *Inscriptions du Cambodge* (Paris, 1937–), VI, p. 9, n. 3.
4. Coedès, "La tradition généalogique des premiers rois d'Angkor," *BEFEO,* XXVIII, p. 142.
5. Inscription of Robang Romeas. Gilberte de Coral Rémusat, Victor Goloubew, and Coedès, "La date du Tà Kèv," *BEFEO,* XXXIV, p. 422.
6. Coral Rémusat, Goloubew, and Coedès, "La date du Tà Kèv," p. 422.
7. See *ibid.,* p. 423, and Coedès, *Inscriptions du Cambodge,* I, p. 189. L. P. Briggs, "The Khmer Empire and the Malay Peninsula," *FEQ,* IX (1950), p. 285, n. 125, identifies Jayavīravarman with Narapativīravarman, elder brother of Udayādityavarman (of the inscription of Prasat Khna; see above, n. 2). He accepts the hypothesis of F. D. K. Bosch identifying Narapativīravarman with Narottama, prince of Bali (see above, p. 314, n. 79).
8. Coedès, *Inscriptions du Cambodge,* III, pp. 205 ff.
9. See Coral Rémusat, Goloubew, and Coedès, "La date du Tà Kèv," p. 424.
10. *Ibid.,* p. 425; Coedès and Pierre Dupont, "Les stèles de Sdok Kak Thom, Phnom Sandak et Prah Vihar," *BEFEO,* XLIII, p. 122.
11. Louis Finot, "L'inscription de Praḥ Khan," *BEFEO,* IV, p. 676.
12. Coral Rémusat, Goloubew, and Coedès, "La date du Tà Kèv," p. 427.
13. Coedès, "Les deux inscriptions de Vat Thipdei," in *Mélanges d'Indianisme offerts par ses élèves à M. Sylvain Lévi* (Paris, 1911), p. 216.
14. *Ibid.* and *Inscriptions du Cambodge,* I, p. 196.
15. Probably a daughter, as Pierre Dupont suggests in "La dislocation du Tchen-la," *BEFEO,* XLIII (1943–46), p. 36, n. 2.

16. See above, pp. 120–21.
17. Louis Finot, "L'inscription de Sdok Kak Thom," *BEFEO,* XV, 2, p. 91. Coedès and Dupont, "Les stèles de Sdok Kak Thom," p. 121.
18. *Ibid.*
19. Coral Rémusat, Goloubew, and Coedès, "La date du Tà Kèv," p. 401.
20. Described by Henri Marchal, "Pavillons d'entrée au Palais Royale d'Angkor Thom," *Et. Asiat. EFEO,* II, p. 57.
21. Georges Groslier, "Le temple du Phnom Chiso," *Arts et archéologie khmèrs,* I (Paris, 1921), p. 65.
22. Henri Parmentier, *L'Art khmèr classique* (Paris, 1939), I, p. 338.
23. Henri Mauger, "Prah Khan de Kompong Svay," *BEFEO,* XXXIX, p. 197.
24. E. Lunet de Lajonquière, *Inventaire descriptif des monuments du Cambodge* (Paris, 1902–11), III, pp. 427, 432.
25. Etienne Aymonier, *Le Cambodge* (Paris, 1900–1904), III, pp. 500–502.
26. *Annual Report on Indian Epigraphy* (1949–50), p. 4.
27. "The Overseas Expeditions of King Rājendra Cola," *AA,* XXIV (1961), p. 341.
28. Coedès, "Documents sur l'histoire politique et religieuse du Laos occidental," BEFEO, XXV, p. 158. Camille Notton, *Annales du Siam* (Paris, 1926–32), II, pp. 34–35.
29. Coedès, "Documents . . . Laos," p. 80.
30. Perhaps earlier than the two other texts. Bangkok edition, 1939, pp. 182–83.
31. According to the *Chāmadevīvaṃsa.* See Coedès, "Documents . . . Laos," p. 159.
32. At the beginning of the eleventh century, before its annexation by Cambodia, Lavo still constituted an independent state (heir of the kingdom of Dvāravatī?). It is mentioned under the year 1001 by the *History of the Sung* (Paul Pelliot, "Deux itinéraires de Chine en Inde à la fin du VIIIe siècle," *BEFEO,* IV, p. 233).
33. Dupont, "La dislocation du Tchen-la," pp. 68–70.
34. Coedès, *Recueil des inscriptions du Siam* (Bangkok, 1924–29), II, pp. 21–31.
35. Georges Maspero, "La géographie politique de l'Indochine," *Et. Asiat. EFEO,* pp. 94–103. Notton, *Annales du Siam,* I.
36. Paul Lévy, "Les traces de l'introduction du bouddhisme à Luang Prabang," *BEFEO,* XL, p. 411.
37. See below, p. 195.
38. Coedès, *Recueil des inscriptions du Siam,* II, p. 10.
39. The eighth day of the crescent moon of *phālguna* 971, according to the inscription of Prasat Roluḥ (Aymonier, *Le*

Cambodge, II, p. 326, and Coedès, *Inscriptions du Cambodge, VII).*

40. Finot, "L'inscription de Sdok Kak Thom," p. 93; Coedès and Dupont, "Les stèles de Sdok Kak Thom," pp. 121, 126.
41. Barth and Bergaigne, ISC, p. 139.
42. Coedès, "La date du Baphuon," *BEFEO,* XXXI, p. 18.
43. Paul Pelliot, trans. and ed., "Mémoires sur les coutumes du Cambodge," *BEFEO,* II, p. 142.
44. Victor Goloubew, "La double enceinte et les avenues d'Angkor Thom," *Cahiers EFEO,* 14 (1938), p. 33; "L'hydraulique urbaine et agricole à l'époque des rois d'Angkor," *Bulletin économique de l'Indochine* (1941), p. 5.
45. "Chronique," *BEFEO,* XXXVI, p. 611, pl. 93.
46. Inscription of Preah Ngôk, in Barth and Bergaigne, ISC, p. 140. Georges Maspero, "Le connetable Sangrāma," *Revue indochinoise,* I (1904), p. 8.
47. Aymonier, *Le Cambodge,* III, p. 507.
48. Coedès, *Inscriptions du Cambodge,* I, p. 222.
49. Above, p. 125.
50. Georges Maspero, *Le Royaume de Champa* (Paris, 1928), p. 132.
51. *Ibid.*
52. A very questionable restoration. See *ibid.,* p. 132.
53. A very questionable restoration. See *ibid.,* p. 134.
54. Maspero, *Le Royaume de Champa,* pp. 134–36.
55. Louis Finot, "Pāṇḍuranga," *BEFEO,* III, p. 645.
56. *Ibid.,* p. 646.
57. Etienne Aymonier, "Première étude sur les inscriptions tchames," *JA* (January-February, 1891), p. 29.
58. Maspero, *Le Royaume de Champa,* pp. 138–39.
59. *Ibid.,* pp. 139–40.
60. *Ibid.,* pp. 141–42.
61. In the subtitle of the Tibetan translation of this work, called *Durbodhāloka* (a translation by Atīśa, the future reformer of Buddhism in Tibet), it is said that it was composed "during the reign of Śrī Chūḍāmaṇivarmadeva, of Śrīvijayanagara, in Malayagiri, in Suvarṇadvīpa." (For this information, we are obliged to J. Naudou.)
62. W. P. Groeneveldt, *Notes on the Malay Archipelago and Malacca* (Batavia, 1876), p. 65. See also Gabriel Ferrand, "L'empire sumatranais de Çrīvijaya," *JA* (July-September, 1922), p. 19.
63. O. W. Wolters, "Tāmbralinga," *BSOAS,* XXI (1958), p. 604.
64. See above, p. 109.
65. Perhaps it still existed in the middle of the last century (Sir Walter Elliot, "The Edifice Formerly Known as the Chinese or Jana Pagoda at Negapatam," *Indian Antiquary,* VII [1878], p.

224) and was destroyed by the Jesuits in 1868. See K. V. Subrahmanya Aiyer, "The Larger Leiden Plates," *Epigraphia Indica,* XXII, p. 229. On the date of the construction, see K. A. Nilakanta Sastri, *History of Śrīvijaya* (Madras, 1949), p. 76.

66. On the Choḷas, from whom the Coromandel (Choḷamaṇḍala) Coast derives its name and whose rise at the expense of the Pallavas dates from the middle of the ninth century, see Louis de La Vallée-Poussin, *Dynasties et histoire de l'Inde* (Paris, 1935), p. 271.
67. The *History of the Sung* shortens his name to Ssu-li Ma-lo-p'i (i.e., Śrī Māravi). On the identification of this name and that of his predecessor, see Coedès, "Le royaume de Çrīvijaya," *BEFEO,* XVIII, p. 7.
68. Published by Subrahmanya Aiyer in "The Larger Leiden Plates," p. 213. See K. A. Nilakanta Sastri, "Śrī Vijaya," *BEFEO,* XL, p. 281.
69. According to Nilakanta Sastri, *History of Śrīvijaya,* p. 79, n. 3.
70. Above, p. 130.
71. R. C. Majumdar, *Ancient Indian Colonies in the Far East,* II: Suvarṇadvīpa (Dacca, 1937), p. 171. According to K. A. Nilakanta Sastri (*The Cōḷas* [Madras, 1935–37], I, p. 220, and *History of Śrīvijaya,* p. 79, n. 13), these were the Maldives.
72. Majumdar, *Ancient Indian Colonies,* II, p. 171, n. 2. Nilakanta Sastri (*The Cōḷas,* I, p. 254, and *History of Śrīvijaya,* p. 79, n. 13) questions that this expedition ever occurred and asserts that the arguments of R. C. Majumdar are unfounded. But Majumdar has given new epigraphic arguments in favor of his thesis in "The Overseas Expeditions of King Rājendra Cola," pp. 338–42.
73. The king who sent an embassy to China in the same year, 1017, is called Hsia-ch'e-su-wu-cha-p'u-mi, that is, Haji Samudrabhūmi ("King of Sumatra"), by the *History of the Sung.* (Groeneveldt, *Notes on the Malay Archipelago,* p. 65; Ferrand, "L'empire sumatranais," pp. 19–20.) According to N. J. Krom in "De naam Sumatra," *BKI,* 100 (1941), pp. 5–25, Sumātra, synonym for Suvarṇa, may have become popular because it was homonymous with Samudra, the name of a port located in the north of the island.
74. Published in E. Hultzsch, *South Indian Inscriptions* (Madras, 1891), II, p. 105, and *Epigraphia Indica,* IX, p. 231. See Coedès, "Le royaume de Çrīvijaya," pp. 4–5, 9 ff., and Nilakanta Sastri, "Śrī Vijaya," p. 286.
75. This list has been studied by Coedès, "Le royaume de Çrīvijaya," pp. 9 ff.; G. P. Rouffaer, "Was Malaka emporium voor 1400 A.D. genaamd Malajoer?" *BKI,* 77 (1921), pp. 76 ff.; Ferrand, "L'empire sumatranais," p. 45; Majumdar, *Ancient Indian Colonies,* II, pp. 175 ff. In the inscription, each name is accompanied by an epithet. But the documentary worth of

these epithets is extremely doubtful, for they constitute sorts of puns, playing on the meanings of the component parts of the geographic terms. Thus, to cite only two examples, Talaittakkolam is called "praised by great men versed in the sciences" because in Tamil *kalai* = science and *takkor* = scholar, and Vaḷaippandūru is described as "possessing both cultivated and uncultivated land" because *viḷaippu* = *sowing* and *tūru* = bush.

76. See below, p. 184. *Mā-,* here and in the other words in this list, equals the Sanskrit *mahā* ("great"). Māyiruḍingam has been located by Paul Wheatley (*The Golden Khersonese* [Kuala Lumpur, 1961], p. 71) in the neighborhood of Ligor.
77. Above, p. 39.
78. "Pré-aryen et pré-dravidien dans l'Inde," *JA* (July-September, 1923), p. 43. But Wheatley (*The Golden Khersonese,* p. 200) rejects this identification as "a flight of fancy" and seems inclined (p. 257) to see in Kāma*langka* an equivalent of *Langka*suka.
79. Rouffaer, "Was Malaka emporium," pp. 78, 81. J. L. Moens, "Śrīvijaya, Yāva en Katāha," *TBG,* 77 (1937), p. 468. The identification is rejected by Wheatley in *The Golden Khersonese,* p. 200.
80. Above, p. 39. In 1001, a "Tan-mei-liu" sent an embassy to China (Pelliot, "Deux itinéraires," p. 233). On this embassy, actually sent by Tan-liu-mei ("Tan-mei-liu" probably being the result of an error by the scribe), and in general on the complicated question of the possible relationships between these various place names, see Wolters, "Tāmbralinga," pp. 587–607, and Wheatley, *The Golden Khersonese,* pp. 65–67.
81. On this name, see H. K. J. Cowan, "Lāmurī," *BKI,* 90 (1933), p. 422.
82. Pāṇḍuranga (Phan-rang) is located outside the circuit, but the identification of Vaḷaippandūru is anything but certain. The opinion expressed above is challenged by Wolters ("Tāmbralinga," p. 601), who observes that some of the places listed, notably Tāmbralinga, may have been independent states.
83. John Leyden, trans., *Malay Annals* (London, 1821).
84. Groeneveldt, *Notes on the Malay Archipelago,* p. 65. Ferrand, "L'empire sumatranais," p. 20.
85. Translated by Sarat Chandra Das, *Indian Pandits in the Land of Snow* (Calcutta, 1893), p. 50.
86. Around 1030, Al-Bīrūnī said that the islands of Zābag were called *Sūwarndīb* in India (i.e., *Suvarṇadvīpa;* see Ferrand, "L'empire sumatranais," p. 64) in conformity with the usage of Atīśa (above, p. 323, n. 61).
87. This King Dharmapāla, whom the Tibetans call the guru Dharmapāla of Suvarṇadvīpa, may also have been the

teacher of Atīśa and of Kamalarakshita and the author of various works related to the *Bodhicharyāvatāra.* (For this information, we are obliged to J. Naudou.)

88. J. L. A. Brandes, in *Notulen van de Directievergaderingen van het Bataviaasch Genootschap* (1887), p. 176.
89. Alfred Foucher, *Etude sur l'iconographie bouddhique de l'Inde,* Bibliotheque de l'Ecole des Hautes Etudes, XIII (Paris, 1900), pp. 105 and 193, n. 23.
90. Above, p. 129.
91. Perhaps it was this circumstance that earned him the name Airlanga, the most probable meaning of which is "he who crossed the water," that is, the strait separating Java from Bali. See R. Ng. Poerbatjaraka, "Erlangha," *Djawa,* X (1930), p. 163, where earlier interpretations are summarized.
92. C. C. Berg, "De Arjunawiwāha, Er-langga's levensloop en bruiloftslied," *BKI,* 97 (1938), pp. 49–64.
93. The date established by L. C. Damais, "Liste des principales inscriptions datées d'Indonésie," *BEFEO,* XLVI (1952), p. 64, n. 2. The inscriptions in the name of Airlanga date from 1019 to 1042 (*ibid.,* pp. 62–65).
94. P. V. van Stein Callenfels, "De veroveraar van Dharmmawangça's kraton," *Oudheidkundig Verslag* (1919), p. 156.
95. Rouffaer, "Was Malaka emporium."
96. N. J. Krom, *Hindoe-Javaansche Geschiedenis* (The Hague, 1931), pp. 241–42.
97. H. Kern, "De steen van den berg Penanggungan (Surabaya), thans in't Indian Museum te Calcutta," *Verspreide Geschriften* (The Hague, 1913–29), VII, p. 83. B. R. Chatterjee, *India and Java* (Calcutta, 1933), II, Inscriptions, pp. 63–74. R. Ng. Poerbatjaraka, "Strophe 14 van de Sanskritzijde der Calcutta-oorkonde," *TBG,* LXXXI (1941), pp. 424–37.
98. W. F. Stutterheim, "Oudheidkundige Aanteekeningen," *BKI,* 92 (1934), pp. 200–201.
99. Berg, "De Arjunawiwāha," p. 82.
100. Kern, *Verspreide Geschriften,* VII, p. 83.
101. G. P. Rouffaer, in *Notulen van de Directievergaderingen van het Bataviaasch Genootschap* (1909), p. 180.
102. Stutterheim, "Oudheidkundige Aanteekeningen," p. 406.
103. W. F. Stutterheim, "De Beelden van Belahan," *Djawa* (1938), p. 307.
104. Berg, "De Arjunawiwāha," p. 92.
105. Krom, *Hindoe-Javaansche Geschiedenis,* p. 262.
106. Berg, "De Arjunawiwāha," p. 64. It is also possible that she was the widow of Sangrāmavijayottungavarman and that Airlanga, following a custom of which we have seen earlier examples, married the king's widow in order to justify eventual claims on Śrivijaya.
107. And even in the west of the island of Java, for up to the

beginning of the thirteenth century Sunda remained a vassal of Śrīvijaya. See below, p. 184, and F. D. K. Bosch, "Een maleische inscriptie in het Buitenzorgsche," *BKI,* 100 (1941), pp. 49–53.

108. Kern, *Verspreide Geschriften,* III, p. 71; VII, p. 30. Krom, *Hindoe-Javaansche Geschiedenis,* p. 264.
109. Stutterheim, "Oudheidkundige Aanteekeningen," p. 196.
110. *Ibid.* and Stutterheim, "De Beelden van Belahan," p. 299.
111. On the literature in Old-Javanese, see Himansu Bhusan Sarkar, *Indian Influences on the Literature of Java and Bali* (Calcutta, 1934).
112. See above, p. 130.
113. Edited by R. Ng. Poerbatjaraka, "Arjuna-Wiwāha, Tekst en vertaling," *BKI,* 82 (1926), p. 181.
114. Berg, "De Arjunawiwāha," p. 19.
115. Unless the hypothesis of C. C. Berg (*ibid.,* p. 92) is confirmed. According to this hypothesis, Mahāmantri i Hino Śrī Samaravijayadharma . . . suparṇa . . . uttungadeva, who from 1037 on replaces the Sumatranese princess in the charters of Airlanga, was none other than his son.
116. Krom, *Hindoe-Javaansche Geschiedenis,* pp. 272 ff.
117. N. J. Krom, *Inleiding tot de Hindoe-Javaansche Kunst* (The Hague, 1923), II, p. 50.
118. Stutterheim, "Oudheidkundige Aanteekeningen," p. 101.
119. For Janggala, we have only epigraphic documents of questionable date, notably one of 1060 (?), an ordinance concerning works of irrigation that emanated from King Rakai Halu, lord Juru Śrī Samarotsāha Karṇakeśana Dharmavaṃśa Kīrtisiṃha Jayāntakatungadeva.
120. P. V. van Stein Callenfels, "Epigraphia Balica," *VBG,* LXVI, 3 (1926). W. F. Stutterheim, *Oudheden van Bali* (Singaradja, 1929), I, p. 190. Damais, "Liste des principales inscriptions," pp. 88–93.
121. J. L. A. Brandes, "Bijschrift bij de door den heer Neeb gezonden photo's van oudheden in het Djambische," *TBG,* 45 (1902), p. 128; *Notulen van de Directievergaderingen van het Bataviaasch Genootschap* (1902), p. 34. Krom, *Inleiding tot de Hindoe-Javaansche Kunst,* II, p. 425.
122. Groeneveldt, *Notes on the Malay Archipelago,* p. 66. Ferrand, "L'empire sumatranais," p. 20. O. W. Wolters has kindly pointed out to me, in a letter of December 4, 1963, that Groeneveldt committed an error in writing that an embassy from Śrīvijaya was sent to China in 1067. The correct date, provided by Ma Tuan-lin, is 1077. This is the same year that Choḷa also sent an embassy.
123. S. Krishnaswami Aiyangar, "Rajendra, the Gangaikonda Chola," *Journal of Indian History,* II (1922–23), p. 353. R. C. Majumdar, *Ancient Indian Colonies,* II, p. 186. Nilakanta Sastri, "Śrī

Vijaya," p. 290. In his *History of Śrīvijaya,* however (p. 84, n. 22), Nilakanta Sastri abandons this hypothesis in favor of the interpretation of the Chinese name as Divākara, for he no longer believes that Kulottunga made a voyage abroad before his accession.

124. Friedrich Hirth and W. W. Rockhill, *Chau Ju-kua: His Work on the Chinese and Arab Trade in the Twelfth and Thirteenth Centuries* (St. Petersburg, 1911), p. 100.
125. The country between the Godavari and the Krishna.
126. For the correct interpretation of this text, see Nilakanta Sastri, "Śrī Vijaya," p. 289, n. 1.
127. Since Ti-hua-ch'ieh-lo was in China in 1067 on behalf of San-fo-ch'i, I cannot see how S. K. Aiyangar, *Ancient India* (London, 1911), p. 130, and Nilakanta Sastri, "Śrī Vijaya," p. 290, can suggest that Devakula, the future Rājendradevakulottunga, could have come to Malaya in the expedition of Vīrarājendra, which took place the following year. Nilakanta Sastri has, moreover, renounced this idea (above, p. 327, n. 123). But see Wolters' correction of the date 1067 above, p. 327, n. 122.
128. Ma Tuan-lin, *Ethnographie des peuples étrangers à la Chine,* trans. Marquis d'Hervey de Saint-Denys, II: Méridionaux (Geneva, 1883), p. 586. Nilakanta Sastri, *History of Śrīvijaya,* p. 84, writes on this subject: "This can only be explained as the result of a wanton misrepresentation on the part of the envoys of Śrī Vijaya who perhaps represented the party that gained the upper hand for a time in that country and against whom the other side had appealed to the Choḷa emperor Vīrarājendra."
129. *History of Burma* (London, 1925), p. 17.
130. By G. H. Luce and his school, in the most recent issue of the *JBRS.* Pe Maung Tin and G. H. Luce have assembled, under the title *Inscriptions of Burma,* published by the University of Rangoon in its Oriental Studies Publications (Nos. 2–6) between 1933 and 1959, five large folios containing excellent facsimiles of 609 inscriptions dating from 1131 to 1364. This collection constitutes the basic material on which this team of researchers is working.
131. Condensed in *Hmannan Yazawin,* part of which appeared as the *Glass Palace Chronicle of the Kings of Burma,* trans. Pe Maung Tin and G. H. Luce (London, 1923).
132. This Burmese pronunciation corresponds to the Pali *Anuruddha* ("calmed, pacified"), but on the votive tablets (*ARASB,* 1906, p. 10; 1912, p. 19; 1915, p. 15) he is called Aniruddha ("without obstacle").
133. The dates given for Anôratha differ from one text to another. Those that have been adopted here are based on epigraphy (Charles Duroiselle and C. O. Blagden, ed., *Epigraphia Bir-*

manica [Rangoon, 1919–36], I, p. 4) and have been accepted as definitive by historians. See Maung Hla, "The Chronological Tables of the Kings of Burma who reigned at Thayekhittagu (Ancient Prome) and at Pagan," *JBRS,* XIII (1923), pp. 82–94.

134. J. A. Stewart, "Kyaukse Irrigation, Side-Light on Burmese History," *JBRS,* XII (1921), p. 1.

135. On Burmese Buddhism, see Than Tun, "Religion in Burma, A.D. 1000–1300," *JBRS,* XLII (1959), pp. 47–69, and "Religious Buildings of Burma, A.D. 1000–1300," *JBRS,* XLII (1959), pp. 71–80.

136. Above, p. 17.

137. H. G. Quaritch Wales, "Anuruddha and the Thaton Tradition," *JRAS* (1947), pp. 152–56.

138. Shin Arahan is a title. His religious name seems to have been Silabuddhi or Dhammadassi (*Glass Palace Chronicle,* pp. 71–72, 74).

139. Very little is known about the history of the Mons. W. Schmidt published in 1906, in the *Sitzungsberichte* of the Academy of Vienna (vol. CLI), a Mon chronicle, the *Slapat Rājāwang datow smim rong,* translated by him in the same volume, and more recently by Robert Halliday in *JBRS,* XIII (1923), p. 1. The *Sudharmavatīrājavaṃsa* and the *Siharājarājavaṃsa* were published in 1910 at Paklat, and the *Dhammachetikathā* was published in 1912. These texts await a translator.

140. The name of Manuha, usually given to this king, is the result of a false reading. See C. W. Dunn, "Dr. J. A. Stewart," *JBRS,* XXXII (1948), p. 89.

141. Duroiselle and Blagden, *Epigraphia Birmanica,* I, p. 6.

142. With the exception, perhaps, of Pegu, which the chronicles do not mention and to which emigrants from Haripunjaya, who settled at first in Thaton, went for refuge at the time of the conquest of that city by Anôratha (Coedès, "Documents . . . Laos," pp. 24, 80).

143. Śrīkshetra (Prome) and four principalities situated in the region of Rangoon: Pokkharavatī, Trihakumbha, Asitanjana, and Rammanagara (Duroiselle and Blagden, *Epigraphia Birmanica,* I, p. 6).

144. On this alleged Tantrism, see above, p. 106.

145. The authenticity of this inscription (*Original Inscriptions Collected in Upper Burma* [Rangoon, 1913], no. 1) is contested. It has not been included in volume I of the *Inscriptions of Burma* of Pe Maung Tin and G. H. Luce. See Duroiselle and Blagden, *Epigraphia Birmanica,* I, pp. 67, 73.

146. V. C. Scott O'Connor, *Mandalay and Other Cities of the Past in Burma* (London, 1907), pp. 245, 249, 283–85. Léon de Beylié, *L'Architecture hindoue en Extrême-Orient* (Paris, 1907), p. 283. On the monuments of Pagan in general, see

R. S. le May, "The Development of Buddhist Art in Burma," *Journal of the Royal Society of Arts,* XCVII (1949), pp. 535–55, and Lu Pe Win, *Pictorial Guide to Pagan* (Rangoon, 1955).

147. Harvey, *History of Burma,* pp. 29–30.
148. Coedès, "Documents . . . Laos," pp. 113–14.
149. Harvey, *History of Burma,* p. 30.
150. *ARASB,* 1906, p. 10; 1912, p. 19; 1915, p. 15. U Mya, *Votive Tablets of Burma* (Rangoon, 1961), part I (in Burmese; with reproductions).
151. On these dates, see Senerat Paranavitana, "Panākaḍuva Copper-Plate Charter of Vijayabāhu I," *Epigraphia Zeylanica,* V (1955), pp. 10 ff.; *A History of Ceylon* (Colombo, 1960), II, pp. 419, 436; *A Concise History of Ceylon* (Colombo, 1961), pp. 187, 198.
152. *Cūlavaṃsa,* LVIII, translated by Wilhelm Geiger (Colombo, 1953), I, p. 202.
153. *Ibid.,* LX, p. 214; C. Rasanayagam Mudaliyar, "Vijaya Bāhu's Inscription at Polonnaruwa," *JRASCB,* XXIX (1924), p. 274; *Epigraphia Zeylanica,* II, pp. 246, 253–54.
154. *Glass Palace Chronicle,* p. 87. O'Connor, *Mandalay,* p. 247. De Beylié, *L'Architecture hindoue en Extrême-Orient,* p. 255. According to G. H. Luce, Zigōn is a corruption of Zibōn (i.e., Jayabhūmi). See his *Mons of the Pagan Dynasty* (Rangoon, 1950), p. 13.
155. *Glass Palace Chronicle,* pp. 96–97.

Chapter X

1. Auguste Barth and Abel Bergaigne, ISC, p. 176. Etienne Aymonier, *Le Cambodge* (Paris, 1900–1904), III, p. 508. Coedès, *Inscriptions du Cambodge* (Paris, 1937–), I, p. 221.
2. Louis Finot, "Les inscriptions de Mi-sơn," *BEFEO,* IV, p. 938.
3. *Ibid.,* p. 945.
4. Henri Maspero, "La frontière de l'Annam et du Cambodge du VIIIe au XIVe siècle," *BEFEO,* XVIII, 3, p. 33.
5. Inscription of Samrong (Coedès, *Inscriptions du Cambodge,* IV, p. 175). A bad reading by Aymonier, *Le Cambodge,* II, p. 391, made it seem that he had reigned until 1089, which made it necessary to consider Jayavarman VI as a usurper who was reigning in the north while Harshavarman reigned at Angkor.
6. Inscription of Prè Rup. See Coedès, "Nouvelles précisions sur les dates d'avènement de quelques rois des dynasties angkoriennes," *BEFEO,* XLIII (1943–46), p. 14.
7. Stele of Phnom Rung (Coedès, *Inscriptions du Cambodge,* V, p. 297).
8. Coedès, "La stèle de Ta Prohm," *BEFEO,* VI, p. 72; "Nouvelles données chronologiques et généalogiques sur la dynastie de Mahīdharapura," *BEFEO,* XXIX, p. 297, n. 1.
9. Aymonier, *Le Cambodge,* I, pp. 395–96; III, p. 510. His bi-

ography is presented in two parallel inscriptions of Preah Vihear and of Phnom Sandak published in Coedès and Pierre Dupont, "Les stèles de Sdok Kak Thom, Phnom Sandak et Prah Vihar," *BEFEO,* XLIII (1943–46), pp. 134–54.

10. At Prè Rup. Aside from the inscription of Nom Van of 1082, we know of only two others dating from his reign: the first, that of 1101, comes from Preah Phnom, fifty kilometers northwest of Angkor (Coedès, *Inscriptions du Cambodge,* III, p. 121); the second is an inscription of Phnom Da in the far south of the country that dates from 1106 (*ibid.,* V, p. 278).
11. Coedès, *Inscriptions du Cambodge,* VI, p. 294.
12. The inscriptions in his name come from Phnom Sandak (1110, Coedès, *Inscriptions du Cambodge,* VI, p. 300) and from Phimai (1109, Coedès, "Epigraphie du temple de Phimai," *BEFEO,* XXIV, p. 345) in the north; from Prasat Trau (1109), thirty kilometers northwest of Angkor (Coedès, *Inscriptions du Cambodge,* III, p. 97); and from Phnom Bayang (1107) in the far south of Cambodia (*ibid.,* I, p. 267). The presence of inscriptions of Jayavarman VI and of Dharaṇīndravarman I in the south makes it necessary to revise the opinion that I earlier expressed ("Nouvelles données chronologiques," pp. 299–300) on the area over which these two exercised their authority. Nevertheless, their principal constructions were located in the north.
13. All these monuments are described in Henri Parmentier, *L'Art khmèr classique* (Paris, 1939).
14. Coedès, "Nouvelles données chronologiques," p. 302.
15. Inscription of Phnom Sandak (Coedès, *Inscriptions du Cambodge,* I, p. 267, and III, p. 121).
16. Louis Finot, "L'inscription de Ban That," *BEFEO,* XII, 2, p. 26.
17. Coedès, "Nouvelles données chronologiques," p. 302, n. 1.
18. Finot, "L'inscription de Ban That," p. 27.
19. Finot, "Les inscriptions de Mi-sơn," pp. 937–38.
20. Georges Maspero, *Le Royaume de Champa* (Paris, 1928), p. 143.
21. *Ibid.,* p. 145.
22. Finot, "Les inscriptions de Mi-sơn," p. 940.
23. Maspero, *Le Royaume de Champa,* p. 147.
24. Finot, "Les inscriptions de Mi-sơn," p. 949.
25. Maspero, *Le Royaume de Champa,* p. 148.
26. Etienne Aymonier, "Première étude sur les inscriptions tchames," *JA* (January-February, 1891), pp. 33–36.
27. Maspero, *Le Royaume de Champa,* pp. 148–49.
28. *Ibid.,* p. 150.
29. The epigraphical data have been utilized by Than Tun in "History of Burma, A.D. 1000–1300," *Bulletin of the Burma Historical Commission,* I (1960), pp. 39–57.
30. *Glass Palace Chronicle of the Kings of Burma,* trans. Pe Maung Tin and G. H. Luce (London, 1923), p. 65.

31. G. E. Harvey, *History of Burma* (London, 1925), p. 316. Charles Duroiselle and C. O. Blagden, ed., *Epigraphia Birmanica* (Rangoon, 1919–36), I, pp. 4, 155.
32. *Glass Palace Chronicle,* p. 66. In fact, Kyanzittha did not claim to be descended from Anôratha in any of his inscriptions; he only claimed to belong to the solar race through his father's family.
33. To whom magicians had announced the birth of an infant destined to rule. *Ibid.,* p. 67.
34. *Ibid.,* p. 93.
35. Probably under the name Bajrābharaṇa, which appears on the votive tablets and on a stele found at Mergui (Louis Finot, "Inscriptions du Siam et de la Péninsule Malaise," *BCAI* [1910], p. 153).
36. *Glass Palace Chronicle,* p. 100.
37. *Ibid.,* p. 101 (Raman Kan).
38. *Ibid.,* p. 104.
39. The name *Kyanzittha,* by which he is usually designated, is a corrupted pronunciation of *Kalan cacsa,* which means "soldier-official."
40. Duroiselle and Blagden, *Epigraphia Birmanica,* I, pp. 4, 89.
41. *Glass Palace Chronicle,* p. 104.
42. *ARASB* (1916–17), p. 19; Duroiselle and Blagden, *Epigraphia Birmanica,* I, p. 4. In any case, before 1093 (Duroiselle and Blagden, *Epigraphia Birmanica,* III, p. 3).
43. *Glass Palace Chronicle,* p. 105.
44. At least that is what the *Chronicle* says, but Than Tun, "History of Burma, A.D. 1000–1300," p. 47, suggests that this daughter actually married Nāgasman, a great-grandson of the Mon king Makuṭa. Their son Alaung-sithu would be Mon through his father and Burmese through his mother, which would have assured him a legitimacy which Kyanzittha seems to have lacked.
45. *Glass Palace Chronicle,* p. 105.
46. *Ibid.,* p. 93.
47. *Ibid.,* p. 107.
48. Duroiselle and Blagden, *Epigraphia Birmanica,* I, p. 5.
49. *Ibid.,* p. 6.
50. *Glass Palace Chronicle,* p. 110. Léon de Beylié, *L'Architecture hindoue en Extrême-Orient* (Paris, 1907), p. 265.
51. Harvey, *History of Burma,* p. 40.
52. Charles Duroiselle, "The Ananda Temple at Pagan," *Memoirs of the Archaeological Survey of India,* 56 (1937). S. K. Saraswati, "Temples of Pagan," *JGIS,* IX (1942).
53. Harvey, *History of Burma,* p. 41.
54. Duroiselle and Blagden, *Epigraphia Birmanica,* I, p. 90.
55. *Ibid.,* I, pp. 154, 164.
56. *Ibid.,* III, p. 5. This building was dedicated according to Vishnuite rites, the place of honor being reserved for the

Mons (Than Tun, "History of Burma, A.D. 1000–1300," p. 46).

57. Duroiselle and Blagden, *Epigraphia Birmanica,* I, p. 74. Just as the explanatory captions of the scenes taken from the Jātakas represented on the ceramic plaques that decorate the Ananda and are published in Duroiselle and Blagden, *Epigraphia Birmanica,* vol. II, are in the Mon language. See Edouard Huber, "Les bas-reliefs du temple d'Ananda à Pagan," *BEFEO,* XI, pp. 1–5.
58. De Beylié, *L'Architecture hindoue en Extrême-Orient,* p. 267.
59. Duroiselle and Blagden, *Epigraphia Birmanica,* I, pp. 164, 165.
60. Nihar-Ranjan Ray, *Brahmanical Gods in Burma: A Chapter in Indian Art and Iconography* (Calcutta, 1932).
61. Duroiselle and Blagden, *Epigraphia Birmanica,* III, p. 4.
62. Friedrich Hirth and W. W. Rockhill, *Chau Ju-kua: His Work on the Chinese and Arab Trade in the Twelfth and Thirteenth Centuries* (St. Petersburg, 1911), p. 59. I do not know what basis G. E. Harvey (*History of Burma,* p. 43) has for saying that this embassy did not pass through Yunnan.
63. Above, p. 148.
64. Ma Tuan-lin, *Ethnographie des peuples étrangers à la Chine,* trans. Marquis d'Hervey de Saint-Denys, II: Méridionaux (Geneva, 1883), p. 586. For the account according to the *History of the Sung,* see Hirth and Rockhill, *Chau Ju-kua,* p. 59.
65. Duroiselle and Blagden, *Epigraphia Birmanica,* I, p. 1.
66. W. P. Groeneveldt, *Notes on the Malay Archipelago and Malacca* (Batavia, 1876), pp. 66–67. Gabriel Ferrand, "L'empire sumatranais de Çrīvijaya," *JA* (July-September 1922), pp. 21–22.
67. Inscription of Labu Tuwa. K. A. Nilakanta Sastri, "A Tamil Merchant Guild in Sumatra," *TBG,* 72 (1932), p. 314.
68. Above, p. 148.
69. An inscription known by the title "the smaller Leyden grant," published in K. V. Subrahmanya Aiyer, "The Smaller Leiden Plates (of Kulotungga I)," *Epigraphia Indica,* XXII (1934), p. 267. See K. A. Nilakanta Sastri, "Śrī Vijaya," *BEFEO,* XL, p. 299.
70. Above, p. 141. On the history of this *vihāra,* after its conversion to Theravada Buddhism, see Senerat Paranavitana, "Negapatam and Theravāda Buddhism in South India," *JGIS,* XI (1944), pp. 17–25.
71. Groeneveldt, *Notes on the Malay Archipelago,* p. 19.
72. Himansu Bhusan Sarkar, *Indian Influences on the Literature of Java and Bali* (Calcutta, 1934).
73. J. L. A. Brandes, *Beschrijving van de ruine de desa Toempang, genaamd Tjandi Djago* (The Hague, 1904), p. 77.
74. N. J. Krom, *Inleiding tot de Hindoe-Javaansche Kunst* (The Hague, 1923), II, p. 250. P. V. van Stein Callenfels, "De Kṛṣṇāyana aan Pantaran," *TBG,* 64 (1925), p. 196.
75. Īśānaguṇadharma Lakshmīdhara Vijayottungadevī.

76. N. J. Krom, *Hindoe-Javaansche Geschiedenis* (The Hague, 1931), p. 280.
77. Groeneveldt, *Notes on the Malay Archipelago,* p. 110.
78. Inscription of Vat Ph'u. Coedès, "Nouvelles données chronologiques," pp. 303, 304; *Inscriptions du Cambodge,* V, p. 292.
79. Inscription of Prasat Chrung. Coedès, "Nouvelles données chronologiques," p. 307; *Inscriptions du Cambodge,* IV, p. 230.
80. Finot, "L'inscription de Ban That," p. 27.
81. Above, pp. 152–53.
82. Coedès, "Nouvelles données chronologiques," pp. 303–304.
83. Finot, "L'inscription de Ban That," p. 27.
84. Pp. 155–56.
85. Maspero, "La frontière de l'Annam et du Cambodge," p. 34, explains that "the Cambodians, having come through Champa, probably crossed the Annamite Chain by way of Lao Bao (Savannakhèt-Hué)."
86. Maspero (*ibid.*) thinks that this time the Cambodians must have passed "by way of Ha-trai (Kèo Nưa pass), or perhaps the Mu-gia pass, since Champa was closed to them."
87. This occupation has left traces in Cham art, notably at Hưng Thanh (Philippe Stern, *L'Art du Champa* (*ancien Annam*) *et son évolution* [Paris, 1942], pp. 65, 108; Jean Boisselier, *La Statuaire du Champa* [Paris, 1963], pp. 303 ff.).
88. Inscription of Da-nê or Batau Tablah (Aymonier, "Première étude," p. 39).
89. Finot, "Les inscriptions de Mi-sơn," p. 965.
90. Aymonier, "Première étude," p. 40.
91. Finot, "Les inscriptions de Mi-sơn," p. 965.
92. *Ibid.*
93. On the dates of these events, see Louis Finot, "Les inscriptions de Jaya Parameçvaravarman I," *BEFEO,* XV, 2, p. 50.
94. Maspero, "La frontière de l'Annam et du Cambodge," p. 34.
95. Above, p. 77.
96. Above, pp. 136–37.
97. Coedès, "Documents sur l'histoire politique et religieuse du Laos occidental," *BEFEO,* XXV, p. 168.
98. *Ibid.,* pp. 83–86. Camille Notton, *Annales du Siam* (Paris, 1926–32), II, pp. 39–53. J. Y. Claeys, "L'Archéologie du Siam," *BEFEO,* XXXI, pp. 429–53.
99. Coedès, "Documents . . . Laos," p. 23.
100. *Ibid.,* pp. 82–83, 162–71. Notton, *Annales du Siam,* II, pp. 36–40.
101. Reproduced in Ma Tuan-lin, *Ethnographie,* p. 487.
102. Below, pp. 179, 181, 183–84.
103. On this name, which must actually have been a title or a polite form by which the Khmer king was designated in his messages, see Coedès, "Nouvelles données chronologiques," p. 304.

104. Ma Tuan-lin, *Ethnographie,* p. 487.
105. Coedès, "A propos de la date d'édification d'Angkor Vat," *JA* (January-March, 1920), p. 96.
106. Coedès, "La destination funéraire des grands monuments khmèrs," *BEFEO,* XL, pp. 339 ff. (with a bibliography of works on this subject).
107. See the five volumes on the ornamental sculpture and the bas-reliefs in Ecole Française d'Extrême-Orient, *Mémoires archéologiques,* II: Le temple d'Angkor Vat (Paris, 1929–32).
108. René Grousset, *Philosophies indiennes* (Paris, 1931), Chapter XI.
109. Inscription (lost) of Vat Sla Ket. Etienne Aymonier, *Le Cambodge,* II, p. 287. Published in Coedès, *Inscriptions du Cambodge,* VI, p. 312.
110. The exact origin mentioned by the *History of the Sung* is not certain, for it is attributed to Chen-la Lo-hu (O. W. Wolters, "Tāmbralinga," *BSOAS* [1958], p. 605).
111. Coedès, "Nouvelles données épigraphiques sur l'histoire de l'Indochine centrale," *JA,* CCXLVI (1958), p. 139.
112. His father, Mahīdharāditya, was the brother of Narendralakshmī, mother of Sūryavarman II. This princess was the daughter of a sister of Kings Jayavarman VI and Dharaṇīndravarman I (Coedès, "Nouvelles données chronologiques," p. 301).
113. Stanza 17 of the inscriptions of Jayavarman VII. Coedès, "La stèle de Ta Prohm," *BEFEO,* VI, p. 72; "La stèle du Prah Khan d'Aṅkor," *BEFEO,* XLI, p. 285.
114. For this reign and those following, see Coedès, "Nouvelles données chronologiques," pp. 304 ff.
115. A period during which, however, great monuments such as Beng Mealea and Banteay Samrè were constructed.
116. Coedès, "Nouvelles données chronologiques," p. 324.
117. Below, p. 166.
118. Maspero, *Le Royaume de Champa,* p. 151.
119. Finot, "Les inscriptions de Mi-sơn," p. 954.
120. *Ibid.*
122. Above, p. 160.
121. Aymonier, "Première étude," p. 37.
123. We now have a tendency to attribute the characteristics of the architecture of the monuments of Binh-đinh and the importation of Khmer sculptures in Champa to this first Khmer occupation, which was followed a half-century later by a second occupation.
124. Finot, "Les inscriptions de Mi-sơn," pp. 959, 961. Aymonier, "Première étude," p. 39.
125. *Ibid.*
126. Finot, "Les inscriptions de Mi-sơn," p. 965. Aymonier, "Première étude," p. 42.
127. Maspero, *Le Royaume de Champa,* p. 158.
128. Finot, "Les inscriptions de Mi-sơn," p. 965.

129. Aymonier, "Première étude," p. 42. See Maspero, *Le Royaume de Champa,* p. 159.
130. Aymonier, "Première étude," p. 41.
131. Finot, "Les inscriptions de Mi-sơn," pp. 965, 966, 968. Aymonier, "Première étude," p. 42.
132. Maspero, *Le Royaume de Champa,* p. 160.
133. Finot, "Les inscriptions de Mi-sơn," p. 973.
134. Finot, "Les inscriptions de Jaya Parameçvaravarman I," p. 50.
135. Maspero, *Le Royaume de Champa,* p. 162.
136. *Ibid.*
137. *Ibid.,* p. 163.
138. According to information from the *Ling-wai Tai-ta,* cited in *ibid.,* p. 164.
139. Ma Tuan-lin, *Ethnographie,* p. 557.
140. Above, p. 332, n. 44.
141. *Glass Palace Chronicle,* p. 119.
142. *ARASB* (1919), p. 23.
143. Above, p. 149.
144. *ARASB* (1919), p. 22.
145. *Glass Palace Chronicle,* pp. 120–21.
146. *ARASB* (1911), p. 18.
147. Camille Sainson, trans., *Nan-tchao Ye-che: Histoire particulière du Nan-tchao* (Paris, 1904), p. 102.
148. *Glass Palace Chronicle,* p. 122.
149. G. H. Luce, "The Shwegugyi Pagoda Inscription," *JBRS,* X, (1920), p. 67, gives 1141, but see Than Tun, "History of Burma, A.D. 1000–1300," p. 47.
150. De Beylié, *L'Architecture hindoue en Extrême-Orient,* p. 278. V. C. Scott O'Connor, *Mandalay, and Other Cities of the Past in Burma* (London, 1907), pp. 257, 259, 263. Lu Pe Win, *Pictorial Guide to Pagan* (Rangoon, 1955), p. 32.
151. Mabel Haynes Bode, *The Pali Literature of Burma* (London, 1909), p. 16. Helmer Smith, *La Grammaire palie d'Aggavaṃsa* (Lund, 1928).
152. On life in Pagan in this period, see Than Tun, "Social Life in Burma, A.D. 1044–1287," *JBRS,* XLI (1958), pp. 37–47.
153. *Glass Palace Chronicle,* p. 126.
154. *ARASB* (1919), p. 22.
155. *Glass Palace Chronicle,* p. 127.
156. This princess was offered to King Alaung-sithu by her father and seems, as was the custom, to have subsequently been married by Narathu. Pateikkaya (Patikāra) has sometimes been placed to the west or southwest of Pagan, but it was more probably north of Chittagong, in the district of Tipperah. See G. E. Harvey, *History of Burma,* p. 326; Nihar-Ranjan Ray, *Sanskrit Buddhism in Burma* (Calcutta, 1936), pp. 93–94.
157. *Glass Palace Chronicle,* p. 133.
158. De Beylié, "*L'Architecture hindoue en Extrême-Orient,* p. 287.

O'Connor, *Mandalay,* p. 221. Lu Pe Win, *Pictorial Guide to Pagan,* p. 48.

159. *Glass Palace Chronicle,* pp. 134–38.
160. *Cūlavaṃsa,* trans. Wilhelm Geiger (Colombo, 1953), II, pp. 64–70.
161. Than Tun, "History of Burma, A.D. 1000–1300," p. 48.
162. Groeneveldt, *Notes on the Malay Archipelago,* p. 67. Ferrand, "L'empire sumatranais," p. 22.
163. Ma Tuan-lin, *Ethnographie,* p. 566.
164. Ferrand, "L'empire sumatranais," p. 66.
165. Krom, *Hindoe-Javaansche Geschiedenis,* pp. 289–97. On their names and their dates, see L. C. Damais, "Liste des principales inscriptions datées d'Indonésie," *BEFEO,* XLVI (1952), pp. 66–69.
166. His complete name was: Śrī Bāmeśvara Sakalabhuvanatushṭikāraṇa Sarvānivāryavīrya Parākrama Digjayottungadeva.
167. Groeneveldt, *Notes on the Malay Archipelago,* p. 19.
168. Śrī Varmeśvara Madhusūdanāvatārānindita Suhritsingha Parākrama Digjayottungadeva.
169. Edited by J. G. H. Gunning (The Hague, 1903). See Himansu Bhusan Sarkar, *Indian Influences on the Literature of Java and Bali,* p. 249. This poem is replete with allusions to contemporary historical facts. See C. C. Berg in F. W. Stapel, ed., *Geschiedenis van Nederlandsch Indië* (Amsterdam, 1938–40), II, pp. 62–64. J. E. van Lohuizen-de Leeuw, "The Beginnings of Old-Javanese Historical Literature," *BKI,* 112 (1956), p. 384.
170. Sarkar, *Indian Influences on the Literature of Java and Bali,* p. 261.
171. Śrī Sarveśvara Janardhanāvatāra Vijayāgrajasama Singhanādānivaryavīrya Parākrama Digjayottungadeva.
172. Śrī Aryeśvara Madhusūdanāvatārārijaya Parākramottungadeva.
173. Śrī Kronchāryadīpa Haṇḍabhuvanapālaka Parākramānindita Digjayottungadeva.
174. P. V. van Stein Callenfels, *Epigraphia Balica* (Batavia, 1926), pp. 33–35.

Chapter XI

1. Inscription of the Phimeanakas, in Coedès, *Inscriptions du Cambodge* (Paris, 1937–), II, p. 117.
2. For the biographical details that follow, see Coedès "Nouvelles données chronologiques et généalogiques sur la dynastie de Mahīdharapura," *BEFEO,* XXIX, pp. 304–28; *Pour mieux comprendre Angkor* (Paris, 1947), pp. 176 ff. B. R. Chatterjee has devoted an article to "Jayavarman VII, the Last of the Great Monarchs of Cambodia," in *Proceedings of the Indian History Congress* (Calcutta, 1939), pp. 377–85.
3. Coedès, "Quelques suggestions sur la méthode à suivre pour

interpréter les bas-reliefs de Banteay Ch'mar et de la galerie extérieure du Bayon," *BEFEO,* XXXII, pp. 76–78.

4. Coedès, "La date du Bayon," *BEFEO,* XXVIII, pp. 88–89.
5. *Ethnographie des peuples étrangers à la Chine,* trans. Marquis d'Hervey de Saint-Denys, II: Méridionaux (Geneva, 1883), p. 487.
6. Coedès, "Quelques suggestions," p. 80, n. 1.
7. Louis Finot, "Les inscriptions de Mi-sởn," *BEFEO,* IV, p. 974.
8. Etienne Aymonier, *Le Cambodge* (Paris, 1900–1904), III, p. 527.
9. Finot, "Les inscriptions de Mi-sởn," p. 975. Georges Maspero, *Le Royaume de Champa* (Paris, 1928), p. 161, identifies Jaya Indravarman ong Vatuv with Jaya Indravarman (IV) of Grāmapura, instigator of the aggression of 1177. Louis Finot, "Les inscriptions de Jaya Parameçvaravarman I," *BEFEO,* XV, 2, p. 50, n. 2, has cast doubt on the accuracy of this identification, but it nevertheless remains plausible.
10. Etienne Aymonier, "Première étude sur les inscriptions tchames," *JA* (January-February, 1891), p. 48.
11. These events are related in an inscription of Mi-sởn translated in Finot, "Les inscriptions de Mi-sởn," p. 975.
12. *Ibid.*
13. *Ibid.,* p. 940. For the date, see Maspero, *Le Royaume de Champa,* p. 367.
14. Aymonier, "Première étude," p. 48.
15. *Ibid.,* p. 51.
16. Philippe Stern, *L'Art du Champa (ancien Annam) et son évolution* (Paris, 1942), pp. 65–66, 108–109.
17. Friedrich Hirth and W. W. Rockhill, *Chau Ju-kua: His Work on the Chinese and Arab Trade in the Twelfth and Thirteenth Centuries* (St. Petersburg, 1911), pp. 53–54. See below, p. 181.
18. That of Preah Khan. See Coedès, "La stèle de Prah Khan d'Aṅkor," *BEFEO,* XLI, p. 299.
19. Published in Coedès, *Inscriptions du Cambodge,* II, p. 161.
20. In "Nouvelles données chronologiques," p. 328, I thought I could conclude, from an embassy attributed to Cambodia and sent to China in 1200 by a king who had been reigning twenty years, that Jayavarman VII was definitely still reigning at that date. But this embassy actually came from Chen-li-fu (below, p. 181), at that time a dependency of Cambodia (see O. W. Wolters, "Tāmbralinga," *BSOAS* [1958], p. 606).
21. Below, p. 189.
22. Ecole Française d'Extrême-Orient, *Mémoires archéologiques,* I: Le temple d'Īçvarapura (Paris, 1926), p. 91, n. 2.
23. References in Coedès, "Quelques suggestions," pp. 71 ff.
24. Coedès, "Le portrait dans l'art khmèr," *RAA,* VII (1960), p. 179.
25. Coedès, "La stèle de Prah Khan," p. 285.
26. Louis Finot, "Inscriptions d'Aṅkor," *BEFEO,* XXV, p. 402. Ecole

Française d'Extrême-Orient, *Mémoires archéologiques,* I, p. 102.

27. Finot, "Inscriptions d'Aṅkor," p. 396.
28. For a description of them, see Aymonier, *Le Cambodge,* III; E. Lunet de Lajonquière, *Inventaire descriptif des monuments du Cambodge* (Paris, 1902–11), III; and the *Guides archéologiques d'Angkor* by Jean Comaille (1912), Henri Marchal (1928), Henri Parmentier (1936), Maurice Glaize (1948), etc. See also Jean Boisselier, "Réflexions sur l'art de règne de Jayavarman VII," *BSEI,* XXVII (1952), pp. 261–70; Philippe Stern, "Le problème des monuments khmèrs du style du Bayon et Jayavarman VII," *Actes, XXI*[e] *Congrès International des Orientalistes* (Paris, 1948), p. 252.
29. See, however, above, p. 335, n. 115.
30. Below, p. 212.
31. Above, p. 98.
32. Coedès, "La stèle de Prah Khan," p. 298, n. 2.
33. Coedès, "La stèle de Ta Prohm," *BEFEO,* VI, p. 75.
34. Coedès, "La stèle de Prah Khan," p. 288.
35. Louis Finot and Victor Goloubew, "Le symbolisme de Neak Peân," *BEFEO,* XXIII, p. 401.
36. Henri Parmentier, "Modifications subies par le Bayon au cours de son exécution," *BEFEO,* XXVII, p. 149; "La construction dans l'architecture khmère classique," *BEFEO,* XXXV, p. 281. Coedès, "Excavations at the Bayon," *ABIA,* XII (1937), p. 42.
37. Uncovered in 1933. See "Chronique," *BEFEO,* XXXIII, p. 1117.
38. Paul Mus, "Le symbolisme à Angkor Thom," *CRAIBL* (1936), p. 57; "Angkor vu du Japon," *France-Asie,* 175–76 (1962), p. 521. The decorative motif of human faces is doubtless Indian in origin; it is noted by I-ching at Nālandā (H. Parmentier, "Les bas-reliefs de Banteai-Chmar," *BEFEO,* X, p. 206, n. 1). According to Jean Boisselier, "Vajrapāṇi dans l'art du Bayon," *Actes, XXII*[e] *Congrès International des Orientalistes* (Istanbul, 1951), p. 324, these faces were those of Vajradhara in the form of Vajrapāṇi, the form assumed by Lokeśvara teaching the Law.
39. Reproduced by the Commission Archéologique de l'Indochine, Henri Dufour and Charles Carpeaux, *Le Bayon d'Angkor Thom, bas reliefs* (Paris, 1910).
40. Coedès, "Les inscriptions du Bayon," *BEFEO,* XXVIII, p. 104; "L'épigraphie des monuments de Jayavarman VII," *BEFEO,* XLVI, p. 97.
41. Paul Mus, "Angkor in the Time of Jayavarman VII," *IAL,* XI (1937), p. 65. Martti Räsänen, "Regenbogen-Himmelsbrücke," *Studia Orientalia,* XIV (1950), pp. 1–11.
42. Coedès, "La stèle de Prah Khan," pp. 295–96.
43. Lunet de Lajonquière, *Inventaire,* I, pp. 37, 92.
44. *Ibid.,* III, p. 391.

45. Above, p. 163.
46. Coedès, "La stèle de Prah Khan," pp. 296–97. See also Coedès, "Les gîtes d'étape à la fin du XIIe siècle," *BEFEO,* XL, p. 347.
47. Paul Pelliot, trans. and ed., "Mémoires sur les coutumes du Cambodge," *BEFEO,* II, p. 173.
48. The number given by the stele of Ta Prohm. See Coedès, "La stèle de Ta Prohm," p. 80.
49. Louis Finot, "L'inscription sanskrite de Say Fong," *BEFEO,* III, p. 18.
50. Coedès, "Les hôpitaux de Jayavarman VII," *BEFEO,* XL, p. 344.
51. Coedès, "L'assistance médicale au Cambodge à la fin du XIIe siècle," *Revue médicale française d'Extrême-Orient* (March-April, 1941), p. 405.
52. Paul Pelliot, "Le Bhaiṣajyaguru," *BEFEO,* III, p. 33.
53. *Glass Palace Chronicle of the Kings of Burma,* trans. Pe Maung Tin and G. H. Luce (London, 1923), pp. 138–39.
54. *Cūlavaṃsa,* LXXVI, trans. Wilhelm Geiger (Colombo, 1953), II, pp. 65–70.
55. *Glass Palace Chronicle,* p. 133.
56. *Cūlavaṃsa,* LXXVIII, p. 103.
57. *Glass Palace Chronicle,* p. 142.
58. *Cūlavaṃsa,* LXXVI, p. 70.
59. *Glass Palace Chronicle,* p. 142.
60. Above, p. 149.
61. On these events, see Taw Sein Ko, "A Preliminary Study of the Kalyani Inscriptions," *Indian Antiquary,* XXII (1893), pp. 17, 29–31.
62. Mabel Haynes Bode, *The Pali Literature of Burma* (London, 1909), pp. 17–18.
63. Emile Forchhammer, *An Essay on the Sources and Developmen of Burmese Law* (Rangoon, 1885), pp. 35–36. Bode, *The Pali Literature of Burma,* pp. 31–33.
64. G. H. Luce, "Note on the Peoples of Burma in the 12th–13th Century A.D.," *JBRS,* XLII (1959), p. 67.
65. *Glass Palace Chronicle,* p. 141.
66. Léon de Beylié, *L'Architecture hindoue en Extrême-Orient* (Paris, 1907), p. 271. V. C. Scott O'Connor, *Mandalay, and Other Cities of the Past in Burma* (London, 1907), pp. 269, 280. Lu Pe Win, *Pictorial Guide to Pagan* (Rangoon, 1955), pp. 41, 63.
67. *Glass Palace Chronicle,* p. 141.
68. *Ibid.,* p. 151.
69. On these works, see Paul Wheatley, "Geographical Notes on Some Commodities Involved in Sung Maritime Trade," *JRASMB,* XXXII, 2 (1959).
70. Hirth and Rockhill, *Chau Ju-kua,* p. 66, n. 18.
71. *Ibid.,* pp. 67–72.

72. *Ibid.*, p. 71.
73. As I did in 1927, "A propos de la chute du royaume de Crīvijaya," *BKI,* 83 (1927), p. 459. R. C. Majumdar (*Ancient Indian Colonies of the Far East,* II: Suvarṇadvīpa [Dacca, 1937], p. 197) and K. A. Nilakanta Sastri ("Śrī Vijaya," *BEFEO,* XL, p. 296) propose reacceptance of this date.
74. Such a shift would explain why the title Chan-pei ([king of] Jambi) was given to the king of San-fo-ch'i in the *History of the Sung* in an account that must date from the period of Chao Ju-kua (W. P. Groeneveldt, *Notes on the Malay Archipelago and Malacca* [Batavia, 1876], p. 63; Gabriel Ferrand, "L'empire sumatranais de Çrīvijaya," *JA* [July-September, 1922], p. 66). See Paul Pelliot, "Les grands voyages maritimes chinois," *TP,* XXX (1933), p. 376; J. L. Moens, "Srīvijaya, Yāva en Katāha," *TBG,* 77 (1937), p. 459.
75. Coedès, "Le royaume de Çrīvijaya," *BEFEO,* XVIII, 6, p. 34, and *Recueil des inscriptions du Siam* (Bangkok, 1924–29), II, p. 45. For the date, see Coedès, "A propos de la chute du royaume de Çrīvijaya," p. 468. The *nāga* is of this period; the statue of the Buddha may be later (Pierre Dupont, "Le Buddha du Grahi," *BEFEO,* XLII, p. 105). On the Mahāsenāpati Talānai named in the inscription, see Coedès, "Talanai," *JGIS,* VIII (1941), p. 61. On Grahi, see above, pp. 161–62, and below, pp. 181, 184.
76. Below, p. 201.
77. Hirth and Rockhill, *Chau Ju-kua,* p. 23.
78. N. J. Krom, *Hindoe-Javaansche Geschiedenis* (The Hague, 1931), p. 298. Complete name: Śrī Kāmeśvara Trivikramāvatāra Anivaryavīrya Parākrama Digjayottungadeva. L. C. Damais, "Liste des principales inscriptions datées d'Indonésie," *BEFEO,* XLVI (1952), pp. 68–71.
79. Edited by R. Friederich, *VBG,* XXII (1849). See Hendrik Kern, *Verspreide Geschriften* (The Hague, 1913–29), IX, p. 70; Himansu Bhusan Sarkar, *Indian Influences on the Literature of Java and Bali* (Calcutta, 1934), pp. 115–17.
80. Published and translated by R. Ng. Poerbatjaraka, *Bibliotheca Javanica,* III (Bandung, 1931). See Sarkar, *Indian Influences on the Literature of Java and Bali,* p. 307.
81. J. E. van Lohuizen-de Leeuw, "The Beginnings of Old-Javanese Historical Literature," *BKI,* 112 (1956), p. 385. *Smara* is another name for *Kāma,* first element of the name of the king, and *-dahana* is an allusion to *Daha,* the other name of Kaḍiri.
82. R. Ng. Poerbatjaraka, "Pandji-verhalen," *Bibliotheca Javanica,* IX (Bandung, 1940). R. O. Winstedt, "The Panji Tales," *JRASMB,* XIX (1941), p. 234.
83. Part of the text of the Siamese drama composed by King Phra Phuttha Loet La at the beginning of the nineteenth century was published in Bangkok in 1921 by Prince Damrong with

a historical introduction. See Dhani Nivat, "Siamese Versions of the Panji Romance," *India Antiqua* (Leyden, 1947), p. 95.

84. Jean Moura, *Le Royaume du Cambodge* (Paris, 1883), II, pp. 416–45.
85. Damais, "Liste des principales inscriptions," pp. 69–73; "Epigrafische Aantekeningen," *TBG,* LXXXIII (1949), pp. 10–15.
86. Hirth and Rockhill, *Chau Ju-kua,* p. 23.
87. Damais, "Liste des principales inscriptions," p. 95.
88. P. V. van Stein Callenfels, *Epigraphia Balica* (Batavia, 1926), pp. 35–59. Damais, "Liste des principales inscriptions."
89. N. J. Krom, *Inleiding tot de Hindoe-Javaansche Kunst* (The Hague, 1923), II, pp. 52, 420. W. F. Stutterheim, *Oudheden van Bali* (Singaradja, 1929), I, pp. 86, 145, 192, considers this place the funerary site of the king "younger son" (*anak wungśu*) mentioned above, p. 147.
90. Coedès, "La stèle de Ta Prohm," p. 81.
91. Coedès, "La stèle de Prah Khan," pp. 269, 301.
92. Coedès, *Inscriptions du Cambodge,* II, p. 176. See also Coedès, "Nouvelles données chronologiques," p. 326.
93. Coedès, "Nouvelles données chronologiques," pp. 309–19.
94. *Ibid.*
95. Finot, "Inscriptions d'Aṅkor," pp. 296, 394.
96. Henri Maspero, "La frontière de l'Annam et du Cambodge du VIIIe au XIVe siècle," *BEFEO,* XVIII, 3, p. 35.
97. Aymonier, "Première étude," p. 51.
98. Above, p. 171.
99. Coedès, "L'année du lièvre 1219 A.D.," in *India Antiqua* (Leyden, 1947), p. 83.
100. Hirth and Rockhill, *Chau Ju-kua,* p. 54.
101. Above, pp. 161–62, 179, and below, p. 184.
102. Paul Pelliot, "Deux itinéraires de Chine en Inde à la fin du VIIIe siècle," *BEFEO,* IV, p. 233. If this country is really Tāmbralinga (which is not certain, for Tāmbralinga is elsewhere called Tan-ma-ling by Chao Ju-kua), we must conclude that it had already absorbed Chia-lo-hsi (Grahi). It certainly must have by 1280 (below, p. 184) because we cannot see how Grahi could have been a dependency of San-fo-ch'i if Tāmbralinga (Ligor) was dependent on Cambodia.
103. An identification challenged by G. H. Luce in "The Early Syām in Burma's History; A Supplement," *JSS,* XLVII (1959), p. 60.
104. O. W. Wolters, "Chên-li-fu," *JSS,* XLVIII (Nov., 1960), pp. 1–35. Aside from an embassy in 1200, this country also sent missions to China in 1202 and 1205 (O. W. Wolters, "Tāmbralinga," p. 606, n. 2).
105. Above, p. 171.
106. Finot, "Inscriptions d'Aṅkor," pp. 296, 394.
107. Aymonier, "Première étude," p. 51.

108. *Ibid.*
109. Above, pp. 171, 180–81.
110. *Le Royaume de Champa,* p. 169.
111. Finot, "Les inscriptions de Mi-sởn," p. 976.
112. Maspero, *Le Royaume de Champa,* p. 172.
113. Aymonier, "Première étude," p. 57. For the date, see Louis Finot, "Les inscriptions de Jaya Parameçvaravarman I," *BEFEO,* XV, 2, p. 51.
114. Finot, "Les inscriptions de Mi-sởn," p. 954.
115. Finot, "Les inscriptions de Jaya Parameçvaravarman I," p. 51, n. 1.
116. *Glass Palace Chronicle,* p. 153.
117. His official title was Tribhavanāditya Pavaradhammarāja. See Than Tun, "History of Burma, A.D. 1000–1300," *Bulletin of the Burma Historical Commission,* I (1960), p. 50. The Pali chronicle *Jinakālamālī* attributes to him the composition of a commentary (*ṭīkā*) on the *Bodhivaṃsa* (Coedès, "Documents sur l'histoire politique et religieuse du Laos occidental," *BEFEO,* XXV, p. 11, note).
118. De Beylié, *L'Architecture hiṇdoue,* p. 299. O'Connor, *Mandalay,* pp. 221, 270, 275. Lu Pe Win, *Pictorial Guide to Pagan,* p. 44.
119. O'Connor, *Mandalay,* p. 260. Lu Pe Win proposes to see in the name of this monument an erroneous reading of a Mon expression representing Tilokamangala (*Pictorial Guide to Pagan,* p. 25).
120. *Glass Palace Chronicle,* pp. 155–56.
121. Tribhavanāditya Pavaradhammarājādhirāja Dānapati (Than Tun, "History of Burma, A.D. 1000–1300," p. 51).
122. Tribhavanāditya Pavarapaṇḍita Dhammarāja (*ibid.,* p. 53).
123. Bode, *Pali Literature of Burma,* p. 25. A mission of monks went to Ceylon between 1237 and 1248. It returned accompanied by Singhalese monks who helped purify the Buddhism of Pagan by drawing on Singhalese rites (Than Tun, "History of Burma, A.D. 1000–1300," p. 53).
124. *Glass Palace Chronicle,* pp. 156–58.
125. Than Tun, "History of Burma, A.D. 1000–1300," p. 54. Title: Tribhavanāditya Dhammarāja Jayasūra.
126. *Glass Palace Chronicle,* p. 161.
127. *Ibid.,* p. 162.
128. *Ibid.,* p. 171.
129. Hirth and Rockhill, *Chau Ju-kua,* p. 62. Ferrand, "L'empire sumatranais," p. 13. Majumdar, *Ancient Indian Colonies,* II, p. 193. Nilakanta Sastri, "Śrī Vijaya," p. 294.
130. A point located about thirty miles upstream on the Trengganu River, where the oldest remains of Islam on the peninsula have been discovered. Paul Wheatley, "Geographical Notes," p. 11; *The Golden Khersonese* (Kuala Lumpur, 1961), p. 70.

131. Above, p. 143.
132. Wheatley, *The Golden Khersonese,* pp. 71–72.
133. See above, pp. 161–62, 179, 181.
134. Chao Ju-kua ends his account of San-fo-ch'i by saying that "This country to the east is conterminous with Jung-ya-lu," that is, Janggala. We shall see that, in fact, in his period, in 1225, the former Janggala, eclipsed at the outset by Panjalu, or Kaḍiri, had just regained supremacy with Tumapel as capital. This is not to say that the dependencies of San-fo-ch'i comprehended the west and the center of the island up to the borders of Janggala, for Chao Ju-kua mentions only Sin-t'o, i.e., Sunda, among the vassal states. For him, Jung-ya-lu (Janggala) no doubt corresponded to the whole Javanese kingdom that was heir to that of Airlanga. See Moens, "Srīvijaya, Yāva en Katāha," pp. 410, 414.
135. Hirth and Rockhill, *Chau Ju-kua,* p. 62. Ferrand, "L'empire sumatranais," p. 13.
136. Wheatley, "Geographical Notes," p. 12, has remarked in this connection that, although we do not know just when the transfer of the capital from Palembang to Jambi took place, this transfer had taken place by the thirteenth century when the expedition of Kṛitanagara to Sumatra was led against Jambi (below, pp. 198, 201).
137. Coedès, *Recueil des inscriptions du Siam,* II, p. 41.
138. Perhaps he recognized the suzerainty of Cambodia, if the country of Teng-liu-mei, mentioned by Chao Ju-kua among the dependencies of Cambodia (above, p. 181), corresponded wholly or in part to his kingdom.
139. Louis de La Vallée-Poussin, *Dynasties et histoire de l'Inde depuis Kanishka jusqu'aux invasions musulmanes* (Paris, 1935), pp. 251 ff.
140. Discussion of these texts in: N. J. Krom, "De ondergang van Çrīvijaya," *MKAWAL,* 62 (1926), series B, no. 5; Coedès, "A propos de la chute du royaume de Çrīvijaya," p. 459; K. A. Nilakanta Sastri, "Śrīvijaya, Candrabhānu and Vīra-Pāṇḍya," *TBG,* 77 (1937), p. 251.
141. Coedès, "Documents . . . Laos," p. 99.
142. *Ibid.* On these events according to Singhalese sources, see C. W. Nicholas and Senerat Paranavitana, *A Concise History of Ceylon* (Colombo, 1961), pp. 281–89.
143. Coedès, "Documents . . . Laos," p. 99.
144. At least this is the opinion of F. H. Giles, "The Koh Lak Tradition," *JSS,* XXX (1938), pp. 18–21.
145. C. C. Berg has published a series of studies on the end of the kingdom of Kaḍiri and the beginning of Singhasāri. These studies are listed in F. D. K. Bosch, "C. C. Berg and Ancient Javanese History," *BKI,* 112 (1956), p. 1. The last and most important of these memoirs has appeared recently in the

VKNAWAL, LXIX, 1, under the title *Het rijk van de Vijfvoudige Buddha* (Amsterdam, 1962). Undoubtedly many readers will wonder why I do not utilize these scholarly works of Berg, works in which there is much of value. The reason is that they depart from the "events" concept of history. Their object is not to reconstruct the drama of events by utilizing the contemporaneous indigenous documents and reliable foreign sources. Berg adheres to the principle (revealed in his article "Javanese Historiography" in D. G. E. Hall, *Historians of South-East Asia* [London, 1961], p. 13) that the history that we can reconstruct according to known epigraphic and annalistic texts does not correspond to what really happened but is only what the kings and their historiographers wanted their contemporaries to believe. Berg therefore tries to determine what the political and religious principles are that have been responsible for the alleged "falsification" of the history. This reconstruction, which is of great interest for a study of the sociology and psychology of the ancient Javanese, is foreign to my conception of history properly defined. Reluctant to take part in a polemic bearing on an area outside of my competence, I shall be content to reproduce the judgment of L. C. Damais ("Etudes javanaises," *BEFEO*, L [1962], p. 416):

"It is necessary, before developing bold theories, to examine *without preconceived ideas* the contemporaneous documents that have come down to us and to determine from them if possible the concrete facts by means of paleographic and philological study as careful as their state permits, instead of seeking to support one's own theories at any cost, for one cannot fail, in the process, to accord unique trust to those among them that seem to corroborate the said theories and to consider those that are in flagrant contradiction with them as spurious sources, whose evidence must be rejected."

146. On the identity of Śṛinga and of Kṛitajaya, see above, p. 180.
147. Above, pp. 147, 158.
148. Hirth and Rockhill, *Chau Ju-kua*, pp. 75–82.
149. B. Schrieke, "Prolegomena tot eene sociologische studie over de volken van Sumatra," *TBG*, 65 (1925), p. 126, n. 36. On Su-ki-tan and Ta-pan, see also R. A. Kern, "Joartan wedergevonden?" *BKI*, 102 (1943), pp. 549–51.
150. Hirth and Rockhill, *Chau Ju-kua*, p. 83.
151. *Ibid.*, p. 62.
152. This list has been studied by Hirth and Rockhill, *Chau Ju-kua*, p. 86; G. P. Rouffaer, "Was Malaka emporium voor 1400 A.D. genaamd Malajoer?" *BKI*, 77 (1921), p. 137; Krom, *Hindoe-Javaansche Geschiedenis*, p. 309.
153. On the last two identifications, see Gabriel Ferrand, "Le

K'ouen-louen et les anciennes navigations dans les mers du sud," *JA* (March–April, 1919), p. 281.

154. Edited by J. L. A. Brandes, *VBG,* 54 (1902), and translated by H. Kern, *Verspreide Geschriften* (The Hague, 1913–29), VII and VIII (reedited by N. J. Krom in 1919). Under the title *Java in the 14th Century* (The Hague, 1960–63), Theodore G. Th. Pigeaud has provided a third edition in five volumes.
155. Edited by J. L. A. Brandes, *VBG,* 49 (1896). Reedited by N. J. Krom, *VBG,* 62 (1920). The references that follow are to the Krom edition.
156. *Nāgarakṛitāgama* (H. Kern, *Verspreide Geschriften,* VIII), p. 7.
157. *Pararaton,* p. 61. It was probably this woman who is represented in the form of the famous Prajñāpāramitā of the Museum of Leyden (N. J. Krom, *Inleiding tot de Hindoe-Javaansche Kunst* [The Hague, 1923], pl. 54).
158. *Pararaton,* p. 62.
159. *Ibid.,* p. 63.
160. *Ibid.,* pp. 64–65.
161. *Ibid.,* p. 72.
162. Krom, *Inleiding tot de Hindoe-Javaansche Kunst,* II, p. 55.
163. *Pararaton,* pp. 73–76.
164. *Ibid.,* p. 77.
165. *Nāgarakṛitāgama,* p. 12.
166. *Ibid.,* p. 13. On the archeological remains of this site, see J. L. A. Brandes, *Beschrijving van Tjandi Singasari* (The Hague, 1909); Krom, *Inleiding tot de Hindoe-Javaansche Kunst,* pp. 68–93; Jessy Blom, *The Antiquities of Singasari* (Leyden, 1939).
167. *Nāgarakṛitāgama,* p. 14. See Krom, *Hindoe-Javaansche Geschiedenis,* p. 327.
168. Kern, *Verspreide Geschriften,* X, pp. 1–76. Sarkar, *Indian Influences on the Literature of Java and Bali,* pp. 83–87.
169. Sarkar, *Indian Influences on the Literature of Java and Bali,* pp. 224–78.
170. Above, p. 147.
171. Sarkar, *Indian Influences on the Literature of Java and Bali,* pp. 322–23.
172. J. L. A. Brandes, *Beschrijving van de ruine bij de desa Toempang, genaamd Tjandi Djago* (The Hague, 1904). Krom, *Inleiding tot de Hindoe-Javaansche Kunst,* pp. 95–136.
173. Above, p. 33.
174. Tāranātha says that at the time of the conquest of India by the Turushkas (this was the invasion of Muhammad-i-Bakhtiyar in the last years of the twelfth century) a number of Buddhist scholars, including Sangama Śrījñāna, Raviśrībhadra, Chandrakaragupta, sixteen *mahāntas,* and 200 minor pandits fled to Pukkam (Pagan), Munjan (Haripunjaya?), Kamboja, and other countries. See Nihar-Ranjan Ray, *Sanskrit Buddhism in Burma* (Calcutta, 1936), pp. 76, 81, 85.

Chapter XII

1. On the theories concerning the dispersion of the Thai, see L. P. Briggs, "The Appearance and Historical Usage of the Terms Tai, Thai, Siamese, and Lao," *JAOS,* LXIX (1949), pp. 60–73; Jean Rispaud, "Introduction à l'histoire des Tay du Yunnan et de Birmanie," *France-Asie,* n.s. XVII, no. 166 (1961), pp. 1849–79.
2. G. H. Luce, "The Early Syām in Burma's History," *JSS,* XLVI (1958), p. 141. See Hsü Yün-ts'iao, *JSSS,* IV, 2 (December, 1947), p. 11.
3. Above, p. 10.
4. P. Lefèvre-Pontalis, "Les Younes du royaume de Lan Na ou de Pape," *TP,* XI (1910), p. 107. These dates are challenged by G. H. Luce in "The Early Syām in Burma's History," p. 126; he asserts that the prestige of Pagan remained intact throughout the thirteenth century and that there is epigraphic evidence demonstrating Burmese sovereignty over the provinces of the north.
5. Camille Notton, *Annales du Siam* (Paris, 1926–32), III, p. 20.
6. *Mission Pavie, Etudes diverses,* II (Paris, 1898), pp. 7–17. Louis Finot, "Recherches sur la littérature laotienne," *BEFEO,* XVII, 5, pp. 160–64.
7. Above, p. 140.
8. Ecole Française d'Extrême-Orient, *Mémoires archéologiques,* II: Le temple d'Angkor Vat (Paris, 1929–32), pls. 558, 559, 572, 573.
9. Luce, "The Early Syām in Burma's History," p. 140.
10. Jean Rispaud, "Les noms d'éléments numéraux des principautés taï," *JSS,* XXIX (1937), p. 77. P. Lévy, "Doublets onomastiques au Laos," *Bulletin de l'Institut Indochinois pour l'Etude de l'Homme,* V (1942), p. 139.
11. Pierre Grossin, *La Province Muong de Hoà-binh* (Hanoi, 1926). Charles Robequain, *Le Thanh-hoa* (Paris, 1929), I.
12. Paul Pelliot, "Deux itinéraires de Chine en Inde, à la fin du VIIIe siècle," *BEFEO,* IV, p. 162.
13. Coedès, "Les collections du Musée de Bangkok," *Ars Asiatica,* XII, p. 31; "India's Influences upon Siamese Art," *IAL,* IV (1930), p. 36. Reginald le May, *A Concise History of Buddhist Art in Siam* (Cambridge, England, 1938), p. 103.
14. *History of the Yuan,* according to information we owe to the kindness of Mr. Trân Van Giap.
15. Henri Maspero, "La frontière de l'Annam et du Cambodge du VIIIe siècle," *BEFEO,* XVIII, 3, p. 35.
16. According to Chou Ta-kuan. See Paul Pelliot, trans. and ed., "Mémoires sur les coutumes du Cambodge," *BEFEO,* II, p. 140; "Deux itinéraires," p. 240, n. 5. In his posthumous edition of Chou Ta-kuan (Paris, 1951), pp. 119 ff., Paul Pelliot expresses doubt concerning the veracity of this assertion.

17. Pelliot, "Deux itinéraires," p. 240, n. 5.
18. Louis Finot, "Les inscriptions de Jaya Parameçvaravarman I," *BEFEO,* XV, 2, p. 51, n. 1.
19. Etienne Aymonier, "Première étude sur les inscriptions tchames," *JA* (January-February, 1891), p. 58. For the dates, see Finot, "Les inscriptions de Jaya Parameçvaravarman I," p. 51.
20. For this episode, see Georges Maspero, *Le Royaume de Champa* (Paris, 1928), pp. 175–87.
21. "The King," says Marco Polo, who visited Champa in 1285 (*The Travels of Marco Polo,* edition of L. F. Benedetto, translated into English by Aldo Ricci [New York, 1931], p. 278), "who was exceedingly old, and had by no means as large an army as the Great Kaan's, being unable to defend himself in the open, held out in his cities and towns, which were so very strong, that he needed fear no one." According to Benedetto, the name Accambale given to the Cham king by certain texts of Marco Polo was the result of a mistake. This opinion is shared by A. C. Moule and Paul Pelliot, *Marco Polo: The Description of the World* (London, 1938), I, p. 366, n. 5.
22. Maspero, *Le Royaume de Champa,* p. 186.
23. *The Travels of Marco Polo,* p. 278.
24. For the relations of the Burmese with the Mongols and the fall of Pagan, see Edouard Huber, "La fin de la dynastie de Pagan," *BEFEO,* IX, p. 633, and especially G. H. Luce, "The Early Syām in Burma's History," *JSS,* XLVI (1958), p. 123, and XLVII (1959), p. 59, and Than Tun, "History of Burma, A.D. 1000–1300," *Bulletin of the Burma Historical Commission,* I (1960), p. 39. It is from these two important articles that the historical and chronological facts pertaining to Burma in this chapter and the ones following are taken.
25. *The Travels of Marco Polo,* p. 196.
26. Huber, "La fin de la dynastie de Pagan," pp. 679–80.
27. *Ibid.* The frescoes decorating the monument known as the "vault of Kyanzittha," near the temple of Shwezigon at Pagan, have preserved curious representations of a Mongol chief and of an archer (*ARASB* [1922], p. 17, pl. 1).
28. Coedès, "Documents sur l'histoire politique et religieuse du Laos occidental," *BEFEO,* XXV, pp. 19–22, 189–94. Robert Halliday, "Les inscriptions Môn du Siam," *BEFEO,* XXX, p. 86.
29. Above, p. 161.
30. Coedès, "Documents . . . Laos," p. 86.
31. *Ibid.*, p. 87.
32. *Ibid.*, p. 88.
33. For the first mentions of the Syāṃ in the epigraphy of Cambodia and Champa, see above, p. 190. They appear for the first time in Burmese epigraphy (as *Rham*) in 1120 (Luce, "The Early Syām in Burma's History," p. 124). In China, the first

mention of the Thai under the name Pa-yi is found in the *History of the Yuan* under the date 1278 (*ibid.*, p. 125).

34. Jean Yves Claeys, "L'archéologie du Siam," *BEFEO,* XXXI, pp. 410–20.
35. Coedès, "Les origines de la dynastie de Sukhodaya," *JA* (April-June, 1920), p. 233; *Receuil des inscriptions du Siam* (Bangkok, 1924–29), I, pp. 7, 49.
36. An unidentified locality, perhaps on the upper course of the Nam Sak.
37. Perhaps the death of Jayavarman VII. R. C. Majumdar, "The Rise of Sukhodaya," *JGIS,* X (1943), pp. 44–51, suggests that Pha Mưang Śrī Indrapatīndrāditya was none other than the son-in-law of the Khmer king Jayavarman VIII, the future Śrīndravarman, and the liberation of Sukhothai thus constituted an episode in his struggle with his brother-in-law and might be dated before 1275. But this hypothesis lacks firm foundation.
38. Pelliot, "Deux itinéraires," p. 241.
39. Coedès, *Receuil des inscriptions du Siam,* I, p. 37.
40. Present-day Rahaeng. Mưang Chọt corresponds to present-day Mae Sọt, north of Rahaeng.
41. This passage resembles the oath of the electors of Genghis Khan too closely to be coincidental: "We shall march at the front in battle; if we win women and girls, we will give them to you. We shall go to the hunt in the first ranks; if we catch game, we will give it to you" (René Grousset, *L'Empire des steppes* [Paris, 1939], p. 258).
42. Named above Ban Mưang, "protector of the kingdom"; the Pālarāja of the Pali chronicles. Coedès, "Documents sur la dynastie de Sukhodaya," *BEFEO,* XVII, 2, pp. 34–44.
43. Grousset, *L'Empire des steppes,* p. 281.
44. *Ibid.*
45. This is the same semantic evolution that the word "Frank" underwent at the beginning of the feudal era. Since only free men composed the "populus Francorum," the legal status and the national name became synonymous. See Marc Bloch, *La société féodale* (Paris, 1939), p. 390.
46. Grousset, *L'Empire des steppes,* p. 282.
47. H. G. Quaritch Wales, *Ancient Siamese Government and Administration* (London, 1934). But this system may also have been of Indian origin.
48. Coedès, *Receuil des inscriptions du Siam,* I, p. 37.
49. J. Burnay and Coedès, "The Origins of the Sukhodaya Script," *JSS,* XXI (1928), p. 87.
50. Probably Wat Chang Lọm. See Claeys, "L'archéologie du Siam," pp. 411–12.
51. Brought back to Bangkok by King Mongkut at the same time as the stele and preserved in the Royal Palace (*JSS,* XVII [1923],

pp. 117–18 and the plates facing pp. 120 and 165), where it is used in the coronation rites.

52. The "Thai who live under the canopy of heaven" were perhaps the Thai living in China, since the Chinese expression *T'ien-hsia* ("under heaven") at that time designated the Chinese Empire.
53. Below, pp. 205–206.
54. N. J. Krom, *Hindoe-Javaansche Geschiedenis* (The Hague, 1931), pp. 328–30.
55. *Nāgarakṛitāgama,* trans. H. Kern, *Verspreide Geschriften* (The Hague, 1913–29), VIII, pp. 15–16; *Pararaton,* ed. N. J. Krom, *VBG,* 62 (1920), p. 79.
56. *Ibid.* See also, below, p. 204.
57. *Nāgarakṛitāgama,* p. 17. According to N. Venkataramanayya, "Tripurantakam Inscription of Vikramottunga Rājendra Cakravarti" (*JGIS,* XIV [1955], pp. 143–49), the author of this inscription, suzerain of four islands, was none other than Kṛitanagara. But the date of his offering to the god of Tripurāntaka, Monday 5 Pusya 1214 *śaka,* i.e., December 15, 1292 A.D., must have been after the death of Kṛitanagara; see p. 199.
58. *Nāgarakṛitāgama,* p. 17.
59. On the relations of Java with the Mongols in this period, see F. G. Kramp, "De zending van Meng K'i naar Java en de stichting van Madjapahit," in *Opstellen geschreven ter eere van Dr. H. Kern* (Leyden, 1903), p. 357; W. W. Rockhill, "Notes on the Relations and Trade of China with the Eastern Archipelago and the Coast of the Indian Ocean during the Fourteenth Century," *TP,* XV (1914), pp. 444–45.
60. Krom, *Hindoe-Javaansche Geschiedenis,* pp. 341–42. Reproduction in *TBG,* 52 (1910), p. 108. The inscription has been published by H. Kern, *Verspreide Geschriften,* VII, p. 190; B. R. Chatterjee, *India and Java* (Calcutta, 1933), II, Inscriptions, p. 75.
61. To whom Kṛitanagara consecrated a temple, Chandi Jawi. Krom, *Hindoe-Javaansche Geschiedenis,* pp. 328–29, 340–41; *Inleiding tot de Hindoe-Javaansche Kunst* (The Hague, 1923), II, pp. 138–50. J. L. Moens, "Het buddhisme op Java en Sumatra in zijn laatste Bloeiperiode," *TBG,* 64 (1925), p. 522; "Het Berlijnsche Ardhanārī beeld en de bijzettingsbeelden van Kṛitanagara," *TBG,* 73 (1933), p. 123. See W. F. Stutterheim, "Nachschrift," *TBG,* 73 (1933), p. 292. On the Śiva-Buddha syncretism, see also H. Kern, "Java, Bali, and Sumatra," in *Encyclopaedia of Religion and Ethics* (New York, 1910–27), VII, p. 495, and Himansu Bhusan Sarkar, "Śiva-Buddha in Old-Javanese Records," *Indian Culture,* I (1934), p. 284. P. H. Pott, "Le bouddhisme de Java et l'ancienne civilisation javanaise," *Conferenze,* Serie Orientale Roma V (Rome, 1952), p. 109.
62. *Pararaton,* p. 79.

63. *Nāgarakṛitāgama,* p. 24. J. E. van Lohuizen-de Leeuw, "Was het optreden van Jayakatwang een usurpatie of restauratie?" *Wegens zijn bizondere verdienste opgedragen aan J. P. Suyling* (Amsterdam, 1949), pp. 151–62.
64. P. 79. L. C. Damais, "L'expédition à Java des troupes de Qubilai Qagan et la date de fondation de Majapahit," *Actes, XXIIe Congrès International des Orientalistes* (Istanbul, 1951), p. 322. The chronology adopted in the following pages is taken from this article.
65. His complete name was Narāya Sangrāmavijaya (*Pararaton,* p. 98).
66. These events are described in detail in an inscription of 1294, edited and translated by J. L. A. Brandes in "Pararaton," *VBG,* 49 (1896), pp. 94–100.
67. The *Pararaton* says he thus feigned submission to Jayakatwang, but this is not what seems to be indicated by the Chinese sources. See R. C. Majumdar, *Ancient Indian Colonies of the Far East,* II: Suvarṇadvīpa (Dacca, 1937), p. 315.
68. Below, p. 217.
69. The Chinese characters represent an original *Yighmiš* (information due to the kindness of L. Hambis).
70. *Nāgarakṛitāgama,* pp. 28–29. R. Ng. Poerbatjaraka, "Vier oorkonden in koper," *TBG,* 76 (1936), pp. 380–81.
71. This follows from an inscription published in Poerbatjaraka, "Vier oorkonden in koper," p. 381, and strongly contradicts the *Pararaton* (pp. 92, 123), which says that the mother of Jayanagara was a Sumatranese princess, Dara Peṭak, brought from Malāyu following the Javanese expedition.
72. *Nāgarakṛitāgama,* p. 31.
73. W. W. Rockhill, "Notes on the Relations and Trade of China," p. 446.
74. "Chronologie van de oudste Geschiedenis van Maja-pahit," *BKI,* 97 (1938), p. 135.
75. Inscription of Padang Rocho, published by N. J. Krom in *VMKAWAL,* 5th series, II (1916), p. 306. See Gabriel Ferrand, "L'empire sumatranais de Çrīvijaya," *JA* (October-December, 1922), pp. 179–81.
76. On this image, see C. M. Pleyte, "Over een paar Hindoe beelden van Padang-tjandi," *TBG,* 49 (1906), pp. 171, 177; Krom, *Inleiding tot de Hindoe-Javaansche Kunst,* pp. 131–33; and F. M. Schnitger, *The Archaeology of Hindoo Sumatra* (Leyden, 1937), pl. XVI, and *Forgotten Kingdoms in Sumatra* (Leyden, 1939), pl. IV.
77. C. O. Blagden, "The Empire of the Maharaja," *JRASSB,* 81 (1920), p. 25.
78. Pelliot, "Deux itinéraires," p. 242.
79. *Ibid.,* p. 326.
80. *The Travels of Marco Polo,* p. 282.

81. *Rapporten van den Oudheidkundigen Dienst in Nederlandsche-Indië* (1913), p. 1. R. O. Winstedt, "The Chronicles of Pasai," *JRASMB,* XVI, 2 (1938), p. 25, says that Pasai was the first Malay kingdom to embrace Islam, during the second half of the thirteenth century.
82. *The Travels of Marco Polo,* pp. 279–80.
83. Pelliot, "Deux itinéraires," pp. 326–27. The *History of the Yuan* specifies elsewhere (W. P. Groeneveldt, *Notes on the Malay Archipelago and Malacca* [Batavia, 1876], p. 30) that the states in question are Nan-wu-li, Su-mu-tu-la, Pu-lu-pu-tu, Pa-la-la, and Mu-lai-yu, which are exactly the states mentioned by Marco Polo.
84. Gabriel Ferrand, "Malaka, le Malāyu et Malāyur," *JA* (July-August, 1918), p. 138.
85. *The Travels of Marco Polo,* p. 280.
86. *Ibid.,* p. 281.
87. *Ibid.,* p. 282. This is the Pa-la-la of the Chinese. Under the name of Pieh-li-la, the *History of the Yuan* attributes to it an embassy in 1284 (W. W. Rockhill, "Notes on the Relations and Trade of China," p. 439). See Paul Pelliot, "Les grands voyages maritimes chinois au début du XVe siècle," *TP,* XXX (1933), p. 308, n. 3.
88. *The Travels of Marco Polo,* p. 282. Paul Pelliot (*Notes on Marco Polo* [Paris, 1959–63], I, p. 86, under the word "Basman") is of the opinion that Marco Polo visited neither Basman nor Fansur (below).
89. See above, p. 324, n. 73. This state, founded around 1250, sent an embassy to China in 1294 (Pelliot, "Deux itinéraires," p. 327 and n. 4).
90. *The Travels of Marco Polo,* pp. 284–85.
91. *Ibid.,* pp. 285–86. Dagroian is perhaps a coypist's error for Damian, present-day Tamiang (between Deli and Achin), named in the *Nāgarakṛitāgama* under the form Tumihang and in the Chinese texts under the form T'an-yang or Tan-yang (Pelliot, "Deux itinéraires," p. 328, and Ferrand, "Malaka," p. 65). T'an-yang sent an embassy to China in 1294.
92. *The Travels of Marco Polo,* p. 287. The Nan-wu-li of the Chinese also sent embassies in 1284 (W. W. Rockhill, "Notes on the Relations and Trade of China," p. 439) and in 1294 (Pelliot, "Deux itinéraires," p. 327 and n. 3).
93. *The Travels of Marco Polo,* pp. 287–88.
94. Pelliot, "Deux itinéraires," pp. 243, 328.
95. Above, p. 198.
96. The Tan-ma-hsi of the Chinese. Pelliot, "Deux itinéraires," p. 345, n. 4.
97. G. P. Rouffaer, "Was Malaka emporium voor 1400 A.D. genaamd Malajoer?" *BKI,* 77 (1921), pp. 35–67, 370–72, 404–406. On the history of Singapore before the founding of

Malacca, see W. Linehan, "The Kings of Fourteenth Century Singapore," *JRASMB,* XX (1927), 2, pp. 117–26, and on Tamasik, see Roland Braddell, "Lung-ya-man and Tan-ma-hsi," *JRASMB,* XXIII (1950), pp. 37–51.

98. Pelliot, "Deux itinéraires," p. 242.
99. Coedès, *Receuil des inscriptions du Siam,* I, p. 48.
100. Pelliot, "Mémoires . . . du Cambodge," pp. 173, 176.
101. There may be traces of the memory of this penetration in local legend. See F. H. Giles, "The Koh Lak Tradition," *JSS,* XXX (1938), p. 1.
102. Pelliot, "Deux itinéraires," p. 242.
103. *Ibid.*
104. Communication from Paul Pelliot (letter of March 10, 1928).
105. C. Hardouin, "Légendes historiques siamoises: Légende de Makkatho," *Revue indochinoise* (February, 1904), p. 121.
106. Notton, *Annales,* III, pp. 30–34.
107. Below, p. 225.
108. Pelliot, "Deux itinéraires," pp. 240–43. G. H. Luce, "The Early Syām in Burma's History," p. 140. (The name of the city of Sukhothai is mentioned under the date of June 15, 1299.)
109. Pelliot, "Deux itinéraires," p. 242.
110. Jean Baptiste Pallegoix, *Description du royaume Thai ou Siam* (Paris, 1854), II, p. 66. Camille Notton, *Légendes sur le Siam et le Cambodge* (Bangkok, 1939), pp. 21–23.
111. On the ceramics of Sukhothai and Sawankhalok, see R. S. le May, "The Ceramic Wares of North-Central Siam," *Burlington Magazine,* LXIII (July-December, 1933), pp. 156–66, 203–21; P'raya Nak'on P'ra Ram, "Tai pottery," *JSS,* 29 (1937), p. 13.
112. Coedès, *Receuil des inscriptions du Siam,* pp. 44–45.
113. Claeys, "L'archéologie du Siam," p. 417.
114. *Khpong* is a Khmer word that means "mountain crest." Phra Khaphung is the lord of the heights, the lord of the summit. This name evokes at once that of the Nat, or Burmese spirit, Mahāgiri, who, it is said, lived on Mount Poppa, the sacred mountain located southeast of Pagan, and whose installation marked the reuniting under the authority of a single chief, the chief of Pagan, of many territorial entities, each possessing its own spirit. We have seen in Funan that the mountain from which the country derived its name and upon which a powerful divinity was supposed to have been enthroned, also symbolized the union of various populations assembled under the authority of a single sovereign, "king of the mountain." And the establishment in 802 by the Khmer king Jayavarman II of the royal linga on the hill of Kulèn coincided with the reunification of the country, which had been split up in the preceding century. We are thus led to consider Phra Khaphung of Sukhothai, the lord of the summit, "superior to all

the spirits of the country," as playing the same role of protector and unifier as the Burmese Mahāgiri on Mount Poppa and the royal linga of the Khmers installed on the Kulèn. The spirit brought about the reunion, on a magico-religious plane, of territories conquered and united by Rāma Khamhaeng. He was a sort of national spirit, dominating from his heights, near the royal city, all the other local spirits. His cult, during the reign of Rāma Khamhaeng, was purely animistic, but this national cult over the centuries came to be integrated with Buddhism, and the powerful spirit "superior to all the spirits of the country" became incarnated in a statue of the Buddha and identified with it (Coedès, *Les Peuples de la péninsule indochinoise* [Paris, 1962], p. 136).

115. Celebrated in Siam until the nineteenth century. See H. G. Quaritch Wales, *Siamese State Ceremonies* (London, 1931), pp. 288–94.
116. Below, p. 215.
117. Pelliot, "Deux itinéraires," pp. 241–43.
118. Coedès, "Documents . . . Laos," p. 88. Notton, *Annales,* III, pp. 34–44. I am adopting the dates of the Pali chronicle *Jinakālamālī.*
119. Coedès, "Documents . . . Laos," p. 90, n. 1. Notton, *Annales,* III, pp. 61 ff.
120. Coedès, "Documents . . . Laos," p. 89, n. 1. Notton, *Annales,* III, pp. 54–61. Inscription of Wat Chiang Man, in *Mission Pavie, Etudes diverses,* II, p. 308.
121. Coedès, "Note sur les ouvrages pālis composés en pays thai," *BEFEO,* XV, p. 39.
122. Bingaraṭṭha designates especially the region of Chiangmai and Yonaraṭṭha, the old principality centered on Chiangrai (Coedès, "Documents . . . Laos," p. 91, n. 2).
123. Pelliot, "Deux itinéraires," p. 244, n. 4. G. H. Luce, "The Early Syām in Burma's History," p. 186.
124. Notton, *Annales,* III, pp. 47–52.
125. Above, p. 194. We must not confuse this Burmese prince with one of the three Thai brothers bearing the same name.
126. A. P. Phayre, *History of Burma* (London, 1883), p. 64. G. E. Harvey, *History of Burma* (London, 1925), p. 75.
127. Published by John Jardine, *King Wagaru's Manu Dhammasattham: Text, Translation and Notes* (Rangoon, 1892). See Emil Forchhammer, *An Essay on the Sources and Development of Burmese Law* (Rangoon, 1885), pp. 36–42.
128. Robert Lingat, *L'Influence hindoue dans l'ancien droit siamois* (Paris, 1937).
129. With the title Tribhavanāditya Pavarapaṇḍita Dhammarāja. The history and chronology of the events that follow are essentially based on the works of G. H. Luce ("The Early Syām in Burma's History") and Than Tun ("History of Burma, A.D. 1000–1300").

130. Tribhavanāditya Pavaradhammarāja.
131. Ecole Française d'Extrême-Orient, *Mémoires archéologiques*, I: Le temple d'Īçvarapura (Paris, 1926), p. 89.
132. *Ibid.*, p. 105. Auguste Barth and Abel Bergaigne, ISC, p. 584.
133. Ecole Française d'Extrême-Orient, *Mémoires archéologiques*, I, pp. 80–81.
134. Pelliot, "Mémoires . . . du Cambodge," p. 176.
135. Ecole Française d'Extrême-Orient, *Mémoires archéologiques*, I, p. 89.
136. *Ibid.*, p. 80.
137. Above, p. 173.
138. Henri Marchal, *Guide archéologique aux temples d'Angkor* (Paris, 1928), pp. 136–38. Maurice Glaize, *Les Monuments du groupe d'Angkor* (Saigon, 1914), pp. 179–80.
139. Louis Finot, "Inscriptions d'Aṅkor," *BEFEO,* XXV, pp. 395–406; Ecole Française d'Extrême-Orient, *Mémoires archéologiques*, I, pp 95–106.
140. Barth and Bergaigne, ISC, p. 579.
141. *Ibid.*, p. 584. On this inscription, see below, p. 228.
142. Above, p. 178.
143. Pelliot, "Mémoires . . . du Cambodge," p. 141.
144. *Ibid.*, p. 131.
145. *Nouvelles annales des voyages,* III; reprinted in *Nouveaux Mélanges Asiatiques,* I (Paris, 1829), pp. 100–52.
146. "Mémoires sur les coutumes du Cambodge," *BEFEO,* II, pp. 123–77. See Coedès, "Notes sur Tcheou Ta-kouan," *BEFEO,* XVIII, 9, p. 4; "Nouvelles notes sur Tcheou Ta-kouan," *TP,* XXX (1933), p. 224. A new translation, copiously annotated, has appeared in Vol. III (Paris, 1951) of the posthumous works of Paul Pelliot. It has been used here in every case where it represents an improvement over the old.
147. *Ch'a-nan* is *Kompong Ch'nang,* whose fresh-water shrimps are still as large as in the time of Chou Ta-kuan ("The shrimp of Ch'a-nan weigh a pound or more"); *Mo-liang* is *Malyang* (above, p. 170); *P'u-mai* may be *Phimai;* the other names are not identifiable at the moment.
148. "In his right hand he holds the lance, in his left hand the shield," which is in conformity with what is shown in the bas-reliefs. But when he adds "The Cambodians have neither bows, nor arrows, nor arbalests, nor shot, nor cutlasses, nor helmets," he is in error, or else armaments had suffered a serious regression in his time as compared with the period of Angkor Wat, when warriors wore helmets and cutlasses, and the period of the Bayon, on which are depicted curious arbalests of Chinese origin (Paul Mus, "Les balistes du Bayon," *BEFEO,* XXIX, pp. 331–41).
149. Maspero, *Le Royaume de Champa,* p. 188.
150. *Ibid.*, p. 392.
151. *Ibid.*, pp. 189–90.

152. Etienne Aymonier, "L'inscription chame de Po Sah," *BCAI* (1911), p. 15.
153. Henry Parmentier, *Inventaire descriptif des monuments čams de l'Annam* (Paris, 1909–18), I, pp. 81–95.
154. *Ibid.*, pp. 557–59.

Chapter XIII

1. Paul Pelliot, "Deux itinéraires de Chine en Inde, à la fin du VIIIe siècle," *BEFEO*, IV, pp. 243, 251.
2. Prince Damrong, "Siamese History prior to the Founding of Ayudhya," *JSS*, XIII (1919), p. 51.
3. *Ibid.*, p. 52.
4. Georges Maspero, *Le Royaume de Champa* (Paris, 1928), pp. 196–97.
5. Camille Notton, *Légendes sur le Siam et le Cambodge* (Bangkok, 1939), p. 26.
6. *Mission Pavie, Etudes diverses,* II (Paris, 1898), p. 235. See Coedès, "Documents sur la dynastie de Sukhodaya," *BEFEO,* XVII, 2, p. 5.
7. A. P. Phayre, *History of Burma* (London, 1883), p. 66.
8. *Ibid.*, p. 67.
9. Henri Maspero, "La frontière de l'Annam et du Cambodge," *BEFEO,* XVIII, 3, p. 35.
10. Coedès, "Documents sur la dynastie de Sukhodaya," pp. 9, 45
11. On this point I adopt the conclusions of P'raya Nak'on P'ra Ram, "Who Was Dharmarāja I of Sukhothai?" *JSS,* XXVIII (1935), p. 214.
12. Coedès, *Receuil des inscriptions du Siam* (Bangkok, 1924–29), I, pp. 89–90, 127–29. In agreement with the article cited in the preceding note, I now attribute the construction of these prints to Loe Thai and not to his son Lư Thai.
13. *Ibid.*, pp. 49–75.
14. *Ibid.*, pp. 145–49. P'raya Nak'on P'ra Ram, "Who Was Dharmarāja I of Sukhothai?" pp. 218–20.
15. Lucien Fournereau, *Le Siam ancien* (Paris, 1895–1908), I, p. 257 (under the name of Vat Jai).
16. Reginald le May, *A Concise History of Buddhist Art in Siam* (Cambridge, England, 1938), pp. 114–19.
17. Above, p. 219.
18. Published in Bangkok in 1912; see Coedès, "Documents sur la dynastie de Sukhodaya," pp. 4–6; "The Traibhūmikathā, Buddhist Cosmology and Treaty on Ethics," *East and West,* VII (1957), p. 349.
19. Coedès, "Documents sur la dynastie de Sukhodaya," pp. 13, 45.
20. Coedès, *Receuil des inscriptions du Siam,* I, pp. 98–99.
21. *Ibid.*, p. 107.
22. Above, p. 208. The *Tao-i Chih-lioh* of Wang Ta-yüan (1350)

names among its dependencies certain countries that are rather difficult to identify but that the *Chu-fan-chih* of Chao Ju-kua in the preceding century listed among the dependencies of Cambodia.

23. Summarized and discussed by Prince Damrong, "Siamese History prior to the Founding of Ayudhya," pp. 35–40.
24. H. G. Quaritch Wales, *Towards Angkor* (London, 1937), Chapter IX ("A Cholera-Stricken City"), pp. 132–46; "Some Notes on the Kingdom of Dvāravatī," *JGIS,* V (1938), pp. 24–32.
25. Prince Damrong, "Siamese History prior to the Founding of Ayudhya," pp. 63–66.
26. On this name, in which I believe it is possible to discern a survival of the name of the kingdom of Dvāravatī, whose center was indeed in the lower Menam (above, p. 76), see Prince Dhani Nivat, "The City of Thawarawadi Sri Ayudhya," *JSS,* XXXI (1939), p. 147.
27. The date given by the *Tao-i Chih-lioh,* according to Edouard Huber's review of Nai Thien's *Burmese Invasions of Siam, BEFEO,* IX, p. 586. On the evidence from the Pali chronicles concerning this battle, see Coedès, "Documents sur la dynastie de Sukhodaya," pp. 40, 43.
28. Coedès, *Les Peuples de la péninsule indochinoise* (Paris, 1962), pp. 136–38; "L'art siamois de l'époque de Sukhodaya," *Arts Asiatique,* I (1954), p. 281. On art, see A. B. Griswold, "New Evidence for the Dating of Sukhodaya Art," *AA,* XIX (1956), p. 240.
29. "La frontière de l'Annam et du Cambodge," *BEFEO,* XVIII, 3, p. 36.
30. "The annals of Wiangčhan and of Luang Phrabang," writes Henri Maspero (*ibid.*), "attribute the conquest of Wiangčhan to King Fa Ngum and place these events in the second half of the fourteenth century; since the successor of this Fa Ngum, King Sam Saen Thai, received the Chinese title of *Süan-wei-shih* in 1404, the date of the Laotian chronicles must not be too inaccurate. All these foreign documents, by complementing each other, enable us to identify—if not precisely, at least approximately—the moment when Cambodian domination in Laotian territory came to an end."
31. "Recherches sur la littérature laotienne," *BEFEO,* XVII, 5, pp. 164–65.
32. Below, pp. 228–29.
33. Translated in *Mission Pavie, Etudes diverses,* II, pp. 1–77. For Fa Ngum, see pp. 17–38.
34. Above, p. 206.
35. Utilized by Paul Le Boulanger, *Histoire du Laos Français* (Paris, 1930), pp. 41–51.
36. On this name, see Coedès, "A propos des anciens noms de Luang Prabang," *BEFEO,* XVIII, 10, pp. 9–11.

37. Coedès, *Receuil des inscriptions du Siam,* I, p. 129.
38. Paul Lévy, "Les traces de l'introduction du bouddhisme à Luang Prabang," *BEFEO,* XL, p. 411. Above, p. 137.
39. In 1311 according to the *Jinakālamālī* (Coedès, "Documents sur l'histoire politique et religieuse du Laos occidental," *BEFEO,* XXV, p. 91); in 1317 according to the *Chronicle of Chiangmai* (Camille Notton, *Annales du Siam* [Paris, 1926–32], III, p. 74).
40. Notton, *Annales,* III, p. 72.
41. Coedès, "Documents . . . Laos," p. 92, n. 2. Notton, *Annales,* III, p. 73.
42. Notton, *Annales,* III, p 71.
43. Coedès, "Documents . . . Laos," pp. 91–92. Notton, *Annales,* III, p. 74.
44. Coedès, "Documents . . . Laos," p. 92, Notton, *Annales,* III, p. 75.
45. Coedès, "Documents . . . Laos," pp. 92–93. Notton, *Annales,* III, pp. 75–77.
46. The first date is that of the *Jinakālamālī* (Coedès, "Documents . . . Laos," p. 93); the second date is that of the *Chronicle of Chiangmai* (Notton, *Annales,* III, p. 77).
47. See n. 46.
48. See n. 46.
49. Coedès, "Documents . . . Laos," p. 93. Notton, *Annales,* III, p. 80.
50. In 1336 according to the *Jinakālamālī* (Coedès, "Documents . . . Laos," p. 94); in 1345 according to the *Chronicle of Chiangmai* (Notton, *Annales,* III, p. 85).
51. Coedès, "Documents . . . Laos," p. 94.
52. *Ibid.* Notton, *Annales,* III, pp. 84–85. The urn containing these ashes was discovered in 1925 (see Notton, *Annales,* III, plate facing p. 84, and *L'Illustration,* Sept. 5, 1925, p. 238).
53. The history of this miraculous statue is told in the *Jinakālamālī* (Coedès, "Documents . . . Laos," pp. 97–103).
54. In 1355 according to the *Jinakālamālī* (Coedès, "Documents . . . Laos," p. 94); in 1367 according to the *Chronicle of Chiangmai* (Notton, *Annales,* III, p. 85).
55. Above, p. 219.
56. Phayre, *History of Burma,* pp. 67–68. G. E. Harvey, *History of Burma* (London, 1925), pp. 111–12.
57. By taking the title of Anantasīhasūra Jeyyadeva.
58. Under the name of Tribhavanāditya Pavarasīhasūra Dhammarāja.
59. Phayre, *History of Burma,* p. 59. Harvey, *History of Burma,* pp. 78–79.
60. The Sawyun of Phayre, *History of Burma,* p. 59, and Harvey, *History of Burma,* p. 79.
61. Phayre, *History of Burma,* p. 63. Harvey, *History of Burma,*

p. 80. On this whole period, see Than Tun, "History of Burma, A.D. 1300–1400," *JBRS,* XLII, 2 (1959), pp. 119–33, and Tin Hla Thaw, "History of Burma, A.D. 1400–1500" *JBRS,* XLII, 2 (1959), pp. 135–50.

62. Phayre, *History of Burma,* p. 83. Harvey, *History of Burma,* p. 123.
63. Coedès, "La plus ancienne inscription en pali du Cambodge," *BEFEO,* XXXVI, p. 15.
64. *Ibid.,* pp. 14–21.
65. Louis Finot, "Inscriptions d'Aṅkor," *BEFEO,* XXV, pp. 403–406. Ecole Française d'Extrême-Orient, *Mémoires archéologiques,* I: Le temple d'Īçvarapura (Paris, 1926), pp. 103–106.
66. Pelliot, "Deux itinéraires," p. 240, n. 5.
67. Coedès, "La date d'avènement de Jayavarmaparameçvara," *BEFEO,* XXVIII, p. 145.
68. Coedès, *Inscriptions du Cambodge* (Paris, 1937–), II, p. 187.
69. Published by Auguste Barth and Abel Bergaigne, ISC, pp. 560–88.
70. Finot, "Inscriptions d'Aṅkor," p. 365.
71. Barth and Bergaigne, ISC, pp. 585–88.
72. Adhémard Leclère, *Cambodge, Fêtes civiles et religieuses* (Paris, 1917). For the Brahmans at the court of Siam, see H. G. Quaritch Wales, *Siamese State Ceremonies* (London, 1931).
73. Pelliot, "Deux itinéraires," p. 240, n. 5.
74. Above, p. 219.
75. Below, p. 236.
76. W. W. Rockhill, "Notes on the Relations and Trade of China with the Eastern Archipelago and the Coast of the Indian Ocean during the Fourteenth Century," *TP,* XVI (1915), p. 106. The passage of the *Tao-i Chih-lioh* has been translated anew and more accurately by Paul Pelliot in the notes of his *Mémoires sur les coutumes du Cambodge de Tcheou Ta-kouan,* Posthumous Works of Paul Pelliot, v. III (Paris, 1951), pp. 136 ff.
77. *Le Royaume de Champa,* p. 193.
78. Above, p. 217.
79. Maspero, *Le Royaume de Champa,* p. 195.
80. Above, p. 219.
81. Maspero, *Le Royaume de Champa,* pp. 197–98.
82. *Ibid.,* pp. 199–200.
83. Henri Cordier, ed., *Les Voyages en Asie au XIVe siècle du bienheureux frère Odoric de Pordenone* (Paris, 1891), p. 187. [Ed. note: English translation from Henry Yule and Henri Cordier, ed., *Cathay and the Way Thither* (London, 1913), II, pp. 166–67.]
84. The Latin and Italian texts say Zampa, Zapa, Campa, Canpa, and Capa.

85. This passage concerning *sati* is translated directly from the Old French. The Latin text says more exactly that his living wife was burned with him: *comburitur ejus corpus una com uxore viva.* See the note in Yule and Cordier, *Cathay and the Way Thither,* II, p. 167.
86. Tatsuro Yamamoto, "On Ṭawālisī Described by Ibn Baṭūṭa," *Memoirs of the Research Department of the Toyo Bunko,* 8 (1936), p. 93. The proposed identification is based upon an ingenious tie-in with the princely title *taval* then in use in Champa, which would be precisely represented by the transcription *trae hoa* (*bô-dê* = *pati*) of the Vietnamese annalists.
87. Maspero, *Le Royaume de Champa,* pp. 201–203.
88. Above, p. 205.
89. Rockhill, "Notes on the Relations and Trade of China," p. 100.
90. Tumasik, the site of Singapore. See above, p. 204.
91. Rockhill, "Notes on the Relations and Trade of China," p. 118.
92. *Ibid.,* p. 120.
93. *Ibid.,* p. 121.
94. *Ibid.,* p. 123.
95. *Ibid.,* p. 125. See Paul Pelliot, "Les grands voyages maritimes chinois au début du XVe siècle," *TP,* XXX (1933), p. 330, n. 3.
96. H. S. Paterson, "An Early Malay Inscription from Trengganu," *JRASMB,* II (1924), p. 252. C. O. Blagden, "A Note on the Trengganu Inscription," *JRASMB,* II (1924), p. 258.
97. On this country, see Paul Wheatley, *The Golden Khersonese* (Kuala Lumpur, 1961), pp. 224–28.
98. Gabriel Ferrand, *Relations de voyages et textes géographiques arabes, persans, et turks relatifs à l'Extrême-Orient du VIIIe au XVIIe siècles* (Paris, 1913–14), II, p. 450.
99. J. P. Moquette, *Rapporten van den Oudheidkundigen Dienst in Nederlandsch-Indië* (1913), p. 11. Gabriel Ferrand, "Malaka, le Malāyu et Malāyur," *JA* (May-June, 1918), pp. 474–75. But see N. J. Krom, *Hindoe-Javaansche Geschiedenis* (The Hague, 1931), p. 396.
100. Ferrand, *Relations de voyages,* II, p. 440.
101. H. K. J. Cowan, "Een interessant getuigenis betreffende de vroegste Islām in Noord-Suṃatra," *BKI,* 117 (1961), pp. 410–16.
102. J. P. Moquette, "De graafsteenen te Pasé en Grissee vergleken met dergelijke monumenten uit Hindoestan," *TBG,* 54 (1912), pp. 536–48. But this opinion is challenged by G. E. Marrison ("The Coming of Islam to the East Indies," *JRASMB,* XXIV [1951], pp. 28–37), who gives confirmation for the Malay tradition that Islam came from the Coromandel coast. See Raden Abdulkadir Widjojoatmodjo, "Islam in the Netherlands East-Indies," *FEQ,* II (1942), pp. 48–49.
103. Cordier, *Les Voyages en Asie,* p. 136.

104. *Ibid.*, p. 153. [Ed. note: English translation from Yule and Cordier, *Cathay and the Way Thither,* II, pp. 147–50.]
105. Rockhill, "Notes on the Relations and Trade of China," p. 148.
106. *Ibid.*, p. 151.
107. *Ibid.*, p. 143.
108. *Ibid.*, p. 134. Gabriel Ferrand, "L'empire sumatranais de Çrīvijaya," *JA,* (July-Sept., 1922), p. 30.
109. Pelliot, "Les grands voyages maritimes chinois," p. 376.
110. Rockhill, "Notes on the Relations and Trade of China," p. 135. Ferrand, "L'empire sumatranais," p. 31.
111. H. Kern, *Verspreide Geschriften* (The Hague, 1913–29), VII, p. 219.
112. J. L. A. Brandes, *Beschrijving van Tjandi Singasari* (The Hague, 1909), pp. 99–116.
113. Krom, *Hindoe-Javaansche Geschiedenis,* pp. 392–93. K. A. Nilakanta Sastri, "Śrī Vijaya," *BEFEO,* XL, p. 303.
114. Hendrik Kern, "De wij-inscriptie op het Amoghapāça-beeld van Padang Chandi," *Verspreide Geschriften,* VII, p. 163. B. R. Chatterjee, *India and Java* (Calcutta, 1933), II, Inscriptions, pp. 79–84.
115. Above, p. 201.
116. J. L. Moens, "Srīvijaya, Yāva en Katāha," *TBG,* LXXVII (1937), p. 457.
117. Sylvain Lévi, *Sanskrit Texts from Bali* (Baroda, 1933).
118. J. L. Moens, "Het buddhisme op Java en Sumatra in zijn laatste bloeiperiode," *TBG,* LXIV (1924), pp. 558–79.
119. Hendrik Kern, "Het zoogenaamde rotsinschrift van Batu Beragung in Menangkabau," *Verspreide Geschriften,* VI, p. 249.
120. C. C. Berg, "Opmerkingen over de chronologie van de oudste geschiedenis van Maja-pahit," *BKI,* 97 (1938), p. 135. See also Berg's *De middeljavaansche historische traditie* (Santpoort, 1927).
121. *Pararaton,* ed. J. L. A. Brandes (*VBG,* 62 [1920]), p. 125. C. C. Berg, *Rangga Lawe, middeljavaansche roman* (Weltevreden, 1930).
122. *Pararaton,* p. 125.
123. *Pararaton,* pp. 125–26.
124. N. J. Krom, *Inleiding tot de Hindoe-Javaansche Kunst* (The Hague, 1923), pp. 159–66.
125. *Ibid.*, pl. 65.
126. K. A. Nilakanta Sastri, "Agastya," *TBG,* 76 (1936), p. 502. See also his "Origin of the Çailendras," *TBG,* 75 (1935), p. 611.
127. *Pararaton,* p. 125. This place has not been identified exactly. N. J. Krom, *Hindoe-Javaansche Geschiedenis,* p. 345.
128. *Pararaton,* p. 126.
129. *Pararaton,* pp. 126–27. *Nāgarakṛitāgama* (trans. Hendrik Kern, *Verspreide Geschriften,* VIII), p. 34.
130. *Pararaton,* pp. 127–28.

131. Cordier, *Les Voyages en Asie,* pp. 161–62. [Ed. note: English translation from Yule and Cordier, *Cathay and the Way Thither,* II, pp. 151–55].
132. Rockhill, "Notes on the Relations and Trade of China," *TP,* XV (1914), pp. 446–47.
133. Below, p. 243.
134. *Pararaton,* pp. 128–29.
135. Krom, *Inleiding tot de Hindoe-Javaansche Kunst,* II, pp. 245–84. M. E. Lulius van Goor, "Notice sur les ruines de Panataran," *Et. Asiat. EFEO,* II, p. 375.
136. *Nāgarakṛitāgama,* p. 257.
137. With the title Tribhuvanottungadevī Jayavishṇuvardhanī. Krom, *Hindoe-Javaansche Geschiedenis,* p. 383. *Nāgarakṛitāgama,* p. 257.
138. *Pararaton,* p. 129.
139. Krom, *Hindoe-Javaansche Geschiedenis,* p. 384.
140. *Pararaton,* p. 139.
141. Krom, *Hindoe-Javaansche Geschiedenis,* p. 387.
142. *Ibid.,* p. 390.
143. *Ibid.,* p. 391. *Nāgarakṛitāgama,* p. 37.
144. Rockhill, "Notes on the Relations and Trade of China," *TP,* XV (1914), p. 447.
145. *Ibid., TP,* XVI (1915), pp. 236–37.

Chapter XIV

1. On the various recensions of the Cambodian chronicle, see Coedès, "Essai de classification des documents historiques cambodgiens conservés à la bibliothèque de l'EFEO," *BEFEO,* XVIII, 9, p. 15. The recension of Vongsa Sarpéch Nong (1818) has been translated by Francis Garnier, "Chronique royale du Cambodge," *JA* (October-December, 1871), p. 336. See also Georges Maspero, *L'Empire khmèr* (Phnom Penh, 1904), and Adhémard Leclère, *Histoire du Cambodge* (Paris, 1914). For the Chinese sources, see J. P. Abel Rémusat, *Nouveaux mélanges asiatiques* (Paris, 1829), I, pp. 90–97. All the dates given below, except those taken from Chinese sources, are subject to revision.
2. W. A. R. Wood, *A History of Siam* (London, 1926), p. 65. The account that follows is based on the *Annals of Ayutthaya* and assumes that there were two seizures of Angkor before the final abandonment of the capital in 1431. These occupations of Angkor, however temporary, seem quite certain, and resolve textual difficulties. They have been challenged by L. P. Briggs, in an article entitled "Siamese Attacks on Angkor before 1430" (*FEQ,* VIII [1948], pp. 1–33); his conclusions, if not proved, have at least some probability.
3. Garnier, "Chronique royale," pp. 341–42. Leclère, *Histoire du Cambodge,* pp. 195–207.

4. Rémusat, *Nouveaux mélanges asiatiques,* I, p. 91.
5. *Ibid.,* p. 92.
6. Garnier, "Chronique royale," p. 343. Leclère, *Histoire du Cambodge,* p. 211.
7. Rémusat, *Nouveaux mélanges asiatiques,* I, p. 93.
8. Wood, *A History of Siam,* p. 76.
9. Garnier, "Chronique royale," p. 344.
10. Rémusat, *Nouveaux mélanges asiatiques,* I, p. 95.
11. Leclère, *Histoire du Cambodge,* p. 215, mentions two reigns between the second conquest of Angkor and the accession of Chao Ponhea Yat.
12. Rémusat, *Nouveaux mélanges asiatiques,* I, p. 96.
13. Garnier, "Chronique royale," p. 344. Maspero, *L'Empire khmèr,* p. 56. Leclère, *Histoire du Cambodge,* p. 216.
14. Coedès, "La fondation de Phnom Penh," *BEFEO,* XIII, 6, p. 6.
15. Etienne Aymonier, "Légendes historiques des Chames," *Excursions et reconnaissances,* XIV, No. 32 (1890).
16. Georges Maspero, *Le Royaume de Champa* (Paris, 1928), p. 203.
17. *Ibid.,* p. 204.
18. *Ibid.,* p. 205.
19. *Ibid.,* p. 206.
20. *Ibid.,* pp. 209–10.
21. *Ibid.,* pp. 211–12.
22. *Ibid.,* p. 214.
23. *Ibid.,* pp. 216–17.
24. *Ibid.,* p. 217.
25. Louis Finot, "Les inscriptions du Musée de Hanoi," *BEFEO,* XV, 2, pp. 13–14; Finot's review of Maspero's *Le Royaume de Champa, BEFEO,* XXVIII, p. 291.
26. Maspero, *Le Royaume de Champa,* p. 220.
27. Finot, "Les inscriptions du Musée de Hanoi," pp. 13–14.
28. Maspero, *Le Royaume de Champa,* p. 221.
29. *Ibid.,* p. 224.
30. A. Cabaton, "L'inscription chame de Biên-hoa," *BEFEO,* IV, p. 687.
31. Maspero, *Le Royaume de Champa,* pp. 226–27.
32. *Ibid.,* p. 228. N. J. Krom, *Hindoe-Javaansche Geschiedenis* (The Hague, 1931), pp. 452, 463.
33. Bi-cai (Chinese Pi Kai = Vijaya), 1441–46, nephew of Indravarman VI; Qui-lai (Chinese Kui-lai), 1446–49, son of Indravarman VI; Qui-do (Chinese Kui-you), 1449–58, younger brother of Qui-lai; Ban-la Tra-nguyêt (Chinese P'an Lo-yue), 1458–60, son-in-law of Vijaya; Ban-la Tra-toan (Chinese P'an-lo T'u-ch'üan), 1460–71, brother of Ban-la Tra-nguyêt. Maspero, *Le Royaume de Champa,* pp. 230–39.
34. *Ibid.,* p. 231.
35. *Ibid.,* pp. 237–39.

36. Jeanne Leuba, *Un Royaume disparu: Les Chams et leur art* (Paris, 1923).
37. Inscription of Batu Tulis at Buitenzorg. The most recent work on this inscription, which is one of the oldest known, is R. Ng. Poerbatjaraka, *TBG,* 59 (1921), p. 380.
38. João de Barros, *Da Asia* (Lisbon, 1778–88), IV, I, chapter 12.
39. *Pararaton,* ed. J. L. A. Brandes (*VBG,* 62 [1920]), pp. 157–58. C. C. Berg, "Kidung Sunda," *BKI,* 83 (1927), p. 1. Krom, *Hindoe-Javaansche Geschiedenis,* pp. 402–404.
40. Trans. Hendrik Kern, *Verspreide Geschriften* (The Hague, 1913–29), VIII, pp. 240–42, 278–79.
41. See below, p. 244, the list of the dependencies on Sumatra and on the peninsula, corresponding to the ancient possessions of Śrīvijaya.
42. W. F. Stutterheim, *Oudheden van Bali* (Singaradja, 1929–30), I, p. 191.
43. Krom, *Hindoe-Javaansche Geschiedenis,* p. 410.
44. G. P. Rouffaer, *Notulen van de Directievergaderingen van het Bataviaasch Genootschap* (1910), pp. 110–13. F. H. van Naerssen, "Hindoe-Javaansche overblijfselen op Soembawa," *TKNAG* (1938), p. 90.
45. P. 279.
46. W. P. Groeneveldt, *Notes on the Malay Archipelago and Malacca* (Batavia, 1876), pp. 35–36. *Pararaton,* p. 164.
47. Restored by Groeneveldt (*Notes on the Malay Archipelago*) as Bogindo Bongkit, and by Gabriel Ferrand ("L'empire sumatranais de Çrīvijaya," *JA* [July-September, 1922]) as Bhra Wangye. Neither of these names corresponds at all to known ones. Ferrand thinks that the second character *yüan* should be deleted, which is probable. *Wang-chieh* appears to be the conventional transcription of *Wengker.*
48. Edited and translated by Hendrik Kern, *Verspreide Geschriften,* VII and VIII. New edition, with translations and commentary, in Theodore G. Th. Pigeaud, *Java in the 14th Century* (The Hague, 1960–63). See Himansu Bhusan Sarkar, *Indian Influences on the Literature of Java and Bali* (Calcutta, 1954), p. 385.
49. Krom, *Hindoe-Javaansche Geschiedenis,* pp. 419–21. On the capital, see W. F. Stutterheim, *De kroton van Majapahit,* VKI, VII (The Hague, 1948).
50. *Pararaton,* p. 196.
51. H. B. Sarkar, *Indian Influences on the Literature of Java and Bali,* pp. 230, 318–22.
52. Above, p. 234.
53. In his *Ying-yai Sheng-lan,* Ma Huan, who accompanied the eunuch Cheng Ho on his journey of 1413, distinguishes three types of inhabitants on Java: the Westerners (Muslims), who came to establish themselves as merchants; the Chinese, who

follow the customs of the Muslims; and the natives (W. W. Rockhill, "Notes on the Relations and Trade of China with the Eastern Archipelago and the Coast of the Indian Ocean during the Fourteenth Century," *TP,* XVI [1915], p. 242).

54. J. P. Moquette, *Handelingen van het Eerste Congres voor de Taal-, Land- en Volkenkunde van Java* (Weltevreden, 1921), p. 31. Paul Ravaisse, "L'inscription coufique de Léran à Java," *TBG,* 65 (1925), p. 668.
55. Bertram Schrieke, *Het boek van Bonang* (Utrecht, 1916), p. 28.
56. *Pararaton,* pp. 177, 180. Krom, *Hindoe-Javaansche Geschiedenis,* pp. 430–32. The *History of the Ming* (Groeneveldt, *Notes on the Malay Archipelago,* p. 36) notes under the year 1403 the division of the country between the king of the West, the prince of Tu-ma-pan (Tumapel), and the king of the East, P'u-ling Ta-ha, Bhreng (or Putreng) Daha. The eunuch Cheng Ho, sent by the Ming emperor Yung Lo, in the course of his first journey abroad found himself in the kingdom of the East in 1406 at the moment of its fall and received the apologies of the conqueror for the death of 170 persons in his entourage (Groeneveldt, *Notes on the Malay Archipelago,* pp. 36–37).

    We learn from this text that the prince of Tu-ma-pan (Tumapel) must be identified with Vikramavardhana, or perhaps with his son who actually bore the title of Bhre Tumapel and whom P'u-ling Ta-ha (Putreng Daha) called Vīrabhūmi (Krom, *Hindoe-Javaansche Geschiedenis,* pp. 431–32). The abstruse and confused data of the *Pararaton* concerning the genealogical lines among the members of the royal family of Majapahit make it quite difficult to reconstruct the history of that period; the data are susceptible to divergent interpretations. Thus, R. C. Majumdar (*Ancient Indian Colonies of the Far East,* II: Suvarṇadvīpa [Dacca, 1937], pp. 339–45) has formulated a theory that Vikramavardhana abdicated in 1400 in favor of his wife, who died in 1429. Vikramavardhana must have assumed power again around 1415, for the *History of the Ming* (Groeneveldt, *Notes on the Malay Archipelago,* p. 37; Paul Pelliot, "Notes additionelles sur Tcheng Houo et sur ses voyages," *TP,* XXXI [1935], p. 301) says that in that year the king took the name Yang Wei-si-cha, Hyang Viśesha, which was actually one of the names of Vikramavardhana. He appears to have reigned not merely until 1429 as has been believed, but until 1436, and he apparently was succeeded at that date by a daughter named Bhre Daha, another name of the princess Suhitā.
57. Below, pp. 245–46.
58. On the voyages of Cheng Ho between 1405 and 1433, see Groeneveldt, *Notes on the Malay Archipelago,* pp. 41–45; Rockhill, "Notes on the Relations and Trade of China," pp.

81–85; J. J. L. Duyvendak, *Ma Huan Re-Examined,* VKNAWAL, XXXII, No. 3 (Amsterdam, 1933); Paul Pelliot, "Les grands voyages maritimes chinois au début du XVe siècle," *TP,* XXX (1933), p. 237; Tatsuro Yamamoto, "Chêng Ho's Expeditions to the South Sea under the Ming Dynasty," *Toyo Gakuho,* XXI (1934), pp. 374–404, 506–54; Pelliot, "Notes additionelles sur Tcheng Houo," p. 274; J. J. L. Duyvendak, "The True Dates of the Chinese Maritime Expedition in the Early Fifteenth Century," *TP,* XXXIV (1938), p. 341.

59. Krom, *Hindoe-Javaansche Geschiedenis,* p. 439.
60. *Pararaton,* pp. 177–90. Krom, *Hindoe-Javaansche Geschiedenis,* pp. 429–32, 444–46.
61. N. J. Krom, *Inleiding tot de Hindoe-Javaansche Kunst* (The Hague, 1923), II, pp. 325 ff. W. F. Stutterheim, "The Exploration of Mount Penanggungan," *ABIA,* XI (1936), pp. 25–30. F. M. Schnitger, "Les terrasses mégalithiques de Java," *RAA,* XIII (1939–42), pp. 105–12.
62. *Pararaton,* p. 199. Krom, *Hindoe-Javaansche Geschiedenis,* p. 448.
63. Krom, *Hindoe-Javaansche Geschiedenis,* pp. 449–50.
64. *Ibid.,* pp. 450–51.
65. Groeneveldt, *Notes on the Malay Archipelago,* p. 39.
66. Krom, *Hindoe-Javaansche Geschiedenis,* p. 458.
67. C. Hooykaas, "Kamandakīya Nītisāra etc., in Old-Javanese," *JGIS,* XV (1956), p. 21.
68. Hendrik Kern, *Verspreide Geschriften,* VI, pp. 257–61.
69. F. M. Schnitger, *The Archaeology of Hindoo Sumatra* (Leyden, 1937), p. 8, pls. XIII–XVI.
70. N. J. Krom, *VMKAWAL,* 5th series, II (1916), p. 338.
71. Groeneveldt, *Notes on the Malay Archipelago,* p. 68. Ferrand, "L'empire sumatranais," p. 24.
72. This name, which is undoubtedly only a simple transcription of *mahārāja,* has been read by J. L. Moens ("Śrīvijaya, Yāva en Katāha," *TBG,* 77 [1937], p. 456) as Haji Dharmāśraya, with the inversion of the two words following Chinese syntax. It will be recalled that Dharmāśraya designates the region of the upper Batang Hari where the statue of Amoghapāśa that was brought from Java was erected in 1286 (above, p. 201).
73. Groeneveldt, *Notes on the Malay Archipelago,* p. 69. Ferrand, "L'empire sumatranais," p. 25.
74. Groeneveldt, *Notes on the Malay Archipelago,* p. 69. Ferrand, "L'empire sumatranais," p. 25.
75. Moens, "Śrīvijaya, Yāva en Katāha," p. 457, proposes that this name be read as Sang Ādityavarman, but this reading is difficult to justify phonetically.
76. Above, p. 234.
77. Groeneveldt, *Notes on the Malay Archipelago,* p. 69. Ferrand, "L'empire sumatranais," pp. 25–26.

78. Krom, *Hindoe-Javaansche Geschiedenis,* p. 412.
79. Groeneveldt, *Notes on the Malay Archipelago,* p. 69. Ferrand, "L'empire sumatranais," p. 26.
80. On the changing of this name, see Pelliot, "Les grands voyages maritimes chinois," pp. 274, 372–79.
81. Groeneveldt, *Notes on the Malay Archipelago,* p. 71. Ferrand, "L'empire sumatranais," pp. 27–28.
82. The Palatine law (Koṭ Maṇḍirapāla), published in volume I of the edition of Siamese laws of D. B. Bradley (Bangkok, 1896) and in volume I, p. 58, of the edition of Robert Lingat (Bangkok, 1938). See G. E. Gerini, *Researches on Ptolemy's Geography of Eastern Asia* (London, 1909), pp. 531–32, and C. O. Blagden, review of Krom's *Hindoe-Javaansche Geschiedenis* in *JRAS* (1928), p. 915.
83. On this place name, which has not yet been identified, see above, pp. 144, 145 (Wurawari).
84. Kern, *Verspreide Geschriften,* VII, pp. 241, 278–79. Krom, *Hindoe-Javaansche Geschiedenis,* pp. 416–17. No explanation is given here for names still in use or easily recognizable.
85. On the history of some of the small Sumatran states in the first half of the fifteenth century, we find some details in the *History of the Ming,* as well as in the *Ying-yai Sheng-lan* of Ma Huan and the *Hsing-ch'a Sheng-lan* of Fei Hsin, both written following the voyages of the eunuch Cheng Ho (Groeneveldt, *Notes on the Malay Archipelago,* pp. 77–101; Rockhill, "Notes on the Relations and Trade of China," pp. 129–59; Pelliot, "Les grands voyages maritimes chinois," pp. 275, 290–94).
86. Rockhill, "Notes on the Relations and Trade of China," pp. 141, 150.
87. But not as political center, since, according to Tomé Pires (*The Suma Oriental of Tomé Pires,* ed. Armando Cortesao [London, 1944], I, p. 108; II, p. 248), the kingdom of Kedah retained supremacy over the tin-bearing districts until its conquest by Mansur Shah (below, p. 246). See, however, R. O. Winstedt, "Did Pasai Rule Kedah in the Fourteenth Century?" *JRASMB,* XLVIII, 2 (1940), p. 150.
88. R. O. Winstedt, "The Advent of Muhammadanism in the Malay Peninsula and Archipelago," *JRASSB,* 77 (December, 1917), p. 171. On the propagation of Islam on Sumatra, this author adds that Islam spread from Achin to Ulakan, then to Minangkabau. In the seventeenth century, the peoples on the coast of the district of Lampong began to be converted, and in the eighteenth century Islam spread into the interior. In the middle of the sixteenth century, a missionary from Palembang went to Borneo and propagated the religion at Sukadana and at Madan. In 1606, a merchant of Minangkabau converted the Raja of Pallo in the Celebes.

89. C. O. Blagden, "The Mediaeval Chronology of Malacca," in *Actes, XIe Congrès International des Orientalistes* (Paris, 1897), II, pp. 239–53. Gabriel Ferrand, "Malaka, le Malāyu et Malāyur," *JA* (May-June, 1918), pp. 391–484; (July-August, 1918), pp. 51–154. G. P. Rouffaer, "Was Malaka emporium voor 1400 A.D. genaamd Malajoer?" *BKI, 77* (1921), pp. 1–174, 359–604. R. J. Wilkinson, "The Malacca Sultanate," *JRASMB,* XIII, 2 (1935), pp. 22–67.
90. *Historical Guide to Malacca* (Singapore, 1936), p. 25.
91. Krom, *Hindoe-Javaansche Geschiedenis,* pp. 436–37. R. O. Winstedt, *History of Malaya* (Singapore, 1962), p. 45. P. V. van Stein Callenfels, "The Founder of Malacca," *JRASMB,* XV (1937), p. 160. For the history and chronology of events, I adopt the views of R. O. Winstedt in his "The Malay Founder of Medieval Malacca," *BSOAS,* XII (1948), p. 728, and his *History of Malaya.*
92. Pelliot, "Les grands voyages maritimes chinois," p. 397. The *History of the Ming* calls him Pai-li-mi-su-la (*ibid.,* p. 389); another text of the sixteenth century calls him Si-li-pa-erh-su-la (J. J. L. Duyvendak, "Sailing Directions of Chinese Voyages," *TP* [1938], p. 366, n. 3).
93. Pelliot, "Les grands voyages maritimes chinois." On the exchanges of embassies between China and Malacca, see Victor Purcell, "Chinese Settlement in Malacca," *JRASMB,* XX (1947), pp. 115–25.
94. Description in the *Ying-yai Sheng-lan* (Rockhill, "Notes on the Relations and Trade of China," pp. 114–17). For the commercial reasons for the founding and prosperity of Malacca, a port of exchange and a port of call commanding the straits, as Śrīvijaya had been before it, see Paul Wheatley, *The Golden Khersonese* (Kuala Lumpur, 1961), Part VII, p. 306.
95. Pelliot, "Les grands voyages maritimes chinois," pp. 397–98, 451.
96. Krom, *Hindoe-Javaansche Geschiedenis,* pp. 438–39. Winstedt, *History of Malaya,* p. 49.
97. The *History of the Ming* (Groeneveldt, *Notes on the Malay Archipelago,* p. 130; Ferrand, "Malaka, le Malāyu et Malāyur," p. 403) calls him Mu-kan Sa-yü-ti-erh Sha, which must surely be corrected to Mu-wo Sa-kan-ti-erh Sha. According to a communication from R. O. Winstedt, it is this change in name which has caused the Chinese sources to regard a single individual as two separate kings.
98. Pelliot, "Les grands voyages maritimes chinois," p. 398. The *History of the Ming* (Groeneveldt, *Notes on the Malay Archipelago,* p. 130; Ferrand, "Malaka, le Malāyu et Malāyur," p. 403) calls him Si-li Ma-ha-la.
99. Winstedt, *History of Malaya,* p. 50.

100. Groeneveldt, *Notes on the Malay Archipelago,* p. 131.
101. Ferrand, "Malaka, le Malāyu et Malāyur," p. 404.
102. Winstedt, *History of Malaya,* p. 50.
103. This is the Su-lu-t'an Wu-ta-fu-na Sha of the *History of the Ming* (Groeneveldt, *Notes on the Malay Archipelago,* pp. 131–32; Ferrand, "Malaka, le Malāyu et Malāyur," p. 404). On the hostilities with Ayutthaya, see G. E. Marrison, "The Siamese Wars with Malacca during the Reign of Muzaffur Shah," *JRASMB,* XXII (1949), pp. 51–66, and XXIV (1951), p. 191.
104. Su-tan Mang-su Sha (Groeneveldt, *Notes on the Malay Archipelago,* p. 132; Ferrand, "Malaka, le Malāyu et Malāyur," p. 404).
105. *The Suma Oriental of Tomé Pires,* II, p. 248.
106. Krom, *Hindoe-Javaansche Geschiedenis,* p. 453. Winstedt, *History of Malaya,* p. 55.
107. "The Grave Stone of Sultan Mansur Shah of Malacca," *Malaya in History,* I (February, 1959), p. 36.
108. Krom, *Hindoe-Javaansche Geschiedenis,* pp. 453–54. Winstedt, *History of Malaya,* pp. 57–60. In the *History of the Ming,* Mahmud is called Ma-ha-mu Sha (Groeneveldt, *Notes on the Malay Archipelago,* p. 133; Ferrand, "L'empire sumatranais," p. 18).

Conclusion

1. "Although the decline of Indian civilization in all of Southeast Asia in the thirteenth century may have been accelerated by the impact of the Mongols, it was not directly caused by them, for we see symptoms of it in the preceding century. The underlying causes of this decline were the adoption of Indian civilization by an increasingly large number of natives who incorporated into it more and more of their original customs, and the gradual disappearance of a refined aristocracy, the guardian of Sanskrit culture. Hinduism and Mahayana Buddhism, in the special form of royal and personal cults, were religions that were hardly suited to the masses; this explains the ease and speed with which the masses adopted Singhalese Buddhism. The disruption caused by the Mongol conquests simply succeeded in breaking up old political groups, old cultural complexes: the Khmer empire, the Cham kingdom, and the Burmese kingdom. Their dissociated elements were finally regrouped to form the combinations we see taking their places: the Burmese kingdoms of Ava and then Pegu, the Thai kingdoms of Ayutthaya, Lan Na, Lan Chang." (Coedès, *Les Peuples de la péninsule indochinoise* [Paris, 1962], p. 128.)
2. The expression is from Paul Mus, "L'Inde vue de l'est: Cultes indiens et indigènes au Champa," *BEFEO,* XXXIII, p. 367.

3. Valuable leads can be found in K. A. Nilakanta Sastri, "Agastya," *TBG,* 76 (1936), p. 533; W. F. Stutterheim, *Bulletin of the Raffles Museum,* ser. B, I (1937), p. 148.
4. W. F. Stutterheim, *Indian Influences in Old-Balinese Art* (London, 1935). K. C. Crucq, *Bijdrage tot de kennis van het Balisch Doodenritueel* (Santpoort, 1928). P. de Kat Angelino, *Mudrās auf Bali* (The Hague, 1923). R. Goris, *Bijdrage tot de kennis der Oud-Javaansche en Balineesche Theologie* (Leyden, 1926). Sylvain Lévi, *Sanskrit Texts from Bali* (Baroda, 1933).
5. Antoine Cabaton, *Nouvelles recherches sur les Chams* (Paris, 1901). Jeanne Leuba, *Un Royaume disparu: Les Chams et leur art* (Paris, 1923).
6. Adhémard Leclère, *Cambodge, Fêtes civiles et religieuses* (Paris, 1917). H. G. Quaritch Wales, *Siamese State Ceremonies* (London, 1931).
7. W. F. Stutterheim, *Rāma-Legenden und Rāma-Reliefs in Indonesien* (Munich, 1925).
8. Robert Lingat, "L'influence juridique de l'Inde au Champa et au Cambodge d'après l'épigraphie," *JA,* CCXXXVII (1949), pp. 273–90; "Evolution of the Conception of Law in Burma and Siam," *JSS,* XXXVIII (1950), pp. 9–31; "La conception du droit dans l'Indochine hīnayāniste," *BEFEO,* XLIV (1951), pp. 163–88. F. H. van Naerssen, "De Ashtadaçawyawahāra in het Oudjavaansch," *BKI,* 100 (1941), pp. 357–76.
9. *L'Inde civilisatrice* (Paris, 1938), p. 28. On sculpture, see Dora Gordine, "Sculpture in Indochina, Siam and Java," *JRAS* (1942), pp. 132–38; R. O. Winstedt, "Buddhist Images from Malaya and Sumatra," *IAL* (1942), p. 41.
10. F. D. K. Bosch, "Een hypothese omtrent den oorsprung der Hindoe-Javaansche Kunst," in *Handelingen van het Eerste Congres voor de Taal-, Land- en Volkenkunde van Java* (Weltevreden, 1921)—translated into English in *Rūpam,* XVII (1924). Henri Parmentier, "Origine commune des architectures hindoues dans l'Inde et en Extrême-Orient," *Et. Asiat. EFEO,* pp. 199–251. A. K. Coomaraswamy, *History of Indian and Indonesian Art* (London, 1927), Chap. VI. Henri Marchal, *L'Architecture comparée dans l'Inde et l'Extrême-Orient* (Paris, 1944). H. G. Quaritch Wales, "Culture Change in Greater India," *JRAS* (1948), pp. 2–32; "The Dong-So'n Genius and the Evolution of Cham Art," *JRAS* (1949), pp. 34–45; *The Making of Greater India* (London, 1951). See above, p. 267, n. 3.
11. Paul Mus, "Barabuḍur," *BEFEO,* XXXII–XXXIV; "Le Symbolisme à Angkor Thom," *CRAIBL* (1936), pp. 57–69. Coedès, *Pour mieux comprendre Angkor* (Paris, 1947); *Angkor, an Introduction* (Hongkong, 1963). J. E. van Lohuizen-de Leeuw, "South-East Asian Architecture and the Stūpa of Nandangarh," *AA,* XIX (1956), p. 279.
12. Above, p. 34.

INDEX

I. GEOGRAPHIC, ETHNIC, AND ARCHAEOLOGICAL TERMS

II. PERSONAL NAMES

III. RELIGIOUS NAMES AND TERMS

IV. TEXTS

V. FOREIGN TERMS

CAMBODIA
DANGREK MOUNTAINS
Mun River
UBON
Phimai
Nom Van
KHORAT
BURIRAM
SURIN
BASSAC
Vat Ph'u
(Lingaparvata)
Ban That
Preah Vihear
Banteay Ch'mar
Phnom Sandak
Prasat Khna
Khon Falls
Sdok Kak Thom
MONGKOLBOREI
MT. BANTEAY NEANG
Preah Phnom
Prasat Ta Keâm
Pr. Roluh
Koh Ker
(Ch'ok Gargyar)
MLU PREI
MT. KULÈN
(Mahendraparvata)
Pr. Trau
Banteay Srei
(Īśvarapura)
ANGKOR
(Yaśodharapura)
Beng Mealea
STUNGTRENG
SIEM REAP
ROLŪOS
(Hariharālaya)
Preah Khan
Vat Ek
BATTAMBANG
Baset
MT. KROM
Great Lake or Tonle Sap
Sambor Prei Kuk
(Īśānapura)
KOMPONG THOM
Sambor
(Śambuphura)
CHANTHABUN
PURSAT
KRATIÉ
Samrong Sèn
P. Preah Vihear
Kompong Ch'nang
Mekong
THBONG KHMUM
KOMPONG CHAM
SREI SANTHOR
Preah Theat Preah Srei
B. Prei Nokor
Vat Sithor
PHNOM PENH
KANDAL
PREI VÊNG
BANAM
BA PHNOM
(Vyādhapura)
TAY-NINH
Ta Prohm
BATI
Pr. Neang Khmau
MT. CHISOR
Ta Kèo
Angkor Borei
PHNOM DA
Asram Maharosei
CHAUDOC
SAIGON
Thap Mươi
PLAINE DES JONCS
Kuhea Preah
MT. BAYANG
HATIEN
LONG-XUYÊN

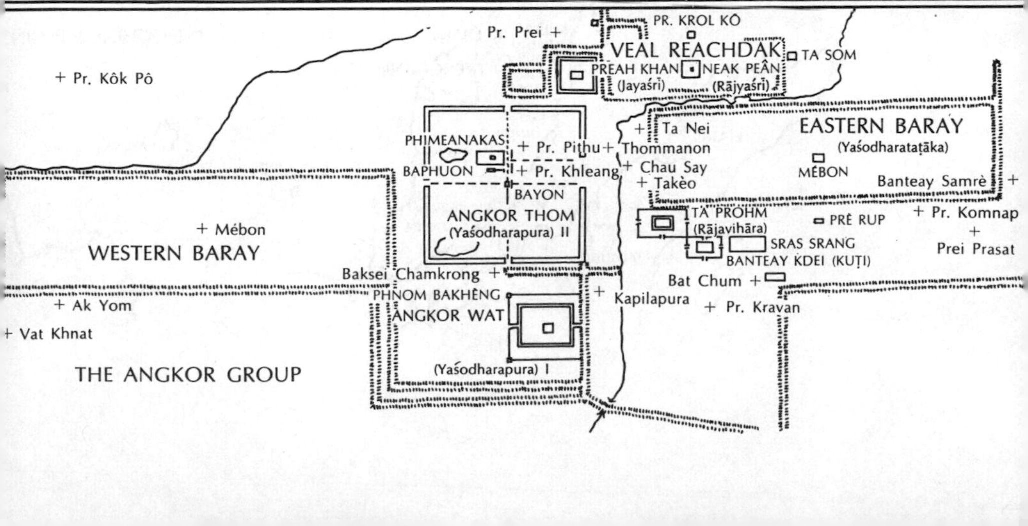

THE ANGKOR GROUP
Pr. Prei
PR. KROL KÔ
VEAL REACHDAK
TA SOM
Pr. Kôk Pô
PREAH KHAN
(Jayaśrī)
NEAK PEÂN
(Rājyaśrī)
EASTERN BARAY
(Yaśodharataṭāka)
PHIMEANAKAS
Ta Nei
Pr. Pithu
Thommanon
MÉBON
BAPHUON
Pr. Khleang
Chau Say
Takèo
Banteay Samrè
BAYON
TA PROHM
(Rājavihāra)
PRÉ RUP
Pr. Komnap
ANGKOR THOM
(Yaśodharapura) II
Mébon
WESTERN BARAY
SRAS SRANG
BANTEAY KDEI (KUṬI)
Prei Prasat
Baksei Chamkrong
Bat Chum
PHNOM BAKHÈNG
Kapilapura
Pr. Kravan
Ak Yom
ANGKOR WAT
Vat Khnat
(Yaśodharapura) I

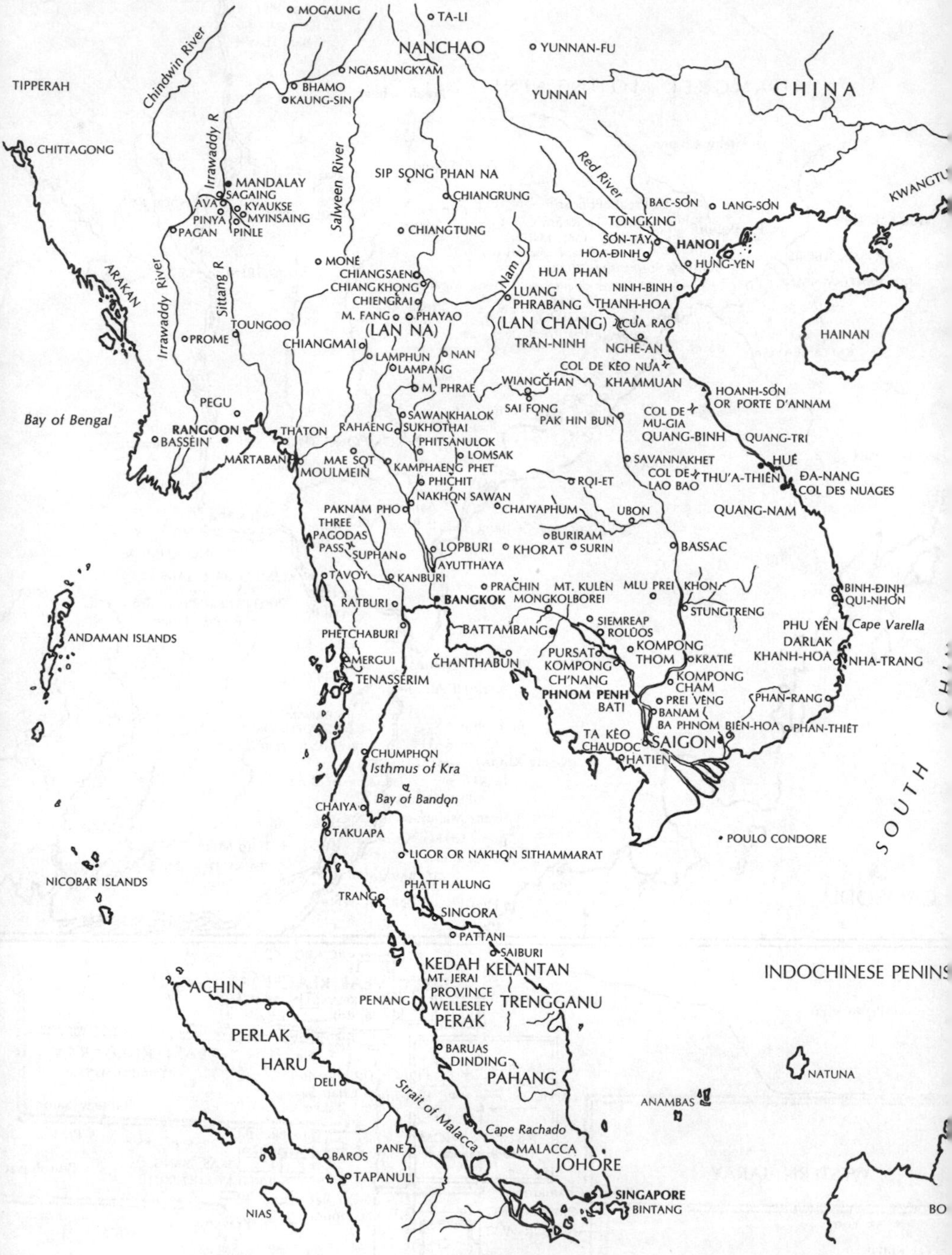
MOGAUNG
TA-LI
NANCHAO
YUNNAN-FU
TIPPERAH
Chindwin River
NGASAUNGKYAM
BHAMO
KAUNG-SIN
YUNNAN
CHINA
CHITTAGONG
Irrawaddy R
Salween River
Red River
SIP SONG PHAN NA
MANDALAY
SAGAING
AVA
KYAUKSE
PINYA
MYINSAING
PAGAN
PINLE
CHIANGRUNG
BAC-SON
LANG-SON
KWANGTU
TONGKING
CHIANGTUNG
SON-TAY
HOA-ĐINH
HANOI
HUNG-YEN
MONÉ
CHIANGSAEN
CHIANG KHONG
CHIENGRAI
M. FANG
PHAYAO
(LAN NA)
Nam U
LUANG PHRABANG
(LAN CHANG)
HUA PHAN
NINH-BINH
THANH-HOA
CUA RAO
ARAKAN
Irrawaddy River
Sittang R
TOUNGOO
PROME
CHIANGMAI
LAMPHUN
NAN
LAMPANG
TRẤN-NINH
NGHỆ-AN
COL DE KÈO NUA
KHAMMUAN
HAINAN
M. PHRAE
WIANGČHAN
SAI FONG
PAK HIN BUN
HOANH-SON OR PORTE D'ANNAM
PEGU
Bay of Bengal
RANGOON
BASSEIN
THATON
MARTABAN
MOULMEIN
RAHAENG
SUKHOTHAI
SAWANKHALOK
PHITSANULOK
LOMSAK
MAE SOT
KAMPHAENG PHET
PHICHIT
NAKHON SAWAN
COL DE MU-GIA
QUANG-BINH
QUANG-TRI
SAVANNAKHET
COL DE LAO BAO
THU'A-THIÊN
HUÉ
ĐA-NANG
COL DES NUAGES
ROI-ET
CHAIYAPHUM
UBON
QUANG-NAM
PAKNAM PHO
THREE PAGODAS PASS
SUPHAN
BURIRAM
LOPBURI
KHORAT
SURIN
BASSAC
AYUTTHAYA
TAVOY
KANBURI
PRAČHIN
MT. KULÊN
MLU PREI
KHON
BINH-ĐINH
QUI-NHON
RATBURI
BANGKOK
MONGKOLBOREI
STUNGTRENG
ANDAMAN ISLANDS
PHETCHABURI
BATTAMBANG
SIEMREAP
ROLŪOS
PHU YÊN
Cape Varella
DARLAK
KHANH-HOA
NHA-TRANG
MERGUI
ČHANTHABUN
PURSAT
KOMPONG CH'NANG
KOMPONG THOM
KRATIÉ
TENASSERIM
KOMPONG CHAM
PHNOM PENH
BATI
PREI VENG
BANAM
BA PHNOM
BIÊN-HOA
PHAN-RANG
PHAN-THIÊT
TA KÈO
CHAUDOC
HATIEN
SAIGON
CHUMPHON
Isthmus of Kra
SOUTH
Bay of Bandon
CHAIYA
TAKUAPA
POULO CONDORE
LIGOR OR NAKHON SITHAMMARAT
NICOBAR ISLANDS
PHATTH ALUNG
TRANG
SINGORA
PATTANI
SAIBURI
KEDAH
MT. JERAI
KELANTAN
INDOCHINESE PENINS
ACHIN
PROVINCE WELLESLEY
PENANG
TRENGGANU
PERAK
PERLAK
BARUAS
DINDING
HARU
PAHANG
NATUNA
DELI
Strait of Malacca
ANAMBAS
Cape Rachado
MALACCA
BAROS
PANE
JOHORE
TAPANULI
SINGAPORE
BINTANG
NIAS
BO

INDOCHINESE PENINSULA
ANCIENT PLACE NAMES
AND ARCHAEOLOGICAL SITES

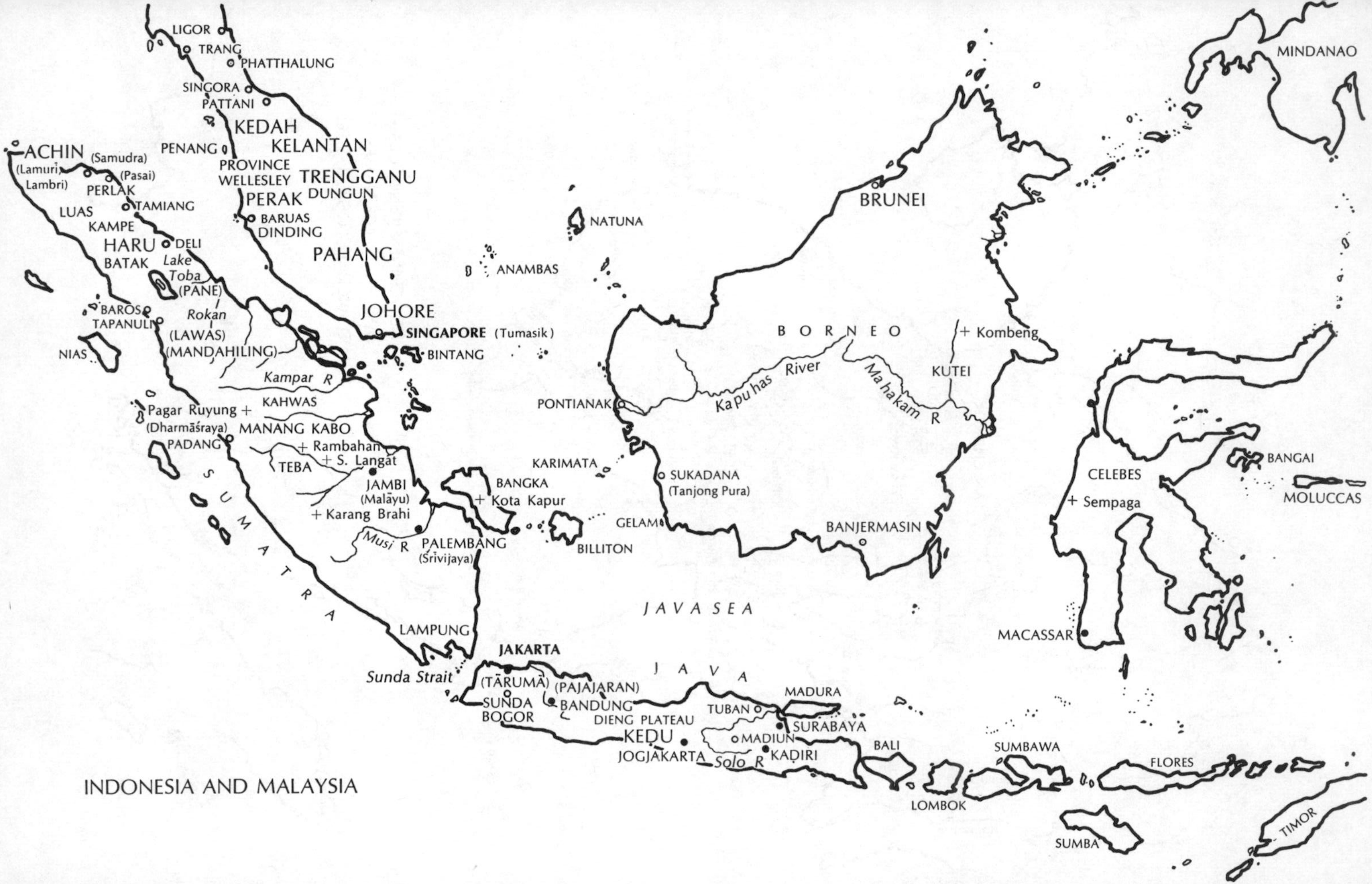

INDONESIA AND MALAYSIA

CENTRAL AND EASTERN JAVA

GENEALOGY OF THE KINGS OF MAJAPAHIT

according to N. J. KROM

(*The names of the kings are in capitals.*)

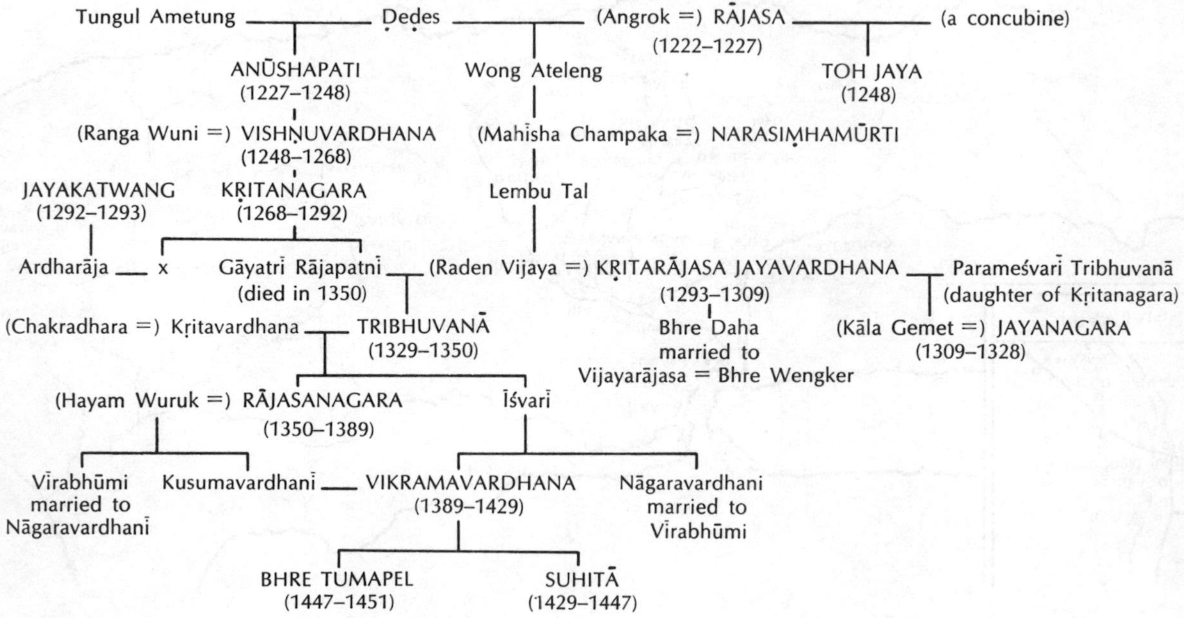

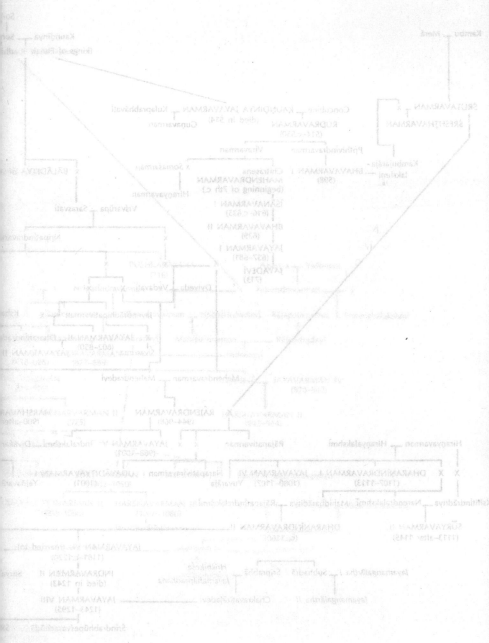